McGowan on Alcohol Licensing Law in Scotland

McGowan on Alcohol Licensing Law in Scotland

Stephen J McGowan

EDINBURGH
University Press

Edinburgh University Press is one of the leading university presses in the UK. We publish academic books and journals in our selected subject areas across the humanities and social sciences, combining cutting-edge scholarship with high editorial and production values to produce academic works of lasting importance. For more information visit our website: edinburghuniversitypress.com

Edinburgh University Press Ltd
The Tun – Holyrood Road
12(2f) Jackson's Entry
Edinburgh EH8 8PJ

Typeset in 10/11 Plantin by
Servis Filmsetting Ltd, Stockport, Cheshire,
and printed and bound in Great Britain

A CIP record for this book is available from the British Library

ISBN 978 1 4744 8364 3 (hardback)
ISBN 978 1 4744 7391 0 (paperback)
ISBN 978 1 4744 9036 8 (webready PDF)
ISBN 978 1 4744 9037 5 (epub)

Contents

Foreword

Energy, enthusiasm and expertise: a potent combination evident on every page of this important new book. An exploration of alcohol licensing in Scotland faces significant challenges: it must address the law's myriad complexities in a readable fashion, making sense of provisions that habitually tax the intellect of those experienced in the field. In that endeavour, Stephen McGowan conspicuously succeeds, aided by a novel, almost conversational writing style, particularly when he recounts his own experiences in the trenches. In the first chapter, the reader will also gain valuable insights into the history of alcohol regulation: a scholarly journey, rigorously researched, taking us from the Home Drummond Act 1828 to the present day, which might of itself form the foundation for a valuable separate work.

It is to the author's credit that even the seasoned practitioner may find settled views on areas of particular difficulty challenged by penetrating analyses. And while a work of this nature dare not fall between two stools – attempting to address an unrealistically broad audience – there is valuable assistance here for novice and expert alike.

From my own authorship experience over many years, I am fully seized of the diligence required to produce such a substantial text. This is not a venture to be embarked upon lightly: it requires a quite extraordinary time commitment, scrupulous attention to detail and the courage to throw one's hat in the ring. I have no doubt that a legion of licensing practitioners will find themselves grateful to Mr McGowan for completing this daunting task.

Jack Cummins
Glasgow
November 2020

Preface

In 2014 I was asked by Margaret Cherry of Avizandum Publishing (now EUP) to commence writing a second edition of my book *Licensing and Gambling Law in Scotland* (2009). Even at that stage, the world of alcohol licensing law had moved on apiece, and at a rate of knots, so I knew I had a considerable task before me. The tenth anniversary of the 2005 Act then passed in 2019 with little fanfare and we had witnessed no less than four new Acts, countless secondary instruments, guidance and policy, and umpteen appeal decisions, all of which I was endeavouring to capture. Even ignoring the plethora of Covid-19 regulations, can there be any area of Scots law subject to such continual and significant change?

I (mis)spent what now seems a significant portion of my life reviewing all of these parliamentary debates and papers to fathom the policy origin of these legion provisions so I could encourage the reader to pursue a deeper appreciation of the purpose of the law, as well as its practical effect. The sheer volume of the law is partly the reason why the book is focused on alcohol licensing – to do it proper justice. My best wishes to the wretch who attempts to author *Gambling Law in Scotland.*

The audience I speak to throughout the book are licensing practitioners of all sorts – police, council officers, licensing standards officers, solicitors, advocates, paralegals, government officials, ministers, health professionals, trainers, other stakeholders, as well as the good people of the licensed trade itself. I have tried to make the style fluid, the language accessible, and with a dash of personality wherever possible whilst relaying anecdotes from "the front". I hope I have succeeded.

I have on my desk a well-thumbed copy of the second edition of *Licensing Law in Scotland*, by Jack Cummins (2000). Twenty years on, it is remarkable to think how much of what Mr Cummins had to digest and interpret is prescient even now. The winding path between that text and the one you now hold is a constant reminder to me, and therefore to you, that the world of licensing is both cyclical and volatile, governed by the keen desires of successive lawmakers; influenced by the aspirations of interest groups and trades. But oh, how the wheel has spun with stinging velocity. Long after this book is published, it will be spinning still.

Stephen McGowan
Strathbungo, March 2021

Acknowledgments and Dedication

I have leaned upon a vast array of fellow professionals in the writing of this book, keen to ensure any sense of perspective I may have had did not completely evaporate across the seven years or so it has taken to deliver it.

These hardy "volunteers" included Scott Blair, Peter Clyde, Dougie Frood, Janet Hood, Archie MacIver, Mairi Millar, William O'Brien and Fiona Stewart. They were all able to propose insights, capture errors, and shine a light on those darkened areas where perhaps I had lost my way, and have my thanks. Very special thanks to Tom Johnston who proofread the entire text at considerable injury to his own sanity, making many sensible corrections and suggestions. I am of course especially grateful to Jack Cummins for also reviewing the entire text, making a number of sage corrections and suggestions; and I am honoured to have him provide the Foreword.

I want to pay considerable thanks to my colleagues at TLT LLP who have supported me in this endeavour personally as well as professionally, especially my comrades in the licensing team Caroline Loudon, Michael McDougall (who reviewed the proofs), Alison Smith, Nicky Corletto and Alice McLaughlin. Niall Hassard merits a special mention for reviewing the entire text, and joint-authoring the chapter on Occasional Licences.

Thank you to the team at Edinburgh University Press including Laura Williamson for their efforts, and of course a special nod to Margaret Cherry. This may well be the last or one of the last books she has had a hand in publishing. She has had a remarkable career driving the publication of innumerable legal texts over many years whilst at Avizandum. I am grateful to her for believing in me back in 2007, and again in 2014 when the work on this book commenced.

Finally, I wish to thank my beloved wife Angie, who has been a source of profound and tremendous inspiration. During the writing of this book and against no small odds she brought about a much lovelier contribution to the world, our beautiful daughter Abigail – to whom this book is dedicated.

Author's Notes

(1) The word "premises" is perhaps the second most abundant in this book, after "licensing". What fun I have had grappling with whether an establishment should be referred to as "a premise" or "a premises". Feedback from peers on this has been split down the middle. In the result, I have followed the language of the 2005 Act which, rightly or wrongly, uses "premises".

(2) As if in answer to my own cries regarding the volatility of Scottish licensing, just before the book went to publication a new appeal was determined, *viz* Keasim Ltd v City of Glasgow Licensing Board, Glasgow Sheriff Court, 8 June 2021 (unreported at date of publication). I understand it is the first appeal in relation to an occasional licence under the 2005 Act. The case surrounds the use of continuous or "back-to-back" occasional licences for an outdoor hospitality facility known as Festival Village in the Candleriggs area of Glasgow. Issues at play included whether an "event" is needed to justify an occasional licence and whether a longer term use was circumvention of procedure. Sheriff Reid quashed the refusals and ordained the board to grant the licences. A brief examination of the general topic of concurrent occasional licences is on p 467. Examination of Sheriff Reid's reasoning, now of some import to this little corner of licensing law, has evaded this text, but will no doubt be ventilated in conference and seminars soon.

Table of Statutes

Table of Orders, Rules and Regulations

Table of Cases

List of Abbreviations

1976 Act	Licensing (Scotland) Act 1976
1982 Act	Civic Government (Scotland) Act 1982
2003 Act	Licensing Act 2003 [England & Wales]
2005 Act	Licensing (Scotland) Act 2005
2011 Regulations	Licensing (Minor Variations) (Scotland) Regulations 2011 (SSI 2011/151)
2012 Act	Alcohol (Minimum Pricing) (Scotland) Act 2012
2015 Act	Air Weapons and Licensing (Scotland) Act 2015
2020 Act	Coronavirus (Scotland) Act 2020
ABV	alcohol by volume
AGCs	adult gaming centres
ACPOS	Association of Chief Police Officers in Scotland
AFS	Alcohol Focus Scotland
ASA	Advertising Standards Agency
AWPs	amusements with prizes
BACTA	British Amusement Catering Trades Association
BBPA	British Beer and Pub Association
BEDA	Bar Entertainment and Dance Association
BHA	British Hospitality Association
BII	British Institute of Innkeepers
CISWO	Coal Industry Social Welfare Organisation (Scotland) [11/8]
Clayson Report	Report of the Departmental Committee on Scottish Licensing Law (Cmnd 5354) (1973) (chaired by Dr Christopher Clayson)
CLSO	Civic Licensing Standards Officer
CRESH	Centre for Research on Environment, Society and Health (Institute of Health and Wellbeing, University of Glasgow)
DPO	Deputy Presiding Officer
DPM	designated premises manager
ECHR	European Convention on Human Rights and Fundamental Freedoms
FECs	family entertainment centres
FOBT	fixed odds betting terminal
HMO	House in Multiple Occupation
LDN	Licence Dispensation Notice
LPGMP	licensed premises gaming machine permit

LSO	Licensing Standards Officer
MSP	Member of the Scottish Parliament
MUP	minimum unit pricing
Nicolson Report	Review of Liquor Licensing in Scotland – the Nicholson Committee (AN501-2003)
NLAG	National Licensing Advisory Group
NUS	National Union of Students
PEL	Public Entertainment Licence
Procedural Regulations	Licensing (Procedure) (Scotland) Regulations 2007 (SSI 2007/453)
QLTR	the Queen's and Lord Treasurer's Remembrancer
SALAF	Scottish Alcohol Licensing Advisory Forum
SCVO	Scottish Council for Voluntary Organisations
SGAIP	Scottish Government Alcohol Industry Partnership
SGF	Scottish Grocers Federation
SHAAP	Scottish Health Action on Alcohol Problems
SIA	Security Industry Authority
SLTA	Scottish Licensed Trade Association
SRC	Scottish Retail Consortium
SWPs	skills with prizes
Transfer Regulations	Licence Transfer (Prescribed Persons) (Scotland) Regulations 2007 (SSI 2007/34)

Chapter 1

The Long and Winding Road – a Brief History of Licensing Law in Scotland

1 WELCOME, TRAVELLER

Alcohol is a topic of considerable interest in Scotland. I welcome those who have taken the time to look at the opening chapter of this book as you are amongst those who would seek to fathom, and take some small pleasure in exploring, the history of licensing law in Scotland – a gritty yet rewarding journey, with both thorn and bloom. It snakes through *terra infirma* and *incognito*; it circles and devours itself even whilst finding bold new direction. We are not alone in our endeavour. The number of hardy travellers on our path in the first quarter of the twenty-first century shows no signs of diminishing and I hope this book may act as a guide and companion.

There is no doubt that alcohol has persisted as one of the most oft-exhorted topics in the Scottish Parliament, since it was reconvened in 1999. It is a topic which attracts colour and controversy, supporters and detractors. There are, it is suggested, three main factors in the discussion of the regulation of alcohol: (1) to control the extent to which the population consumes alcohol; (2) taxation; and (3) wider sociological and economic levers. Analysing much of this is, sadly, outwith the scope of this book and this introductory chapter does not purport to provide an in-depth sociological analysis of Scotland's relationship with alcohol either now or then, as much as I would like it to.

However, I do aim to enlighten as to the origin of the modern licensing laws of Scotland, as well as to their practical application. Whilst the key function of this book is (I hope) to provide practical insight, can one truly comprehend without that deeper history?

Licensing law has forever been a legislative patchwork quilt that has been ripped up, darned and knitted anew. It is of keen interest not just to the alcohol historian or policy maker but also to you, the licensing practitioners – that is, those who live and breathe the practice of licensing law itself – be you solicitors, paralegals, local authority administration workers, police officers, health officials, licensing standards officers or of course people who work and operate business within the licensed trade. Whilst I hope to help you understand the practical application of the law, please first accompany me down our mysterious path, which may yet lead us blinking and in awe, to the Licensing (Scotland) Act 2005.

2 THE EVOLUTION OF LICENSING LEGISLATION

The earliest recognisable legislation (in comparison with current regulation) for licensing in Scotland is probably the Home Drummond Act of 1828.[1] There have been licensing Acts in Scotland since the fifteenth century, and then notably in 1756[2] and 1808,[3] but it was the 1828 Act that introduced the idea of meetings (half yearly in those days) at which the licensing board members of their day, the justices, could grant certificates. The 1828 Act had transfer and appeal facilities, and justices could attach conditions to the certificates they issued. There were penalties for selling without a certificate and for a breach of conditions. Then came the Forbes Mackenzie Act in 1853,[4] which introduced the notion of having separate concepts like "public house" and "off-sale" licences as well as a terminal hour of 11pm, and robbed the unfortunate blacksmiths of Scotland of their historical ability to sell spirits from their smithy or residence.

Taxation was, of course, a key factor in these earlier legislative forays. The plain fact was (and is) that Scotland as a nation enjoyed buying and consuming alcohol, and without regulation the government was missing out on significant revenue when people chose to spend their earnings on moonshine and other illegal liquor. Bootlegging[5] was common and there were many shebeens[6] to be found across Scotland. Customs duty was introduced as far back as 1644, and the proceeds used to fund the English Civil War, and in 1713 a Scottish riot over malt duty was suppressed by English infantry.

Then there is the "social" control element; several reports in the nineteenth century pointed to the social problems caused by alcohol. The Enquiry into Drunkenness of 1834[7] was appointed to:

> "enquire into the extent, causes and consequences of the prevailing vice of intoxication among the labouring classes of the United Kingdom in order to ascertain whether any legislative means can be devised to prevent the further spread of so great a national evil."

Then came the Public Houses Report of 1852–53 in which it was found that one in twenty-two Glaswegians had been convicted of an offence relating to drunkenness (trumped only by Dublin with one in twenty-one) and that Glasgow had the least licensing regulation compared with other British cities. A multitude of other reports along this line were published in the late nineteenth century.[8]

1 Licensing (Scotland) Act 1828 (9 Geo IV c 58).
2 Alehouses Act 1756 (29 Geo II c 12).
3 48 Geo III c 143.
4 Licensing (Scotland) Act 1853 (16 & 17 Vict c 67).
5 The term "bootlegging" arises from North America. Bandits would attempt to cross the Mexican and Canadian borders into the US with liquor hidden in their boots, usually in hip flasks and similar receptacles.
6 A shebeen is an illicit drinking den. The term is often associated with Scotland and Ireland but is also used in South Africa and New Zealand.
7 Report from the Select Committee (1834) vol VIII, 455pp (Sessional no. 559).
8 Intoxication (Scotland) Report, Accounts and Papers (1858) vol XLVII, 6pp (Sessional no. 154); Habitual Drunkards Report (1872) vol IX, xxviii, 249pp (Sessional no. 242) (in this report, a certain Dr Alexander Peddie refuted the suggestion that the levels of drunkenness in Edinburgh could be attributed to the city's poor drinking water); The laws regulating the sale

State intervention was also used to alleviate the problems that the grain industry was experiencing. The government at the time was keen to increase the sales of grain, as it was a commodity Britain could produce in abundance. However, there was not a great market for it, so they relaxed the rules surrounding the production and sale of beer and the number of breweries increased substantially.[9] The infamous "Gin Alley" by Hogarth is one of the most enduring images of the antisocial effects of alcohol consumption – but the sketch was actually one of two, accompanied by another, often overlooked, sketch of "Beer Street", where life is a mite rosier. The parallel to be drawn here, somewhat ironically to twenty-first-century eyes in an age when "craft" gin and other spirits is at an apogee, is that gin consumption was depraved; but that beer consumption, which helped the grain industry at that time, was an entirely jovial pastime.

There were several other legislative changes after that[10] and the Forbes Mackenzie Act was drastically altered. But, then, a most significant change came with the passing of the Licensing (Scotland) Act 1903. The 1903 Act consolidated all the previous legislation, spread across numerous Acts of Parliament, and provided a host of new facilities, powers and offences which are more familiar in modern times, such as requiring layout plans for premises for which a licence was sought and the registration of clubs (which was borrowed from the equivalent English system), and some others which may now be considered antiquated, such as the right of a man to obtain separation from his wife should she be a "habitual drunkard", although not, it would seem, the other way around.

The 1903 Act really did not have much time to settle in before continental war was upon Europe and this gave rise to a number of changes to alcohol sale and supply as a result of wartime government. A Liquor Control Board was established with the onset of the Great War under the Defence of the Realm (Liquor Control) Regulations 1915, in order to control consumption and, amongst other measures, banned the practice of buying "rounds" (or "treating" as it was known then). State control was removed after the war in the Licensing Act 1921[11] (although it persisted, for political, defence and

and consumption of excisable liquors sold not for consumption on the premises in Scotland Report, Minutes of Evidence, Appendix and Index (1878) vol XXVI, xxvii, 563pp [C 1941]; Intemperance Report, Fourth report from the Select Committee of the House of Lords, Minutes of Evidence and Appendix (1878) vol XIV, iv, 691pp, maps (Sessional no. 338); Treatment of Inebriates Report from the Departmental Committee, Minutes of Evidence, Appendices and Index (1893) 1893–94, vol XVII, Report 9pp [C 7008].

9 According to the Scottish Beer and Pub Association, in 1841 there were 1,085 brewers and 498 maltsters registered in Scotland.

10 These included: (1) the Public Houses Acts Amendment Act 1862 (25 & 26 Vict c 35), which introduced the power of entry for police and the offences of "hawking" and of a person other than a traveller obtaining drink on a Sunday; (2) the Publicans' Certificates (Scotland) Act 1876 (39 & 40 Vict c 26), which, for the first time, borrowed some of the English licensing laws, discussed "table-beer" licences, and absolved the certificate holder from any need to personally appear at a meeting; (3) the Inland Revenue Act 1880 (43 & 44 Vict c 20), which stole the idea of a "six day" licence from English law; (4) the Public Houses, Hours of Closing (Scotland) Act 1887 (50 & 51 Vict c 38), which permitted the terminal hour to be reduced to 10pm except for certain cities; and finally, of some historical note, is (5) the Child Messenger Act 1901 (1 Edw VII c 27), which prohibited the sale of alcohol to children under the age of 14 "except in quantities not less than one reputed pint, and in corked and sealed vessels".

11 11 & 12 Geo V c 42.

social reasons, in certain key areas where there remained a significant military presence, such as in the Cromarty Firth and Gretna districts).

The 1920s and 30s saw the rise of the temperance movement, which, although it had existed in Scotland for some time, dating back decades, saw perhaps its largest triumphs with the eventual commencement of the Temperance Scotland Act 1913, the effect of which had been delayed by fighting on the continent. The 1913 Act allowed for a form of proto-overprovision, where local communities could vote directly on the numbers of licensed premises in their area. People could vote for "no change", meaning licensed premises would stay the same, "no licence", meaning closure of all licensed premises in that area, or for a reduction in numbers. A number of votes resulted in the creation of "dry" areas in certain parts of Scotland in 1920. Many publicans were given payments as compensation for losing their business.[12] A further round of voting occurred in 1927 when the number of dry areas fell.

Despite some further changes[13] and the Second World War, the next major development for legislative reform in the world of licensing was the establishment of two committees as the fifties turned to the sixties, the Guest Committee and the Clayson Committee.

The Guest Committee was appointed in 1959 and produced two reports: the first was in respect of Sunday trading and permitted hours, and led to the standardisation of opening hours throughout Scotland (including Sundays), extended hours where table meals were taken, and the creation of restaurant and restricted hotel licences, all introduced in the Licensing (Scotland) Act 1962. The second report was in relation to the function of the then licensing courts, but did not lead to any legislation.

This leads us to the report of Dr Christopher Clayson, which would go on to inspire the Licensing (Scotland) Act 1976, a statute which requires a more comprehensive analysis as we approach the 2005 Act.

3 INTRODUCTION OF THE LICENSING (SCOTLAND) ACT 1976

The Clayson Committee was established in 1971 and reported in 1973. It was in this report that the idea of balanced community involvement was explored, away from the polarised approach from the temperance years and, in turn, it spurred the administration of liquor licensing to be removed from the burgh licensing courts and placed in the hands of a body composed of local authority councillors – the licensing board. Not all of Clayson's recommendations were taken forward, but his report led to the passing of the 1976 Act[14] and for the first time in the United Kingdom placed the power in the hands of a local licensing "authority", the licensing board, as distinct from the local council authority.

12 Those payments continued in the form of pensions derived from investments until those individuals had perished, and thereafter were subsumed into temperance organisations.

13 The Intoxicating Liquor (Sale to Persons under Eighteen) Act 1923 (13 & 14 Geo V c 48), which established the rule for 16- and 17-year-olds consuming alcohol with a meal; New Towns Act 1952; Licensing (Seamen's Canteens) Act 1954; and Licensing (Scotland) Act 1959.

14 Dr Clayson CBE (1974) OBE (1966) passed away on 17 January 2005. His obituary was published at 29 SLLP 16, and as I recall was dictated by Sir Menzies Campbell, QC, over the phone to a certain tenderfoot paralegal working at R & JM Hill Brown & Co.

The 1976 Act homologated the patchwork of legislation that had gone before and created seven types of liquor licence: (1) public house; (2) hotel; (3) entertainment; (4) restaurant; (5) refreshment; (6) off-sale; and (7) restricted hotel. These licences were complemented by a number of other permissions such as regular extensions to the permitted hours; occasional extensions; table meal declarations (which allowed extensions on Sunday trading); children's certificates[15] and so on. The 1976 Act provided for licences to be suspended, to be transferred from one party to another, and for occasional licences and occasional permissions for special events on unlicensed premises.

The 1976 Act initially appeared to be well received. Research by the *British Medical Journal* in 1986 found that "the changes introduced since 1976 appeared to be popular as there was a widespread perception that public drunkenness had become common-place",[16] in reference to the seemingly successful liberalisation of the law. But, as with many aspects of life, the devil was in the detail, and the day-to-day workings of the 1976 legislation proved far from trouble-free. As the 1980s moved into the 90s and beyond, the Act was castigated by many as obscure and unnavigable.

4 THE PATH TO REFORM: MODERNISATION AND THE HEALTH AGENDA

A number of commentators were voluble in their diatribes against the operation of the 1976 Act, typified in the now ubiquitous words of Lord Clyde:

> "It does seem to me to be at least difficult to find a clear pattern or consistent philosophy in the legislation embodied in the Licensing Act."[17]

Jack Cummins, editor of *Scottish Licensing Law and Practice* and subsequently author of the *Licensing (Scotland) Act 2005 Greens Annotated Statutes*, wrote in 1993:

> "Nothing less than the meticulous construction of a completely new code of alcohol regulation will properly serve the interests of the public and operators of licensed premises."[18]

Perhaps two of the biggest concerns with the operation of the 1976 Act were the antiquated terminology[19] and the varying ways in which the Act was

15 Although children's certificates were not catered for in the original 1976 Act, they were a Clayson creation, and eventually were introduced by the Law Reform (Miscellaneous Provisions) (Scotland) Act 1990.

16 Br Med J (Clin Res Ed) 1986 Jan 4; 292(6512): 36–39. Interestingly, an article published later that year in the same journal did not appear to display the same positivity about the 1976 changes. Discussing the interplay between the liberalised laws and admissions for "self-poisoning" through alcohol abuse in West Fife, the authors said: "Analysis showed a dramatic increase in the frequency of alcohol taken in association with self-poisoning, in both sexes, after the liberalisation of Scotland's liquor licensing laws": Br Med J (Clin Res Ed) 1986 Dec 6; 293(6560): 1466–1468.

17 *Argyll Arms (McManus) Ltd v Lorn etc Divisional Licensing Board* 1988 SCLR 241 at 243.

18 J C Cummins, *Licensing Law in Scotland* (1993) Preface to the 1st edition.

19 Provisions regarding such things as seamen's canteens (Part III); orders for athletic clubs to have alternative licensed hours during winter in order to cater for outdoor sports (s 56); and exemptions for theatres erected prior to 1 January 1903 (s 138), whilst eminently evocative, perhaps served to disenfranchise many of the more modern users of the Act.

interpreted from board to board. From a board's point of view, the members simply applied and interpreted the Act as they saw fit, so long as the board acted *intra vires*. But for the private practitioner, police and licensed trade this meant coping with more than forty differing interpretations and confusion often abounded. Harmonisation was therefore seen as a holy grail.[20]

Modernising and updating the legislation was the primary spur that led to the 2005 Act. In fact, there had been numerous cries during the mid-1990s for change; in September 1997 the then Minister for Home Affairs, Henry McLeish, told the National Licensing Conference in Dundee that he was not aware that the 1976 Act had fallen into disrepute, but conceded that he was "not hostile" to change. Then, in May 1998 the English Home Office Minister George Howarth told a meeting of the BII (British Institute of Innkeeping) that the English liquor licensing laws were to be revamped.[21] It was clear that something was in the air.

In 1999 a number of licensing boards submitted a joint statement to Mr McLeish underlining the problematic aspects of the 1976 Act – looking for a level playing field, greater ease of applications and greater teeth for boards. Mr McLeish's response was lukewarm but indicated the matter could be looked at by the new Scottish Parliament.[22] Those boards then sent a booklet to each of the newly appointed MSPs.

Conservative MSP Keith Harding submitted a motion to the Scottish Parliament in 2000 seeking a review of the 1976 Act.

Perhaps the ultimate catalyst was, in fact, a series of proposals by Liberal Democrat MSP Donald Gorrie, who created a "shopping list" of ideas which he believed should be considered by a "Clayson style" commission, which he originally released in October 2000.[23] Many of these proposals went on to feature in the 2005 Act.

Up to this point, the focus of these pleadings had been modernisation. It was, however, probably the health agenda that finally got things moving as "Binge Britain" was very much in the headlines. One of the first tasks of the new Scottish Parliament was to agree on a national framework for dealing with alcohol abuse, so the calls in 1999 by Scottish licensing boards to review the law fell directly into the Parliamentary lap of those seeking to have Parliament take action on alcohol abuse.

Donald Gorrie lodged a motion, which was debated by the Scottish Parliament on 9 November 2000, in the following terms:

20 This was not a universally held view. Phyllis Wilson, then Clerk to the Motherwell District Licensing Board, said in an article in 1995, "Idiosyncrasies are not developed by clerks or boards without reasons", and blamed the failings in the Act itself as the reason why differing approaches arose: [1995] 1 SLLP 19.

21 England, of course, later saw the introduction of the Licensing Act 2003.

22 "Boards press McLeish for 'urgent action' on licensing law reform" [1999] 12 SLLP 3.

23 Gorrie's "shopping list", as it was, makes for interesting reading now that the 2005 Act has come to fruition. His sixteen proposals included: immediate suspension notwithstanding any appeal; a broadening of the categories of objectors; publication of licensing board policy statements; annual fees; the training of board members; and bringing clubs into the licensing mainstream. For the full "shopping list", see "MSP calls for immediate suspension powers" [2000] 17 SLLP 3.

> "That the Parliament agrees that everything possible should be done to ensure that alcohol abuse and the issues of health and violence arising from it receive greater attention, and urges the Executive to promote civilised social drinking and to reduce excessive and underage drinking through any means available, including administrative action, publicity, education and legislation."

During the debate he said:

> "Either the Executive – or, if it has the resources, the Parliament – should set up a new, Clayson-type commission. That inquiry was so long ago that our press officer could not even spell his name right, as he had never heard of him. In the 1970s, the Clayson commission did really good work and helped reform the Scottish licensing laws. We need a new look at the problem now; there are many aspects to it and life has moved on over the past 30 years. We need a new Clayson-type commission . . . I believe in the need for a member's bill. Following considerable research, I gave Jim Wallace a preliminary shopping list of 16 issues that could be included in a bill. I have spoken to people with opinions on all aspects of the licensing of alcohol and I have found a great deal of agreement. I would be happy to co-operate with other people who I know have great interest in the subject and who come at it from different angles. They will be able to voice other useful ideas. We can draw up a member's bill that commands a great deal of consensual support in the Parliament and among all the organisations that have to deal with matters of licensing and alcohol. It would make some important changes while longer-term consideration was being undertaken by the Clayson-type commission."

By pressing for his Member's Bill, Mr Gorrie alerted the then Executive to take some action and it seemed he was pushing at an open door. Minister Malcolm Chisholm, in responding to the Gorrie motion, said:

> "Liquor licensing and the Licensing (Scotland) Act 1976 is a complex area on which people have widely differing views. People argue for different strategies only to arrive at the same conclusions. A great deal of work must be done on that area, but we accept the need to consider a review of licensing within the context of developing our national alcohol misuse strategy."

The liquor licensing laws for Scotland were therefore a topic that the new Scottish Parliament could really get its teeth into and consolidate a number of related workstreams, and this was moved forward quickly. The first suggestion by the Executive that licensing laws in Scotland would be formally reviewed by the new Scottish Parliament came only next month, on 7 December 2000. During Parliamentary debate that day, Minister Malcolm Chisholm announced:

> "There is strong support for an overhaul of current licensing law. Licensing laws have generally stood the test of time and are not systematically failing. Nevertheless, we have looked carefully at all the arguments. I am pleased to announce that we have decided that the time has come for a comprehensive review of licensing laws. An independent committee with a fairly wide-ranging remit will conduct the review. Full details of the membership of the committee and how the review will be conducted will be announced in due course."

The responses to this announcement from a wide variety of MSPs in the debate indicate that the context for this review was not simply modernisation, but wider public health concerns. Donald Gorrie had this to say at this debate:

"In the short term, my research and the polls that have been carried out by a magazine[24] that circulates among people who deal with licensing – as well as what has been said in this debate and in the recent members' business debate on alcohol – show a consensus on a number of points, which could rapidly be incorporated into a bill and which would offer a quick improvement to our whole attitude to alcohol. It is important that we pursue that; we could show that we are in earnest by having a bill dealing with alcohol as soon as possible. There is a lot of support for that among all parts of the licensed trade, lawyers, licensing people and the groups involved in trying to reduce the amount of alcohol that is consumed."

The matter continued to be debated behind closed doors until the fateful day of 28 June 2001, when the then Minister for Justice, Jim Wallace, announced that a committee was to prepare a report, under the stewardship of Sheriff Principal Gordon Nicholson CBE QC. The committee was to review liquor licensing "with particular reference to the implications for health and public order". According to the *Regulatory Impact Assessment for the Licensing (Scotland) Bill*:

"the Nicholson Committee received over 200 written submissions and held 8 days of oral evidence sessions with representatives from 23 organisations. Publication of the report was followed by a period of public consultation on its 90 recommendations which attracted over 160 responses".

Not content with this driving force behind the ultimate report, the government then announced a second, short-life committee[25] to look specifically at the regulation of off-sales, the impact of alcohol on communities and antisocial behaviour. By this time, the devolved Scottish Administration was in full swing and when it came to fresh legislation, the Scottish Executive (as it was then) was revelling in the novelty of passing Scottish Acts. In due course, both the Nicholson and Daniels Reports were issued and promulgated amongst stakeholders and those with an interest.

Eventually, the Scottish Executive issued a White Paper that was put out for consultation, and the Licensing (Scotland) Bill was prepared and published. The Bill was debated by the Executive through a series of committees and votes (some more controversial than others[26]). During this time, the first iteration of a "National Licensing Forum" was mooted (a body which has since been attempted and abandoned on multiple occasions – see Chapter 5 below), following a proposal from Nicholson, in order to guide the Executive – although their proposals did not appear to be acted on – and the Forum was eventually dissolved.[27]

Meanwhile, *vox academia* from the discipline of public health was heard loudly via advocates within the Scottish Parliament, and this narrative certainly influenced the terms of the new Act (and its subsequent regulations), and with

24 The august *Scottish Licensing Law and Practice*, of course, edited by Jack Cummins. SLLP stopped appearing as a published magazine around 2012 but the conferences and website (www.sllp.co.uk) live on.

25 The Daniels Committee headed up by Peter Daniels, the then Chief Executive of Renfrewshire Council.

26 See, e.g., "Off-sales hours slashed as last-minute amendments tarnish final Bill debate" [2005] 32 SLLP 1.

27 See http://www.scotland.gov.uk/Topics/Justice/Licensing/Alcohol-licensing/NationalForum. Nicholson had not envisaged the National Licensing Forum to be a "short life" committee: see Chapter 10 of the Report of the Nicholson Committee (2003).

such alleged "novel" considerations as wider community involvement (notwithstanding this had been introduced by Clayson) and a greater emphasis on overprovision (notwithstanding the now antique temperance legislation and the existence of overprovision in the 1976 Act). It suited some to hail these as an innovative and progressive approach to the regulation of the sale of alcohol in a more modern time. Of course, there was nothing especially new in any of this for those who had pondered the history of licensing regulation in Scotland, as the wheel turned and cycle of trends and patterns in regulating the sale of alcohol was about to reinvent itself again.

5 THE LICENSING (SCOTLAND) ACT 2005

All of this finally leads to the introduction of the Licensing (Scotland) Act 2005. The 2005 Act fundamentally altered the scope of regulation in Scotland; gone were the seven types of licence, replaced with one supposedly generic, catch-all, licence referred to as a premises licence, alongside the creation of a separate personal licence for individuals working in the licensed trade, whilst retaining the occasional licence introduced by the 1976 Act. Licensing boards were also retained but complemented by licensing forums and new specialist officers called Licensing Standards Officers. Underpinning the whole system was the creation of five licensing objectives, which set the stall and indicated the purpose of the entire Act.

The licensing objectives (as amended) are laid down in section 4 of the 2005 Act and are:

- Preventing crime and disorder
- Securing public safety
- Preventing public nuisance
- Protecting and improving public health
- Protecting children and young persons from harm.

These objectives mirror those implemented in the English Licensing Act 2003,[28] minus the reference to young persons (which was only added to the Scottish system by the Air Weapons and Licensing (Scotland) Act 2015) and of course the public health objective, which was a Scottish creation. In fact, a number of aspects of the 2005 Act appeared to mirror the 2003 Act – which was an unhappy development for some contemporary commentators, who argued that elements of the English provisions should not take root in Scottish soil.

One might look first at the Regulatory Impact Assessment (RIA) which accompanied the Licensing (Scotland) Bill, which was published on 30 March 2005. The RIA says the purpose of the Bill is to:

> "To modernise the present licensing regime for the sale of alcohol. Offering a balanced package which reflects the needs of individuals, communities, business and consumers, underlined by a consistent philosophy provided through the licensing objectives".[29]

28 For an expansive guide to English licensing laws after conversion, see Philip Kolvin QC, *Licensed Premises: Law and Practice* (Tottel Publishing, 2005).

29 RIA, Licensing (Scotland) Bill, March 2005: para 1.

It also acknowledges the modernisation element of the proposal:

> "Failure to modernise in this area could inhibit the development of the hospitality, late night refreshment and leisure industries, hindering their attempts to diversify and to become more attractive to families, tourists and to children. Diversification is also important to rural life where village pubs are often the social hub of the area, and more will close if they are unable to use the premises for a wide range of purposes."[30]

The Policy memorandum to the original Licensing Bill is also instructive and sets the stall for the key aims of the legislation:

> "There are four key issues that underline the approach the Executive has taken in proposing the new licensing system for Scotland. They are: reducing underage drinking, reducing binge drinking, providing a voice for communities, and modernisation. Specifically the Bill aims to:
> - simplify and modernise the existing legislation (the Licensing (Scotland) Act 1976 as amended);
> - balance the rights of the majority of people who drink responsibly against the need to protect local communities from nuisance and crime associated with misuse of alcohol;
> - provide strong monitoring and enforcement powers;
> - establish a more inclusive system for all those with an interest;
> - support responsible members of the licensed trade; and
> - allow local flexibility balanced with consistency of decision making."

The Parliamentary history of the Act, along with some excerpts from the principal debate on 22 June 2005, is found at Appendix A.

6 NEVER-ENDING REFORM

The Licensing (Scotland) Act 2005 was given Royal Assent on 21 December 2005. Practitioners expected a slew of secondary legislation to fill out the various gaps, but I doubt anyone could have foreseen the sheer volume of instruments, orders, regulations, reports, reviews, new primary legislation, further secondary legislation to fill out the new primary legislation, more reports, regulations amending previous regulations, regulations amending errors in previous regulations, emergency regulations for issues which had not been thought of, guidance and sundry information which emanates from the 2005 Act in one form or other.

To be blunt, the 2005 Act (as amended) has been an excellent example of how not to legislate. Any reasonable person who peruses Appendices A and B can reach but one conclusion: that the current Scottish alcohol licensing law, even as comparative youngling, is a nebulous and tortuous maze. It is difficult to accept that a sensible, responsible licensee can understand the extent of law which underpins their business, or an experienced police officer or licensing standards officer enforce it, when it is virtually impossible for even specialist licensing solicitors to locate, penetrate, fathom, tie together and comprehend the law.

If there is one piece of legislation which the Scottish Parliament badly

30 Ibid para 9.

needs to scrutinise, not through its policy or aims, but through its construction and delivery (or non-delivery) of that policy and those aims, it is the Licensing (Scotland) Act 2005. The root of this sits at the feet of a number of characters, such as those who would espouse reactionary politics, as well as an unfortunate serial unwillingness over long periods to listen to those who have painstakingly highlighted the practical and technical issues with the Act, and the need by successive Governments to be seen to do something about problematic alcohol consumption in Scotland, thus sacrificing the quality of legislation that this area so badly deserves for ill-fated haste.

It is depressing to appreciate that, whilst commendably seeking to deal with the harms which arise from the irresponsible sale or consumption of alcohol, our Parliament has, on so many occasions it has legislated in this field, given us bad law.

In 2019 and 2020 there were calls for a full consolidatory Act as well as post-legislative scrutiny, although all that fell by the wayside (along with much of normal life) with the onset of the Coronavirus pandemic, and yet further amendments to the 2005 Act, which were occasioned as a result of the crisis, in the Coronavirus (Scotland) Act 2020.[31] We shall have to wait to see how the wheel turns again, as it no doubt will,[32] but for those looking to explore a full timeline of the various amendments to the 2005 Act, and all secondary legislation pertaining thereto, you will find a detailed and comprehensive list at Appendix B.

31 For the purposes of this book, and my own sanity, I have decided to deal with the 2020 Act amendments in a vacuum, given the statutory shelf-life of those amendments; and the fact that by the time the book is in your hands, these changes will have likely reverted. The 2020 Act amendments are detailed at Appendix I.

32 "Ka was a wheel; its one purpose is to turn" (Stephen King, *The Wastelands*, first published 1991 by Grant).

Chapter 2

The Licence Requirement

1 WHEN IS A LICENCE NEEDED AT ALL?

Prior to turning our gaze towards the intricacies of the 2005 Act, it would also be useful to provide an analysis of the licence requirement itself. What I mean by that is to discuss when a licence might be needed at all – a question which is perhaps more complex than might first appear. At its most basic, the entire purpose of the 2005 Act is to create a structure within which alcohol can be sold and consumed legally. It does so by creating a general criminal offence in section 1(1) of sale of alcohol without a premises licence or occasional licence. This licence requirement does not apply to exempt premises or where the sale is sale of alcohol to trade. The law surrounding exempt premises, and what is meant by selling alcohol to trade, is examined in Chapter 11, at Sections 6 and 8 respectively.

So far so good, one would hope. But outside of these concepts there are some underlying key definitions which need to be explained. The first of these is what is meant by "alcohol" itself, before considering definitions of what might constitute a licensable sale or supply of alcohol, or to be more accurate, what might not constitute such a sale or supply.

2 WHAT IS ALCOHOL FOR THE PURPOSES OF LICENSING LAW?

Alcohol is a common term in everyday use, but it has a clear definition for the purpose of licensing law and not all forms of alcohol, or products with an alcoholic content, are actually treated as alcohol under the 2005 Act and therefore no licence is needed to sell those exempted products. Alcohol for the purposes of the 2005 Act is defined in detail at section 2(1) as follows:

> "In this Act, 'alcohol'—
> (a) means spirits, wine, beer, cider or any other fermented, distilled or spirituous liquor, but
> (b) does not include—
> (i) alcohol which is of a strength of 0.5% or less at the time of its sale,
> (ii) perfume,
> (iii) any flavouring essence recognised by the Commissioners of Customs and Excise as not being intended for consumption as or with dutiable alcoholic liquor, [...]
> (v) alcohol which is, or is included in, a medicinal product,
> (vi) denatured alcohol,

(vii) methyl alcohol,
(viii) naphtha, or
(ix) alcohol contained in liqueur confectionery."

Note the absence of a (iv) in the above list – this now deleted entry previously related to angostura bitters which, at the time of commencement of the 2005 Act, was also included as a product outwith the scope of the licensing definition of alcohol. This was reversed in section 54 of the Air Weapons and Licensing (Scotland) Act 2015 as of 15 May 2017.[1] In the absence of any particular licensing desire, one way or other, to have bitters covered by the 2005 Act, it appears that the product was re-classified for duty-related reasons.

The Act goes on to appropriate definitions for "beer", "cider" and "wine" from the Alcoholic Liquor Duties Act 1979, which are as follows:

- "Beer" includes ale, porter, stout and any other description of beer, and any liquor which is made or sold as a description of beer or as a substitute for beer and which is of a strength exceeding 0.5 per cent, but does not include black beer the worts whereof before fermentation were of a specific gravity of 1200° or more.
- "Wine" means any liquor which is of a strength exceeding 1.2 per cent and which is obtained from the alcoholic fermentation of fresh grapes or of the must of fresh grapes, whether or not the liquor is fortified with spirits or flavoured with aromatic extracts.
- "Cider" means cider (or perry) of a strength exceeding 1.2 per cent but less than 8.5 per cent obtained from the fermentation of apple or pear juice without the addition at any time of any alcoholic liquor or of any liquor or substance which communicates colour or flavour other than such as the Commissioners may allow as appearing to them to be necessary to make cider (or perry).

It should also be noted that, as far as trial proceedings for certain offences under the Act are concerned, the contents of containers which bear a description purporting that the liquid therein is alcoholic, shall be taken as said alcohol.[2] This rule even applies where the container is empty, or almost empty to the point that an anlaysis of the contents is not possible. The presumption may be rebutted at trial.[3]

2.1 "Alcohol free" products

It is common to see training materials and other alcohol-related guidance documents which discuss "alcohol free" and "low alcohol" products. The 2005 Act does not provide any definition of "alcohol free" or "low alcohol". As far as Scottish licensing law is concerned, the position is that a product is either alcohol, or it is not; and in relation to the ABV the activation point is 0.5%. In other words, a product is licensable if it is above 0.5%, and is not licensable if it is at or below that point. Separate understandings of what might be meant by "alcohol free" or "low alcohol" are therefore irrelevant as far as Scottish licensing law is concerned, but do require some context given their prevalence in the market.

1 As repealed under the Air Weapons and Licensing (Scotland) Act 2015 (Commencement No. 6 and Saving Provisions) Order 2017 (SSI 2017/119) art 2.
2 2005 Act, s 140.
3 Ibid s 140(4) – although if seeking to do so, the party must give at least seven days' notice of their intention to do so (s 140(5)).

The descriptor "alcohol free" typically relates to a product which is 0.05% or less, and the descriptor "low alcohol" typically relates to a product which is 1.2% or less. These two expressions originally emanate from the Food Labelling Regulations 1996.[4] Schedule 8 to the 1996 Regulations, which deals with "Misleading Descriptions", had the following to say:

> The description "alcohol-free". Shall not be applied to any alcoholic drink from which the alcohol has been extracted, unless—
> (a) the drink has an alcoholic strength by volume of not more than 0.05 per cent, and
> (b) the drink is marked or labelled with an indication of its maximum alcoholic strength (in one of the forms specified in regulation 30(1) immediately preceded by the words "not more than") or, in an appropriate case, with an indication that it contains no alcohol.
>
> The description "low alcohol" or any other word or description which implies that the drink being described is low in alcohol. Shall not be applied to any alcoholic drink unless—
> (a) the drink has an alcoholic strength by volume of not more than 1.2 per cent, and
> (b) the drink is marked or labelled with an indication of its maximum alcoholic strength (in one of the forms specified in regulation 30(1) immediately preceded by the words "not more than").

The 1996 Regulations were revoked as of 13 December 2018[5] leaving Westminster to pick up the pieces in England and Wales, and the Scottish Government to sort out what would be done north of the border. In England and Wales the Westminster Government launched a consultation[6] as to whether they should legislate to keep these terms, or continue on a "guidance only" basis, and the outcome of this was to deregulate and proceed on the basis of guidance. The guidance – called the Low Alcohol Descriptors Guidance – was published as of 13 December 2018 but it must again be noted that this applies to England and Wales only. The descriptors adopted in the guidance are as follows:

- Low alcohol – the drink must be 1.2% alcohol by volume (ABV) or below and an indication of its maximum ABV should be included on the label.
- Alcohol free – this should only be applied to a drink from which the alcohol has been extracted if it contains no more than 0.05% ABV, and the products should also include the ABV (or state that they contain no alcohol) on the label in order to use the descriptor.

The Scottish position is that the 1996 Regulations were also repealed as of 13 December 2018 but without an alternative put in place. This issue was recognised in the Scottish Government Alcohol Framework 2018.[7] A consultation about what to do with the descriptors was run by Food Standards Scotland and this closed in November 2018. Amongst other matters, the consultation said:

> "The popularity and sales of low and non-alcoholic drinks in the UK is on the rise with a 20.5% increase in sales over the 12 months to July 2017. The market and product range is diversifying: beers, lagers, stouts, wines and even some mixed

4 SI 1996/1499.
5 By virtue of the Food Information Regulations 2014 (SI 2014/1855).
6 "Local Alcohol Descriptors", Department of Health and Social Care, March 2018.
7 Scottish Government Alcohol Framework 2018, published 20 November 2018: see paras 101–3.

> spirits are available, with some retailers dedicating shop aisles in supermarkets to stock such products. Organisations such as Club Soda (a mindful drinking forum) are helping to educate the public and retailers to promote non-alcoholic alternatives. Figures provided to FSS by NHS Health Scotland have shown that overall Scottish sales of low alcohol and non-alcoholic beers have increased by 14% in the period 2009–2016.
>
> Low alcohol products may have fewer calories than regular strength alcoholic drinks and could help reduce calorie intake as part of a healthy diet. The switch to lower and non-alcoholic beverages may have a positive effect in helping achieve public health gains in reducing UK alcohol consumption and help support people to move towards drinking less than 14 units a week as outlined in the UK Chief Medical Officer's low risk drinking guidelines published in 2016. Since December 2014, the legal drink-drive alcohol limit in Scotland has been lower than in the other countries of the UK. This may be an additional reason to retain the alcohol descriptors for beverages less than 1.2% ABV."

Despite this excerpt recognising the clear and growing consumer interest in such products, no measures have been put forward or put in place since the consultation closed, meaning the terms have no legal or even quasi-legal status at all in Scotland. The FSS website simply says:

> "No decisions have been taken but in the meantime we recommend that businesses use the terms contained in regulations 42 and 43 and Schedule 8 of the Food Labelling Regulations (FLR) 1996 (as amended)."

The relationship between these descriptors and the 2005 Act is therefore perfunctory at best; they are simply matters which licence holders need to be aware of in the labelling or advertising of products that it is suggested they should have regard to; and there is certainly no licensing breach committed if the descriptors used on products are missing or erroneous in some way. It is difficult to see what penalty, if any, might exist in regulatory law terms given the absence of both regulation and even of guidance, whilst the matter remains outstanding.

The key element of considering "alcohol free" products in the world of licensing comes down purely to whether they are alcohol for the purposes of the Act or not. If a product is 0.5% or less, no licence is needed to sell it. Notwithstanding this, I am aware of the practice in some retailers that alcohol branded products which are 0.5% or less will still activate the age verification checks on tills and so on. To be clear, there is no age verification required under law as regards a product which is 0.5% or less, but one can go further and confirm that the licensing laws simply do not apply to such products at all. In other words, products with an ABV of 0.5% or under can be sold without a licence, at any time, to any person, and displayed in any location. If a retailer chooses to restrict these products, that may be as a result of confusion, but the matter is one for them to take a view on and maintain a policy if they wish.

2.2 Alcohol food products

Food or other non-liquid products that contain alcohol are not alcohol for the purposes of the 2005 Act. Examples might include brandy butter, rum-raisin cakes or Irish cream-liqueur ice cream, frozen cocktails,[8] flavoured condiments like a bourbon BBQ sauce, or even gin-infused jams or Jarl-infused marmalade.

8 That is, an ice-lolly style product designed to be eaten in a frozen state.

There is no doubt that alcohol is a constituent part of the product and in some cases there might even be an ABV displayed. However, these types of products are not, in my view, alcohol for the purposes of licensing law.

The licensing laws are designed to apply to free-flowing liquid products that are designed to be drunk. Alcohol that is part of a food-based product that is in a solid or semi-solid state does not require a licence to sell and no part of the 2005 Act applies to such products. It is then a matter for individual retailers to take a decision about whether they wish to adopt age verification processes, but if they do, that is a matter for the retailer and their own internal policies. If a retailer does wish to adopt such restrictions, then key messaging to customers is sensible to prevent any confusion and embarrassment at the tills.

2.3 Liqueur confectionery

As is made clear at section 2(1)(ix) of the Act, liqueur confectionery is not alcohol for the purposes of licensing law – meaning you don't need a licence to sell it, there is no control over where it can be displayed and there are no other licensing controls (such as bans on promotions and so on) which apply to it. Liqueur confectionery is defined at section 147(1) of the Act as follows:

> " 'liqueur confectionery' means confectionery which—
> (a) contains alcohol in a proportion not greater than 0.2 litres of alcohol (of a strength not exceeding 57%) per kilogramme of the confectionery, and
> (b) either consists of separate pieces weighing not more than 50 grammes or is designed to be broken into such pieces for the purposes of consumption."

However, the Act does impose one special rule about liqueur confectionery and that is it is illegal to sell it to a child (someone aged 15 or below). In other words, it is lawful to sell these products to persons aged 16 years and above. The usual rules about age verification and due diligence then apply.

3 WHAT IS A SALE OR SUPPLY OF ALCOHOL FOR THE PURPOSES OF LICENSING LAW?

Section 147(1) contains the following definition of "sell":

> " 'sell', in relation to alcohol, includes barter and expose to or offer for sale, and related expressions such as 'sale' are to be construed accordingly".

So the sale of alcohol includes not just the ordinarily understood meaning of sale in that it is a form of exchange for money (or money's worth); it also includes barter and, crucially, the offer to sell.[9] So if alcohol is merely offered for sale, that is still classed as a sale even if no sale has actually taken place.

In relation to "supply" of alcohol, section 3 of the 2005 Act says:

> **"3 Certain supplies of alcohol to be treated as sales**
> (1) A supply of alcohol which is not otherwise a sale of the alcohol is, in the circumstances described in subsection (2) or (3), to be treated for the purposes of this Act as if it were a sale of the alcohol.

9 It is also likely to include a "sale" to a test purchaser: see *Wm Morrison Supermarkets PLC v Reading Borough Council*, 9 February 2012 (as reported at [2012] 51 SLLP 6).

(2) The first set of circumstances is where the supply is by or on behalf of a club to, or to the order of, a member of the club.
(3) The second set of circumstances is where the supply is made to, or to the order of, a person pursuant to a right acquired by the person under a contract."

I deal with section 3(2) in relation to clubs in Chapter 11 at Section 2. The purpose of section 3(3) is to deal with what happens when alcohol is supplied as part of a wider contract and where the contract is not a "direct" purchase of alcohol for money or money's worth. The provision exists to ensure that such supplies are caught by the licensing law and that such supplies are treated as sales. It is worth exploring this further by way of example.

- **Alcohol free of charge**: If alcohol is provided free of charge, then there is no licence requirement. A famous case here is that of *Macdonald v Skinner*[10] in which an operator decided to give out free drink to customers, having lost his licence. There was no evidence of any hidden payment for the drink and therefore no licensing offence had occurred.
- **Bring your own bottle**: If premises allow alcohol to be brought by customers and consumed by them, then there is no licence requirement. The addition of a corkage fee does not activate the licence requirement. In this case, the premises have not supplied the alcohol at all, but are supplying other services such as glassware, ice and so on, which is what the corkage relates to.
- **Alcohol by donation**: If, at a charity event, there is a provision of alcohol which is not paid for *per se*, but is left open to people to make a donation of their choosing, this would not necessarily activate the licence requirement. However, the arrangement would need to be carefully worded. If it is left for people to obtain alcohol and a donation is encouraged but not mandatory, then in my view it is arguable that section 3(3) is not engaged as no contract is formed. This assumes, of course, that no contract is in place in terms of the wider event. This example might also be reflected in the practice of an "honesty bar", although, in the charity event example, the alcohol is not the primary purpose of attendance whereas an "honesty bar" existing of its own accord, adjunct to some other free-to-attend occurrence, may be a less attractive argument to make under section 3(3).
- **Alcohol ancillary to a paid-for event or activity**: If alcohol is provided as part of an event or activity, where one has paid in order to participate, then section 3(3) would be activated and therefore a licence would be required. If I pay for a ticket for a brewery tour, and I am given beer as part of the tour, this would be a classic section 3(3) example, even if the beer is labelled as a free sample. The quantity is irrelevant, even a "tasting" of small measures of different beers or spirits would be caught. It is not free even if labelled as such; for you have only been able to access it by buying a ticket for the tour. Other examples might be the hire of a vehicle such as a party bus or hen-party limousine, where alcohol is provided as part of the service. Alcohol is clearly being supplied pursuant to a contract, so section 3(3) is activated and a licence would be required. This rule applies regardless of

10 1979 JC 29.

whether the alcohol is described as free, or where the specific price of the alcohol might not be clear.[11]

- **Alcohol paid for in advance and then "re-sold"**: I have come across examples where a company will have ordered a stock of alcohol, say for an office party, and will run a cash bar, which may make a profit or a loss – in other words, the cost is subsidised to some extent. The stock has been bought from a licensed retailer so that separate sale is clearly covered. But what of the "subsidised" sale by the company to its staff at the office party? That is clearly another sale. Profit or loss is irrelevant. If a company sells its employees alcohol, that is a sale of alcohol and would require a licence.
- **Free alcohol on licensed premises**: What of the free glass of prosecco, e.g. on arrival at a celebration such as a family party? First of all, in many cases it is likely that the "reception drinks" have been paid for as part of a wider package. As the premises are licensed, the real issue here is whether the provision of any free alcohol might be in breach of the licence, especially the mandatory conditions in relation to irresponsible conditions. These are explored in detail in Chapter 8 at Section 2.1.9.

11 This is a long-established rule: see *Scott & Co v Solomon* [1905] 1 KB 577; *Taylor v Smetten* (1883) 11 QBD 207; and *Doak v Bedford* [1964] 2 QB 587.

Chapter 3

The Licensing Objectives

1 ORIGIN OF THE LICENSING OBJECTIVES

Underpinning the whole licensing system are five licensing objectives, which collectively are the prism through which one must view the purpose of the 2005 Act, and represent the five foundations on which the licensing law is built (a "clear pattern and unifying philosophy", perhaps). The licensing objectives are laid down in section 4 of the 2005 Act and are:

- Preventing crime and disorder
- Securing public safety
- Preventing public nuisance
- Protecting and improving public health
- Protecting children and young persons from harm.

These objectives (save the public health objective) are almost identical to those implemented in the Licensing Act 2003 which covers England and Wales, and which was going through its own transitional process around the same time that the Nicholson Committee was meeting to discuss Scottish reform. So from where did the 2003 Act obtain its own objectives?

The 2003 Act was sparked by the publication on 10 April 2000 of the *Time for Reform* White Paper by the Home Office. One of the key threads in the paper was the recognition that the English licensing laws were burdensome, complex, and in some cases "obscure and deeply confusing".[1] The White Paper tackles this head on by saying:

> "The Purposes of the current arrangements for licensing leisure and entertainment outlets are not expressly stated in the legislation: this is itself a drawback. They should, we think, be judged against the following main objectives:
> (Alcohol)
> - Protecting the public from crime or disorder
> - Protecting children from too early an exposure to alcohol
> - Preventing public nuisance and disturbance to the public
>
> (Public entertainment (including theatres and cinemas))
> - Protecting the public and minimising nuisance as above
> - Assuring public safety (because events can attract large numbers of people)."[2]

The separate references to alcohol and entertainment stem from the separate English licensing regimes which the White Paper sought to bring together, but one can clearly see the etymology of the 2003 Act licensing objectives and in

1 So sayeth the then Home Secretary Jack Straw, in his Foreword to the White Paper.
2 *Time for Reform* (2000) p 6.

turn the five Scottish licensing objectives with regard to the wording used here. The Licensing Act 2003 objectives were ultimately prescribed under section 4(2) of that Act as follows:

(a) the prevention of crime and disorder;
(b) public safety;
(c) the prevention of public nuisance; and
(d) the protection of children from harm.

Again one can see the clear resemblance to four of the five Scottish objectives here.

The use of an overarching set of licensing objectives within a UK licensing regime was fortified with the publication of the Budd Report on gambling in the UK in 2001, the year after publication of *Time for Reform*.[3] Although neither the term "objective" nor "principle" is used in the body of the Budd Report, in his introduction Sir Alan Budd refers to a note he circulated to his Committee members as his "dream", which said: "I hope we shall be able to establish principles which are acceptable to all sensible people and shall make proposals consistent with those principles". There can be no doubt Sir Alan Budd was aware of the *Time for Reform* White Paper and it is, of course, referred to in the report itself. The Budd Report, very early on, makes clear that all of its recommendations seek to ensure that three main aims are met:

- permitted forms of gambling are crime-free, conducted in accordance with regulation and honest
- players know what to expect, are confident they will get it and are not exploited
- there is protection for children and vulnerable persons.

The UK Government response to this, the 2002 White Paper *A Safe Bet for Success*, is the second time we see a specific Government reference to "licensing objectives", with the three aims above endorsed. The paper says: "These objectives are not new, but the current law provides only an approximate fit with them".[4] Again, we see a real willingness to create a concise list to summarise the central philosophy of what regulation, in this case gambling regulation, is designed to achieve.

The reader is left with no doubt about the import of the gambling objectives when section 1 of the Gambling Act 2005 steams ahead by proclaiming:

> "In this Act a reference to the licensing objectives is a reference to the objectives of—
> (a) preventing gambling from being a source of crime or disorder, being associated with crime or disorder or being used to support crime,
> (b) ensuring that gambling is conducted in a fair and open way, and
> (c) protecting children and other vulnerable persons from being harmed or exploited by gambling."

The specific wording chosen by the Parliamentary draftsmen has altered some from the Budd versions of these objectives, but the thrust is of course the same.

3 Sir Alan Budd, *Gambling Review Report* (Cm 5206, 2001).
4 *A Safe Bet for Success* (Cm 5397, 2002) para 1.10, p 4.

Although the Licensing Act 2003 and Gambling Act 2005 objectives are not on all fours with the 2005 Act objectives, it is perhaps no great contention to suggest that their underlying philosophy or utility was informed by the lessons of the 2003 Act and Gambling Act to endeavour to have Scottish alcohol licensing achieve clarity, transparency and simplicity in what had been historically a very complex area of law.

The 2005 Act licensing objectives can be traced back to the Nicholson Report. Nicholson, in conducting his report, identified a number of principles to which he tasked his Committee. One of these was:

> "Any restrictions imposed by law should be those which are necessary in order to promote public health, public order and safety, a nuisance-free environment, and the protection of children from harm."[5]

It takes no leap of imagination to see the immediate comparison between this founding principle of the Committee, and the eventual objectives of the 2005 Act, and it is clear that the Committee was well aware of the English licensing objectives.

After listing various other principles to which the Committee was to have regard (such as "Legislation should be framed in a way which will make it possible for young people to be introduced to licensed premises in a responsible and supervised manner"), Nicholson goes on to say:

> "We then go on to propose that in future certain of the foregoing principles should be enshrined in statute, and that the promotion of those principles should determine the approach of licensing boards and others to all matters arising under licensing law. The 'licensing principles' which we propose are: the prevention of crime or disorder; the promotion of public safety; the prevention of public nuisance; the promotion of public health; and the protection of children from harm."

Note in particular that the "promotion of public health" ultimately translated to the much wider "Protecting and Improving Public Health" when it reached the statute book.

This first reference to the licensing principles is followed by no less than sixty-seven further occasions when the term is referred to; such as with regard to policy statements, refusal of applications and so on. It is clear that Nicholson saw his principles as the central pillars of the proposed new licensing system in Scotland.

The Explanatory Notes to the 2005 Act underline the importance of what became the licensing "objectives" after they were enshrined in statute:

> "This section [s 4] establishes 5 high level 'licensing objectives' that represent the values on which the Scottish licensing system would be based, the parameters against which everyone would measure the elements of that system and the solid foundation which local authority Licensing Boards must have regard to in carrying out their functions under the Act."

If one peruses the Guidance to Licensing Boards[6] further wisdom is apparent. Paragraphs 1 to 4 state:

> "1. The Act complements the wider policies of the Scottish Executive. This includes measures to tackle antisocial behaviour, and the programme of work set out in the

5 Nicholson Report, p 2.
6 Guidance to Licensing Boards (2007).

> Plan for Action on Alcohol Abuse, which seeks to tackle underage drinking, binge drinking, and the wider problems associated with alcohol misuse.
> 2. Act establishes a national policy framework to provide an appropriate level of consistency across Scotland on the implementation of licensing policy. Within that national framework, Licensing Boards will have flexibility to take local decisions in light of their own area's particular circumstances.
> 3. The Act sets out 5 high level 'licensing objectives'. These represent the principles on which the new licensing system is based, and provide Licensing Boards with a solid foundation on which to build their own local policies. These objectives are not ranked in order of importance. Each has equal weighting and all must be paramount considerations when Licensing Boards are carrying out their responsibilities. [The objectives are then listed.]
> 4. As well as complementing the wider policies of the Scottish Executive these objectives aim to improve the environment for social drinking to one which is safe and welcoming for all."

As with the Licensing Act 2003 in England and Wales and the Gambling Act 2005, the use of licensing objectives is linked to a wider aspirational policy position. The Guidance confirmed that each objective is of equal importance and no one objective is rated higher than any other. It is also interesting to note the reference to "improving the environment" for social drinking in the above excerpt, which underscores the legitimacy of alcohol consumption as a lawful activity.

The inferences to be drawn here are, in my submission, that the objectives are: (1) aspirational; (2) designed to instil an overarching sense of public safety within the operation of licensed premises; and (3) designed to support the socially acceptable responsible sale and consumption of alcohol. This final inference is drawn from the concomitance of the objectives and is a recognition that the role of alcohol in society can be a positive force ("social drinking which is safe and welcoming for all") and is often lost in translation when one only seeks to view the subject of alcohol licensing through the recognised undesirable impact that alcohol can have. In order to truly understand the licensing objectives, one must consider both the merits and demerits.

To approach the licensing objectives as purely negative considerations and view licence applications or the conduct of licence holders through the solitary prism of "harm" is in my view flawed: first, because the Act is not a refusing Act (see my opening discussion on the grounds of refusal in Chapter 10 at Section 1), but, ultimately, because as a matter of natural justice and proportionality a licensing board should consider both the potential benefits and the potential costs of the grant of a licence application, with regard to the licensing objectives.

Neither the sale of alcohol nor the consumption of alcohol is illegal save in certain circumstances and is not therefore inherently irresponsible. Alcohol is a legal product which is enjoyed in moderation by many without issue or harm. The objectives then speak to a wider sense of what licensing is all about: it is about accepting that an activity can, does and should occur (in this case the sale and consumption of alcohol), but that it requires be regulated in the public interest.

2 THE NATURE OF LICENSING OBJECTIVES

Before turning to discuss each of the licensing objectives in turn, it is important to understand their contextual importance both in terms of where they are referred to in the 2005 Act, but also in relation to their interpretation and application at the coal face of licensing and in the appeal courts. We need to understand not just the history or context but the "nature" of the licensing objectives to truly appreciate their import.

Appendix C contains a full list of the references to the licensing objectives throughout the 2005 Act for those who wish to see the prevalence and location of their existence within the Act, but it is worth stating that, if we leave aside the specific references, fundamentally they overarch the whole system and are therefore a continuous theme in the Act, with duties placed on licensing boards, licence holders, applicants, the police and licensing standards officers connected to them. The significance of the licensing objectives cannot, therefore, be understated, but we must start this analysis by understanding what the law means when it prescribes an "objective".

The legal nature of an "objective" as a stand-alone concept is something which is examined in the environmental law case of *R (Thornby Farms Ltd) v Daventry District Council.*[7] In this case, the court held that an "objective" in law was something other than what might be material considerations before an authority with a regulatory task to exercise. A prescient passage from the case is as follows:

> "An objective in my judgement is something different from a material consideration . . . it is an end at which to aim, a goal. An objective which is obligatory must always be kept in mind when making a decision even while the decision maker has regard to other material considerations."[8]

The key nature of the objective is within its obligatory status. It is something to be achieved. This quality chimes with licensing law in the test purchasing decision from the Court of Session, *Lidl UK GmbH v City of Glasgow Licensing Board*[9] in that the premises licence review process involves ensuring the objectives are met and not imperilled in the future. This is discussed in greater detail in Chapter 14 at Section 12.1.

Whilst the objectives are sometimes referred to as "high-level" objectives, case law under the 2005 Act indicates, quite firmly, that the objectives are not general public interest objectives but *licensing* objectives and, as the form of licensing the 2005 Act relates to is the sale of alcohol, the licensing objectives are inextricably linked to the sale of alcohol.

There is no better place to commence an exploration of this idea than with *Brightcrew Ltd v City of Glasgow Licensing Board.*[10] The *Brightcrew* case, an Inner House decision (ultimately) is probably the most quoted appeal decision to have arisen from the 2005 Act and although I am one of those who has added to these quotes,[11] reflecting on the decision leads me to the view that

7 [2003] QB 503.
8 Ibid para 53.
9 [2013] CSIH 25.
10 [2011] CSIH 46.
11 Examples of my commentary on Brightcrew include: "The Future is Brightcrew?" *Journal of the Law Society of Scotland*, January 2012; "New Proposals Fail to Cheer" *Scottish Licensed*

it is no more than a modern re-statement of the extent of a licensing board's powers and, therefore, is fundamentally about *vires*.

The case itself relates to a Glasgow lap-dancing club, whose application to "convert" from the old licensing system to the 2005 Act was refused on the grounds that the premises were in breach of the board's policy on adult entertainment. The case was covered in the mainstream press due to allegations about full-frontal nudity and other matters, which were outlawed by the policy, and has since attracted much comment and further media attention as it has been put forward as the driving force behind the introduction of Sexual Entertainment Venue licensing, a separate regime to license sexual entertainment venues, which was legislated for under the Air Weapons and Licensing (Scotland) Act 2015 as an amendment to the Civic Government (Scotland) Act 1982.

The importance of the case apropos the licensing objectives is that it confirms that licensing boards should not step outwith their "essential function" of the control of the sale of alcohol, and that where a board has regard to the licensing objectives, they should only do so if the objectives are influenced by the sale of alcohol – and not as freestanding, general public interest objectives. As Lord Eassie says, in one of the key paragraphs of the judgment:

> "inconsistency with a licensing objective is inconsistency flowing from the permitting of the sale of alcohol on the premises in question. The fact that [the licensing objectives] are all desirable in a general sense does not empower a licensing board to insist on matters, which, while unquestionably desirable in that sense, are nevertheless not linked to the sale of alcohol. For a licensing board so to insist would be to divert a power from its proper purpose".

The general proposition is fortified by section 27(7) of the 2005 Act, which prohibits licensing boards from attaching conditions that relate to matters regulated under other law, but this is very often ignored in practice – see Chapter 8 at Section 6.1.3.

But is *Brightcrew* really such a quantum leap? It seems to me to be a reminder of long-established principles about how far licensing authorities can go in the exercise of their powers. This arose under the old Licensing (Scotland) Act 1976 in the form of *Applegate Inns Ltd v North Lanarkshire Licensing Board*,[12] in which the *vires* of what a licensing board could control beyond the sale of alcohol was debated (in that case, it was certain forms of entertainment).

In the celebrated case of *Gerry Cottle's Circus Ltd v City of Edinburgh District Council*,[13] Edinburgh Council had refused an application for a temporary public entertainment licence on the moralistic grounds that it would lead to unfair treatment of the animals. The court held that the council was acting outwith its powers by refusing an application based solely on a view that the concept of performing animals was wrong. The decision is now considered to be the classic example of one of the grounds of judicial review, namely "improper purpose" – where an authority uses a power to support a purpose other than that for which it was intended.

Trade News, 21 February 2013; "Licensing and the Carpets of Dundee", Stephen McGowan's Licensing Blawg, 26 September 2012, www.licensinglaws.wordpress.com

12 [1997] 7 SLLP 10.

13 1990 SLT 235.

In the "burger van" case *McCluskey and Others v North Lanarkshire Council*,[14] a decision to ban snack vans from being located near schools was overturned by the court as the local authority had acted *ultra vires* by using the licensing system to impose nutritional standards of its own choosing and by using the licensing system to achieve a non-licensing aim, in this case to take measures "to address the issue of child obesity". Sheriff Smith said:

> "Imposing a condition because one has to be seen to be doing something is an ulterior purpose and not a licensing purpose."[15]

There is also authority from south of the border. In *Peck v Amber Valley Borough Council and Allured (Miles from Nowhere)*[16] and *Developing Retail Ltd v South East Hampshire Magistrates' Court and Usher and Portsmouth City Council*,[17] the question was whether the English authorities could condition "non-licensable" activities. The result seems to be that if the activities occur as a direct result of the licensable activities, then conditions may be appropriate.

Finally, in the case of *R (on the application of Bristol City Council) v Bristol Magistrates' Court and Somerfield Stores (interested party)*,[18] Somerfield appealed the imposition of certain conditions attached to their premises licence. These conditions related to general health and safety matters. Again, the court found that licensing conditions should not duplicate other legislation. There is a concurrent theme here, which chimes with *Brightcrew*.

Taking these together with the purpose of the anti-duplication provision in section 27(7) of the 2005 Act, *Brightcrew* is not in uncharted waters at all – far from it. I would suggest that it is a timely reminder that the *raison d'être* of alcohol licensing law is the regulation of the sale of alcohol, and that licensing law should not be used as a panacea for general public interest concerns which are regulated elsewhere.

But with all this in mind, one must yet explore the view that there is a *Brightcrew* "spectrum", or perhaps a connectedness, which should be considered. *Brightcrew* does not completely strip licensing boards of their ability to hear and consider certain issues. It would take a strong argument, in my view, to convince a board not to take steps where the licence holder was allowing open drug dealing and use, whilst having no particular issue with sale or consumption of alcohol; but, on the other hand, I for one have argued that calling a review of a licence because the electricity meter has been tampered with is outside the jurisdiction of a licensing board. Having said all of that, you never can tell how a particular board may react to a case.[19]

A number of cases under the 2005 Act have complemented or otherwise supported the general notion that licensing boards should stick to licensing, and not stray into other matters. In *Northset Ltd v City of Glasgow Licensing*

14 [2016] SC HAM 3.

15 Ibid para 96.

16 Derby Magistrates' Court, 17 April 2008, unreported.

17 [2011] EWHC 618 (Admin).

18 [2009] EWHC 625 (Admin).

19 Janet Hood and I acted for separate clients in premises licence reviews at the same board hearing in June 2020 following "lockdown lock-ins". In my case the police had discovered a baker's dozen of patrons enjoying the hospitality of the pub manager notwithstanding the social distancing requirements invoked under the Coronavirus (Scotland) Act 2020. Janet's case, which was heard first, was dismissed on a *Brightcrew* motion, and I followed suit with the same outcome.

Board,[20], an application for major variation for the Rufus T. Firefly bar on Hope Street, to license an enclosed rooftop external area space, was refused on the basis that the stairs leading to the area were too steep. Yet the stairs had been built in accordance with appropriate planning and building regulations. The steepness of the stairs was a not a licensing matter, so the appeal succeeded. Sheriff Principal Bowen pulled no punches:

> "[t]he first ground of refusal as stated appears to reflect a view on the part of the board that the stairs leading to and from the external drinking area were too steep having regard to the fact that they might be used by persons who had consumed alcohol. This seems to suggest that, albeit the stairs are good enough to comply with the relevant building regulations, they do not comply with some other standard. That standard is unascertainable. If the stairs comply, in all respects, with detailed building regulations it cannot be correct for a licensing board to regard them as inadequate as a matter of general impression."

In *Bapu Properties Ltd v City of Glasgow Licensing Board*,[21] an application for major variation to permanently license an external pavement area at The Dhabba restaurant on the corner of Bell Street and Candleriggs was refused because the board members who visited the premises did not like the amount of space the proposed area would take up on the pavement and it would therefore be, in their eyes, unsuitable for the sale of alcohol. Yet the area had been approved and given a permit under the Roads (Scotland) Act 1984 by the roads department of Glasgow City Council and had full planning permission. The case has much to say on the "leaps of logic" taken by the board in reaching a view that the area would be unsuitable, but Sheriff Reid also looks at the link (or absence of such) between the licensing objective of preventing public nuisance, founded upon by the board in refusing the major variation, and the sale of alcohol. This case is looked at in more detail under the public nuisance heading below.

Then we have *Kell (Scotland) Ltd v City of Glasgow Licensing Board*,[22] which relates to another Glasgow lap-dancing club. This case was perhaps somewhat overshadowed by *Brightcrew* but is worth reading again as the court held that a licensing board was not entitled to impose conditions in relation to sanitary conveniences.

A wider point about the proper purpose of licensing was elaborated in the important civic case we should return to, which was noted above, namely *McCluskey and Others v North Lanarkshire Council*,[23] in which a number of street traders had been forced to move their snack vans away from the locality of local primary schools by imposition of a licence condition. At paragraph 65, Sheriff Smith says:

> "That obesity among the general population and children especially is considered problematic is not in dispute. That elected representatives wish to confront this problem and take steps to promote healthier lifestyles is to be commended. Neither of these is the issue in this case. The issue is whether the defender, as a licensing authority, has the power to impose this particular condition upon the licences of street traders. In my judgement it does not."

20 Glasgow Sheriff Court, 22 March 2012, unreported.
21 Glasgow Sheriff Court, 22 February 2012, unreported.
22 [2010] ScotSC 23.
23 [2016] SC HAM 3.

He later adds at paragraph 96:

> "The sub-committee had an ulterior purpose which was expressed at p4 of the statement of reasons where reference was made to 'their general wish that they had to be seen to be taking measures, from a regulatory perspective, to address the issue of child obesity.' In addition there was a purpose to promote and encourage the uptake of school meals which involved the removal of snack vans which it considered traded in less healthy food than that to be found in a secondary school. Imposing a condition because one has to be seen to be doing something is an ulterior purpose and not a licensing purpose."

This *dictum* chimes neatly with what the Court of Session says in *Brightcrew* about desirability versus ability. A licensing authority may wish to take an action, but are they legally able to? This brings us back to considering the "objective" and "purpose" of the 2005 Act itself: to regulate the sale and consumption of alcohol. In turn, the five licensing objectives must live within that habitat.

Brightcrew has certainly not turned licensing boards into lame ducks and any solicitor who practises at the licensing bar will confirm that. The ultimate *Brightcrew* legacy may not be what it had to say about licensing objectives, but that it ultimately convinced the Scottish Government that adult entertainment required to be regulated separately.

Moving away from *Brightcrew*, another key case here, and for Scottish licensing law generally, is *Lidl UK GmbH v City of Glasgow Licensing Board*.[24] This landmark case from the Court of Session concerned test purchase failure and suspension. A Lidl store in Glasgow failed a single test purchase. They passed a follow-up test. There were no other issues before the Board. On the basis of that single test purchase failure, the Board suspended the licence for 5 days, having been asked to review the licence by Strathclyde Police (as was). Lidl appealed to the sheriff court, where Sheriff Mitchell rejected the appeal and said that the Board was entitled to impose a sanction such as a suspension as a "deterrent" to ward off other licence holders from acting unlawfully. Lidl appealed to the Court of Session. The original sheriff court decision was at odds with decisions from other courts, for example in the unreported case of *Co-operative Group Ltd v Inverclyde Licensing Board*,[25] in which a suspension was overturned on appeal as "disproportionate" following a single test purchase failure, the Sheriff taking the view that a written warning was the correct disposal.

What is of jurisprudential significance to the licensing objectives, is the interesting things *Lidl* has to say about the process of premises licence reviews:

> "the process of review is essentially forward looking. It involves examining whether the continuance of the particular premises licence in issue, without taking any of the steps listed in section 39(2) [that is, the sanctions open to a Board, e.g. suspension, revocation etc], would be inconsistent with endeavouring to achieve the licensing objective in question. The process of review is therefore not directed to imposing a penalty in respect of some past event which is not likely to recur to an extent liable to jeopardise the licensing objective."

24 [2013] CSIH 25.
25 Greenock Sheriff Court, 8 October 2010, unreported, but see [2010] 46 SLLP 6.

This was a clear statement that the sanctions open to a Board at review should not be used to penalise for retrospective detriment, but rather deployed where it is necessary in order to "future proof" the licensing objectives. Thus, where a licensing board wishes to suspend a licence, it must do with some sort of clear aim as to what the period of suspension is designed to achieve, with regard to the relevant licensing objectives which may have been at play in the particular case. For example, if a review was brought due to an absence of staff training records then a suspension might be imposed to allow staff to be trained properly; or if a premises had been subject to incidents of proxy purchasing of alcohol by adults for under-agers, perhaps the suspension might be to allow the installation of a CCTV system covering external areas to premises.

Having dissected the DNA of the licensing objectives as a generality, let us turn to examine each one in turn.

3 PREVENTING CRIME AND DISORDER

If one is to reflect on preventing crime and disorder as a result of the sale or consumption of alcohol, this can lead to a wide consideration of matters indeed, and, despite my comments about what might be described as the narrowness of the licensing objectives further to *Brightcrew*, it is clear that a significant number of examples can be given of either crimes or disorder arising from alcohol.

In my mind, the starting place here is consideration of offences under the Act itself. I would suggest that it is doubtful there is any merit in an argument that an offence under a licensing Act is not relatable to at least one of the licensing objectives. So when we consider how the crime and disorder objective might be imperilled, we should first consider licensing offences: sale of alcohol to a drunk person, sale of alcohol to a child or young person, operating outwith the licence, and so on.

Then there is a wider consideration of crimes and disorder arising from the sale or consumption of alcohol which are not explicit licensing offences. One might suggest, for example, that an assault which occurs in a licensed premise as a result of intoxication coupled with indifferent management might be sufficient to suggest this objective can be engaged.

On the other hand, if an applicant has criminal convictions, this does not necessarily mean he or she should be denied a licence with regard to this objective. The particulars of the conviction, severity, link to alcohol, vintage, may all be important.

In *Kennedy v Angus Licensing Board*,[26] the question of linking convictions to the licensing objectives was explored. A personal licence holder was convicted of drink driving in February 2012. She reported the conviction to the licensing board as required under the 2005 Act. Separately, the police reported the matter to the licensing board under the auspices of section 83 of the Act and recommended that the personal licence be revoked having regard to the licensing objective of preventing crime and disorder.

26 Forfar Sheriff Court, 22 August 2012, unreported.

The personal licence holder had been witnessed leaving the pub she operated in the small hours of the morning, entering her vehicle and driving into a parked car twice, not far from the premises. She was later found to be over the legal limit and indicated that after clearing up for the night she had had consumed two or three glasses of wine. In suspending the personal licence for 6 months as a result of this, the Board wished to "send a message" to other licensees. In the statement of reasons the board said that it considered the following matters to be relevant:

- That the licence holder had a previous conviction for drink driving
- That the alcohol had been consumed in licensed premises
- The offence was a "serious disregard for the law"
- If she was unfit to drive, how would she have been able to attend to her responsibilities as a personal licence holder?
- On any view she should not have been consuming alcohol on the actual premises even though it was closed to the public.

The board therefore took the view that a lengthy 6-month suspension was commensurate with the crime prevention objective and the decision would "send a message to deter other licensees". In the view of Sheriff Veal, who upheld the appeal, this approach was wrong. The Board erred in law by taking the view that the mere existence of the conviction impinged upon the capability of the licence holder to fulfil her duties as such. In other words, there was no link between the conviction and her status as a personal licence holder.

Sheriff Veal also considered the suggestion that the crime prevention objective under the 2005 Act can be read widely enough to include "deterrence" as false; diverging at that time from the still live view of Sheriff Mitchell in the *Lidl* case, prior to that view being overturned by the Court of Session.

He also stated that the Board should take into account the sanction already imposed under the criminal courts and consider whether that is sufficient; and seems to my mind to have regard to the *Brightcrew* position when he says:

> "I am unable to identify any relevant connection between the commission of this offence and the 'licensing objectives' set out in section 4 of the 2005 Act. I am not persuaded that the very fact of the existence of this conviction should automatically incur an additional discretionary penalty at the hands of the Licensing Board. I consider that the reference to 'deterrence' . . . is . . . inappropriate."

The case appears to me to follow *Arora v City of Glasgow Licensing Board*,[27] the first personal licence appeal under the 2005 Act.[28] In that case Mr Arora had applied for a personal licence. He had a conviction for drink driving but the police did not recommend refusal. The Board refused the application as a result of the presence of the conviction. This was overturned on appeal, and although the Sheriff was critical of the Board for not lending greater weight to the absence of a police recommendation to refuse, he also said:

27 Glasgow Sheriff Court, 17 May 2010, unreported.

28 This case was conducted by John Batters, a renowned licensing solicitor; a colleague, influence and friend, he retired in 2015 having practised licensing law for over 35 years.

> "The mere existence of the offence . . . did not justify the conclusion that it was necessary to refuse the application. There required to be a discrete reason for the board's conclusion that it was so necessary and that reason required to be properly explained. No such reason or explanation appears."

This, in my view, bears comparison with *Kennedy*. In both cases the board fail to create a link between the mere existence of the conviction and how that link imperils the licensing objective of preventing crime and disorder. This link is described as the "licensing nexus"; and is the "connectedness" to which I refer in this chapter.

Of importance in weighing up the prevention of crime and disorder must be the views of the police. Case law suggests that the views of the police should be given particular consideration when this objective is invoked, and certainly that the absence of any suggestion from the police that there is harm or that the objective is imperilled is a matter the board should consider attaching appropriate weight to in its deliberations. That can be seen from the *Arora* case noted above but there is further jurisprudence on this point.

In *Kaur v City of Glasgow Licensing Board*,[29] an off-sale conversion application had been refused on the grounds of the licensing objectives of crime and disorder and public nuisance. The applicant had sought 10am to 10pm and the application had attracted objections which proposed a terminal hour of 8pm because the premises had historically traded till 8pm and, according to the objectors, there had been less antisocial behaviour. To be clear, the premises remained opened until 10pm albeit alcohol sales ceased at 8pm, and there had been issues arising from the general closing time of 10pm. The applicant refused to concede the hours back to 8pm and the application was refused. Sheriff Scott upheld the appeal because the police antisocial behaviour report indicated that there had been no rise in reported difficulties or incidents since the premises had traded (albeit unlicensed) till 10pm, and the board did not explain why it preferred the objectors' views over that of the then Strathclyde Police.

Similarly, in *Shafiq v North Lanarkshire Licensing Board*,[30] the board had refused an application for a premises licence on the basis of a single conviction for under-age sale of alcohol. However, despite the presence of the conviction the police had not recommended refusal of the licence and the licensing board erred by not taking that absence into account when founding on the crime prevention objective to refuse the licence.

Another useful way of exploring this objective is with regard to the production of antisocial behaviour reports. These reports are produced in connection with new licence applications where requested by the board (or sometimes the applicant) or where the police themselves feel it appropriate so to do. Antisocial behaviour reports will list incidents and crimes which have occurred in the locality over a 12-month period. These incidents and crimes cannot be said to be linked to the applicant, as he is not yet in possession of a licence and not trading. They may, on the other hand, have occurred as a result of the mismanagement of other licensed premises in the locality and therefore may provide useful context as to the nature of the locality from a general crime perspective. But how many of the incidents on the report are of relevance to

29 [2010] 44 SLLP 14.
30 [2009] 42 SLLP 44.

the licensing objective? Is a "fender bender" of any interest? Perhaps, if the road traffic accident had occurred as a result of drink driving. What about incidences of abuse in private premises? Perhaps, if there is evidence that the perpetrator of violence or abuse has consumed alcohol at identifiable premises.

In one case I am aware of, a report listed a murder of a young person outside a licensed premises. The owner of the premises was entirely unaware of the incident and, after querying this, it transpired that the murder had actually occurred on the top deck of a bus which happened to be at a bus stop outside the premises at the time of the attack, and the premises address was given as a locus in the crime report as a point of geographical reference.

The conclusion I ask the reader to reach is that not all crime and disorder is relatable to a licence application. The "connectedness" of crimes and disorders must be considered not simply with regard to whether or not they arise from alcohol *per se*, but the other external factors that may be at play, which would include geographic, demographic, and temporal connectedness.[31]

4 PREVENTING PUBLIC NUISANCE

There are several of what one might describe as "common sense" or generally understood examples of public nuisance emanating from licensed premises. Intoxication can lead to high spirits, elevated noise levels, good natured mischief, and, at the other end of that spectrum, shouting and swearing, aggression and nuisance from altercations. In addition, nuisance can arise from dispersal of persons from licensed premises, from persons making use of smoking areas or simply standing outside to smoke, or from the sound of entertainment being provided for the amusement of patrons.

A reminder of the necessary link between the sale of alcohol and public nuisance is perhaps appropriate as we begin to analyse this objective, and assistance comes in the form of *Bapu Properties*, where the Sheriff looks specifically at the link between the licensing objective of preventing public nuisance, and a more general understanding of public nuisance. In upholding the appeal, he said:

> "I conclude that, to the extent that the Board's decision proceeds under Section 30(5)(b) of the 2005 Act, the apprehended 'public nuisance', upon which the Board's decision was predicated, was not related to the sale of alcohol. The single function of a Licensing Board under the 2005 Act is that of the licensing of the sale of alcohol. The powers to licence the sale of alcohol cannot be deployed to effect objectives not related to the sale of alcohol, but which the Licensing Board might yet find desirable. The objectives listed in Section 4 of the 2005 Act, though striking in their apparent generality, are not 'free-standing' objectives. They are 'licensing' objectives. The objectives, if they are to be relied upon to refuse a licence, must be 'linked to the sale of alcohol'."

He goes on to say:

> "It cannot be enough for a Board to identify a tenuous, incidental, ancillary, indirect, or immaterial connection with a perceived mischief, or licensing objective,

31 See also *Pagliocca v Glasgow District Licensing Board* 1995 SLT 180 in relation to crime and causal connection with licensed premises.

to justify the refusal of a variation application by reference to Section 30(5)(b) (or, as in *Brightcrew*, by reference to Section 23(5)(c)). The supposed 'link' must be subject to a qualitative assessment . . . In the present case, the Board founds upon the licensing objective of 'preventing public nuisance' (section 4(1)(c)). The supposed 'public nuisance' arises from the apprehended pedestrian congestion on the footpath. However, in my view, the apprehended pedestrian congestion is not directly or materially linked or related to the permitting of the sale of alcohol on the premises. Put another way, the perceived inconsistency with the licensing objective does not flow (directly or materially) from the licensing of the sale of alcohol. The pedestrian congestion (and resulting apprehended public nuisance), if it exists at all, would be attributable to the physical presence of tables and chairs forming part of, and the barriers delineating, the pursuers' external restaurant operation, as already sanctioned by the Section 59 Agreement (item 5/4 of process) and the planning consent (item 5/5 of process), by which the pursuers were granted permission by Glasgow City Council to occupy and use this same section of footpath as an extension to its Indian restaurant business, at defined times and on stated conditions. In other words, the supposed congestion (and resulting apprehended public nuisance) would occur whether or not alcohol was permitted to be sold on the external footpath area. The supposed congestion (and resulting apprehended public nuisance) would be precisely the same whether the external area was being used for the sale of curry and water, or for the sale of curry and lager. The perceived congestion (upon which the public nuisance is predicated) has no direct, material or necessary link with the permitting of the sale of alcohol on the premises. The Board is not concerned with preventing public nuisance generally. The Board is only concerned with the prevention of public nuisance so far as referable to the sale of alcohol. The impact of the external licensed area upon pedestrian traffic on the footpath is exactly the same, whether or not alcohol is permitted to be sold in that area. Therefore, the congestion (and perceived resulting apprehended nuisance) has no direct or material connection with the sale of alcohol."

4.1 Nuisance from external areas/outside premises

Let us explore a hypothetical scenario. Two teetotallers attend a pub to socialise and drink lemonade. During the course of their socialising, they fall out, decide to leave and have an argument standing outside the premises which results in fisticuffs, and noise and disturbance to the young family who live in a flat above the premises. Let us say that in our scenario there is no doubt that the level of noise and nuisance is extreme – but is the licensing objective of preventing public nuisance engaged?

Our two lemonade-drinkers have not attended the premises because it is licensed, for they take no drink. They have attended because it is a social space. No alcohol has been sold to them or consumed by them. Alcohol has no part to play at all. The fact that the altercation occurred outside a licensed premises can be said, therefore, to be incidental. The nuisance has not arisen because the premises are licensed. In this type of illustrative scenario, I would suggest that the correct regulatory route to interfere with the nuisance is the general common law crime of breach of the peace, a police matter.

Turning to another fictional (yet none-to-difficult to imagine) episode, if a group of hen-party revellers, having attended a nightclub and having consumed alcohol at the premises across a number of hours, are creating havoc in a smoking area outside the club at 2.30am, and the pensioner who lives across the road is disturbed, is the public nuisance objective engaged? In this case it might be far easier to argue that it should be, and one can argue that it matters not whether the havoc is good natured, high spirits, or genuinely fractious.[32]

Yet, that analysis only takes us so far. Recalling that the specific wording of the objective is "Preventing Public Nuisance", the real test is not whether the nuisance occurred, but what the premises licence holder did to *prevent* the nuisance in the first place. What policies were in place? What staff training was deployed? What level of staff presence was there in the outside area? Was there CCTV covering this area which could be viewed internally by staff in order to respond to an incident? Had the licensee taken steps in the past to deal with noise outside its premises? Had the licensee liaised with the licensing standards officer or the neighbours previously? Were there any complaints made at all to the premises?

4.2 Nuisance from entertainment noise

One of the controversial areas which sits beneath this objective is audibility, or inaudibility, of noise or sound from licensed premises in neighbouring properties. Perhaps the most famous example of this specific debate is the Edinburgh noise condition.

Following the onset of the 2005 Act, all on sales licensed premises in Edinburgh that permitted the playing of recorded music or live entertainment had a condition attached to the licence as follows: "all amplified music and vocals must be inaudible in any neighbouring residential premises". This condition was attached as a local condition which Edinburgh Licensing Board developed as part of the conversion to the 2005 Act regime. It has been argued by commentators that the condition is extreme, disproportionate, unenforceable, arbitrary, but alternatively welcome, necessary, sensible and obvious. The idea of an "inaudibility condition" is an example of a dichotomy within the public nuisance objective.

Notice that the condition referred to "amplified" music and vocals, and this caught music played through speakers and even vocals from televised sport as a form of amplification. Truly unamplified music such as an *a capella* barbershop quartet, or an acoustic guitarist who sings unamplified would not be caught at that time, as neither would (perhaps conversely) a Jon Bonham-style[33] solo drum performance with a twenty-piece kit which is not amplified through microphone use.

Within the bounds of the public nuisance objective, is an expectation of total inaudibility going too far or even lawful? We know that conditions have to be enforceable, understandable and proportionate. We also know that section 27(7) of the 2005 Act makes it clear that conditions cannot relate to another enactment – licensing conditions should be about licensing the 'essential function' of what the licensing Act is aiming to regulate, and that is the sale of alcohol.

32 Although, there is a separate point about whether a single complaint is sufficient to activate the notion of 'public'.

33 I say Jon Bonham. I could just as easily have referred to Ginger Baker here, or possibly Jon Hiseman. Or Keef Hartley or Keith Moon. I was tempted to take it back to Buddy Rich or Art Blakey. This was a matter of some debate on my part as those of you who know me best will forgive. I eventually plumped with Bonham, having regard to the live version of *Moby Dick*.

Is there not an argument that a condition about entertainment noise is *ultra vires* given noise is regulated under the Environmental Protection Act 1990?

This is why the Edinburgh condition is so interesting to the debate, because it is about technology, and amplified music is not affected by alcohol (unless one argues that the band is intoxicated and cranks up the volume). One might also argue the condition is 'practically' unenforceable because the only way amplified music can truly be inaudible is if it does not occur at all. One might also argue it was disproportionate: it was simply going too far. Edinburgh Licensing Board ultimately softened the condition moving from an "inaudibility" test to an "audible nuisance" test; and required licence holders to apply to take advantage of the new condition. Many applications to change the condition were unsuccessful based on concerns raised by residents or others. True inaudibility is, in my view, a fiction.

In *R (Developing Retail Ltd) v East Hampshire Magistrates' Court*,[34] an English High Court licensing judicial review case, this issue was discussed. A licence was granted but subject to certain conditions. One of the conditions with which the judicial review was concerned was: "All noise arising from regulated entertainment at the premises shall be inaudible 1 metre outside any noise sensitive premises." Clare Montgomery QC, sitting as Deputy High Court Judge, found:

> "without clarity as to the premises or location intended to be protected by this condition, and without some degree of specificity as to what is meant by inaudibility, the condition is in my judgment so vague as to be unenforceable. In those circumstances I consider that the noise condition is liable to be quashed. There was, however, clear evidence before the magistrates' court that would have justified the imposition of a condition protecting nearby residential properties from noise generated by licensed activities on the site. This could lawfully have been prevented by the imposition of a condition that specified the particular nearby locations (presumably residential premises) intended to be protected, and required that noise from the licensable activities did not exceed a specified level of decibels measured at a particular location over a particular period."

4.3 Non-noise nuisance?

Is it possible that other forms of nuisance might be caught by the licensing objective? I have dealt with cases involving what one might refer to as "personal" nuisance, that is, where the nuisance alleged is unwanted attention or interference. I would suggest that this type of matter is one for the police to investigate under criminal law. I have also dealt with cases where licensing has been used to make complaints about "smell" nuisance. This again, in my view, is not a licensing matter. Smell nuisance is very clearly a matter which is regulated under the Environmental Protection Act 1990 and any complaints about smells should be dealt with under that legislation.

A judicial expression of this under the public nuisance bracket can be found in *Maresq T/A La Belle Angele v Edinburgh Licensing Board*.[35] In this case the operators of a nightclub had applied for a regular extension under the 1976 Act. This allowed the premises to operate to 3am instead of 12 midnight.

34 [2011] EWHC 618 (Admin).
35 2001 SC 126.

These extensions were heard annually under the old system. Edinburgh City Council had objected to the application for the extended hours on the basis that there had been illegal fly-posting for events at the clubs, which they claimed constituted a public nuisance. The board granted an extension, but till 2am only instead of the existing and proposed 3am which the club had enjoyed. The court upheld the appeal on the basis it was irrational to restrict hours of trade from 3am to 2am when that would have no impact on the fly-posting; and that fly-posting was not a "public nuisance" in relation to the relevant statutory provision under the Licensing Act.

5 SECURING PUBLIC SAFETY

I have found that "public safety" is a much wider idiom to endeavour to harness and define for the purposes of this book. Public safety in the general sense suggests something that is in the wider interests of society, about the welfare and protection of the public. In natural conversation the concept could easily be said to apply to matters which relate to licensed premises such as the safety of pressurised gas canisters or fake alcohol, but such matters are not licensing matters, and the public is protected from these issues under other law.

We therefore need to think about safety in relation to the supply and consumption of alcohol. Taking a simplistic approach, I would seek to explore this objective by supposing that there are two groups of people that the term "public" might be said to refer to, namely (a) customers of a licensed premises; and (b) the wider public. I have found it helpful to consider this objective with regard to a licensing version of a legal "duty of care" to these two subsets of the public. The general duty of care under the Scots law of delict is not one I can sensibly discuss in detail here but the general principles which arose from the most famous case of all, *Donoghue v Stevenson*,[36] are of interest in this licensing context, and with some historic irony, as I do believe that Mrs Donoghue had her infamous bottle of ginger beer sitting outside a licensed café in Paisley.[37]

Looking after one's own customers should not and does not result from the regard of this bespoke objective alone. It should be the default approach of the right-minded and professional licence holder. To explore examples of what this might mean in day-to-day practice, we can start by suggesting that securing the safety of one's own customers in respect of alcohol would necessarily then link to drunkenness offences. It would link to knowing when to refuse the sale of alcohol. It would link to refusing entry to intoxicated members of the public. It would link to knowing the difference between looking after an inebriated customer who may be vulnerable, or sending them off into the night without regard for their safety. There is an overlap in this to the public health objective noted below, when thinking about "securing" the objective being a way in which the licence holder "controls" consumption of alcohol so that the person does not harm themselves or others.

From practice, it is clear that the duty of care in relation to the licensing objective of securing public safety does not end at the front door of the licensed premises. There is a wider duty of care, but it has its limits. Securing

36 1932 SLT 317.

37 One can only hope that Mr Stevenson had the necessary permits in place for outside seating.

public safety does not require a licence holder to endeavour to secure the safety of the entire public; there must be a causal link between the "footprint" of his or her licensed premises and the safety of members of the public whom have some connection to the premises. Let us analyse this further by example.

If a person has been sold alcohol irresponsibly and comes to some harm as a result of their intoxication, then one might be able to argue strongly that the objective has not been upheld. However, there is clearly in my view a "connectedness" test here. If a person has been served alcohol when he should have been refused, and on leaving the premises is unable to walk sensibly, falls into a river and drowns, then that is a different matter to someone who has had one pint in a pub and several hours later and several miles along the road, trips and falls into oncoming traffic. Similarly, if an intoxicated patron leaves a premises and five minutes later assaults their partner in the street, it might be that creates sufficient nexus to link the incident to the premises. On the other hand, if two people meet in a restaurant, have one drink and leave, and later that evening one sexually assaults the other, it may be more difficult to make out the nexus or causal link to that licensed premises.

What is clear, is that I doubt it can be said that certain incidents can or should only fit under the auspices of one of the objectives. In terms of decision-making, the licensing board can certainly seek to engage "one or more" of the objectives in refusing an application or upholding a review. If there is evidence of a pattern of children and young persons persistently obtaining alcohol from a local retailer who is selling alcohol to a proxy purchaser, then that is a scenario where the public safety objective could be engaged, as the sales of alcohol may impact on the safety of the proxy purchaser, who may be a vulnerable person, the safety of the children and young persons, and perhaps the safety of members of the wider public in the vicinity of the shop, even though there is some obvious overlap with the other licensing objectives.

6 PROTECTING CHILDREN AND YOUNG PERSONS FROM HARM

This objective started life as "Protecting children from harm". It may seem odd that there was no initial consideration for "young persons" within the objective (or even adults, for that matter) and whilst children and young persons are defined separately (children are aged 15 and under; young persons are aged 16 and 17[38]), I do not believe there was any real intention to exclude young persons from the protection of a licensing objective *per se*. There are only two provisions within the Act which separate children and young persons: one relating to the sale of liqueur confectionery and chocolates (see Section 8.13 below), and one concerning the consumption of alcohol ancillary to a meal (discussed in more detail later in this book). I think instead that this was an oversight by the draftsmen who can perhaps be forgiven because of the interchangeability of the generic short-hand use of the term "children" which even Nicholson fell afoul of, referring in parts to "children" when he actually meant "children and young persons".

The change to include "young persons" occurred directly as a result of

38 2005 Act, s 147.

the decision in *Tesco Stores Ltd v Midlothian Licensing Board*.[39] This case concerned the suspension of a Tesco store in Dalkeith following a single failed test purchase. The licensing board moved to suspend the licence for 7 days with immediate effect. The immediacy of this step is severely criticised by the Sheriff and that aspect is discussed in Chapter 14 at Section 2.1. In the context of the licensing objective of preventing children from harm (as was), one of the grounds of appeal which was upheld was that the test purchaser was not a child but a young person – a 16-year-old. In founding on the "children from harm" objective, the licensing board had erred in law because no child had been involved.

This eventually resulted in section 41 of the Air Weapons and Licensing (Scotland) Act 2015, described thus by the explanatory notes to the Act:

> "Section 41 amends the licensing objective at section 4(1)(e) of the 2005 Act to include young persons. The term young person is defined at section 147 of the 2005 Act and means a person aged 16 or 17. Under the legislation, Boards must ensure that their decision making is underpinned by the five licensing objectives, including the existing objective 'to protect children from harm'. This amendment expands this requirement so that Boards must also consider protecting 'young persons' from harm."

The starting point to understand the application of this objective in practice is to remember that the Act itself contains a number of provisions concerning activities which are prohibited concerning children and young persons. There are several offences under the Act such as selling alcohol to a child or young person, delivering alcohol to a child or young person, and so on. These are all discussed in detail in Chapter 19.

The next thread to pull is the specific provisions contained within the operating plan of premises licences. An applicant for a premises licence where on sales is proposed must confirm whether they intend to allow children and young person's access to the premises, and if so, on what terms, and in what areas, and what ages, and at what times. There is an underlying assumption that there should be no blanket permission of children and young persons to be on licensed premises[40] and, where they are, this should be controlled.

This has led to most licensing boards developing their own approach to access by children and young persons, detailed in their Statement of Licensing Policy, and attaching local conditions. So, we have a series of separate rules for children and young persons applying across the thirty or so licensing boards. In Glasgow, the board will not normally allow children or young persons in a bar style premises after 9pm. In Edinburgh, this can be as late as 1am for young persons on some licences although that board has pulled back from a previously more relaxed approach since the adoption of new local licensing policies in 2018/2019.

We then have differentiation between children and young persons on a set of premises: so, for example, children may not be able to attend unaccompanied by an adult, but young persons might be allowed to attend without such supervision.

We then move into the realm of separate rules for separate premises within

39 2012 SCLR 575.

40 At least, in relation to on-sales premises. There is no such restriction in relation to off-sales only premises.

the same licensing board depending on the style of premises, and this aspect links to a wider discussion of the purported move away from licence categorisation under the 1976 Act.[41] When one considers that there is almost a standard approach to applications either by way of policy or the imposition of what are effectively standard conditions, then categorisation is alive and well.

It is also within the reams of conditions and requirements pertaining to children and young persons that one can easily point to a dichotomy: where licensing boards are looking to achieve desirable outcomes, but outcomes which nevertheless may sit outwith the licensing objective, because the mischief is not linked to the sale of alcohol. North Ayrshire licensing board looks to impose the following conditions where it is proposed children are to be admitted:[42]

"• No Child shall be permitted to operate any amusement-with-prizes machine or video/DVD/electronic machine which is in the Premises, except mobile telephones or other hand-held electronic devices owned by the Child.
- All heating appliances must be adequately guarded;
- All electrical sockets must be fitted with a safety cover when not in use;
- Where meals are provided a Children's menu must be available at all times, or alternatively the main menu must show that half portions are available for Children;
- The playing of darts, pool, snooker or any other game is prohibited;
- There shall be no dartboard, pool table or other facilities for such activities in those area(s);
- There must be available (for sale or supply) for consumption by Children meals and beverages other than alcohol;
- Drinks supplied to Children under 12 must be served in non-glass containers;
- Straws must also be available to Children free of cost;"

Several of these relate to general health and safety matters and are governed under another enactment. The first one strays well into the territory of the Gambling Act 2005, in which, certain gaming machines (or Amusements with Prizes as described above) can be played by any person of any age. I can discern no link between the sale of alcohol and the provision of free straws, and, further, that condition is at odds with the prevailing views on single-use plastics.

The Perth and Kinross Licensing Board policy statement contains the following:

"The Licensing Board expects premises with the facility for on consumption which permit entry to children aged 5 or under to have the following:—

(i) provision of a safe high chair facility
(ii) provision for heating customer supplied children's food at no extra cost
(iii) all heating sources adequately protected
(iv) all electrical sockets covered
(v) safety film placed on glass doors or BS standard safety glass
(vi) the times at which children will be permitted to be on the premises or any part thereof appropriately displayed."

One might ask the question: how is a rule requiring licensed premises to heat up food brought to the premises by a supervising adult linked to the sale of alcohol and in turn the licensing objective? In some cases, the rules which are applied are particularly detailed. The West Dunbartonshire approach is as follows:

41 See Chapter 7, at Section 2 on categorisation and the relevance of local licensing policy.
42 Statement of Licensing Policy, North Ayrshire Licensing Board (2018–2024).

> "The Board's Policy is that children and young people under the age of 18 will only be permitted into licensed premises which are considered to be restaurants or into other licences premises where:—
> (a) The primary purpose of allowing them access is to consume a meal; or
> (b) To attend a pre-booked function; or
> (c) Hotels – the Board accepts that children and young persons under the age of 18, who are resident in the premises, are allowed free access throughout the premises with the exception of the bar area. No children and young persons will be permitted in the bar area except where the primary purpose of allowing them access is to consume a meal or to attend a pre-booked function. Within the bar area, children and young persons will not be permitted to remain after 10 p.m. other than in exceptional circumstances, for example a wedding or other pre-booked function being held in the bar where the presence of children or young people after 10 p.m. can be justified. A condition to this effect will be imposed by the Board on the licences of all premises where children may be resident; or
> (d) In tourist areas children may be present in premises other than for the purpose of attending a pre-booked function or having a meal providing that individual premises can satisfy the Board that tourism is a very significant part of their trade. In such cases children shall not be entitled to remain after 10 p.m. nor to remain in the vicinity of the bar.
> (e) In relation to clubs whose primary object is sport, children and young persons under the age of 18 are permitted to have the following access to the premises:-
> - Children and young persons who are junior members of such a club, plus junior guests, are permitted to access all areas of the premises (excluding the bar) until half an hour after closure of the sporting facilities to which they have access;
> - In relation to the bar area, children under 16 are permitted to purchase non alcoholic drinks at the bar area but are not permitted to drink in the bar area. Young persons aged 16 to 18 are permitted to purchase and consume non alcoholic drinks in the bar area providing there are no gaming machines or pool tables in the area;
> - Children and young persons are not permitted to access any area of the premises in which gaming machines are located.
> - Children under 16 are permitted to remain in the bar area in compliance with paragraph 5.5 of the Board's Licensing Policy Statement (i.e. for the purpose of consuming a meal or attending a pre-booked function).
>
> (f) Children should be accompanied by an adult whilst, on the Premises and this should be specified in the operating plans. Separate criteria apply to sports clubs as specified at paragraph (e) above."

To spare the reader thirty-five different approaches to rules concerning children and young persons, each of which has rules within rules, the overall impression given is that, in practice if not enshrined in the Act, there is a form of unascertainable (and therefore unlawful) or extra-statutory "suitability" test occurring here, which is perhaps connected to the wider licensing objective of protecting children and young persons from harm, but in some cases goes beyond direct harm associated with a child or young person being provided with alcohol. One then wonders therefore about the consideration of the overall *ambience and atmosphere* of a licensed premises.

Just because no specific licensing offence is committed does not mean that it is desirable that children or young persons should be able to attend a set of premises. If the atmosphere is especially adult, such as a hypothetical traditional "boozer" where the average customer might be a boor, this might impact upon the objective, whilst the gastropub across the road, which has the same licence, operating plan and conditions (but different clientele), might not. Granted, it is unusual to see a new licence application for a wet-led pub these days, but nevertheless it seems to me to be appropriate for a licensing board to interrogate this dimension of a proposed operation in order to satisfy themselves that the proposal is not inconsistent with the licensing objective, and because this type of atmosphere arises from the sale and consumption of alcohol on the premises, the nexus is forged. West Dunbartonshire Licensing Board poses this interrogation thus:

> "The Board encourages licence holders to demonstrate both within their Operating Plan and in their everyday practice the measures which will be put in place to protect children and young people from harm."[43]

But this must be applied reasonably. In one case in which I appeared, a request to allow children and young persons into an area which was to be used for dining was met with concern from a board member because the kitchen was at the opposite end of the premises and hot food or liquids might be spilled onto children as it was delivered to the tables. This type of approach from local members, which can be experienced from time to time, links us back to remember the ethos of the licensing objectives and the "essential function" of the licensing board as the regulators of the sale of alcohol – not as general public guardians.

As with the other objectives and the general application of the licensing law, a licensing board must, in deciding to refuse an application with regard to this objective, do so based on relevant material which will justify a refusal. In the case of *NATL Amusements (UK) Ltd v North Lanarkshire Licensing Board*,[44] a cinema had applied for permission to allow customers to consume alcohol within the hall after 7pm but the board refused this, saying those "under 18 should not be placed in an environment where films were being exhibited when alcohol could be freely consumed in a dark environment". Sheriff Kelly upheld the appeal. He said:

> "The concerns which the Board had for children in darkened cinemas when alcoholic drinks were being consumed might well be commendable. However, grounding a decision upon them would require clarity as to what formed their basis, which would have to be capable of enunciation and elucidation. If the concerns are vague and resistant to articulation they are more likely to be risks to which attention ought to be afforded than imminent, tangible dangers. While the Board have expressed a discomfiture which they feel and concerns which they harbour, it is not possible to detect any justifiable, objective material which forms the basis for them and thereby for the decision taken by them. Were there any actual instances of harm to be drawn from cinemas elsewhere, none were alluded to. Were the particular locality such as to render it sensible to treat it differently from elsewhere, no mention was made of it. While the concerns might have been real in that they were genuinely held, they have not been demonstrated to be real in that any rational or discernible explanation was evident for them."[45]

43 West Dunbartonshire Licensing Board Statement of Licensing Policy 2013–2016, para 16.2.
44 2018 SLT (Sh Ct) 89.
45 Ibid para 9.

7 PROTECTING AND IMPROVING PUBLIC HEALTH

The so-called "fifth licensing objective" is easily the most controversial and yet remains the least understood. The Nicholson Committee remit specifically contained reference to health, in the words of then Justice Minister Jim Wallace, on 28 June 2001:

> "To review all aspects of liquor licensing law and practice in Scotland, with particular reference to the implications for health and public order; to recommend changes in the public interest; and to report accordingly."

But public health was not the sole marker for the review of the law in this area. As Nicholson points out, the purpose was a full review and:

> "It is our hope that our report contains a substantial package of measures which will simplify and improve licensing law and practice; which will give consumers a wider range of choice, but which will at the same time provide means for controlling undesirable and irresponsible behaviour on the part of some licensees; which will increase community involvement in the licensing process; and which will take full account of the health and public order issues which are mentioned specifically in our terms of reference."[46]

A number of issues arise here, not simply health, and of course one must remember that the original impetus for the 2005 Act came from licensing boards seeking a modernisation and simplification of the licensing laws of Scotland. However, there is no doubt that public health was a key factor in the ultimate review:

> ". . . there has been growing concern in recent years about the health implications of, for example, binge drinking on the part of the young of both sexes and about the growth of alcohol related illnesses, affecting all ages. Additionally, those with a concern for public order have become increasingly alarmed at the links between over-consumption of alcohol and the commission of crimes, in particular crimes of violence."[47]

In the foreword to the document issued by the Scottish Executive (as was) to licensees, the then Justice Minister Kenny MacAskill underlined this in somewhat balder terms:

> "The Licensing (Scotland) Act 2005 aims to help address the problems created by alcohol misuse and tackle Scotland's drinking culture to create a better environment for everyone. While the new Act will be a major change, it is a change for the better."[48]

So there is no doubt that health is an important factor in the contextualisation of the 2005 Act. It is not, however, the primary or sole driver for the legislation. It is one of five licensing objectives, each with equal weighting, and "health" considerations must be taken into account within the legal framework and rule of law which underpin the 2005 Act alongside any other consideration.

Early attempts at interaction with the licensing system from health practitioners proved somewhat ineffectual, with many representations to licence applications erroneous, unspecific, with submissions rejected with alacrity

46 Nicholson Report, p 12.
47 Ibid p 39.
48 "What Licensees Need to Know", February 2008.

within a quasi-judicial setting that must have been a steep learning curve for those brave representatives. The public health vanguard learned that a licensing board hearing is not like an academic debate, hustings, conference or exchange of policy ideas. The conflict of what constitutes "evidence" in the world of academic papers and research, compared with a hearing of a licensing board, has proven to be a complex field to furrow.

This tension has been explored in academic papers by leading health authors and it is useful to explore these perceptions. A study by Dr Niamh Fitzgerald from 2015,[49] which examined "how public health actors have attempted to influence local alcohol licensing policies and decisions in Scotland to ensure that the licensing objective of 'protecting and improving public health' is met", sought to explore this issue by interviewing individuals within the public health sphere who had interaction with the licensing system. Some of the comments which draw out the complexity of adopting standard public health approaches within a bespoke quasi-judicial system include:

- "One of the most challenging aspects for public health actors was being clear on what overprovision actually meant, and what evidence might demonstrate that it did or did not exist."[50]
- "It was considered challenging by many to gather and analyse robust data, one noted that 'all the datasets are slightly not quite what we need' and another noted clear weaknesses in the data, in particular the ability to link alcohol-related harm to any specific premises or even geographic area."[51]
- "Some participants reported a considerable degree of shock and frustration the evidence they presented 'didn't result in the outcome we were hoping'. One key informant felt that "if the licensing board had the full data of the extent of alcohol problems in the area they generally would be horrified. They would think 'we have to do something'."[52]
- "Interviewees reported that councillors did not always have a good understanding of health data, or of what constituted good evidence."[53]

In an Alcohol Focus Scotland publication from 2014, the authors said:

> "While impact has been demonstrated with regards to increased engagement of public health in the licensing process, the evaluation has shown that overall, the extent to which health data is used in practice continues to be subject to varying interpretations of the evidence by licensing board members and officials. The licensing policy outcome therefore does not always reflect the health evidence presented."[54]

What is clear from these types of articles and comments is that there is a different understanding as to what may or may not constitute evidence in the licensing sphere, and a frustration from public health actors that the evidence they seek to rely on and present is not resulting in their desired outcomes of a more rigid licensing policy or greater numbers of refused applications. This "different understanding" is discussed in detail below but perhaps one of the primary elements is grasping why some types of evidence are better than

49 Niamh Fitzgerald, "Influencing the Implementation of a Public Health Objective in Scottish Alcohol Licensing: A Qualitative Interview Study" (University of Stirling, 2015).

50 Ibid p 10.

51 Ibid.

52 Ibid p 11.

53 Ibid.

54 Laura Mahon and James Nicholls, "Using Licensing to Protect Public Health" (Alcohol Focus Scotland, 2014) p 1.

others, and an important part of this is the legal requirement for licensing decisions to be reached with regard to *causal* evidence.

7.1 The public health objective and causality

Causal evidence is a linchpin of licensing decisions. It is long established in licensing law matters that there is a difference between *causation* and *correlation*, and this is very relevant in licensing decisions. The weight to be attached to that strength of evidence is a key part of a licensing board's decision making. The starting point, therefore, should be the apparent observation that "causal" evidence should attract more weight than "correlative" evidence when a licensing board deliberates on the outcome of applications as well as on policy.

The fact that causality is a higher level of evidential threshold was criticised in the Alcohol Focus Scotland publication "Review of Statements of Licensing Policy 2013–2016" as setting the bar "too high". The presence of a causality test is also described by Alcohol Focus Scotland in public briefings as "unhelpful". This view appears to be because, anecdotally, licence applications are granted because there is no causal evidence of public health harms and therefore boards are unable to refuse, even though it is suggested that they might want to (and overlooking the other reasons why a board may reach a view).

The (un)helpfulness of a causality test to the stated aim of seeking greater numbers of refusals or to nurture a more restrictive policy environment is neither here nor there, however. First, seeking merely to create a hostile environment for existing or new licensed premises is not the purpose of the 2005 Act, nor is it the function of the licensing board to seek to do so as a default aim or end. It is the function of the board to make decisions and decide on policy based on material fact and other evidence that can lawfully be relied upon and justified. Secondly, the licensing board is not governed by aspirational or positional policies favoured by either public health actors or any other stakeholder including the trade – what they are governed by is the rule of law.

Many critics of the causality test point to the 2007 Scottish Government Guidance to Licensing Boards, where there is a clear reference to causal evidence, having fallen into disrepute, as if that prejudices the requirement for causality, or that this is the origin of the test, which of course it is not. The Guidance certainly discusses causality in the context of assessing overprovision, but it should be remembered that as a fundamental rule of law it applies not just in assessing overprovision but in relation to any evidence presented to a board alleging detriment. The causality test does not exist because it is referred to in this document, and would exist in law even if it was not mentioned in that publication.

The relevant section of the Guidance is from paragraph 47 to paragraph 50 and is in the following terms:

> "47. The results of all consultation should be evaluated to identify robust and reliable evidence which suggests that a saturation point has been reached or is close to being reached, <u>always provided that a dependable causal link can be forged between that evidence and the operation of licensed premises in a locality</u>. Factors which the Licensing Board may take into account include:
>
> - the information provided by the chief constable;

- subject to the constraints of data protection legislation, CCTV footage supplied by the chief constable or another source which illustrates disorder associated with the dispersal of customers in any locations;
- evidence from the licensed trade that the density of licensed premises in the locality has resulted in levels of competition which have applied downward pressure on the price of alcohol;
- evidence gathered from local residents of antisocial behaviour associated with licensed premises;
- information from the local authority's Environmental Health Department about noise complaints which can be attributed to the operation of licensed premises in a locality;
- data supplied by the NHS Board or other health bodies, for example, local Accident and Emergency Departments or Alcohol Action Teams.

48. It will not normally be appropriate to arrive at a decision based on one particular factor alone; but rather consideration should be given as to whether aggregated information and evidence from a number of sources points compellingly towards a particular conclusion.

49. The Licensing Board should not take into account:

- the manner in which individual premises in a locality are managed, since it is possible that well-managed premises may act as a magnet for antisocial behaviour, or may eject a substantial number of customers who collectively produce disorder and nuisance to a degree which is unacceptable;
- any concerns as to the quality of management of individual premises, which should separately be addressed through other statutory mechanisms;
- the need or demand for licensed premises in the locality. Commercial considerations are irrelevant to a policy which is designed to protect the wider public interest; or
- the hours during which licensed premises in the locality trade, since these will be controlled through operating plans.

50. The Licensing Board's policy should be expressed in such a way that interested parties are left in no doubt as to the reasons for its adoption, including the evidence upon which the Board relied and the material considerations which were taken into account."

Note that the sentence underlined at the start of paragraph 47 which refers to causality is emphasised in this way by the Guidance, not in the reproduction for this book. By highlighting the sentence it is therefore clear that the issue of proving a causal link is a very important one to the Government. Here is a key point: this axiom is not a creation of the Scottish Government for the purposes of this Guidance. The reason it exists in the guidance is because of decades worth of licensing jurisprudence – the case law and decisions which underpin the rule of law. Readers will have noted my references to the causal link in connection with the public safety objective in preceding paragraphs. The underlying law of causality applies to all of the objectives; it is not a doctrine affecting public health alone.

It may be that the causality test is unhelpful to those who wish to see more applications refused, but that is not the point. The point is that licensing boards must observe the correct legal tests in their decision-making. In their publication "Using Licensing to Protect Public Health: From evidence to practice",[55] Alcohol Focus Scotland conducted research amongst certain

55 Laura Mahon and James Nicholls (published by Alcohol Focus Scotland, August 2014, funded by Alcohol Research UK).

groups as to what impact the public health objective was having. They found, amongst other outcomes, that:

> "Interviewees were asked whether any progress had been made over the past two years with regards to licensing boards' understanding and promotion of the public health objective. Without exception they reported an improved general awareness of the public health objective and an appreciation of alcohol harm in a wide sense. None, however, felt that improved awareness and understanding was necessarily being translated into licensing decision-making."

They then quoted a licensing clerk who contributed to the study as saying:

> "The board is well aware of the concept of the public health objective . . . So far as month to month board business is concerned, other than representations about particular applications, there is very little mention of the public health objective. Much of the consideration of their business is more focused on the other licensing objectives. This is possibly because it is difficult to make a direct link in terms of individual applications."

The idea that improved awareness and understanding did not translate into licensing decision-making is an interesting one. That a board might fathom the health evidence does not equate to them acting upon it, because the evidence might not be of sufficient weight in their independent assessment to influence their decision. This does not mean the licensing board did not comprehend the health evidence, but that, having comprehended it, they took a view on it and in turn made a decision with regard to that view, within the legal parameters in which a decision can be made. If a health representative is aggrieved with a decision of the board, perhaps taking the view that the evidence has not been understood or properly listened to, then the correct remedy is to seek judicial review, as is the case for the establishment of a licensing policy.

A separate issue in this debate is that this requirement to have a higher threshold of evidential burden is presented as weighted in favour of the licensed trade. First, the Guidance makes it clear that commercial considerations such as demand should not be taken into account, and neither should economic considerations such as the viability of a business. The existence of a causality principle is not about promoting the alcohol industry: it is about observing the rule of law. I do not espouse the view that a licensing board should close its mind to health evidence or academic studies, simply that in considering what weight to attach to that evidence or those studies, as with any evidence of any nature, it must do so within a legal framework, just like it must do when contemplating all of the other objectives.

It may be worth noting for ease of reference the five grounds of appeal under the 2005 Act:

- That the board erred in law
- They based their decision on an incorrect material fact
- They acted contrary to natural justice
- They exercised their discretion in an unreasonable manner
- And, in the case of review hearing, that the decision was disproportionate.

A licensing board therefore has a very difficult job to do. They must weigh up such evidence as is presented to them, and then consider whether to grant the application or not, but in doing so must not err in law, must not base their decision on incorrect material facts, must not contrary to natural justice, must not exercise their discretion unreasonably and in the case of a review hearing must act proportionately (albeit there is an argument that proportionality could apply to other decisions because of underlying human rights considerations).

This brings me to the next point about the rule of law and the health objective. As I say elsewhere in this book, the 2005 Act is not a refusing Act. The Act is there to regulate the sale of alcohol but it also recognises that there is a place in Scottish society for the grant of new licences. Section 23(4) of the Act states:

> "The Board must, in considering and determining the application, consider whether any of the grounds for refusal applies and—
> (a) if none of them applies, the Board must grant the application, or
> (b) if any of them applies, the Board must refuse the application."

If no ground of refusal applies, the board *must* grant the application. And the opposite is also true. It is therefore neither a granting nor a refusing Act. It is neutral, based on the merits or demerits of the particular application. To put it another way, it is *directory not discretionary* for both grant or refusal depending on whether a ground of refusal applies. This is not the same in every licensing regime in Scotland. Under the Gambling Act 2005, for example, a licensing board "must aim to permit"[56] the grant of a new gambling licence – the default position is therefore that the gambling licence should be granted. Clearly, that is not the case in the alcohol licensing system. A balance requires to be struck. This balance must be underpinned, therefore, by properly evidenced reasoning and that is where the requirement for causal evidence comes into play, and has permeated licensing decisions for decades.

So what do the courts say on the causality principle? In *Deejay's Nightclub v Aberdeen Licensing Board*,[57] the board had rejected a regular extension application for a nightclub in Fraserburgh under the old 1976 regime seeking 2am opening, following police objections about vandalism. The court, in upholding the subsequent appeal says:

> "Here the issue, thrown into stark relief by the vandalism offences report, is whether the material put before the board does show any causative link between the premises being open and the incidents of vandalism reported. By causative link I do not mean necessarily that the applicants are to be considered at fault. It may be . . . that the vandalism occurs simply because at certain times a large number of people, possibly the worse for wear, are leaving the premises. The question at issue here is not whether, if such causative link is shown, the applicants can show in respect of individual cases that they were not at fault. Rather, it is whether the material put before the board demonstrates any causative link."

And then:

> "It is plain from looking at the vandalism offences report that it provides no evidence of any causative link between vandalism and the applicants' premises. The report states that during a period of one year from 1 June 2006 to 31 May 2007 there had been 161 reported vandalism offences "in proximity to" the applicants' nightclub. This is shown graphically by the superimposition of a series of rings on a town plan of the area, with the applicants' premises at the centre. The locations of the

56 Gambling Act 2005, s 153.
57 [2007] CSOH 188.

> incidents are marked and are mainly within the shaded area next out from the bulls eye. The top segment of the town plan covered by these circles is made up of sea and industrial and commercial estates. Unsurprisingly the vandalism incidents are marked mainly in the lower part. I am told, however, and it was not disputed before me, that almost all the licensed premises in Fraserburgh are within the same area. Accordingly, that geographical spread shows nothing of any relevance."

This is important because it reminds us of the requirement to look at the specific premises and the alleged detriment arising from those specific premises. It is also an early pre-2005 Act warning about the use of general or generic statistics. The debate can be widened out to consider the role of policy. A licensing board must remain open to the individual merits of an application. It must not, in adopting a policy, fetter its own discretion. There are numerous cases on this point including *Elder v Ross and Cromarty Licensing Board*[58] and *Aitken v City of Glasgow District Council*.[59]

It is also worth noting that efforts to suggest a "wider approach" through the lens of the licensing objectives allowed a board to "decouple" the causal link did not meet with success: see *Kaur v City of Glasgow Licensing Board*.[60]

The first appeal decision which looked at the public health objective under the 2005 Act was *Galloway v Western Isles Licensing Board*.[61] *Galloway* specifically deals with the issue of a refusal based on the health objective. In this case, an application seeking Sunday opening was refused on the grounds that more licensed hours would lead to greater availability, which in turn could lead to more harm. Whilst the case has a religious subtext, it discloses a number of points that are of clear interest to those seeking to grasp the health objective:

It is not for the applicant to demonstrate that greater availability would not be inconsistent with the public health objective: "it is clear from the passage from the Statement of Reasons which I have quoted above . . . that having apparently decided that granting the application would result in the increased availability of alcohol, (which the Board says would not be consistent with protecting and improving public health) the Board has qualified that by saying that the applicant had not demonstrated that such increased availability would be consistent with that licensing objective. That qualification leads me to the view that the Board has introduced into its exclusive decision-making process a requirement on the applicant which has no basis in the statutory formula. It discloses a clear error of law."

Licensing boards must base their policies on causality: "it is essential that when applying its licensing policy a Licensing Board must find and demonstrate a causal link between the particular mischief apprehended and the general terms of the policy itself".

In order to make a decision based on health evidence, it must be focused on the particular premises: "The Board did not focus (as it should have done) on the Club itself, its members and guests and its activities; and it failed to explain how granting the application would

58 1990 SLT 307.
59 1998 SCLR 287.
60 [2009] 44 SLLP 14.
61 [2011] LR 814.

> be detrimental to public health. Now I accept that a part of the Board's Licensing Policy is to protect and improve the health and welfare of patrons of licensed premises; and of course such a policy is laudable. But to apply that general policy to a particular application without examining its specific merits (or demerits) amounts to an arbitrary application."

So the requirement for boards to make decisions regarding the health objective based on the presence of probative causal evidence has not been plucked from the air, nor is it simply because it is in Government guidance or policy. It is the rule of law.

Another example of this is to be found in the case of *Martin McColl Ltd v Aberdeen City Licensing Board*.[62] This case, which is probably best remembered in relation to overprovision, also has important points to make about causality and the dichotomy of possibility and probability. In this case, an off-sale application for an RS McColl shop was refused on the grounds of overprovision and the licensing objective of protecting and improving public health.

The appeal as regards the public health objective was upheld by the sheriff court: in refusing the application based on the licensing objective of protecting and improving public health, the board looked to whether the application "may" be inconsistent with that objective; whereas the legal test in section 23(5)(c) is that the grant "would" be inconsistent. The difference between "may" and "would" is critical. The Sheriff says:

> "It is very clear that [the Board] require, when applying such factors as are relevant, to come to a view that these would be inconsistent with one or more of the licensing objectives (Section 23(5(c)) and in that event that the board must refuse the application. That is, however, a completely different test from a set of circumstances which may be so inconsistent. This is the difference between possibility and probability. The defenders have adopted a substantially lower test than required."

In short, speculation about potential health harm (or indeed, speculation about imperilment of any of the objectives) is not sufficient grounds on which to refuse an application. Refusing a licence on the basis that it is possible that it may lead to inconsistency with the licensing objective is therefore not good enough. A board requires to have sufficient evidence that that the inconsistency is not merely possible but is probable. Considering the wider jurisprudence, such evidence would have to be targeted in terms of the specific application and premises, and would also require to be probative and capable of independent assessment even where concerns are "real and genuinely held". This brings sharply into focus the contrast of certainty and speculation; the contrast between causation and correlation. There is a higher evidential threshold to demonstrate causation and probability as compared with correlation and possibility.

Another judicial example of the requirement for causal evidence can be found in the earlier case of *Maresq T/A La Belle Angele v Edinburgh Licensing Board*,[63] mentioned at Section 4.3 above. The judicial review was won on a number of grounds but one of these was that there was no causal connection between the sale of alcohol during the extended period of hours, and the alleged public nuisance of fly-posting which had been conducted by a third

62 30 November 2016, unreported.
63 2001 SC 126.

party. Referring to the need for the causal link, the Court of Session accepted the argument by the appellant that:

> "there had to be a causal connection between the mischief perceived and the use of the premises for the licensed activity" [said] "the objectionable activity . . . was not a consequence of the use of the premises for the sale of alcoholic liquor during any extension of permitted hours".[64]

The requirement for a causal connection is also discussed in *Aquilla Clark v North Ayrshire Licensing Board*,[65] and, of course, another seminal licensing decision, *Risky Business Ltd v City of Glasgow Licensing Board*,[66] in which Lord Prosser famously said:

> "the mere possibility of some undesirable sequel to the grant of the application [is] not a ground for refusal: the test [is] one of likelihood or probability".[67]

Linking this issue specifically to the public health objective, I encourage readers to reflect on what I say is a difference between licensing policy and alcohol policy. What is often entirely overlooked is that the licensing system is not designed with an aim of controlling licence numbers, nor is it simply to ensure that alcohol is sold responsibly (although each of these is incredibly important): it also is a framework to administer the business environment in which lawful alcohol retailers must exist. In other words, the global aim of licensing may be to ensure public safety and standards, but licensing regimes must also by their very nature allow for the operations which are licensed to be able to go about their business successfully within the approved regulatory environment. Not every licence process is about how the alcohol is actually sold or consumed. For example: transfer applications; minor variations to reconfigure the layout of premises; major variations to allow activities not connected to the sale of alcohol such as early opening for breakfasts, or to allow a grocer shop to open at 6am to sell milk and newspapers; the list goes on and in these processes it is difficult to see how the public health objective could be engaged.

Licensing boards are both the administrators and the regulators of the licensing regime. They must shoulder that burden fairly. To ask a licensing board to look only at the negative aspects, or demerits, whilst ignoring the merits such as job creation, tourism, community, amenity and the human happiness which responsible alcohol consumption can bring, perhaps betrays a disconnect in realising why successive Parliaments have over centuries entrusted licensing to local elected bodies: accountability to local people and interests; and therefore the recognition that responsible licensed premises can be a positive aspect of our society. Interestingly, Nicholson commented on the possibility that one of the licensing objectives which was discussed as a possible option was making people drink less:

> "When we worked out what we thought should be the licensing objectives – which are now enshrined in the bill – we felt that we could not specifically say that making people drink less should be a licensing objective. If we make that an objective for

64 Ibid at para 134.
65 28 January 1998, unreported.
66 2000 SLT 923.
67 Ibid at para 15.

> licensing premises, we will need to shorten licensing hours, never mind maintaining or even increasing them. I suspect that you will say that this is not the whole answer, but cutting the time that people are allowed to drink could have an impact on total consumption. Indeed, one could go further and introduce draconian laws under which a premises, licence holder or person serving in a bar is entitled to serve no more than two drinks to any customer. All sorts of measures can be taken to cut down drinking. The Executive's approach – which I agree with – is that the bill must be seen as part of a wider picture. Licensing can do only so much to persuade people to cut down their drinking; other measures to tackle that issue might be introduced, for example, by the Health Department or through educating children in schools. Our report tried to do what I think the bill is now doing, which is to provide a statutory licensing framework that will assist, not hinder, such initiatives. I believe that that is what we have achieved."[68]

I say that a licensing board must apply section 23(5); but in doing so it should be open to hearing submissions about the positive aspects of a case so long as those submissions are not legally incompetent in some way, such as a time-barred representation.

The Scottish courts recognise this balancing act. Lord Hodge, sitting in the Court of Session in the minimum pricing appeal, said:

> "The industries which the petitioners represent include companies which make a substantial contribution to the national economy and their products when used responsibly contribute to human happiness. But the abuse of alcoholic drinks and the harm which the abusers cause to themselves and others is a matter of general public concern both in this jurisdiction and throughout the United Kingdom."[69]

The Scottish Government also recognises the balancing act, in addition to numerous public statements on the benefits of licensed industry, as well as in the licensing guidance, which contains the following:[70]

Para 19: benefit of later hours to the night-time economy
Para 23: relationships with other strategies including tourism
Para 25: tourism needs to be taken into account when formulating local policy
Para 51: positive benefits for the locality in introducing new licensed premises
Para 52: some premises may have benefits to the local economy.

This balancing act – the weighing up of the good and the bad – is done with regard to deeply embedded principles.

7.2 The public health objective and quality of evidence

It is worth exploring, in the context of the public health objective, the debate on the presence or absence of evidence at hearings under the 2005 Act, as in the decision in *Ask Entertainment Pub Ltd v Aberdeen City Licensing Board*.[71] This case supports the ongoing requirement of a board to make decisions

68 Local Government and Transport Committee, 22 March 2005.
69 [2012] CSOH 156.
70 Guidance to Licensing Boards (2007).
71 2013 SLT (Sh Ct) 94.

based on bald facts and not supposition or conjecture. This again requires the board to be able to forge a link, or what is referred to in this case and others as a "nexus", between the alleged harm and the sale of alcohol from particular premises. In *Ask*, the issue was whether there was evidence that the licence holder had links to organised crime and might thus engage the licensing objective of preventing crime and disorder. As no probative evidence was independently assessed, the revocation of this licence was overturned on appeal.

Similar lines can be drawn to an earlier case, another appeal following revocation of a licence under the 2005 Act, *Melville v City of Glasgow Licensing Board.*[72] *Melville* deals with the awkward situation when a board is faced with two competing and conflicting versions of what the facts are: in this case, whether a pub was open outside its licensed hours or not. The board accepted the police version that it was, and rejected the licence holder and customer testimonials that it was not. In doing so, they fell into error, the Sheriff saying:

> "Neither account can be said to be more likely than the other. Each version is as likely as the other. On the material before me, without having heard from the witnesses, I cannot resolve which of these two irreconcilably different accounts should be preferred."

The quality of the evidence is therefore central. The better the quality of the evidence, the more robust the decision made by a board based on that evidence.

It may also be instructive to look further afield, as one might consider decisions such as *Brewdog Bars Ltd v Leeds City Council*,[73] in which the court held that if an applicant could demonstrate that the application would not add to perceived problems in an agreed cumulative impact zone (the English equivalent of overprovision zone), then the licence should not have been refused. The *Brewdog* case reminds us that the individuality of the applicant and the application should always be considered; and although an English case it does link to the Scottish approach of having a "rebuttable presumption" against the grant of a licence in an overprovision zone: in other words, that a new licence can be granted on cause shown.

And just like the Scottish case law, this type of consideration in English decisions is not new: in *Lees-Jones v Chester Licensing Justices*[74] the question of amenity and detriment is considered and the case reminds us of the need for licensing authorities to remember the range of controls on issues resulting from a vibrant night-time economy, not simply licensing controls, as factors which may be relevant to alleged detriment.

There is a rich thread of case law which creates clear precedent on how a licensing board should deal with evidence and on what legal basis decisions can therefore be made.[75] Licensing boards have a difficult job not simply in making their decisions but in having to act in an arena where many are ignorant about the *vires* of a Board.

72 [2012] LR 907.
73 6 September 2012, unreported.
74 [2001] LR 642.
75 See, for example, *JAE (Glasgow) Ltd v City of Glasgow District Licensing Board* 1994 SCLR 333 in relation to competing *ex parte* "evidence".

In the July 2014 issue of the *Journal of the Institute of Licensing*, Frances Carbery from the Public Health team in Bury discusses her experiences of appearing at a licensing committee. She says:

> "I have learnt that solicitors are paid to do a job, the same as I am, and while we have different agendas, in some ways we are similar. As a public health professional, I look for evidence to support decisions that reduce health inequalities and improve quality of life. A solicitor also uses evidence to support his or her case. We have a different understanding of evidence, but ultimately we both want our evidence to be strong enough for the right decision to be made by the licensing panel."[76]

That "different understanding" of evidence is a fascinating one and debate is yet in its infancy. It is only now that licensing boards in Scotland are starting to pay real attention to the public health objective and public health evidence. Public health practitioners are getting more familiar with the licensing system. Many scholarly articles have been published exploring these issues from a public health perspective. Licensing practitioners are all on a journey, one which may be signposted by academic studies, research, and other evidence which may be "for" or "against" depending on the subject matter and your own personal view.

So how have academic studies been used at licensing hearings? It is clear that there is a sizeable body of academic research in relation to alcohol, some of which has been quoted in this book, and also (but perhaps less so) in relation to how the licensing system affects health harms. It also seems to me that the robustness of research can vary greatly and that there are studies which reach different outcomes on the same topic. How any of this might assist a licensing board remains to be seen: one might argue that studies can be presented to argue both sides of a debate. Ultimately, and as a matter of law, academic studies are of lesser evidential value than material fact because there are always subjectivities, whereas a material fact is black and white: either it is or it isn't.

An interesting example of disparity in relation to academic studies and licensing law in Scotland is the alleged effect of the introduction of the "multi-buy" ban condition which came into effect on 1 October 2011. The multi-buy ban is a mandatory premises licence condition which was imposed on Scottish licences by virtue of the Alcohol etc (Scotland) Act 2010 and was designed to ban alcohol deals such as "three bottles of wine for a tenner" or "buy two get one free". It was noticed at the time that some retailers replaced their three bottles of wine for a tenner with individual bottles at £3.33, and so on.

However, there are two studies into the effect of this ban on alcohol sales, and they reach different conclusions. The earlier study, Nakamura et al, "Impact on alcohol purchasing of a ban on multi-buy promotions: a quasi-experimental evaluation comparing Scotland with England and Wales"[77] is from April 2014 and found that: "there was no significant effect of the multi-buy ban in Scotland on volume of alcohol purchased either for the whole population or for individual socio-economic groups", concluding, "Banning multi-buy promotions for alcohol in Scotland did not reduce alcohol purchas-

76 "Public Health Impact in Bury" (2014) 9 JoL 41.

77 (2014 Apr;109(4):558–67. doi: 10.1111/add.12419. Epub 2014 Jan 12).

ing in the short term. Wider regulation of price promotion and price may be needed to achieve this."

The second study, from December 2014, Robinson et al, "Evaluating the impact of the alcohol act on off-trade alcohol sales: a natural experiment in Scotland"[78] reached a different conclusion:

> "[t]he introduction of the Alcohol Act in Scotland in 2011 was associated with a decrease in total off-trade alcohol sales in Scotland, largely driven by reduced off-trade wine sales."

It does seem to me that the more recent study can perhaps be said to be more robust as it deals with a longer period of time but both are simply studies: both have limitations and caveats; and there will always be more studies. One can take from them what one wishes and that, I argue, underlines my point above about any comparison between academic study and material fact for evidential value.

In August 2014, Alcohol Focus Scotland published a paper entitled "Using Licensing to Protect Public Health: From evidence to practice".[79] This interesting paper posits a smart summary of the dilemma thus:

> ". . . licensing board members often appear to struggle to apply scientific evidence to policy and decision-making in practice. There are also challenges in effectively merging the perspectives and practices of licensing and public health: public health considerations tend to concern population-level indicators and long-term trends, whereas licensing operates in an environment characterised by case-by-case decision-making, negotiated settlements and complex legal argument."[80]

The study also gives a clear indication of the progress of influence of health information on licensing boards, particularly in relation to their statements of licensing policy, at that time:

> "Scottish statements of licensing policy in 2013 show an increased use of health evidence in comparison to the previous statements published in 2010. Nine percent of policies in 2010 cited the use of health evidence in comparison with thirty-six percent in 2013."[81]

They go on to say:

> "the extent to which health data is used in practice continues to be subject to varying interpretations of the evidence by licensing board members and officials. The licensing policy outcome therefore does not always reflect the health evidence presented."[82]

This last sentence is of particular interest in hinting at a possible disconnect in understanding how individual or policy decisions are reached by licensing boards or even a frustration that licensing boards do not slavishly adopt the policy positions put forward to them by health actors in the licensing system. It is not the job of the licensing board to adopt policy positions put to them by any stakeholder group. It is the job of the licensing board members to

78 (2014 Dec;109(12):2035–43. doi: 10.1111/add.12701. Epub 2014 Sep 12).

79 Laura Mahon and James Nicholls, published by Alcohol Focus Scotland and funded by Alcohol Research UK.

80 Ibid p 1.

81 Ibid p 3.

82 Ibid p 4.

independently assess such evidence and draw their own conclusions insofar as they may lawfully do so.

A key academic paper in this area, which is referred to in various licensing policy statements and often in public health representations, is commonly referred to in licensing circles as the "CRESH Report". This is a reference to the academic paper "Alcohol-related illness and death in Scottish neighbourhoods: is there a relationship with the number of alcohol outlets?"[83] This report was commissioned by Alcohol Focus Scotland, which was particularly interested in obtaining better evidence on the relationship between alcohol availability, alcohol-related harm and outlet density. The report found that:

> "[c]ompared with datazones with the lowest outlet availability, alcohol-related death rates were significantly higher in datazones with higher outlet availabilities, and the differences increased markedly as availability increased."[84]

Comparing this with alcohol-related hospitalisations, the report had this to say:

> "The alcohol-related hospitalisation results suggest the existence of outlet availability thresholds – over 6 off-sales, 9 on-sales, or 14 total outlets within 800 m – below which hospitalisation rates did not differ, but above which rates increased significantly. Such a threshold was not found for alcohol-related deaths – each increase in outlet availability was associated with a higher death rate."[85]

The basic proposal here is, of course, that the greater the concentration of licensed premises in a particular locality, the greater numbers of negative health outcomes there will be. The authors go on to propose an explanation for this by linking the density of outlets to encouraging irresponsible sales practices by licence holders:

> "Locations with high concentrations of on-sales outlets may encourage harmful drinking episodes through the coming together of drinkers and competitive drinks markets. High concentrations of off-sales outlets also create more competitive markets, with alcohol promotion tactics such as loss-leading and discounting used to compete with other stores. Competitive pressures on smaller convenience stores can also result in alcohol being sold to street drinkers, or sold as single cans."

This comment is speculative, as far as my reading of the report goes, and appears to me to proceed on an assumption that the market place does more to influence the sales practice of an operator than any desire to operate within the law and conditions of a licence, which, in the absence of evidence in the report, is an unwarranted inference.

The CRESH Report, which was often presented to licensing boards to encourage them to adopt policies of overprovision, is often criticised by licensing solicitors on several grounds. There is a disconnect between the amount of alcohol available and the amount consumed in that the data of how much alcohol is actually sold from premises in a locality is not available. There is also a disconnect in displacement of purchasing trends: if there are two shops where before there was one, this does not mean I will buy twice the amount of alcohol. The report also suffers from a further disconnect with licensing policy

83 Elizabeth A Richardson, Niamh K Shortt, Jamie Pearce and Richard Mitchell (Centre for Research on Environment, Society and Health (CRESH), Institute of Health and Wellbeing, University of Glasgow, 2 October 2014).

84 Ibid p 6.

85 Ibid p 10.

in that it only looked at numbers of premises licences, and not capacity (of any hue). The report also pre-dated the impact of the minimum pricing condition, which did not come into effect until 1 May 2018, and which may have had some tempering influence on the reference to loss-leading, but it does not pre-date the multi-pack ban condition which came into effect in 2011.

The most commonly cited passage at licensing board hearings, however, was the following caveat:

> "Finally, we should caution that our study was cross-sectional – it looked at a single point in time – hence while it suggested significant associations between outlet availability and alcohol-related harm we cannot conclude that the relationship is causal. Further analyses over time will be required to establish whether the links are causal, but currently alcohol outlet data for Scotland are only available for a single point in time. Better quality time-series licensing statistics, disaggregated into finer categories than simply on- or off-sales, would allow for research into longitudinal relationships between availability and harm."[86]

This concession brings us to the point that academic studies can only take a licensing board so far.[87] In my experience of appearing in licensing board hearings, board members are less reluctant to place credence in more targeted forms of evidence such as witness testimony – for example, a neighbour who has actually witnessed an operator sell alcohol to "street drinkers" as the CRESH Report puts it, or on a police report detailing persistent complaints of such activity with dates and times.

Responding to criticisms that the report did not do enough to equate its findings with particular named localities and thus be of better use to licensing boards and their decisions, Alcohol Focus Scotland commissioned an updated research exercise in 2018 and the result of that was a tailored report, authored by Alcohol Focus Scotland directly: "Alcohol Outlet Availability and Harm in Scotland".[88] This report, and the individual authority findings, were sent to licensing boards as part of their consultation exercise in formulating the licensing policies which covered the period 2018–2023 and thus a reader of the policies will most likely find reference to this updated report and the individual findings.

This report was no doubt of greater help to licensing boards in considering outlet density. There is no reference at all to the previous caveat on causality in the 2014 CRESH report, with Alcohol Focus Scotland preferring to instead use the term "a clear and statistically significant relationship" to describe outlet density and alcohol harms. Notwithstanding that the updated research is of interest to licensing boards, the underlying caveat remains, even if conspicuous by its absence from the 2018 report.

An additional contextual observation is that the authors state that looking at trends of outlet availability over time is important, and in doing so run their findings from 2012 to 2016. This allows them to state that numbers of licensed premises have increased, and in particular that off-sale licence numbers had increased by 4 per cent. This is, of course, a material fact, as

86 Ibid p 10.

87 The evidential strength of academic studies is gently derided by Sheriff Principal Murray in *Martin McColl Ltd v West Dunbartonshire Licensing Board* 2018 SLT (Sh Ct) 322 (at 331).

88 Published April 2018.

the numbers had risen from 16,157 to 16,629 over that period. However, a more balanced picture could have been presented in that in 2009 the number of licences was approximately 22,500. This represents an overall drop in alcohol outlet availability of approximately 26 per cent over the period 2009 to 2016.

Taking a step back on this issue, it would not be correct to say that it is only now that such studies are influencing policy. Studies into alcohol have been published for decades. What might be correct to say is that the quality of the information is better and it is clear that Alcohol Focus Scotland and various other health academics have put considerable effort into seeking to produce robust health information.

Clayson, in his report which led to the Licensing (Scotland) Act 1976, dedicates the whole of Part VI of his report to "The Need for Research", scathingly concluding:

> "this absence of knowledge is insupportable and [the] opportunity it gives for tendentious opinion is itself a contributory factor to the serious problem of misuse of alcohol in Scotland".

I have a copy of a health paper by the then Scottish Home and Health Department entitled "Scottish Licensing Laws", by Ian Knight and Paul Wilson, which was published in 1980, no doubt commissioned as a result of the Clayson rebuke, and it makes for interesting reading. For example, in relation to 11pm closing instead of 10pm, the authors conclude there was "no statistically reliable evidence of an overall increase (or decrease) in consumption after the extra hour", but that there is evidence of additional Sunday consumption following the relaxation of Sunday restrictions.

Nicholson was also not blind to such considerations. His report deals with health research and analysis and numerous studies between paragraphs 2.2 and 2.13. In the latter paragraph however, Nicholson says:

> "We have encountered difficulty in obtaining reliable Scottish data on matters such as [public health and disorder], and we venture to hope that in future such data may be compiled [in Scotland] in a systematic way."

The lack of probative data was an issue for Clayson and for Nicholson. But times and technology have moved on even since Nicholson and I have no doubt that research will continue and hope that this will help inform the decisions of licensing boards.

There is no doubt that licensing boards have regard to health data zone[89] information especially in relation to the formulation of their overprovision policies, so it is clear that this type of information is being presented to them in consultation or otherwise, such as with the 2018 report noted above. Appearing at licensing hearings across the country on a regular basis, the licensing practitioner can see this in action and see these reports being discussed. However, what one can also see is that the quality of health evidence also varies across the country, that some licensing boards are more amenable to health evidence than others and that each NHS health board and representatives who appear on their behalf have their own individual approaches.

89 Health "data zones" arise from the use of the Scottish Index of Multiple Deprivation, and are extremely localised geographical areas. See www.simd.scot

In some areas my experience is that the NHS representative will comment on any new licence application, citing local health statistics. Some will comment on all new licence applications but in a more measured way, having regard to the specific nature of the application. Some make no representation at all. In some areas, a representative from the NHS sits alongside Police Scotland and Licensing Standards Officers at just about every hearing. In other areas, an appearance by a representative from the NHS health board is a rarity.

Thinking again about Clayson's rebuke, what is certainly the case is that licensing boards, in addition to Government, are now being asked to consider, and are referring to, more of this type of information and more frequently than ever before. The difficulty comes in perhaps expecting licensing boards to respond or behave in the way that Government can when the legal framework within which they must exist is constructed with a unique and interesting apparatus. Government can take high-level policy approaches: licensing boards by their nature and by the legal system within which they operate must consider the fine detail and the local issues. It is also worth remembering that there are factors involved in any particular licence application beyond perceived health harms (if any).

West Dunbartonshire Licensing Board, for example, amended its now famous policy on overprovision, which is probably still the most robust in Scotland, to acknowledge that the grant of a licence could bring public health benefits through increased employment.[90] They did so having regard to Waddell and Burton's "Is Work Good for your Health and Well-Being?" (2006)[91] and other research.

Trying to draw all this together, I think it is fair to say that the public health objective has attracted the most commentary out of all the objectives. Increasingly beneficial health evidence and studies should be an accepted and welcome part of the process. The best decisions of a licensing board are almost always the best-informed decisions. The public health objective is of course central to licensing, but licence applications should not be viewed through the prism of the public health objective alone. There are five licensing objectives under the 2005 Act and each has an equal footing; it is the job of the licensing board to independently assess all information put before it, and add such weight to that information as it thinks appropriate.

The application of the public health objective and all of the objectives is not ultimately governed by academic studies, media or popular opinion but by the rule of law, and therefore evidential principles which underpin that rule: causality, sufficiency, probativity, reasonableness, natural justice and proportionality.

90 The acceptance of employment as a benefit to the public health objective was later endorsed by Sheriff Principal Murray in *Martin McColl Ltd v West Dunbartonshire Licensing Board* 2018 SLT (Sh Ct) 322 (at 332).

91 Gordon Waddell and Kim Burton, "Is Work Good for your Health and Well-Being?" (The Stationery Office, 2006).

8 IS THERE ROOM FOR A SIXTH LICENSING OBJECTIVE?

In debates surrounding the Air Weapons and Licensing Bill, Patrick Harvie MSP had proposed an amendment to the 2005 Act to introduce a sixth licensing objective, namely: "Promoting social and cultural life". This unsuccessful attempt was inspired by the closure of Glasgow arts and music venue The Arches, which resulted from a review hearing at which the City of Glasgow Licensing Board had decided to vary the hours of the premises to cease at 12midnight instead of 3am, following evidence of drug taking and deaths during the use of the venue as a late night club venue. The net effect of losing the nightclub business of the venue meant that the daytime activities could not be supported and the venue closed. This created a passionate backlash from the artisitic and cultural community of Glasgow as well as commentators on drug policy and laws.

When the amendment was debated in Holyrood, Patrick Harvie said:

> "[The existing licensing objectives] are important factors and licensing boards should take them into account, but positive factors can come from licensed venues and their cultural and social benefit to a community. Those factors should also be taken into account."

Under a wider concern that closing venues like the Arches would lead to the use of illegal drugs going underground, he later added:

> "By taking our current approach to licensing, we risk increasing the incentive for such irresponsible behaviour. [My amendment] asks that we balance the decision about individual premises with the wider impact on the community."

The then Justice Minister, Michael Matheson, was having none of it. He responded:

> "I am concerned that, while the aim is laudable, we should not be charging licensing boards with the promotion of social and cultural life. The existing licensing objectives concern themselves with mitigating the effects of alcohol. However, the proposed new objective does not have that same concern as its primary aim . . . [the amendment] would undermine the entire alcohol licensing regime and all that it sets out to achieve."

Harvie pressed the amendment(s) but was defeated 109 votes to 9.

Reflecting on this, it is my view, as I have expressed above, that a licensing board is perfectly entitled to consider the positive aspects of a licence application through the prism of the existing five licensing objectives, just as they are entitled to consider the injury an application may do to them. In *SCS Retail (No. 1) Ltd v South Lanarkshire Licensing Board (East Kilbride Division)*,[92] an application to increase the terminal hour of an off-sale licence from 8pm to 10pm had been refused at an original hearing with regard to the objective of protecting public safety and preventing crime and disorder. In doing so the board had relied on suggestions from objectors that the later hour would increase antisocial behaviour, and attract under-age drinkers to congregate at the premises and consume alcohol in a nearby underpass, noting that the general area was poorly lit and not well covered by public CCTV.

On a joint motion to remit the case for a re-hearing, the board agreed with

92 2013, unreported – remit agreed on joint motion.

submissions that in fact the applicant was prepared to invest heavily in the amenity of the premises and the adjacent locality such as in installing new CCTV systems (to cover a larger part of the surrounding area including the area around the premises itself), which would act as a deterrent to proxy purchasing, as well as installing public lighting and alarms to deter persons who may have sought to drink in the street and underpass. The board agreed that these efforts would support the objectives in a positive way and the application was granted.

Chapter 4

Licensing Boards

1 THE HISTORY OF THE LICENSING BOARD

The licensing board is a long-established part of the national framework for the regulation of licensed premises in Scotland. The modern iteration of the licensing board is a Clayson[1] invention, when boards as we know them now came into being with the onset of the 1976 Act, and ultimately retained through conversion into the 2005 Act. Prior to the 1976 Act the licensing laws had been regulated by "justices", a short-hand reference to Justices of the Peace, who in many cases were also local government representatives and therefore fulfilled a dual role. Justices of the Peace carried out a judicial function below that of the modern Sheriff Court, dealing with petty crimes and offences in a local geographical area as well as what we now might refer to as regulatory offences such as breaching local byelaws. They also dealt with licensing sessions – hearings – where permits might be issued or cancelled and prior to the onset of the 1976 Act, which introduced quarterly hearings, these earlier licensing justices sessions would happen annually or bi-annually.

This is in contrast to the position in England and Wales, for example, where licensing was in the gift of the Magistrates' Courts under the Licensing Act 1964 and was only replaced with local authorities as licensing authorities, and therefore with local councillors dealing with licensing decisions, with the passing of the Licensing Act 2003.[2] Having local representatives, as opposed to the senior judiciary in Sheriff Courts, deal with the regulation of licensing in Scotland is therefore an institutional position which is long established, underpinned by structures which go back to the nineteenth century if not before.[3]

Notwithstanding this, part of the remit of Nicholson was to take a fresh look, and establish whether the local licensing board should remain the appropriate regulator for licensed premises in what was at that point to be a "brave new world" of licensing in Scotland. For the most part, there was a consensus that licensing boards should be retained; they had been doing the business of liquor licensing for decades, had vast experience in the area, knowledge of licensees and licensed premises, as well as staff and systems in place. In par-

1 See Chapter 1 at Section 3.

2 The 2003 Act came into force on 24 November 2005.

3 Although, it should be noted that under the old 1976 Act the then "registration" for private members clubs was dealt with by the sheriff courts (under Part III of the 1976 Act), albeit applications for Regular Extensions – annually set permissions for later hours (and even Sunday afternoon trading hours) were within the remit of the licensing board. Club registration with the Sheriff Court was eradicated when clubs were brought into the 2005 Act licensing regime.

ticular, the fact that the licensing board under the 1976 Act as a collective of local government councillors brought "local knowledge" to the table was seen as something to be retained in the wider spectrum of seeking greater involvement from the community in the new licensing landscape. The importance of "local knowledge" had been given judicial expression for some time, and, as a licensing concept, is discussed elsewhere in this book; in particular, in relation to overprovision as a ground of refusal in Chapter 10 at Section 3.4.3.

The Nicholson Committee, during meetings and research, heard views that the licensing board might be replaced with some sort of tribunal with a number of people from different backgrounds, but this was dismissed. The relevant extract is worth repeating here for further elucidation:

> ". . . some of our consultees suggested that licensing boards should in future be replaced by a new kind of tribunal which would be composed of representatives from a range of bodies and organisations which have an interest in the operation of licensing law. That, it was suggested, could include representatives from the licensed trade, from local residents' groups, from the police, from public health, and so on. By contrast, licensing boards themselves argued strongly for the retention of the present position on the basis that members of licensing boards have a unique knowledge of the locality which they represent and, moreover, are ultimately answerable to their constituents at the ballot box. We are not persuaded that a representative body, drawn from a variety of backgrounds, would in fact be an effective and coherent decision-making tribunal. It would inevitably, we think, create a risk of competing sectional interests. Moreover, there is, we believe, a difficulty in that, once one tries to establish a representative body, it may be difficult to determine its membership with any certainty since some bodies who have initially been omitted may continue to press for representation. It is also perfectly possible that the actual representatives from constituent bodies might themselves be replaced by others from time to time. That, of course, would adversely prejudice the continuity, and consistency of decision-making, of any new tribunal. That is something which would be undesirable. We consider that on the whole the present system for providing the membership of licensing boards has worked fairly well: and we can see considerable force in the argument that councillors are well suited to being members of the boards on account of their local knowledge and their democratic accountability to the electorate."[4]

To that end, under the 2005 Act the "licensing board" is retained as a creature of statute which is a politically independent body of councillors who sit on the board and oversee applications and the licensing process. It is essential to understand that the licensing board is not a local authority body. It is not a committee of the council. This is discussed in detail below. The individual councillors who sit on the boards are subject to rules and Codes which did not exist in 1976,[5] but the overall function of the board remains broadly the same. There has been, however, substantial changes for those who administer the work of the board, which is dealt with below at Section 5.

The real novelty then, looking back to the period pre-2005 Act, was the introduction of the local licensing forum, a hitherto unknown beast and statutory creation of the 2005 Act. Forums have had a mixed response from licensing stakeholders, with some more effective than others. The purpose of

4 Nicholson Report, para 3.3, p 46.

5 For example, the Code of Conduct for Councillors introduced by the Ethical Standards in Public Life etc (Scotland) Act 2000.

the forums is discussed further in Chapter 5, but in general terms the main thrust of this new entity was to support the community involvement principle which Nicholson had referred to, perhaps best described as a "silent" licensing objective.

2 WHAT IS THE LICENSING BOARD?

As I explain above, the licensing board of the 2005 Act is substantially the same entity as it was under the 1976 Act; that is, a body representing a council area (or a portion of that area), made up of elected local councillors, whose job it is to decide upon licensing applications by granting or refusing, to apply measures to existing licence holders where necessary and proportionate, and generally to oversee the application of licensing law in its area. The key thing to note here is that the licensing board is a separate legal entity from the council. The licensing board may have policies which are separate from and in opposition to the council and they may in fact be on opposite sides of an action. For example, in *Glasgow City Council v City of Glasgow Licensing Board and For Your Eyes Only*,[6] the council unsuccessfully objected to the grant of an entertainment licence, on the basis that the venue was to be used as an adult entertainment venue. The licensing board granted the application even though the council was opposed. The council appealed the decision and lost.

The make-up of the board tends to be decided after a local government election and the 2005 Act provides no special process for this, meaning that it is left to councillors to decide for themselves who will sit on the board. The fact that the board members are councillors does, however, impact on the political make-up of the board – if a political party is strongly represented in the council, it is likely that the board will reflect that, having the largest representation of members on the board and perhaps the convenor, although that is not always the case. It may be that a councillor from a minority party is elected convenor due to particular experience, or for some other expedient reason.

There is a licensing board for each council area in Scotland. Some of the council areas have decided to divisionalise their governance, so that, for example, Dumfries & Galloway Council is divisionalised into four licensing board areas. A council may make a determination to divisionalise its area for the purposes of the 2005 Act under section 5(2). Where such a step is taken, each division has its own licensing board.[7]

Noting that the members of the board are local politicians, it is important to stress that the board does not make its decision on a partisan or party political basis – each application is treated on its own merits and, as a councillor, each member is bound by the councillors' code of conduct introduced by the Ethical Standards in Public Life etc (Scotland) Act 2000. Bias shown by a board member may result in a decision of the board being overturned on appeal.[8]

6 Glasgow Sheriff Court, 5 May 2005, unreported.

7 There is also provision to revoke a determination to divisionalise, so that a council area that has established divisions may remove them and revert to being a single area (s 5(4) and (5)).

8 See, e.g., *Mahmood v West Dunbartonshire Licensing Board* 1998 SCLR 843 and as digested

The public or perceived function and powers of a board stand to bear further scrutiny. Much of the media coverage of the powers of a licensing board is ignorant of the *vires* of a Board. In addition, the increasing role of health in the licensing arena has placed a considerable amount of public pressure on licensing boards, with many health commentators calling for the boards to take actions which, it can be suggested, are beyond their powers. The very nature of what a licensing board is, or should be, is being called into question here. In my mind, there is a difference between *licensing* policy and *alcohol* policy. What is often entirely overlooked in the wider public rhetoric surrounding alcohol is that the licensing system is not simply designed to ensure that alcohol is sold responsibly; it is also a framework to adminster the business environment in which lawful operators must exist.

Licensing boards are the administrators of this particular licensing regime. They must shoulder that burden fairly. They must examine closely the possible demerits that the grant of a licence might bring; but they must also examine the merits; and apply the results of those interrogations to the grounds of refusal. It is for the licensing board to take an independent assessment on a case-by-case basis, and not act as a cheerleader for the trade or any other interest group. There is some overlap here between the "local knowledge" of the licensing board and the aim of greater community involvement. When one reads a critique of lack of community engagement in the licensing system in Scotland, this is often purely from the perspective of those who have negative views on licensed premises or on new licensed premises; the fact that new licences are granted at all is said to demonstrate the lack of community voice. This assumes the community is always opposed to licences, which is an unwarranted inference.

The properly understood aim of greater community involvement is to allow that community to have an independent voice; which is as likely to support licensed premises as to decry them. This chimes precisely with why Parliaments have entrusted licensing to local elected bodies: independence of mind, and accountability to the community.[9]

at [1998] 11 SLLP 23, in which a board convenor visited an objector's business and, upon leaving, gave a "friendly wave". This action was substantial enough to derail the refusal of the application. In *Cameron v Fife Council* 2005 SLT (Sh Ct) 115 a licensing committee decision was reversed on the basis that there was a reasonable suspicion that some of the councillors might be biased; in this case, one of the councillors on the licensing committee was involved in a school board meeting in which he had openly expressed an opposition to the grant of a street trader licence near the school premises, and the chair of the committee had also been present at that school board meeting.

9 The respect which licensing authorities are shown as the correct decision-makers is reflected in the refusal of courts to entertain discussion on the merits of a decision – see, e.g., *Middleton v Dundee City Council* 2001 SLT 287, where the Inner House said (at 290): "Parliament has left the decision on propriety and fitness to hold a taxi licence to local committees because they are considered to be best placed to assess the needs of, and standards of service appropriate to their area . . . the court should be slow to lay down hard and fast rules of general application as to the matters which are relevant or irrelevant to the consideration of these questions by committees."

2.1 The "legal DNA" of the licensing board

The licensing board has been considered a "special tribunal" for one hundred years and more.[10] A licensing board is not a judicial body, but a quasi-judicial administrative body. As such, it is under a legal duty to deal with all parties fairly and equally: this, for the avoidance of doubt, includes the applicant. This was so even prior to the creation of licensing boards under the 1976 Act. As discussed above, pre-Clayson, the administration of licensing was dealt with by licensing "courts" (referred to as justices), but the licensing court was a court covering a particular burgh, and made up of elected councillors and justices of the peace. Before the onset of the Licensing (Scotland) Act 1976, there were sixty-seven separate licensing courts in Scotland. The origin of these courts goes back to at least 1756, and they evolved principally as local government evolved. The Guest Committee, a predecessor of Clayson, stated clearly that licensing was an administrative and not a judicial system. As Clayson later put it:

> "although [licensing] decisions are not judicial, it is desirable that they should be approached in the judicial spirit."

This Clayson vignette remains entirely valid.

Since that time, a significant change which has tugged at the edges of the licensing board is the Human Rights Act 1998 (and, of course, section 29 of the Scotland Act 1998) in relation to Article 6(1) of the European Convention on Human Rights and Fundamental Freedoms (ECHR), known generally as the right to a fair trial. The more exact wording is:

> ". . . everyone is entitled to a fair and public hearing within a reasonable time by an independent and impartial tribunal established by law".

It has been established for some time that a licence is a property right.[11] It is also clear that Article 6(1) does not just apply to civil or criminal courts in the traditional sense but also to administrative bodies, and this would include a Scottish licensing board.[12]

So the licensing board has to be independent and impartial – independent from Government, from the health professionals, and from the trade. The board also has to act lawfully as regards the legal principles underpinning the right to appeal: they may not "err in law", base their decision on an incorrect material fact, act contrary to natural justice, exercise their discretion in an unreasonable manner, and, in the case of a sanction resulting from a review hearing, act disproportionately. And the board also has a duty to make decisions based on an evidential basis; and such evidence must be probative; and the decision reached must journey through an independent assessment of any evidence, and not blind acceptance of assertion or speculation. These

10 *Lundie v Falkirk Magistrates* (1890) 18 R 60.

11 *Tre Trektorer Aktiebolag v Sweden* (1989) 13 EHRR 309; the famous so-called "*Three Tractors*" case.

12 It should be noted, however, that Article 6(2) and (3) do not apply to matters before a licensing board as they only deal with criminal jurisdictions. This means, for example, a licence holder or applicant may not exercise a true "right of silence" in responding to *sub judice* matters, although clearly they cannot be forced to comment, and the absence of comment will have such weight attached to it as the board deem fit.

parameters are part of the licensing board "rule book" often overlooked by those unhappy at decisions which make headlines.

This brings me then to look more closely at the administrative, but also quasi-judicial nature of the board. In *Kieron v Adams*,[13] which considered an appeal following rejection of a Sunday opening application under the old 1976 Act, Sheriff Principal Reid said:

> "The proceedings before the licensing board are, no doubt, administrative in character although they require to be conducted in a quasi-judicial way."

Why might this be so? It is first of all "administrative" because the board members are the ultimate administrators of a licensing system within which lawful businesses must be able to operate; and, secondly, "quasi-judicial" because the board, in dealing with hearings, must act under the above legal strictures and ultimately must weigh up all submissions placed before it in a way that provides an equality of treatment to all parties, including the applicant.

The 2005 Act is not a "refusing" Act. It is not the job of the board to look to refuse applications. The 2005 Act is by its very nature permissive as it creates a system under which alcohol may lawfully be sold and consumed. It reflects Parliament's acceptance that alcohol should be sold and enjoyed responsibly. That the board enjoys an inherent discretion to consider both positive and negative aspects of an application as put forward at the hearing, has perhaps been most recently affirmed in *Tesco Stores Ltd v City of Glasgow Licensing Board*:[14]

> "While s.23 does not permit discretion in applying the tests ('must grant'; 'must refuse') it does not prescribe what the board must do in 'considering' the test. To this extent, the 2005 Act is no more prescriptive, in relation to the approach to decision making, than previous licensing legislation, and the pre-2005 authorities still apply."[15]

To put it another way, boards cannot ignore the "equality of treatment" principle, as it refers back to the underlying principle of natural justice to which they are bound.

One example of this is bias, and even the appearance of bias.[16] In some cases, a member of a licensing board may declare an interest and step down from a particular application. Examples of this can range from membership of a local bowling club to holding shares in an applicant company. There may be a personal connection. What is important in this test is not that there is bias, but that there is the appearance of bias.

Other adverse conduct by a licensing board member during a hearing can prejudice the decision made by a board. In *Epic Group (Scotland) Ltd v Aberdeen Licensing Board*,[17] a member of the board was seen to have fallen asleep during the course of submissions, and then later voted. On appeal, Sheriff Principal Derek Pyle criticised the Board, saying:

> "It scarcely needs to be said that these are serious breaches of natural justice . . . it is surprising that having presumably realised that she had missed some of the

13 1979 SLT (Sh Ct) 13.

14 2013 SLT (Sh Ct) 75.

15 Ibid at para 40.

16 *Law v Chartered Institute of Patent Agents* [1919] 2 Ch 276, as followed by *Blusins Ltd v City of Dundee Licensing Board* 2001 SLT (Sh Ct) 176 and countless others.

17 2013 GWD 8-182.

> exchanges during the hearing she still thought it appropriate to participate in the deliberations and vote in favour of the decision reached by her colleagues. It is equally surprising that apparently no other member of the defenders either noticed that she had fallen asleep or, if they did notice, did not consider the inappropriateness of her being involved further in the proceedings. I do not know what the quorum is for such hearings but if the member's disqualification from further participation in the hearing would have meant that the hearing would have to be adjourned, then that was the decision the defenders ought to have made."[18]

In May 2014, a member of the Stirling Licensing Board was censured by the Standards Commission for Scotland, having been adjudged to have broken the Councillors Code of Conduct with respect to his alleged behaviour towards objectors to an application, which the Commission found was "aggressive".

The other side of this licensing coin is of course the conduct of applicants as regards dealings with board members. Section 8 makes it an offence for an applicant to attempt to influence a member of the board. The offence does not extend to other parties such as objectors, who can (it would seem) quite happily try to influence a member without committing any offence. At first blush, it may appear odd that only one type of party to the process (the applicant) should be covered by such a rule, but in my understanding the Scottish Parliament felt that if the offence extended to objectors, this would effectively stop residents from speaking to their own councillor about matters of amenity that affect them and their locality. Nevertheless, there are some who believe this is inequitable.[19]

In summary, in order to properly understand the role and remit of the licensing board, one must accept that the primary factor in their governance is the rule of law.

3 TRAINING OF LICENSING BOARD MEMBERS

Thinking back (often fondly) to my earliest involvement in this world of licensing in the old 1976 Act days, it is not difficult to recall one of the bugbears of many a licence holder (speaking to whilst I stood at the public counter of the Glasgow Council licensing section), aggrieved that the board did not see eye to eye with his or her proposals or business operation, which was that the councillors had little or no experience of how the trade actually worked. In some cases, that was no doubt true, but there are of course many licensing board members with substantial understanding of the licensed trade even if no direct experience.

However, towards the twilight years of the 1976 Act there was clear evidence of a knowledge gap in the absence of formal training. When the Scottish Parliament was in its infancy, and originally turned its attention to reviewing

18 Ibid at para 8.

19 A clerk tells me that is not unusual to have members seek guidance where a constituent has discussed the matter with them, on the basis that they are concerned this prior knowledge might lead to disqualification from involvement in the case. Members might be advised in such circumstances that knowledge of a case is not an automatic bar: the test is of course to avoid a reasonable perception of bias. "Fact finding" about the local issues pertinent to a case is not the same thing as taking a view or position on that case; but such approaches must come with a health warning.

the licensing laws, a great many of the newly elected Ministers of the Scottish Parliament had been serving councillors and would have sat on licensing boards and licensing committees. During a debate on 7 November 2000, Jamie Stone MSP said:

> "Those of us who have been councillors have sat on licensing boards. We know that members sit like a row of tatties, the clerk says: 'Is that agreed?' and members nod in agreement."

The knowledge gap was something that Nicholson recognised and addressed in suggesting that the board members should have to undergo statutory training. This suggestion made it to the statute books. Schedule 1 paragraph 11 to the 2005 Act and the Licensing (Training) (Scotland) Regulations 2007[20] require licensing board members to undergo appropriate accredited training within 3 months of election.[21] Members are elected every 4 years, normally at the "First Statutory" meeting of the newly elected council following local government elections.[22]

The board member training course was one of the first to be developed by training providers and the courses started rolling out in mid-2007. A member of a licensing board may not take part in proceedings unless he or she has complied with these provisions. The latest version[23] of the course features many aspects of licensing law similar to those taught to personal licence applicants, such as the nuts and bolts of the 2005 Act, but it goes beyond that too, into the realm of the administrative and quasi-judicial principles which have been discussed above.

4 MEMBERSHIP AND QUORUM OF LICENSING BOARDS

A licensing board must be made up of a minimum of five and no more than ten councillors. The number of councillors sitting on a licensing board under the 1976 Act varied wildly – larger cities such as Edinburgh argued that they needed a large number of members in order to represent the city appropriately,[24] but other commentators found having a board of some ten or twelve members to be unwieldy. It was also felt that the applicants, objectors, the general public and dare I say it even licensing solicitors could be frightened by the sheer number of people before them.

The opposite end of this argument is that the council staff who administered the meetings can sometimes have real problems locating enough councillors to make the board quorate, and there are many examples of board meetings being called off on the day because there were not enough councillors, much

20 SSI 2007/95.

21 There is no provision in the Licensing Act 2003 for English licensing committee members to undergo training.

22 The training rule might mean a very experienced licensing board having to resit the training, and might also mean a new member who has perhaps just been put in place on the board a few months prior to a local government election, also having to resit the course.

23 The training course itself was last updated following a Scottish Government working party in 2011 in which the author participated along with licensing colleagues from a trade, trainer, health and local authority background. A new working group was established at the start of 2021 to review and update the course specification.

24 See also "Board sizes 'ridiculous'" [2005] 30 SLLP 4.

to the dismay of all involved. To reflect this reality, the specific rule is that there must be one-half of the number of members present in order for the meeting to be quorate, but in any case not fewer than three.[25] This means that, whilst a board for a particular area may as a whole have a maximum of five members, three would be needed for a quorum.

4.1 Election, disqualification, removal and tenure

Election to the board is decided internally by the councillors themselves, and must be done at the first meeting after each ordinary election of the council. There are some statutory disqualifications from a councillor being appointed to the board. These are if the councillor is:

- a premises licence holder,
- an employee of a premises licence holder and works as such in licensed premises,
- engaged in the business of producing or selling alcohol, whether alone or in partnership with another person,
- a director or officer of a company engaged in the business of producing or selling alcohol, or
- an employee of any person engaged in the business of producing or selling alcohol and works as such in that business.

The role of member lasts until the next ordinary election, typically every four years.[26] He or she may be re-elected at the next election to the board. A member may resign (perhaps to move to another local government committee), and automatically ceases to be a member of the board if he ceases to be a councillor or is disqualified. A member may be removed from office if he is unfit by reason of mental or physical inability.[27]

4.2 *The convenor*

The convenor of the board is the chairperson and must be elected at the first meeting of the licensing board following its inception. If a vacancy arises, it must be filled at the next available licensing board meeting. The convenor is subject to the same rules on disqualification and tenure as a normal councillor, although the removal of a convenor may proceed only where the number of councillors in favour of the move exceeds one half of the total number of members.[28] If the convenor is not able to preside at a particular meeting, another councillor must be elected as convenor for the purposes of that meeting.[29]

25 2005 Act, Sch 1 para 12(1).

26 The cycle was interrupted by the Scottish Local Government (Elections) Act 2009; elections after 2007 were held in 2012 and then 2017, and have returned to four-yearly, so that in doing so local government elections would fall between elections for the Scottish Parliament. Licensing policy statements now follow the four-year cycle (see 2005 Act, s 6 – as amended by the Air Weapons and Licensing (Scotland) Act 2015).

27 2005 Act, Sch 1 para 5.

28 Ibid para 7(2).

29 It should be noted that the rules which apply to 1982 Act committees, where an appointed deputy convenor would automatically take the position in absence of the convenor, do not apply with licensing boards, and election of an acting convenor should be the first item of business at the start of a licensing board meeting if the usual convenor is not available – and

Crucially, if there is a split decision (on which see below) and equality of votes arises, the convenor (or whoever is chairing the meeting) has a casting vote.[30] Where a split vote occurs, the typical procedure would be for the clerk to perform a "roll call" of members who support each motion and then, if necessary, the convenor can cast the final vote. If a casting vote is made, the convention is typically to see the convenor follow their original vote.[31]

5 THE CLERK OF THE BOARD AND ASSISTANTS

For every licensing board there is a clerk. The clerk must be a solicitor or advocate and their job is to oversee the administration of the applications made to the board, run the board meetings and (crucially) to provide legal advice to the board on any and all matters arising. Most boards also have assistant or depute clerks due to the high level of work involved in this role, and in many cases the individual who fulfils the role of clerk will have that as one of many duties as a solicitor for the local authority. Schedule 1 paragraph 8 also provides that the board and clerk be provided with "such other staff, property and services as are required for their purposes". The staff who work in this capacity are council employees (as is, of course, the clerk). Staffing numbers vary from board to board. In some cases, there will be a team of people but in others only one or two.

5.1 The day-to-day work of a licensing board, and how hearings are conducted

The main thrust of the work for the board, clerk and staff is of course dealing with applications that have been made under the Act. Schedule 1 paragraph 9 gives the board power to appoint committees to assist with the exercise of any of its functions; for example, there could be a complaints committee which would hear premises licence review applications. In practice, I am unaware of any significant examples of this use of "sub-committee" powers, with most work being done by the full board itself.

A great deal of board work will be dispensed with at a hearing of the licensing board. The hearings will normally take place in a hall or court of the relevant local authority, at which applications will be called and heard. Applicants (and others) may be represented by another person at a hearing held by the board, but the board may be disinclined to hear representations from a person claiming to represent another without written authority.[32] The "feel" of a licensing board hearing can vary drastically depending on geographical location. In some areas, the hearings are conducted in locations

the election must be in public (2005 Act, Sch 1 para 12(2)). If the convenor is *in absentia,* then the clerk should convene the start of the meeting until the motion to appoint an acting convenor has been approved at which point business as normal should resume.

30 2005 Act, Sch 1 para 6(6). For a discussion of the operation of a "casting vote" under the 1976 Act, see *Strathtay Retail Ltd v Perth and Kinross Licensing Board* [1998] 11 SLLP 20.

31 It should, however, be stated that, notwithstanding convention, convenors are not obliged to follow their original vote: see, e.g., *R (Hewitson) v Guildford Borough Council* [2011] EWHC 3340 (Admin); [2012] JPL 951.

32 SSI 2007/453, reg 14.

which create an atmosphere similar to that of a court, whereas in other cases the hearings are conducted in what some may describe as a more collegiate format.

The meetings must be held in public, but the board may retire to consider an application before returning to declare its decision in public.[33] There is not always a need to declare how each councillor has voted, if indeed there is a vote, unless there is a division.[34] Otherwise, the decision by way of a motion and seconder might simply reflect the collective will of the board, for example to grant, or refuse,[35] and the absence of any counter motion should be taken as assent *qui tacet consentire videtur*. If a dissenting member fails to attract a seconder, that motion would fall. If there were a supported division, typically a roll-call would then occur with clerk asking each councillor in turn to declare their position. In some case, there may even be three separate motions (which I have experienced on a few occasions but it is generally rare).

In practice each board has its own way of dealing with this. In Glasgow, for example, every application is discussed but then adjourned for the members to consider in private. In Edinburgh, on the other hand, almost every application is debated fully in public and only on rare occasions do they retire to consider an application. In many areas, such as Aberdeen, Renfrewshire, South Lanarkshire divisions and many others, the members will retire if an application is contentious or if a member has asked for legal advice. In those cases, it is not uncommon for the clerk to confirm the detail of the legal advice provided once the board has returned to the public so that parties are aware.[36]

Another often discussed aspect here is the fact that councils themselves can hold a licence. There are numerous examples of this in Scotland and

33 On decisions being made in public following discussion in chambers, see *City Leisure Musselburgh (Ltd) v East Lothian Licensing Board*, digested at [2004] 28 SLLP 47.

34 A division may become apparent in private debate, in which case a roll-call would be conducted once back in public session. One can contrast this with the equivalent provisions under the 1976 Act, where the lack of a vote was generally considered to be fatal: see *Simpson v Banff and Buchan District Licensing Board* 1990 SC 347; 1991 SLT 18 and *McKay v Banff and Buchan Western Division Licensing Board* 1991 SLT 20; *Sood Enterprises Ltd v City of Glasgow Licensing Board* 1999 SLT (Sh Ct) 51; although in the later case of *City Leisure (Musselburgh) Ltd v East Lothian Licensing Board*, 2004 SLT 1210, Lord Emslie declined to support this view, saying (at para 13): "The only requirement is that, by one means or another, the Board must be seen to reach their decision in public. The members must no doubt have an opportunity to indicate dissent or to advance a contrary proposal if they wish, but, provided such an opportunity is given, their assent to an uncontradicted motion may be indicated according to whatever practice the chairman may habitually recognise."

35 On the issue of "collective will", see *Piper v Kyle and Carrick District Council* 1988 SLT 267 (2D), where the apparent bias of a single member of a committee was not held to have interfered with collective will as the committee had, as a whole, exercised discretion reasonably. See also 2005 Act, Sch 1 para 13 as to defects in decision-making.

36 See, e.g., *Clark v Kelly* 2000 SLT 1038 for a discussion on airing legal advice provided to the decision-maker in private. It has been put to me that a clerk may decline to confirm the legal advice given at the time of the hearing, on the basis that the 2005 Act allows a relevant party to request a full statement of reasons; but that approach precludes an instant rebuttal (if the board is prepared to entertain it) on legal grounds, which an applicant might wish to get "on the record"; and it robs the parties of some level of transparency as to the advice given at the pivotal moment. This might interfere in particular with a premises licence review hearing outcome that could be subject to interim recall, where an appeal will necessarily be lodged prior to the receipt of any statement of reasons.

some have questioned whether the licensing board, made up of councillors, should be allowed to make decisions on applications by the council, or perhaps an arm's-length entity which holds a licence, to which they belong.

The format can also vary in terms of the calling of applications. In the majority of board areas, applicants are cited to attend at a particular time and then wait till their case is called to make submissions. As a licensing board hearing is a public forum, many applicants and other parties will sit patiently in a gallery awaiting their case to be called. In some board areas, however, the applicants and other parties will be asked to wait in a sort of "holding" area and then called in on an individual basis.

A common complaint in England and Wales is lack of time to present submissions. I understand that there is a practice in certain licensing authorities of giving a licence holder or, in most cases, all parties, a clear steer on a maximum speaking time, even where the matter at hand is a review of the licence and possible suspension. This practice, it can be argued, might effectively stop the licence holder from having his case heard in full, which would seem to be at odds with the right to a fair hearing. In Scotland, applicants are usually given fair time to speak but there are plenty of examples where verbose submissions are hurried along by the board, perhaps especially towards the end of a meeting. It is also relatively common to see a convenor, or perhaps a clerk, provide certain instructions to parties not simply in terms of format, but in terms of content – for example, many boards will inform parties present but not overly familiar with the licensing hearing processes not to introduce "new material" which was not part of their representation. This, of course, is on the basis of "fair notice" to the applicant. It is also proper that a convenor may intervene where case management considerations make intervention proper, as where submissions are repetitive or a party introduces irrelevant matters such as a moral opposition to alcohol *per se*.

The frequency of hearings also varies across Scotland. In larger city boards, a monthly hearing is typical, whereas in some of the smaller jurisdictions hearings may be bi-monthly or at times even farther apart. Most of the licensing boards endeavour to publish a list of their meeting dates for the coming year, although this can be subject to change. In rare cases, hearings may have to be abandoned where a quorum is not possible.

In most cases, applicants will be represented by a solicitor or agent, but they may represent themselves. There are no rights of audience requirements for an agent appearing before a licensing board, so a qualified solicitor, trainee solicitor, paralegal, or other type of agent may represent the applicant. It is, of course, a matter for the applicant to decide upon the best representation for them. One matter which may benefit exploration is what the law says on a last minute "continuation" of the case. It is not altogether uncommon for an agent to find themselves at the bar, about to present the case, but be unable to do so, perhaps because the client has not appeared, or perhaps they have only recently been instructed and do not have the full facts to hand in order to represent the client properly.

I have certainly been in this predicament on a few occasions. If one is unable to proceed with the case then the agent should seek continuation. In most cases a licensing board would consider that to be a fair approach so that the applicant is best represented. In the case of *Havenbrook Ltd v City of Glasgow*

Licensing Board,[37] a request by an agent to adjourn was dismissed and the application was subsequently refused. The appeal was upheld, but on the related but separate matter that the board ought to have adjourned as a result of matters which emerged in the course of the hearing which "were so material as to merit an adjournment in the interests of natural justice". On the discrete point of refusing an agent's request, the court said:

> "I find the reasons in support of an adjournment advanced at the outset less than compelling. Whether I would be persuaded to adjourn is, of course, beside the point. The matter involved an exercise of discretion. I consider that the Board was entitled to refuse to adjourn at that juncture in the exercise of its discretion. The Board had been given no explanation as to why the applicants had not given adequate instructions to their appointed agent in advance of the quarterly meeting. If this criticism were to be viewed in isolation I respectfully accept the reasoning of Sheriff Mitchell [in *Mohammed v City of Glasgow Licensing Board* [1998] 6 SLLP 14] and the limitations upon the scope for appeal."[38]

In this case the agent had not, it would seem, offered any particular reasoning beyond a general request to adjourn. It is therefore sensible to lead reasons as to why a continuance is merited, when asking a board to do so.

The hearing will almost always feature contributions from officers. It is commonplace to find Police Scotland, licensing standards officers, a representative from the local health board, and other officials such as from building standards, who may all have something to say about the application. The legal status of these standard reports is of interest. Whilst the Act talks of "representations", and sets timelines under which these must be received and intimated, in practice it seems to be the case that reports from local authority departments have some sort of quasi-representation status not provided for under the Act itself. Reports from building standards, for example, which may pass comment on the proposed capacity of premises as well as on wider building and structural issues, may not be treated by the board as falling within the terms of what the Act deals with as representations. That does not mean, of course, that the board should not have regard to these reports,[39] but merely that the status of them within the structure of the Act could be clearer, and it is accepted that a board will seek additional guidance or input from the officials and ask for the views on certain matters which may go beyond what was stated in the report or representation.[40]

In order to minimise the amount of work that has to be decided upon by a board at a hearing, a lot of the decisions can be made under "delegated powers": in other words, decisions made outside a meeting. The board may authorise the clerk, a member of the board, a committee or even support staff, to make decisions in this fashion. There are, however, some types of application and function that may not be delegated and must be considered at a meeting. These are:

37 [2009] 40 SLLP 22.
38 Ibid at 23.
39 As is said in the famous case of *J & J (Inns) Ltd v Angus District Licensing Board* 1992 SLT 930 at 935: "It would be absurd if a board was required to exercise its discretion by having to work in the dark because it could not entertain any information which might be available."
40 This might be especially true in review hearings where boards are specifically entitled to seek and obtain further information from any source; but prior notice of such additional information obtained prior to any hearing should certainly be given to the licence holder or agent.

- determining the board's policy for the purposes of the licensing policy statement
- the overprovision assessment
- premises licence applications
- "major" variation applications
- transfer applications where the applicant has been convicted of a relevant or foreign offence
- personal licence applications or renewals where the applicant has been convicted of a relevant or foreign offence
- conducting a hearing (and any steps which may arise from the hearing, such as suspension or revocation)
- making a closure order; and
- refusal of confirmation of a premises licence.

Finally, an occasional licence application may be delegated only where there is no objection or representations to the application.

Other than the processing of applications, the 2005 Act has tasked licensing boards with producing four key reports or papers:

(1) the overall statement of licensing policy
(2) an overprovision assessment (which, in practice, sits within the policy statement)
(3) an Annual Functions report; and
(4) an Annual Financial report.

We will now look at each of these in turn.

6 THE STATEMENT OF LICENSING POLICY

The statement of licensing policy is in fact one of the cardinal features of the licensing regime, albeit tucked away at section 6 of the Act. The statement acts as a guide and rulebook as to how a licensing board is likely to go about its business, not simply for the board itself but also for licence holders, agents and the public and other interested persons. The statement can be of use to all and, for private practitioners, can be a positive tool in considering the chance of success or otherwise for a client's potential application. When the 2005 Act was originally enacted, it called for the statement to be produced every three years,[41] although there was provision for it to be added to or amended during that time by way of supplementary statements.[42] Under the terms of the transitional arrangements to the 2005 Act, the first statement of licensing policy was to be published by each licensing board by 30 November 2007.[43] While most boards managed to achieve this, several were unable to produce a statement and in many cases were extremely understaffed as the work increased to a level never seen before.[44] This was unfortunate for applicants in the March and even June conversion tranches, who were left to lodge their premises

41 2005 Act, s 6(1).
42 2005 Act, s 6(2).
43 Licensing (Appointed Day and Transitional Provisions) (Scotland) Order 2007 (SSI 2007/128).
44 See, e.g., "Falkirk 'in breach' by missing deadline" [2007] 38 SLLP 9.

licence applications without the guidance of the statement. Another unfortunate development at that time was that many of the statements themselves appeared to be remarkably similar, not simply in form and content but striking word-for-word exactness, as a number followed perhaps a little too closely the template provided by the then Scottish Executive.

These first policies ran from 2007 to 2010, noting that the Act came into force on 1 September 2009 but that applications could be made from 1 February 2008 for personal licences and conversion applications. The second round of policies, covering 2010 to 2013, were more developed and we began to see some clear divergence in different board areas as the new system had bedded in, and boards began to display their own personalities under the 2005 Act strictures. The third round of policies was initially supposed to cover the period 2013 to 2016 but this was ultimately extended to 2018 with the later onset of the Air Weapons and Licensing (Scotland) Act 2015. Section 42 of that Act replaced the specific reference to "three years" with the blander "licensing policy period", such period requiring to commence on the date:

> "occurring 18 months after an ordinary election of councillors for local government areas takes place under section 5 of the Local Government etc. (Scotland) Act 1994".

The wider "policy" position behind the extension of the policy period is to tie this into the local government elections. Certain licensing boards argued that the triennial review meant they were hamstrung by the policies of their predecessors, and following elections with new intake of eager and fresh-faced councillors ready to make their mark, this would be the appropriate time to update the policy. An early example of a board disagreeing with the policy of its predecessors is in Edinburgh, where the licensing board elected following local elections in 2012 disagreed with its previous iteration on the issue of commencement of on-sales licensed hours on a Sunday remaining at 12.30pm, and began to allow 11am commencement bringing it into line with the majority of Scotland even though the policy, which was due to run until 2013, stated the old 12.30pm start.

This change in licensing policy periods was one of the first changes brought about by the Air Weapons and Licensing (Scotland) Act 2015, coming into effect as it did on 30 September 2016.[45] The transitional provisions applicable to the Order which enacted this provision provided that existing licensing policy statements in place prior to 30 September 2016 remained in force until such times as a new policy is published. This meant that the policies brought into effect to cover the period November 2013 to November 2016 were effectively extended until approximately eighteen months after the 2017 local government elections (albeit boards could bring their new policies into effect prior to that ultimate deadline if able to). The current run of statements covers the period 2018 to 2022.

The statement itself must be prepared in such a way that it seeks to promote the licensing objectives[46] and the licensing board must also have regard to the Scottish Government Guidance to Licensing Boards in preparing and

45 Air Weapons and Licensing (Scotland) Act 2015 (Commencement No. 4, Transitional and Saving Provisions) Order 2016 (SSI 2016/132), art 2.

46 2005 Act, s 6(3)(a).

adopting the guidance, a requirement imposed on them under section 142(3). The role of the statutory guidance in adopting policy has met with controversy over the years, not least because that even as at 2020 it had not been updated since the first edition was launched in 2007. The Guidance therefore has attracted opprobrium because of its vintage, coming into being over two years before the Act itself did, but also because some elements of the guidance are disputed in the licensing community.

What is accepted, or at least should be, is the primacy of statute. The guidance is of relevance, but does not supersede the law:

> "It is important to remember that, while regard must be had to the guidance, it should not be allowed to usurp the clear language of the statute."[47]

However, although the primacy of statute is key, there is no doubt that regard must be given to the Guidance, and any decision or policy where this has not occurred would be open to challenge.

When the draft guidance was approved by the Scottish Ministers on 20 February 2007, its status and role within the licensing system was debated. MSP George Lyon said:

> "We are not producing guidance that tells boards exactly how to make the Act work. Some people would like us to give boards a script and provide guidance that anticipates every scenario, but we are not going to do that. We want boards and, just as important, their clerks to be creative and innovative and to implement the Act in a way that meets local needs and circumstances. There is always a danger that too prescriptive guidance would hinder that. We are also not using guidance as an alternative to secondary legislation or as a lawyer's guide to the 2005 Act . . . I make it clear that we will always be open to suggestions from people who are directly involved in the licensing process about how the guidance might be revised in future. Any revised or new guidance will, of course, be laid before the Parliament, as the 2005 Act requires."

It is open, therefore, to licensing boards to have regard to the guidance, but then ignore it. The Act goes so far as to create a requirement under section 142(4), which states:

> "Where a Licensing Board decides not to follow any guidance issued under subsection (1), the Board must give the Scottish Ministers notice of the decision together with a statement of the reasons for it."

However, whilst many licensing board policies do not slavishly follow the guidance, and whilst many individual decisions by licensing boards do not slavishly follow the guidance, I am not aware of a single instance of a licensing board complying with section 142(4). What is clear is that there are appeal cases where the board has not had regard to the Guidance and that this omission has been upheld as an error in law.[48]

The Scottish Government established a working group to review the Guidance through the Institute of Licensing.[49] The work of that group occurred towards the end of 2017 and into Spring 2018. The remit was to feed back on the aspects of the guidance which required to be updated. The group

47 *R (4 Wins Leisure Ltd) v Blackpool Council* [2007] EWHC 2213 at 2224 (para 15).

48 See, e.g., *Aldi Stores Ltd v Dundee Licensing Board*, Dundee Sheriff Court, 12 August 2016, unreported.

49 On which I must declare an interest, as I chaired this group.

returned those views, and the Scottish Government later produced a draft second version of the guidance which went out for public consultation from 19 March 2019 to 19 May 2019. In the early part of 2020, there were signs that a final version, having taken account of feedback during the consultation, would finally be published. This timeline disappeared with the onset of Covid-19 and so the second edition is still awaited.

Coming back to the process to agree licensing board policy, the board must consult with the local licensing forum, such other persons as appear to the board to be representative of interests not represented by the forum, and any such other persons that the board deems appropriate. After the statement has been published the board *must* have regard to the policy in exercising its functions.[50]

In day-to-day terms the policy is a very useful guide to all. It will indicate what a licensing board believes are the appropriate on- or off-sales hours in its area. It will indicate what the board believes to be suitable access arrangements for children and young persons in certain types of premises. It will put in place rules concerning how the board expects licensed outdoor areas such as beer gardens to be operated. In doing so, however, the policy should also specify the basis and reasoning for those views being reached.

Noting this, it should be remembered that the statement of policy is open to challenge – the board cannot create a policy that is *ultra vires* of its remit[51] and of course if the policy is not properly supported by probative evidence then that too could lead to a successful challenge.[52]

However, whilst it is true to say that a decision reached in reliance on a flawed policy is challengeable, one should be clear that to seek an appeal based on the lawfulness of the statement of licensing policy requires careful consideration. The strength of policy was examined in the decision of *Kell (Scotland) Ltd v City of Glasgow Licensing Board*.[53] The *Kell* case was another lap-dancing refusal, now much overshadowed by its sister case, *Brightcrew*. As the exact facts of the two cases are different, so too are the *dicta*, and there are some interesting observations on this wider point of the weight a board will attach to its own policy, to be taken away from Sheriff Principal Taylor's opinion:

> "It is quite clear that the Act has changed the manner in which Licensing Boards must operate. The requirement to publish a policy statement, and to consult before

50 2005 Act, s 6(4).

51 An example of this at the time the new Act was being passed in Parliament was a proto minimum pricing appeal, namely *Mitchells & Butlers Retail Ltd v Aberdeen City Licensing Board* [2005] SLLP 24. In this case the Aberdeen attempt to introduce a minimum price was ruled unlawful as the 1976 Act did not give boards such powers. Licensing solicitor Andrew Hunter said in 2007 that it was only a matter of time before licensing board policy statements faced judicial review or appeal: see "Premises licence applications, licensing board policies and vires" [2007] 38 SLLP 21.

52 An English expression of this view can be considered in *Daniel Thwaites plc v Wirral Borough Magistrates' Court* [2008] EWHC 838 (Admin). In this case a licence holder had successfully proposed to vary his licence to have a later terminal hour but a subsequent appeal by objectors was upheld. The licence holder then sought judicial review on the grounds that the magistrates had based their decision on the mere possibility that his later trading hours may attract noise problems. This was successful; the judge held that a decision should not be made on speculation and that the magistrates had (at para 63) "proceeded without proper evidence and gave their own views excessive weight".

53 2000 SLT (Sh Ct) 197.

> publication, has also altered the previously established legal framework. Mr Skinner is correct in submitting that when refusing an application made under the Licensing (Scotland) Act 1976, a Licensing Board required to give proper reasons with a satisfactory evidential basis. However, now that every Licensing Board requires to have a policy statement, it seems to me that it is sufficient for a Board to refuse a licence on the basis that the application breaches that policy statement always providing that the Board is prepared to admit exemptions to the policy if there is specific justification for departing from it."[54]

This supports the general expression that courts are and should be slow to intervene in matters which rightly sit with the licensing board[55] and there are numerous cases of failed policy challenges especially in relation to licensed hours. Advocate Scott Blair, a renowned licensing expert, has frequently commented that with any new policy "there are winners and losers". In other words, the fact that someone loses out does not, of itself, justify a challenge.

Fortifying this is the accepted position that each case is always on its own merits and there is no "comparative principle" in licensing law – where one might argue that an unreasonable exercise of discretion has occurred where other similar cases have been successful – even where such decisions are made at the same hearing.[56]

The year 2010 was a strong one for licensing policy and in particular policy on licensed hours, with no less than four appeal cases concerning refused hours, all of which failed. In each of these cases, the licence holders had been "losers" in the Scott Blair sense, in that they had previously enjoyed certain licensed hours which were removed from them by the operation of policy rather than on an individual case basis. One such case was *Carmunnock Village Recreation Club v City of Glasgow Licensing Board*[57] where the club had, for some time, operated with a 1am licence without any particular difficulty or complaint. During the transition hearing, the club was forced to accept a terminal hour of midnight as this was the new Glasgow Licensing Board policy. They later sought to recover the 1am by way of a major variation, which was refused. That decision led to the appeal and whilst I think it was accepted that there were no issues which pertained to the specific premises, the sheriff rejected the appeal on the basis that the board was entitled to reach a policy view on hours, had consulted on the matter and was entitled to give significant weight to its own policy.[58]

54 Ibid. He continues to unravel the thread of keeping an open mind to exceptions in a later paragraph, stating: "when the Board is exercising its functions under the Act it is only provided that it 'must have regard to the licensing policy statement'. It does not provide that the Licensing Board is obliged to slavishly follow what is contained in the licensing policy statement."

55 See, inter alia, *Associated Provincial Picture Houses Ltd v Wednesbury Corporation* [1948] 1 KB 223 (CA), *Holmes v Hamilton District Council* 1987 SCLR 407 (Sh Ct), *Ranachan v Renfrew District Council* 1991 SLT 625, *Hughes v Hamilton District Council* 1991 SLT 628, *Latif v Motherwell District Licensing Board* 1994 SLT 414, *Middleton v Dundee City Council* 2001 SLT 287, *Mejury v Renfrewshire Council* 2001 SC 426, and *Chief Constable v Renfrewshire Council and Caldwell* Paisley Sheriff Court, 8 November 2002, unreported.

56 See the principal cases of *Cashley v City of Dundee District Council* 1994 SLT 1111 (ED) and *Fife Council v Ewing* [2011] CSIH 45; but *also Loosefoot Entertainment Ltd v City of Glasgow District Licensing Board* 1991 SLT 843 (ED); 1990 SCLR 584 and *Sangha v Bute and Cowal Divisional Licensing Board* 1990 SCLR 409 at 412FG. The principle is also reinforced in *Martin McColl Ltd v West Dunbartonshire Licensing Board* 2018 SLT (Sh Ct) 322.

57 9 July 2010, unreported.

58 This approach is consistent with *Ahmed v North Lanarkshire Council* 1999 SLT 1064, which

In the same year and at the same licensing board, we have the decision in *Drinkcafe Ltd v City of Glasgow Licensing Board*[59] which also covers a case where premises lost existing hours due to a change in licensing policy as opposed to individual concerns about the operation of the premises. Here, nightclub premises Boho traded in the west end of Glasgow and had enjoyed a 3am licence for some years. The Glasgow board brought in a policy whereupon nightclub venues outside the city centre would only be allowed to trade until 2am. Boho therefore sought to challenge this in order to preserve their existing 3am licence. However, the Sheriff upheld the decision of the board – they were entitled to adopt a policy, and in doing so necessarily to take account of a wider picture which led them to the view that the policy was lawful and necessary. That individual premises had no history of difficulty was, in effect, neither here nor there as a policy had been adopted and the licence holder had not convinced the board why it should operate as an exception to that policy.[60]

This was followed by *WWMC Ltd v Renfrewshire Licensing Board*[61] which related to a policy decision by the board to allow later hours on the provision of significant entertainment. In general terms, the board had adopted a policy whereby an operator who could show that they provided significant entertainment could take advantage of a later terminal hour. Again, the licence holder "lost out" in respect of this but the court held the view that the board was entitled to reach a view on this differential and had had regard to the licensing objectives in doing so.

There then followed two cases concerning multiple pub operator Greene King. In *Greene King v North Lanarkshire Licensing Board*[62] the operator had lodged a major variation application for a premises called the Horseshoe Bar, seeking an 11am commencement hour on Sunday, where the local policy at that time was still 12.30pm. This was refused based on the operation of the policy. In refusing the appeal, the Sheriff had similar regard to the fact the policy had been properly adopted with regard to wider concerns, in this case in relation to the licensing objective of preventing crime and disorder. The applicant had attempted to make a case for an exemption, including an offer to restrict the hours so that they would not be operated on occasions when two football teams based in Glasgow might be playing against one another. The board had listened to the case but having done so still applied its own policy, which it was entitled to do.

Finally, in *Greene King Brewing and Retailing Ltd v Dundee Licensing Board*[63] another "policy hours" case was considered. Whilst the appeal was rejected, and the details are broadly aligned to the cases above, the decision allows us to explore and speculate on what the limits of this approach might be to provide some balance to the concomitance of these "Policy Hours" cases. Here, Greene King had premises, the Old Bank Bar, where they wanted to

related to a change in policy on late hours catering licences following Local Government reorganisation.

59 2011 SLT (Sh Ct) 5.

60 Following the earlier decision of *Cinderella's Rockafella's Ltd v City of Glasgow Licensing Board* 1994 SCLR 591. See also "Brightcrew judgement sinks hours variation" [2010] 45 SLLP 4 for a discussion of the decision.

61 3 November 2010, unreported.

62 23 December 2010.

63 24 February 2011.

trade from 10am to 11pm whereas the existing hours were 11am to 12midnight, which were the hours agreed in terms of the licensing policy. The board refused the application on the grounds of the public health objective albeit that the overall number of hours traded would remain the same. Their view was that allowing the 10am start might send a message to other licence holders that this commencement hour would be "normalised" in some way. The Sheriff, in rejecting the appeal, appears to have agreed that allowing the 10am start would create a "precedent" which other premises might seek to take advantage of, without necessarily agreeing to the linked earlier terminal hour. This might be described as a concern over some sort of indirect impact on the wider policy aims.

Whilst the case does have some merit in the wider discussion of the weight a board should attach to its own policy, my own view is that the decision is erroneous, and has two key issues. First, the idea that a decision can be made so as to "set a precedent" is almost certainly a mis-step, with regard to a wide body of case law requiring the licensing board to take each case on its own merits and not allow its own discretion to be fettered – which would of course include not adopting or applying a policy too rigidly. Secondly, when one reviews the idea of "sending a message", it is doubtful that this *dicta* can have too much bearing in the wider jurisprudence, noting the later decision from the Court of Session in the case of *Lidl UK GmbH v City of Glasgow Licensing Board*,[64] which of course overturned the previous decision of the Sheriff that the board was entitled to suspend a licence following a failed test purchase in order to act as a sort of deterrent to other licence holders.

The idea of using a decision to create a deterrence was also looked at in the decision of *Kennedy v Angus Licensing Board*.[65] In this case Sheriff Veal was in disagreement with the board in its decision to revoke a personal licence where one of its reasons was that this would "send a message to other licensees" concerning behaviour linked to the licensing objective of preventing crime and disorder. He rejected the idea that the objective should be read widely enough so as to consider forms of deterrence, saying:

> "I am unable to identify any relevant connection between the commission of this offence and the 'licensing objectives' set out in section 4 of the 2005 Act. I am not persuaded that the very fact of the existence of this conviction should automatically incur an additional discretionary penalty at the hands of the Licensing Board. I consider that the reference to 'deterrence' . . . is . . . inappropriate."

Looking down south there are a couple of earlier English cases which are of interest as we consider the legal position of policy. In one of the leading English policy cases, *British Beer and Pub Association v Canterbury City Council*,[66] the council's policy was challenged on the grounds that it sought to place additional burdens on licence holders. In the result the council amended its policy during the challenge; but the judge, Richards J, held that the policy was:

> "over prescriptive in a number of places, suggesting the existence of requirements that cannot lawfully be imposed . . . it is for applicants to determine the contents of their applications."[67]

64 [2013] CSIH 25.
65 22 August 2012, unreported.
66 [2005] EWHC 1318 (Admin).
67 "Trade bodies claim victory in policy challenge" [2005] 31 SLLP 13.

There is a point to be made here about licensing boards "micro-managing" premises through policy, although a separate Scottish decision on the imposition of conditions where such a challenge was made, did not curry favour with the courts.[68]

Whilst a licensing policy may of itself be challenged under judicial review,[69] it is also important to note that it is now settled law that a policy can also be challenged in summary application for appeal, where the board for example refuses an application having regard to its policy. Notwithstanding the cases noted above, the matter was also confirmed in the Court of Session in the leading case of *Brightcrew*, which is of course discussed in significant detail elsewhere in this book. There are numerous examples of appeals where the unsuccessful applicant has drawn attention to some flaw in policy, which could include a flaw in material fact. Such challenges perhaps most commonly appear in relation to overprovision, to which we now turn.

7 THE OVERPROVISION ASSESSMENT

Overprovision is without doubt one of the most controversial elements of the 2005 Act and has generated a number of appeal cases, perhaps more than any other discrete area of jurisprudence. Those who practised prior to and during the 2005 Act transition may recall incorrectly reported media comment suggesting that boards could not refuse licences on the grounds of overprovision. Of course, they could and often did.[70] Nevertheless, the creation of the "overprovision assessment" as a specific part of the new licensing regime seemed in part to emanate from this misunderstanding, coupled with a general feeling in Holyrood that there were simply too many licensed premises in Scotland. Historically, this may have been accurate. According to the Scottish Beer and Pub Association, in 1800 Glasgow had one inn for every 130 Glaswegians and there were so many pubs that the hanging signs had to be removed because they were darkening the city streets.

In more recent times, however, the number of licences has dropped significantly. At the last count of licences (including members' clubs[71]) under the 1976 regime, around 2008, there were in the region of 22,500 licensed premises. After the 2005 Act had bedded in, the first round of liquor licensing statistics confirmed that this number had dropped to 16,305 licences. This severe drop has been attributed to the economic downturn, the rise in off-sale

68 *BM Taverns Ltd v Perth and Kinross Licensing Board* 19 October 2012, unreported.

69 There is, of course, a consideration as to whether a judicial review may be deemed premature: see *Wm Morrison Supermarkets plc v South Aberdeenshire Licensing Board* [2010] 45 SLLP 29, although of course that case did not concern a policy in the statutory sense; cf *obiter* of the Sheriff Principal in *Kell (Scotland) Ltd v City of Glasgow Licensing Board* 2000 SLT (Sh Ct) 197 at para 14.

70 1976 Act, s 17(1)(d). For an interesting précis of the history of overprovision in Scottish licensing law, see "Explaining overprovision" [1996] 5 SLLP 16. To read trade reaction to the new approach to overprovision as the Act was first published, see "A trade divided: Overprovision" [2005] 30 SLLP 5; and in relation to problems assessing overprovision at that time, see Stewart Ferguson, then Clerk to the City of Glasgow Licensing Board, "Assessing overprovision: problems ahead?" [2005] 31 SLLP 27.

71 According to the Explanatory Notes to the Licensing Bill (22 February 2005), there were 2,349 registered clubs.

Table 4.1 Licence numbers

Year	*Total Licences*	*On Sales*	*Off Sales*
2018/19	16,722	11,631	5,091
2017/18	16,696	11,595	5,101
2016/17	16,742	11,625	5,117
2015/16	16,704	11,593	5,110
2014/15	16,663	11,537	5,096
2013/14	16,520	11,476	5,044
2012/13	16,396	11,475	4,921
2011/12	16,338	11,482	4,856
2010/11	16,305	No data	No data

consumption (stay-at-home consumption/pre-loading), supermarket alcohol purchasing, the smoking ban, and to the 2005 Act itself, which resulted in a number of operators choosing simply to allow their old licence to lapse due to expense and complexity of conversion to the new system.

The numbers of licences as confirmed by the Scottish Government since the inception of the 2005 Act are as shown in Table 4.1.

Interestingly, one of the "options" considered by the Parliament following the publication of the Nicholson Report was whether to introduce a moratorium on new licence applications – the ultimate overprovision policy. This was addressed in the Regulatory Impact Assessment to the Licensing (Scotland) Bill published in March 2005 as follows:

> "A moratorium on new licences would act as a brake on the introduction of new venues into the market. If the market place is crowded, then providers may resort to irresponsible promotions to maintain their profitability. The introduction of a moratorium would prevent such a situation arising. However, it would not solve the problem in areas where the market may be regarded as already overcrowded both in relation to off-sales and on-sales and would not allow development in areas not presently overprovided for. A moratorium is also likely to lead to an artificial value for those places already holding a licence, imposing a greater cost on those wishing to enter the market place. If no new licences were forthcoming this could encourage those places already holding a licence to apply to enlarge their premises leading to the rise of more high volume vertical drinking establishments compared to smaller bars. A pro-active overprovision assessment by Licensing Boards would enable more focused action to be taken in specific areas where overprovision was causing local problems."

The concept of overprovision is, in my view, underpinned by a perceived notion of harm. If a locality is "overprovided" with licensed premises, then that is deemed to be a negative feature of that area. This presupposes that harm such as in the form of prejudice to the licensing objectives through public nuisance, crime, health and so on will arise simply because of the number of licensed premises in that area. The first edition of the Guidance to Licensing Boards says that the 2005 Act approach to the overprovision assessment:

> "recognises that halting the growth of licensed premises in localities is not intended to restrict trade but may be required to preserve public order, protect the amenity of local communities, and mitigate the adverse health effects of increased alcohol consumption resulting from growing outlet density."[72]

72 Guidance to Licensing Boards (Scottish Government, April 2007) para 34.

However, on one view, that is a blunt approach which pays no heed to any independent assessment or evidence, but instead pre-supposes harm. There are any number of variables which should be taken into account in this and the matter is complicated to say the least. As far as this chapter is concerned, we will be focusing on the statutory duty placed on licensing boards in their assessment of overprovision, but readers should also refer to Chapter 14, at Section 3.4, which explores overprovision as a concept and as a ground of refusal in some detail.

The 2005 Act requires every licensing board to conduct an assessment of overprovision. The overprovision assessment is in fact an element of the statement of licensing policy. The provision detailing this process was amended by section 54 of the Air Weapons and Licensing (Scotland) Act 2015 with respect to an alleged *lacuna* concerning "locality" (as noted below) so that section 7(1) and (2) (as amended) now provides:

> "(1) Each licensing policy statement published by a Licensing Board must, in particular, include a statement as to the extent to which the Board considers there to be overprovision of—
> (a) licensed premises, or
> (b) licensed premises of a particular description,
> in any locality within the Board's area.
> (2) It is for the Licensing Board to determine the 'localities' within the Board's area for the purposes of this Act, *and in doing so the Board may determine that the whole of the Board's area is a locality* [my emphasis]"

This latter statement contains the principal addition to these elements of the provision, clarifying the position that a board was entitled to define its whole area as a locality. This followed the evidence of several licensing boards who submitted during the Call to Evidence period in Autumn 2014 that the plural use of "localities" plus one reading of the word "within" could be taken to mean that a locality had to be a subset of the principal locality, that being the entire jurisdiction. Many practitioners disagreed that such a clarification was necessary, but the matter is now put beyond doubt with this amendment.

An additional change which was made to the definition came in via an amendment to section 7(3) which widened the scope of what was to be assessed in determining whether there was overprovision. The amended provision, which was enacted on 30 September 2016,[73] reads:

> "(3) In considering whether there is overprovision for the purposes of subsection (1) in any locality, the Board—
> (a) must have regard to the number and capacity of licensed premises in the locality,
> (aa) may have regard to such other matters as the Board thinks fit including, in particular, the licensed hours of licensed premises in the locality, and
> (b) must consult the persons specified in subsection (4)."

The persons to be consulted are the chief constable, such persons as appear to the board to be representative of the interests of the licensed trade in the locality, residents in the locality and such other persons as the board thinks fit.[74]

73 Air Weapons and Licensing (Scotland) Act 2015 (Commencement No. 4, Transitional and Saving Provisions) Order 2016 (SSI 2016/132) art 2.

74 2005 Act, s 7(4).

The key changes, however, concern the three pillars of assessment. Note that the board:

- "must" have regard to the number and capacity of licensed premises (this does not include occasional licences),
- "must" consult certain persons (noted below),
- but "*may*" have regard to such other matters as the board thinks fit, including licensed hours (my emphasis).

The ability of the board to consider what it likes in reaching an assessment of overprovision is novel and may be said to strike a fatal blow to a two-dimensional "numbers game" analysis of the concept.

It must be the case, however, that boards had already taken into account various matters beyond the mere number of licensed premises in the overprovision policies which pre-dated this change. That much can be read from the policies themselves. When the City of Glasgow 2013–2016 policy came into force, that board had taken a markedly different approach to establishing which areas it considered to be overprovided. In the Glasgow 2010–2013 policy, some of the areas had been identified as those which were considered with significant late-time activity – areas like Shawlands Cross, John Street, Byres Road and the Charing Cross end of Sauchiehall Street. Yet when the 2013–2016 policy was adopted, all four areas were dropped in favour of areas where evidence had indicated there were the most significant issues in the city concerning public health and public nuisance, which it was felt could be linked or attributed to a concentration of licensed premises.

In relation to the consultation process itself, the Guidance to Licensing Boards is worth repeating in full here:

> "The results of all consultation should be evaluated to identify robust and reliable evidence which suggests that a saturation point has been reached or is close to being reached, *always provided that a dependable causal link can be forged between that evidence and the operation of licensed premises in a locality*. Factors which the Licensing Board may take into account include:
>
> - the information provided by the chief constable;
> - subject to the constraints of data protection legislation, CCTV footage supplied by the chief constable or another source which illustrates disorder associated with the dispersal of customers in any locations;
> - evidence from the licensed trade that the density of licensed premises in the locality has resulted in levels of competition which have applied downward pressure on the price of alcohol;
> - evidence gathered from local residents of anti-social behaviour associated with licensed premises;
> - information from the local authority's Environmental Health Department about noise complaints which can be attributed to the operation of licensed premises in a locality;
> - data supplied by the NHS Board or other health bodies, for example, local Accident and Emergency Departments or Alcohol Action Teams.
>
> 48. It will not normally be appropriate to arrive at a decision based on one particular factor alone; but rather consideration should be given as to whether aggregated information and evidence from a number of sources points compellingly towards a particular conclusion.
>
> 49. The Licensing Board should not take into account:
>
> - the manner in which individual premises in a locality are managed, since it is possible that well-managed premises may act as a magnet for anti-social behaviour,

or may eject a substantial number of customers who collectively produce disorder and nuisance to a degree which is unacceptable;

- any concerns as to the quality of management of individual premises, which should separately be addressed through other statutory mechanisms;
- the need or demand for licensed premises in the locality. Commercial considerations are irrelevant to a policy which is designed to protect the wider public interest; or
- the hours during which licensed premises in the locality trade, since these will be controlled through operating plans.[75]

50. The Licensing Board's policy should be expressed in such a way that interested parties are left in no doubt as to the reasons for its adoption, including the evidence upon which the Board relied and the material considerations which were taken into account."

A key expression in these excerpts is of course the reference to the causal link. The issue of causality in the licensing process has been a controversial one for some stakeholders and is discussed at length in Chapter 3 at Section 7.1 in relation to the meaning of the licensing objective of Protecting and Improving Public Health.

The importance of following the correct protocol in carrying out the overprovision assessment and consultation cannot be underestimated. Errors in the process will allow the policy to be challenged on appeal. In *Aldi Stores Ltd v Dundee Licensing Board*,[76] a new off-sale licence for Aldi was refused on the overprovision ground having regard to the board's adopted policy which included the creation of an overprovision zone in which the proposed premises were located. There was significant critique of the adopted policy and the appeal was upheld. A key part of this critique was that the board had erred in law by not following the Act or indeed the Guidance to Licensing Boards as regards how to go about creating the overprovision assessment. The board lapsed into a "basic and early" error by not identifying a locality and then consulting upon that locality. Instead, they provided a list of options as to which locality or localities people considered to be overprovided. Other errors were made, such as not identifying the specific capacities of all on- and off-sales premises in the locality (they had only identified the off-sale capacity).

Whilst the first edition of the Guidance to Licensing Boards has been criticised by many licensing practitioners, primarily due to its vintage, the primacy of statutory guidance is underlined in case law by *Daniel Thwaites plc v Wirral Borough Magistrates' Court*,[77] and appeals such as the *Aldi* case and others[78] reinforce the need for the licensing boards to ensure they follow the correct processes.

75 This bullet point is now incorrect, noting the subsequent amendment to the Act to allow licensing boards to take account of licensed hours as part of the overprovision assessment, as discussed above.

76 Dundee Sheriff Court, 12 August 2016, unreported.

77 [2008] EWHC 838 (Admin).

78 *Marini v South Lanarkshire Licensing Board (Hamilton Division)* 2019, unreported. In this case refusal of a new premises licence in the overprovision zone of Bothwell led to a joint motion on appeal of an agreed remit for reconsideration. One of the grounds of appeal in the case was that the board had not followed the correct process in the formulation and consultation of its policy.

7.1 Overprovision and determining localities

"Locality" for these purposes is entirely within the hands of the board.[79] As is made clear above, the 2015 Act has confirmed that the locality can be the entire jurisdiction of the board. In selecting any locality, a licensing board must do so with regard to probative evidence and not select areas arbitrarily. The Guidance to Licensing Boards says:

> "The identification of localities could be approached in a number of ways. The Licensing Board may consider that information which the chief constable is capable of providing is a reasonable starting point. The chief constable will be able to:
> - identify 'hotspot' areas within the Licensing Board's area where it can demonstrate that crime, disorder and nuisance are caused by customers of a concentrated number of licensed premises;
> - suggest other areas in which the number of licensed premises or premises of a particular description is moving closely towards overprovision; and
> - provide the Licensing Board with the geographical boundaries of those areas."[80]

This was addressed in the case of *Martin McColl Ltd v Aberdeen City Licensing Board*.[81] This case concerns the refusal of an off-sale licence by the Aberdeen board for a proposed RS McColls premises in Kinkorth. The application was refused based on overprovision and the public health objective.

At the time of the decision the Aberdeen board had a virtual blanket overprovision zone across its whole jurisdiction in respect of off sales, save a forested area and a green field site used for farming (Anguston and Kirkhill). It is worth considering what the policy had to say about its assessment of overprovision at that time:

> "Having excluded these two localities, the Board identified the rest of its area as a locality which has overprovision of off sales premises. The Board, having regard to the number and capacity of liquor licensed premises in this locality and, with the supporting evidence provided by consultees, adopted this locality as having an overprovision of liquor licensed premises for off sales. The Board realised that there were premises which sold alcohol for off consumption only and other premises which sold alcohol for both off and on consumption. It decided to restrict overprovision to premises that sold alcohol for off consumption only which, according to the information from the Health Board, is where the source of cheap alcohol lies."

They go on to say:

> "The Board also realised that this figure was likely to change in future should any off sales premises close by way of surrender or revocation. The Board was also aware from the Health Board's advice that described their evidence as 'the tip of the iceberg' and that there was a lot of under-reporting. The Board therefore considered that this would not automatically lead to a successful application for a new licence on the basis that an existing licence had been surrendered or revoked. Should that occur the Board may consider carrying out a further overprovision assessment before determining such future application."

79 2005 Act, s 7(2). Licensing boards have always had quite a wide discretion in determining what area(s) they wish to define as a locality: see *Lazerdale v City of Glasgow Licensing Board* 1996 SLT 451 and *Caledonian Nightclubs Ltd v City of Glasgow District Licensing Board* [1996] 4 SLLP 11.

80 Guidance to Licensing Boards (April 2007) para 43.

81 Aberdeen Sheriff Court, 26 August 2015, unreported (but digested at [2016] LLR 725).

The board also said:

> "The Board realised that the terms of section 7 of the 2005 Act did not support calculating overprovision to cover its entire area."

In this case, the applicant sought an off-sale display area of $10m^2$ for the shop premises. The application drew representations from Police Scotland and the Licensing Standards Officer, both of which merely pointed the board's attention to their own policy. The application was refused.

The sheriff granted the appeal, saying that the selection of the Anguston and Kirkhill localities amounted to excluding two areas:

> "of no consequence, in an effort to present the resulting locality as other than covering the whole area".[82]

He later said that the subtraction of these two areas was a "*cosmetic exercise*" and therefore the 2005 Act had not been followed, requiring as it does localities to be identified and assessed. The Sheriff recognised that the Air Weapons and Licensing (Scotland) Act 2015, which was enacted but not yet commenced at the time of the decision, clarified that a board was entitled to adopt its entire jurisdiction.

Importantly, the Sheriff also criticised the Board for the absence of dealing with the steps required under section 23(5)(e) in order to find a ground of refusal with regard to overprovision, namely to have regard to the number and capacity of licensed premises, or licensed premises of the same or similar description as the subject premises in the relevant locality.

Further criticism is levied in that the board did not refer to the locality within its policy (that is, the whole jurisdiction minus Anguston and Kirkhill), but instead chose to consider a second locality which was determined at the hearing (1 kilometre from the application premises). The statement of reasons did not specify in which of these localities overprovision would have been created following grant of the licence.

There are a number of lessons to be learned here, the foremost of which I would suggest is that the selection of localities for overprovision purposes should be based on probative evidence and policy should be set based on where the evidence leads. Another key lesson is to ensure that particular localities are accepted and understood in translating the policy to the consideration of individual applications. It is common practice in certain board areas to provide information by way of maps and statistical information. At the North Lanarkshire Licensing Board, for example, an applicant is provided with a highlighted plan in advance of the hearing, clearly indicating what the locality will be in terms of the board's assessment of the application as a whole but with particular regard to overprovision. That communiqué will also include a list of all licensed premises within that zone and indicate capacity details.

In contrast, the Renfrewshire Licensing Board takes a "Goldilocks" approach, offering an applicant three options as to locality at the time of the hearing, taking into account a "small, medium and large" radial area. Applicants can have their say on which of the three is most appropriate as it relates to that particular application. Other parties may also have a say on

82 Ibid at para 17 of the judgment.

this. The board then decides which locality is "just right" – and the hearing continues.[83]

The issue of determining localities in the context of a licensing hearing is explored at length in Chapter 10 at Section 3.4.2.

7.2 Overprovision and capacity

Once the board has identified its localities it must assess whether there is overprovision by looking not just at the numbers of licensed premises, but also their capacity. The capacity element is, perhaps, one of the more confusing aspects of the 2005 Act regime for the uninitiated. Capacity is defined in section 147(1) and, for on-sales purposes, means the maximum number of persons who may be accommodated in the premises at any one time and, for off-sales purposes, the amount of space given over to the display of alcohol for sale. So there are in fact two types of capacity, and some premises may have both – it is not uncommon for a pub, hotel or bar to also wish to have an off-sale offer for customers which may not be in the form of a traditional shop or separate area, but perhaps may simply relate to where a customer has enjoyed a particular glass of wine with a meal and wishes to buy a bottle to take home.

It therefore follows that there are a number of different classes of potential overprovision: an overprovision of licensed premises; an overprovision of licensed premises of a particular type,[84] an overprovision of a particular portion of the licensed hours, an overprovision of people (on sales capacity) in a locality; and, finally, an overprovision of space across all the premises in a locality given over to the display of alcohol (off-sale capacity).[85] How the board reaches a view on each of these positions can be coloured by any matters it sees fit but its decision must be based on probative evidence.

8 ANNUAL FUNCTIONS REPORTS

The Annual Functions Report requirement was introduced at section 9A of the 2005 Act following the passing of the Air Weapons and Licensing (Scotland) Act 2015 and the obligation to produce the reports commenced from financial year 2017/18. Paragraph 184 of the Explanatory Notes to the 2015 Act states the purpose of this was to require licensing boards:

> "to produce an annual report on the exercise of their functions, summary of decisions made by the Board and information about the number of licences held under the Act.; and an annual financial report on their alcohol licensing activities".

The report must be produced annually, within three months of the end of each financial year.[86] There are three key elements which must be included in the report:

83 Sadly, there is no porridge.
84 See the *Caledonian* case in which overprovision was described not simply on economic factors but on amenity; it can also relate to existing forms of entertainment on premises within a locality compared with the proposed form in an application before the board.
85 Difficulties with on- and off-sale capacities are discussed further in Chapter 8 at Section 3.11.
86 Section 9A(1).

"(a) a statement explaining how the Board has had regard to—
(i) the licensing objectives, and
(ii) their licensing policy statement and any supplementary licensing policy statement (including the Board's statement under section 7(1) (duty to assess overprovision)),
in the exercise of their functions under this Act during the financial year,
(b) a summary of the decisions made by (or on behalf of) the Board during the financial year, and
(c) information about the number of licences held under this Act in the Board's area (including information about the number of occasional licences issued during the year)."[87]

The board may also include such other detail and information as the licensing board consider appropriate, and they are also given a power to request certain details from the local authority, thus: "At the request of a Licensing Board the relevant council must provide the Board with such information as the Board may reasonably require for the purpose of preparing a report under this section."[88] The annual functions report may be issued in a conjoined format with the annual financial report (discussed below).

The origin of this requirement lies with concerns raised by Alcohol Focus Scotland over the transparency of the work of licensing boards on the basis that the absence of a formal reporting function made it difficult for members of the public to understand the licensing system and therefore to interact with it successfully. In a 2015 study on the public health objective, Dr Niamh Fitzgerald stated:

> "Progress towards protecting and improving public health is being made within the current Scottish licensing system, but requires extensive effort with no guarantee of success. Action by government could shore up the system by introducing greater clarity particularly in relation to determinations of overprovision. This ought to give proactive Licensing Boards the confidence to act decisively, support greater consistency in practice, and justify the introduction of greater accountability, for example through detailed annual reporting which ought to nudge other Boards along the same path".[89]

At Stage 3 of the Air Weapons and Licensing Bill on 25 June 2015, the then Justice Minister explained to Parliament the intention of introducing the functions report requirement:

> "[This] addresses a concern first raised by Alcohol Focus Scotland and others, supported by the Local Government and Regeneration Committee, about the need for licensing boards to provide greater clarity about how they carry out their business . . . John Wilson moved a non-Government amendment at stage 2 to oblige licensing boards to lodge annual reports on the exercise of their functions. The Government is sympathetic to the views that were expressed during the bill process, and I am grateful to Mr Wilson for agreeing to withdraw his amendment at stage 2 to allow my officials to carry out some informal stakeholder engagement before lodging the Government amendment. Section 55 already imposes a duty on licensing boards to produce an annual financial report. Amendment 12 imposes a further duty on boards to prepare and publish an annual report on the exercise of their functions no

87 Section 9A(2).
88 Section 9A(4).
89 Niamh Fitzgerald, "Influencing the Implementation of a Public Health Objective in Scottish Alcohol Licensing: A Qualitative Interview Study" (University of Stirling, 2015) p 15.

later than three months after the end of each financial year. The amendment sets out what generally should be included in the report and what boards should have regard to in its compilation . . . The annual reports will ensure increased accountability and transparency from licensing boards so that the public can see how they go about their business."[90]

The first functions reports were issued by licensing boards for the 2017/18 financial year. Alcohol Focus Scotland conducted an analysis[91] of all the functions reports they could locate (not all were produced or released). Amongst a variety of observations, the report noted:

"There is a wide variation between the reports in the depth and breadth of detail provided and the way in which information is presented. Nevertheless, the majority allow for some scrutiny and analysis of the board's decision making, to varying degrees and with differing levels of ease, and outline the evidence that has been used to develop policy and inform decision making. However, while there are many examples of good practice, a number of the reports contain only minimal information and are unlikely to enable communities/stakeholders to assess and understand the operation of the licensing system in their local area."

As these reports are now, or should be, an annually occurring feature of the licensing system in Scotland, it is expected that they will grow in sophistication and may become useful resources for those seeking to understand the wider role and decisions of the board, such as local licensing forums (discussed in detail below). The annual reports will continue to be analysed by Alcohol Focus Scotland and others.

9 ANNUAL FINANCIAL REPORTS

The sister provision for the Annual Functions Report is the Annual Financial Report which is found at section 9B of the 2005 Act. By way of background, the Policy Memorandum to the Air Weapons and Licensing Bill had this to say on Annual Financial Reports:

"The 2005 Act enables the Scottish Ministers to make provision for the charging of alcohol licensing fees . . . The fees regime is intended to reflect the Scottish Government's intention to make the system self-funding i.e. to cover both direct and indirect costs incurred by Licensing Boards. In other words, the money raised by fees should be broadly equivalent to the expenses incurred by the Board and the council for that area of the Board, in administering the licensing regime during that period. After the fees regime came into effect in 2009, stakeholders in the licensed trade queried the disparities between fee levels in different local authorities and suggested that Boards should be transparent about these figures to demonstrate that their fees regimes are based upon cost recovery (unless they choose to make a deficit). Consequently, this Bill creates a duty on Licensing Boards to produce an annual financial report and provides for what information should be included in such a report. As Licensing Boards are already under an obligation to ensure their fee income is broadly equivalent to their costs, this duty will require them to make public the calculations that are already being carried out."

90 Official Report, Stage 3 of the Air Weapons and Licensing Bill, 25 June 2015, pp 63–5.

91 "Review of Licensing Board Annual Functions Reports 2017–2018" (Alcohol Focus Scotland, March 2019).

The specific requirement of what the report must include is found at section 9B(2), which states:

> "(2) A report under this section must include—
> (a) a statement of—
> (i) the amount of relevant income received by the Licensing Board during the financial year, and
> (ii) the amount of relevant expenditure incurred in respect of the Board's area during the year, and
> (b) an explanation of how the amounts in the statement were calculated."

The expressions "relevant income" and "relevant expenditure" are defined thus:

> "'relevant income', in relation to a Licensing Board, means income received by the Board in connection with the exercise of the Board's functions under or by virtue of—
> (a) this Act, or
> (b) section 14(1) of the Alcohol etc. (Scotland) Act 2010 (social responsibility levy) in so far as relating to holders of premises licences or occasional licences, and
> 'relevant expenditure', in relation to a Licensing Board, means any expenditure—
> (a) which is attributable to the exercise of the Board's functions under or by virtue of—
> (i) this Act, or
> (ii) section 14(1) of the Alcohol etc. (Scotland) Act 2010 (social responsibility levy) in so far as relating to holders of premises licences or occasional licences, and
> (b) which is incurred by—
> (i) the Board,
> (ii) the relevant council, or
> (iii) the Licensing Standards Officer (or Officers) for the Board's area."[92]

Two particular items of note here are (1) the reference to costs incurred by the "relevant council" – this, of course, recognises the practical reality that the licensing board does not of itself administer the system on a day-to-day basis and it is reliant on the local authority to provide staff, administration and other support; and (2) the reference to the social responsibility levy. The levy is discussed in detail elsewhere, but it does at least limit the reference to income and expenditure arising from the 2005 Act, as opposed to other forms of licence under the Civic Government (Scotland) Act 1982 which are caught by the levy. The levy has not, at the time of writing, been commenced.

As with the annual functions report, there is a power created to require the local authority to assist the licensing board in this matter:

> "the relevant council must provide the Board with such information as the Board may reasonably require for the purpose of preparing a report under this section."[93]

The timescale for production of the report is normally within 3 months of the end of the financial year.[94] I am aware that some clerks believe this to be unrealistic given the time it takes for a local authority to prepare accounts, which may not be finalised within that timeframe.

92 Section 9B(3).
93 Section 9B(4).
94 2005 Act, s 9B(1).

10 POWER TO RELIEVE PROCEDURAL FAILINGS

One of the intriguing sections of the 2005 Act is 135, which introduced what may be shortly termed as a "slip rule" or "dispensing power", a power which allows the board to ignore procedural failings in connection with any relevant procedural provision of the Act. This is perhaps the closest equivalent of section 13(2) of the 1976 Act, which operated to allow late applications,[95] but section 135 is much wider and significant in its terms – for example, it could potentially be used to ask a board to consider an application lodged outwith a statutory deadline (such as the 28-day deadline for a transfer application), to ignore defective display of a site notice, and so on. But it does not just apply to an applicant: it may also be used by any party to a proceeding except the board itself. One example of this is that Police Scotland may seek to rely on the provision where it fails to lodge any comment or objection within the relevant timescale.

In order to relieve any procedural failing, the board must be satisfied that the failure is due to "mistake, oversight or excusable cause", and consider it appropriate in all the circumstances to relieve the failure. As the power under section 135 is entirely discretionary, the acceptance of its invocation varies across Scotland.[96] From my own experience, I would suggest that the most common case where section 135 might be relied on is in relation to transfer applications where the 28-day deadline has been missed. Licensing boards will take diverging approaches to this. Some will not contemplate the use of section 135 under any circumstances, perhaps taking the view that "procedural provision" in section 135(3) limits the application of the dispensing power to excuse failures compliance in secondary legislation (whether Regulations or the Board's own rules), as opposed to failures to meet primary legislation. Some are prepared to allow section 135 to operate where the applicant is an insolvency practitioner and that practitioner may have been appointed sometime after the insolvency event for various reasons.

Finally, it should be noted that, in comparison to accepting "late" transfer applications where section 34 uses the word "may" as to the making of such an application, it seems clear that section 135 cannot be used to allow something where the Act requires a board to do something by use of the word "must" or "shall", such as granting a minor variation or refusing an application seeking off sales outwith 10am to 10pm; and so on.

11 DUTY TO KEEP A PUBLIC REGISTER

Section 9 of the Act requires the licensing board to keep a register containing information relating to premises licences, occasional licences and personal licences, and decisions made in relation to specific applications, as required under the Licensing Register (Scotland) Regulations 2007.[97] These were amended to include details provided by applicants in their Disabled Access and Facilities Statement, on which see Chapter 8 at Section 6.

95 Although only to applications for grant and renewal of licences, not to transfers under that Act.
96 A decision not to invoke s 135 would have to be challenged by way of judicial review.
97 SSI 2007/33.

The regulations require the register to include copies of operating plans and layout plans, details of conditions, transfers and variations, reviews and extensions for premises licences (as well as details for occasional licences, personal licences and closure orders). Practically, this may be difficult to achieve. A "public register" which contains the operating plan and layout plan for all premises in a board's area would be of considerable size. Thankfully, the register can be in physical or electronic form.[98]

The register must be available for public inspection at all reasonable times. In practice, many licensing boards have made an online resource available and some of these are fairly sophisticated and up to date[99]. It can only be hoped that all licensing boards are ultimately able to provide an online resource, which would be of benefit to many parties interested in the licensing system.

Regulation 9 requires that information must be kept on the register for a period of five years after the relevant licence or application becomes inactive: that is, after the refusal of an application or after a licence has ceased to have effect, been revoked or surrendered. The licensing board should also publish details of application fees.[100]

98 Ibid, Regulation 2.

99 The presence of certain data online was considered relevant in rebuffing a Freedom of Information request by an LSO as to the reasons behind delays in processing a personal licence application by a separate licensing board. See Decision 053/2017: Mr Paul Fair and the City of Glasgow Licensing Board, Scottish Information Commissioner, 18 April 2017.

100 Licensing (Fees) (Scotland) Regulations 2007 (SSI 2007/553), reg 18.

Chapter 5

Licensing Forums

1 LOCAL LICENSING FORUMS

Section 10(1) of the 2005 Act simply states: "Each council must establish a Local Licensing Forum for their area."[1] The origin of the local licensing forum is twofold: first, a number of unofficial forums already existed in certain local authority areas; and, secondly, they were a response to what Nicholson reviewed in relation to alternatives to the licensing board itself. Whilst dismissing the idea that a wider forum or tribunal was the correct body to regulate the licensing system, Nicholson recognised the benefit in having a body which represented wider views and could air such views, to allow the licensing board as an independent decision-maker to inform itself. The Nicholson report said:

> ". . . we consider that local licensing forums of the kind we have just been describing could have a useful, and indeed democratic, role to play in ensuring that any board policies are well-informed and are based on an appreciation of the concerns of the wider community. We therefore consider that there would be advantage if local licensing forums of the kind that already exist in some areas were to be extended throughout the country. It is our view that such forums should be established by legislation and that, in terms of the legislation, licensing boards should be under a duty to meet their local forum."[2]

The overall idea fits well with what I have described as the "silent" licensing objective, that of greater community involvement in licensing. Note that the independence of the board is crucial and that the provision above under section 10(1) requires the local authority, that is, the council, to establish a licensing forum – not the licensing board. Having this separation is essential for transparency and for that reason I take the view that a licensing board member should not sit on the licensing forum. A licensing board member may very well attend a licensing forum meeting, give evidence, answer questions and respond to queries or explain policy, but should not be a member of the forum itself, in my view.

The Guidance to Licensing Boards confidently asserted that:

> "An effective Local Licensing Forum should be widely recognised as being both independent and expert. As such it will enjoy the trust of all those whose interests are affected by licensing."[3]

It goes on to proclaim:

1 Divisionalised areas may have divisional forums.
2 Nicholson Report, para 3.18, p 52.
3 Guidance, para 347.

> "The Local Licensing Forum must also strive to develop the trust of the licence holders and the licensing board by producing impartial and effective advice to the Board."[4]

The independence of the licensing forum was a consideration put directly to Nicholson in person when he gave evidence at the Scottish Parliament. He said:

> "[The independence of the forum] is important as a matter of principle. As the committee probably knows, even before the Nicholson report was published, there were local licensing forums in some parts of the country, albeit that they were set up informally. I think that I am right in saying that the Edinburgh licensing forum was chaired by the chairman of the local licensing board. As far as I understand, that arrangement worked well. Nonetheless, although it may work well in some instances, there can be no guarantee of it doing so in all areas, which is my reason for saying that, as a matter of principle, it is better that the forums are independent. Obviously, they should meet the licensing board fairly frequently."[5]

2 ADMINISTRATION OF LICENSING FORUMS

The rules regarding memberships, meetings and so on for licensing forums are to be found in Schedule 2 to the 2005 Act. A licensing forum will consist of several members to be decided on by the council, so long as the number is not less than five and not greater than twenty-one.[6] Each member is an individual invited by the council to join the forum, with the aim that "the Forum is representative of the interests of persons or descriptions of persons who have an interest which is relevant to the Forum's general functions". These persons include:

- the licensed trade
- the chief constable
- health, education or social work officers
- young persons[7]
- residents.

The only statutory prescription over whom the council must appoint to the local licensing forum is that they must ensure that at least one of the members of the forum is a LSO for that area,[8] and, following the enactment of the Alcohol etc (Scotland) Act 2010 and the inclusion of health boards as statu-

4 Paragraph 350.

5 Local Government and Transport Committee, 22 March 2005.

6 See Sch 2 para 2(1) for the original provision which created a maximum of 20; but note that SSI 2011/130 raised the maximum to 21 to allow a "new" member of the forum to be appointed in order to represent the local health board. This followed the Alcohol etc (Scotland) Act 2010 inclusion of health boards as statutory consultees within the licensing system.

7 The use of the phrase "young persons" in this context is unhelpful given the Act defines this as a person aged 16 or 17, thereby excluding anyone under that age, or preventing ongoing participation where someone reaches their eighteenth birthday. This cannot have been the intention of Parliament and it is submitted that the intention was to capture "young persons" in a broader, non-legal sense.

8 Schedule 2 para 2(3).

tory consultees, a person nominated by the health board for that forum's area must also be included.[9]

The forum will have a convenor who will be elected on terms and conditions as the council sees fit. The council picks up the bill for the administration of the forum and any staff, property or services required in order for it to function appropriately. The forums must meet no less than four times a year (although in practice this is not always observed – see below), and the quorum is one half of the number of members. Other than the rule that the meetings must be held in public, the rest of the arrangements are entirely within the power of the council. Section 10(3) of the Act provides that the licensing board must hold a joint meeting with the forum at least once a year.

3 THE PURPOSE OF LOCAL LICENSING FORUMS

Local licensing forums have three main functions:

- to keep under review the operation of the Act in the forum's area,
- to keep under review the way the licensing board exercises its functions under the Act, and
- to give advice and make recommendations to the board as the forum considers appropriate.

Importantly, none of these functions stretches to allow a forum to make recommendations in relation to a particular case or singular application, nor do they imbue the forum with any power to change policy. I understand that, in some areas, members representing the trade or public have declined to attend future meetings once they realise that the forum cannot discuss individual cases.

The licensing board must merely have regard to any advice or recommendation given by the forum, and, if the board elects not to follow that advice or recommendation, it must give the forum reasons for its decision,[10] but there the matter ends and there are numerous examples of forum recommendations consigned to the licensing dustbin.[11]

There is a requirement for the board to produce statistical information when required by the forum although there are also examples of licensing boards asking forums to examine certain matters, conduct research, and report their findings back to the board.

4 LOCAL LICENSING FORUMS IN PRACTICE

Back in 2008, it was expected that there would have been the mandatory four meetings of each forum on an ongoing basis across Scotland and

9 This amendment was achieved through s 11(7) of the Alcohol etc Scotland Act 2010 and commenced by SSI 2011/130.

10 2005 Act, s 12(2). The reasons must be given within 42 days of the decision being made: Procedural Regulations (SSI 2007/453) reg 17.

11 This was described by an unnamed LSO as an "epic fail in the Act" in an NHS evaluation in 2013. Examples of failed recommendations include the Edinburgh forum attempt at asking for a condition requiring premises to have a working defibrillator, and the Dundee forum attempt to have premises subject to a condition requiring carpets to be shampooed (see www.licensinglaws.wordpress.com/2012/09/26/licensing-and-the-carpets-of-Dundee/).

that these would continue, and forums would be a significant part of the licensing landscape. Looking back at my research of forums at that time, the initial formation of some forums appeared to be "top-heavy" with the licensed trade, and community and health representation was perhaps under-represented. Over the decade or so since that time, this has changed back and forth in various local areas, and forums now can be very centred on the health agenda, or focused on the voice of the trade, or somewhere in the middle. There is a perceived tension, which it is said has resulted in some forums working less efficiently than others, and some being abandoned altogether.

In and around 2010 a website was created to act as a national resource for local forums, set up by Alcohol Focus Scotland, which also produced a "Training Resource" including a DVD for forums to train their own members. This was put in place in an effort to create some sort of national support landscape for forums, which would provide an answer to the difficulties many had experienced in even getting off the ground, by being able to access a free shared resource.

Whilst well intentioned and of clear assistance to forums, these resources appear to have been withdrawn and anecdotally there appears to have been a view espoused from trade quarters that these efforts had perhaps strayed too far in potentially fettering the independence of the forum by creating a framework which some forum members took to mean that Alcohol Focus Scotland should "take the lead" in forum activity. If such a view was taken by forum members, that perception would run counter to the Scottish Government Guidance in its discussion of "an inclusive approach to involvement" and a "balanced representation of all 'communities of interest'". In order for a forum to remain effective, it has been argued that no one interest group should seek to own the structures or provide a secretariat function for the forum, but that groups should restrict themselves to acting as interested and engaged members. It is of course, under law, for the local council to provide the structure and support within which the forums must exist.

Over the next few years there is evidence that some forums worked well, and one can locate multiple minutes from a number of local forums which evidence an ongoing and healthy working pattern. However, there is also evidence that some forums retained practical difficulties.

In 2013 the NHS commissioned a report[12] on the implementation of the 2005 Act. It had this to say about local licensing forums: "[There has been] a hardening of attitudes towards Forums, with a number of interviewees describing them as having stalled or failed completely." The report goes on to explore this in more detail:

> "Licensing Forum members who took part in the case study phase thought that there were advantages and disadvantages in such a diverse group working together. On the one hand, bringing together people with a range of expertise and knowledge was seen as valuable in itself. However, not all Forums had managed to achieve a good working relationship between members of different bodies, and struggled to achieve a consensus. Members of one Forum, for example, alluded to fundamental differences between those representing a health agenda and those representing

12 A MacGregor et al, "An evaluation of the implementation of, and compliance with, the objectives of the Licensing (Scotland) Act 2005: Final Report" (May 2013).

business interests. It was suggested that this had resulted in some issues effectively becoming 'off limits' for discussion.

Board respondents and LSOs also stated that Forums had the potential to become 'bogged down' in conflict, which was unsurprising given the different constituent groups represented on the one body. The issue of independence was touched upon indirectly by representatives of one Forum among whom there were differences of opinion about whether the appropriate balance had been struck between the level of licensed trade involvement and that of community and health representation."[13]

The report is critical of the effectiveness of local licensing forums, blaming their inactivity or lack of success on the divergence of views of those at the table, a clouded remit, and disinterest from licensing boards themselves.

In 2014 the Glasgow Centre for Public Health in partnership with Alcohol Focus Scotland produced a report entitled "Strengthening the community voice in alcohol licensing decisions".[14] This report analysed the performance of the Glasgow Licensing Forum at that time, and commented:

> "There were mixed views among Glasgow stakeholders regarding the city's Forum. Some stakeholders felt it was struggling to find its purpose and although forum discussions and presentations were described as interesting, its overall impact was frequently questioned. One stakeholder described it as a 'constructive talking shop'. There was a general perception among a number of stakeholders that trade representatives had a strong presence on Glasgow's Forum."[15]

The report described one Licensing Standards Officer as saying the Forum was "wandering aimlessly and no-one is entirely sure what they're there for".

An academic paper by leading health expert Dr Niamh Fitzgerald from 2015 looked at this further:

> "Many participants reported ongoing problems with forums. These included that forums had not met for a long time, were not representative, or were not able to function well when they did meet. Some were described as 'top heavy with trade' or 'a forum of licensees basically' or 'full of trade who try to protect the trade' or 'very heavy trade representation . . . dominated to a large degree by trade'. They noted that it was often difficult to get community representation onto forums: one commenting that 'I think they'd bite the arm off anybody who wanted to step forward as a member'."[16]

It is unclear if any special progress has been made since the publications noted here. Anecdotally, the overall constant appears to remain: some licensing forums are incredibly active and manage to engage positively with their licensing board and manage to find a way to work as a collective notwithstanding that there may be conflicting approaches or views (what Nicholson may have termed "competing sectional interests", perhaps); other forums are fractured, and yet other forums simply do not exist at all.

13 Ibid p 54.

14 November 2014.

15 Page 21.

16 Niamh Fitzgerald, "Influencing the Implementation of a Public Health Objective in Scottish Alcohol Licensing: A Qualitative Interview Study" (University of Stirling, 2015) p 14.

5 THE NATIONAL LICENSING FORUM?

The local licensing forum should not be confused with any reference to the National Licensing Forum (in whatever iteration) or doomed successor groups such as the National Licensing Advisory Group (NLAG) and the Scottish Alcohol Licensing Advisory Forum (SALAF). At the time of writing there is no National Licensing Forum but it is perhaps worth noting that a national forum did exist and explore these attempts.

These "national" licensing bodies, such as they were, had (and have) no statutory place or function under the 2005 Act but when the first one was established it was considered to be an appropriate step in order to follow through on a Nicholson recommendation:

> "A National Licensing Forum should be established. Its members, who should be appointed individually by the Minister for Justice or the Minister for Health, should be drawn from a wide range of relevant backgrounds. The Forum should meet periodically under the chairmanship of the Minister for Justice and the Minister for Health, or one or other of them, and its task should be to keep licensing law and practice under constant review, and to offer advice to Ministers as to ways of dealing with emerging problems or difficulties."[17]

The first National Licensing Forum was established by Government prior to the onset of the commencement of the 2005 Act with the purpose of creating a high-level panel of experts in order to help understand the practice of licensing law, but it did not get properly off the ground and was abolished in February 2007 principally because of a lack of agreement as to who should Chair the Forum.

On 5 January 2009 the then Justice Minister Kenny MacAskill said, in response to a Parliamentary question about reforming a national forum:

> "The National Licensing Forum was abolished by the previous administration. At a meeting with the Convention of Scottish Local Authorities and Alcohol Focus Scotland on 12 June [2008], I made clear that the Scottish Government would welcome the sharing of good practice between licensing boards and would further welcome any effort by COSLA to establish an appropriate mechanism for doing that."

In an interview with MacAskill on 24 January 2013, the *Scottish Licensed Trade News* asked "Do you support the creation of a new national licensing forum?" to which he replied:

> "We do think there should be a national forum. [In] the discussions we've been having with COSLA [Convention of Scottish Local Authorities] we've never felt that we should set it up, because there are things where they may disagree with us. To some extent the debate has been about who is going to host it or convene it. One of the work strands of the Scottish Government Alcohol Industry Partnership involves setting up a national licensing forum. We've arranged meetings with a sub-group of interested people and we're at the stage now of trying to find a mutually acceptable chair. The concept is right, because the more we can engage in talks, the more the trade can speak to government, the more that trade can speak to licensing boards and the more, in particular, board members can speak to each other. It has been a matter of some frustration that we have not been able to establish this, but I think we will get there."

17 Nicholson Report, recommendation 47, p 128.

At that time, the group referred to as the Scottish Government Alcohol Industry Partnership (SGAIP) was a forum for discussion between several large alcohol producers and bodies representing the licensed trade, and Scottish Government, who convened the Partnership and attended meetings. Although originally set up in February 2007, as a response to the abolition of the original National Licensing Forum, the Partnership was revitalised in 2013 under a new partnership agreement which outlined its purpose and aims as follows:

> **"Purpose**
> The Scottish Government Alcohol Industry Partnership (SGAIP) is a vehicle for Government and Industry to work together to address the complex issues surrounding alcohol misuse and promote responsible drinking in Scotland. The Partnership also serves as an industry consultative forum on alcohol legislation.
> **Aim and Objectives:**
> The aim is to deliver a long term collaborative approach to fostering a culture which recognises that a healthy society is one in which alcohol is consumed responsibly and in moderation.
> **The main objectives of the Partnership are:**
> 1. to deliver joint initiatives to tackle alcohol related harm and promote responsible drinking, including the specific initiatives which may involve working with other key stakeholders;
> 2. to be a constructive sounding board and consultative forum on alcohol misuse policy, and in particular on alcohol legislation."

With this background of partnership in mind, when responding to concerns that the trade would have their voice stifled on the new National Licensing Forum, MacAskill said:

> "If the trade wasn't there, there would be a real problem. This has to be a partnership – it can't be diktat. Getting people in the room is important. While there is a clear reason for me to speak to the licensing board convenors, speaking in the absence of the trade would frankly be a bit daft."

Despite MacAskill's efforts, he could not convince health groups to sit at the same table as the alcohol industry and so the new 2013 iteration of the National Licensing Forum was also doomed to failure. Around this time, health groups were alleging that the alcohol industry had misrepresented evidence in relation to evidence sessions on minimum pricing and appeared to have convinced Government that a body which would influence national policy on alcohol should not include the alcohol industry. Rightly or wrongly, MacAskill, and Government, moved away from the idea of a national forum and it has not been attempted since. Government subsequently went further, removing their official connection with the SGAIP in 2015, albeit indicating they would continue to listen to the voice of that organisation. The Scottish Government said in September 2015:

> "The Scottish Government and Alcohol Industry Partnership members have agreed to find new, lighter-touch ways of collaborating on measures to reduce alcohol harm. The Scottish Government will continue to work with members of the alcohol industry where aims align."

Subsequently, the SGAIP decided to continue on and was reconstituted as the Scottish Alcohol Industry Partnership.[18] It has since led a number of initiatives

18 www.saip.org.uk

including the 125ml wine measure campaign to publicise the presence of smaller wine measures in pubs and bars, the "You're Asking for It" campaign designed to target under-age drinking and in particular proxy purchasing, and the Drinkaware at Work campaign to support knowledge sessions on informed choices surrounding alcohol consumption.

A National Licensing Forum may have had its uses, but these attempts all failed due to conflicting interests and groups, partisan politics, and apathy; all of which contributed to the blurring of the remit of what a National Licensing Forum might be, rendering it inert.

Chapter 6

Licensing Standards Officers

1 OVERVIEW

Perhaps the most obvious result of the aim of greater ongoing involvement and interaction with licensed premises was the creation of the position of licensing standards officer (LSO), a person employed by the council (not the board), who in short may be described as a sort of gateway between the board, licence holders and of course the public and other persons. LSOs have special powers and abilities under the 2005 Act including enforcement powers. So, what is the background to the creation of this role? The Explanatory Memorandum to the 2005 Act has this to say:

> "Subsection (1) places a duty on local authorities to appoint one or more officers to be known as Licensing Standards Officers ('LSOs') whose general statutory functions are those set out in section 14 of the Act. This is a new role. The Civic Government (Scotland) Act 1982 empowers the police and authorised officers of licensing and fire authorities to enter and inspect premises, vehicles or vessels of a licence holder or applicant for a licence. With respect to liquor licensing, however, there is currently no such provision."[1]

This, of course, only takes us so far in seeking to properly understand the origin of the role. Under the 1976 Act, the operation of licensed premises was broadly speaking only interrogated every three years when the licence was due for renewal, albeit that the police had a special power to bring a suspension hearing, and, in some areas, the annual renewal of "regular extensions", that is, additional hours which became to be (in practice) the standard and accepted hours, might be used to threaten action in a particular issue. One of the flaws, it was perceived, in this type of system was the lack of "ongoing" interaction which might raises issues or actions outwith these specified structures.

It is always instructive to go back to Nicholson. In the chapter headed "Supervision and Compliance", Nicholson teases out a number of strands which ultimately thread together to support the concept of specialist licensing officers. Part of this is that Nicholson wanted his licensing system to support the idea that there would be "in the public interest . . . greater scrutiny than was previously the case before a licence is granted". He went on to underline how not just this wider principle, but that of ongoing compliance, would be achieved:

> "We consider that, if the operation of the licensing system is to be adequately supervised by licensing boards, it will be desirable that there should be an appropriate

1 Explanatory Memorandum to the Licensing (Scotland) Act 2005, para 31.

number of officers, answerable to their local licensing board, who can actually carry out that task. There is some comparable provision to that effect under the Civic Government (Scotland) Act 1982, and we note that the current Licensing Bill for England and Wales makes reference to an 'authorised person', a term which includes 'an officer of a licensing authority . . . who is authorised by that authority for the purposes of this Act'. Our understanding is that it is intended that such officers will carry out a supervisory and advisory function on behalf of licensing authorities."[2]

Nicholson also paid particular regard to a similar role in place in British Columbia during his period of research, noting that the job of the Canadian licensing standards officers in that province was not necessarily to spend all their time "seeking out wrong-doers", but to build relations with the licensed trade and to employ a sensible, pragmatic approach:

"not every transgression will automatically be reported to the licensing authority: instead, the enforcement officers will usually work with the licensee in question in order to bring about a more compliant operation in the premises in question. The enforcement officers also work in close cooperation with the police both in uncovering instances of non-compliance but also in trying to bring about improvements by informal means."

It is clear to divine that Nicholson wanted to engender a spirit of partnership and the sense of working sensibly in order to help achieve compliance with the new licensing system, as a sort of shared goal, especially where the premises licence is designed to last in perpetuity, creating a reason for ongoing support, assessment, and compliance. In rejecting the idea that the officers should be called "licensing enforcement officers", Nicholson said:

"We think, however, that the term 'enforcement officer' gives a less than comprehensive, and possibly misleading, indication of the kinds of functions which we envisage; and we therefore suggest that an alternative name might be 'Liquor Licensing Standards Officer'."

A central point about LSOs is that they are independent. Independent from the licensing board, from the trade, and from other stakeholders. They are not answerable to the licensing board. They carry out a function on behalf of the local authority as provided for under the legislation. Parliament examined this relationship and debated it during the progress of the Licensing Bill and came to this conclusion. Nicholson had originally suggested that LSOs be officers of the licensing board, but Parliament ultimately rejected that.

2 APPOINTMENT OF LICENSING STANDARDS OFFICERS

Prior to the onset of the 2005 Act, many councils across Scotland had appointed at least one LSO, as there were in fact already several people in positions not too dissimilar to the LSO before the Nicholson Committee even released its report. I can certainly recall alcohol licensing enforcement or policy monitoring officers in place at two board areas – South Ayrshire and Glasgow – going back to 2000. My recollection is that South Ayrshire has the

2 Nicholson Report, para 7.3, p 106.

best claim to having had the first ever LSO.[3] Of course, under the 2005 Act, the appointment of such officers is now prescribed in the statute.

Section 13(1) of the 2005 Act states that each council must appoint at least one LSO, with the actual number left to the council to decide.[4] Different approaches are evident in this regard. In some cases there is a ratio effect based on numbers of licensed premises; in some areas the minimum is observed based purely on resource. The reality, therefore, is that the numbers of LSOs appointed much depends on the council area, and since the Act came into force in 2009 this has fluctuated hither and thither.[5] It is competent for an individual to be an LSO for more than one council area,[6] although as yet I am unaware of this practice occurring.

Those carrying out the role of LSO have come from a variety of backgrounds including former licensing board administration staff, retired police officers, housing officers, council enforcement officers from other departments such as environmental health, and there is at least one serving LSO at the time of writing[7] whose background comes from the licensed trade itself.

2.1 Training of LSOs

Section 13(5) and (6) provide for a training requirement. The accredited training courses available were originally offered back in 2007/8 by the British Institute of Innkeepers (BII) and ServeWise, the training arm of Alcohol Focus Scotland, but owing to lack of ongoing numbers the BII course fell away and now only the Alcohol Focus Scotland course is available to sit for new LSOs looking to take up the position. Under the Licensing (Training) (Scotland) Regulations 2007[8] each LSO must undertake and pass the training within 18 months of his appointment to the position, and if the LSO does not comply with this, his or her employment must be terminated by the council.[9]

The training itself is a two-day course and contains details on the 2005 Act; the role and responsibility of an LSO; the role of the LSO in relation to the licensing board, the local authority and the licensing forum; powers of other statutory bodies; details of premises, personal and occasional licences; dealing with and managing conflict; assertiveness; offences; control of order; associated law; social responsibility; the effects of alcohol; and other relevant areas.

In the Stage 2 Report to the Licensing Bill, the Subordinate Legislation Committee looked at the issue of providing for the training by way of secondary legislation so that the specification of the training could be more easily updated. The report says:

3 An honourable mention, therefore, for Catriona Andrews, who remains in the role of LSO for South Ayrshire Council at the time of writing.

4 2005 Act, s 13(4).

5 At the time of writing, I think the record number is still held by Edinburgh City Council who at one point had nine LSOs, although some of these were part-time positions. Glasgow City has had as many as four at one time, albeit again not all working full time. Some areas such as Falkirk, North Lanarkshire and Aberdeen City have two LSOs, and a good number of areas such as North Ayrshire, West Lothian, Clackmannanshire and beyond have only one (hopefully not too lonely) LSO.

6 2005 Act, s 13(2).

7 An honourable mention to Peter Clyde from West Dunbartonshire.

8 SSI 2007/95.

9 2005 Act, s 16(2).

> "Section 13(4) of the Bill already enabled Scottish Ministers to prescribe the qualifications a Licensing Standards Officer would need, but did not allow Scottish Ministers to prescribe the training a Licensing Standards Officer should undertake. The National Licensing Forum agreed, when giving consideration to Licensing Standards Officers, that any training regarded as mandatory should be prescribed in order to ensure consistency across the country. Such training is considered likely to change as the Licensing Standards Officer's role develops and was therefore considered to be best suited to being set out in regulations. As these regulations will be mainly procedural and technical and will not change the application of Bill policy it was felt the use of negative procedure was the most appropriate."[10]

It is perhaps regrettable, then, that it was not until early 2021 that efforts were finally made to commence an update of the LSO training specification (the outcome of which is awaited at the time of writing). I am aware that many LSOs take it upon themselves for professional development purposes to follow an ongoing personal requirement for para-statutory training. A great many LSOs have, for example, undertaken the personal licence training course, and a cadre of LSOs have undertaken the Central Law Training (CLT) Paralegal Qualification in Licensing Law which is accredited through the University of Strathclyde.

3 THE WORK OF A LICENSING STANDARDS OFFICER

There are two aspects of the day-to-day reality of the work of an LSO: those ascribed by the statute, and then the duties that they may actually carry out in addition to the statutory ones. The 2005 Act simply states that an LSO is to "exercise . . . the functions conferred on a Licensing Standards Officer by virtue of this Act". It may be mischievous to suggest, but one wonders whether an action by an LSO which is not specifically catered for in the statute would then fall to be considered *ultra vires*, and potentially challengeable. The Guidance to Licensing Boards had this to say about LSOs:

> "It is imperative that Licensing Standards Officers have a good understanding of the needs and aspirations of the licensed trade and work to build respect for the role by the judicious application of their powers. LSOs will require to be able to work with persons from every background. They will require to have diversity training to ensure their ability to properly handle themselves in different and potentially sensitive or difficult situations."[11]

This, of course, links back to Nicholson's vision. There are some further interesting notes about the general function of the LSO in the Explanatory Memorandum:

> "LSOs do not act as policemen with regard to licensing, but they will liaise with the police and other relevant officials such as environmental health officers in ensuring the licensing objectives are adhered to and solutions found to problems involving licensed premises. LSOs will act as a source of advice and guidance for licensees and for the community; mediate between communities and the trade or between

10 Scottish Parliament, Subordinate Legislative Committee, 40th Report 2005 (Session 2), 14 November 2005, at para 5.

11 Guidance to Licensing Boards (April 2007) para 263.

> any two parties where there is a need to resolve a local problem and develop a local solution and supervise compliance with licence conditions by the relevant licence holders."[12]

The specific functions are provided for in section 14(1) and are as follows:

- providing to interested persons information and guidance concerning the operation of the Act in the area,
- supervising the compliance by the holders of premises or occasional licences in respect of premises in their area with the conditions of their licence and other requirements of the Act,
- providing information to Licensing Boards about any conduct of holders of, or persons applying for, personal licences in the area, which is inconsistent with the licensing objectives,[13] and
- providing mediation services for the purpose of avoiding or resolving disputes or disagreements between licence holders and any other person in relation to compliance.

We will look at each of these principal functions in turn.

3.1 Providing to interested persons information and guidance

This power requires to be analysed in three parts.[14] The first question one must ask is, who are "interested persons"? The 2005 Act does not provide a definition of this phrase either generally or under this particular section. One must therefore give a broadly general and common-sense interpretation to the phrase, which I suggest is, very simply, any person who is interested in the 2005 Act. This would include, of course, the general public, but also licence holders and persons working within the licensed trade, and any other stakeholder or group, including the local licensing forum.

Secondly, what do we mean by "information"? Again, there is no statutory definition provided. Information would therefore be in the broadest sense whilst relevant to licensing, such as information which might be available on the public register, information on fees, and information on the schedule of licensing board hearings or licensing forum meetings, ought to be within the grasp of the LSO to direct the person to the correct resource, or provide the information directly if that were reasonable.

Thirdly, what do we mean by "guidance"? One thing which is for sure, is that "guidance" does not extend to providing legal advice. The Guidance to Licensing Boards states:

> "LSOs will not be expected to give legal advice or make applications or objections on behalf of any party. Care should be taken in training to ensure that is understood by the LSOs and their customers. It is not anticipated that LSOs will be legally qualified, although this would not be a barrier to application, however their role must not be to give legal advice as this could lead to conflict of interest in any subsequent action by the LSO or the Board."[15]

12 Explanatory Memorandum to the Licensing (Scotland) Act 2005, para 32.
13 This power was added as of 15 May 2017, by operation of s 57(2) of the Air Weapons and Licensing (Scotland) Act 2015 and commenced under SSI 2017/119.
14 I am grateful to my colleague Niall Hassard in encouraging me to adopt this approach here.
15 Paragraph 266.

There is a clear distinction to be made in relation to offering "guidance" on an application, for example, and offering legal advice. A difficulty may arise where a licence holder takes guidance from a LSO in good faith as formal advice, that is, as if the LSO were an agent for the licence holder, and does not appreciate the need for independence. There are cases of LSOs certainly providing advice on applications such as telling a licence holder what the licensing board will or won't accept; or encouraging them to apply for matters as part of a major variation application which were not part of the original variation the licence holder wanted to achieve. It is also understood that there are examples of LSOs who have gone as far as assisting applicants and licence holders in the completion of forms and what to do and say at licensing hearings. LSOs who indulge in this type of activity are well-meaning and trying to assist people by giving them a steer, but they do so at their peril, as operating on the verges of what is legal advice might create a false impression.

In my view this type of practice is fraught.[16] There is no doubt a LSO will know their board well, and have good intentions in assisting someone, but it is not their job to advise someone on an application beyond outlining the basics as this (a) creates a conflict of interest, as it is not the job of the LSO to represent any party, and (b) will create difficulties for both the applicant and the LSO – I have witnessed hearings where an applicant has represented themselves and, upon facing some sort of backlash from a member of the board on a particular aspect, provides what they believe to be the simple explanation that the LSO told them it would all be fine, much to the embarrassment of several parties. I have also seen cases where an LSO has advised an applicant that the application would never be granted, only to see it granted; or where an LSO does not tell an applicant with premises in an overprovision to seek independent advice notwithstanding the presumption against the grant; and I have also seen cases where an application in which an LSO has been "involved" ends up in difficulty and an independent solicitor is required to step in. The *bona fides* of the LSO is not the key concern – the issue is the impression which may be created in the mind of the licence holder.

The LSO must maintain a relationship with the board as well as the trade and other parties, and in order to do so must ensure impartiality. Impartiality disappears when the LSO has been assisting the applicant with their application. In addition to this it must be remembered by LSOs that the perception of bias is sufficient to derail an application even when assistance is offered in good faith. At all times, it is incumbent upon the LSO to ensure the applicant is advised that they can seek independent legal advice.

Similarly, it is not for the LSO to "take the side" of an objector such as an aggrieved neighbour. The LSO cannot become an advocate for any party and must endeavour to plough that middle ground as best they can.

A good LSO will know implicitly when to draw the line in providing guidance, and a sensible applicant should understand the remit of the LSO can only go so far and that they are not a free legal resource. Members of the public may be less aware of this, which makes it all the more important that the LSO ensures parties understand the extent and remit of their role. None of this, of course, should be read as detracting from the exceptional work that

16 See, for example, Janet Hood, "Standards officers crossing boundaries" [2011] 47 SLLP 8.

LSOs do up and down the country, and the examples I narrate above are the exception, not the rule.

Lastly, it is perhaps instructive that a clear origin of the "providing information and guidance" power related to the period *prior* to the commencement of the 2005 Act; that is, the function would be to use LSOs to convey information to interested parties about the then new licensing system and help with a smooth transition period:

> "Advice would also be available from the new Licensing Standards Officers, part of whose role would be to provide information and guidance on the new system. The early availability of this information should enable businesses to prepare applications in line with Board policy which are therefore more likely to be approved by the Board"[17]

This power is very much a creature influenced by its genesis, to provide a human face and impartial resource to assist with the transition to a new licensing system. That impartiality must persist.

3.2 Supervising compliance

In a preceding paragraph I described the compliance function as a "shared goal". This approach implies a joined up, positive trajectory whereupon the LSO will work with a licence holder to go on a journey to help them achieve compliance with the Act, should they have stepped out of line in some way. This, of course, depends entirely on the trust and relationship between the two parties, and frankly the willingness of the licence holder to adhere to the terms of the licence and to listen carefully to the views of the LSO who will be trying to help.

Having dealt with dozens of LSOs in each local authority area and knowing most of them very well, it is only fair for me to acknowledge that this approach, that of constructive and good-natured assistance, is uniformly the one taken. Of course, there are always difficult scenarios. It is also the case that sometimes there can be a genuine and perhaps even good-natured disagreement on what compliance looks like. In some instances, the licence holder will be entirely wrong, and in some cases, dare I even say it, the LSO may themselves have flirted with an erroneous interpretation of what the Act requires. This depends on your viewpoint!

The specific function here is narrated under section 14(1)(b) of the Act as follows:

> "(b) supervising the compliance by the holders of—
> (i) premises licences, or
> (ii) occasional licences,
> in respect of premises in the area with the conditions of their licences and other requirements of this Act".

So, there is a double header here – first of all, supervising compliance means making sure that licence holders are observing the conditions of their licence; and separately supervising "other requirements of this Act". With respect to licence conditions, these are discussed in detail in Chapter 15, but any

17 Regulatory Impact Assessment, Licensing (Scotland) Bill (30 March 2005) para 66, p 22.

licence holder should (must) know the mandatory conditions which attach to their licence as well as any additional local conditions. Whilst the concept of *ignorantia juris non excusat* may reign, it is to be accepted that some of these conditions can be difficult to interpret and also that the wording of the Act is not always comprehensible.

With respect to "other requirements of this Act", I think that needs a little more exploration. My starting point would be to suggest that this does not include two key areas, namely the control of order and criminal offences. I suggest that those matters should sit squarely with the police and whilst there will always be some overlap, and whilst LSOs will of course work closely with the police, it would in my view be outwith the remit of LSOs to involve themselves in disorder-related issues, or the alleged commission of criminal offences (other than reporting such matters to the police and assisting them with their enquiries). Similarly, whilst the breach of a licence condition is of itself a criminal offence, the Act clearly envisages a structure to allow the licence holder to fall back into compliance through the efforts of the LSO and if this does not occur, then yes, ultimately the police might look to charge a licence holder with the relevant offence.

There are too many licence conditions to explore in detail here (see Chapter 15 for a much wider explanation) but a couple of examples may be of some assistance to explore the principle. One of the conditions that LSOs are tasked with engaging is payment of the annual fee. I have no doubt this might be seen by some elements in the licensed trade as a "debt collection" function and in turn I am also sure that LSOs could spend their time more productively if only licence holders would pay their fees on time – but it is certainly a typical task for LSOs to be asked to visit premises if the fee has not been paid and to encourage compliance with the condition.[18]

Perhaps the most common condition that LSOs are tasked with monitoring is the one concerning irresponsible promotions. The licensed trade will grow and evolve and in doing so will always come up with new and wonderful ways to promote their premises and the products they sell. Sometimes, these innovations can lead to certain promotional activities occurring which might be in breach of the Act. LSOs may discover this through a random visit, or more likely by way of a complaint made by competitor premises or member of the public.

So what might "other requirements" mean? A good example of this is ensuring that notification requirements have been met. These are discussed in detail in Chapter 9 at Section 2 as regards new licence applications (for example), but it is certainly the case that one of the jobs of the LSO would be to ensure that an applicant has properly displayed a site notice in connection with the application, and to report to the licensing board on any issues. LSOs would also liaise with the applicant or their agent should there be an issue with the site notice and ultimately, if necessary, the notice may have to be re-displayed.

Might "other requirements" also extend to interrogating the competence of applications? This is an interesting question. On the face of it, I would argue that it is not the job of the LSO to assess the competence of applications nor

18 This approach, it might be argued, pays no heed to the fact that the non-payment of the annual fee is a criminal offence as it a breach of a licence condition and therefore a breach of s 1(1). That would make it a police matter!

is it their job to take a view on whether an application can be processed. It is surely correct that the LSO must remain independent and that means independent of the processing of the applications in any respect. Any decision on the competency of an application should sit with the clerk and their assistants in the licensing team, and any decision on the merits sits with the board. The LSO should be seen in the same light as the police: a separate, independent party. The LSO can comment on an application, in respect of their duties and obligations under the Act, but that is where it should end.

Now that I have stated what I think the properly understood role of the LSO is, it would be churlish of me to hide from the practical reality that many LSOs will often contact an applicant or agent in an effort to be helpful to move the application along. For example, if the application has been lodged with some mistake in the accepted address of the premises, or if the layout plan submitted does not conform with the requirements; it would not be unheard of for the LSO to lift the phone and ask for the matter to be resolved. These "assistances" are often welcome. However, as with the point above concerning legal advice, there must be a note of caution here. Decisions about applications, even decisions on whether the application is competently made, do not sit with LSOs, but with the clerk, and, in some cases, not even with the clerk, but with the board. A decision by a LSO to reject or refuse to process an application would be *ultra vires* and therefore unlawful.

Thinking back to the "journey" of compliance, I would suggest that the generally expected approach follows this sort of path, in my experience:

- LSO becomes aware of a possible breach of a condition, either through visiting the premises or complaint by third party
- LSO will approach licence holder, typically in person or over the phone, to make them aware of the issue and discuss it
- LSO will take the view of the licence holder and third parties as necessary and reflect on the matter
- LSO will reach a view. If LSO satisfied, that is the end of the matter and communications would be made as such to relevant parties. If LSO not satisfied, further communication with the licence holder will occur
- LSO will likely issue a verbal, informal request to take certain steps to ensure compliance
- If these steps are taken, that is the end of the matter – but LSO may keep under review
- If the steps are not taken, the LSO may issue a formal written notice under section 14 of the Act indicating what the licence holder must do and, typically, within what timescale, although noting a timescale is not a specific requirement under section 14
- If the terms of the section 14 notice are not met, the LSO can instigate a premises licence review.

One last technical point to be made here is that this "supervising compliance" function extends only to holders of premises or occasional licences (although worth noting there is no mechanism for a LSO to review an occasional licence), and perhaps surprisingly, does not extend to personal licence holders, albeit LSOs may now comment on personal licence applications (see Chapter 17 at Section 2.1.2) and instigate personal licence reviews (see Chapter 17 at Section 5.4). The salient point here in terms of practical application is that the

LSO must ensure that whoever he or she is engaging with is the premises (or occasional) licence holder or someone authorised by the holder of that licence to deal with them. For example, if premises are leased out to a third party who runs the premises on a day-to day-basis, whilst it is entirely necessary for the LSO to engage and communicate with the people in charge, they must include the premises licence holder in those conversations or communications and not assume or accept that the tenant will inform the landlord, notwithstanding they may be under an obligation to do so under their lease. Ensuring ongoing monitoring of personal licence holders is dealt with under the next heading.

3.3 Providing information on conduct inconsistent with the licensing objectives

Section 14(1)(ba) is in the following terms:

> "(ba) providing information to Licensing Boards about any conduct of holders of, or persons applying for, personal licences in the area, which is inconsistent with the licensing objectives".

This provision was inserted in 2017 and emanates from a request from the National LSO Liaison group;[19] which had the benefit of being requested at the same time as the re-introduction of the so-called "fit and proper" test under the Air Weapons and Licensing (Scotland) Act 2015 (and is discussed in detail elsewhere), and sat neatly in that context. Part of the "suite" of amendments to achieve a fitness test was the corollary acceptance that LSOs should have more powers in relation to dealing with non-compliance by personal licence holders, or dealing with behaviours by personal licence holders which struck at the licensing objectives. The Explanatory Memorandum to the 2015 Act states:

> "This provision makes it clear that Licensing Standards Officers have a new general function of being able to provide information to Licensing Boards about the conduct of personal licence holders or applicants for a personal licence which is inconsistent with the licensing objectives."

This, it is therefore suggested, was inserted to "close the gap" under the "supervising compliance" function which only relates to premises and occasional licence holders; but in doing so speaks to that wider accepted desire for LSOs to have a greater say in the general "fitness" of personal licence holders.

The second aspect of this provision is to clarify that this investigative power, and the power to put across views, applies not only to existing personal licence holders but also to applicants – that is, to prospective personal licence holders. This is important because it allows the LSO to raise concerns, genuinely held,

19 In the formal response to the Air Weapons and Licensing (Scotland) Bill, the then group co-ordinator Douglas Frood (at that time of Falkirk Council but latterly West Lothian Council) said: "Currently, should a holder of a personal licence be found, by an LSO, to be acting in a manner inconsistent with the licensing objectives, the only route to make the appropriate licensing board aware is through a premises licence review application under section 36. This approach is cumbersome and in the case of an Occasional Licence applied held under a personal licence, not applicable. We feel that, notwithstanding the normal process of guidance and advice carried out by LSOs, it would be beneficial to be able to bring a personal licence holder before the issuing board."

Table 6.1 Sliding scale

Low	→	→	*High*
Meeting the Licensing Objectives	Inconsistency with the Licensing Objectives	Prejudicing the Licensing Objectives	Breaching the Licensing Objectives

perhaps about the applicant's behaviour in licensed premises of which they have some awareness or insight. There are numerous examples of persons which LSOs will interact with who have a *prima facie* management role in a licensed premises and who, perhaps at an earlier time, did not hold a personal licence, and of those examples I am sure that LSOs can give examples of poor practice, shoddy management practices or specific examples where, as an unlicensed member of staff, the person has acted in a manner which has been inconsistent with the licensing objectives. This provision allows the LSO the latitude to air such matters, should they choose to.

A wider discussion about what might happen with such information is dealt with elsewhere, but it is clear that the provision is to allow LSOs to present material (a) which might form a report in connection with an application for a personal licence application, or (b) where the LSO wishes to make the board aware of ongoing matters which may be leading to a personal licence review; but it is perhaps worth saying here that the burden or test which the LSO has to keep in mind in providing information to the licensing board under this heading is that of "inconsistency" with the objectives.

This threshold is relatively low, meaning the evidential burden on the LSO is not, in turn, especially high. If one compares the interpretation of an action which is "inconsistent" with the objectives, to one which "breaches" or "prejudices" the objectives, you can see that the language used suggests that there is a sliding scale, which might look something like Table 6.1.

The language is therefore important in this context. By the use of "inconsistency", as opposed to a form of wording which would imply a higher bar, this allows the LSO latitude to raise issues in a fairly broad sense.

3.4 Providing mediation services

The last "principal" power of the LSO is to provide mediation services. Interestingly, there is no specific mention of "mediation" as a power for LSOs in Nicholson. It does discuss, in generalities, the LSO co-operating with other enforcement officers and acting as a conduit for that other officer to deal with the licence holder. Reviewing the Parliamentary progress of the then Licensing Bill, there is clear discussion concerning the "silent" objective of increasing community participation in licensing with respect to the position of LSO, and it is with this in mind that I believe the mediation power was proposed and, ultimately adopted.

The precise wording of the Act (at section 14(1)(c)) is as follows:

> "providing mediation services for the purpose of avoiding or resolving disputes or disagreements between—
> (i) the holders of the licences referred to in paragraph (b), and
> (ii) any other persons,
> concerning any matter relating to compliance as referred to in that paragraph."

Paragraph (b) referred to at section 14(1)(c)(i) and (ii) as narrated above, is of course the power of supervising compliance with respect to premises and occasional licences. This initial observation should provide some LSOs with comfort that the extent of their mediation services is that which is within their remit as alcohol licensing standards officers – in other words, this power does not mean that LSOs should be mediators in *any* dispute which happens to be between a licence holder and, say, their next-door neighbour. It is *not* the job of the LSO to mediate in relation to property disputes, littering disputes, cooking smells and other errata that happen out there in the real world. It *is* the job of the LSO to mediate in relation to a dispute concerning compliance with the terms of a premises or occasional licence.

This is a good example of where the law may not sit with the practical reality. The LSO will be seen by the public to be someone that they can bring issues in front of, even if not necessarily a licensing issue, because their issue, whatever it may be, relates to a licensed premises. The law, however, confirms that a problem may not be a licensing problem just because it emanates from licensed premises. The erroneous nature of this understandable "wider" perception is also, perhaps unhelpfully, reflected in other resources pertaining to the Act. For example, the Explanatory Notes to section 14(1)(c) suggest a slightly more flexible interpretation of this point:

> "[LSOs will] mediate between communities and the trade or between any two parties where there is a need to resolve a local problem and develop a local solution".

However, that must be read through the lens of the language which is used in the Act.

Taking an even more liberal approach on this issue is the Guidance to Licensing Boards, which states (at paragraph 271):

> "LSOs will require to have some mediation skills. It is considered that in most cases these skills would involve the application of common sense. Examples of this would be when complaints were received from neighbours about noise problems at premises caused by the late-night deposit of bottles in bottle banks. An LSO may be able to persuade the licensee to carry out this task at a more reasonable hour to resolve the issue."

This type of language, whilst aiming to be helpful, indicates what I believe to be a disconnect between the statutory function, and a genuinely held expectation of how a LSO might interact on a wider basis. The issue of noise nuisance from bottle collections is not, for me, a licensing issue. It is very clearly a matter regulated under the Environmental Protection Act 1990, and it is to that piece of legislation that a person unhappy with noise from bottle bins should resort. However, it is easy to understand how a well-intended person might suggest that this be picked up sensibly by a LSO to find a favourable outcome without taking formal actions. Indeed, it is not uncommon for this sort of thing to be discussed and argued at a licensing hearing as that is the practical reality (if not the lawful reality) of the experience of people in their day-to-day lives.

At the other end of the scale, it may be that other aspects of noise nuisance are matters which sit with the LSO, such as entertainment noise. Leaving aside the wide-ranging *Brightcrew* debate for one moment, it is clear that any licence authorises certain activities and it must surely be sensible that a LSO be allowed to mediate between parties where there is some suggestion that those activities are causing mischief to the licensing objectives. Another way to put this is to say that it is useful to consider that LSO mediation might relate to matters which are narrated in the licence. This would include entertainment noise, but exclude noise from emptying bottles; and so on.

From an agent's perspective, my own experience is that you come to accept that people raise these issues and, depending on your style of advocacy, it may be sensible to respond and offer compromise to build rapport with the authorities and those making the representations instead of rebuffing the topic by quoting case law or even licensing law textbooks. Of course, that strategy may not always be appropriate and depends on the circumstances of the case.

The Guidance to Licensing Boards suggested the following points would be instructive for LSOs in conducting mediation:

- Be confident working with a range of difficult people
- Understand the pitfalls of working in situations where alcohol is a significant feature
- Remain calm and professional during difficult encounters
- Communicate effectively and build rapport under pressure
- Have a range of ways of handling upset, aggressive and other difficult behaviour
- Understand the personal safety issues involved in carrying out their role
- Understand how to resolve disputes using a mediation-style dispute resolution
- Remain impartial
- Help people assess different ways of moving their situation forward
- Encourage parties to resolve disputes by dialogue where appropriate
- Be able to set up, structure and run a joint, face-to-face dispute resolution session
- Understand when mediation-style dispute resolution is appropriate and when it is not.

There comes a time when mediation can only take the LSO so far. First, we have noted that there is a limit to what the LSO should actually be seeking to mediate, which might be described as broadly equivalent to the properly understood meaning of *licensing objective*. Secondly, there are cases where mediation will not work, perhaps due to one or both parties simply being unwilling to enter into the process, or, having done so, where the process fails. I have been involved in cases where licence holders have instructed the services of a trained independent mediator, where, for example, the relationship between a resident and the LSO has broken down. LSOs will do their best to find solutions, but they are not miracle workers.

4 SPECIFIC POWERS OF A LICENSING STANDARDS OFFICER

Having looked at four main "general" powers of the LSO, we now turn to some more specific powers catered for (or not) under the Act, which are as follows:

- Powers in relation to entry, inspection and seizure
- Powers in relation to unlicensed premises
- Powers in relation to occasional licences.

We will examine each of these in turn.

4.1 The power of entry, inspection and seizure

Section 15 states:

> "(1) A Licensing Standards Officer for a council area may, for the purpose of determining whether the activities being carried on in any licensed premises in the area are being carried on in accordance with—
>
> (a) the premises licence or, as the case may be, occasional licence in respect of the premises, and
>
> (b) any other requirements of this Act,
>
> exercise the powers specified in subsection (2).
>
> (2) The powers referred to subsection (1) are—
>
> (a) power to enter the premises at any time for the purpose of exercising the power specified in paragraph (b),
>
> (b) power to carry out such inspection of the premises and of any substances, articles or documents found there as the Officer thinks necessary,
>
> (c) power to take copies of, or of an entry in, any document found on the premises, and
>
> (d) power to seize and remove any substances, articles or documents found on the premises."

Paragraphs (c) and (d) were added to section 15 by way of section 197 of the Air Weapons and Licensing (Scotland) Act 2015 and commenced as of 29 June 2018.[20] Let us break this down in more detail to analyse the constituent parts, and first let us look at the difference between these powers and licensed versus *unlicensed* premises.

4.2 Power of entry to unlicensed premises and premises subject to application

The starting point here is confirm that LSOs do not have any power to enter or inspect unlicensed premises (but note the section 137 caveat discussed below). The original Licensing Bill had in fact proposed such powers. Interestingly, during the debates surrounding the passage of the Licensing Bill, the police had lobbied Parliament not to give LSOs the same rights to enter premises as the police had and would enjoy. On 22 June 2005 during a Parliamentary debate, Tavish Scott MSP said:

> "Police evidence to the committee suggested that we should reconsider allowing licensing standards officers to enter unlicensed premises. The Association of Chief Police Officers in Scotland stressed the potential for licensing standards officers to become involved in dangerous situations that would be best left to trained police officers. I confirm that I am happy to lodge suitable amendments at stage 2 to deal with that issue."

20 Criminal Justice and Licensing (Scotland) Act 2010 (Commencement No. 15 and Saving Provision) and the Air Weapons and Licensing (Scotland) Act 2015 (Commencement No. 8) Order 2018 (SSI 2018/102) art 2(b).

George Lyon on 20 September 2005 said:

> "ACPOS and the committee expressed concern at stage 1 about the right of licensing standards officers to enter and inspect unlicensed premises. I agree that we should not place LSOs in situations that could expose them to danger, so we have lodged amendment 15 to remove that power."

Compare section 15 with the equivalent section relating to police powers of entry, section 138, which states:

> "(1) A constable may at any time enter and inspect any licensed premises.
> (2) A constable may—
> (a) if the condition in subsection (3) is satisfied, and
> (b) subject to subsection (4),
> at any time enter and inspect any premises (other than licensed premises) on which food or drink is sold for consumption on the premises.
> (3) The condition referred to in subsection (2)(a) is that the constable has reasonable grounds for believing that alcohol is being sold on the premises in breach of section 1(1)."

Section 138(2) clearly allows the police to enter and inspect unlicensed premises under the circumstances narrated, and by comparison this is a power which is clearly not afforded to LSOs and was indeed actively lobbied against and rebuffed. Police powers of entry and other powers are discussed in more detail in Chapter 19.

Whilst the comparison is instructive, it is not the whole story. There is a separate power of entry hidden away at section 137 of the Act, and that is the power to enter and inspect premises for the purpose of determining a pending licence application or where there has been a review application in relation to an existing premises licence. This power applies equally to the police and LSOs. Section 137 states that this power applies where the following applications have been made:

(a) a premises licence application,
(b) a premises licence variation application,
(c) a premises licence review proposal or application,
(d) an application under section 47(2) for a temporary premises licence,
(e) an occasional licence application, or
(f) an extended hours application.

This power is also different to the general power under section 15. First of all, the power under section 138 applies "at any reasonable time" as opposed to "any time" under section 15. There is no further legislative guidance on what might constitute a "reasonable" time under these circumstances, so I would hazard a guess that this *may* be read to infer that a reasonable time would be when premises are open, that is, during what might be described as normal business hours, if the premises are trading unlicensed: for example, a "bring your own bottle" style restaurant. In this regard, if the premises are already functioning, I would also propose that a reasonable time would be a time which is sensible and appropriate for the operator of the business to properly deal with the LSO's enquiries. Using our example of the "bring your own bottle" restaurant, perhaps it would not be reasonable to expect a business person to attend to queries at the height of the lunchtime service, and that a reasonable approach would be to arrange a later time when the premises are less busy.

This more restrictive power of entry is also linked to a particular purpose, namely that the LSO is wishing to assess the likely effect on the licensing objectives if the application were to be granted, or, in the case of a review, "the effect which the selling of alcohol in accordance with the premises licence is having on those objectives".[21] In practice, the LSO will produce a report in relation to applications and reviews, even if to confirm that they have no particular view one way or the other, and it makes sense that this inspection power be used to help them in the preparation of such reports.

Acting almost as an opposite provision to that of having to attend at a reasonable time, is the power that LSOs can use "reasonable force" if necessary in conducting their assessment, and a person who obstructs an LSO from carrying out the visit and inspection commits a criminal offence. It is curious to note that this potential use of reasonable force does not exist in the "standard" right of entry, inspection and so on in relation to premises which are licensed, whilst the linked offence of obstruction does. I have yet to discover why Parliament saw fit to grant a power to use reasonable force in an unlicensed premises, but not in a licensed premises.

Putting that statutory conundrum to one side, I cannot imagine a circumstance when a LSO would ever contemplate the use of reasonable force when conducting an assessment of this nature. I wonder if the reference to this ought to have been restricted to the police. The Guidance to Licensing Boards states (at paragraph 274):

> "LSOs will have the power of entry at all reasonable times and otherwise should require a warrant. LSOs will not have the power to force entry to premises."

This is, unfortunately, a confusing paragraph which appeared to erroneously conflate both the provisions concerning access at "any time" and a "reasonable time" along with saying they cannot force entry albeit we know they can use reasonable force in conducting an assessment for a prospective application.

4.3 Power to inspect, seek and remove items

LSO powers to generally inspect, seek items, take copies, and remove items are replete. The first element of this is that LSOs can "carry out such inspection of the premises and of any substances, articles or documents found there as the Officer thinks necessary". The "such inspection of the premises" part relates to a wider inspection of the premises, so the officer has a power to do a full "walk round" of the premises – which means all parts within the licensed area. In the majority of cases, the extent of the licensed area should be the entire footprint of the premises, which would include non-public areas.

The general approach to licensing premises in Scotland is that it is the full footprint of the premises which is "within the red line," indicating the licensed area. In other words, when we discuss the notion that a LSO can carry out an inspection of the premises, this relates to the demise of the *licensed premises*. In most cases the delineation of the entire premises will also be the licensed premises but, to give one example, if the premises are a pub with a manager's private flat above it, then that private flat is unlikely to be part of the licensed premises and therefore the LSO cannot insist on access or inspection.

21 2005 Act, s 137(2)(b).

Non-public areas, with the exception of genuinely private areas like residential dwellings, are most likely to be a part of the licensed premises and this would include areas such as the cellar, staff room, kitchen, or any other back of house/staff area.

During the inspection the LSO can inspect any substances, articles or documents he or she may find. They can also seize and remove these mysterious substances, articles and documents, and even take copies of the documents or entries in those documents.

Let us examine this part a little closer. In relation to substances, one would assume that this includes alcohol although as the word "substance" is not defined in the Act it could literally mean anything.[22] In practical terms, however, I am not aware that the inspection of substances is something which occurs with regularity, never mind the seizure of such items. If, for example, the LSO came across a substance which looked like fake alcohol, would that be something they would take action on, or would it more properly sit with some other regulatory officer? Similarly, if the LSO came across substances in a staff area which appeared to be illegal drugs, would it really be expected that the LSO would try to remove the drugs, or instead report this to the police at that time?

Inspection of articles or documents is another matter. An absolutely central part of the day-to-day experience of the LSO is checking compliance with documentary matters, which would include checking that the mandatory signage is on display: the summary of the licence; the notice under section 110 of the Act; the notice under Schedule 3 to the Act. The officer would also check that other documents are available such as full copy or certified copy of the licence, policy documentation such as the "Challenge 25" policy, and, of course, staff training records.

Why might a LSO seize and remove documents? The records may be incorrect. The records may be flawed in some way. The quality of records may lead to suspicions. There are, unfortunately, examples of fraudulent papers being discovered where staff training declarations have been signed and/or countersigned where the member of staff has not actually received the training or may not even exist. If the LSO is seeking to build a case of sharp practice and non-compliance to put to the licensing board then it makes sense that the officer has a power to seize suspect documents. I am aware of at least one case where a LSO discovered that a summary licence had been "doctored" so as to show a premises manager who had not been officially named on the premises by way of a minor variation application.

4.4 Power to issue a compliance notice

Section 14(2) ascribes a particular power in relation to the compliance function noted above. If an LSO believes a condition to a premises or occasional licence has been or is being breached, he or she may issue the licence holder with a notice requiring that licence holder to take any such action to remedy the breach as may be specified in the notice. If the notice is not complied with

22 The *Collins Dictionary* defines a substance as a "a solid, powder, liquid, or gas with particular properties", whilst the *Cambridge Dictionary* suggests it is a "material with particular physical characteristics".

to the satisfaction of the LSO, he or she may then make an application to the board for a review – note that the LSO can only instigate a review in relation to a premises licence, not an occasional licence, but perhaps of more importance here is to recognise that the Act has created this route as a step which should be carried out prior to going to review.

I have discussed at length the notion of the LSO working with the licence holder to bring them into compliance. This includes the LSO following the steps available to them in the correct order as the Act envisages. In other words, that the LSO should only seek a review of a premises licence in relation to a breach of conditions where he or she has first endeavoured to resolve the matter by way of the section 14(2) compliance notice (and, I would suggest, even before that by trying to resolve the matter informally) – this appears to me to be the clear intention of section 14(2)(a)(ii). In other words, if a premises licence review is sought in relation to a breach of conditions without the notice having been issued first, then the licence holder can fairly argue that he or she has not been afforded the appropriate route and opportunity to bring themselves into compliance. One might go further and say a review request absent a section 14(2) notice which has not been complied with, is not competent.

The detail of the notice is not prescribed. In practice, it takes the form of a letter, although in some cases LSOs in certain council areas have developed a "style" notice which is issued. The wording of the notice and the matters to be attended to are therefore left to the style of the individual officer. In most cases the notice will specify which condition is relevant and will go on to narrate the officer's position as to how this condition has been breached. This may go into granular detail if required but if the correct process has been followed then the licensee will be well aware of the issues and should be expecting the notice to be issued having hopefully engaged with the officer on the matter, even if parties are not in agreement. The notice might also give a timescale to allow compliance, although the Act does not explicitly cater for this approach.

Whether a timescale for compliance is proposed is therefore, it would seem, in the gift of the LSO. For example, if the LSO has reported that the breach related to the condition requiring installation of baby changing facilities, then one would expect the notice might give a period of time to allow the licence holder to arrange for facilities to be installed. On the other hand, if the premises are running a clearly unlawful irresponsible promotion then the notice might demand immediate compliance with no grace period.

If the terms of the notice are not agreed, that is, if the licence holder simply disagrees that the condition has been breached as a matter of fact or law, then they have two options. The first is that they allow the LSO to take the matter further, to a premises licence review hearing, and argue their case in front of the board, as happened in the case of *Mitchells & Butlers Retail Ltd v Dundee City Licensing Board*,[23] which is discussed in detail in Chapter 15 at Section 4.8. The second option is to challenge the notice directly, which would have to be by way of a judicial review as there is no formal appeal procedure within the Act; it is therefore the less likely of the two options.

23 2011 SLT (Sh Ct) 53.

4.5 Licensing standards officers and occasional licences

LSOs have some particular powers set out under the Act in respect of occasional licences. On receipt of a competent occasional licence application, the licensing board must serve notice of it on the LSO (as well as the police). The Act does not provide a deadline for the board to serve notice on the LSO but one would normally expect this to happen with a matter of some days given that the events which are proposed to be licensed might only be some weeks away. Section 57(3) says that the LSO *may* submit a report with their views on the application and if doing so this should be within 21 days of the date they received the notice. This power, to report on occasional licences, is therefore discretionary but the LSO should ensure their report is with the board before the 21-day deadline. If a report is submitted, then the licensing board must take account of it in reaching their decision. As is discussed in more detail elsewhere, it is possible that the board may require a hearing and if so, that the LSO attend to speak to their report and perhaps answer questions.

5 LSOS AND PREMISES OR PERSONAL LICENCE REVIEWS

LSO powers in relation to premises licence reviews are examined in Chapter 14 at Section 5. LSO powers in relation to instigating personal licence reviews are examined in Chapter 17 at Section 5.4.

6 POWERS IN RELATION TO GAMBLING ON ALCOHOL LICENSED PREMISES

The Guidance to Licensing Boards boldly stated (at paragraph 281):

> "It would be appropriate for LSOs to monitor Gaming premises. However, this should be left to the discretion of local authorities."

This statement was issued several months prior to the onset of the Gambling Act 2005, which came into force on 1 September 2007, and clearly was made without taking into account the technical difficulties that ultimately came to the fore on this topic.

Under the Gambling Act 2005, in order to conduct enforcement activity an officer has to meet the definition of an "authorised person" for the purposes of that Act. My view has been that LSOs appointed under the Licensing (Scotland) Act 2005 cannot meet the definition of "authorised person" under section 304 of the Gambling Act 2005 because they are not officers of the licensing authority (the licensing board), but the local authority, which is not a licensing authority for the purposes of alcohol licensing – and these are separate legal entities. This is a drafting error which emanates from the Parliamentary draughtsmen's lack of understanding of the separate Scottish licensing system, and poor oversight at Westminster level.

I raised this issue subsequent to the onset of the Licensing (Scotland) Act 2005 on 1 September 2009 in articles and at conferences. The earliest versions of the Gambling Commission's Guidance to Licensing Authorities did not recognise the issue at all and it was not heeded until the consultation to update that Guidance in 2012, but even then the treatment was not satisfactory.

The Gambling Commission was frustrated by the lack of enforcement activity in Scotland and ultimately proposed a "workaround" in the publication of its advice note "The Role of Authorised Persons in Scotland", from July 2013. The Commission wisely opened that document with the following caveat: "The interpretation of the Act and powers of authorised persons is ultimately a matter for the courts".

The Commission conceded that LSOs do not meet the definition under section 304 and this is confirmed at paragraphs 2.4 and 2.5 of the guidance note. The "workaround" it proposed was to have LSOs assigned dual or multiple roles for the local authority; in other words, if the LSO also has other duties such as having been authorised to conduct functions in relation to public/environmental health, then they might fall into the definition having been authorised for a non-licensing function. The Gambling Commission was forced to construct an inelegant solution to this issue and this remains its position on the matter.

The practical reality is that, at time of writing, most licensing boards disagree with the Gambling Commission "solution". There are also examples of LSOs conducting gambling enforcement visits in certain local authority areas where those authorities have satisfied themselves on the "workaround" point. Speaking with LSOs, I know that there is a divergence of views, with many concerned not just at the technical issue, but that, in being asked to conduct enforcement under the Gambling Act, they do not have the necessary tools or equivalent training that they do under the Licensing Act, which may leave them open to criticism or challenge.

The waters were muddied somewhat with the statutory creation of "civic licensing standards officers" (CLSOs) under the Civic Government (Scotland) Act 1982. To be clear, this is a separate legal role under the 1982 legislation. A "2005 Act LSO" is not a "civic" LSO unless approved as such. The Air Weapons and Licensing (Scotland) Act 2015 amended the Civic Government (Scotland) Act 1982 by introducing a new section 45G, which required Scottish local authorities, as licensing authorities under the 1982 Act, to appoint a CLSO with effect from 1 May 2017. A number of local authorities modelled this new role on the 2005 Act LSO in terms of job description and, as I understand it, some LSOs have also been made CLSOs, but in other cases separate individuals have been appointed to that role. One can now state that a CLSO is an officer of a licensing authority and therefore could meet the definition of "authorised person" under the Gambling Act 2005 in a cleaner way; however, the central issue remains that the licensing authority for alcohol and gambling in Scotland is the board, not the council.

Depending on which construction of these terms you seek to follow, it is at least possible to argue that CLSOs might conduct gambling enforcement. However, it is indelicate at best that civic officers are being asked to deal with gambling, and then have to report such issues to the licensing board, a body against which they have no remit.

For my part, I would prefer that Westminster corrected this to put the matter beyond doubt. Until it does, I believe that any action conducted by a LSO or even a CLSO which pertains to the Gambling Act 2005 is potentially challengeable. This is a highly regrettable state of affairs, because we all agree that clearly there needs to be licensing authority enforcement of gambling premises and if this *lacuna* were corrected it would make life easier for all stakeholders to get on with it.

Chapter 7

Premises Licences – Part 1 Origins and Effect; Duration and Duties

1 THE ORIGIN OF THE PREMISES LICENCE

Part 3 of the 2005 Act deals with premises licences, a central pillar of the Scottish alcohol licensing system. Cutting to the chase, it may be helpful to state that a premises licence is defined in section 17 as:

> "... a licence issued by a licensing board ... authorising the sale of alcohol in relation to specific premises".[1]

In other words, a premises licence is an alcohol licence which will relate to a set of premises (and the phrase "premises" can be widely interpreted – as discussed later), regardless of the business type or style of alcohol trading conducted on the premises. It may seem eminently sensible to enjoy a licensing system whereby there is simply "a licence" to sell alcohol, but to properly understand the mechanics of the premises licence, and before examining application processes and so on, one must contextualise the 2005 Act approach, as this unitary system was preceded by legislation which created many forms of alcohol licence.

For those practising licensing law at the time of transition to the 2005 Act, the idea of moving to a single type of permanent licence that authorised the sale of alcohol with no differentiation in terms of business model, and no separate nomenclature such as "public house", "hotel" or "restaurant", was bold and controversial. If one did not operate with a "public house" licence in contrast to a "restaurant licence", how would the difference in particular rules or laws pertaining to certain premises be discerned by the operator, the authorities, and the general public? Would there be any difference at all? There is no doubt the move to a single premises licence represented a major shift in the regulation of licensing in Scotland, which had created the notion of separate public house and "grocer's certificates" (off-sales) at least as far back as 1853, and therefore categorisation was systemic. On the other hand, the utility of having seven separate types of alcohol licence as was the case under the 1976 Act, each with their own rules and foibles,[2] was questioned towards the end of the twentieth century and many found the definitions confusing, especially in relation to which premises may or may not have a "bar", and differing rules concerning children's access. The Regulatory Impact Assessment

1 The term also applies to temporary licences under s 47, as discussed in Chapter 11 at Section 4.

2 The seven types of alcohol licence were: Public House, Hotel, Restricted Hotel, Entertainment, Refreshment, Restaurant, and Off-sale.

to the Licensing Bill captures this public detachment from the 1976 Act licensing laws in the following example:

> "The law concerning the sale and consumption of alcohol by children is deeply confusing to parents, other members of the public and visitors to this country, and is largely discredited. In particular, the law governing the consumption of alcohol by minors relates only to the area in licensed premises described as the bar area, leaving children at liberty to consume alcohol in other areas of licensed premises."

There were also concerns from some quarters that the licence categories offered a somewhat underhand way of seeking approval for what one might shortly refer to as a "Trojan horse" licence – for example, asking for a hotel licence for premises which in fact would principally trade as a public bar, on the basis that a "hotel" branded application might attract fewer objections than a "public house" branded application. Nicholson referred to this sort of thing as "licensing by stealth", citing the following examples:

> "cases where a hotel licence has been granted on the basis that the premises will be used primarily as a hotel with a small bar area for patrons. What later happens, however, is that the bar area is extended inexorably both within the premises and sometimes in the open air outside with the result that the premises effectively become a large super-pub, attracting many hundreds of patrons at a time, with a few letting bedrooms attached. Another example which has been given to us involves the small grocery shop which seeks an off-sale licence ostensibly to enable it to carry a small stock of beer, wine and spirits in addition to its main stock of groceries. In some such cases, however, we have been told that what has happened thereafter is that the groceries virtually disappear and the whole shop is turned into a large off-sales emporium."[3]

In addition to the potential for public confusion over rules for different licence types, and machinations over sharp practice from some operators seen to be "gaming the system", a further issue with the old-style categorisation needs to be identified – namely, innovation. The reality of lawful commercial business practice was (and is) that blurred lines already existed in terms of how premises actually operated – long before urbane phrases such as "casual dining", "small plates" and "street food" became commonplace in the trade and even among the public. Whilst for many people it remains perfectly obvious to identify a pub or a restaurant, it is suggested that the same people would concede that new licensed spaces have evolved and broken free of these traditional descriptors. Innovation in the licensed trade continues, for example the rise of the so-called "restaurant with rooms" premises, or where retail operators give space to "food-to-go", or where a premises might offer "competitive leisure" or "experiential facilities", and is unlikely to relent.

If that statement is accepted, then it can be understood why the idea of a single flexible premises licence would be the answer to all of this, as it would allow for new developments in change within industry as well as within law. To put it another way:

> "Most would agree that the licence types no longer reflected modern licensing practices and were inappropriate in light of the development and growth of licensed premises, particularly the night-time economy"[4].

3 Nicholson Report, para 4.2, pp 55–6.

4 Mairi Millar, "Operating Plans: a recipe for uncertainty?" [2008] 39 SLLP 19.

Thinking back to the practice of licensing law under the 1976 Act, whilst some solicitors generally approved of categorisation, as it assisted them in advising their clients, many found that the restrictive nature of seven classes of licence began to cause problems for clients looking at these more modern and innovative business models, such as hybrid night venues which seemed to fall somewhere between public house and entertainment, or the more relaxed dining bars and eateries which in some cases also morphed into night-time entertainment spots, or even with artistic, community or cultural centres, which might do all of these things and more. In this climate, it is not difficult to divine how the sense arose that a single, generic licence could be the best way forward. This thinking was not too bold a step, with more than just a furtive glance to the system south of the border where the single premises licence was already in place.

Nicholson summarised this as follows:

> "it will obviously be in everyone's interests (including those of the licence holder) if the precise nature of the licensed operations are prescribed with clarity at the stage when the licence is first granted. For the foregoing reasons we consider that the time has come to depart from the present system of seven somewhat ill-defined types of licence to a system where each licence will clearly state the nature of the operations which may be undertaken by the licence holder."[5]

Thus, the single premises licence was born, with good intentions in mind.

2 THE SINGLE PREMISES LICENCE IN PRACTICE

As we have explored above, all premises can, theoretically at least, have a licence tailored to their specific needs, meaning all licences across Scotland could be individually created to fulfil the desire of the applicant, assuming the licensing board was in agreement with the requests. Whether that has proven to be the case in reality, is suspect.

First, it is worth observing that the Nicholson flexibility led to a media outcry at the time of the Licensing Bill, proclaiming it would result in 24-hour drinking, as in theory people could apply for any hours they wished. This ignored the fact that the application process did not result in a "deemed grant" – the terms of the licence including trading hours did, of course, require to meet the approval of the licensing board and could be commented on by the police, local residents and indeed any person. The hullabaloo over this issue even led to amendments during the passing of the Bill which left us with the provision under section 64, *viz* that which created a presumption against the grant of a 24-hour licence. This provision, and controversial scenes in the Scottish Parliament which created it, are often criticised and are examined elsewhere in this book; but ultimately this licensing vignette indicated that Parliament could not stomach a *carte blanche* approach.

What one should reflect upon in relation to this, to my mind at least, is that the philosophical construct of the single premises licence was not in fact to create a "one licence fits all" system, but rather the opposite – a system in which the licensing board can be in no doubt as to the exact details of a

5 Nicholson Report, para 4.3, p 56.

proposed operation and grant a licence on the basis of that unique offer. In doing so, the detail offered by the applicant is "captured" in such a way that the licence would be stamped accordingly; thus, detracting from the ability of that licence holder to trade in a way that was on the verges or even completely outside a certain category or style, in a fully or quasi-clandestine manner. Having the licence tailored and unique to a single set of premises created the additional safety net that, in order to amend it, the holder of the licence would have to go back to seek permission of the licensing board.

So, with that in mind, it is no great leap of logic to query whether those who dreaded the idea of the "blank canvas" approach had their fear, that licences would become all things to all people, realised. At the time of conversion to the new system, many licensing boards simply applied blanket policy conditions and hours to the new premises licences as they were considered through the transitional period, and as applicants were wary of seeking specifics for fear of losing their 'grandfather' status, these were by and large accepted without debate, although in some cases there were operators who lost trading hours because of a new policy being adopted.[6]

Whilst it is therefore true to state that the transition to the 2005 Act did not leave us with thousands of "open ended" licences, the opposite is also true, in that it also did not leave us with a kaleidoscope of varied and various licences across the land. The result instead was that licences were transitioned on a quasi-category basis and what we ended up with were lots of licences which broadly looked exactly like they did before, especially in relation to trading hours. Whilst it is now true that a licensed premises can be said to hold a "premises licence" as opposed to a "public house" or "off-sale" licence, what we saw was a more subtle categorisation of another type, through the vagaries of local licensing policy statements holding sway. Licences were being converted from the old system to the new within local policy artifices which, in their own way, maintained the old-fashioned separations of style and type.

Since transition back in 2009, it might be said that this policy-led approach to category has become entrenched to some degree, for as licensing board policies have become more informed and advanced, there has been a visible creep towards blatant categorisation.[7] Whilst it could be argued that this has had the effect of potentially undermining a suggested wider goal of flexibility within the system for local premises and individual cases, the counter to that is of course that it is perfectly acceptable for a board to consider how best to carry out its functions and agree upon a general approach, and in doing so to follow the statutory requirement to create a policy and look to follow that policy, which includes adopting a policy position on how they expect certain styles of business to trade and what hours of operation they should benefit from.

As readers will know, each application is taken on its own merits – a steadfast axiom of the licensing system in Scotland, and exceptions to policy can be and are granted, but, as is their nature, by exception rather than rule!

Let us examine this point a little more closely. I have suggested that the categorisation can be seen most openly in the discussion of licensed hours in

6 See Chapter 4 at Section 6 on the reference to various so-called "policy hours" cases.

7 An example where this has not been the case is Aberdeen City Licensing Board, whose policy 2018–2024 introduced a blanket on sales licence policy allowing 3am terminal hour – to the delight of many publicans and bar owners, and the derision of many nightclub operators.

various board policy statements, where it is not untypical to find a graph, box or paragraph confirming what hours a licensing board is likely to approve for a "restaurant" style premises or a "late night entertainment" style premises, and such language and terms are used. Some boards have taken this further by introducing certain qualifications or hurdles which an applicant must negotiate before they can unlock the hours they wish, such as that certain forms of entertainment must be available, or that a minimum percentage of the layout of the premises must be used for a particular activity.

This suggests that categorisation has actually become more profound than under the old 1976 approach. Under that Act, you were a public house or hotel or entertainment premises because that was the type of licence you had. Under the 2005 Act approach, your premises and style of operation must meet several conditions and tests and observe certain rules before the licensing board will approve your licence in terms of policy.

The issue of categorisation has even moved beyond licensing board consideration in certain local authority areas, where one might not even leap the planning section 50[8] hurdle unless certain wording is used in the general description or certain hours are sought, or certain activities provided for – based on a draft application and comparison to the underlying planning permission.

What this brings us to is a system where different trading practices are still controlled but not by separation of licence type, rather by the application of local licensing policy and then by decision-making on a case-by-case basis and agreeing licences with regard to that policy.

This alternative approach to categorisation is not necessarily unwelcome. It can be suggested that that by housing the concept of category within policy, as opposed to statute, this should create an atmosphere where the system can "react" to innovation as well as issues of concern by amending policy to take account of new concepts and fears, as opposed to a rigid set of licence types.

On the other hand, re-examining my earlier references to public confusion over different licence types in comparison to the 2005 Act system does suggest at least one practical issue which I and many others have encountered, and that relates to the statutory form of the site notice displayed at premises to advertise an application. The language used in the notice can lead to general confusion from members of the public, who see the phrase "premises licence" in bold type and despite a list of sought-after activities being listed on the notice, might often assume that the premises will become the lowest common denominator, or rather, will be the least favourable to the local area because the true nature of the business being proposed is not properly explained.

This introduction is an effort to provide context to the axiom of the single premises licence. Let us move on to less existential matters.

2.1 The duration of a premises licence

A premises licence, once granted, is of indefinite duration. It does not require to be renewed.[9] The abandonment of any renewal process (licences were renewed triennially under the 1976 Act), leaving licences "open ended", was

8 Planning certificates and the relevance of s 50 are discussed in detail at Section 3.8 below.

9 Although note the obligation to pay an annual licensing fee, on which see Chapter 15 at Section 4.12.

criticised during evidence sessions at the Scottish Parliament in the passing of the 2005 Act. These concerns were ultimately dismissed by the Local Government and Transport Committee:

> "The Committee notes the concerns expressed by some witnesses about the proposed end to the three-year renewal process. The Committee notes that the Deputy Minister's position is that the new licensing regime will allow stronger community involvement in the licensing process via the local licensing forums, and that complaints about anti-social behaviour associated with a licensed premises could be made known quickly via the Licensing Standards Officers. The Committee notes, however, that it is difficult to assess how effective the new arrangements will be in addressing local concerns about licensed premises, and therefore recommends that the new National Licensing Forum reviews and monitors this aspect of the new licensing regime. The Committee further recommends that Ministers should ask the National Licensing Forum to co-ordinate a public information campaign designed to inform the public about their rights under the new licensing system and the procedures by which the public can highlight concerns about licensed premises."[10]

Of course, the National Licensing Forum never took hold (see Chapter 5 at Section 5) so an assessment of whether open-ended licences were really countered by greater community involvement was never undertaken.

A premises licence will cease to have effect only if one of the following events occurs:

- if the premises licence is suspended by the board, it ceases to have effect during the currency of the suspension period;[11]
- revocation of the licence;
- the premises cease to be used for the sale of alcohol;
- the licence holder dies, becomes incapable, or becomes insolvent (under s 28(7) an individual or partnership is held to become insolvent on the approval of a voluntary arrangement, being adjudged bankrupt, sequestration, entering a deed of arrangement, or granting a trust deed; a company is held to become insolvent on the approval of a voluntary arrangement, the appointment of an administrator or administrative receiver, and liquidation); or
- surrender of the licence.

Let us look at some of these events more closely.

2.1.1 Suspension or revocation of the licence

The effect of suspension and revocation, and the law surrounding these processes, is discussed in detail in Chapter 14 at Section 4.1.

2.1.2 When does a licence "cease to be used for the sale of alcohol"?

The Act provides no particular detail as to any determinant period of time on this point. There is, for example, no statutory provision discussing closure of premises whether temporary, semi-permanent or permanent. There has been

10 Stage 1 Report to the Licensing (Scotland) Bill, Local Government and Transport Committee, para 37.

11 Note that the suspension of a licence does not affect the requirement to pay an annual fee: see Licensing (Fees) (Scotland) Regulations 2007 (SSI 2007/553) at regulation 7(1).

no case law under the 2005 Act on this point as yet. However, it can be noted that, under the 1976 Act, in the case of *Mount Charlotte Investments plc v City of Glasgow District Licensing Board*[12] a prolonged period of closure justified the refusal of a renewal application.

The phrase "cease to be used for the sale of alcohol" in my mind implies permanency. It would be absurd to suggest that the provision would apply when a pub closes its doors at 1am for the night.[13] The premises have ceased to be used for the sale of alcohol, it is true, but clearly that is not what this provision is intended to strike at. Similarly, I do not see that this is designed to capture a number of other scenarios such as where premises are closed for refurbishment, or have been damaged in some way, or where a tenancy is changing hands. I suggest that the provision is aimed at a definitive cessation of alcohol sales where there is no likelihood that sales will recommence. An example would be where premises have been sold and the new business is clearly not a licensed business – perhaps a former pub has been turned into a bank; or perhaps a former convenience store has been turned into a salon. In these types of cases there is a clear "break".

What might be more difficult to fathom is when the provision may activate should a licensed premises be subject to a period of closure over a longer time frame. It is entirely probable, and indeed factually correct, to suggest that, in some cases, premises which are not trading may be closed for some time even though the owner has every intention of retaining the licence. Think of a scenario where a pub is on the market for sale but has failed to attract interest, or perhaps offers have fallen through. Extraneous market forces may be to blame for a delayed sale, despite the owner's best efforts. The presence of the licence is essential and has an intrinsic value to the overall commercial value of the premises. There is no doubt the premises have ceased to be used for the sale of alcohol, but these wider factors might be taken into account. There are also cases where a licence holder may "sit on" an unused licence to maintain the licence numbers underpinning a local overprovision policy and thus keep potential competitors out.

There is a separate question about the actual operation of section 28(5)(b) – how does the determination that the licence ceases to have effect occur? This is not something that can occur organically. A definitive stance requires to be taken by the licensing board. In most cases this will happen through a premises licence review proposal brought by the licensing board themselves under section 37 although there are also examples of boards *ex proprio motu* taking a decision to declare that the premises licence has ceased to exist without having followed the formal review procedure. In the absence of any formal process in place to deal directly with section 28(5)(b) I tend to the view that a review hearing is the safer approach as this at least affords the licence holder a right to be heard and a right of appeal, and therefore the process is less likely to offend natural justice.

Of some import to these deliberations might not be simply the actions of the licence holder but also the actions of the board members themselves. In one case I witnessed, a proposal to revoke a licence on the basis the premises had ceased to trade, which was brought by a clerk under section 37, was rejected

12 1992 SCLR 311.

13 Or, for that matter, a prolonged period of enforced closure as a result of a global pandemic.

by the licensing board at the hearing, upon learning that the licence holder had continued to pay the annual fee, and the council had taken the payment.

2.1.3 Transfer of the licence following named events

A licence ceases to have effect where certain events occur as narrated above. The premises licence may be "saved" if, within 28 days from the date of certain prescribed events, an application to transfer the licence has been lodged with the board.[14] Thereafter, if the application for transfer is refused, the premises licence ceases to have effect on the date of the refusal. A detailed examination of the transfer provisions is provided in Chapter 12.

2.1.4 Surrender of a premises licence

Section 28(6) makes specific provision for the surrender of a premises licence, which was perhaps a novel consideration back in 2009, as there was no procedure on a statutory footing under the previous regime.[15] In order to surrender the licence, the licence holder must give to the board a notice stating that he wishes to surrender the licence, along with the principal licence itself (or a statement of reasons as to why the licence cannot be produced).

The ability to surrender the licence informs part of the debate over who should actually hold the premises licence in a landlord and tenant set-up. On the one hand, the landlord (such as a pub company) may wish to avoid possible vicarious liability for offences whilst named as the premises licence holder;[16] on the other, if the tenant or lessee is named as the premises licence holder then they could surrender the licence out of spite, should the parties have a disagreement. I have come across cases where an individual holds the licence "in trust" for the company. In these circumstances, the trust deed would make provisions to ensure that the individual would not surrender the licence, but having a guarantee on paper does not mean it could not be done.

In *London and Edinburgh Inns Ltd v North Ayrshire Licensing Board*,[17] a tenant surrendered a public house licence. The landlord lodged a temporary transfer that was rejected by the board on the ground that there was no licence to transfer, following receipt of the letter of surrender from the tenant. The landlord argued that "surrender" was incompetent under the Act, and that the licence was the landlord's "possession" for the purpose of Article 1 of the European Convention on Human Rights. The court held that the Act envisaged that there was a licence subsisting when the transfer application was made, and instructed the board to convene a hearing to consider the application; but at the same time the decision confirmed that the concept of surrender, in relation to the 1976 Act, was competent.[18]

14 2005 Act, s 28(2).

15 The practice is, however, well established: *D & A Haddow Ltd v City of Glasgow District Licensing Board* 1983 SLT (Sh Ct) 5; *Connelly v Glasgow Licensing Authority* 1964 SLT (Sh Ct) 77; *W S Murphy Ltd v Alloa Burgh Licensing Authority* 1973 SLT (Sh Ct) 2. See J C Cummins, *Licensing Law in Scotland* (2nd edn, 2001) pp 164–6.

16 One should, of course, remember the terms of s 141B of the 2005 Act in relation to whether a tenant operator is an "employee or agent" of the licence holder.

17 [2004] 29 SLLP 30.

18 Alan Barron argues that this decision is consistent with the view of Lord Gill in *Datelock Ltd v*

This case makes one ponder the reaction to what might be termed a "vexatious surrender" under the 2005 Act. Unlike under the 1976 Act, where there was no surrender provision, a surrendered licence cannot now, in my view, be brought back to life. The licence can only be surrendered by the licence holder, so a purported attempt to surrender may be blocked where a board is not satisfied that the person seeking to make the surrender has authorisation. It is at least theoretically possible for a board to reverse a surrender retrospectively where it is satisfied that the surrender should be treated as "not made", but, as the Act is silent on this, that is a matter for the board to take a view on. However, there is the issue of the terms of section 28(6)(a) to contend with, requiring a statement as to the reasons for failing to provide the principal licence at the time the surrender is made. If this statement is not made, or is not satisfactory, then again the board could take the view that the purported surrender has not met the terms of the Act and is therefore "not made".

During the passage of the Air Weapons and Licensing Bill, the Institute of Licensing and Law Society of Scotland argued that some provision should be made to deal with vexatious surrender of a licence, which would allow a board a power to treat the surrender as not made. The Local Government and Transport Committee heard evidence from the author on this point and subsequently asked the Scottish Government for views, to which the response was that the introduction of such a power had the "potential to undermine facets of the existing regime . . . the proposal would not be widely supported by others."[19]

If a licence has been surrendered vexatiously, such as by a tenant who has fallen out with a landlord, the only remedy may therefore be through the civil courts, but the licensing board should be approached to at least confirm a view.

3 ADMINISTRATIVE DUTIES OF A PREMISES LICENCE HOLDER

The 2005 Act contains a number of administrative duties that apply to the holder of a premises licence. These principally revolve around keeping information up to date and display of certain documents, or notifications relating to offences. These might be best considered as "record keeping" related duties; as opposed to duties that engage the licensing objectives directly.

3.1 Duty to notify changes to connected persons

Under section 40A of the Act, the premises licence holder is required to give the licensing board a formal notification of when a person becomes or ceases to be a connected person.[20] Connected persons are as defined in section 147(3) as follows:

Bain 1998 SLT 381, when he says (at 382): "where a licence has ceased to have effect, it does not follow that it is 'irretrievably lost'" ([2004] 29 SLLP 38), but that dictum does of course relate to the 1976 Act and may be of lesser value as a result.

19 Stage 1 Report, Air Weapons and Licensing Bill, 23 March 2015, para 250, p 44.

20 In broad terms, the existence of connected persons as a concept is to allow the police to run checks against those individuals, in case they may wish to object to a licence being granted to an applicant where a connected person is of concern to them, or to raise review proceedings where such a person is convicted of a relevant offence.

> "a person is, in relation to a partnership, a company, a club or other body (whether incorporated or unincorporated), a connected person if the person—
> (a) in the case of a partnership, is a partner,
> (b) in the case of a company—
>   (i) is a director, or
>   (ii) has control of the company,
> (c) in the case of a club, is an office bearer of the club,
> (d) in any other case, is concerned in the management or control of the body."

There is no statutory form for this, and there is no fee required. All that is required is an email or letter with the relevant details provided. Unlike the provisions under section 48 (on which, see below), there is no requirement to return the principal licence to the licensing board when providing a notification of these changes. The names and addresses of the connected persons do not appear on the licence document itself – they will simply be retained on the administrative system the board uses for internal purposes.

A typical example of this process is where a company director resigns. In that case, then the licence holding company (or their agent) must notify any relevant licensing board of this within one month. Failure to make the notification without a reasonable excuse within that period is a criminal offence.[21] Where the company (or partnership, etc) holds licences in more than one board area, each of those licensing boards must be notified.

3.1.1 Interested parties – a phantom provision?

Readers of the Act either in print or online may see the heading of section 40A referred to as "Connected persons *and interested parties*: licence holder's duty to notify changes" (my emphasis). The phrase "interested parties" is not included in the section heading at 3.1 for reasons explained below, but the phrase is scattered throughout parts of the 2005 Act, the Criminal Justice and Licensing (Scotland) Act 2010, and attendant law and regulations. Many of these references defy comprehension as to whether they have legal effect, so some explanation is necessary.

We should start in understanding the origin of the concept. This lay with the desire of Police Scotland to see behind a licence holder where they believed there could be nefarious individuals who, whilst not "connected persons", were nevertheless connected. The process of notification under section 40A apropos interested parties would allow the police, it was therefore argued, to be aware of such persons, and scrutinise their involvement. This aspiration should be read in the context of the absence, at that time, of a wider "fit and proper" test (on which, see Chapter 10 at Section 3.1), and related concerns that the police could not properly shine a light on criminal elements who may have some connection to licensed premises. This concern was further ameliorated by the contemporaneous creation in 2010 of section 141B,[22] which extended the concept of vicarious liability to include these interested parties.

When the "fit and proper" test was reintroduced to the 2005 Act, further amendments were introduced in relation to interested parties to augment the ability to assess such individuals as part of licensing processes (see below).

21 Liable on summary conviction to a fine not exceeding level 2 on the standard scale.
22 See s 195(3) of the Criminal Justice and Licensing (Scotland) Act 2010.

The definition of interested party was provided for at section 184(4) of the Criminal Justice and Licensing (Scotland) Act 2010, by creating a new section 147(5) of the 2005 Act as follows:

> "a person is an interested party in relation to licensed premises if the person is not the holder of the premises licence nor the premises manager in respect of the premises but—
> (a) has an interest in the premises as an owner or tenant, or
> (b) has management and control over the premises or the business carried on on the premises."

Whilst no doubt wishing to bolster transparency, and therefore reduce prospects of infiltration by serious and organised crime (a noble pursuit), the concept of "interested parties" was pilloried as it evaded purposeful definition.[23] In addition, the section 40A notification requirement would mean significant burden on not just licence holders but also licensing boards (who were required under section 40A(3) to give a copy of the notification to the police). There would, it was feared, be inevitable argument around who may or may not be a person with "management and control" over (a) the premises and (b) the business carried on on the premises; and the numbers of notifications (given how widely the definition is drawn) could have been staggering.

Due to the multifarious concerns over all of this, the wording which referred to "interested parties" in section 40A was never commenced, albeit confusion reigned for 8 years whilst the wording remained seemingly alive in print and online versions of the Act, a lurking yet visible spectre. The wording which related to "interested parties" in section 40A (notifications) and section 141B(2), (3) and (4) (vicarious liability) was excluded from the initial commencement of those wider provisions,[24] and although the section 141B provisions were later commenced in 2011,[25] they could not be relied upon, due to the fact the underlying section 147(5) definition had not itself been commenced.

The first step towards exorcising this licensing demon occurred with the passing of section 59 of the Air Weapons and Licensing (Scotland) Act 2015. The purpose of this section was twofold. First, to remove the reference to

23 Persons with control over the premises itself may include, it was argued, security or management companies who have nothing to do with the licensed premises but might be in charge of access arrangements to the building that the licensed premises are within, for example. And what of control over the business? That could capture a plethora of persons from other management individuals beyond the premises licence holder or premises manager who may or may not run a business, or even area managers for a company who oversee the operation of particular premises amongst others. Even the reference to "owners" and "tenants" is of poor construction, given they themselves may be a legal entity like a company with directors and shareholders and so on, and, before we know it, we are truly down the rabbit hole.

24 The generality of s 40A and s 141B was commenced as of 13 December 2010 under the Criminal Justice and Licensing (Scotland) Act 2010 (Commencement No. 6, Transitional and Savings Provisions) Order 2010 (SSI 2010/413), however, a close inspection of Column 4 of the Schedule to the Order in relation to those sections notes that the commencement excludes the wording relating to interested parties.

25 This happened on 1 November 2011 by way of the Criminal Justice and Licensing (Scotland) Act 2010 (Commencement No. 9, Transitional and Savings Provisions) Order 2011 (SSI 2011/354), which commenced s 195 of the 2010 Act (which included the new s 141B of the 2005 Act) "For all purposes insofar as not already in force" (see Column 4 of the Schedule to the Order as it pertains to s 195).

interested parties in section 40A, meaning there would be no notification requirement where such parties changed. Secondly, section 59 tinkered with the yet to be commenced definition of interested party under the proposed section 147(5), so that a premises manager could be treated as an interested party for the purposes of the vicarious liability provisions in section 141B.

Simultaneously, the 2015 Act breathed further life into the concept by creating a number of additional amendments to the 2005 Act under the general banner of the reintroduction of the "fit and proper" test, which referred to interested parties. These were:

- Section 43 of the 2015 Act – a new section 22(1A) of the 2005 Act which allows an objector to a premises licence application to have regard to "any information that the person considers may be relevant to consideration by the Board of any ground for refusal" including reference to any person who would become an interested party if the application were granted.[26]
- Section 44 – a new section 33(7A) of the 2005 Act which allows the police to give any information they consider to be relevant to consideration of the application by the board in respect of a person who would become an interested party if the transfer were granted.[27]
- Section 45 – a new section 36(5A) of the 2005 Act which allows a person making a review proposal to include any information that person considers relevant to the ground of review including in relation to any person who is an interested party.[28]

At this stage, none of the earlier law surrounding interested parties was "live" because the underlying definition remained uncommenced. The 2015 Act provisions noted above awaited their own commencement, but this occurred by way of the Air Weapons and Licensing (Scotland) Act 2015 (Commencement No. 6 and Saving Provisions) Order 2017,[29] meaning the new ss 22(1A), 33(7A) and 36(5A), all of which reference interested parties, were commenced as of 15 May 2017. At this stage, however, none of these provisions could yet be relied upon because the underlying section 147(5) definition was not in force.

It was not until 2018 that further movement occurred, with the passing of the snappily titled Criminal Justice and Licensing (Scotland) Act 2010 (Commencement No. 15 and Saving Provision) and the Air Weapons and Licensing (Scotland) Act 2015 (Commencement No. 8) Order 2018.[30] This Order carried out two key tasks:

- It commenced section 184 of the Criminal Justice and Licensing (Scotland) Act 2010 insofar as not already in force – thereby commencing, finally, the notification requirements in relation to "interested parties" in sections 40A and 48, and the definition of interested party itself in the new section 147(5).

26 On which, see Chapter 9, Section 4.1.
27 On which, see Chapter 12, Section 3.
28 On which, see Chapter 14, Section 3.
29 SSI 2017/119.
30 Article 3 of the Criminal Justice and Licensing (Scotland) Act 2010 (Commencement No. 15 and Saving Provision) and the Air Weapons and Licensing (Scotland) Act 2015 (Commencement No. 8) Order 2018 (SSI 2018/102).

- It then commenced section 59 of the Air Weapons and Licensing (Scotland) Act 2015, thus immediately repealing the just commenced references to interested parties in sections 40A and 48.

It is thought that this "commence and repeal" approach for section 40A notifications (adding or removing an interested party) and section 48 notifications (change of name or address of an interested party) was preferred to leaving them uncommenced, where there might always be some doubt about their future status. For the avoidance of doubt, the effect of the 2018 Order is that all references to interested parties under section 40A and section 48 are expunged (hence why it does not appear in my section heading or explanatory text at Section 3.1 above).

Crucially, the 2018 Order finally commenced the definition under the proposed section 147(5) as of 29 June 2018 (as well as the corollary amendment to the section 141B provision, to capture premises managers as persons who could be vicariously liable). This meant that the amended section 141B provision, as well as the 2015 Act references to interested parties in relation to objections, transfers and reviews, were finally brought to life.

3.2 Duty to notify court where a premises licence holder

Section 41 creates a reporting obligation (failure to observe being a criminal offence[31]) upon the holder of a premises licence to produce their licence to a court where the licence holder has been charged with a relevant offence,[32] "not later than the person's first appearance or, as the case may be, next appearance in court in connection with the offence".

There is provision for where a court process has begun and the licence is granted at a stage where the outcome has not been reached, so that the reporting obligation applies there too.

Whilst the Act requires the principal premises licence to be produced to the court, there is a saving provision if the licence is unavailable, where, if the production of the licence is not practicable, the licence holder must notify the court (at section 41(2)(b)) of:

"(i) the existence of the premises licence,
(ii) the identity of the Licensing Board which issued it, and
(iii) the reasons why it is not practicable to produce the licence."

The purpose of this is to ensure that the court is aware of the licence holder's status as a premises licence holder, so that the court may in turn observe the obligation to report the outcome to the licensing board. This requirement is contained in section 42 and requires the clerk of a Scottish court to give notice of the conviction to the licensing board which issued the licence as soon as reasonably practicable. This means that the licensing authorities are aware of criminal proceedings which result in a conviction, to ensure that any further steps in relation to the licence might be considered as a result of that conviction.

Note that this obligation does not extend to connected persons so there is no need for, say, a director of a company which holds a premises licence, to report this, where that director is charged as an individual.

31 Conviction of which will lead to a fine not exceeding level 2 on the standard scale (s 41(4)).
32 See Chapter 19, Section 2.1, on the definition of "relevant offence".

3.3 Duty to notify the licensing board of convictions

The flip side of the above reporting obligation to the court is this: an obligation upon premises licence holders themselves to report convictions of relevant or foreign offfences to the licensing board, which is contained within section 43. This notification must be done within one month of the date of conviction. There is no formal process or fee in relation to this notification, so an email or letter from the licence holder or their agent will suffice.

This obligation applies not just to the holder of a premises licence, but also to connected persons. So, for example, if I am a director of a company which holds a premises licence and I am convicted of a relevant offence, then I must inform the licensing board of this conviction within the one-month period.

Failure to meet the one-month deadline is itself an offence.[33]

3.4 Duty to update changes to names and addresses

Section 48 creates a series of notifications requirements where one of the following has occurred:

- the licence holder's name has changed;[34]
- the address of the licence holder has changed (in relation to a company, for example, this would be the registered company address);
- the name of the premises manager has changed (not to be confused with changing the premises manager altogether);
- the home address of the premises manager has changed;
- the name or address of any connected person has changed.

It is important to differentiate these processes from those potential amendments which might be made under the minor variation procedure, especially as some licensing boards have, erroneously, conflated the two. The above processes are catered for separately under the Act and the licensing board has a legal obligation to update any licence documentation following receipt of one of these changes.[35] There is no statutory fee (although some boards might charge a "duplicate" fee to print an updated licence) and no formal application for any of these notifications. Instead, it is simply a matter of writing or emailing the licensing board to confirm whatever the new details might be. However, the principal licence needs to be returned to the board, so, if emailing the board, it should be made clear that the licence is being returned under separate cover. If the licence cannot be produced, a statement of reasons as to why that is the case should be provided. This might be a simple case of stating that the licence has been lost or misplaced (on which see Section 3.6 below), or perhaps that it is already with the board for a separate application

33 See s 43(6). A person convicted of this offence is liable to a fine not exceeding level 4 on the standard scale.

34 Where a change of company name occurs, the s 48 process is the one to follow. The company is, of course, the same legal entity regardless of the name. On a rare occasion, a board might suggest an application for transfer would be required. That is not correct. Once it is explained, perhaps by reference to the company number or by showing the change of name extract from Companies House (if necessary), the s 48 notification should be accepted.

35 2005 Act, s 49(1)(a).

to be updated. In these circumstances, a licensing board might charge an administrative fee to produce a duplicate licence.

The premises licence holder should note that the changes which relate to the premises manager will also affect the same details on that individual's personal licence, and there is a separate notification process to be followed in relation to that licence, although the duty to follow this sits with the individual personal licence holder, not the premises licence holder where that individual may be named as the premises manager.[36]

3.5 Duty to keep, display and produce premises licence

The requirement to keep, display and produce the licence might sound like it could be a licence condition, but it does in fact sit with the "Miscellaneous" groupings of sections under Part 3, and, in particular, section 52. These duties should not, however, be taken lightly by the premises licence holder as failure to observe them is a criminal offence.[37]

The first requirement under section 52 is that the premises licence – often referred to in practice as the "principal" premises licence – should be kept on the premises under the control of the premises licence holder or the premises manager. The requirement also allows a "certified" copy of the licence to be so kept, in lieu of the principal.

It is worth stating at this juncture what is actually meant by "the licence". The licence is a collective term for a series of documents: the licence, the operating plan, the summary document, and the premises layout plan. Whilst each of these documents exists and is referred to separately within the Act, it is not prudent to think of them as a collection of separate documents: instead, the correct approach is to think of them as the singular licence. The document is therefore normally over a dozen or more pages when one takes into account the various details, including the list of mandatory and local conditions.

The reference to the "principal" premises licence is essentially a reference to the original copy printed and produced by the licensing board. A "certified" copy, on the other hand, means a photocopy of the document, which has been certified by a solicitor or notary public. The certification is a confirmation that the copy is a true copy of the original document. Although the exact form of wording is not prescribed, it might say something simple like: "I certify that this is a true copy of the principal licence". That statement would be accompanied by the signature and name of the solicitor or notary public conducting the certification.[38]

Section 52(2) creates a separate obligation to display the summary of the licence (or a certified copy of the summary). This document is usually only two or three pages long. The document should be "prominently displayed on the premises so as to be capable of being read by anyone frequenting the premises". This means, practically speaking, that it cannot be in a back of house office, or should not be behind the bar next to the gantry unless the

36 On which, see Chapter 17, Section 3.

37 A person guilty of an offence under s 52 is liable on summary conviction to a fine not exceeding level 3 on the standard scale.

38 My own view is that every page of the licence should be certified in order to provide the fullest confidence that each page is correct.

licence holder is sure it can be read from that distance. To put the matter beyond doubt, my recommendation is that it should be on display out in the open areas where the public can circulate freely and read the details of the licence up close.

The final strand of this grouping of duties imposed on the premises licence holder is the requirement to produce the licence – and that is a reference to the full licence, not just the summary – when asked to do so by a licensing standards officer, or a police officer. Failure to produce the licence when asked to do is a criminal offence, unless there is a reasonable excuse. A reasonable excuse would include, in my view, that the licence is with the licensing board to be updated (perhaps following a variation application or section 48 notification).

3.6 Theft, loss etc of premises licence or summary

During the normal course of day-to-day life, whether or not there is any live application or notification, a licence or the licence summary might be lost. It may be moved around a public house or supermarket and become dog-eared, damaged or misplaced, or perhaps lost in the mail from a solicitor to his client. Where a duplicate copy is required, section 53 allows for this; but if the licence is lost or stolen, that has to be reported to the police first. The typical approach here is to dial 101 and report the licence as lost or stolen, providing the police with the licence number/details. In turn the police will provide an incident reference number and this should be stated on the request to the licensing board, made along with payment of any administrative fee the board may charge.

Chapter 8

Premises Licences – Part 2 Application

1 APPLYING FOR A PREMISES LICENCE

There are some initial details one must examine when making an application for a premises licence. A good application, properly prepared, will take into account not just the obvious statutory requirements and process and the filling of forms, but a wider view of context and aims, and the sensible applicant will have explored a handful of more fundamental questions of competency, such as:

- What and where are the premises and how are they identified or delineated?
- What is the appropriate licensing board to which the application should be made?
- Who is the appropriate person to make the application?

1.1 What and where are the premises?

Identifying the premises may not be as simple as it first appears! One must consider whether the premises are a physical construct such as a building, or a vehicle of some sort; or, if a building, does the "premises" have outdoor areas and spaces, or does it relate to perhaps more than one structure or building? These are all questions which must be explored with the eager applicant. If the premises to be licensed is an existing unit or building, say premises trading as an unlicensed café or restaurant, then matters may be straightforward, and there will at least be an accepted address . . . or will there?

1.1.1 The address of the premises

Let us look more closely at the question of the premises address. It is not uncommon to encounter several examples of premises with two, three and even four separate addresses used by different people or agencies: for example in the title deeds or land certificate, licensing, rates and building control, or the planning and other departments of the local authority. This always makes for great sport with an applicant when trying to tie down what the appropriate address is.

For the purpose of the 2005 Act, the correct address is the one as given on the valuation roll; in other words, the rates address. This is because application dues are based on rateable value and boards will need to check the valuation roll to ensure that the fee submitted with the application is correct. The rates address can be determined by using the search facility on the Scottish

Assessor's website,[1] or by checking the premises' rates bill. The key figure is the "rateable value", as opposed to how much is actually owed annually.

I have been involved in cases where objectors have sought to derail an application on the basis that they do not like or agree with the address stated on the application form; perhaps it does not match the address on their title deeds if they live next door, and they spy a chance to suggest incompetency. Sadly for the energised objector, none of that is relevant. The only test for a licensing application is that the address must be the address the local authority uses for rates and therefore it is the address on the assessor's valuation roll. There can, however, be occasions where the address is not on the roll.

1.1.2 Problem scenarios where there is no entry on the valuation roll

So, we are agreed that the budding applicant must cast aside any address other than the one on the valuation roll. But what if the premises have no entry on the valuation roll? It is actually common for this to be the case. Perhaps the premises were a private residence such as an old country castle which is to be converted into a wedding hotel, or a town house which is to be converted into an uber-trendy speakeasy, and have therefore not been assessed for business rates. Perhaps the premises have not yet been constructed so valuation has not yet occurred. Perhaps the premises were or are part of a larger set of premises, and the larger premises have an entry but our little premises do not.

If the application premises exist but are a private residence, then one can at least determine the correct local authority by identifying to whom the council tax is paid. I would also suggest that the address which is used for the property against the council tax seems likely to be the one used when the building and business are assessed for rates and would use that address in any initial application. If the rates address for some reason proved to be slightly different, that should be dealt with further down the line.

It is possible that a tweak to the address could be dealt with by a sensible communication with the clerk, assuming the application is in process, or perhaps at the time of the hearing, if any amended address is known by then. It ought to be achieved with little difficulty, although some clerks may take the view that if the licence has been granted and the rates address subsequently changes, a minor variation might be needed to correct the address; in my view that is incorrect and the correct process is simply an administrative change on the licensing database system – perhaps with a fee for a duplicate, updated licence with the correct address shown.

If the application premises have not yet been constructed, then one must use an address other than the rates or other tax address at the time of application; it is suggested that the address given at the time of the planning permission approval is the best candidate, as this will at least link to the relevant certificate of suitability. The fee regulations do, of course, allow for such circumstances and, where no rateable value has been set, the applicant pays an initial fee with their application (up to £200, maximum fee for lodging a provisional licence application, as in this scenario it must surely be), and in turn a quantum at either: (a) the confirmation of the licence, if the rateable value has been fixed; or (b) at such other time once the rateable value has been fixed.

1 www.saa.gov.uk

If the application premises are part of larger existing premises with an entry in the valuation roll, this can be a headache. It is possible that the smaller premises might attract a separate valuation and indeed that may be the plan of the operator or proposed operator. On the other hand, if the licence is for some form of concession unit within a larger retail or commercial environment, a separate rateable value may not be possible for any number of reasons and the applicant may have to simply accept this, the most obvious difficulty being that it means paying a higher fee. If the proposal is to apply to the assessor to carve out a separate entry, then it may be sensible to decide that the appropriate course of action for a new licence should be to pursue a provisional licence and lodge the initial fee (up to a maximum of £200), with the balance being paid once the valuation roll has been updated.

1.1.3 Where the premises comprise more than one building

If the application proposes to capture more than one building, one must establish whether the buildings have different entries in the valuation roll. If they do, that might cause some licensing boards a concern and they may insist on separate licences. That is not always the case, however. It is, of course, easier to adopt an approach of allowing multiple buildings to be covered by a single licence where the wider "campus" is covered under a single rates address. A good example of this might be a whisky distillery and visitors centre, which might have a number of a buildings all of which need to be covered by a licence such as the despatch facility, perhaps a separate bar and tasting room in another building, and perhaps even a further building which serves as a tourist attraction and may have a café or restaurant. Another common example is in golf courses where a single licence might cover the clubhouse as well as a halfway house at the ninth for refreshments.

There is certainly nothing to prevent a licence covering more than one building in law, noting that the definition of "premises" in section 147(1) is:

> "any place and includes a vehicle, vessel or moveable structure".

A "place" may certainly be a location with more than one building. There are numerous examples of this, such as educational establishments, distilleries (as detailed above), or in tourist and leisure attractions. Whether such a type of facility could all be captured under a single licence or not will come down to the approach taken by the individual licensing board and it would be prudent to consult the licensing board clerk in advance of making any application.

1.1.4 Does the premises include outdoor or external areas?

Lastly, in relation to defining "the premises" we must consider the use or proposed use of any existing outdoor or external area; and there may be some special concerns and considerations to be aware of here.

First, I should state that if an outdoor area is to be a permanent part of the licensed space, there is nothing inherently wrong or unlawful with that, so long as certain matters are in place. One of the key elements is planning permission. If applying for a premises licence with a beer garden at the rear, the applicant will need to produce a certificate of suitability under section 50 of the 2005 Act to confirm they have the appropriate planning permission for the licensed premises – and as the licensed premises include the beer garden, the planning permission must reflect this also.

If the area is owned privately then one assumes permission has been obtained to use the area and in most cases the proprietor or occupier is also the applicant.[2] If the area is owned by a local authority, then of course the operator would need to obtain permission to use the outdoor area from that local authority, which would include planning permission and may also include permission in the form of a permit under section 59 of the Roads (Scotland) Act 1984, commonly referred to in the licensing world as a "tables and chairs permit" – albeit section 59 of the 1984 Act covers the use of pavements and council land for a multitude of reasons such as the placing of skips, as well as use of such space for the placement of outdoor dining and drinking areas.

There is also a question concerning whether there are any local byelaws in relation to the consumption of alcohol outdoors. A great many local authorities have passed byelaws which prevent alcohol consumption (or the possession of alcohol in an open container) outdoors in public places.

Is a beer garden or other external licensed space a "public place"? In *Vannet v Burns*[3] a public house car park was considered to be a "public place" for the purpose of the Road Traffic Act 1988 and in *The Queen on the application of Lewis v The Director of Public Prosecutions*[4] another pub car park was held to be a public place. There is no doubt that a beer garden is public in the sense that the public may frequent and make use of the area. However, for licensing purposes in Scotland, if the area in question is covered by the licence, then it ceases to be a public place in the legal sense, all the while remaining such in the ordinarily understood sense of the word. In other words, a byelaw on alcohol consumption in public areas would not apply to an outdoor area which has been covered by a licence under the 2005 Act. This is because whilst the licence is in force, the licence holder is given a presumptive control over the area and persons are there at the invitation of the licence holder. In other words, whilst the location remains a public place in that members of the public may resort to it, it is not a place where the public have unfettered access.

Whether the outdoor area *should* be licensed is a matter, of course, for the licensing board on a case-by-case basis on the merits.

1.2 What is the correct licensing board to apply to?

The term "appropriate licensing board' is defined in section 18(1) as the licensing board in whose area the premises are situated. This may appear obvious, but of course there are examples of premises on the county lines or which may even straddle local authority jurisdictions, so it is not always immediately apparent. When an applicant puts forward a proposed set of premises, whilst it can be instructive to look at maps and assess the geography, the sure

2 It is possible to come across cases where a licensed external area is under shared or dual ownership, e.g. a "back court" arrangement. There is nothing per se to prevent the area being licensed, but the licensing board may desire to see some form of agreement that consent is in place, perhaps especially where residents are objecting.

3 1998 SCCR 415.

4 [2004] EWHC 2081.

solution is to refer back to the valuation roll. A simple check of the address on the assessor website will confirm the position.

There are rare cases where premises might sit across the boundary line, and where this might occur the Act provides a solution – section 18(1)(b)(i) states that the applicant should apply to "the Board in whose area the greater or greatest part of the premises is situated". If there is no way to determine this, then the fallback position is simply that the applicant may then experience the unique joys of choosing which licensing board to apply to.[5]

1.3 Who should make the application?

The next step is to check who is making the application. There is only one statutory requirement in relation to lawful competence: the applicant cannot be an individual under the age of 18.[6] In theory, therefore, any legal person whether natural or non-natural could make an application for a premises licence. Whilst the Act does not explicitly consider or restrict the notion of legal *personae* in relation to who may or may not apply for a licence, this is of course implicit and the Act does detail further requirements based on the type of legal person applying in relation to notification and further information to be provided in the guise of "connected persons", such as directors of a limited company. These provisions are explored in detail below.

There is a further basic point about the competency of any applicant, which is whether it is appropriate for a licensing board to accept, far less grant, an application unless it is satisfied that the applicant has a legal right to occupy or govern who occupies the premises, and I do stress the word "occupy" as opposed to "trade". Upon examining this issue, it is not a statutory requirement or test and the 2005 Act is in fact silent on the issue of "right to occupy". On the other hand, it surely cannot be correct as a matter of law, for example, that a person could have a licence application considered on the merits when that person has no claim or future claim which would allow him to occupy or have a right over the premises. If that were not so, then persons of ill intent could seek to apply for licences for established businesses with which they have no connection, out of mischief or vexation. The right to occupy, or the right to grant occupation, is, in the practical reality of the licensing world, therefore a relevant consideration in relation to the competency of the application.

Identifying whether the applicant has a right to occupy has been something which the police have investigated as part of their vetting process for some time, although the practice appears to ebb and flow and, despite the single police force in Scotland, there are geographical variations on how forcefully these details are pursued. It is correct to say that the police have no statutory power to compel the applicant to produce a right to occupy, but despite that they will often ask for such evidence, and may go further into requesting details which may be commercially sensitive such as term of lease or quantum of rent. It is a matter for the applicant to decide how to deal with such queries.

5 2005 Act, s 18(2).

6 2005 Act, s 20(1). Although note that under the proposed Immigration (Alcohol Licensing and Late Hours Catering) (Scotland) Regulations 2018, a new s 20(1A) would create an "entitlement to work in the United Kingdom" test for applicants. This instrument exists in draft form only and it is not known, at the time of writing, when or if it will be laid before the Scottish Parliament.

What is clear, is that, in determining who should hold the licence, there is no legal requirement for that person to have a financial relationship with the alcohol transactions that will occur under the licence. In other words, the party to whom the profits go need not be the licence holder. Thus, a bar which is owned by a company may have an individual holding the premises licence, or vice versa, and so on. The 2005 Act is disinterested when it comes to who makes money from the sale of alcohol, save where perhaps it can be shown that the profits are being used in some criminal enterprise.[7]

Lastly, is there any benefit in making the application in the name of an individual, as opposed to a limited company or other body corporate? There is perhaps no real licensing law gain save avoiding some technical gremlins noted elsewhere such as failure to intimate a change in registered address and that sort of thing. In practice some operators choose to use a limited company for the purposes of holding licences alone. That licence-holding company, whilst not trading or operating in the commercial sense, would still be subject to the requirements under the Companies Act 2006 such as annual returns and so on. However, it is perfectly acceptable to have the licences in the name of a company which is not the company that actually trades the business. This might be the case where, as I mention above, an operator has a trading company, and a separate company to hold the licence (for their own reasons), but it may also be the case where the premises are owned by a party other than the day-to-day operator and the premises owner may wish to retain control of the licence. This is a common set-up in so-called "pubco" models where a brewery or pub company might own the pub and hold the licence but lease the pub to a tenant who runs the business on a day-to-day basis.

One reason for holding the licence in a company separate to the trading arm, or perhaps separate to licences held elsewhere, is to avoid the administrative headache of dealing with the notification of convictions for that other party or its connected persons. On the other hand, if a company operates multiple premises with multiple subsidiary or sister companies as licence holders, then it has given itself additional work in relation to notification of change of director's details, should this occur. All of this really is a matter for the applicant to take a view on.[8]

Lastly, we should acknowledge that an unscrupulous person may propose that the application be made in a name other than their own, for fear of police scrutiny, or perhaps in the name of a limited company where he or she is not a shareholder or director but retains control in other ways. In my view such attempts are invariably ill fated, and if there were an attempt to apply for a licence clandestinely in this manner, it may well be argued that the police would be entitled to object and perhaps raise the "fit and proper" test. There have certainly been cases where licensing boards have taken an extremely dim view of having the wool pulled over their eyes.

Having examined these initial thoughts, let us get back to basics and now turn to look at what the Act requires in order to make a competent application. Section 20(2) of the Act sets out the following requirements:

7 A useful comparator to this might be, for example, the additional provisions one might find under the Civic Government (Scotland) Act 1982 as regards second hand dealer or metal dealer licences, in relation to ensuring reset is not occurring when items are bought or sold.

8 It is worth observing that the position was otherwise under the 1976 Act, since a licence authorised the sale of alcohol "by that person", i.e. the holder.

- A description of the premises must be given
- An operating plan must be provided
- A layout plan must be provided
- A disabled access and facilities statement must be provided
- Certificates of suitability under s 50 must be provided
- The appropriate fee must be paid.

We will now look at all of these requirements in turn and begin by taking a close look at the application for itself.

2 THE APPLICATION FORM

The application form for a premises licence is laid down in Schedule 3 to the Premises Licence (Scotland) Regulations 2007[9] and is six pages long. The first page of the application form should identify which licensing board the application is to be made to, and whether the application is for a full or provisional premises licence. The applicant is required to strike out the option which does not pertain to his application – whether a "full" premises licence, or a provisional licence. The difference between these two options is discussed in detail in Chapter 11 at Section 3. The form itself (together with the operating plan, see below) gathered detractors during conversion; with many participants saying that it was too long and unwieldy, whilst others were of the view that it did (and does) not provide enough detail.

The application form was originally designed by a sub-group of the first National Licensing Forum in May 2006. In a debate on the Premises Licence (Scotland) Regulations 2007 on 13 November 2007, the then Justice Minister Kenny MacAskill said:

> "The sub-group included representatives from the licensed trade, the police, licensing boards and other stakeholders. The forms were not simply dreamed up by us, but were developed by those who will use them. They were revised and refined over a long period."

So now we know who to blame for the form – ourselves!

The Scottish Parliament indicated, even at such an early stage, that it would be prepared to review the form after 1 September 2009 but two attempts to do so in the early years of the Act were aborted, including one which had reached the stage of producing fully detailed drafts of applications for various processes. Despite these valiant efforts, the application form has therefore remained unchanged since the onset of the Act.

2.1 Question 1: Details of premises

Question 1 requires applicants to give details of the name, address and postcode of the premises. Remember that the address to be used should be the address on the valuation roll wherever possible and noting the comments above.

Although there is no specific "box" or area to state the name on the form, common practice amongst licensing solicitors is to have the name entered here prior to stating the address. The name is not always known, and it is not

9 SSI 2007/452.

generally a problem to give no name, or to use a generic descriptor instead of a name, such as "despatch premises" or the like. Not all boards specify the premises name on the premises licence they issue (Edinburgh Licensing Board, for example, does not use names) so in some jurisdictions there may be little point in putting a name down. In addition, if a name is stated, then to change it requires the submission of a minor variation application (see Chapter 7, Section 10.1.4) which attracts a cost. It is not unknown for some premises to change names on a semi-frequent basis as new owners or operators come and go, so for those board areas where no name is stated on the licence, the cost of the minor variation is unnecessary.

It is unlikely that a premises operator who has re-invented the branding of his premises but has not updated the licence with the new name, is going to face enforcement action. As a matter of law, the minor variation application should of course be lodged, but I have yet to encounter the police officer, licensing standards officer or clerk who has raised an issue over an old name appearing on the licence, other than to suggest that it be swept up the next time a more significant change is to be made, for example a premises manager change or a major variation.

Having the name as part of the licence is also useful when it comes to public access of the register and for persons looking to establish who may hold the licence for a particular set of premises. The address may well be known, but the name makes it all the more identifiable.

2.2 Question 2: Details of applicant

The particulars of the applicant are required in question 2 and there are separate boxes to be used depending on the legal status of the applicant – whether an individual, partnership or company, or club or other body. In each case address details will be required, for example the registered address of a limited company. In the case of an individual, date and place of birth are also required. If the applicant is a non-natural person, then details will need to be given for "connected persons". This term is defined in section 147(3) of the Act as:

- in the case of a partnership, a partner;
- in the case of a company, a director or person who has control of the company;
- in the case of a club, an office bearer of the club; and
- in any other case, a person concerned with the management or control of the body.

The details required for these persons are full name, address, date of birth and place of birth.

There is a question as to whether company directors are required to give their personal details. Section 243 of the Companies Act 2006 allows for a company director to nominate a "service address" to be named on the company books instead of his own personal address, generally for reasons of privacy or confidentiality.

The service address option, if used, typically means that the address given is the company's registered address, or perhaps their solicitor's office or their own head office address, if not the registered address. But the 2005 Act requires applicants to declare the full *home* address, and other personal details, of company directors.

So, does the 2005 Act trump the Companies Act 2006? The privacy afforded under section 243 only goes so far. It does not necessarily apply where the information is requested by prescribed "public authorities". These are prescribed under the Companies (Disclosure of Addresses) Regulations 2009[10] which came into force on 1 October 2009. This instrument provides a comprehensive list of bodies treated as "public authorities", which includes the Gambling Commission, the Scottish Ministers, the Security Industry Authority, and many more. It also includes "a local authority within the meaning of s.54(2) of the Act" ("the Act" being the Companies Act). Section 54(2), in turn, describes a local authority in the Scottish context as "a council constituted under section 2 of the Local Government etc (Scotland) Act 1994".

A licensing board is not a public authority under the 2006 Act so, at first blush, it would seem that using a service address may be done without rebuke. However, it is not altogether straightforward in the real world of licensing. It seems that there may be a subtle difference between providing the information at the time of application, or where it is requested further down the chain when the application is in process.

Included on the list of prescribed "public authorities" is "a police force", which includes Police Scotland. All new premises licence applications which go to the licensing board are notified by the board to Police Scotland – so, even if indirectly, the home address may be requested by the Police in order to allow them to comply with their own legal obligations under the Act, and the applicant would have to provide it to allow that process to be completed. It is the police who will be most interested in the home address in order to verify identity – and the presence or otherwise of relevant or foreign offences.

There is a practical dimension to consider. Does it benefit the applicant to simply provide the home address from the outset in order to short-circuit the process? It may be that the application is time sensitive and it may be that something like a police report will appear all the faster if they have all the information at hand without resorting to following procedures to request the information be extracted from Companies House.

It is not uncommon for a solicitor to discuss this with the client and perhaps decide to simply provide the home address on the form or on a paper apart, or perhaps submit the application with the service address but an additional statement confirming that the home address can be provided under separate cover on demand. The home address details would not appear on public notification of the application, or on the public record of applications or indeed granted licences. This is all a matter for the applicant.

2.3 Question 3: Previous applications

Question 3 is about previous applications under the 2005 Act and asks whether the applicant has already been refused a premises licence in respect of the application premises. In the earlier days of the 2005 Act, one or two impish licensing boards changed this question to require details of any other

10 SI 2009/214.

applications made by the applicant under the 2005 Act. In some cases this could have led to having to provide details of hundreds of other applications: for example, for a supermarket chain or pub company. As stated elsewhere, such information is not required and the board should not be changing the statutory form in order to ask different questions. If an applicant comes across an amended form, this should be disregarded in my view, and only the details of refused applications should be provided.

That being said, it is not uncommon for the police to ask about other licences that an applicant may hold as part of their investigatory activities in the licensing process. Providing clarifications to the police along these lines can be of some assistance in establishing the existing experience of an applicant as well as the wider context and can therefore be of assistance to an applicant wishing to provide comfort to the police that a proposed application will be in a safe pair of hands.

2.4 Question 4: Convictions

Question 4 relates to previous convictions. The applicant and connected persons (if applicable) must declare any relevant or foreign offence. This does not currently relate to spent convictions considered as such under the Rehabilitation of Offenders Act 1974. Section 129(4) of the 2005 Act specifically stated that "for the purposes of this Act, a conviction for a relevant offence or a foreign offence is to be disregarded if it is spent". Post 2009, there were examples of licensing boards ignoring this and asking for spent convictions, and some even sought to rely on the fact that the 1974 Act allows a licensing authority to take account of spent convictions, where the authority is satisfied that justice cannot otherwise be done. However, despite such dalliances, I think the general licensing community consensus came to be that section 129(4) should be the end of the matter. There is a separate discussion to be had on whether the police could provide detail in relation to spent convictions in any representation or objection they seek to provide in relation to an application, discussed later.

We certainly know that the police and others were unhappy with section 129(4) as they actively lobbied to have it removed, and indeed this resulted in section 52 of the Air Weapons and Licensing (Scotland) Act 2015, which proposes to repeal section 129(4) entirely, thus having the effect that spent convictions would no longer be disregarded, or as the Explanatory Notes to the 2015 Act state:

> "This amendment will make it possible for spent convictions to be brought to and considered by Boards as part of their decision-making."

Part of the philosophy of reintroducing spent convictions is noted in paragraph 124 of the Policy Memorandum to the 2015 Act, which states:

> "Within this Bill there are a range of provisions to help ensure that people live their lives safe from crime, disorder and danger".

Paragraph 132 elaborates further:

> "The Bill provides Licensing Boards with powers to consider a broader range of information when making decisions regarding the alcohol licensing regime. These additional powers help Boards to protect the public by ensuring that only appropriate

persons can gain a personal or premises license. To this end, the Bill expands the remit of what Boards may consider."

The Memorandum goes on to explore this in more detail at paragraphs 140 and 141:

"Key stakeholders have argued that it is imperative that Boards have as much information as possible at their disposal to allow them to make a considered decision on an application. Limiting Boards to the consideration of a definitive and restricted list of convictions for relevant offences permits unsuitable persons to operate within licensed premises and may contradict the five licensing objectives upon which the Act is founded (particularly preventing crime and disorder).

Consequently, this Bill repeals section 129(4) of the 2005 Act to allow Boards to consider spent convictions. Although the proposed changes would enable Licensing Boards to consider spent convictions for relevant offences, the existence of such convictions would not necessarily prevent an applicant from getting a personal licence. The fact that an applicant has convictions, whether spent or otherwise, may or may not act against them and this will be dependent on the nature and timing of the offence. The Board will consider each case on its own merits as they do with unspent convictions for relevant offences."

Licensing authorities in Scotland are used to dealing with spent convictions. Under the 1982 Act it is not uncommon for spent convictions to be considered, and under the old 1976 Act licensing boards did have the power to consider spent convictions so long as a two-step process was followed. The board was required to make a conscious decision to admit consideration of the offences prior to hearing them and taking them into account, and then could only do so if satisfied at any stage that justice could not otherwise be done. This two-step process is most commonly associated with *O'Doherty v Renfrewshire Council*[11] but is also explored in other cases such as *Adamson v Waveney District Council*[12] and *Kelly v City of Glasgow Licensing Board*.[13]

This repeal has yet to be commenced despite being placed on the statute book in 2015 and was delayed in particular because of the issues surrounding the 10-year renewal of personal licences around 2018/19. It was thought that introducing spent convictions at the time tens of thousands of existing personal licence holders were struggling to renew their licences would create further strife. Given that the *dicta* of *O'Doherty* relate to underlying matters of natural justice, and section 129 has not been amended other than to repeal subsection (4), one must assume that the old two-step test will return and boards would do well to follow it once the repeal is commenced.

If the applicant has a conviction, then the form provides for detail of the type, date and court where the person was convicted to be supplied. In many cases an applicant may not properly understand if some misdemeanour was a formal criminal conviction or may not appreciate that an admonishment is still a conviction. In other cases, an applicant may know of the presence of a conviction but be hazy on the details such as the penalty of the date of the conviction. If an applicant is unsure, it is best to state the position to the best

11 1998 SLT 327; [1997] 7 SLLP 6.
12 [1997] 8 SLLP 17.
13 [2004] 27 SLLP 43.

of their recollection as far as the form allows. Failure to declare a criminal conviction is itself an offence.[14]

The requirement to notify the board of convictions subsists past the date that the application has been lodged, and, if the applicant is convicted after lodging the application, they have one month to declare this to the licensing board by giving notice of the nature of the offence and the date of conviction. There is no statutory form of notification here; all that is required is a written or electronic communication to the board providing the detail. If the board receives a notification of this sort, it must suspend consideration of the application until such times as they have alerted the police, and the police have been allowed to check and report themselves. For this purpose, the police are given 21 days to provide a notice back to the licensing board following receipt by them from the board of confirmation that the conviction notice has been received from the applicant. Failure to notify the licensing board of a conviction which has occurred after a licence application has been lodged is itself an offence under section 24(10).

2.5 *Question 5: Description*

Question 5 is the description of the premises, as discussed at Section 3.5 below.

2.6 *Question 6: Clubs*

Question 6 relates to members' clubs only and requires the applicant to confirm that the constitution and rules of the club are compliant with the Licensing (Clubs) (Scotland) Regulations 2007[15] (the position of clubs under the 2005 Act is discussed in detail in Chapter 11 at Section 2).

2.7 The signed declaration

Finally, there is a declaration to be signed by the applicant or his agent. A licensing board must assume, where the form is signed by a solicitor, that he or she has the authority to act on behalf of that applicant. If the form is signed by a non-solicitor agent, again a board will normally assume that the agent has the authority to do so. If the form is signed by an employee of the applicant, again it can only be assumed that the signatory has the authority to sign: for example, on behalf of a company. These matters are unlikely to be flagged up in the normal course of things; however, if an application were made by a company and the signatory was not a director or recognised solicitor, a licensing board may question the validity of this before accepting the application. There are examples, perhaps in relation to variations as opposed to premises licence applications, where a party has attempted to lodge an application, but they do not have the necessary authority to sign.

14 2005 Act, s 24.
15 SSI 2007/76.

2.8 The description of the premises

Section 20(2) requires the application to "contain" a description of the premises. This is catered for in question 5 of the application form. The description of the premises is not the address – it is, in most cases, a short paragraph identifying the type of business which might be operated as well as the physical nature of the premises and indicating the surroundings and environment. Examples of what may constitute a description of the premises may include:

> "A traditional public house style premises set within a row of commercial properties in a tenement brick-built building, with residential flats above. The premises have a main public bar, a lounge bar, and a beer garden to the rear."

> "A stand-alone country hotel with 8 letting rooms, of stone-build construction and within private grounds. The premises have a dining room, a function room, a pool/snooker room, and a public bar with small snug area."

> "A single-storey community grocery store with small off-sales facility."

> "A nightclub premises with dancing, entertainment and live music provision. The main entrance is on the ground floor of the High Street and leads to the basement where the principal public part of the premises is located."

Of course, the description may be more complicated than these examples, especially for facilities such as sports/arts or leisure complexes which might have multiple buildings and uses, and practitioners will come across multi-layered descriptions as well as those which cut neatly to the point, such as a real life case I came across where the general description was simply put as "Basic Public House".

My view on how to frame a general description is that applicants should take care not to make the description too detailed, in order to avoid the need for any variation arising in the future if there is an innocuous change of some sort. There are some anecdotal examples of variations being required where the general description had included references such as "just across from the Woolworths" or other local landmarks which no longer exist and in turn mean the description is wrong as it is out of date, thus meaning the licence holder is asked to submit an application to correct the description.[16] This is unfortunate for the licence holder, as the process is dealt with by way of a major variation meaning a full process including a hearing is required for what may be a very anodyne amendment.

There is also a chance that the description might have to have regard to the underlying planning permission which will have a description attached to it. This is important in at least one licensing board area, where a section 50 request must be accompanied by a draft licence application, and the planning department may refuse to issue the section 50 certificate of suitability if the wording in the draft application does not appear to sit well with the planning use class.

16 In one case my colleague Niall Hassard recalls, the new owner of a restaurant appeared at a licensing board to change the description of his premises from "Chinese restaurant" to "Italian restaurant". We can only hope that, should any future owner wish to run it as a Greek restaurant, advices are taken on this.

Finally, the description section of the application may also provide an opportunity to "set in stone" a specific element of the proposed operation, which may or may not assist in convincing a licensing board to issue a licence. There are examples where an application for an off-sales has been allowed where the applicant has proposed or agreed to a general description which specifies the national origin of the products. This strategy has sometimes been employed to show faith that a specialist style of operator has no ulterior motive. These efforts are not always well-met. If the general description is proposed to be used as a tool in this way, the applicant would do well to seek advice.

Were I to be asked to carry out a health check on an existing premises licence, and the holder wished to seek some changes, I would certainly take the opportunity to update the general description as part of any wider variation.

3 THE OPERATING PLAN

The operating plan could have a chapter in its own right, such is the importance and significance of this aspect of the licensing regime under the 2005 Act. But the operating plan is rightfully a part of the premises licence itself and so is considered here. The origin of the operating plan is found in section 20(4) of the 2005 Act, which outlines the following:

> "(4) An 'operating plan' in relation to any premises is a document in the prescribed form containing—
> (a) a description of the activities to be carried on in the premises,
> (b) a statement of the times during which it is proposed that alcohol be sold on the premises,
> (c) a statement as to whether the alcohol is to be sold for consumption on the premises, off the premises or both,
> (d) a statement of the times at which any other activities in addition to the sale of alcohol are to be carried on in the premises,
> (e) where alcohol is to be sold for consumption on the premises, a statement as to whether children or young persons are to be allowed entry to the premises and, if they are to be allowed entry, a statement of the terms on which they are allowed entry including, in particular—
> (i) the ages of children or young persons to be allowed entry,
> (ii) the times at which they are to be allowed entry, and
> (iii) the parts of the premises to which they are to be allowed entry,
> (f) information as to the proposed capacity of the premises,
> (g) prescribed information about the individual who is to be the premises manager, and
> (h) such other information in relation to the premises and the activities to be carried on there as may be prescribed."

The actual format of the operating plan is provided for in the Premises Licence (Scotland) Regulations 2007.[17] The premises licence application form does not become the licence, once granted. There is a separate statutory form for the licence itself, which will use details from the application form, but is not a carbon copy. On the other hand, the operating plan element of

17 See Schedule 5 to those Regulations.

the premises licence application will become part of the actual licence once granted (assuming of course what has been sought is approved).

Looking at the terms of section 20(4) noted above, one can see that the operating plan is a sort of manifesto that outlines the extent to which the premises may operate, not just in relation to the sale of alcohol but also for any other activities that take place of any kind. What is crucial to appreciate is that as the operating plan is a part of the premises licence section 1(1) comes into play, *viz*:

> "alcohol is not to be sold on any premises except under and in accordance with a premises licence."

A breach of this could lead to six months' imprisonment, a fine up to £20,000, or both.[18] As the operating plan is a part of the premises licence, in turn, a breach of the terms of the operating plan could have severe consequences as it would be an offence under section 1(1).

Now consider that the operating plan may feature mundane activities which have little or no direct link to the sale of supply of alcohol, such as "selling groceries" or "open from 6am to sell milk and newspapers" and it can be seen how important it is that the operating plan is prepared in a thorough and measured manner. Getting it right in the first instance is doubly important because any change to the operating plan, with few exceptions, is going to require a major variation application meaning cost, time, and a public hearing with no guarantee of approval.

The operating plan itself has eight questions, which are addressed in turn, in order to provide the detail as required under section 20(4) and (5) of the Act.

3.1 Question 1: On- and off-sales

Question 1 requires the applicant to indicate whether alcohol will be for sale for consumption on the premises, off the premises, or both. For the avoidance of doubt, "on-sales" means that alcohol will be sold for consumption on, that is within, those licensed premises. This indicates an immediate or nearly immediate consumption of the alcohol purchased within the boundary of those licensed premises. Off-sales means that alcohol will sold on the premises but consumed "off the premises". So, for the avoidance of doubt, with an off-sale purchase, alcohol cannot be consumed on those licensed premises but is sold to be taken away and consumed at another location at an indeterminate time.

It is possible for a premises to have both on- and off-sales, and even if one of the options is ancillary or even only a remote possibility, the prudent applicant should consider whether or not to include the option at the stage of application to avoid having to go back to add it at a later date.

It may not always be sensible to include one or the other, however. If we take the example of a restaurant which is proposed to open in an area of designated overprovision where there are significant levels of alcohol health harm, whilst the proposed business of a *bona fide* restaurant may not provide people with difficulty, including "off-sales" may attract concern. From the proposed operator's perspective, it may be that he only wishes off-sales to cover the possibility that a patron, having enjoyed a particular glass of fine wine, asks to

18 2005 Act, s 1(4).

buy a bottle to take home. That level of detail is not shown on the site notice, so the reference to off-sales may pique the interest of the local health board or some other party concerned about drinking levels in residential premises in the locality. These are questions for the applicant to consider.

There is a debate about whether "tastings" of alcohol on off-sale premises might require the licence to also cater for on-sales. In this context, we are usually talking about something akin to, for example, a craft beer masterclass or a "meet the distiller" event, where the product may be showcased within an off-sale environment in order to allow customers to experience or sample the product. The approach on this varies from board to board. My position is that tastings of alcohol which are provided for free do not require to take place on premises which have "on-sales" on the licence. If there is no sale, then it is not an "on-sale". However, one must remember the terms of section 3 of the 2005 Act and the concept of sales pursuant to a contract. If the alcohol provided in samples or tastings is accessed by the customer having paid some form of money or money's worth to attend the event, then section 3 clearly makes that a licensable event.

So, for example, if I attended my local craft beer shop and the owner had some small samples of a new beer to try as a matter of courtesy, that in my view is perfectly lawful and would not attract the need to have "on-sales" stated on the operating plan. On the other hand, if I pay a sum of money to obtain a ticket to a more structured event where access is by said ticket and I gain "free" samples or tastings within that event, then I think section 3 is activated and on-sales would be needed. This difference is of particular relevance when one goes on to consider what adding "on-sales" to an off-sale licence in order to allow "money's worth" tastings might mean for that operator.

To add on-sales, it is at the least a major variation application meaning several months of processing, cost, and a public hearing which may attract concerns or representations and some of these representations may go further in airing matters which are perhaps unrelated to the request of the variation, albeit such matters might not be relevant to the licensing board. At worst, however, adding on-sales to an off-sale licence can be cost-punitive because the addition creates a need to state a licensed on-sale capacity, in other words, to state how many people can occupy the premises. This means that sanitary capacity and escape provision is suddenly an issue and some off-sale retailers might find that in order to simply allow tastings they need to install additional toilets, and this may prove costly or logistically impossible.

A separate point is whether "tastings" or "sampling events" need to be listed in the operating plan as a separate bespoke activity. My approach in a new licence would certainly be to capture such events if that is what is proposed. Whether the wording needs to appear on an existing licence is a matter of interpretation on a local level. Some licensing boards are relaxed about this and do not feel the need to have "tastings" stated specifically. Other boards, however, do wish to see that level of detail. This is just one reminder as to why it is so important to take proper advice and get your operating plan fit for purpose.

3.2 Question 2: On-sale hours

Question 2 consists of a table of the days of the week, in which the applicant must indicate the times he intends to be open for the sale of alcohol for consumption on the premises. The decision as to what hours to propose will of course be heavily influenced by what the licensing board statement of licensing policy indicates are the boards "preferred" operating hours for particular types of premises within their jurisdiction. For example, the hours sought might be something of the order of 11am to midnight seven days a week or 1am at the weekends, for pub-style premises, or it might be that the hours sought are something like 7pm to 3am or 4am for a nightclub, although obviously there are a number of variations on this.[19]

So the prudent thing for a new applicant to do is to check the relevant licensing board's policy statement, as there will invariably be a note on what the board considers to be the appropriate times, and take matters from there.

3.3 Question 3: Off-sale hours

Question 3 is the same as question 2, only in relation to the hours for off-sales. Section 65 of the 2005 Act provides that any application which is made seeking off-sales hours outside 10am to 10pm must be refused. In the result, any new premises licence application seeking off-sales is likely to simply request 10am to 10pm seven days a week; however, such shorter periods as may be appropriate depending on the actual trading hours of the premises might also be stated, if that is what the applicant wishes. Where the application relates to premises that want to offer both on- and off-sales, it is not uncommon to find that licensing boards will insist that the start time for off-sales matches that of the on-sales hours – in other words, that off-sales commence at, say, 11am instead of 10am.[20] Again, reference should be made to the licensing board's policy statement. If an applicant unwittingly applies for off-sale hours outwith 10am to 10pm, it is open to the licensing board to ask for a correction rather than simply refuse the application outright. Section 23(7) states:

> "Where the Licensing Board considers that—
> (a) they would refuse the application as made, but
> (b) if a modification proposed by them were made to the operating plan or layout plan (or both) for the subject premises accompanying the application, they would be able to grant the application,
>
> the Board must, if the applicant accepts the proposed modification, grant the application as modified."

The reference to the "layout plan (or both)" in subsection (b) above was added by way of s 181 of the Criminal Justice and Licensing (Scotland) Act

19 During the transition process to the 2005 Act in 2008 and 2009, several boards insisted on the hours being the exact hours that were currently operated by the premises including any regular extension; other boards took a slightly more pragmatic approach and accepted later closing times as "like for like" in order for the application to be grandfathered into the new system, and some decided that they would accept applications from 11am on Sunday mornings (where the "traditionalists" insisted on the 12.30pm start).

20 It should be noted, however, that with the rise of remote retail sales, there may be a legitimate reason for an ostensibly on-sales premises to seek an earlier commencement for off-sales in order to facilitate remote orders and despatch.

2010 and brought into force on 13 December 2010;[21] however, in practice such proposed amendments were already being proposed and accepted.

A proposal to amend the licensed hours in the context discussed above may typically happen during the application process by mutual consent but perhaps prior to the consultation period (i.e. that it is agreed prior to the site notice being displayed) or it may even be proposed and agreed at the hearing by asking the applicant to accept 10am instead of 9am, for example. It should be noted, however, that I have had the experience of licensing boards forcing a continuance of an application, to allow a re-run of the consultation process with the amended version of the operating plan even where the applicant is agreeing to lesser hours than those sought. It is therefore a scenario that must be considered thoughtfully by the applicant as a delay until the next hearing of the licensing board, which could be some months.

3.4 Question 4: Seasonal variations

Question 4 allows the applicant to give information about seasonal variations to the licensed hours. "Seasonal demand" in this context could mean a number of things, depending upon the interpretation which is now applied to the concept on a local licensing board basis. It has been taken by the vast majority of licensing boards to include and perhaps almost explicitly focus upon the additional hours typically traded during the festive season, and locally approved festivals or events which attract extra hours. In the early period of the Act, there were examples of licensing boards that did not accede to that general view and continued to ask for and expect extended hours applications. As time has marched on, most licensing boards now no longer expect applications for the festive period and are content to deal with them under the seasonal variation provisions in the operating plan. Falkirk remains a notable exception to this rule.

The general effect of this approach is therefore that any premises which have the appropriate wording within the seasonal variation part of the operating plan will automatically be entitled to trade such additional hours as is specified in the licensing board policy statement or such supplementary statement as may be issued from time to time. Many premises will therefore be able to enjoy those additional hours. If a premises licence is silent on the issue of seasonal variations, it is still open to that operator to seek one-off extended hours applications but, in addition to that, my advice to the licence holder would be to look to correct the matter on a more permanent basis by seeking a major variation of the licence.

The festive period is not the whole story of seasonal variations, however. Some licensing boards extend the concept and use of the seasonal variations provision to a more commonly understood explanation of what "seasonal trading" might mean – that is, "seasonal demand" as a concept is more in line with situations such as licensed premises in holiday or caravan parks which are closed for certain parts of the year, or perhaps for small hotels or guest houses which have restricted opening times during the "low" season.

21 As provided for in the Schedule to the Criminal Justice and Licensing (Scotland) Act 2010 (Commencement No. 6, Transitional and Savings Provisions) Order 2010 (SSI 2010/413).

It is common that boards with significant rural areas where there is expected, and traditional, seasonal closures will have policy wording which relates to use of the seasonal variation section to "capture" the details of that seasonal opening.

My view is that the original intention of the section on "seasonal variations" was to capture the details of premises which may only trade seasonally in the sense I have described here, that is, certain premises which are closed over a particular period of time such as remote guest houses or holiday parks. The etymology of the phrase "seasonal variations" in the operating plan certainly originates from the previous provision under the old 1976 Act, which provided for special "seasonal licences" under section 62 of that Act, allowing an applicant to propose that the licence would not have effect for certain periods.

All that being said, there is no doubt that the use of this provision within the operating plan to cater for the accepted later hours for certain periods of the year and certain locally approved events and festivals is helpful and welcome, not just to the licensed trade, giving them the certainty they need to take bookings and anticipate demand, but also to the licensing board administration staff, as well as police staff, in removing the burden of processing multiple extended hours applications the vast majority of which would always be granted in any event.

There are some additional quirks to examine. At least one board uses the seasonal variation part of the operating plan to require operators to state the actual trading hours as opposed to the licensed hours which the premises may enjoy but not typically use. Aberdeenshire divisional boards adopt this practice, where, for example, a retailer will be granted an off-sale licence from 10am to 10pm but the seasonal variation section will state, for example, that the premises typically trade from 10am to 6pm. This approach is couched in terms of ensuring the public register of licences adequately describes when premises might be likely to open so the public is aware of this, as opposed to enforcing a "duty to trade" *per se*, a controversial topic which is explored in much greater detail in Chapter 16 at Section 9.

Some examples of the sort of terminology that could be used in the application form to describe proposed seasonal variations are as follows:

> "Any additional hours as allowed in terms of the licensing board policy statement, including additional hours for the festive season and during the Edinburgh Festival."

> "The hours given in questions 2 and 3 are those hours of operation during high season. During low season, the premises may open later in the morning and close earlier at night, depending on demand; and the premises are closed altogether in the months of January and February."

> "The premises will not typically trade beyond 8pm except during the festive season when they may remain open till 10pm to cater for additional demand."

Other uses of this section include an approach in some areas to allow for an additional uplift of off-sale capacity during certain times of the year – typically, to allow for additional display of alcohol products during the festive season.

The best guidance for completing this section of the application is then to read and understand the local licensing board approach. Unless the applicant wishes to make a "merits" case on something unusual, it is perhaps best to adopt the licensing policy approach to seasonal variations as regards hours, and, if appropriate, additional off-sale capacity.

3.5 Question 5: Activities

Question 5 is the most detailed part of the whole "premises licence package" and relates to the activities and services that will be provided on the premises in addition to the sale of alcohol. There are many practitioners' views on the utility of this part of the form – some of those involved in the process believe it is far too detailed and others the reverse. All agree that it represented a significant increase in the information provided to the board compared with that under the 1976 Act regime.

The importance of getting this part of the application correct cannot be stressed enough. Once the licence is granted with these activities, they become the activities that the licence holder is allowed to provide; or, to put it another way, the licence holder cannot provide any activity unless it is stated on the licence, and, if he does wish to introduce a new activity, that would require a major variation application to achieve it. As I note elsewhere, the provision of an activity which is not catered for in this part of the operating plan is a criminal offence – a breach of section 1(1) of the Act. The most innocuous of activities could therefore have serious repercussions for a licence holder. Whether certain activities are accepted to be "implicit" is a matter for the applicant to take advice on but my view is that the applicant would do well to ensure that the application is written as broadly as is sensible and reasonable.

There is a point to be made here about control of activities other than the basic act of the sale or consumption of alcohol – given the significant debates on the remit of the licensing board whose "essential function" is to regulate the sale of alcohol discussed through the prism of the *Brightcrew* decision elsewhere in this book. How does the fact that the board regulates these other activities as a part of the premises licence sit within that wider habitat?

The introductory text to the 2005 Act, which may be described as the Act's "mission statement", is that it is:

> "An Act of the Scottish Parliament to make provision for regulating the sale of alcohol, and for regulating licensed premises and other premises on which alcohol is sold; and for connected purposes."

The reference to "regulating licensed premises and other premises on which alcohol is sold" seems to impart the sense that there is a form of regulation of the premises itself beyond that of the mere sale of alcohol, especially as the sale of alcohol is listed within the introductory text separately. It does seem logical that Parliament, in entrusting licensing boards to regulate licensed premises, confers some notion that a board might have an interest in what occurs on those licensed premises other than the sale of alcohol. It would be absurd to expect a licensing board to close its mind to everything that may occur on licensed premises other than the sale and consumption of alcohol.

However, this is clearly an area of some friction, given the courts have ruled that licensing boards cannot stray into non-licensing matters (see the detailed discussion on the purpose of the licensing objectives in Chapter 3) on top of Parliament itself recognising that boards should not be adding terms and conditions to licences which relate to matters or activities that are legislated for elsewhere[22].

There is some distinction to be teased out here, albeit it is not black and white, and I can only offer my own impressions of the matter. One of the most common narrated "activities" is the provision of restaurant facilities or bar meals. I do see a difference in a licensing board seeking to impose conditions or controls on a matter such as the quality of the hygiene or nutritional value of meals which are served in a restaurant, as opposed to wishing to be informed about restaurant facilities taking place and using that information to reach a view on whether a premises should be licensed taking into account the ambience or atmosphere that a food-led business may infer, in a particular case. In this example, there is a difference between a board seeking to comprehend how extensive or significant restaurant facilities will be (as this may influence their thinking on what the appropriate licensed hours or children's access to the premises might be) and a board interrogating the restaurant facilities (on the basis that they query whether drainage or ventilation systems in the kitchen are suitable), or questioning the healthiness of the food on offer.

It follows, then, that it is competent for a board to wish to examine activities so long as the examination of those activities *has a licensing purpose*. If a local convenience store wishes to open at 6am to sell milk and newspapers, then whilst it is accepted that this activity would need to be properly narrated in the premises licence application, it can of itself scarcely concern a licensing board. What may be of relevance, given that alcohol cannot be sold until 10am in an off-sale capacity, is, for example, the board seeking assurance as to how the display of alcohol might be managed or restricted from 6am onwards to prevent customers attempting to purchase it. Thus, a board can be seen to be examining the provision of an activity for a legitimate licensing purpose, albeit the activity per se is not the sale of alcohol.

Taking this understanding further, the interrogation could lead to the denial of certain activities at the time of a new premises licence application, or the removal of activities from a licence on review. Take the scenario where a set of premises has attracted drunkenness and unlawful behaviours as a result of patrons attending some form of live entertainment. If such matters were brought to a review hearing, and it were established that the entertainment provision was a negative influence on patrons' behaviour, it would be possible for the licensing board to remove the activity from the licence by varying it under the auspices of section 39(2)(b) of the 2005 Act. Another example might be the presence of a pool table which is not managed properly by staff – it has attracted an undesirable element to the premises and has led to violence occurring. Perhaps a board might delete "indoor/outdoor sports" from the licence to take the matter out of the licence holder's hands as there is evidence that they are not managing it correctly and this has led to licensing offences occurring.

In terms of how a board navigates these choppy waters, there is surely a balancing act – and whilst practitioners and the trade must concede that a licensing board cannot be expected to put their fingers in their ears and collectively whistle Dixie, so too should licensing board members be mindful (and reminded) of the properly understood interpretation of their quasi-judicial remit.

22 2005 Act, s 27(7)(c).

Bringing this back to the context of making a premises licence application and completing a proposed operating plan: whilst it may jar to acknowledge that a licensing board could have some control over activities which have no bearing on the alcohol side of premises, such as the sale of general groceries in a local convenience store or the sale of sports memorabilia in a gift shop that also offers gift packages of sports-branded alcohol products, nevertheless the applicant must ensure that their application properly reflects what they intend to do. The properly prepared licence holder should understand that whilst it may not seem logical that the licensing board may interrogate mundane activities – even if accepting that there is a judicial limit to that interrogation – the key point in this context is such activities should always be stated on the application form.

There is then a follow-up question as to what level of detail is needed. Does every single occurrence of any sort require to be narrated? A level of common sense should be adopted here and it may not be necessary to go into *minutiae*, albeit that I offer a barometer that the salient activities are ones which are provided or allowed for the purpose of engagement or interaction by the public – in other words, activities occurring which are not designed for public participation surely sit outwith the wider auspices of this section. For example, the collection of bins or disposal of empty bottles is an activity which occurs; stock-taking is an activity which occurs; mopping the floors is an activity which occurs; but these are not activities which I think Parliament intended should be narrated on a licence. It might be helpful to think of the difference as "back of house" activities and "front of house" activities.

So what "front of house" activities should be narrated? The starting point is to consider how the form itself governs the provision of this information. A list of pre-ordained "activities" are laid out in a four-column table on the operating plan application pages:

- the first column indicates the type of activity;
- the second column is used to confirm if the activity takes place or not;
- the third column is used to indicate if the activity takes place within the licensed hours; and
- the fourth column is used to indicate if the activity takes place outwith licensed hours.

Applicants should carefully consider each activity and decide whether it is something they provide and, crucially, whether it will be provided outside the licensed hours.

3.6 Activities in the operating plan

The activities provided for by the form are as follows.

3.6.1 Accommodation

This of course refers to letting rooms and accommodation facilities that one would typically find in hotels, motels, bed & breakfast, guest houses and so on.[23] Unlike the rest of the pre-defined activities, this is the only one where

23 This activity refers to public accommodation such as letting rooms and not private accommodation that may exist such as personal living quarters which happen to form part of the

the third and fourth column are pre-populated with the term "N/A" for "not applicable", as it is to be sensibly understood that accommodation facilities exist 24 hours a day and therefore necessarily outwith the licensed hours. In some cases I have come across licences where this has been inadvertently amended to either "Yes" or "No" but that would be incorrect. In one case I dealt with, the licence said "No" to accommodation outwith core hours and the licensing board insisted on a major variation application to correct the matter. This related to a trading hotel and therefore was of some concern to the operator to say the least. There is no test as to the "standard" of the accommodation, nor is there any test as to the number of rooms which would have to be provided in order for this activity to be rightfully activated on a licence. In other words, the presence of just one letting room of some description is sufficient to seek to tick this box. One still comes across queries from those who believe there is some rule about a minimum number of rooms but that relates to the old system under the 1976 Act.[24] There is now no test of this nature to be concerned with.

3.6.2 Conference facilities

This type of activity links especially to larger premises such as hotels and conference centres that will be used for conference, seminar or training events in event rooms which may be located in the building. It is not uncommon for some smaller licensed premises to have function rooms, or merely parts of the premises that are structurally distinct, which might be used for a conference.[25] Such premises may not host larger international delegations, but in my view there is no mischief in including this activity if premises have appropriate space or facilities, and have some possible inclination towards hosting this type of event. This is a good example of an activity which in the normal way of things is unlikely to attract any special attention from a licensing board.

3.6.3 Restaurant facilities

One of the most common questions I am asked is what is the difference between "restaurant facilities" and "bar meals". One appears to give a more formal impression than the other, but that aside I think it is difficult, and perhaps unhelpful, to be overly prescriptive in this regard. It may be that a board would take the view that "restaurant facilities" is a reference to the provision of a set-aside table dining area where customers are served at the table only;

building that is licensed, such as a pub manager's flat above the premises. In England and Wales, it is incredibly common for pubs to have living quarters of some description as a part of the property, so much so that there is a special rule for rates prorogation known as the 90/10 rule where a 10% discount applies to account for the personal living space. In Scotland, the reverse is true and there is no special rates treatment. Pubs without a flat above, known as "lock-ups", are more prevalent in Scotland.

24 Under s 139 of the Licensing (Scotland) Act 1976, a premises defined as a "hotel" meant "(a) in towns and the suburbs thereof, a house containing at least four apartments set apart exclusively for the sleeping accommodation of travellers; (b) in rural districts and populous places not exceeding 1,000 inhabitants according to the census for the time being last taken, a house containing at least two such apartments".

25 In 2018 I hosted the AGM of the Institute of Licensing Scottish region at Tigerlily, a hotel, bar and nightclub premises on George Street in Edinburgh.

as opposed to a more relaxed bar area where a meal might be taken sitting at tables or perhaps even eaten at the bar or counter.

That interpretation flows from the reference to restaurant *facilities* as opposed to restaurant *meals*, the word facilities suggesting to me an inference of construction, layout and environs as opposed to what food is actually served. I see little success in seeking to discern what might be a "restaurant meal" in comparison to a "bar meal"[26] from a licensing law perspective and so my advice to clients in this situation may be to tick the boxes for both activities.[27]

It is the case that some boards will use the distinction in order to consider children and young person access, perhaps on the basis that a more relaxed access might be suitable in a *bona fide* restaurant, as opposed to a bar which sells food, but in my experience that is normally achieved through a sensible discussion at the hearing and whilst I do have some experience of board members querying the presence of "bar meals" on the operating plan of a proposed restaurant, the interrogation is typically one of curiosity as opposed to a manoeuvre to have the activity removed. There is no specific definition of "a meal" in the 2005 Act, which is unfortunate as Nicholson chided the lack of definition of the term in the 1976 Act and yet provided no proposed definition himself.[28] The term "meal" is referenced in relation to an exception to the offence of consumption of alcohol by a young person where that consumption is "along with a meal",[29] and that exception is discussed in greater detail in Chapter 19 at Section 4.1.5. There is, in some licensing literature and in past legislation,[30] reference to a "table meal" in this context which suggests that a meal is something to be eaten at a table, perhaps implying a plated portion of food which might be consumed with the use of cutlery, but that is not necessarily the case. The Licensing Act 2003 defines "table meal" as:

> "a meal eaten by a person seated at a table, or at a counter or other structure which serves the purpose of a table and is not used for the service of refreshments for consumption by persons not seated at a table or structure serving the purpose of a table".[31]

Whilst the word "table" does not appear in the 2005 Act, the English definition is helpful, and I would argue that it is generally accepted that bar snacks such as crisps and nuts would not be sufficient to constitute a meal, however a serving of a filled roll or baguette with crisps or salad on the side may better fit the description, and to justify the term "meal" the offering need not be *haute cuisine*. Is it the place of licensing law to differentiate between a club sandwich served at the Dormy Clubhouse in Gleneagles and a pre-filled corned beef roll available from

26 Such debates, I might suggest, should be properly left to food critics and bloggers – Tom Johnston take a bow?

27 I think this comment stands, notwithstanding the furore which occurred following the temporary legal definition of "licensed café" in the Health Protection (Coronavirus) (Restrictions and Requirements) (Additional Temporary Measures) (Scotland) Regulations 2020 (SSI 2020/318) in October 2020.

28 Nicholson Report, para 13.2, p 131: in discussing the failings of the 1976 Act approach to children's access, he says, "The clarity of the relevant provisions is not assisted by the absence of any definition of the term 'meal'."

29 2005 Act, s 106(3).

30 Section 1(2) of the Licensing (Scotland) Act 1962 created provision for a restaurant certificate which authorised the holder "to sell or supply excisable liquor in the said premises to persons taking table meals there, for consumption by such a person as an ancillary to his meal".

31 Licensing Act 2003, s 159.

the top of the bar counter at the Press Bar in Glasgow's Albion Street? With the continued popularity of "small plates" and tapas style offerings, I think it a difficult proposition to reach a settled view on quantity, as well as quality, in relation to defining a meal. In *Miller v MacKnight*,[32] the issue of whether a "sandwich" constituted a meal was examined in the context of Sunday drinking rules of the time, which required alcohol to be sold at a meal. The case concerned the Douglas Hotel in Bo'Ness. The Lord Justice-General (Normand) said:

> "There can be no question that a sandwich may constitute a meal, and likewise, there can be no question that a sandwich may be of such exiguous dimensions or be asked for in such circumstances that is it apparent to the landlord to whom the order is given . . . that the request is mere subterfuge to obtain liquor."

He went on to say that the absence of a tablecloth and knives and forks, and the comparative costs of a sandwich versus a more formal meal were immaterial considerations and that:

> "Any hungry man coming into a hotel may want a meal at an irregular hour, and he may want a sandwich instead of an ordinary meal of one or more courses, but nevertheless, what he gets is a meal and he is entitled . . . to ask for a glass of beer along with it."[33]

3.6.4 Bar meals

See above.

3.6.5 Receptions (including "weddings, funerals, birthdays, retirements etc")

This might shortly be termed a "catch-all" activity to cater for various celebratory events which occur on licensed premises. A reception implies a planned gathering of people, typically to celebrate or mark a particular occasion. The occasion need not be one of the four suggested in parentheses as demonstrated by the presence of "et cetera" and also need not be a family-focused event. The "reception" may be any gathering of any sort and should, in my view, be interpreted widely. This activity should be ubiquitous across on-sale premises licences, most of whom must at one time or another play host to an event of some sort. An off-sale premises licence may also feature this activity although it would be considered a rarity by most. In some licensing board areas members would query why, for example, a local convenience store is proposing to play host to weddings and birthdays.

3.6.6 Club and other group meetings

This is another "catch-all" activity which is to be found on various licences purely to cover a licence holder if some form of meeting occurred. Licensed premises could be the host venue for all kinds of clubs and groups such as sporting clubs (e.g. the local football or darts team which meets for a pint

32 1945 SLT 251.

33 There is further wisdom from the English courts. In *Soloman v Green* (1955) 119 JP 289, sandwiches accompanied by "sausages on sticks" were held to be substantial enough to serve ancillary to alcohol; and in *Timmis v Millman* (1965) 109 SJ 31 sandwiches with a garnish of pickles or beetroot were sufficient to constitute a table meal.

after the game), historical appreciation societies, local CAMRA or other drink enthusiasts, walking clubs, fitness classes, knitting classes, and other groups and clubs *ad infinitum*.

3.6.7 Recorded music

This will typically refer to the playing of pre-recorded background music such as a radio, jukebox or a smart device streaming music for the enjoyment of patrons. It would also cover the (sometimes) benign sort of background music one might hear playing over the Tannoy system in a retail store. It would be unusual to advise an applicant not to have this activity engaged in an operating plan, although there are always exceptions. Operators of so-called "micro-pubs", a rarity but not unknown in Scotland, might purposefully choose not to have this activity allowable under their own licence because their operation is designed to encourage the "art of conversation" as the means of entertainment on their premises, and not having the ability to provide it makes for an easy answer when it is requested.

3.6.8 Live performances

A live performance implies a human performer (perhaps even a non-human performer?) who delivers some form of entertainment or action or who interacts with the audience (if there is one) by way of a personal appearance. This could capture a multitude of entertainments from live bands and karaoke to proper DJ sets, comedy, poetry recital, singing, dancing, acting and more. A live performance need not be amplified or altered by electronica in any way for it to be classed as a live performance.

3.6.9 Dance facilities

I take a dance facility to be a formally set aside area of a licensed premises which has the primary purpose of allowing a space for people to get down and boogie. In the sense that I discuss "restaurant facilities" above as relating to something physical, the same ethos applies here. My view is that a dance facility is a permanent or perhaps even semi-permanent area set aside – that is, a dancefloor. I would therefore advise an applicant to add dance facilities to premises which have or propose to have such a feature. It may not be necessary to add dance facilities to premises such as a pub or restaurant if there is no dedicated space for dancing; however, it may be prudent to consider it, in order cover the possibility that dancing may occur. I do not see that an ad-hoc outbreak of boogie-woogie at a table in a bar should be downtrodden if the licence does not activate dance as an authorised activity – a sensible approach should be taken. If a pub has something like a regular talent competition – for example, where the premises are located in a holiday park, whether for the grown-ups or the wee ones – then it would seem to make sense to have it in the licence. Dance facilities might also cover exercise classes or even an event like "Strictly Springburn" where a function room in a community pub is given over to ballroom tutorials. I have also seen cases where dancing events have happened on off-sale premises – in particular, charity fundraising events in large supermarkets. I encourage practitioners to take a relaxed view on such matters.

3.6.10 Theatre

This is an activity which may overlap somewhat with "live performances". It seems to me that any theatrical performance is also a live performance. No doubt premises such as specialist theatre venues will have this activity listed on their operating plan, in addition to live performances. I would also entreat applicants to add the activity as a matter of "best endeavours" to capture the possibility that some form of theatrical show may happen, if only something like a one-person play or performance. It was only in 2020 that the Scottish Parliament finally confirmed that it would commence repealing the licensing requirements under the separate Theatres Act 1968, leaving it up to individual local authorities to decide whether theatre premises should be licensed by way of a special public entertainment licence under the Civic Government (Scotland) Act 1982, if licensed at all. This means that certain premises might be licensed under the 2005 Act but also hold a separate licence under the 1982 Act and this will depend on the individual resolution of local councils. However, it may be instructive to consider the 1968 Act treatment of the art form. "Theatre" is not actually defined under the 1968 Act (nor indeed under the 2005 Act) but section 12 of the 1968 Act created a requirement to hold a theatre licence "for the public performance of any play". The Cambridge *Dictionary* describes theatre as "(the writing or performance of) plays, opera, etc, written to be performed in public". A key consideration for our purposes is to remember that "theatre" on a premises licence operating plan need not appear solely for specialist theatrical premises – it is, of course, well established that some types of performances can occur on premises other than the Lyceum or Pavilion. A most useful example of this is the Edinburgh Festival Fringe's diaspora; as anyone who has some experience of Edinburgh in August will know, there are arts and theatrical performances occurring in all sort of premises including tiny pubs and bars. It makes sense, then, to consider including theatre as an activity for any premises in Edinburgh city centre, and in other areas across Scotland, where there is some tangible expectation that it may occur.

3.6.11 Films

The showing of films on licensed premises is also something which happens regularly and is not of itself one of the possible activities that generally attracts concern or controversy. "Films" is not a defined term and will be taken to mean any form of film showing, be it new cinematic releases from Hollywood or Bollywood or anywhere else, playing DVDs or streaming movies via a projector, or local independent films. It may also be deemed to cover a film which is on a TV screen in the premises whether it just happens to be on a particular channel at that time which no one is especially interested in, or where the film is shown purposely either for background ambience or because it is actually to be viewed as part of the night's entertainment.[34] Noting all of this, it will certainly be the case that a cinema, if licensed for alcohol,

34 There are premises which trade in both Edinburgh and Glasgow under the name "Lebowskis". In both premises, there is normally to be found a TV screen playing the Coen brothers film *The Big Lebowski* in order to supplement the atmosphere the operator seeks to create as part of the background.

should have "films" listed as an activity. You would also expect to see it on other arts or entertainment venues such as stadiums, concert venues, and so on. But you can also expect to see it on the operating plan of a normal high street pub or even retail premises. As "film" is not defined, it may include educational film as well as film for entertainment. This would therefore include films of any length and would include training films or any other form of film, although I caveat that point in that I do not believe the intention is to capture anything other than film which is shown to the public.[35] Adding it to your application for a new licence just to be covered in case it ever occurs is unlikely to attract opposition. All that being said, it should be noted that there is a separate cinema licence requirement under the Cinemas Act 1985 and that Act also provides for certain exceptions and exemptions.[36] There is a general exemption to the cinema licence requirement available for those not showing any more than six films across a calendar year.[37] The 1985 Act was originally applied across England and Wales as well as Scotland but was repealed south of the border following the enactment of the Licensing Act 2003, which makes the provision of films a "licensable activity" along with the sale of alcohol under that Act. In other words, no separate cinema licence is needed in England and Wales as long as one holds a premises licence authorising this as a licensable activity.

3.6.12 Gaming

The word "gaming" is not defined under the 2005 Act and it is important to understand that it may not necessarily mean a form of "gambling". First, we should note that under the Gambling Act 2005, gaming is a subset, that is, just one type, of gambling. Gambling is defined under that Act as "gaming, betting; or participating in a lottery"[38] and gaming is subsequently defined as "playing a game of chance for a prize"[39]. But "gaming" on a premises licence operating plan might also refer to gaming where there is no element of chance and gaming which is not gambling, such as the playing of arcade games, or other "pub" games like Jenga, and possibly even interactive participation in app-based games like Pokemon Go.[40] Again, there is something to be said for a prudent, inclusive approach for the budding applicant in including an activity of this nature which might trap a number of matters. Unlike theatre and

35 Many operators take advantage of training provided by Police Scotland such as that known as "Bystander Training", which involves a film showing scenarios of how to deal with vulnerable customers. This occurs when the premises are closed or in part of the premises which is not accessible to the public at that time.

36 See further, Stephen J McGowan, *Local Government Licensing Law in Scotland* (Institute of Licensing, 2010) ch 23.

37 Cinemas Act 1985, s 7.

38 Section 3 of the Gambling Act 2005.

39 Section 6(1) of the Gambling Act 2005. Further provision is made for what is meant by a game of chance, which "includes (i) a game that involves both an element of chance and an element of skill, (ii) a game that involves an element of chance that can be eliminated by superlative skill, and (iii) a game that is presented as involving an element of chance, but (b) does not include a sport". These definitions are looked at in more detail in Chapter 21.

40 There are, for example, premises whose principal activity is the playing of 1980s retro style arcade games, the type found in a cabinet apparatus like a traditional "pacman" or "space raiders" machine, as well as other worthies like "Street Fighter" and "House of the Dead".

film, however, gaming is a more emotive word and I have seen countless interrogations of this activity, in some cases ill informed. It is up to the applicant to ask for it if he or she does intend to provide gaming, whether it is gambling or non-gambling gaming. It is up to any person to object to that proposal if they wish, and it is up to the licensing board to examine the proposal and reach a view. In many cases the inclusion of gaming relates to pub or bar-style premises in which they might like to provide a typical pub fruit machine, or perhaps offer card games such as poker or other forms of equal chance gaming such as bingo. Note that gaming machines may not be made available outside the alcohol licensed hours,[41] a point often missed by boards and practitioners alike – so, if the operating plan indicates that the gaming activity might occur outwith the licensed hours in the fourth column of the matrix, by operation of the Gambling Act 2005 that cannot be read to include gaming machines, but only other forms of gaming such as poker or bingo, or non-gambling gaming. Whether the licensing board thinks it appropriate to allow poker or other gaming to occur prior to or after the end of licensed hours is a matter for them. The definition of "gaming" as a form of gambling on alcohol-licensed premises is noted in Chapter 21 at Section 4.1.1 and that chapter contains detailed explanations of what forms of gaming may take place.

3.6.13 Indoor/outdoor sports

This entry in the premises licence operating plan activity matrix covers two activities: indoor sports and outdoor sports. An applicant may only wish to offer one, but is forced to go for both, which is surely not cricket. The difference between "indoor" and "outdoor" should need no explanation albeit I would remind readers that as we are discussing activities on a licence, an applicant should only be looking to add outdoor sporting activities if they occur within the area of the licensed premises, that is within the "red line". So, what type of sports might one find on (or outside!) a licensed premises? There is, to some small extent, a possible overlap between "gaming" and "indoor sports" in that it could be read to constitute activities such as dominoes or cribbage but indoor sport certainly relates, in my view, to darts, pool and snooker. A number of competitive entertainment activity premises are back in fashion, such as specialist darts venues, shuffleboard venues, or golf venues where alcohol may even be ancillary to the sport as the key offer to the patron. Indoor sports would also refer to premises such as large sporting arenas or indoor stadiums which may also be licensed for alcohol and therefore would include the full gamut of professional sporting activities. Outdoor sport is perhaps less obvious a topic but I have represented, for example, a rugby and sporting club in the west end of Glasgow for which I obtained a major variation to permanently license the outdoor spectator areas where cricket, tennis and rugby occur. Some licensed premises, boasting very generous licensed outdoor facilities, may have activities such as lawn bowls or croquet available and the licensed area may include the greens (or at least a portion of them, for spectating) and there are hotel premises where one can find giant chess boards and the like in the outdoor grounds, although I will avoid the debate on whether chess is a game or a sport!

41 Gambling Act 2005, s 278(1)(c).

3.6.14 Televised sport

The presence of this activity on the operating plan might, for some, link to concerns over "sports bars" or "football pubs" and that the showing of live football suggests a particular type of atmosphere which may or may not be appropriate for a certain type of licensed premises. The term used, however, is of course "sport" and not just football – and therefore can and does cover all form of sports which may happen to be shown on screens in the premises either as a primary source of entertainment or simply in the background. It is not uncommon to find televised sport as a "catch-all" for premises which would not ordinarily show live football but may wish to have the chance to show other sporting events which, for example, may have some national interest such as a Scottish team or individual playing a final in a particular discipline, or where the sporting event is being hosted in Scotland or the UK such as the Glasgow Commonwealth Games 2014 or European Championship 2020[42]. There is an interesting question as to the interpretation of "televised". The ordinary meaning of the word does of course mean the showing of a sporting event which is broadcast on "television", which is a reference to a particular medium. If a licence holder wished to stream a sporting event over the net and display this on a projector or laptop screen, would that be "televised?" What if the event shown was not live? The word "live" does not appear in the term. If the licence holder was showing a recording of the "Rumble in the Jungle" from YouTube, for example, would that constitute the showing of televised sport? The 2005 Act does not define the term "televised" and whilst it is fair to acknowledge that technology has moved on apiece since the application form was drafted, I would tend to the view that the intention here is surely to capture the showing of sport for entertainment purposes and this would include highlights or reruns.

3.6.15 Outdoor drinking facilities

This refers to any sort of outdoor or external area which may be used for drinking, and the use is not limited to the drinking of alcohol as the word "drinking" is not defined in that restrictive sense. Thus, if one has an external area where it is intended non-alcoholic drinks might be consumed such as teas and coffees or even Irn Bru, then this activity should still be referred to in the operating plan in order to cover the point. The outdoor drinking area should be shown properly on the layout plan attaching to the premises licence and, of course, alcohol may only be sold or consumed within that licensed area. Note that, whilst by definition alcohol cannot be sold outside the licensed hours, column four should be a "Yes" in order to cover the provision of soft drinks etc prior to the commencement of the licensed hours, for example to allow patrons to sit for a coffee prior to 11am. Licensed external areas are discussed in more detail at Section 1.1.4 above.

3.6.16 Adult entertainment

Despite this activity being theoretically capable on any licensed premises, and the activity being one of the pre-defined ones on the activities matrix as part

42 The 2020 Championships were delayed to the summer of 2021 as a result of the Coronavirus pandemic.

of the pre-set operating plan options, "adult entertainment" is not mentioned anywhere under the primary legislation and is actually defined under the Licensing Conditions (Late Opening Premises) (Scotland) Regulations 2007.[43] The definition is as follows:

> "any form of entertainment which—
> (a) involves a person performing an act of an erotic or sexually explicit nature; and
> (b) is provided wholly or mainly for the sexual gratification or titillation of the audience."

The definition of adult entertainment is provided as part of these regulations because the provision of this activity is one of the features of what is treated under the wider ambit of the 2005 Act as a special type of licensed premises attracting additional conditions and regulation. The Act terms these "late opening premises", and the purpose of these regulations is to fortify licences which relate to nightclub or similar late-night venues where it is deemed additional public safety conditions are merited because of the unique nature of these venues. The late-night conditions are discussed at length in Chapter 15 at Section 8.

For the purposes of exploring the requirement to activate this activity on the premises licence operating plan, applicants should note that the frequency of the activity is irrelevant. Whilst an obvious candidate premises for this type of activity will be a lap-dancing or strip club style premises, on the basis that the adult entertainment is the primary activity of the premises, the activity should also be listed on the operating plan for less specialist premises such as pubs, bars and clubs where it is envisaged by the operator that adult entertainment may occur every so often – even if just once a year.

The definition itself is drawn fairly widely. There is no reference to nudity being a prerequisite *per se*, and no reference to the gender of the performer or audience, and so an applicant who believes that they may wish to allow some variant of activity which could be caught by the definition should certainly seek advice. The *Cambridge Dictionary* defines "erotic" as "relating to sexual desire and pleasure"; both states of mind and body which the reader may agree can be achieved whilst fully clothed. "Sexually explicit", on the other hand, connotes something beyond humble eroticism, where there may be simulation of a sexual act or display of the sexual organs.

Of importance is to note that the salient construction of the definition is that the constitution of adult entertainment is either erotic *or* sexually explicit; it need not be both. However, whilst that part of the definition creates a stratification of sorts, it also adds a further evidential test which must exist for the definition to engage, in the use of the word "and" in the next line: "*and* is provided wholly or mainly for the sexual gratification or titillation of the audience". Sexual gratification in this part of the definition should be interpreted, in my view, as including an initial or ongoing heightened state of arousal – that is, that it should include the process of gratification, as opposed to the culmination or completion of being gratified.

The phrase "titillation" implies a less heated form of excitement; and may imply a form of entertainment which is on the bawdy side instead of something more overtly carnal; but is nevertheless some form of arousal. Lastly,

43 SSI 2007/336, reg 1(2).

the "wholly or mainly" element should, it is argued, allow for some flexibility where the activity is perhaps not the essential element of a performance such as the performance of a theatrical play which may contain a sexual scene of some sort, as well as possibly creating some space to allow for a more comedic style performance. An existing licence holder who wishes to add adult entertainment to a licence must surely do so in the knowledge that it is bound to attract representations in the public consultation, and therefore seeking advice is again a sensible course. Applicants should note, at the least, that without any special reference to nudity some forms of entertainment may well be caught by the definition, such as a "burlesque night" or similar event. Hosting a "ladies night" event which features male strippers, even if the performance is more one of comedy than of genuine arousal, may also be trapped by this definition.

Of some interest, of course, is the separate definition of "sexual entertainment" which now exists as a legal construct in relation to the civic licensing of sexual entertainment venues under the 1982 Act. Section 76 of the Air Weapons and Licensing (Scotland) Act 2015 creates a new section 41(2)(ab) of the 1982 Act which provides for a subset of public entertainment licence known as a "sexual entertainment venue". The definition of "sexual entertainment" is found in the new section 45A(3) of the 1982 Act and is as follows:

> " 'sexual entertainment' means—
> (a) any live performance, or
> (b) any live display of nudity,
> which is of such a nature that, ignoring financial gain, it must reasonably be assumed to be provided solely or principally for the purpose of sexually stimulating any member of the audience (whether by verbal or other means)."

This introductory part of the definition for sexual entertainment of itself creates a difficulty with the contrary definition of "adult entertainment". On the basis one must assume that premises which are sexual entertainment venues will also sell alcohol, you then have an operator who is providing a form of entertainment which has two different meanings under two different yet overlapping licensing regimes. Until this matter is reconciled it is the definition of adult entertainment under the 2005 Act which is to be preferred, as regards with compliance with this Act.[44]

3.7 Activities outside the licensed hours – additional information

If the applicant intends any of these activities to take place outside the licensed hours, then this should be indicated in the fourth column of the operating plan matrix, which is set aside for that specific purpose – but they must also give further details, which can be provided in a free text box which is located below the activities matrix on the operating plan. To give an example of this, say an application is for a premises licence for a restaurant style premises that also seeks to open at 8am to provide breakfasts, teas and coffees. The statement required should be something along the lines of:

44 The Scottish Government have noted this issue and propose to replace the 2005 Act definition of "adult entertainment" with the 1982 Act definition of "sexual entertainment", see "Provisions for licensing of sexual entertainment venues and changes to licensing of theatres: Guidance" (Scottish Government, 28 March 2019).

> "Bar snacks and breakfasts will be sold from 8am to cater for local demand from workers and passing trade, and in connection with funerals, club meetings and other functions. Where the premises are open from 8am, recorded music and televised sport may be made available. No alcohol will be served before the commencement of core hours without the benefit of an approved extended hours application."

Another example of activities outside the licensed hours may relate to activities which might occur after the terminal licensed hour. Whilst not as common as licences which allow activities pre-licensed hours, there are numerous examples of premises where activities may be permitted after the bar is closed at the end of the night, and these may have wording such as the following for a post-club "cool down" facility:

> "The club will provide a meal facility from 4am to 6am, providing hot meals, soft drinks, teas and coffees. No alcohol will be served during this time."

Another example might be where a rugby club or sports bar has convinced the licensing board that it can safely offer an unlicensed facility for live sporting events which may be occurring at odd hours such as the Superbowl, or perhaps a Lions tour of Australia or New Zealand, or a World Cup hosted by a nation in the Southern Hemisphere.

The point of this "free text" box concerning activities outwith the licensed hours is that it provides certainty for the licensing board as well as other interested parties such as local residents as to the extent of what the licence permits even although this particular element of the operating plan relates to activities which will occur when no alcohol is sold. The wording in the box will, once the licence is granted, become a part of that licence and therefore the holder of that licence would have to obey those terms.

3.8 Other non-prescribed activities

The next part of question 5 allows the applicant to give information about other activities which are not catered for in the application. This is the opportunity for applicants to specifically list any unusual or specialist activities which they would like to cater for. The box can typically be used to enter categories of activity which may fall under some of the specific activities noted in the matrix, such as "quiz nights" or "karaoke", which one might suggest would fall with the definition of a "live performance" but in practice are often caught here for the avoidance of doubt. It is not uncommon to see other activities such as "charity nights", "psychic nights", "knitting club" and the possibilities are endless. One might also see reference here to "home deliveries" to capture a premises which is offering takeaway food and drink (whether alcohol or not),[45] or reference to

45 It is suggested by some that the activity of "home delivery" of alcohol might not be required as a separate activity by virtue of the fact that the presence of an off-sale licence *of itself* must include that, as a form of purchase for consumption off the premises. This position is fortified by the presence in the Act of rules and regulations as to the delivery of alcohol, supporting the view that home delivery is implicit. Many boards have, notwithstanding this, insisted operators seek major variation applications so that the phrase "home deliveries" (or even "click and collect" for that matter) is expressly shown; primarily to have assessed the robustness of how such a function is carried out. The irony of this point is that the implicit consent for delivery may be interpreted as only relating to alcohol; and therefore, delivery of other products such as food or non-alcoholic beverages would need to be expressly stated. The Coronavirus (Scotland) Act 2020 relaxed these rules on a temporary basis: see Appendix I. Note that,

non-alcohol retail sales such as general grocery items or sports memorabilia. As to how far one should go in the application, my general approach is to capture what the applicant wants, perhaps along with some additional wording that I know will be acceptable in a particular licensing board area. It is probably unhelpful to festoon this part of the application with a plethora of colourful and unusual activities where there is no real prospect of them occurring.

3.9 "Late opening" questions

The final part of this element of the operating plan, namely Question 5(g), relates to "late opening" premises – in other words, certain premises which open after 1am. This question is designed to ensure that those premises for which the late opening conditions would apply are "caught" in the application form asking whether the premises have live or recorded music with a decibel level exceeding 85dB, and whether, when fully occupied, there are likely to be more customers standing than seated.[46] By confirming these matters, this allows certainty as to the additional conditions which may be applicable and allows those who report on the applications such as the licensing standards officer to reflect properly on what is being proposed before drawing up their reports.

3.10 Question 6: Children and Young Persons

Question 6 relates to the terms on which children and young persons will be allowed access to the premises. Note that the heading states "Question 6 (On-sales Only)". In other words, the whole of question 6 applies only to premises for which it is intended that alcohol will be sold for consumption on the premises. This stems from section 20(4)(e) of the 2005 Act which states:

> "(e) where alcohol is to be sold for consumption on the premises, a statement as to whether children or young persons are to be allowed entry to the premises and, if they are to be allowed entry, a statement of the terms on which they are allowed entry including, in particular—
> (i) the ages of children or young persons to be allowed entry,
> (ii) the times at which they are to be allowed entry, and
> (iii) the parts of the premises to which they are to be allowed entry,".

The reference to "on the premises" in the opening part of this subsection confirms that there is no need or requirement for an off-sale application to provide any of this detail. These elements should be left blank where the application is for off-sale only; and in turn there is no specificity of regulation as to access by children and young persons in an off-sale premises licence[47] when considered through the prism of the detail of the operating plan. That being said,

where the home delivery is of a pre-mix cocktail product, a separate HMRC permission called a compounder licence is also required.

46 Late opening conditions are discussed in Chapter 15.

47 Whilst this is currently the case, I would not be surprised to see some lobby to have this amended and to allow licensing boards greater control over access by children and young persons in an off-sale environment, noting the concerns that some stakeholders appear to have over the mere display of alcohol and how that may create a negative impression on those aged under 18. If this were to be amended, then one might expect proposals such as banning those under the age of 18 from accessing the aisle where alcohol is displayed, for example – or indeed going further and creating a "shop within a shop" style approach.

it would not be correct to imply that licensing boards are "lame ducks" with respect to the access of retail and off-sale premises by those aged under 18. It is open to a licensing board to consider adding a local condition of some sort where it is felt that evidence has been presented that the licensing objective of protecting children and young persons will not be met if the application were to be granted.[48]

Let us now consider the detail required in this part of the operating plan. The first part of the question pertains to whether or not children and young persons will be allowed. Nicholson had recommended that there should be a presumption that children and young persons would be allowed to access all licensed premises, with an opt-out feature.[49] Nicholson chose to quote Clayson in this regard:

> "We would hope that [allowing under 18s to access licensed premises in a regulated manner] would tend to reduce the possibility of children regarding (as some no doubt do at present) drinking, particularly in a public house, as a symbol of adulthood which is desirable in itself. We are firmly of the view that it is much better that they should come to see drinking in the right conditions as simply an incidental part of normal social activity."[50]

Nicholson goes on to elaborate upon the justification for the "opt out" scheme he proposed as follows:

> "... we consider that there would be advantage if, in future, there were to be a statutory presumption in favour of allowing children and young persons into all parts of licensed premises. Plainly, of course, there will be some licensed premises of a kind where it would not be appropriate for entry to be permitted. Premises offering extreme adult entertainment, including for example nudity, would be an obvious example of that. However, it is our view that for the future it should be for premises licence holders, if so advised, to opt out of the presumption in favour of children and young persons having a full right of entry rather than for them to have to seek express permission for such entry to take place. Premises licence holders should have an absolute right to opt out of the presumption, and licensing boards should not, in our view, have any entitlement to impose it on unwilling licence holders."[51]

48 For example, I have witnessed a handful of cases where a retailer who is located near a school and has a significant customer base of children from that school over the lunch break, has applied for a licence and this has drawn objection due to the preponderance of under 18s during that time. I have witnessed different licensing boards interrogating how the premises will be managed when there are large numbers of teenagers on the premises. I have seen a licensing board consider imposing a condition that alcohol not be sold during that particular period, for example "Alcohol shall not be sold during the school term period between the hours of 12noon and 1pm". I have also seen a separate licensing board consider imposing a condition on having the alcohol removed/covered during these "school break" periods.

49 This, of course, is in stark contrast to the 1976 provisions. The rules regarding children on licensed premises under that Act were deceptively simple, but remarkably misunderstood. Aside from refreshment licensed premises, the general rule was simply that children under 14 were not allowed in the bar area. In other words, it was perfectly fine for persons of 14 years and older to be in any part of licensed premises at any time, and for those aged 13 and under the only restriction was being in the bar area. The 1976 Act had provision for a special "children's certificate" which was a Clayson invention, although not adopted until 1990, and it was introduced to allow children aged 13 years and younger in the area to which the certificate applied – usually to include the bar area in order to circumvent the general restriction.

50 Clayson Committee Report, para 11.10; as quoted in the Nicholson Report at para 13.3, p 132.

51 Nicholson Report, para 13.7, p 133.

This liberal approach is perhaps reflected in the original terms under the Licensing Bill for the proposed operating plan, which made no reference at all to having to indicate the terms on which under 18s would have access to licensed premises.[52] This approach was not favoured as the Bill passed through Parliament, however. The Stage 1 Report from the Local Government and Transport Committee had this to say on the matter:

> "The Committee notes the comments from Sheriff Principal Gordon Nicholson and others in relation to the lack of a policy on the face of the Bill relating to the access of licensed premises by children. If the Executive has a clear position that an opt-in approach to the access of children is desirable, the Committee would question why this clear principle has not been included in the Bill. In relation to the relative advantages of an opt-in versus an opt-out approach, the Committee is persuaded that many licensed premises in Scotland are not suitable for children and so an 'opting-out' approach to access by children would not be appropriate.
>
> However, the Committee does accept that establishing a 'family friendly' atmosphere in some pubs and certain other licensed premises is a desirable objective and could help change Scotland's drinking culture. The Committee recommends that the Executive should consider whether it can do more to encourage licensed premises, where appropriate, to become more 'family friendly' with appropriate facilities for children and families."[53]

After all the hue and cry, amendment 22 was passed and the Bill amended at Stage 2 to require the information on access being inserted into the operating plan, thus "inverting the onus" which Nicholson had originally proposed.

What all of this means is that it is up to the applicant to propose the ages of children and young persons allowed, and the areas in the premises where they will be allowed, and under what terms.[54] It is then up to the licensing board to determine to agree with those proposals, or not.

52 Clause 19(4) of the Licensing Bill as introduced on 22 February 2005.

53 Stage 1 Report from the Local Government and Transport Committee, paras 52 and 53, published 13 June 2005. The matter was debated in a meeting of the Local Government and Transport Committee on 20 September 2005. The then Deputy Minister for Finance, Public Service Reform and Parliamentary Business, George Lyon, led amendment 22 which sought to require the terms of children and young person's access to be stated on the operating plan. He said:

> "...we would like licensed premises to allow access to children, but only where access is suitable and appropriate. There is to be no presumption that premises are suitable. The fact is that many on-sales licensed premises are unsuitable for children. We therefore propose that applicants who apply for a premises licence must specify in the operating plan their proposals for the access of children. The type of activities to be carried on in the premises in addition to the sale of alcohol will be relevant to the board's consideration of the issue. Not all entertainment may be suitable for children or for children of a certain age, so the operating plan must detail those activities and the ages of the children. The size of the premises and the times at which children are to be allowed access – it might just be lunch time – are relevant, as is whether an area for children can be segregated off. When the licensing board is armed with that type of detailed information, it can make the kind of informed decision in the best interests of children that all of us want to see being taken."

This was debated, with some members suggesting it was "too restrictive". Tommy Sheridan, then MSP for the Scottish Socialist Party, said:

> "I am troubled that we are encouraging licensed premises to be more child friendly. I am worried that we are forgetting the type of substance that is being sold on those premises. It is a dangerous substance that we do not want to normalise. We should not make it part and parcel of everybody's life or bring up children to accept that it is part and parcel of life. I would like to hear from the minister that the Executive recognises that we are talking not about bread and milk, but about a dangerous substance. That must be taken into account when we are thinking about children and normalisation. It should not be taken as read that children should be encouraged to be in licensed premises."

54 Interestingly, during the transitional period some boards insisted that if the applicant intended

Having noted this genesis of the statutory provisions, let us turn back to examine the operating plan application form and consider the practicalities. Question 6(b) requires an applicant to give details of the "terms" under which children and young persons will be allowed. Examples of the sorts of "terms"of entry may include:

> Children and young persons will be admitted only for the purposes of taking a meal when accompanied by an adult.
>
> Children and young persons will be admitted when accompanied by an adult to attend a function.
>
> Children and young persons may be admitted when they are resident on the premises.

The terms which are relevant to a particular applicant will of course be influenced by the type of operation he or she proposes to run and a sensible approach here would be to seek the terms which are those genuinely sought after.

Next, the applicant must identify the ages of children or young persons to be admitted. It may be appropriate simply to state something along the lines of 'children and young persons as defined in the Licensing (Scotland) Act 2005', or even a simple "Ages 0 to 17", but of course this will very much depend on the circumstances of the premises and it may be suitable or desirable to a particular business person to identify a specific age group for their own reasons. Note that, if the proposal is to include allowing children aged five or under, then the licence will be subject to a mandatory condition requiring baby-changing facilities to be accessible to persons of either gender.

There is an interesting dimension to consider in relation to the overlap between this element of a premises licence, which purports to allow a licence holder *carte blanche* over what ages of person may be admitted (so long as the licensing board agrees with it!), and the provisions under the Equality Act 2010 concerning "age" being a protected characteristic under section 5 of that Act. Does a licensee offend the terms of the 2010 Act if they choose not to have persons under the age of 14 for example, or chooses not to have anyone aged under 18 at all for that matter? This general point might be prefaced with the context of the common law right of refusal, which includes a right of refusal not just to serve a person, but to prohibit entry to licensed premises; however, that common law only reaches so far as it does not offend the 2010 Act.

Interestingly, the Schedule of exceptions to the 2010 Act[55] which relate to age include "Age restricted services" which specifically mentions the provision of a service (which, for our purposes, is access to licensed premises by under 18s) in relation to licensed premises – however, the definition of "licensed premises" only refers to premises under the Licensing Act 2003, despite the Schedule applying as law in Scotland. This appears to be an oversight. One can imagine that the general proposition would be that if a supervening statutory requirement is imposed on a provider of services, then that "trumps" the protection of the characteristic. That is particularly so where that supervening requirement – the obligation to observe the terms of one's premises licence – is

that children would be allowed in the "bar" area, then that would prevent the "like for like" status and remove the grandfather rights.

55 Paragraph 30C, as inserted into Schedule 3 to the Equality Act 2010, by art 6 of the Equality Act 2010 (Age Exceptions) Order 2012 (SI 2012/2466).

a legal duty the breach of which is a criminal offence under the 2005 Act and can deprive the licence holder of his liberty. However, there does appear to be a legislative *lacuna* here as no specific provision has been made for licensed premises in Scotland.

Notwithstanding this gap, an application which proposes restricted access by reference to age is not necessarily a breach of the 2010 Act. First of all, it is a hypothetical. It is an application for the possible future provision of services which cannot come to pass unless and until it has approval from a licensing board. If I want to open a nightclub and make it over 18s only because I don't believe the atmosphere would be conducive to children or young persons, I don't see that the application process in which I propose that restriction could be successfully subject to challenge under 2010 Act grounds when law exists to support the restriction[56] – and once the licence is granted on those terms, then of course I am bound by that licence in any event.

Discrimination on age, in this context, is legitimate and can be distinguished from, say, an application for a hotel which purports to restrict access to heterosexual guests only, because there is no statutory (far less moral) basis for that restriction – whilst there is an absolute statutory basis for preventing persons under 18 from accessing premises, where it is illegal for persons under 18 to buy, consume or be sold the principal product available, and where there is a wider objective of protecting children and young persons from harm.

Moving on, the next part of question 6 requires the applicant to identify the times when children and young persons may be admitted. It is not always the case that the full licensed hours will mirror the hours of access for children and young persons. It would be fairly unusual to see a licence which allows children and young persons access till 3am, for example, unless that premises were perhaps a bona fide restaurant. The type of simple wording one might see here could be:

> "Children and young persons will be allowed on the premises till 10pm."
>
> "Children and young persons are allowed at all times."
>
> "Children and young persons are allowed until 10pm Sunday to Thursday and 8pm on Friday and Saturday."

It may be that different times are submitted for different age groups, for example:

> "Residents will be allowed entry at all times; children and young persons attending for a function will be allowed entry until 11pm; and children and young persons attending for the purpose of taking a meal will be allowed entry until 9pm."

Again, this is very much a matter of fact and degree and the individual needs of the applicant, in reference to the licensing board's policy statement and what the board is prepared to grant.

Finally, the applicant is also required to identify the part(s) of the premises to which the children will have access. This may simply be the entire premises, but where there are specific area(s) these will need to be identified on the layout plan and described at this section of the operating plan, for example by saying something like:

56 See also s 13(2) of the Equality Act 2010.

> "Children and young persons will be allowed access to the main bar and raised seated area to the rear of the premises, as shown on the attached layout plan."
>
> "Children and young persons are permitted entry to the restaurant dining area only."
>
> "Children and young persons are allowed throughout the premises including the licensed external area."

It is important to make sure that whatever is proposed in the operating plan is on all fours with what is shown on the layout plan. If the application is amended in some way, perhaps at the hearing, to restrict the areas proposed, it is not unheard of for a licensing board to grant the licence subject to an amended layout plan being produced to reflect what was agreed, although some boards may wish to continue the application to the next available hearing to allow a revised layout plan to be reviewed and reported on by the statutory consultees.

3.11 Question 7: Capacity

Capacity is one of the most problematic areas of the 2005 Act. It caused tremendous difficulties for applicants, clerks, agents, architects and officers in building standards during the transitional period and continues to pose problems for applicants unhappy with the capacity which may be imposed on them, as well as wider philosophical issues over how capacity affects alcohol harms; and how such harms can be evidenced in a licensing board hearing.

Perhaps surprisingly for those who did not experience the 1976 Act, there was no stated capacity on licences under that regime, save for amended entertainment licences that were subject to a swathe of public safety conditions which were brought in to the old licensing system in 1990 following public and parliamentary concern over the illegal rave culture of the late 1980s. Public house, hotel and restaurant premises did not have a capacity stated on their licence at all. When Nicholson reviewed this aspect of the old liquor licensing regime, he found this to be unsatisfactory and focused particularly on the issue of fire safety. Fires in licensed premises was clearly part of the collective consciousness of the Nicholson Committee as the researches were occurring around the same time as the infamous Cowgate fire in Edinburgh on the night of 7 December 2002 which destroyed a number of licensed premises including, perhaps mostly famously, a club premises known as La Belle Angele, as well as the Gilded Balloon. Nicholson proposed allowing licensing boards to add a capacity to a licence as a condition of the licence through the auspices of the fire authority:

> "In appropriate cases a licensing board should be entitled to require the fire authority to specify a safe maximum capacity for specified premises and, where that has been done, a board should be entitled to make it a condition of a premises licence that the specified maximum capacity should not be exceeded."[57]

He had, in fact, gone as far as suggesting that a certificate of suitability under what is now section 50 of the 2005 Act should be produced by the fire authority as a part of the new licence application process, but that was not taken for-

57 Nicholson Committee Report, para 4.18, p 65.

ward formally, as readers will note in the relevant paragraphs below discussing section 50 certificates. Of this purported fire certificate, Nicholson said:

> "Such a certificate would take account, among other things, of suitable emergency exit routes, adequacy of lighting, and so on. In appropriate circumstances it should also, we consider, specify a maximum number of people that the premises should be permitted to accommodate at any one time. Given the current proliferation of very large licensed premises which are intended to attract considerable numbers of customers at any one time, we consider that this is an aspect of public safety which should not be ignored."[58]

Although there is no provision for a special fire certificate which governs the capacity of a premises as he had proposed, Nicholson's desire to have a stated capacity was ultimately carried through as it became one of the features of the operating plan and therefore breach of a capacity is a criminal offence.[59] Capacity was not defined in the original Licensing Bill albeit there were numerous references to capacity such as for calculating overprovision. South Ayrshire Council, in their written evidence on the draft Bill at Committee stage, pointed to the lack of definition. At Stage 2, in response to this, the definitions we now have (as noted below) were proposed by minister George Lyon.[60]

So how does the operating plan actually deal with the question of capacity? This appears under Question 7, which requires applicants to state the "proposed capacity" of the premises. There are, following the George Lyon amendment, two types of capacity under the 2005 Act: an on-sale capacity, and an off-sale capacity. These terms are defined in section 147(1) of the Act as follows:

> "(a) in relation to licensed premises (or any part of such premises) on which alcohol is sold for consumption on the premises (or, as the case may be, that part), the maximum number of customers which can be accommodated in the premises (or, as the case may be, that part) at any one time, and
> (b) in relation to licensed premises (or any part of such premises) on which alcohol is sold for consumption off the premises (or, as the case may be, that part), the amount of space in the premises (or, as the case may be, that part) given over to the display of alcohol for sale."

Let us explore the definition of each in turn.

3.11.1 On-sale capacity

Licensed premises, like any other building in Scotland, are required to meet the provisions of the Building (Scotland) Act 2003 and the Building (Scotland) Regulations 2004.[61] It has become accepted therefore that the on-sale or

58 Ibid para 4.16, pp 63–4.

59 The disengagement of a special certificate from the fire authority, or a special process for the fire authority to govern capacity of licensed premises, was debated during Stage 2 of the Bill. On 3 October 2005, Andrew Arbuckle moved "Amendment 187" which would have created a special role for the fire authority, but he subsequently withdrew this following submissions from George Lyon that any safety concerns could be raised via the general application consultation, noting that the fire authority is one of the consultees.

60 3 October 2005, amendment 110, which was agreed unanimously by the Local Government and Transport Committee.

61 SSI 2004/406.

Table 8.1 Occupancy load factors

Area	*Load factor*
Standing spectators' area	0.3
Amusement arcade, assembly hall (including a general-purpose place of assembly), bar (public area), bingo hall	0.5
Concourse, dance floor, queuing area	0.7
Committee room, common room, conference room, dining room, licensed betting office (public area), lounge (other than a lounge bar), meeting room, reading room, restaurant, staff room, waiting room	1.0
Exhibition hall	1.5
Shop sales area (supermarkets, department stores, hairdressers, etc)	2.0
Art gallery, dormitory, factory production area, museum, workshop	5.0
Office	6.0
Kitchen, library, shop sales area (furniture, floor coverings, cycles, domestic appliances, etc)	7.0
Bedroom or study bedroom	8.0
Bed-sitting room, billiards room	10.0
Car park, storage and warehouse accommodation	30.0

occupancy capacity should be calculated by reference to the *Non-Domestic Technical Handbook*, which is a government-issued handbook for building control officers issued under the 2004 Regulations. This document is subject to ongoing update. The version in force at the time of writing was that issued to take effect from 1 October 2019.[62]

Agreeing the on-sale capacity is not as simple as agreeing the maximum number of customers. There are two different types of capacity which may be looked at in order to reach the magic number:

- occupancy capacity
- sanitary capacity.

Occupancy capacity is dealt with in section 2.9.2 of the *Technical Handbook*. The occupancy capacity of licensed premises is determined by dividing the area in square metres by a special measurement known as a "load factor". The "load factor" is different depending on the type of premises and use to which they are put. The occupancy load factors are as shown in Table 8.1.

The most common occupancy load factors connected to licensed premises are:

- restaurants/dining areas (1),
- public bar areas (0.5) and
- dance floors (0.7).

To give an example, if public house premises had a bar area of 40 square metres, then a basic occupancy capacity calculation would be 40 divided by 0.5 = 80 persons. Licence holders may refer to these for general information but should avoid making calculations on their own. The capacity calculation is not straightforward as certain parts of the premises are not included for this

62 The document is available at the Scottish Government website: https://www.gov.scot/publications/building-standards-technical-handbook-2019-non-domestic/

purpose, for example hotel bedrooms, toilets or the area behind the bar, and certainly a decision on the capacity is not one for a solicitor to make, but an architect or similarly qualified person.

Underpinning these numbers is a wider general philosophy of safe escape from a fire. Building standards reports can therefore sometimes refer to "escape" capacity as a separate construct to the occupancy capacity. This is because there may be some wider issue with the construction or layout of the premises which limits the number of people for fire safety reasons, regardless of the load factor calculation above. It is worth noting the relevant part of the non-domestic handbook on this issue, here:

> **"2.9.1 Escape Principles**
> The occupants should be able to leave the building or part of the building in relative safety during the outbreak of a fire without assistance from the fire and rescue service. Designers generally achieve this by providing independent routes of escape either directly to a place of safety, or through an adjacent compartment or protected zone. The time available to leave a room or compartment of fire origin before being overcome by fire or smoke is dependent on a number of key factors:
>
> - the number and mobility of occupants in the compartment or room of fire origin
> - the containment measures of the room or compartment of fire origin
> - the geometry of the room or compartment
> - means of early warning of fire
> - the fire dynamics (e.g. the fire load and the rate of fire growth)
> - the distance to reach a place of safety, a protected zone or another compartment, and
> - the number and width of exits.
>
> There are many options available to designers when considering escape from buildings to a place of safety. However these options can be subdivided into 3 broad categories:
>
> - direct escape
> - internal escape
> - external escape.
>
> Direct escape means that occupants can escape from a building directly to a place of safety by way of a final exit door without using an internal or external escape route. Whilst direct escape to a place of safety is preferable, this is not always possible or convenient, for example, in hospitals or multi-storey buildings with many floors high above the ground.
>
> Internal escape is perhaps the most common method of escape from buildings. Occupants escape from fire using enclosed corridors and stairs inside the building to reach a final exit door from the building, which leads to a place of safety.
>
> External escape routes are wholly or partially open to the external air therefore the risk of smoke logging is reduced compared with enclosed escape routes inside the building. External escape routes include external escape stairs, access decks and flat roofs. In certain circumstances, an escape route from a building may be by way of a flat roof or an access deck."

Putting all of this into practice in the context of a licensing application, a basement restaurant may have a potential occupancy capacity of 200, but an "escape" capacity of only 60 because there is only one way in or out of the premises to the street level. In these circumstances, building standards officers will report both figures but will be looking to the licensing board to agree the lower figure as the "on-sales" capacity stated on the licence. It may be that the technical "escape" capacity of 60 can be improved upon by having other measures in place.

This brings us on to one of the less glamorous aspects of the practice of licensing law which is the amount of time one spends counting toilets to obtain a "sanitary capacity". The standard for sanitary facilities is laid down at section 3.12 of the *Handbook*, and the standards vary depending on the type of premises and operation, although the *Handbook* does concede that certain premises may not fall easily into the categories suggested. The general principle seems to be that "facilities should be sufficient in number to prevent queuing, other than in exceptional circumstances", and that the facilities should be calculated with regard to the maximum number of persons the building is likely to accommodate, based on the normal use of the building.

Licensed premises will normally fall to be considered under section 3.12.5 of the *Handbook*, "Provision for public in entertainment & assembly buildings", which is as follows:

> **"Buildings used for assembly or entertainment**
> Male WC provision: 1 for 1 to 100 men; 1 for 101 to 250 men; plus 1 for each extra 500 males over 250, or part thereof
> Male urinal provision: 2 for 1 to 100 men; plus 1 for each extra 80 men, or part thereof, over 100
> Female WC provision: 3 for 1 to 40 women; 4 for 41 to 70 women; 5 for 71 to 100 women; plus 1 for each extra 35 women, or part thereof, over 100
>
> **Restaurants, cafes, canteens and fast food outlets (where seating is provided)**
> Male WC provision: 1 for every 100 men up to 400, thereafter 1 for each further 250 men, or part thereof
> Male urinal provision: 1 per 50 men, or part thereof
> Female WC provision: 2 for 1 to 20 women; 3 for 21 to 50; 4 for 51 to 100; 5 for 101 to 150; 6 for 151 to 200; and 1 for each further 100 women over 200, or part thereof
>
> **Public houses and licensed bars**
> Male WC provision: 1 for 1 to 75 men; 1 for 76 to 150; and 1 for each extra 150 men over 150, or part thereof
> Male urinal provision: 2 for 1 to 75 men; 3 for 76 to 150 men; and 1 for each extra 75 men, or part thereof
> Female WC provision: 2 for 1 to 25 women and 1 for each extra 25 women, or part thereof."

The *Handbook* also goes on to provide a number of other points in relation to sanitary provision for licensed premises, which include:

- There should be one hand wash basin per watercloset, or one hand wash basin per 5 urinals.
- Numbers of customers should be calculated at four persons per 3 square metres of the "effective drinking area".
- Public houses with restaurants should be provided with sanitary facilities as for licensed bars.
- Public houses with public music, singing and dancing licences should be as for licensed bars. The licensed area for public music, singing and dancing should be separated for calculation of numbers of persons and the provision of sanitary facilities in such areas should be calculated as for buildings used for public entertainment.

When an application for a premises licence is made, the building standards report may contain reference to the sanitary capacity. As with the interplay between occupancy capacity and escape capacity, so too is there some interplay or overlap between the occupancy capacity and the sanitary capacity. Typically, the building standards officer will be asking the board to agree the lowest figure. So, for example, if the officer agrees with the applicant that the occupancy capacity for their shiny new bar is 250 people, but that the number of toilets means the sanitary capacity can only reach 200, then 200 is the number that the officer will ask the licensing board to impose on the licence.

It is unusual in the extreme to see a licensing board grant an occupancy higher than the one proposed by the building standards officer. It may be that, if the applicant has had sight of the report in time, perhaps a compromise position can be reached, especially where the premises are under construction. Perhaps the applicant can slightly modify the layout to add an additional toilet or wash hand basin to get to the magic number. If this is achievable, and parties agree, then a revised layout plan would need to be lodged showing the updated layout with additional toilet facilities.

The crucial thing for applicants to note is that capacity is not the number of people they think they can accommodate, but a number based on a proper calculation which should have regard to the non-domestic handbook. It should be left to a professional to make the appropriate calculation.

3.11.2 Off-sale capacity

The off-sale capacity of a licensed premises is where things take a more complicated turn. The "capacity" here is actually the area given over in premises to the display of alcohol. For ease of reference, the section 147(1) definition is as follows:

> "in relation to licensed premises (or any part of such premises) on which alcohol is sold for consumption off the premises (or, as the case may be, that part), the amount of space in the premises (or, as the case may be, that part) given over to the display of alcohol for sale".

A critical point to note here is that this definition does not simply relate to traditional off-sale premises but premises for which it is indicated that off-sales will occur. This means that public house, restaurant or bar premises where it is proposed that off-sales might also occur, would (in most cases) have to give both the on-sales capacity (or "occupancy capacity") and an off-sale capacity too.

For supermarkets, grocers and off-sale premises, this will usually mean the shelving and other display areas. For on-sales premises, such as bars and hotels, this will usually mean the gantry area behind the bar[63]. In gift shops it might mean miniatures on display in a glass case.

It is at this point that the novice applicant takes a deep breath and asks: "Why do they need this information?" It may be wise to take a step back from the technicalities of this to gain the answer. Remember that, under section 7 of the Act, licensing boards have a new duty to assess overprovision. Section 7(3)(a)

63 In my view this is a wholly unsatisfactory convention. Alcohol on a gantry is rarely a display from which products will actually be available for off-sale purchase. Yet, those figures are now part of overprovision assessments, and the wider statistic of how much alcohol is "on display" for off-sales in a local area is in part contributed to by this fiction.

says that the board, in considering whether there is overprovision, must have regard to the number *and capacity* of licensed premises in the locality.[64]

So, overprovision is not just overprovision in relation to numbers of licensed premises or the number of people that may frequent these premises, but there can also be an overprovision of areas given over to the display of alcohol. The thinking behind this does of course relate to the proposal that there is some form of link between the availability of alcohol, and alcohol harms. This idea is one that is all too familiar to those practising licensing law either on behalf of a health board or the trade, given there has been significant attention given to this issue and that of causality – a debate I explore in detail in Chapter 3 on the licensing objectives and elsewhere in this book. However, one should note that the concern over displays of alcohol leading to problematic behaviours is one which pre-dates the 2005 Act, and it certainly informed discussions surrounding the drafting of the Act, and the use of the term capacity, at the time. For example, in July 2005, the then Deputy Leader of Glasgow City Council said:

> "Placing alcohol around the store encourages people to buy on impulse."[65]

So exactly what information is needed? Regrettably, there are varying interpretations as to what constitutes a display and therefore an off-sales capacity.[66] The practical consensus, with a number of notable dissensions, seems to be that the off-sale capacity is the visible amount of "facing" alcohol which is actually on display to the customer, that is, the façade of the display. This can be calculated simply by multiplying the height of the display by its length and is therefore expressed as an amount of m^2. On the other hand, at least one board requires the display to be stated in linear metres, and at least one insists that the display area is not simply what the customer can see but the depth of the display as well – in other words, a cubic capacity expressed in m^3.

It is instructive to consider what was said by ministers when the off-sale capacity definition was approved at Stage 2 of the Licensing Bill. On 3 October 2005 the insertion of the off-sale capacity definition was discussed at the Local Government and Transport Committee. George Lyon, the Liberal Democrat MSP who led the amendments to the Bill on behalf of the Labour–Lib Dem coalition Government in Holyrood at that time, said:

> "For off-sales, it will be the amount of space in the premises given over to display of alcohol for sale. That will take account of the volume of alcohol on display and will catch not just shelving but other three-dimensional floor space display areas."

Fergus Ewing, the SNP MSP, queried this definition and asked:

> "Does that include shelf and floor space? In most off-sales not only is one greeted with shelves replete with multifarious alcoholic beverages, but one sees the floor jam-packed with large stacks of cans and cheap offers."

George Lyon's response was:

> "The total volume of the shelf space and floor space is included. Members will know from walking around supermarkets or any off-sales premises that they use a mixture of both."

64 Cf the amended s 23(5)(e) where there is no longer a reference to capacity.

65 See "Supermarket displays under attack" [2005] 31 SLLP 15.

66 See Lynn May and Sean Hoath, "Cutting through the capacity confusion" [2009] 40 SLLP 16 for a discussion of the varying approaches at the time of transition.

Whilst it is clear that this discussion was describing the presence of alcohol on display not just on traditional shelves but also on floor space, as opposed to a debate over cubic capacity versus linear capacity or other capacity, Mr Lyon's initial reference to *volume* and *three-dimensional floor space* here suggests that the intention of Government was to include not just a front facing display but the depth of a display too – in other words, not just the five bottles of wine in a row facing the customer, but also the six bottles each behind those five facing bottles. That is not the definitive experience in practice, with only the size of the front face or façade being the measurement used by the majority of licensing boards. Note also that there is no reference to "storage" areas but instead Mr Lyon refers to "floor space", indicating the alcohol which is in public areas only.

The matter is further complicated by regulations relating to "single display" areas. These are discussed in Chapter 15 at Section 4.15 but in short, create a condition which requires off-sale premises to indicate a single display area (a secondary area is allowed where it is inaccessible to the public, e.g. the spirit shelf behind a retail counter) where alcohol may be put on display for sale, and, having done so, that area is set in stone as a condition of the licence and alcoholic products could not be displayed anywhere else without first going back to the licensing board to seek permission to do so by way of a variation to the premises licence.

The debate on what constitutes an off-sale alcohol display is important because these numbers and capacities are used in the formulation of the overprovision assessment and in turn can be had regard to as part of considering new applications. For example, if a local area has three supermarkets and nine convenience stores, and the sum total of all of the displays of these premises amounts to 1,250m^2, and I am asking for an off-sale licence with a proposed display of 250m^2 (or any other size), it is open to the local health board or indeed any person to oppose this additional display with regard to any overprovision policy or with regard to overprovision even if there is no declared policy for that locality, and it is also open to any person to also oppose the display with respect to the public health objective. What weight the licensing board gives such submissions is of course a matter for them.

Practically speaking, what an applicant must do is understand which of the two types of capacity they wish to adopt and state them. If there is to be on-sales, then state a sensible occupancy capacity which can be justified under the building regulations. If there is off-sales, then work out the display capacity as required by the relevant local licensing board, which means getting out the measuring tape if necessary. If a predominantly on-sales premises wish also to offer an off-sale facility, then either there is a dedicated off-sale display area, in which case the measurements for that area should be given, or, if there is no dedicated area, then the likely figure which would be expected from the licensing board is the public display of alcohol within the on-sales premises, and that, in most cases, is the gantry behind the bar. In restaurant premises, for example, with numerous displays of bottles of wine across the premises on shelves or on other displays, these would be caught as they fall to be classed as alcohol which is on public display and can be purchased to take off the premises. An applicant minded to operate in this way should certainly seek advice.

Lastly, what about alcohol which is for sale via off-sales, but is not on display? That, in my view, should certainly *not* be included within the figure.

Take the example of a working brewery where there is no public access. The premises might be licensed because they have a website and take online orders for their beers, therefore selling direct to the public albeit remotely. The despatch facility requires to be licensed, namely the brewery premises, but as there is no alcohol on *public display*, as no members of the public are admitted, then the display capacity given as part of the application should be zero. Similarly, any alcohol stored away from public areas should not be counted as a part of the licensed *capacity* even though the area where the alcohol is stored will be a likely part of the licensed *premises*.

3.12 Question 8: The premises manager

Section 19 of the Act defines a "premises manager" as, in relation to any licensed premises in respect of which a premises licence has effect, the individual for the time being specified as such in the premises licence. He or she must hold a valid personal licence and may not be designated as a premises manager for more than one set of premises.[67] Question 8 requires the applicant for the premises licence to give the details of the individual who is to be nominated as such, including name, address, date of birth, and so on. There is also space to give details of the personal licence that the premises manager must hold in order to be named as such. The details of the proposed premises manager need not be given where the application is for a provisional premises licence, as the person's identity may not yet be known. In such cases, the manager's details are provided at the time of the confirmation of the provisional licence. The processes in relation to provisional licences are discussed in Chapter 11.

3.13 The Declaration

The final part of the operating plan form is another declaration to be signed by the applicant or his agent. Some licensing boards have maintained the unfortunate habit of separating the premises licence application form from the operating plan form and these have to be downloaded separately from a council website. This is confusing for party applicants who may not appreciate that the operating plan document is a part of the application. The person signing the operating plan should, in my view, be the same person who has signed the premises licence application form and it would therefore be helpful to have the two documents downloadable as a single document. Finally, the operating plan declaration makes some stipulations as to the person signing, such as: "If signing on behalf of the applicant please state in what capacity", and contains the caveat: "The contents of this operating plan are true to the best of my knowledge and belief". These simply mirror the wording at the bottom of the premises licence application form. For both, appropriate contact details should be provided.

67 There is an exception to this rule, established under s 19(2), to be found in the Licensing (Vessels etc) (Scotland) Regulations 2007 (SSI 2007/545). Special provisions for vehicles and vessels are discussed in Chapter 11 at Section 7.

4 THE LAYOUT PLAN

The administration of licensing has gone hand in hand with the production of plans for decades, but prior to the 2005 Act the "licensing drawing" was never set in statute: section 10(2)(a) of the 1976 Act simply required "a plan of the premises", and even then, no plan was required at all if the application was for an off-sale premises. This caused problems for architects and lawyers faced with different requirements in respect of detail and information to be shown from the respective Scottish licensing boards. Those who had dealt with such applications knew that the plans had to show construction, layout, drainage, ventilation, lighting, and water supply in connection with sanitary and washing facilities, as these details would be needed in order to procure a section 23 certificate in respect of food hygiene. In the event, the licensing drawing or plan became something similar to a plan for a building warrant, but with extra detail thrown in for good measure.

During the consultation on the Nicholson Report and evidence sessions throughout the passage of the Licensing (Scotland) Bill, practitioners pressed fervently to have a harmonised, legislative description of the layout plan to be used in connection with the 2005 Act. Nicholson went only as far as to suggest that an application should be accompanied:

> "by a layout plan setting out the precise location and extent of items such as bar counters, display shelving, etc."[68]

The suggestion by Nigel Don MSP, during a meeting of the Justice Committee dealing with proposed premises licence regulations (which would contain a definition of the layout plan) that a 2005 Act layout plan could be:

> "generated on a piece of graph paper by anybody with competence to use a sharp pencil and a ruler"[69]

was openly mocked by licensing practitioners at conferences and seminars, however in fairness to Mr Don his point was seeking to attract attention to potential costs to the licensed trade in engaging professional architects. The opprobrium this attracted was later rounded on by Justice Minister Kenny MacAskill, who had a pop at agents criticising this and other elements of the system, calling them "Cassandras" and adding:

> "There have also been cases where operating plans and application forms submitted by agents have fallen short in terms of the quality that might reasonably be expected. Interestingly, board staff have said that in some cases operating plans and layout plans completed by the owner of the premises have been better than those completed by agents. It seems that, while some plans have indeed been prepared by applicants using the sharp pencils and rulers so deprecated last year, it is others that need to sharpen their act."[70]

In response to the issue, Gary Cox, the then civil servant in charge of licensing wrote formally to the Justice Committee on 31 October 2007. He said:

> "I can confirm Mr Don's understanding is correct. Neither the Act nor the regulations require that the layout plan must be completed by a draughtsman or architect.

68 Nicholson Report, para 4.10, p 60.
69 30 October 2007.
70 See "MacAskill: System working well" [2009] 40 SLLP 6.

> It is however likely that many premises will wish to instruct professionals to carry out this task while others will be content to do it themselves. The operator of a large nightclub spread over various floors may be more likely to employ an architect than the owner of a small convenience store, gift shop or restaurant who may choose to prepare their own plans. Indeed, I am aware of at least one trade body that is providing templates to assist its members produce their own plans."[71]

Those who hoped that a proposed harmonisation of layout plan specifications would kick in to provide some relief during the fraught transitional period were to despair. It transpired that production of layout plans was probably the single most difficult aspect of transition, certainly in relation to those applications that were lodged in the initial March and June tranches of 2008, with plans being rejected for a variety of reasons, and each licensing board inventing their own unique set of requirements for what the plan should be, notwithstanding that the Scottish Parliament did produce regulations to detail what would be needed. In the years which have passed, from my own experience it is safe to say that the vast majority of licence applicants I have dealt with has engaged the services of an architect to draw up the layout plan. Sometimes at my urging, but in the main because where the matter relates to a new licence application then the proposed operator will regularly have engaged an architect in any event, perhaps in relation to securing planning permission, building warrants, or advising on the design and layout of the premises.

The relevant regulations are the Premises Licence (Scotland) Regulations 2007[72] and they provide an applicant with the basis of what the plan must show, known as the 'layout plan specification'. This specification, which might be best described as the base requirements given some licensing boards do insist on additional matters, is as follows:

> "(1) A layout plan is to be drawn–
> (a) in a scale where 1 millimetre represents 100 millimetres; or
> (b) in such other scale as may be agreed between the person submitting the plan and the Licensing Board to which it is to be submitted.
>
> (2) A layout plan–
> (a) is to show the matters specified in paragraph (3);
> (b) is to show the matters specified in paragraph (4) in the case of premises to be licensed for the sale of alcohol for consumption on the premises;
> (c) is to show the matters specified in paragraph (5) in the case of premises to be licensed for the sale of alcohol for consumption off the premises; and
> (d) may include a legend through which the matters mentioned or referred to in those paragraphs are sufficiently illustrated by the use of symbols on the plan.
>
> (3) The matters specified in this paragraph are–
> (a) the extent and dimensions of the boundary of the building, if relevant, and any external and internal walls of the building and, if different, the perimeter and dimensions of the premises to be licensed (including outside drinking areas);
> (b) the location and names of any streets surrounding the premises from which members of the public have access to the premises;

71 I am grateful to Adam Sinclair from the Scottish Government for locating a copy of this document for me.
72 SSI 2007 452, reg 5.

(c) the location and width of each point of access to and egress from the premises;
(d) the location and width of any other escape routes from the premises;
(e) the location of any equipment used for the detection or warning of fire or smoke or for fighting fires;
(f) the location of any steps, stairs, elevators or lifts on the premises;
(g) the location of any toilets on the premises (identified as male, female or disabled as appropriate);
(h) any area on the premises set aside specifically for the use of children and young persons; and
(i) any area on the premises to which children and young persons will have access.

(4) The matters specified in this paragraph are the use or uses to which each part of the premises will be put (under reference to the activities identified in the operating plan).

(5) The matters specified in this paragraph are–
(a) the location of the area or areas to be used for the display of alcohol;
(b) the maximum width and height (in metres) of the frontage to be used for the display of alcohol within that area or those areas; and
(c) the maximum linear measurement (in metres) of any displays of alcohol outside the frontage referred to in head (b)."

Most of these provisions have caused concerns and so each is considered in turn below.

4.1 The scale

Regulation 5(1) requires the layout plan to be in a scale of 1:100, or such other scale as the applicant and licensing board may agree on. The 1:100 scale is the most commonly used scale for licensed premises, but the 1:50 scale is often much more appropriate for smaller premises in order to bring out smaller details. It would be, in my view, very draconian for a board to insist upon a scale of 1:100 if the applicant wishes to use another scale, within reason. Some care should be taken when reproducing scaled plans. If an architect has prepared a scaled plan it may not be suitable to print it at A4 or A3 size as this would warp the scale.

4.2 Matters required under paragraph (3)

Paragraph (3) requires all licensed premises to have a layout plan with details of the dimensions of the boundary, internal and external walls, and other areas to be licensed such as external beer gardens and so on. It also requires measurements for access and egress points, and escape routes. This appears quite simple but can cause tremendous difficulty. Imagine if you will a 15-storey hotel complex – every single doorway having to be measured out and shown on the plan. I would be tempted to speak to the licensing board to see if that extreme level of detail was necessary, unless it had already been prepared by the architect.

The requirement to show names of streets from which the public have access then has to be considered. It is not a requirement to have a separate "location plan", in the way, perhaps, that a location plan was required to be submitted with a provisional grant application under the 1976 Act, section 26(2), although there is no harm in providing one if one is available. Having a location plan such as an Ordnance Survey style plan in the top right corner of the layout plan could be informative and useful, but the plan should not be rejected if no location plan is shown – as long as the layout plan itself shows the names of streets from which the public have access to the premises this should be sufficient. In some cases, squeezing a location plan on to the layout plan to fit on the same page would be impossible in any event.

The next requirement under paragraph (3) is for the layout plan to show fire-fighting equipment, smoke detection equipment, stairs, lifts, elevators and toilets. All of that is relatively straightforward, as long as the location is known, and I would only add that the detail of the toilets should include showing the cubicles, urinals, and wash-hand basins.

The final requirement under paragraph (3) is in relation to children and young persons. The layout plan is required to show the area(s) for children and young persons and area(s) to which children and young persons will have access. This may be satisfied by a simple statement on the plan to the effect that children and young persons are allowed throughout the premises. If there is a specific area, for example a raised dining area, then it is helpful to have that area labelled, lined or hatched to signify it as such.

Applicants should take care to note that some boards do have specific requirements about the way in which these areas are labelled on the plan and the licensing board statement of policy should be referred to, and a conversation with the licensing section could prove instructive. Secondly, "access corridors" could be shown on the plan in order to signify those areas that the children and young persons require to have access to, for example to the entrance and exits and toilet facilities. A form of wording I often use which appears to be accepted more often than not is "Children and Young Persons will have access throughout the public parts of the premises",[73] with perhaps the non-public parts hatched as such albeit within the "red line".

4.3 Matters required under paragraph (4)

Where it is intended that alcohol is to be sold for consumption on the premises, this activates the details required on the layout plan under paragraph (4), which are the activities to take place as described in the operating plan. This will usually mean a legend indicating the relevant activities and the areas within the premises where they take place. The requirement could be achieved by labelling each and every room or area with wording or colouring but I find that an "activity" table is much neater and clearer, so long as the rooms are labelled correctly. The most important thing here is to make sure that the descriptors used on the layout plan and any legend are the same as the language which is used in the operating plan and in the premises licence. An example of this is as shown in Table 8.2.

Perhaps a more adroit way of expressing this is to simply add the following wording to the layout plan: "Activities will take place in accordance with the approved operating plan".

73 I have dealt with cases where LSOs suggested that staff ought also to be referenced here, perhaps with wording such as "young persons employed on the premises may have access to non-public areas to carry out their duties", but I would suggest that approach is not one which is widely followed.

Table 8.2 Example wording for activity/location

Activity	*Location*
Live entertainment	Function room
Recorded music	Public bar and function room
Televised sport	Throughout premises
Indoor sport	Pool room
Gaming	Gaming machine locations are shown on plan. Poker nights take place in function room.
Restaurant meals	Raised seating area in public bar

4.4 Matters required under paragraph (5)

Where it is intended that alcohol is to be sold for consumption off the premises, this activates the details required on the layout plan under paragraph (5) – note that this does not just apply to traditional off-sale premises but to premises which have an off-sale facility such as pubs or hotels. Those details relate to the area in which alcohol is displayed (as discussed above), and therefore should indicate the physical part of the premises where alcohol is displayed, perhaps by way of a coloured line or hatching, and separately the dimensions should be shown in accordance with the custom of the relevant local licensing board.[74]

Finally, the regulations state that each premises licence application is to be accompanied by six copies of a layout plan, or such lesser number as the board may specify.[75] Some licensing boards do now accept transmission of a plan electronically, but they are a rare breed.

5 CERTIFICATES OF SUITABILITY

As noted above, an application for a premises licence must be accompanied by certificates of suitability under section 50. Before discussing the certificates, note the term "must be accompanied by" – the certificates therefore require to be obtained in advance and lodged with the application itself.[76] The timing of this is of some importance. If advising an applicant that their application might take four months (for example), has that factored in the time it might take to secure the relevant certificates of suitability? One must have a keen understanding of how each local authority issues these certificates whilst also having one eye on licensing board hearing dates and, for some

74 The rules around "single display areas" are discussed in Chapter 15 at Section 4.15.

75 Licensing (Procedure) (Scotland) Regulations 2007 (SSI 2007/453), reg 5. There is an exception to the need to produce a layout plan in respect of a vessel which is not permanently moored or berthed; a vehicle; or any other moveable structure, under the Licensing (Vessels etc) (Scotland) Regulations 2007, reg 5.

76 This is in contrast to the position under the 1976 regime, where the rule for the equivalent section 23 certificates was that an application "shall not be entertained" unless the certificates are produced to the board. In practice, most boards took the pragmatic view that this meant the certificates could be lodged at any time (within reason) up to the date of the meeting at which the application was to be heard, although one or two boards did insist the certificates were lodged with the application.

boards, last lodgement dates, in order to properly manage the expectations of the applicant.

This may have quite a dramatic effect when it is considered that, in relation to the building standards certificate, an accepted completion certificate has to be in place. In practice, this means that where the application premises are in the process of being built or completed, the applicant should take an extremely early view on the licensing process and go down the provisional premises licence route. Licensing has often been the last piece of the puzzle, after planning and the building warrant process, but it is to be ignored at the businessperson's peril. Even where a licence is being sought for an existing trading business, there could be all manner of reasons why any of the three certificates ought not to be issued. Perhaps premises have, over some time, moved from being a takeaway to a sit-down restaurant, over successive landlords or tenants. Perhaps this has happened without any regard to the Use Class under planning legislation. Applying for a licence can open many a Pandora's box.

The certificates themselves are in relation to planning,[77] building standards[78] and food hygiene.[79] Broadly speaking, the purpose of the certificates is to establish and prove that the premises are compliant with planning law, building law, and food law. To put it another way, the purpose of the certificates is to establish that the premises are safe for the public in non-licensing concerns. These underlying consents are of course necessary for a trading business in any event, but as noted above sometimes activities can go under the radar and it is the licence process that activates requirements to be undertaken such as securing correct planning permission for premises now trading as a public house but which have a Class 3 restaurant planning consent only, or seeking a retrospective building warrant for the mezzanine level which seats fifty people and is very lovely, but has no building permission.[80]

In almost all cases, there will be an application form to complete to apply for the certificate, attracting a fee, which will be sent directly to the relevant authority department. A handful of licensing boards will accept the requests directly, and then pass them on internally, but it is best to check with the board well in advance. In some areas, the planning and building standards certificate are on the same application form. In many areas there are highly specialist council officers who issue these certificates on an ongoing basis and have some experience of the licensing process and how the certificates interact with that process. In other areas, knowledge of the certificates can be hazy and it may take an applicant a few attempts before finding the appropriate officer who knows what a section 50 certificate is, far less being able to assess if one can be issued.

77 2005 Act, s 50(3)(a).
78 2005 Act, s 50(3)(b).
79 2005 Act, s 50(3)(c).
80 Whilst all of these foibles are part of the daily joys of getting through the licensing process, the wider technical issue which some operators appear to overlook is that absence of these checks and certificates would almost certainly invalidate the public liability insurance.

5.1 Certificates of suitability: planning

The purpose of planning, in very basic terms, is to give particular areas of land or premises an approval for their proposed use, so that a regime of control over development and the types of use to which land can be put can be imposed, and once that area of land has been given a particular use, it can only be used for that purpose and no other – unless an application to change the use has been granted. In licensing terms, planning is very much a precursory and prerequisite step, fundamental to the success of any new licence application. Not only will the presence of planning permission be axiomatic to the viability of a new licence application, but the permission itself may have an impact on the ultimate function of the business – for example, the planning permission could have a condition restricting the use of premises after 11pm, which could be a major problem for an operator wishing to run a nightclub.[81]

As stated above, planning permission is permission to use a piece of land or premises for a particular purpose. Those "purposes" are identified by the system of "use classes" laid down in the Schedule to the 1997 Order.[82]. Not all classes will relate to licensed premises, but to form a wider appreciation of how they fit into the use class structure, they are replicated in full here.

> **"Class 1. Shops**
> Use–
> (a) for the retail sale of goods other than hot food;
> (b) as a post office;
> (c) for the sale of tickets;
> (d) as a travel agency;
> (e) for the sale of cold food for consumption off the premises;
> (f) for hairdressing;
> (g) for the direction of funerals;
> (h) for the display of goods for sale;
> (i) for the hiring out of domestic or personal goods or articles;
> (j) launderette or dry cleaners; or
> (k) the reception of goods to be washed, cleaned or repaired;
> where the sale, display or service is principally to visiting members of the public.
>
> **Class 2. Financial, professional and other services**
> Use for the provision of–
> (a) financial services;

81 In *Di Ciacca v Scottish Ministers* 2003 SLT 1031, a wine bar proprietor appealed against a planning condition which restricted the hours of operation to between 11am and 11pm Sunday to Thursday and 11am to midnight Friday and Saturday. One of his grounds of appeal was that the planning system should not be used to regulate hours when another regulatory regime (the Licensing (Scotland) Act 1976) was in place to do just that. The court rejected this, however, holding that the planning authority could not lawfully disregard a material consideration such as the presence of a late-night wine bar on the amenity of the vicinity.

82 Town and Country Planning (Use Classes) (Scotland) Order 1997 (SI 1997/3061). Licensing practitioners may sometimes have to deal with English planning use terminology, as clients with premises on both sides of the border sometimes neglect to appreciate that Scotland has a separate planning system. The English use classes are laid down in the Town and Country Planning (Use Classes) Order 1987 (SI 1987/764) as amended. The classes relevant to licensed premises in England include: A1 (shops and sandwich bars); A3 (restaurants and cafes); A4 (drinking establishments); A5 (hot food takeaways); C1 (hotels); D2 (various leisure premises); and *sui generis* classes for nightclubs, amusement centres and casinos.

(b) professional services; or
(c) any other services (including use as a betting office);
which it is appropriate to provide in a shopping area and where the services are provided principally to visiting members of the public.

Class 3. Food and drink
Use for the sale of food or drink for consumption on the premises.

Class 4. Business
Use–
(a) as an office, other than a use within class 2 (financial, professional and other services);
(b) for research and development of products or processes; or
(c) for any industrial process;
being a use which can be carried on in any residential area without detriment to the amenity of that area by reason of noise, vibration, smell, fumes, smoke, soot, ash, dust or grit.

Class 5. General industrial
Use for the carrying on of an industrial process other than one falling within class 4 (business).

Class 6. Storage or distribution
Use for storage or as a distribution centre.

Class 7. Hotels and hostels
Use as a hotel, boarding house, guest house, or hostel where no significant element of care is provided, other than premises licensed for the sale of alcoholic liquor to persons other than residents or to persons other than persons consuming meals on the premises and other than a use within class 9 (houses).

Class 8. Residential institutions
Use–
(a) for the provision of residential accommodation and care to people in need of care other than a use within class 9 (houses);
(b) as a hospital or nursing home; or
(c) as a residential school, college or training centre.

Class 9. Houses
Use –
(a) as a house, other than a flat, whether or not as a sole or main residence, by–
(i) a single person or by people living together as a family, or
(ii) not more than 5 residents living together including a household where care is provided for residents;
(b) as a bed and breakfast establishment or guesthouse, where at any one time not more than 2 bedrooms are, or in the case of premises having less than 4 bedrooms 1 bedroom is, used for that purpose.

Class 10. Non-residential institutions
Use, not including residential use–
(a) as a crèche, day nursery or day centre;
(b) for the provision of education;
(c) for the display of works of art (otherwise than for sale or hire);
(d) as a museum;
(e) as a public library or public reading room;
(f) as a public hall or exhibition hall; or
(g) for, or in connection with, public worship or religious instruction, or the social or recreational activities of a religious body.

Class 11. Assembly and leisure
Use as a –
(a) cinema;
(b) concert hall;
(c) bingo hall or casino;
(d) dance hall or discotheque; or
(e) swimming bath, skating rink, gymnasium or area for other indoor or outdoor sports or recreation, not involving motorised vehicles or firearms."

In terms of the Licensing (Scotland) Act 2005, we need to examine these different classes to understand how the Use Class system fits into the section 50 structure. Class 1 will cover off-sales premises such as shops or supermarkets; class 3 covers on-sales premises such as restaurants – but not public house style premises (see below). Class 7 relates to hotel premises but uses language more keenly linked to the previous 1976 Act regime, noting the differentiation as to guests; under which there were separate rules for "restricted" hotel licences and "full" hotel licences; and class 11 would seem to apply to some licensed premises where entertainment other than alcohol consumption might be the main purpose of that premises.

One of the most common issues you come up against is where the premises are proposed to operate as a bar or traditional public house. Article 3(5) of the 1997 Order states '*Nothing in any class shall include any use as* [amongst others] *a public house.*' This has led to a *sui generis*, meaning unique or "of-its-own" category – sometimes referred to a "mixed-use development" class use for public houses, and this can lead to complications. The critical point is that class 3 use on its own is not enough to support an application for a premises licence for a traditional bar or pub – it will only be of use for a restaurant or café style offer. The planning permission will typically require special wording to include the words "public house" for the avoidance of any doubt. When applying for the section 50 certificate, the planners might wish to view the proposed operating plan to ensure that it meets their understanding of the existing or proposed use class. If the premises have morphed from an unlicensed restaurant into a bar, and the operator is now seeking a licence, then it is unlikely the section 50 certificate will be issued; and a planning application for change of use would be required. Only after that planning application were approved would the section 50 certificate be issued.

The next issue is the difference in the definitions of hotel premises. As readers may have noted above, class 7 does not relate to premises where the premises licence can be used to serve non-residents as a matter of course. Again, this language harks back to the 1976 Act regime where there was a normal "hotel licence" which allowed non-resident consumption, and a special "restricted hotel licence" on which only residents could consume alcohol, or non-residents where alcohol was consumed with a meal.[83] This

83 In *Donald v Stirling Licensing Board* 1992 SLT (Sh Ct) 75, a hotelier trading from a restricted hotel licence was granted a full hotel licence, and objectors to the application appealed the decision. In order to support the application with the relevant certificates of suitability under the Licensing (Scotland) Act 1976, s 23, the hotelier produced a certificate from planning which, although stating there was permission for a "hotel licence", was defective as the type of hotel licence it referred to was a restricted hotel licence in terms of the class use. The decision to grant the application was therefore based on an incorrect material fact and the decision was reversed.

planning treatment now has no link or nexus with the 2005 Act licensing regime where different categories of licence no longer exist. The planning treatment of what is now a rather old-fashioned construct in relation to hotels and guests has led to another *sui generis* or stand-alone class use to support applications for "full" hotel premises and again the planning permission should specifically reflect this even though it makes *little* technical difference to the licensing regime whether premises are a hotel or a guest house with no public bar.[84]

Finally, there is the question of the use class for a proposal that relates to some form of premises where there is a public entertainment, which might also sell alcohol. As noted above, class 11 covers a wide variety of premises such as nightclubs and concert halls, but alcohol licences may also exist at a myriad of other types of very specific premises such as tourist attractions, arts centres, bowling alleys, cinemas, and so on. What is sometimes required (though not always) is a planning permission which actually incorporates the use of the premises or part of the premises for the sale of alcohol. An example of the wording used in a planning permission in this regard could be: "Community art and theatre venue with licensed bar and café". The key element for our purposes is not necessarily the planning permission for the form of entertainment, but that the planning permission supports a licensed use for that entertainment premises. It could be that planning permission has been granted for some form of entertainment venue but with a specific condition that no alcohol may be sold. If that were to be the case, then clearly the planners would not be issuing a section 50 certificate and the proposed licence applicant would have to apply to the planning department to have the condition removed.

Assuming all is well and the correct planning permission is in place, the section 50 planning certificate must be signed on behalf of the appropriate authority,[85] typically by a head planning officer or a deputy, and may state either that planning permission under the Town and Country Planning (Scotland) Act 1997 has been obtained or that no such permission is required. A separate form of certificate for a provisional premises licence is catered for, where there is provisional planning permission in place; this is discussed further below.

5.2 Certificates of suitability: building standards

The building standards certificate is again signed off by the appropriate authority (or officer on behalf of the authority) and states one of the following:

84 The only slight difference is potentially in relation to fees. There is a possibility that the "guest house" which only serves residents could attract a lower application fee. Whilst there is no other technical or legal difference under the 2005 Act between different classes of commercial accommodation premises such as hotels, guest houses and everything in between, these differences could have an impact on the prospects of any new licence application based on the merits of the application and how it fits with the licensing objectives and the other grounds of refusal of a licence. For example, a neighbouring resident might not oppose a guest house next door having a small alcohol offer for bona fide residents, but may not be best pleased with the idea of the guest house also offering a public bar.

85 The "appropriate authority" is not always a council: e.g. certain areas in Scotland are covered by a park authority.

- a completion certificate has been accepted under the Building (Scotland) Act 2003, s 18 in respect of any construction or conversion of the subject premises in connection with their proposed use as licensed premises,
- permission for the temporary occupation or use of the premises has been granted under the 2003 Act, s 21(3), or
- no such certificate or permission is required.

In short terms, the building standards certificate confirms that the building to which the licence application relates has been built correctly and is safe for the public to be in. The issue of a completion certificate or a temporary occupation certificate relates to a warrant being granted in the first place. When one wishes to construct or carry out warrantable works to premises, an application must be made to the building standards department of the local authority. A building standards officer will review this and if all is well, perhaps after some to-ing and fro-ing and amendment of plans and so on, will issue a warrant, which is the permission needed to start the works.

The "completion" certificate is a certificate lodged to the building standards officer to confirm that the build of the premises has been completed *with respect to the warrant*. If there have been elements of the build which have changed as the project has gone on, these would need to be approved by the warrant officer probably through a formal amendment to warrant application. Lodging a completion certificate is not the same as "accepting" a completion certificate, which is effectively a separate document issued by the building standards officer to confirm that they agree the works have been done and all is well.

The specific building standards officer dealing with the warrant and completion certificate may or may not be the officer who is dealing with the issue of the section 50 certificate, and, if they are not one and the same, then the applicant or his agent has some work to do and needs to make sure communication levels are robust to procure the certificate as early as possible, and that it is not forgotten with the acceptance of the separate completion certificate.

The difference between the issue of a completion certificate and that of a temporary occupation permission comes down to how much of the premises is complete. If the full works are done and all tickety-boo, a completion certificate could be issued. If there are some minor snagging issues which would not affect public safety, then the building standards officer has the flexibility to issue the temporary occupation permission, to allow the premises to open to the public. This flexibility will only be given where the officer is satisfied that the outstanding matters will not impact on the safety of customers and he or she will also no doubt seek undertakings and assurances from the architect or developer that the snagging will be remedied in short order. A temporary occupation permission is sufficient to release the section 50 certificate for licensing, but of course the final works still need to be done so that a completion certificate can be issued to finalise matters from the building regulation perspective.

It may be the case that no completion certificate or temporary occupation permission from building standards is needed. It would only be needed if warrantable works were being done or proposed to be done in order to establish or trade the premises as licensed premises. For example, if the application related to established premises which were trading as an unlicensed restaurant, then it may be sufficient for the building standards officer to simply issue the section 50 certificate stating that no completion certificate is needed – thus giving the "green light".

5.3 Certificates of suitability: food hygiene

The main legislation governing this area is the Food Safety Act 1990 and the Food Hygiene (Scotland) Regulations 2006,[86] although it should be noted that there are vast swathes of EU and national regulations covering food safety and hygiene. Section 1 of the 1990 Act provides that the legal definition of "food" includes drink (that is, all drink including alcoholic and non-alcoholic drink) and at section 3 sets out a presumption that food supplied is to be fit for human consumption. The Act empowers officers of the relevant local authority to enter licensed premises to inspect food intended for human consumption,[87] and to issue notices if the food is found to be non-compliant with food safety requirements.[88] Officers may also issue "improvement notices" where they feel a food business is not complying with regulations, and failure to comply with such a notice is an offence,[89] but note that as with other regulatory regimes discussed in this book, there is a due diligence defence available.[90]

The food hygiene certificate is signed on behalf of the appropriate authority to confirm that the premises comply with the Food Safety Act 1990:

- relating to construction, layout, drainage, ventilation, lighting and water supply or concerned with the provision of sanitary and washing facilities.

Typically, these matters would require to be shown on the layout plan that would be sent in support of a licence application and in turn circulated internally from the licensing section to their council colleagues in environmental standards. The environmental standards officer would then ascertain whether the food preparation areas and so on appear to be in accordance with the regulations.

Is a standard licensing layout plan sufficiently detailed to allow an officer to satisfy himself as to compliance in areas such as drainage or ventilation? In my experience it is not uncommon to have a food officer contact me to ask for layout plans to be amended or to have additional details added to allow them to carry out their tasks. The most common approach here is to apply for a provisional licence, where there is no need to issue a food hygiene certificate at the point of application. Assuming the licensing board grants the provisional licence, the applicant would request the certificate thereafter and deal with the food hygiene officer then. It may be possible to secure a food hygiene section 50 certificate for an existing trading business such as our old friend the unlicensed restaurant. One would hope that the premises are already compliant and therefore there should be no difficulty in issuing the section 50 certificate.

Note that section 50(1)(c) only requires a food hygiene certificate to be produced "if food is to be supplied on the premises". Perhaps this wording

86 SSI 2006/3.
87 Food Safety Act 1990, s 32.
88 Food Safety Act 1990, s 9.
89 Food Safety Act 1990, s 10(2).
90 Food Safety Act 1990, s 21.

was drafted by someone who thought that premises without meals on offer – that is, a wet led bar – could escape this requirement; however, the 1990 Act defines "food" as including drink – this includes alcoholic drink – so the reality is that a food hygiene certificate is required for every single licensed premises, making the section 50(1)(c) qualification redundant.

Operators should note that there is a separate requirement unconnected to the section 50 process or the licensing process known as "food premises registration". This is a requirement to register with the local authority's environmental food hygiene department and is dealt with under the Food Premises (Registration) Regulations 1991,[91] regulation 2 of which states: "No person shall use any premises for the purposes of a food business . . . unless those premises are registered." The registration request should be intimated at least twenty-eight days in advance of the first day of the use of the premises, and will normally be by way of a standard application form attracting no fee. Potential licence holders should refer to their local authority for further information on this process as it is often overlooked.

6 THE DISABLED ACCESS AND FACILITIES STATEMENT

The newest requirement for a premises licence application is that it must now contain a "disabled access and facilities statement", this provision having been inserted into the 2005 Act[92] by virtue of section 179 of the Criminal Justice and Licensing (Scotland) Act 2010 and fortified by the Premises Licence (Scotland) Amendment Regulations 2018,[93] which came into force, and thus commenced the requirement to produce the statement, on 30 March 2018.

For the purposes of the statement, the term "disabled persons" is to be interpreted with regard to section 6 of the Equality Act 2010. Section 6(1) says:

> "(1) A person (P) has a disability if—
> (a) P has a physical or mental impairment, and
> (b) the impairment has a substantial and long-term adverse effect on P's ability to carry out normal day-to-day activities."

The 2018 Regulations prescribe the form of the statement, which are worth noting here to explore. The form asks three key questions:

- Is there disabled access to the premises?
- Do you have facilities for those with a disability?
- Do you have any other provisions available to aid the use of the premises by disabled people?

These initial queries are then supplemented by more open-ended queries with space to provide detailed information. With respect to access, the form states:

> "**Disabled access to, from and within the premises**
> Please provide clear and detailed description of how accessible the premises are for disabled people. e.g. ramps, accessible floors, signage."

91 SI 1991/2825.
92 At section 20(2)(b)(iia).
93 SSI 2018/49.

The type of response you may see in this section could be something along the following lines:

> "The premises have a street level main door which can be opened automatically by way of a panel."

> "The premises are located at the bottom of a set of 14 circular steps leading to the basement where the main door is. There is no wheelchair access to the premises as a result."

The crucial point here is that the purpose of the statement is to provide knowledge of what facilities are there, not to criticise said facilities (see below).

The next part of the form asks for more details on the facilities available:

> "**Facilities available**
> Please describe in detail the facilities provided for disabled people. e.g. disabled toilets, lifts, accessible tables."

Examples of the type of thing you might see here could be:

> "A lift is located on the ground floor allowing access to the mezzanine level, and to the basement. The ground floor is laid out so as to provide plenty of room for manoeuvrability for walking aids and devices."

> "There is no disabled or accessible toilet on the premises."

Again I give these polarised examples to indicate that the statement should be what the fact of the matter is. Premises may have exceptional disabled facilities. They may have no facilities at all. Whatever the factual position is should be stated.

The final part of the statement is about "other provisions":

> "**Other provisions**
> Please provide details of any other provisions made to aid the use of the premises by disabled people. e.g. assistance dogs welcome, large print menus."

Statements here might include confirming that assistance dogs are indeed welcome, or that there is a hearing aid induction loop, or other facilities which are about the customer experience as opposed to access to the premises. The answer to this question could well be "None".

The existence of the disabled access and facilities statement requirement can be traced back and credited to the "Barred!" campaign[94] which highlighted the lack of facilities for disabled persons in bars and pubs, in particular in Edinburgh where the campaign began, but also across Scotland. It is rare that a single-issue campaign, led in the main by one person through social media, achieves legislative reform so the efforts of those involved should be commended. As a person with a close family member who has difficulty walking, it is an issue I keenly understand as it is very frustrating to have

94 See, for example, "Pub disability law passed in Scotland", *Morning Advertiser*, 1 July 2010; "Disability activist gets accessible pubs licensing law passed at the Parliament", *The Guardian*, 2 July 2010. *The Guardian* article includes a quote from then "Labour party activist" Kezia Dugdale, who would go on to lead the party: "We knew it was going to be really hard to get licence holders to change their facilities, as many of the buildings are old and hard to convert." She says that the new law doesn't automatically require pubs to change their facilities, but it does require them to complete a compliance form showing what disabled facilities they do or don't have."

your options limited because of lack of accessibility, and the issues that the unknown can bring.

It is worth discussing how the statement is used at the coal face of licensing hearings. One of the key difficulties could be said to be how a licensing board should deal with the statement. The licensing board itself is not a body entitled to or expected to reach a view on the quality or otherwise of disabled access, so it would be difficult for them to reach a view, if indeed a view were to be reached. There is nothing here which requires the board to "assess" or criticise the statement. One can see how the assessment might be linked to the "suitability" ground of refusal but a refusal based on inadequate disabled facilities is unlikely to sit with the general precept of the 2005 Act and the "essential aim" of the licensing board being about the regulation of alcohol, nor would such a refusal stand up to scrutiny, I would suggest, in relation to the legal concept of "improper purpose" and noting a number of appeal decisions in this regard, not least the infamous *Brightcrew* case.[95]

The reality is that the intention of Parliament was not to introduce an assessment by licensing boards of disabled access and facilities, but instead for the information to be part of the licensing process and therefore publicly available. The Explanatory Notes to the 2010 Act explain it thus:

> "T[he] statement is to contain information about disabled access to the subject premises and the facilities or any other provision available to aid the use of the premises by disabled people. Failure to provide this statement is not a ground for refusing an application. Rather, it would mean the premises licence application would be incomplete. The application could not therefore be considered by the Licensing Board as it would not be a valid application under section 20(2). A premises application which is accompanied by the statement would require to be determined by the Licensing Board in the normal way according to section 23 of the 2005 Act."[96]

The information in the statement will be on the public register and therefore persons interested in knowing what facilities there may or may not be, can take an educated and informed choice about whether a set of premises is appropriate for their needs.

In some cases, licensing boards might ask for a report on the statement to be issued as part of the application process by officers from building standards. But even so, whilst building standards may take a view on physical access issues and building regulations, it is of some doubt that a licensing board can take a view on other "facilities" such as hearing aid loops, braille menus, or even general staff training on how best to facilitate persons with specific disabilities other than one of general and well-intended query.

If a disabled customer believes that they have experienced some form of discrimination because of their disability, or have experienced access or facilities issues, this should be raised with the premises operator directly and perhaps matters can be addressed to the satisfaction of both parties. If necessary, a civil legal action could be raised. Ultimately, however, the Equality and Human Rights Commission[97] was specifically empowered by the Equality Act 2010 to enforce its terms, not a Scottish licensing board.

95 Cf *William Hill (Caledonian) Ltd v City of Glasgow Licensing Board* 2003 SLT 668.

96 Paragraphs 750 and 751, Explanatory Notes to s 179 of the Criminal Justice and Licensing (Scotland) Act 2010.

97 www.equalityhumanrights.com.

When the requirement for the statement was first introduced in 2018, it piqued the attention of some licensing board members and for a while applicants and their agents faced scrutiny over the statement. However, my experience is that this has now largely dissipated and the statement might only be mentioned where a third party has raised an issue such as a resident objecting to a premises licence because he or she does not believe the proposals go far enough to cater for disabled access. Such a resident is likely to be advised by the clerk or the chair of the board that their power as a licensing board can only go so far.

7 SUPPLEMENTARY INFORMATION REQUIRED WITH A PREMISES LICENCE APPLICATION

Some licensing boards, not content with the premises licence and operating plan, have sought further information and detail from applicants, including fire assessments, risk assessments, and "licensing objectives statements". One board even doctored the application form to introduce a new question seeking to establish if a fire assessment had been conducted, and to provide proof – notwithstanding the fact that the format of the application form is laid down in statute and cannot be tinkered with. I have sought to identify these additional documents and details to reflect the reality of what some licensing boards may request, but it should be noted that there is no legal basis to have these accompany a premises licence application.

7.1 Fire assessments

Fire assessments are a legal requirement under the Fire (Scotland) Act 2005. That Act makes several provisions for enforcement of the regime by the relevant fire authority and, in my view, attempts by the licensing board to get involved are unnecessary and a duplication of administration. The applicant, however, should take their own view on this.

7.2 Risk assessments

Risk assessments are required under the general health and safety laws. Some boards used the transition process as a vehicle to enforce other statutory regimes such as this one and asked conversion applicants to produce general risk assessments.[98] This practice died out; up until the onset of the Coronavirus recovery period when operators seeking to take advantage of the ability to utilise new outdoor facilities were tasked with producing "social distancing" related assessments for the use of said areas.[99] In relation to the generality, licensed premises must have a risk assessment in place; but it is not a matter for a licensing board to investigate.

98 See "Risk Assessments" [2008] 39 SLLP 12.

99 See Appendix I on the Coronavirus (Scotland) Act 2020.

7.3 Licensing objectives statements

Several boards require applicants to supplement their application with a statement as to how they will seek to uphold the five licensing objectives. This is not a statutory requirement but as the practice is well established in some areas, many agents will provide a statement in order to smooth the passage of the application. However, it is also true that whilst some boards will ask for the statement they will not actively pursue it, or seek to chastise the applicant due to its absence (making one wonder why they ask for it at all). A licensing board could in theory seek to rely on section 23(5)(c), which states that a ground of refusal for a premises licence is that the granting of the application would be "inconsistent with one or more of the licensing objectives". Asking for the statement, it is argued, assists the board in considering whether that ground of refusal might apply. However, the Act is clear about what documents need to submitted, and there is a further natural law point about the request inverting the onus of the burden of proof: that is, whether it is for the applicant to prove his application is consistent with the objectives, or for the board to find on the basis of the evidence that it is inconsistent with the objectives. It is, of course, for the board to prove inconsistency, but this should be on an evidence-led basis.

The inclusion of such statements was actively rejected as a statutory requirement by the Scottish Government when the application format was adopted under the Premises Licence (Scotland) Regulations 2007. In a debate on 30 November 2007, the then Justice Minister Kenny MacAskill said:

> "Glasgow City Council licensing board asks that a new section be added to the form to require all applicants to write a paragraph stating how they will comply with the licensing objectives. The proposal was considered carefully by the sub-group, but it was rejected. The sub-group took the view that such a section was unnecessary and raised concerns that it would be bewildering for applicants, who would either end up writing meaningless nonsense just to keep the licensing board happy or feel under pressure to go to the otherwise unnecessary expense of employing the services of a legal expert to complete the forms. Such a requirement would be an unnecessary burden on the licensed trade for no apparent advantage. In addition, Scotland's licensing lawyers might simply develop a standard paragraph that could be stamped into every form to comply with the requirements. Nothing has changed since that decision was taken by the sub-group that developed the forms. I am satisfied that the forms as presented provide enough information to enable the licensing board to determine whether an application would compromise its licensing objectives. The new Act also makes sufficient provision for monitoring and inspection to ensure that the licensing objectives are upheld. If the objectives are not upheld, a review of a licence can be initiated."

MacAskill's comment about the use of generic statements is well made. Considering an opposite impact to a "standard" wording adopted by licensing lawyers, if the application is submitted by someone without any proper legal knowledge of the objectives the statement may be poor or worthless. The statement may simply restate what has been entered into the premises licence application and operating plan and is therefore unnecessary repetition, or the content may stray outside the licensing sphere. In all of these cases, I suggest that the utility of the statement is debatable. A final concern is about what happens to these statements after they have been lodged – in what ways could they be relied upon in the future? There was concern that such statements would be turned into conditions on the licence, as happened in some jurisdictions in England.[100] That has not proven to be the case in Scotland but there are examples of licence holders having their statements "read back to them" when perhaps they face scrutiny subsequently to receiving the licence.

The following are generic examples of the types of basic statements that a licensing board might come across, but, as noted above, the value of these is left to the reader to decide.

Preventing crime and disorder

- All staff are trained when they are first employed, and periodically by way of refresher training.
- There is effective supervision of staff at all times by the manager or assistant manager on duty.
- ID is required in the form of passports and photographic driving licences.
- The premises have fixed external lighting on the walls.
- Fixed bins are provided externally for smokers.
- All glasses are made of reinforced glass.

Securing public safety

- The occupancy capacity of the premises will be adhered to.
- The premises are well maintained.
- Escape routes and exits are kept clear at all times.
- The toilets are checked on a regular basis.
- The premises have a glass clearance policy.
- There are training sessions for fire alarm drills and training on equipment.
- First aid facilities are provided throughout the premises.

Preventing public nuisance

- Deliveries are kept to a specific window of time where possible.
- Smokers are provided with fixed bins within a designated area.
- A taxi marshal is used to expedite patrons at closing time.
- The premises are fitted with soundproofing.

Protecting and improving public health

- Staff are vigilant at all times to prevent risks of excessive consumption of alcohol.
- There are no irresponsible promotions.
- There is a wide variety of non-alcoholic beverages available.
- There is a "driver's shelf" in the bar.
- There is a substantial healthy food offer in the premises.

Protecting children and young persons from harm

- No children and young persons are allowed in the premises.
- Children and young persons are monitored by staff at all times.
- Children and young persons are only admitted when accompanied by an adult.

If a licensing objectives statement is required, it should of course be tailored to suit the individual premises, and these are merely given as some illustrative examples I have come across in practice.

100 Note, however, that under the 2003 Act the "operating schedule" (the English equivalent of the operating plan) actively requires applicants to give statements as to how the four licensing objectives will be upheld.

8 PREMISES LICENCE FEES

Under the 1976 Act, a licence in force would attract fees of £86 to renew the licence triennially, £86 annually for a regular extension, and £86 triennially for a children's certificate. Under the 2005 Act, there is a single one-off fee to apply for a premises licence, but then an annual fee that must be paid in order to keep the licence in force.

The fee regime is supposed to be based on an appreciation of how much the local authority incurs in the expense of administering the licensing system.[101] In other words, the administration of the system should be cost-neutral. The 2005 Act proceeded on this basis due to evidence from local authorities that the taxpayer had been subsidising the licensing system for years.[102] However, the Scottish Parliament was quite shrewd and, instead of setting exact fees, set a maximum up to which the boards themselves could determine the fee to be used, much to the chagrin of licensing lawyers up and down the country at that time, who had been looking forward to a uniformity of fees.

The response to this at the onset of the 2005 Act was that some licensing boards simply elected to charge the full amount, but others conducted a cost-analysis exercise and tried to set the fees at a level that would fund the regulation of the licensing system without profit. At the time of conversion to the new licensing system, there were indications that some boards had ingathered a surplus of some consideration.[103] Through the hue and cry of the transitional period, the Scottish Parliament indicated that it would review the fee levels after 1 September 2009, but such attempts have proven ill-fated (see below).

To provide context for the policy objective behind the fee levels in the Regulations noted immediately below, the Executive Note states:

> "The purpose of the instrument is to provide for the fees to be charged by Licensing Boards in relation to various matters under the Licensing (Scotland) Act 2005. The instrument employs a variety of methods – flat-rate fees for personal licences, minor variations, occasional licenses [sic] and applications for extended hours; a capped range of fee values tied to the rateable value of a property for premises licence applications, annual fees, and provisional licence confirmations. It further allows Licensing Boards to set various fees in relation to more routine processes carried out under the Act. This approach is designed to ensure the right balance is achieved between consistency across Scotland, proportionality relative to the size of the premises, and flexibility for each Licensing Board to ensure they can fully meet their running costs from fee income.
>
> …
>
> The method of determining the fees payable with an application for a premises licence is based on the rateable value of the premises. This fulfils the needs for the system to be simple, and, broadly speaking, ensures that businesses which will take up more of the Licensing Boards' time and resources in processing applications pay more than smaller premises.

101 Licensing (Fees) (Scotland) Regulations 2007 (SSI 2007/553), reg 13.

102 In 2003, Brian Adam MSP for Aberdeen North advised that the costs met by Aberdeen City Council were equivalent to £807 for every three-year period: "MSP calls for end to licence subsidies" [2003] 25 SLLP 5.

103 On 17 April 2008, the Edinburgh Licensing Board announced it had made a surplus of some £233,000, procured solely from the new licensing fees it had received from the March tranche of conversion applications. This was despite the fact that the Edinburgh board had set its fees lower than the statutory maximum.

There is a view that some premises with a high rateable value but which only generate a small proportion of their income from alcohol sales are disproportionately affected by these proposals. The independent research which formed the basis of the Government's consideration of fee arrangements accepts that this is possible but concludes that the overall benefits of the system chosen far outweigh the disadvantages.

The research shows that the vast majority of premises (82%) fall into the lowest 3 rateable value categories. Within that, 51% of premises will fall into either category 1 or 2 and will therefore pay application fees up to £200 or up to £800 respectively, and annual fees of up to £180 or up to £220 respectively. It is important to note that category 1 contains premises (as set out in regulation 4) which are to be included in the lowest category regardless of their rateable value. For example, registered clubs are automatically included in the lowest category, along with visitor attractions and Bed and Breakfast type establishments where alcohol is only available to guests. This approach is considered proportionate and equitable. Only the largest premises, for example large supermarkets, are likely to fall into the highest category.

The application fees are capped at a higher level than the annual fee because, as the research points out, the costs of processing an application are likely to be higher than the ongoing costs of monitoring compliance with the new licensing system and the running costs of Boards after completion of the transition period.

The Regulations provide that the annual fee levels quoted are to be the maximum amounts chargeable – there is an expectation that Licensing Boards may require to charge at or close to the full fees quoted to cover their costs initially (as anticipated by the research report), but thereafter may begin to benefit from the efficiencies of the new system and be able to pass these savings on to the trade."

The Executive Note goes on to address impact on small business by declaring:

"The use of rateable values as a determinant of fee level is specifically designed to make the fee proportionate to the size of the business. Small businesses will also tend to have less personal licence holders per premises, minimising the cost arising from personal licence applications and renewals of these licences 10 years thereafter."

Despite these lofty aspirations, the reliance on rateable value meant that some premises, at the time of conversion, simply gave up their licence as alcohol was a small or ancillary part of their business. The sometimes arbitrary approach to how rates are assessed led to calls for the fee system to be abolished, although this came to nought.[104]

In any event, the maximum fees[105] that may be charged are laid down in the Licensing (Fees) (Scotland) Regulations 2007[106] and are shown in Table 8.3.

104 In 2011 the then Justice Minister Kenny MacAskill commented in Parliament to the effect that the use of rateable values had created "distortions" in the then system, and instigated a review. The review was not, however, able to put forward a credible alternative (see "Macaskill promises licensing fees review" [2011] 50 SLLP 5).

105 The costs were described as a "lurking horror" by now-retired licensing solicitor James Scott at [2004] 28 SLLP 10, and on 4 November 2008 Conservative Chris Walker lodged a petition with the Scottish Parliament against the fee levels, on the principal basis that they would hurt rural businesses, but also that the legislation did "not tackle irresponsible drinking, [it] serves only as another stealth tax on an industry already financially stretched. We need to promote tourism not kick it in the teeth": see *Morning Advertiser*, 4 November 2008.

106 See regs 5, 6 and 8.

Table 8.3 Licence fees

Category	*Rateable value*	*Premises licence fee*	*Annual fee*
1	None/Special	£200	£180
2	£1–£11,500	£800	£220
3	£11,501–£35,000	£1,100	£280
4	£35,001–£70,000	£1,300	£500
5	£70,001–£140,000	£1,700	£700
6	over £140,000	£2,000	£900

8.1 Premises licence fees – the "special categories"

Category 1 requires a little elaboration as it is a special category for particular premises, *viz*:

- premises not entered on the valuation roll, or where there is no rateable value or a nil value shown in respect of them on that roll,
- premises whose main function is to provide a visitor attraction and any sale of alcohol is for consumption off the premises only, and is considered by the board to be incidental to other activities on the premises,
  club premises, and
- premises whose main function is to provide accommodation, are not open to the public except to provide accommodation, and any alcohol sold on the premises is to be consumed on the premises by guests accommodated there.

8.1.1 Premises not on the valuation roll

An example of where this may apply could be off-sale premises for a convenience store set within an armed forces facility, but not behind security checkpoints. The shop will likely not have its own entry on the valuation roll, as the facility will have a single entry. I discuss a number of issues arising from the valuation roll earlier in this chapter, but in relation to those premises which are part of larger facilities, as regulation 5(4) states that "appropriate rateable value" of licensed premises means the "rateable value shown on the valuation roll in respect of those premises or of larger premises of which they form part", I am unaware of any successful arguments to reduce the amount.

8.1.2 Premises which are visitor attractions

I have to say that this provision surprised me when I was reviewing the Act in preparation for this book. I am not aware of any examples of licensing boards allowing this dispensation.

8.1.3 Club premises

Whilst club premises – that is, not-for-profit members' clubs and the like – are treated as licensed premises for the purposes of the 2005 Act (as they fall within the legal definition of "licensed premises"), the Act does make several concessions for these premises, including putting them in the lowest fee category regardless of rateable value. The 2005 Act treatment of club premises is covered in detail in Chapter 11 at Section 2.

8.1.4 Guest accommodation

It is interesting to note that the dispensation given here, namely a lower application fee for premises where there is no "public" consumption of alcohol, is perhaps one of the last vestiges of the old 1976 system which separated the concept of "hotel licences" and "restricted hotel licences" to reflect premises which had letting rooms but also perhaps a full bar and restaurant, and other premises which had letting rooms but no public bar or restaurant – that is, where only bona fide residents can consume alcohol. Reflecting on this, I do wonder how many such premises did actually take the benefit of this lower fee. I would not be surprised if many operators of such premises simply paid the higher fee, with both the applicant and indeed the licensing board perhaps overlooking this discount provision.

8.2 The annual fee

The payment of the annual fee, the level of which is noted in Table 8.3, is actually a mandatory condition under Schedule 3. The licensing board must send a notification or reminder to each holder of a premises licence, no later than 30 days before the date on which the fee is due and must specify the level of fee required. The first annual fee falls due on 1 October following the grant of the licence,[107] and subsequent annual fees are all payable on 1 October of each year, or the following Monday if that date is a Saturday or Sunday.[108]

The licensing board may allow payment of the annual fee to be made in quarterly or monthly instalments[109] although this is a rarity. Non-payment of the annual fee is a criminal offence as it is a condition of the licence, and therefore an offence under section 1(1). Many licensing boards will institute review hearings of their own volition under section 37 of the Act, in order to try and deal with non-payment of the fee. Typically, the offending licensees will pay up in advance of the hearing. If this does not occur then some boards will suspend the licence until such time as the fee is paid, or even revoke the licence[110]. In some licensing board areas, an application for transfer may be halted by the board if there are unpaid annual fees, although there is no statutory mechanism for this and it is generally agreed that the debt sits with the licence holder, not the premises.

Notwithstanding the examples of practice I highlight in the preceding paragraph, it should also be noted that using the review mechanism to seek payment of the annual fee is not without its detractors. There is no doubt that non-payment of the fee can be subject to a competent application for review of the licence, or, to use the language of section 37, a competent review

107 Although watch out for a pro rata charge following grant or confirmation of a licence.

108 Regulation 7.

109 Regulation 7(4).

110 The approach in Aberdeen City is to vary the licensed hours to zero, thus preventing trade until such times as the board is happy to grant a section 40 "review" to reverse the variation (on which see Chapter 14 at Section 7.1)

"proposal". It is also clear that breach of a condition, which is what non-payment is, is a specific ground of review under section 36(3), which applies to the review proposal process under section 37. Further, it is also clear that, as a matter of fact, the section 39 requirement for "grounds to be established" is engaged because either the fee has been paid on time or it has not. However, it has been argued that there could be some difficulty in imposing a sanction in these circumstances, because the sanctions under section 39 may only be imposed where the board "considers necessary or appropriate for the purposes of any of the licensing objectives"; and that a technical or administrative issue such as non-payment of the annual fee cannot give sufficient substance to create a lawful link to one of the objectives. To put it another way, how does non-payment detract from public health, or public safety? How does non-payment of an administrative fee relate to the sale or consumption of alcohol, which is the prism through which the objectives are properly understood? Is the purpose of the licensing Act to allow its terms to be utilised to assist in the collection of a civil debt?

It may be argued successfully in response to such suggestions that the non-payment of the annual fee is a licensing offence and therefore a criminal matter, and in turn that the objective of preventing crime and disorder is engaged. The short title of the Act does, of course, refer to those mysterious sounding "connected purposes" which can be read as to relate to the administration of the licensing system. The system is funded through the ingathering of the fees, and on that basis a sanction under section 39 following a review proposal under section 37 would be lawful. The matter may yet be tested in the courts.

Chapter 9

Premises Licences – Part 3 Administration

1 ADMINISTRATION OF A PREMISES LICENCE APPLICATION

Having looked above at the detail of the application form, and the details of the documents and assorted ephemera which must accompany a premises licence application, we now turn to consider how the application is administered and processed.

The 2005 Act has placed a substantial amount of work in the hands of the clerk and their staff and, once the licence application has passed over the counter, they must perform several duties which were not required under the 1976 regime. The first duty after the application has been received is not specifically mentioned in the Act but should be obvious – it has to be checked to ensure that the application has been properly made. In other words, that it is competent. It may be the case that the application has some fundamental flaw and cannot be accepted – for example, if it has been lodged without an operating plan or the appropriate certificates of suitability, or if the incorrect fee has been paid. This checking process is about the competency of the application in terms of the prescribed requirements of the Act, as opposed to the merits of the applicant or their application proposal.

If the application has a fundamental error, for example the fee has not been enclosed, the board may simply reject the application and ask for it to be re-submitted. In some cases, if a minor element of the application has an error, the board may accept the application at the counter with an amending sheet to follow. Many board areas do not have a specialist licensing public counter per se, and applications will be processed by mail receipt upon lodgement at a generic council office facility with a public counter. This scenario does not infer acceptance of the application, which must be checked by the licensing section first, if no specialist licensing officer has received and receipted the application.

Linked to the central notion of competency is the prospective introduction of what will be known as the "period of determination" for applications lodged under the 2005 Act. The Air Weapons and Licensing (Scotland) Act 2015 has made provision for licensing boards to formally acknowledge applications where they meet the prescribed requirements, or to give notice where they do not, indicating what elements may be at fault or missing. These new provisions, which are introduced at sections 134ZA, 134ZB and 134ZC of the 2005 Act by way of section 61 of the Air Weapons and Licensing (Scotland) Act 2015, also create a maximum 9-month processing time for all applications under the 2005 Act (excluding applications for review of a premises or personal licence), which is termed the "period of determination". These yet-to-be-commenced provisions would create a "deemed grant" scenario in that if a licensing board fails to determine an application within the nine-month window, then it will be granted subject to any mandatory conditions. The nine-month window runs from the date of lodgement of the application, if it has met the prescribed requirements, or, if it has not, the date that the applicant has remedied the flaws and the application becomes complete or competent.

The idea of a 9-month "backstop" provision is not unheard of in the world of Scottish licensing. Applications under the Civic Government (Scotland) Act 1982 are also subject to the same 9-month provisions – this period having been increased from 6 months under section 77 of the Air Weapons and Licensing (Scotland) Act 2015.[1]

2 NOTIFICATION AND PUBLICITY FOR THE APPLICATION

The 2005 Act creates a number of ways in which a licence application requires to be advertised or notified to various parties. This, in some respects, carries on the tradition from the 1976 Act which had similar provisions for notification, albeit it is greatly expanded and the burden is on the licensing board to deal with. As the Explanatory Notes to the 2005 Act say: "This is a new duty and a change from what was previously provided for in the Licensing (Scotland) Act 1976." Indeed, the statutory requirement of consultation with certain persons under the Act was created specifically in response to the policy objective of engaging communities under the terms of the Licensing Bill. The Policy Memorandum to the Bill explains the wider aims:

> "There are four key issues that underline the approach the Executive has taken in proposing the new licensing system for Scotland. They are: reducing underage drinking, reducing binge drinking, providing a voice for communities, and modernisation."[2]

Note that of these four key aims for the then Scottish Executive, the aim of "providing a voice for communities" is demonstrated through the proposals for formal consultation with key persons and groups. The Policy Memorandum later focuses on the community aspect, in relation to application consultation, with the following explanation:

> "The Bill provides for better and more effective community engagement in the system . . . This would be supplemented with a system where those with a specific interest are given direct notification of a licence application i.e. the community council, chief constable, fire authority, the local authority and each person having a notifiable interest in neighbouring land to the premises."[3]

This provides some context and background to the notification provisions in the 2005 Act. There are in fact two key processes:

1 The civic 9-month period was commenced as of 1 May 2017 under the Air Weapons and Licensing (Scotland) Act 2015 (Commencement No. 5 and Saving Provisions) Order 2016 (SSI 2016/307) (art 4), and perhaps interestingly is described in the Policy Note attached to the commencement Order as a provision which "modernises and expands the requirement for licensing authorities to deal with matters expeditiously" notwithstanding that it lengthens the period the licensing authority has to consider the application.

2 Paragraph 6, Policy Memorandum to the Licensing (Scotland) Bill, as introduced on 28 February 2005.

3 Ibid paras 104 and 105.

- a prescriptive process for "notification" of the application to certain persons, compliance being entirely in the hands of the licensing board, and
- a separate "notice" process involving the display of a site notice at the premises, which relates to the wider public and is a burden shared between the licensing board and the applicant (as noted below).

We shall address both processes in turn, beginning with those placed in the purview of the licensing board.

2.1 Notification requirements: what the licensing board must do

Section 21 of the Act requires the board to give notice of an application for a premises licence to certain persons, who are as follows:[4]

- each person having a notifiable interest in neighbouring land – "notifiable interest" meaning any occupier of land within a 4-metre radius of the application premises[5] (originally set at 50 metres but the legislators reined this in, much to the delight of every clerk in Scotland),[6]
- any community council within whose area the premises are situated,
- the council within whose area the premises are situated (except where the council is the applicant),
- the appropriate chief constable,
- the fire authority,
- the relevant health board.

Section 21 as originally enacted required the licensing board to give a full copy of the application along with the notice. This created significant logistical difficulties for licensing staff requiring to make multiple copies of many documents and plans to send out to a number of parties; or to facilitate online access of such documents. The requirement was scaled back as a result of section 180 of the Criminal Justice and Licensing (Scotland) Act 2010, which created a new subsection at section 21(2) as follows:

> "(2) On giving notice of an application under subsection (1), the Licensing Board–
> (a) must provide the [appropriate] chief constable with a copy of the application, and
> (b) may provide any other person to whom notice is given with a copy of the application."

4 Interestingly, in his discussion of who a competent objector should be (a point linked, of course, to who should be consulted), Nicholson proposed that "any body representing an established religion where that body owns or occupies property in or near the neighbourhood of the premises to which the application relates" (Nicholson Report, para 6.23) should be considered – a description that was intended to supplant the previous references to "organised church" in the 1976 Act, which was thought not to properly capture a multitude of faith-based organisations. Of course, the 2005 Act does not recognise any faith as a consultee – but does allow for any person to make a representation or objection which includes, of course, any religion or persons representing such a body.

5 The full definition of what amounts to neighbouring land, from the Licensing (Procedure) (Scotland) Regulations 2007 (SSI 2007/453) reg 4 is: "Land is 'neighbouring land' for the purposes of section 21(1)(a) if– (a) it is within 4 metres in any direction of any boundary of the premises to which the application in question relates; and (b) it is not part of– (i) a road (within the meaning of section 107 of the New Roads and Street Works Act 1991); (ii) land covered by water; or (iii) a railway line."

6 See "Executive set to slash red tape" [2007] 36 SLLP 1.

The provision therefore now only requires the board to give a full copy of the application to the police, although they may give anyone else entitled to receive a notice a full copy of the application if they wish. The underlying procedural regulations still provide that:

> "(1) Where a Board is giving a notice of a premises licence application which falls within paragraph (2), it must also–
> (a) send to the person in question a copy of the operating plan and layout plan which accompanied the application; or
> (b) provide that person with information as to where on a website a copy of those plans may be viewed."[7]

However, the operative "may" from the revised section 21(2)(b) means that these regulations only apply where the board wishes them to.

The Procedural Regulations also provide that the notification of the application must be given to these certain bodies within 21 days of receipt of the application.[8] There is nothing to prevent the giving of the notice by way of email and in some cases licensing boards will have established communication channels to the police, fire, health board, community councils and may fall back on traditional mail when writing to local residents.[9]

2.2 Persons to be notified: a closer look

It should be instructive to take a closer look at each of the persons to be notified under section 21. Most of these might shortly be referred to as "responsible authorities" in the way the Licensing Act 2003 or Gambling Act 2005 does.

- **Persons within a 4-metre radius**: this is clearly aimed at including neighbours who might be affected either positively or adversely by the grant of the licence application, but one of the first issues to consider is whether the landlord or tenant of the neighbouring property should be the person to receive the section 21 notification. Whilst the Act refers to "each person", the procedural regulations confirm it is the *occupier* of the land to whom the notification should be sent. In many cases it is not possible for a licensing board to determine this level of detail – for example, where a residential property is rented out, or how many persons actually occupy the land – and the board will have to rely on the information it can obtain from council IT systems as to residential addresses. In most cases, boards have developed a software program which creates a list of all the addresses within a 4-metre radius and letters are generated automatically thereafter, which can be addressed to "The Occupiers" in the way that one might receive a circular relating to the electoral register. This can lead to anomalies from a public or community perspective, where persons who own or live on property might not receive the notification. Other trouble can arise in relation to the geographical extent of the notification area. For example, neighbours who live across the road from a public house might not receive a notice even though they may be directly affected by proposed activities. As their residence is

7 Licensing (Procedure) (Scotland) Regulations 2007 (SSI 2007/453) ("the Procedural Regulations") reg 9.
8 This is a reduction on the original 42-day period which applied during conversion.
9 See further, Paul Romano "It's good to talk: the duty to consult" [2007] 36 SLLP 21.

perhaps beyond the 4 metres, they are not required to be notified. It is not altogether uncommon for a board to be criticised by an objector to a licence application for not having received a notification. In some cases this might be because the notice has gone astray or not been delivered, but is most likely to be because the person lives outside the 4-metre zone which the licensing board has regard to. I have witnessed a number of cases where local residents express grievance at the rule and unfairly blame the licensing board or even the applicant. Some licensing boards do "letter drop" residents in larger perimeters than the statutory 4 metres.

- **Community councils**: in many cases there will be an established community council or perhaps residents' association with which the licensing board will have established links when issuing notices of new premises licence applications. There are a number of very highly informed and active organisations that will appear on multiple occasions to object to new licence applications, and yet others who pay no heed to the process and do not engage. In some cases, when a representative of the community council appears, the licensing board will insist on having something in writing from the community confirming the authority of the person appearing. In many cases the representative is likely to be a "well kent" face and therefore authorisation letters are not asked for. The representation of community council views at a licensing hearing can be subject to some difficulty for the person appearing. It is easy for an individual to lapse into proffering their own view, as opposed to any agreed view of the council. It may also be the case that the community council itself had mixed views about a particular case. It is incumbent upon the community council to agree the remit of the spokesperson, and incumbent upon the spokesperson to observe that remit. It is also especially important that the community council retain a proper agenda and minutes of the meetings where any licensing representation has been agreed or decided upon.
- **The council**: as discussed elsewhere, it is highly relevant to remember that the licensing board is not the council, that is, the local authority. The licensing board is a licensing authority for the purposes of alcohol (and gambling), and is a creature of statute, independent of the local authority. This is discussed at length in Chapter 4. Practically speaking, the staff who administer the licensing regime (and by that I mean the people who deal with the paperwork, process the cheques, copy the applications – in other words, those hardy characters on whose backs the whole system exists) are of course employees of the council, not the licensing board: including clerks, administration staff, and even licensing standards officers. It may be that this notification is done via an internal system or email address; although on the face of it the process appears to be a missive from one department of the council to another, one must remember the independent nature of the licensing board. Although unusual, it is not unheard of for the local authority to take a view on a licence application and to express those views to the licensing board.
- **The appropriate chief constable**: following the unification of the predecessor police forces, the appropriate chief constable is of course the chief constable of Police Scotland. In practice, my understanding is that whilst correspondence may be addressed to the chief constable, it is in reality sent to the local licensing department of the police and picked up on by (in most

cases) specialist officers or civilian police staff who administer licensing on a day-to-day basis on behalf of the police. In turn, whilst reports and letters from the police to the licensing board may be in the name of the Chief Constable as a matter of formality, it is unlikely he or she would have signed off on every single licensing letter and the local licensing Inspector, Sergeant or Constable is the more likely author. The police also have a centralised licensing team and in some cases they will have input to letters which are lodged such as premises licence review proposals. The police have a distinct, special role in the licensing system, and this is discussed in more detail below.

- **The fire authority**: this is as designated under section 61 of the Fire (Scotland) Act 2005, but again, following the unification of the predecessor fire forces, now simply relates to Fire Scotland. It is most unusual, in my experience, to see a fire officer appear at a licensing board hearing, although not unheard of. In some areas, the Firemaster will send an email or letter back to the licensing board in relation to any licence application which has been notified, but the level of engagement varies wildly. In some areas, the Firemaster will take a definitive interest and even inspect the premises and make comments, and report these to the licensing board. In other areas, the Firemaster will submit some generic comments about ensuring the operator meets with fire regulations, and in many cases there will be no comment from the fire authority at all.
- **The relevant health board:** there are fourteen health boards which are noted, as they relate to the various licensing boards, at Appendix D. As the interaction between licensing boards and health boards has proven one of the more textured discussion points of the licensing system, this is discussed in more detail below.

Health board engagement in the licensing process varies from area to area. At certain licensing board hearings, it is not uncommon to see a local health board representative attend and speak in person, having lodged objections or representations to certain applications. In some board areas the NHS will lodge comments but no representative will appear to speak to those representations, and in some board areas no NHS interaction appears to occur at all.

Given the wider controversy of the public health objective, which I have discussed in Chapter 3 at length, this engagement of the NHS as a consultee perhaps requires some additional comment here. Over the years of practice of licensing law at hearings across Scotland since conversion, I think there would be a consensus view from private practitioners that we have observed a gradual improvement in the quality of interaction and engagement. In early forays, some health boards were criticised publicly for lodging illogical objections, such as objecting to a variation to reduce an alcohol display area, or, in a case I was involved with, an objection to a variation relating to an internal reconfiguration of the premises on the basis there were "too many premises in the city centre". A number of other objections in certain board areas appeared to have no relation to the specific application but were statements about general health concerns related to a local area. On numerous occasions I and other practitioners witnessed licensing board members criticising the information brought to hearings by health representatives on the basis that it was imprecise, generic, and could not be reasonably referred to by them in their deliberations.

Whilst we have now moved on from these earlier examples, it can still be said that some of the material put forward by health representatives is difficult for a licensing board to fathom, such as in one case suggesting that a cinema be forced to count units consumed and cut off customers who had reached revised recommended daily limits; or, in another case where a new licence was sought for a restaurant following an insolvency event, where it was claimed that allowing children and young persons into a family friendly environment should be opposed, because it would normalise alcohol.

The fundamental issues I explored in Chapter 3 perhaps explain why engagement by the NHS in licensing is an uneasy challenge. In some areas, there are examples of active health board representatives withdrawing from the process on the basis that their views were being, it was claimed, ignored or overlooked, or because of the prevailing views of leading figures on the licensing board.

From a purely personal perspective, I would observe that the best results in engaging with the licensing board have come from submissions that were balanced and appropriate, and absent of generalisation or scaremongering. It cannot be easy for health representatives to dip themselves into the quasi-judicial world of a licensing hearing and it is important to commend those who do so with reasonableness, respect and proportionality.

The treatment of the NHS representative as an "official" in hearing proceedings also varies. In some licensing board areas, the NHS representative sits in on every hearing, whether or not they are a party to it having lodged a formal objection or representation, and may be asked for their views during the course of an application being considered. In other areas, the alternative approach is taken and the NHS representative, if indeed there is one, will be treated like any other objector.

2.3 Publication requirements: what the licensing board must do

Moving on from the notification of prescribed persons, the task of the licensing board does not end there. There are also additional publication requirements to ensure further publicity for the terms of a licence application. Under the Procedural Regulations, the board must, within 42 days of the date the application is received, give notice of the application on the board's website or a local newspaper. If the notice is on the website, it must remain there for 21 days. It is unusual or even impossible to locate a licensing board willing to incur the cost of a newspaper advert, so not unreasonable to propose that each one utilises a page on the local authority website; and in fact there are no newspaper adverts out there at all.[10] The online publication of pending applications also allows interested parties to keep a watching brief on applications in certain areas, or which may relate to certain applicants, for which they have an interest.

10 This is in contrast to the 1976 Act, s 12(1) of which created a statutory requirement for the clerk of the licensing board to "not later than three weeks before the first day of the meeting of the board at which the applications are to be considered, cause to be published in one or more newspapers circulating in the area of the board a list of all competent applications".

2.4 The site notice requirement: what the licensing board and applicant have to do

There is also a site notice requirement – that is, a public display of an official notice at the "site" of the application premises. There are duties here which sit with the licensing board, and duties which sit with the applicant. Once the board has received an application, it must give the applicant notice of when it intends to advertise the application, as the site notice must be displayed from the same date. It is also up to the licensing board to give the applicant a copy of the actual notice which is to be displayed. There is no provision for how much warning the board need give the applicant in this regard, and in some cases I have received a site notice on the day, or even a day or two after, it is supposed to be displayed. It is hoped by agents such as I that the board will give the applicant fair warning about the start of the display period, especially where the notice might be sent direct to premises without advising the agent. In the vast majority of cases I am aware of, site notices do land at least 7 days ahead of the first date of display, which should be plenty of time for arrangements to be made to have it displayed.

The site notice itself is prescribed in the Procedural Regulations and is an A4-sized notice, with information in relation to the application such as the details of the applicant, the premises address, the licensed hours sought, and activities sought. It is for the licensing board to draft this notice based on the information they have received in the application. Therefore, it is important the applicant checks that the site notice accurately reflects the application which was lodged, and contains no errors. The vast majority of notices which are issued are in good order, but we are all human and sometimes a typographical error may have occurred. If this happens, contact should be made immediately with the licensing board to see if the matter can be remedied *tout de suite* – because that erroneous information might also be on the notifications given to the statutory consultees, or on the website advert.

So, assuming the notice has been issued and all is well, the burden to actually display it then falls to the applicant. The regulations state that the notice must be displayed:

> "at or near the premises to which the application relates and in a place and at a height where the notice can conveniently be read by the public".[11]

The best location will very much depend on the exact nature of the premises but it is good practice for applicants to keep several copies and perhaps display two or three at different locations, for example, if the premises relate to a large undeveloped site, or if the premises have more than one entrance. Some of the most important tools of a licensing lawyer in private practice include an office laminator, gaffer tape, a hole punch and plastic ties. In my experience it is better to have displayed multiple notices where there is any contention, than deal with allegations of no notice being displayed at all. Local knowledge is also a boon here – if the application premises are on a high street with a significant amount of night time activity, perhaps it is more likely that some ruffian will tear down the notice in an act of japery, as opposed to premises located by a field in a remote location.

11 Licensing (Procedure) (Scotland) Regulations 2007 (SSI 2007/453), reg 7(2).

It is good practice for the premises staff to check the notice each day and replace it if it ever becomes defaced, is torn down or lost. A record should be kept of any difficulties. These days it should be relatively easy to take a photo of the notice on a mobile phone and keep copies to confirm the date and time. Relying on this evidence may become essential should someone dispute the notice has been displayed correctly. As it is a requirement that the notice be displayed for 21 days, the board must be satisfied that this has occurred and can reorder display if there is evidence of gaps in the display of the notice, even if this is not the fault of the applicant.

At the end of the site notice period, applicants are required to submit a "confirmation of site notice", the form of which is also set out in the Procedural Regulations, and this should be sent to the board the day after the last date for display where possible. This is also an A4-sized document confirming the details of the applicant, premises, and the dates of display, with a space for the applicant or agent to sign confirming the notice was indeed displayed. If there have been difficulties with the notice, details should be given in this document, for example: "On 4th December we discovered the notice had been torn down by a customer leaving the premises, and immediately replaced it".

If it becomes apparent during the notice display period, or even after it, that there has been a serious issue, it may be prudent to ask for new dates and have the notice re-displayed as soon as known as this may not knock out the timeline of the application reaching a particular hearing if addressed immediately. The alternative is that the competency is discussed at a hearing which may result in continuation of the application, or worse. It is possible for a licensing board to overlook an issue with the display of the site notice and not require a re-run of the display period at all, by invoking section 135 – the power of the board to relieve failure to comply with rules and other requirements, where:

> "(a) the failure is due to mistake, oversight or other excusable cause, and
> (b) the Board considers it appropriate in all the circumstance to relieve the failure."

As with most aspects of the licensing regime, different boards take different approaches to this and some boards will be more willing than others to entertain a section 135 submission.

3 THE SPECIAL POLICE ROLE IN THE NOTIFICATION PROCESS

Section 21 makes specific provision for the police to respond to the notification of an application and details a number of different aspects of police interaction in the licence application process. Within 21 days of the date they have been notified of the application, the police *may* supply the licensing board with a report on antisocial behaviour in the locality to which the application relates, and *must* provide the board with a report regarding convictions.

3.1 The antisocial behaviour report

When the 2005 Act was first enacted, the production of an antisocial behaviour report was mandatory in respect of every single new premises licence application. This led to significant resource issues for the police, having to produce detailed reports which in many cases they did not want or need, and had little if any information that was of possible relevance. Parliament ultimately downgraded the antisocial behaviour report from a mandatory to a discretionary requirement and this change took effect on 13 December 2010.[12]

The antisocial behaviour report provisions now sit within, first, section 24A of the 2005 Act, subsection (1) of which states that:

> "A Licensing Board may, at any time before determining a premises licence application, request the chief constable to give the Board a report detailing [antisocial behaviour]."

Note then, that in the first instance it is a matter for the licensing board at their discretion to obtain the report. In practice, some licensing boards will have a standing arrangement with the police to produce a report where the application falls within an overprovision zone or where other material factors may apply.

The board may also request the report based on observation of local knowledge or noting the receipt of representations, or indeed for any reason. An example of this might be a board member who is the ward councillor for the locality, who has particular knowledge which has been presented to them perhaps at surgeries by members of the community, and the board member believes that the report may be useful or instructive in teasing out some issues which they are aware of locally.

A key element in practice here, perhaps of particular import to the applicant, is how the request of an antisocial behaviour report might impact on the timeline of the application being determined. The board members themselves might, on the first calling of the case, propose a continuance to allow for the production of a report. If the report is disclosed close to a hearing date, the applicant might seek continuation to allow for time to digest the contents of the report. Indeed, the police might also seek a continuation if they need time to produce the report through resourcing issues. Any delay to the determination of the application might not be ideal for an applicant who is likely working to a timeline with conditional funding, building work due to commence, securing employees' start dates, and various other business reasons. The delay may be something which is outwith the applicant's control but if a report is to be produced, and it is thought it would be of some detriment to the success of the application, then of course the ability to properly rebut any adverse inference that the report has created may be more of a priority in order to give the application the best chance of success.

During the transition period, the ability of the police to produce an antisocial

12 Sections 180(3)(b) and 206(1) of the Criminal Justice and Licensing (Scotland) Act 2010 repealed the original s 21(3)(b) of the 2005 Act, which contained the "must" provision for the antisocial behaviour report. This was commenced on 13 December 2010 by operation of the Criminal Justice and Licensing (Scotland) Act 2010 (Commencement No. 6, Transitional and Savings Provisions) Order 2010 (SSI 2010/413) art 2 and Sch.

behaviour report at their own standing was explicitly provided for,[13] but for a short period after commencement the report was mandatory in all cases. This was ultimately corrected as of 13 December 2010 by operation of section 183 of the Criminal Justice and Licensing (Scotland) Act 2010, which inserted section 22(2A) to the 2005 Act:

> "(2A) The chief constable may, under subsection (1)(b), make representations concerning a premises licence application by giving to the Licensing Board a report detailing—
> (a) any cases of antisocial behaviour identified by constables as having taken place on, or in the vicinity of, the premises,
> (b) any complaints or other representations made to constables concerning antisocial behaviour on, or in the vicinity of, the premises."

An antisocial behaviour report could therefore be produced and presented as part of a representation or objection to an application just as the police might seek to place any other material before a licensing board to support their representation or objection. The police frequently will prepare certain background reports or papers, or produce open source material, in order to fortify the point they wish to make. If the police believe that an antisocial behaviour report is instructive in a particular case, then they may choose to prepare and present it.

Interestingly, where the board requests the report, the wording of what should be produced is slightly different to that under section 22(2A). Section 24A(1), which deals with the "board requested" report, states that the police should provide detail as follows:

> "(a) all cases of antisocial behaviour identified within the relevant period by constables as having taken place on, or in the vicinity of, the premises, [and]
> (b) all complaints or other representations made within the relevant period to constables concerning antisocial behaviour on, or in the vicinity of, the premises."

Note that the section 24A wording includes reference to a "relevant period" whilst the section 22(2A) wording does not. The relevant period under section 24A is one year. The absence of this condition from section 22(2A) infers that the police have a wider discretion to produce material over a longer period of time where they choose to present an antisocial behaviour report themselves, albeit one wonders if this is an oversight by the draftsman.

The actual format of the report is in a letter or report which typically will contain two long lists of incidents, the first list being crimes and cases of antisocial behaviour, and the second list being incidents or complaints which have not necessarily resulted in convictions, over a period of one year. The period should run back from the date that the police receive the request from the licensing board.[14] The one-year period is typically used in a section 22(2A) report notwithstanding (as noted above) there is no restriction in comparison to a section 24A report. In one case I was engaged in, the police produced a report over a two-year period instead of the typical one year, at my request, in order to demonstrate a submission I wished to make about the dearth of incidents in a particular locality.

13 Article 9(2) of the Licensing (Transitional and Saving Provisions) (Scotland) Order 2007 (SSI 2007/454).

14 Section 24A(5).

The reference to "vicinity" in relation to the geographical reach of the report is undefined, and is left to local practice and variance. In some licensing board areas, they have pre-determined "localities" which are used – small areas which are defined and agreed down to individual streets, post codes and so on; the terminus points of which may not necessarily be equidistant from the central application premises. For example, premises which abut a forest on one side, and a housing scheme on the other, might have the "vicinity" drawn more widely on one side to capture more of the populated area than the forested region. In other areas, a somewhat blunter approach might be taken with an agreed radius of, say, 50 metres being adopted as the vicinity for the purposes of the report. This type of approach might be seen, for example, in a large city or town area.

It is useful to point out that the antisocial behaviour report "vicinity" may not be the same area as the "locality" for the purposes of overprovision. The "vicinity" may form a smaller part of an agreed overprovision zone, for example, or it may indeed fall partly within an overprovision zone and partly outwith it. It is important that all parties understand what these geographical areas are in order to reach a lawful determination.

The antisocial behaviour report will therefore feature a long list of crimes such as murder, assault, theft, public urination, public intoxication, and so on, and state the number of such incidents during that one-year period. This means that a report could have "zero" beside every single type of offence, but may also have dozens or maybe even a number into the hundreds against a particular offence. An example of what the report might look like is shown in Figure 9.1 below.

The merits of the antisocial behaviour report require some debate. In *Pagliocca v Glasgow District Licensing Board*,[15] it was held that a refusal of a licence under the 1976 Act could not be based simply on a supply of police statistics which had no causal relationship to the application premises, and that logic does of course hold to applications being considered under the 2005 Act.[16] When you examine what information the report must contain, it is readily observable that there could be a substantial amount of information to provide, and that the usefulness of that information can be challenged. During the transition period a representative of the former Strathclyde Police observed at a licensing conference that a report covering a restaurant premises in Sauchiehall Street in Glasgow would dredge up hundreds of incidents, none of which would have any likely practical link to the premises in question, and that point remains sound.

The issue here therefore is not the information, but what weight a licensing board should attach to the information. The most extreme example of questionable utility I came across is one case where, in the list of crimes that had occurred in the locality, a murder had occurred at the address of an application premises. On investigation, it transpired that the offence occurred on the top deck of a passing bus which had stopped near the application premises address as a result of the altercation, and, upon attending, the police officer used a bar next to the incident as a landmark address in his or her reporting notes.

15 1995 SLT 180.

16 I explore the relevance of causality in the licensing system throughout Chapter 3 on the licensing objectives.

Antisocial Behaviour Report
(The Windsor, 121 High Street)
(Dates: 1/1/19 to 1/1/20)

In terms of Section 24A of the Licensing (Scotland) Act, 2005, I now provide, as requested by the Licensing Board, a report detailing all cases, complaints and representations within the relevant period concerning antisocial behaviour on the premises or within a 50-metre radius of the premises:

Incidents	**Count**
Complaints	0
Drugs/Solvent abuse	3
Disturbances	0
Drinking in public places	9
Assault	0
Damage to property	2
Neighbour Dispute	1
Noise Complaint	0

Crime Reports	**Count**
Breach of the Peace [inc. racial etc aggravations and Criminal Justice Licensing (S) Act 2010 Section 38]	2
Culpable and Reckless Conduct	0
Drunk & Incapable [Civic Govt (S) Act 1982 Section 50(1)]	3
Drug-related offences	0
Assaults	0
Indecent Assault	0
Street Drinking	17
Urinating [Civic Govt (S) Act 1982 Section 47]	0
Vandalism (including fire-raising and malicious mischief)	1

Riotous behaviour while Drunk on Licensed Premises[1] [Licensing (S) Act 2005 Section 78]	0
Refusal to leave Licensed Premises [Licensing (S) Act 2005 Section 79]	1

[1] This reference to Section 78, and the following entry referencing Section 79, are both erroneous referrals to the Licensing (Scotland) Act 1976. These entries appeared in a real life report, and I use them here to demonstrate the importance of checking the details of each entry. No doubt the police meant to refer to the equivalent 2005 Act provisions in sections 115 and 116.

Figure 9.1 Example of an antisocial behaviour report

In some circumstances, the police officer attending a hearing may be able to "look behind" the figures and provide raw data about the individual incidents such as specific dates and times – depending on how well briefed she or he is. In addition, it is not uncommon for the licensing board to interrogate the attending officer and probe for details, so being well briefed for attending a hearing is not a task merely for the applicant. The police officer may or may not be in a position to add some colour to the statistics by way of local knowledge or experience – for example, a member of the licensing board might ask the officer to confirm how the number of crimes compares to neighbouring localities in order to get a better sense of whether the figures are extraordinary, and it may be that the officer has experience of these localities.

It is also worth noting that the presence of a report is not of itself necessarily something to be seen as a manifestation of adversity to the success of the application – it may be that the report confirms that the local area is not one of concern for the police, and this information might have some value to an applicant looking to rebut the observations of an objector which purport to be to the contrary. A report populated with significant numbers of incidents could have nothing to say about the individual application, and it also the case, of course, that a "blank" report does not mean the application should be granted.

Looking at the sample report in Figure 9.1, one can see that some of the information presented might have particular import to the licensing board and this is the salient point as to the utility of any report. If the application before the board is for a new off-sale licence, perhaps the board might have little to say in relation to the "Neighbour Dispute" which is listed, but certainly have questions about the seventeen incidences of street drinking. The issue then is for the board to take a view on the connectedness of the incident or incidents to the proposed application and application premises, and the connectedness of these incidents to the five licensing objectives. The report should be interrogated by the applicant and by the board, whose members will then reach a view as to what weight to place upon it.

3.2 The police convictions report

In addition to the discretionary production of the antisocial behaviour report, the police also have a mandatory obligation to produce a report in relation to relevant or foreign convictions of the applicant or connected persons. Note that the Act provides a full statutory list of what constitute "relevant offences" and these are detailed in Appendix G. The convictions report is actually one of two reports required under section 21(3)(a), which are either:

- a notice stating that neither the applicant nor any connected person has been convicted of any relevant or foreign offence, or
- a notice specifying any convictions of the applicant or any connected person.

What is important to note here is that this is designed to be a neutral reporting tool which provides the licensing board with information as to the presence or otherwise of any relevant or foreign convictions. The submission of either report cannot and should not create an inference to mean that the police take one view or another. If the police submit a report confirming that there are no convictions, this does not mean that they cannot also object to the applicant or application. Similarly, if the police submit a report which confirms the presence of convictions, this does not mean the police take a view on these as to whether the application should be granted.

If the police do wish to make a representation or an objection, that should in my opinion be detailed in a letter separate from the convictions report and it is open to the police to make such a representation or objection regardless of the terms of the section 21 notice. However, the practice in this regard does vary because although we have a single police force, the reality is that local officers still retain some control over the style of letters they submit to licensing boards. This means that it is not uncommon to see the police present one letter, which "ticks the box" of the reporting requirement under section 21 by indicating the presence of convictions, before going on to lay out a case that the application should be refused. In some areas, one does see the practice of "two letters" being used: one to satisfy the section 21 reporting requirement; and a separate letter where any representation or objection is outlined, perhaps with or without regard to whatever the section 21 report may be. This latter approach is, in my submission, the correct one.

When the Act was originally passed it was thought that the measure of simply providing one of two reports relating to the presence of convictions represented a substantial erosion of the powers of the police to comment on licensing applications, but that was because any objection flowing from the conviction report could only be where the police were concerned that the the applicant was "involved in serious organised crime", and in turn that the police believed the application should be refused on the basis of the licensing objective of preventing crime and disorder.[17] The specificity of this subsection caused great alarm, as it was felt that this ground of objection was severely limited, and also that because section 22 created special provision for police they could not be classed as "any person" under the general provisions for objections.[18]

This significant curtailing of police views was attacked prior to the commencement of the Act and so the Criminal Justice and Licensing (Scotland) Act 2010 removed those constraints and extended the power of objection to remove the required link to organised crime, and by allowing objection to be made with regard to any of the licensing objectives.[19] Subsequently, the Act was further amended in the Air Weapons and Licensing (Scotland) Act 2015 to allow consideration of whether the applicant is "fit and proper" in addition to objecting on the grounds of the licensing objectives.

These historic limitations were all swept away following the various amendments to the Act noted above, and the police may object or make a representation to an application on any of the grounds of refusal just like any other objector (see below). To summarise, the police can provide three separate documents in relation to a premises licence application: a convictions report, which is mandatory; an antisocial behaviour report, which is discretionary; and any letter where they make a case to object or to make representation to the application, perhaps with regard to the first two reports, or not.

17 In the original s 22 this objective was referred to as the "crime prevention" objective as opposed to its actual wording, which caused further confusion.

18 See further "ACPO(S) brands restriction of chief constable role 'unthinkable'" [2005] 30 SLLP 12.

19 See "Chief Constables to gain new powers" [2008] 41 SLLP 3.

4 OBJECTIONS AND REPRESENTATIONS

The first element to note here is that the 2005 Act provides for two types of interaction: an "objection" to the application; and a "representation" to the application. The origin of this differentiation lies first with the old 1976 provisions for the police to make "observations" as well as "objections",[20] and, secondly, with considerations of Nicholson, who rightly observed that a number of what we might now term to be "responsible authorities" had a sort of special role and a wider interest in the licensing system and whose general views, which might not be objections, would be of some value to the licensing board. Nicholson's proposal was to have a list of statutory persons who might object, and statutory persons who might make "observations".[21] Parliament agreed with the sentiment but, sensibly in my view, cut through this by simply providing that "any person" could make objections or representations.

4.1 Form and content of an objection or representation

There is no particular prescription as to the form of an *objection*, save that it should relate to "any ground relevant to one of the grounds for refusal specified in section 23(5)" (discussed below). Section 22(1A) provides some additional guidance as to what an objection may strike at:

> "A person giving a notice under subsection (1) may include in the notice any information that the person considers may be relevant to consideration by the Board of any ground for refusal including, in particular, information in relation to—
> (a) the applicant,
> (b) where the applicant is neither an individual nor a council, a connected person in relation to the applicant, or
> (c) any person who would be an interested party in relation to the subject premises if the application were to be granted."[22]

It is extremely common for objections to relate to matters which have no bearing on the grounds of refusal, or indeed no bearing on licensing at all. It is not to be expected, I suggest, that members of the public will be familiar with the vagaries of the licensing Act nor of the grounds on which a licence can be refused, nor indeed the *vires* of a licensing board and legal principles such as that under *Brightcrew* and beyond. It is a matter for the applicant to rebut any objection on grounds of competency as well as merit, of course, but a well-drilled licensing board should also be explaining the scope of their remit to objectors, and managing expectations of persons if they are raising issues irrelevant to licensing.

The "any person" rule allows the Act to deliver on the wider policy objective of engaging communities by allowing anyone to say what they wish – whilst, of course, the licensing board retains control over its own view as to whether any information presented in an objection is of relevance.

20 The Licensing (Scotland) Act 1976 as originally enacted did not contain any special provision for "observations" by the police. This was altered as a result of the Law Reform (Miscellaneous Provisions) (Scotland) Act 1990, which introduced a new s 16A to the 1976 Act allowing the police to lodge observations. This was commenced as of 1 January 1991.

21 Nicholson Report, para 6.21, pp 84 and 85.

22 See Chapter 7, Section 3.1.1 in relation to the concept and definition of "interested party".

The Act also provides further detail about what a *representation* might be or be designed to achieve. Section 22(1)(b) says that representations may be:

"(i) in support of the application,
(ii) as to modifications which the person considers should be made to the operating plan accompanying the application, or
(iii) as to conditions which the person considers should be imposed."

It can thus be seen that the purpose of a representation is to allow persons "a say" in relation to a licensing application where they are not in opposition to the application and may welcome it. In addition to letters of "full blown support", it is very common to deal with objections from residents or other parties who are not really opposed to the application in the round, but perhaps might be looking for comfort on a particular issue such as asking for a particular terminal hour to be observed in the use of an external area.

4.2 Who is "any person" in the context of objections and representation?

Under the 1976 Act, there were six specific categories of objector.[23] Under the 2005 Act, "any person" may object to the application, and any person may make representations concerning the application (including in support of it). This was obviously a significant widening of those entitled to be heard in relation to a licence application but is now simply an accepted part of the system. The term "any person" should be read to mean any natural persons, that is, any human being with lawful capacity, and also any non-natural person, that is, a legal entity such as a company or partnership. My reference to "lawful capacity" in relation to individual objectors is designed to tease out a couple of technical points which I have experienced in practice. First, I take the view that "any person" should be read widely to include someone who is lawfully appointed to represent someone without lawful capacity to represent themselves.[24] But does the term "any person" extend to persons of any age? The Age of Legal Capacity (Scotland) Act 1991 provides that no person under the age of 16 may enter into a legal transaction; however, section 2(4A) of the 1991 Act provides:

> "A person under the age of sixteen years shall have legal capacity to instruct a solicitor, in connection with any civil matter, where that person has a general understanding of what it means to do so; and without prejudice to the generality of this subsection a person twelve years of age or more shall be presumed to be of sufficient age and maturity to have such understanding."

Given these provisions were not enacted with the making of objections to licence applications in mind, and given the absence of any case law on the matter, it would seem that "any person", so far as an individual is concerned, could be read to be any person aged 12 to 15, if they have instructed a solicitor, or any person aged 16 and above.

23 1976 Act, s 16. These were neighbours, community councils, an organised church, the chief constable, the fire authority, and the local authority.

24 For example, by operation of a power of attorney, or as a result of a statutory order under the Adults with Incapacity (Scotland) Act 2000.

4.3 Intimation of objections and representations to the applicant

Intimation to the applicant of any objection or representation received is in the hands of the licensing board. Under the 1976 Act, objectors were required to serve their objection on the applicant themselves. That onerous obligation was shifted and now the burden sits with the licensing board. The Act requires the licensing board to send a copy of the objection or representation to the applicant at least 7 days prior to the date of the hearing.[25] In practice, some licensing boards will issue objections and representations to the applicant as and when received, and in other areas the board will send all the papers together in one go, at the time they issue a citation letter to confirm the date and time of the hearing. In some cases this might be several weeks or even months after the end of the site notice period, so this means there are cases where an applicant sees an objection 7 days ahead of a hearing, even where that objection was lodged some weeks prior. From an agent's perspective, it is useful to have sight of objections and representations from any party as early as possible. It is often the case that the terms of the objection might be countered in a sensible way by dialogue, such as where the objector has perhaps misunderstood the application, or where the applicant is prepared to propose certain conditions which are not capable of being outlined in a site notice or notification which a local resident or other party might receive.

The board does have a facility to reject objections and representations – under section 22(4) – if it considers that the objection or representation is "frivolous or vexatious". The board also has a power under section 22(5) to recover expenses from a person who makes an objection or representation which they have rejected on these grounds. This provision is no doubt to strike at "serial" complainers but I am unaware of a licensing board actioning this power. A key element to the power under section 22(4) is to understand the difference between an objection which might be incompetent, irrelevant, or simply not persuasive, and one which is frivolous or vexatious.

4.4 What is a frivolous objection?

The word *frivolous* is described in the *Cambridge Dictionary* as "behaving in a silly way or not taking anything seriously"; "a frivolous activity or object is silly or not important rather than useful or serious". Extending that meaning, one could say therefore that a frivolous objection is an objection which is silly or not important. In licensing terms, one might suggest that a frivolous objection is one which the objector knows is unlikely to be taken seriously or succeed, or is without merit. I am unaware of any licensing board striking out consideration of an objection on the grounds that it is frivolous. It is more likely that the board will allow the objection to be heard and then attach no weight to it in their deliberation.

4.5 What is a vexatious objection?

Whilst there is no specific definition of *vexatious* under the 2005 Act, it is hopefully agreed that the commonly understood concept of a vexatious

25 Licensing (Procedure) (Scotland) Regulations 2007 (SSI 2007/453), reg 11(1).

objector is someone acting *mala fides*, someone who persistently brings objections perhaps without merit or perhaps to harass the applicant or operator of the premises. A vexatious objection might also be one which is deemed to be an "abuse of process". The word "vexatious" is described in the *Cambridge Dictionary* as someone who is "difficult to deal with and causing a lot of anger, worry, or argument", and, in a legal context, something vexatious is something which has "little chance of succeeding in law, but intended to annoy someone or cause problems for them".

Although there are no specific licensing *dicta* on the definition of "vexatious", Scots law does recognise the problematic nature of vexatious individuals and there are some important cases which explore the concept. A key decision is that of *Lord Advocate v McNamara*,[26] in which the court adopted the observations of Lord Bingham of Cornhill in *Attorney General v Barker*[27] that:

> "The hallmark of a vexatious proceeding is in my judgment that it has little or no basis in law (or at least no discernible basis); that whatever the intention of the proceeding may be, its effect is to subject the defendant to inconvenience, harassment and expense out of all proportion to any gain likely to accrue to the claimant; and that it involves an abuse of the process of the court, meaning by that a use of the court process for a purpose or in a way which is significantly different from the ordinary and proper use of the court process."[28]

The Courts Reform (Scotland) Act 2014 makes provision for "vexatious litigation orders", which has the effect of restricting a so-called "vexatious litigant" from instituting civil proceedings unless the person has the permission of a judge of the Outer House.[29] The power exists only where a person has:

> "habitually and persistently, without any reasonable ground for doing so—
> (a) instituted vexatious civil proceedings, or
> (b) made vexatious applications to the court in the course of civil proceedings".

The 2014 act also creates powers to deal with "vexatious behaviour". The Explanatory Notes to the 2014 Act say that this is:

> "designed to empower the courts to deal with vexatious behaviour and abuse of process in a similar way to the use of Civil Restraint Orders (CROs) by the courts of England and Wales".

The most recent judicial examination of the definition of "vexatious" under Scots civil law was in *Lord Advocate v Mohammed Aslam*.[30] In *McNamara*, Lady Dorrian says:

> "The critical finding will be that repeated litigations and applications have failed for reasons of competence, irrelevance and the like. It is the fact that repeated actions were commenced with there being no reasonable grounds for doing so which can render them vexatious."[31]

In the absence of clear licensing dicta on the matter, if one extends the 2014 Act understanding of "vexatious" and the concepts narrated by Lady

26 2009 SC 598.
27 [2001] 1 FLR 759.
28 Ibid para 19.
29 Courts Reform (Scotland) Act 2014, ss 100 and 101.
30 [2019] CSIH 17.
31 2009 SC 598 at para 10.

Dorrian above, this suggests a basic understanding that a vexatious objector in a licensing application might be someone who habitually or persistently lodges objections without having a reasonable ground to do so. This perhaps implies a two-part test: there must be an element of repetition, and there must be an element of unreasonableness. Unreasonable might include successive irrational, irrelevant or incompetent objections. In the licensing context, this may therefore capture objections which contain material or allegations that lie outside the essential remit of the licensing board – that is, material or allegations which are not *licensing* matters. If a licensing board has advised an objector thus, and to take irrelevant remonstrations elsewhere, and the objector continues to make fresh objections on the same grounds, then a board might find this to be vexatious.

There are only a very few anecdotal examples I am aware of where licensing boards have taken a view that certain objections, or objectors, are vexatious, and I suggest that such a stance is rare. In one case I dealt with, I made a preliminary point of competency to attempt to strike out consideration of an objection on the grounds that it was vexatious. The licensing board had heard the view of this particular objector on at least four previous occasions in related hearings for the same premises. I argued that the central point of the objection had been heard and the issue determined on those previous occasions, and that the further objection was therefore vexatious. The board retired to consider this and, in the result, found against me,[32] and the objection was heard. On another occasion, I was able to convince a licensing board that a particular objection was vexatious by evidencing that the individual had been barred from the premises for misbehaviour, and the objection had been made in bad faith as a form of revenge. In this latter case, there was no "repetition" as this was a first-time objection, but the board was satisfied fairly quickly that the objection should be rejected under section 22(4).

4.6 Late objections or representations

The Procedural Regulations provide that a board may treat an objection or representation as not made if it was received after the last date for receiving such objections or representations as specified in the site notice – in other words, the last day of display of the notice (or subsequent redisplay, if appropriate). The board does have the power to accept late objections and representations where there are "good reasons". In that case, the board must consider whether it is in the interests of justice to postpone or adjourn the hearing. In practice, it is common for licensing boards to allow a late objector present at a hearing to state the reasons for the lateness, and then decide whether to allow it or not, also having regard to the view of the applicant. Many boards have a practice whereby, if a late objection or representation has no person to speak to it at the hearing, it simply falls. In all of this, it is critical that late objections and representations are not circulated amongst board members' papers. A decision as to whether the objection or representation is to be received must be made first and this should be done at the hearing and, in the interests of natural justice, the views of the applicant should also be sought.

From a strategic point of view, an agent representing an applicant may

32 Perish the thought!

wish to consider what might be gained by having a battle over whether a late objection should be received in certain circumstances. If the party is present, and their views are perhaps shared by other competent objectors, or perhaps are views which it is felt will not prove fatal to the application, then it may be strategically sensible to allow that person to have their say, and rebut their comments on the merits. It is of course open for an applicant to make a motion that the late objection should not be heard and whether this is appropriate is a matter for an agent to take a view on. If an agent is considering that the matter may end up in an appeal, then it may be prudent to oppose consideration of the late material so that this might be an avenue of attack on appeal.

Chapter 10

Premises Licences – Part 4 Determination

1 DETERMINATION OF A PREMISES LICENCE APPLICATION

Having looked through the form of the application, the consultation and other technical processes in previous chapters, we now come to consider how the application will be determined by the licensing board. Determination is governed principally by the provisions of section 23 of the 2005 Act. A key feature is that for any new licence (including a provisional licence) application a hearing must be held; at said hearing the board must take account of the operating plan, the layout plan, the general description and the certificates of suitability, as well as any report issued by the police, and any other objections or representations competently received.

In relation to the timings of this process, the Act requires that the hearing must be held no later than 119 days after the last date of display of the site notice.[1] Presently, there appears to be no sanction or remedy should the 119-day period be missed. The practical reality is that most licensing boards can take several months to process a new licence application. This can vary wildly and in some cases licensing boards have been known to take six months or even longer to get an application put to a hearing. This all depends on various local foibles and practices. In some cases, the timeline is influenced by the frequency of hearings, which in turn might be influenced by the amount of business a particular licensing board might have to process. It is not uncommon for some licensing boards to sit monthly, such as Edinburgh, Aberdeen, Scottish Borders, and so on, whereas some of the other boards might only sit three or four times a year.

Once a date has been decided for the hearing, the licensing board will issue a citation confirming the date, time and venue of the hearing. The board will issue copies of relevant paperwork which they have received in connection with the application, and the citation will be sent to the applicant as well as to other persons such as objectors who have lodged papers for consideration.

It is typical to receive 7 days' notice of the hearing date, although in many cases the board date might be known well in advance, or the board might confirm the date of the hearing at the time it issues the site notice for display. This is one for private practitioners to be aware of as it is all too easy to focus on the site notice instructions and overlook that the letter might also be a citation.

1 Although, note my discussion in the opening paragraph of Chapter 9 in relation to the yet-to-be enacted provisions which will create a new "period of determination", allowing up to 9 months to reach a conclusion.

The citation should confirm the date, time and location of the hearing. The hearing is usually conducted in the council chamber (or equivalent) in the traditional city chambers or town hall/council facilities, but not always. I have attended hearings in local theatres and even an ice rink.

On attending the hearing, the applicant is most likely to be one of a number of cases to be heard that day and many licensing sections will email an agenda to agents in advance. The agenda is also made available online in many areas, although not all. An application will call, and all relevant parties will have their say. Questions may be asked and answered. It may be that the applicant will face a tough time in what is a court-like formal process. It may be that the applicant is pushing an open door. The process and mechanics of hearings is also discussed in greater detail in Chapter 4 at Section 5.1. Ultimately, the board must come to a lawful decision.

The key consideration in reaching a determination is to establish whether one of the grounds of refusal applies to the application – if one or more grounds do apply, then the application must be refused, but if no ground applies, then the board must grant the application.[2]

The language which is used here is very important and to my mind is an axiomatic element of the whole policy and philosophy underpinning the licensing system in Scotland. As I have discussed elsewhere in this book, the 2005 Act is neither a granting nor a refusing Act,[3] as much as interested parties might like it to be one way or the other. It is not for the licensing board to look to refuse an application, and neither is it for the licensing board to start from a position that an application should be granted (as is the case under the Gambling Act 2005). The licensing board must look to each application with an open mind and consider each application on its own merits or demerits. It cannot refuse an application on a whim or even for "other good reason", as is the case under the Civic Government (Scotland) Act 1982, even if that reason might be a justifiably held and perfectly sensible view far less an irrational or arbitrary one. The board's task is simple in this regard: it must assess the application lawfully and decide if a ground for refusal applies. If a ground applies, the application is refused. If no ground applies, the application is granted.

The grounds for refusal are provided for in section 23(5) and are as follows:

- The premises are excluded premises.
- The application must be refused if it is for premises for which an earlier refusal has been given within the previous year;[4] or the applicant seeks

2 2005 Act, s 23(4).

3 The general expression of licensing law as a merits-based system in which it is to be expected that licences will be granted is one which has subsisted for generations: see, for example, Lord Ormidale in *Baillie v Wilson* 1917 SC 55 at 58:

> "The purpose and the scope of the Act is truly to regulate the sale of exciseable liquors. The right of the public to be supplied with liquors, and the right of members of the public to sell liquors, if only the statutory regulations thereanent are observed, seem to me to be recognised, and that in each licensing area. There is certainly no duty imposed on the licensing tribunals to see that each area is kept supplied with whisky and public-houses, but section 11, which enacts that it shall be lawful for the Licensing Court to grant certificates for the year to such and so many persons as the Court shall think meet and convenient, appears to me to mean that, if there are persons duly qualified according to the statute applying for licences, a duty is imposed on the Court to grant certificates to some at least of the applicants."

4 2005 Act, s 25(2).

24-hour licensing without exceptional circumstances;[5] or the applicant seeks off-sale hours outwith 10am to 10pm.[6]

- The licensing board considers that the granting of the application would be inconsistent with one or more of the licensing objectives.
- Having regard to the nature of the activities proposed to be carried on in the subject premises; the location, character and condition of the premises; and the persons likely to frequent the premises, the board considers that the premises are unsuitable for use for the sale of alcohol.
- Having regard to the number and capacity of licensed premises or licensed premises of the same or similar description as the subject premises in the locality in which the subject premises are situated, the board considers that, if the application were to be granted, there would, as a result, be overprovision of licensed premises, or licensed premises of that description, in the locality.

There is a special provision for those circumstances where the board considers that the application requires a tweak or amendment in order for it to be satisfied that a ground of refusal does not apply under section 27(3). This covers the inevitable horse-trading which occurs at so many licensing hearings across the country and is a natural part of the licensing process. The application, once lodged, is not fixed in tablets of stone. It is possible that some amendment is agreed by all parties, which would allow comfort and in turn allow the application to be granted. An applicant might seek certain hours of trade, which attracts considerable opprobrium, and, upon reflecting on those concerns, agrees or proposes a lesser number of hours. An applicant might seek to have a particular capacity for their premises, only to discover building standards do not agree and propose a smaller capacity, which they can live with and accept. An applicant might originally plan to have a beer garden, but then agree to delete that from their application because objections have been received from residents.[7]

There are innumerable ways in which an application might be tinkered with at the hearing. The way the Act is written implies that the "proposer" of the modification is the board themselves, which is often the case, but the practice in reality is of course that a prudent applicant, seeing which way the wind is blowing, might offer a concession or two of their own volition. The board can listen to such offers and, in the end, it is the board who will formally propose the modification as part of the decision-making process. If the applicant accepts the modification – whether or not it is a modification they have themselves suggested, or one which is grudgingly accepted having been placed before them in the form of an ultimatum – then the board must grant the application.

If the board does decide to refuse the application, it must specify the ground

5 2005 Act, s 64(2).

6 2005 Act, s 65(3).

7 The issue of modifying layout plans as part of this process was one which met with considerable concern from the trade when it was first proposed as part of the Criminal Justice and Licensing (Scotland) Act 2010 amendments to the 2005 Act, with some pointing to this power being a way in which some boards might micro-manage the cosmetic layout of premises. In practice, these modifications are really only where there is some technical issue which is raised by an officer such as from building standards: see further "United trade opposition to plan changes" [2008] 41 SLLP 5.

of refusal, and, if the ground relates to the licensing objectives, it must specify the relevant objective(s). This will be read out formally at the time the determination is announced, or, at least, it should be. Clerks should take care to ensure that a decision to refuse by the board is legitimately based on one of the grounds of refusal to avoid the possibility of a challenge should the decision not go the way that the applicant or any other party wish it to. I have been involved in several cases where individual board members will go "rogue" and narrate their reasons for refusal – sometimes in considerable detail – and watch the clerk squirm as the penny drops that none of the reasons given is lawful grounds of refusal. It is up to a good clerk to marshal the board members and ensure decision-making is transparent and lawful.

When announcing the decision, different approaches are taken across Scotland. In some areas, each case is considered and determined and announced, before moving on to the next case. In other areas, the board will hear a clutch of applications together before retiring in private, and then return to announce the determinations of those applications together in a list.

If the board decides to grant the application, it must issue first a notice of the decision in writing within 7 days, and thereafter must issue the premises licence along with a summary of the licence within 28 days.[8] If the board decides to refuse the application, the applicant must at that moment, even if it means interrupting the flow of the hearing, pipe up and request a determination under section 25 of the Act, if they want the ability to bring the application back for a second crack at the whip within a year. Section 25 provides for a one-year moratorium on a fresh application where a refusal has occurred, unless a "direction" is given at the time of the refusal, or there has been a "material change in circumstances". Of course, the applicant may have no interest in securing this possibility and it is a matter for them to request it or not. It is also a matter for the board to grant or refuse. It may be that, upon a refusal, the applicant seeks a section 25 direction and makes additional submissions as to why the board might allow the fresh application and grant the direction. Licensing board treatment of the section 25 direction requests varies across the country. In some areas, a direction will always be given if sought. In some areas the board will require convincing.

The applicant, police and any party appearing may request a statement of reasons as to how the board reached the decision under section 51(2), whether granted or refused. The request must be lodged with the board no later than 14 days after receipt of the notice and must then be issued within a further 14 days in the form provided in Schedule 4 to the Procedural Regulations.[9] In many cases an agent will request a statement of reasons at the instance of the refusal, in "live time" as it were. Whilst this is accepted practice, and most clerks will note this and therefore crack on with preparing a statement, the correct approach would be to follow up any verbal request with a written one, in order to completely satisfy the terms of section 51. The reference to the request for a statement of reasons is by "giving notice", and the clerk "receiving" such notice. It is implicit, in my view, that this language infers a notice should be in writing and is to best to cover one's posterior.

8 2005 Act, s 26(1) and Licensing (Procedure) (Scotland) Regulations 2007 (SSI 2007/453) ("Procedural Regulations"), reg 20.

9 Regulation 15.

2 GROUNDS OF REFUSAL OF A PREMISES LICENCE: COMPETENCY GROUNDS

Let us now examine the grounds of refusal in more detail. In broad terms, the grounds for refusal can be separated into two categories: (1) competency grounds; and (2) merit-based grounds. The first set of grounds of refusal I have labelled "competency" grounds on the basis that if an application falls into one of these categories a licensing board has no option but to refuse the application because it is technically incompetent under certain terms of the 2005 Act.

2.1 Excluded premises

Section 23(5)(a) of the Act states that an application for a premises licence must be refused by the licensing board if the subject premises are "excluded premises". The term is defined in section 123 of the Act and excluded premises are *motorway service areas* and, with certain qualifications, *garage premises*. The provision therefore, on the face of it, creates an automatic, non-negotiable outcome where an an application is effectively unlawful if it pertains to one of these two classes of premises. However, the Act goes on to confirm a specific definition of each, allowing for debate and, in the case of garage premises, a limbo pole which, should it be negotiated succesfully, would allow the application to be considered on the merits in the usual way.

In these cases then, should an application be lodged for what is deemed to be either a motorway service station or a garage premises, there is a preliminary point to be raised, in most cases at a hearing, as to whether section 123 applies and if so, how.

2.1.1 Excluded premises: motorway service areas

The default position in Scotland is that no premises in a motorway service area can be granted a premises licence. Section 123(2)(a) defines motorway service areas as:

> "premises on land—
> (i) acquired or appropriated by a special roads authority, and
> (ii) for the time being used,
> for the provision of facilities to be used in connection with the use of a special road provided for the use of traffic of class 1 (with or without other classes)".

This is identical to the English provision contained at section 176(2) of the 2003 Act.

The specific definition is important because there are cases where what appears to the general public to be a services facility, as it is commonly understood, may not fit this specific legal definition. In June 2013, JD Wetherspoon attracted some media coverage having successfully applied for a premises licence at Beaconsfield Services by South Bucks District Council, as the first "pub" to be given a licence at services in the United Kingdom. A number of other retail operators had been granted off-sale premises licences under the 2003 Act without too much attention prior to this, all of them overcoming the section 176 hurdle of the 2003 Act on the basis that the specific services point was not covered by the definition as the land had been sold by the Highways Authority to private third parties.

The position is reflected north of the border but on a smaller scale in relation to the numbers of service areas. In April 2016, the Stirling Licensing Board granted a premises licence to M&S for a premises at the Moto services near Bannockburn at the meeting point of the M9 and M80. The land had been sold by the special roads authority to a private company called Granada Services in 1985, and therefore the general prohibition as noted above under section 123 of the 2005 Act did not apply.

So, whilst the general proposition that motorway service areas are excluded remains true, interested parties need to examine the title and definition of the specific roads where the service stations are located.

2.1.2 Excluded premises: garage premises

Section 123 operates to exclude garage premises subject to a special provision under subsection (5), which is in the following terms:

> "premises used for the sale by retail of petrol or derv or which form part of premises so used are not excluded premises if persons resident in the locality in which the premises are situated are, or are likely to become, reliant to a significant extent on the premises as the principal source of—
> (a) petrol or derv, or
> (b) groceries (where the premises are, or are to be, used also for the sale by retail of groceries)."

The source of this provision is the pervasive, but in my view unpersuasive, belief that alcohol should not be sold from premises which people normally attend by motor vehicle[10] because it would in some way influence them to drink and drive.[11] Such logic pays no heed to the many thousands of motorists who attend supermarkets and local stores and complete their shopping without resorting to opening and consuming their alcoholic purchases on the drive home.

Section 123 has proven to be a most unhappy provision, attracting significant opprobrium and case law almost from inception.[12] Note that the provision

10 Under the 1976 Act, some boards had simply refused point-blank to issue a licence to garage premises: see, e.g., *Lamb & Gardiner Ltd v Perth and Kinross District Licensing Board* [1998] 10 SLLP 22, and *Texaco Ltd v North Lanarkshire Licensing Board*, Hamilton Sheriff Court, 10 June 1997; [1997] 8 SLLP 25; others have created a sort of balancing act based on comparison of sales of alcohol and groceries to petrol, as in *Safeway Stores plc v City of Glasgow Licensing Board* 2001 SLT 1115 and in *BP Express Shopping Ltd v Perth and Kinross Licensing Board* [2005] 31 SLLP 34. See also "Should unleaded mean unlicensed?" [1998] 10 SLLP 31.

11 An example of how Parliamentary thinking looked in this direction is from the debate on 7 December 2000, when the review of licensing laws in Scotland was just announced. MSP Mary Mulligan said:

> "A recent example of availability going too far comes from my area, which is West Lothian. An application was made to the licensing board for alcohol to be sold in the shop at a petrol station. The council turned it down, but there might be an appeal. We are all clear about the fact that alcohol and driving do not mix. For those who can take alcohol in reasonable measures, that may not be an issue, but if we put alcohol in a place where it is available to people who are driving, that might prove too great a temptation to some. We should not put people in that position."

12 The provision led to some garage premises being unable to convert their licences during the 2005 transition process. Perhaps embarrassingly for the Scottish Parliament, s 123 had not

creates an inference of reliance on the proposed premises not for the purchase of alcohol, but for the purchase of other groceries or indeed fuel/derv. This is a most unusual provision to take root in a licensing Act for which jurists have been at pains for some time to affirm has a central remit or essential aim, that of the regulation of alcohol. Yet here, we have a provision which is about protecting a community facility if it can be shown local people do rely that on that facility regardless of the sale of alcohol, through the process of securing permission to do that very thing! Section 123 is more akin to a planning law provision than a true licensing provision and perhaps this is part of the reason why it has generated such difficulty.

Section 123 has also probably generated more appeals than any other discrete technical provision of the Act, as courts sought to make sense of the provision. The first of these was in fact the first reported appeal arising from the 2005 Act – *Co-operative Group Ltd v Aberdeen City Licensing Board*,[13] affectionately known as the "Two Old Ladies" case.[14] Sheriff Principal Sir Stephen Young said:

> "As indicated, the question the Board had to consider was whether as a matter of fact persons resident in the locality in which the premises were situated were, or were likely to become reliant to a significant extent on the premises as the principal source of petrol or derv or groceries. I have emphasised the words 'persons resident in the locality' since these are the persons who matter here, and not the local community as a whole. It is not even necessary that all the residents in the locality should be, or be likely to become, reliant to a significant extent on the premises as a principal source of petrol or derv or groceries. All that is required here to satisfy the test is that there are some persons (for example elderly persons who are unable to drive or, as counsel suggested, the residents of a sheltered housing scheme) who as a matter of fact are, or are likely to become, so reliant on the premises."[15]

His reference to elderly residents became referred to shorthand in licensing circles as the "Two Old Ladies" test, indicating if an applicant could demonstrate that even two people were, or likely to become, reliant on the premises, the hurdle would be cleared. Flowing from this, applicants began to conduct market research and present their findings to the licensing board. Further refusals occurred, however, and the next garage appeal resulted in *BP Oil (UK) Ltd v City of Glasgow Licensing Board*,[16] which related to two premises in Glasgow, in which Sheriff Scott allowed both appeals on a similar vein to the Aberdeen case above (this decision was, however, appealed to the Court

actually been brought into effect when conversion applications for garage premises began to be heard. Some commentators argued that a licensing board could not refuse an application for a garage because the provisions for excluded premises were not in force. This did not stop boards taking that very step and many pointed to s 148, with its reference to "excluded premises", which was in force. The matter was brought to the attention of the government at an early stage but was not addressed until the introduction of the Licensing (Scotland) Act 2005 (Commencement No. 5) Order 2008, the sole purpose of which was to enact s 123 as of 5 September 2008. By this time, several garage applications had been refused.

13 [2009] 41 SLLP 16.

14 See also "Co-op victory in garage appeal case" [2009] 41 SLLP 1; and Andrew Hunter "Excluded Premises: Settled Law or One Interpretation?" [2009] 41 SLLP 12 for commentary on the case.

15 [2009] 41 SLLP 16 at para 9.

16 Glasgow Sheriff Court, 17 July 2009, unreported.

of Session and conjoined with two Edinburgh appeals, and that decision is explored in more detail below[17]).

Around the same time, BP also appealed a refusal for an Edinburgh premises[18] and Sheriff Principal Bowen QC took a different approach to the Glasgow and Aberdeen cases, preferring to focus on the premises as opposed to persons who might be reliant on them. His judicial analysis continued in this different direction in *Roc UK Ltd v Edinburgh Licensing Board.*[19] Again, the court was being asked to look at a refusal for filling station premises, in this case an ESSO garage in Canonmills, Edinburgh. Sheriff Principal Bowen QC continued to apply his separate approach in disagreeing with the Aberdeen and Glasgow decisions:

> "I have preferred the view that the focus of section 123(5) is not on a handful of individuals but is on the premises, the question being whether there is a significant degree of reliance on them by persons resident in the locality when viewed as a group."[20]

At this stage, we had several garage appeals all floating around the jurisprudential ether, none of them binding on the other, and reaching different tests and conclusions. Sensibly, parties agreed to run a conjoined appeal to the Court of Session to seek final clarity on the matter and the BP Glasgow and Edinburgh cases were all swept up and culminated in the combined case of *BP Oil (UK) Ltd v City of Edinburgh Licensing Board and City of Glasgow Licensing Board*,[21] with Lords Eassie, Brodie and Wheatley presiding. This case has become the settled law on the matter of what section 123 is supposed to mean. After a wide-ranging review of the legislative background and shrieval decisions, including analysis of aspects specific to each case, the crux of the decision as regards the meaning of section 123(5) is found in the following paragraph:

> "**[51]** Recognising that we have to deal with an unquestionably difficult legislative provision, and having regard to the general nature of the policy apparently underlying the provision, *we have come to the view that what the language of sub-section (5) envisages is that there be a recognisable number of persons in the locality, not necessarily constituted as a group, who as a matter of their purchasing habits see and treat the shop premises in question as the principal source from which they may in ordinary course obtain either groceries or fuel and who would properly consider themselves materially disadvantaged or inconvenienced were that shop not to provide those retail facilities. In judging that matter, evidence of alternative retail outlets for groceries or motor fuel (or the local knowledge of the licensing board to that effect) is plainly not excluded; but the existence of some alternative facilities within the locality will not in itself prevent the giving of a positive answer to the question.* We appreciate that in what we have just said we may be seen as 'glossing the statute'; but given the recognised unclarity of the text, we think we have little alternative but so to express ourselves in deciding these appeals and endeavouring to discern the proper sense in which the legislature should be held to have intended the phraseology which it deployed."

The wording in italic (my emphasis) provides the reader with the *ratio decidendi* of this case, and it is on this wording that all "garage" cases should now

17 See "Petrol station refusals head for appeal" [2009] 40 SLLP 5 for commentary on the appeals at the time.

18 *BP Oil (UK) Ltd v Edinburgh Licensing Board*, 22 December 2009, unreported.

19 2010 SLT (Sh Ct) 21; [2010] LLR 719.

20 Ibid para 13.

21 [2011] CSIH 29.

be assessed – but the surrounding wording book-ending this key text is left here, to demonstrate the judicial view of the quality of the legislation itself. In practical terms, applicants in this scenario will still, as they did in the earlier efforts post 2009, seek to rely on market research as well as other forms of evidence such as affidavits in order to demonstrate that this "principal source" test, as it might be paraphrased, is satisfied in order to jump the section 123(5) hurdle and have the application considered on the merits.

It may be of interest for some readers to note that England and Wales have had a similar journey, of sorts, with their approach to garage licensing. Section 176(2)(b) of the 2003 Act states that "excluded premises" means "premises used primarily as a garage or which form part of premises which are primarily so used". This led to a number of challenges on the use of the word "primarily" and is known as the "primary use" test, where English and Welsh authorities took matters such as footfall and turnover into account.[22] It is, of course, important to realise that the English "primary use" test is not the same as the Scottish "principal source" test, as I have described it above.

2.2 Grounds for refusal: an application made within one year of a previous refusal

As noted above in the discussion concerning the contemporaneous request for a direction under section 25 following a refusal, the Act provides that:

> "the Board must refuse any subsequent premises licence application in respect of the same premises made before the expiry of the period of one year beginning with the date of the earlier refusal".[23]

This creates a one year "moratorium" on applications for the same premises (unless, of course, a direction is granted as discussed).

There are a couple of elements of this to flesh out. First, what is meant by the "same premises"? On the face of it, if a particular set of premises such as a shop unit or a leisure unit like an unlicensed restaurant were refused an application, then it seems likely that a subsequent application seeking to license the same unit would fall foul of this provision. If, however, a party sought to license a larger set of premises which included the former unit previously refused, then there is a real argument that it is not the same premises. This will come down to fact and degree of course.

I would suggest that, if a shop unit at 10 High Street were refused, and a subsequent applicant had possession of both 10 High Street and the shop next door at 12 High Street, and wished to knock them together and seek a licence for the new, larger set of premises, then there is a strong argument that the new 10/12 High Street is not the "same premises". In *Kelvinside*

22 There are a number of English cases exploring primary use: *Green v Justices for the Inner London Area* (1994) 19 LR 13; *R v Liverpool Crown Court, ex parte Kevin John Goodwin* (1998) 38 LR 21; and the influential *R (on the application of Murco Petroleum Ltd) v Bristol City Council* [2010] EWHC 1992 (Admin). In a case from January 2014, Shell UK Oil Products Ltd convinced South Hams District council that the s 176 test should be set aside as it was not compatible with the EU Services Directive: see "Garage forecourts, premises licences and the EU Services Directive", www.localgovernmentlawyer.co.uk, 29 January 2014.

23 2005 Act, s 25(2).

Community Council v City of Glasgow District Council,[24] for example, a second application for premises which purposefully included an additional reference to a beer garden did not constitute the same premises, when the preceding application had not been clear on the inclusion of that area, the Lord Justice-Clerk saying:

> "In the second application, however, the description made it plain that there was to be a beer garden. In these circumstances, I am of the opinion that there was material before the licensing board entitling them to conclude that the premises to which the second application related were different to the premises which were the subject of the first application."[25]

In this case, then, the premises were substantially the same, the only change being that they now included an external area and were still treated as not being the "same premises".

The next ponderation is about the commencement of the one-year period – exactly when does this activate? Note that the wording refers to an application "*made* before the expiry of the period of one year" (my emphasis). The reference to the application being "made" might mean that the one-year time bar relates to the *lodgement* of the application within one year, as opposed to it being determined within that period; but it has also been argued that "made" should refer to the date not when the application is lodged but when the application is presented at a hearing. A cute applicant could not, therefore, lodge the second application 8 or 9 months after the refusal hoping to have it heard just after the one-year period.

What all of this means in the context of our discussion of grounds of refusal is that any application lodged for the same premises up to and including the date of the first anniversary of the refusal of the previous application, will automatically be refused because it is an incompetent application.[26] Unless, of course, the agent appearing has been savvy enough to remember the section 25 direction request, and the board magnanimous enough to grant it!

2.3 Grounds for refusal: an application seeking a 24-hour licence

Section 64 of the 2005 Act is in the following terms:

> **"24-hour licences to be granted only in exceptional circumstances**
> (1) Subsection (2) applies where, in relation to any premises—
> (a) an application of any of the following kinds is made to a Licensing Board in respect of the premises, namely—
> (i) a premises licence application,
> (ii) a premises licence variation application,
> (iii) an occasional licence application, or
> (iv) an extended hours application, and
> (b) if the application were to be granted, the licensed hours in relation to the premises would be such as to allow alcohol to be sold on the premises during a continuous period of 24 hours or more.

24 1990 SLT 726.
25 Ibid at 734.
26 On the issue of a new application competing with a contemporaneous appeal to a previous refusal, see the gambling case of *MAB Bookmakers Ltd v Orkney Islands Area Licensing Board* 2019 SLT (Sh Ct) 18.

> (2) The Licensing Board must refuse the application unless the Board is satisfied that there are exceptional circumstances which justify allowing the sale of alcohol on the premises during such a period."

This provision therefore creates a rebuttable presumption against granting a licence, or a variation or one-off extension of an existing licence, which would allow 24 sequential hours in which sales of alcohol may occur. Unlike some of the other "technical" grounds of refusal we are examining in this section of the book, this ground of refusal is not a black and white competency test – there is a subjective element to this, namely, the "exceptional circumstances" test.

Why was it thought necessary to create this specific statutory provision noting that licensing boards had unfettered control not to grant such applications under the general application of the licensing system?

Nicholson did, of course, discuss this issue. His report reflects on the commercial reality of some premises already trading for 24 hours like supermarkets, albeit with restricted licensing times,[27] and goes on to say that:

> "the time has now come when there should no longer be what many regard as petty and irrational restrictions on the sale and supply of alcohol".[28]

Against the backdrop of a multitude of different licensing hours and possible extensions under the 1976 Act, and the changing attitudes he identifies, he concludes:

> "For the foregoing reasons we have come to the conclusion that the existing system relative to permitted hours should be replaced by one where it is in theory possible for licensed premises to be open 24-hours a day."

This proposal created pandemonium at political levels and was described in the media as a move allowing all pubs to open around the clock, thus creating a narrative of fear. To suggest, however, that Nicholson's proposal was all for deregulation of the Gin Alley type, would do severe injury to his Committee's report and his memory. Shortly after the preceding statement quoted above, Nicholson went on to say:

> "We are in no doubt that licensing boards would operate a system of 'authorised' hours in a responsible and acceptable manner, and their general approach to that should be set out in policy statements . . . If effect were to be given to the foregoing suggestions there might not in fact be a very noticeable difference between the licensing scene as it exists at present and as it might exist in future. We imagine that many operators are reasonably satisfied with their present permitted hours, and would not wish to seek any changes. Moreover, we suspect that in many instances purely commercial considerations, such as staff costs, would dissuade licensees from seeking greatly extended hours. On the other hand, what we are proposing might result in some increases in opening hours in circumstances which are likely to be welcomed by consumers."[29]

It is very clear then, to the informed reader, that Nicholson was not espousing a "wild west" approach to licensing hours, but instead was advocating that licensing boards should be allowed greater flexibility to make local choices which were appropriate for their jurisdictions. He certainly was not advocating

27 Nicholson Report, para 2.17, p 41.
28 Ibid para 5.4, p 72.
29 Ibid paras 5.6 and 5.7, pp 72 and 73.

some form of unrelenting 24-hour licensing in that wider sense. Indeed, in his own written response to the Bill, he said:

> "if this provision is to remain, I would respectfully suggest that the trigger point should be a number of hours just beyond what might normally be regarded as acceptable – say, 18 hours".

In the earliest Parliamentary debates on a proposed Licensing Bill after Nicholson had reported, this "myth" was exposed. The then Minister for Justice Cathy Jamieson said in the debate on 17 September 2003:

> "One significant myth that has grown around the recommendations is the much-publicised, so-called free-for-all on opening hours. I will be clear in dispelling that myth. Sheriff Principal Nicholson and his committee have not opened up Scotland to 24-hour drinking as a matter of course. The recommendations suggest a move from the present piecemeal position of fixed opening hours with locally agreed extensions to a more tailored, premises-by-premises approach that is founded on the proposed new legislative principles. Each set of premises will have an operating plan that sets out its operating hours and conditions. Those will be tailored to ensure that the new licensing principles are not put at risk. We should pause and ask those who might peddle the idea of routine 24-hour opening to consider how any establishment could have a routine 24-hour licence and still meet its obligations of promoting public order and public health and protecting children."

When challenged on allowing an "American" style system for 24-hour supermarkets, Cathy Jamieson said:

> "My point is that we must work on a premises-by-premises basis. Contrary to what was suggested in some sections of the media, we are not proposing a free-for-all or saying that pubs and other premises could routinely be open 24-hours. It is important to get the framework right and to have localised decision making. I expect a range of issues to be taken into account in making those decisions. The Executive sees little or no argument for any premises routinely to sell alcohol throughout the day and night. Sheriff Principal Nicholson has been striving publicly to correct the misinterpretation of his recommendation."

In the same debate, MSP Kenny MacAskill, who would of course go on to become the Justice Minister who delivered the 2005 Act, said on this point:

> "I regret that the hares have been set running as regards the idea of 24-hour operation, which is unfortunate, unfair and fundamentally untrue."

Notwithstanding these assurances, the Local Government and Transport Committee, which steered the Bill, ultimately maintained concerns over the concept of 24-hour licensing, even having heard oral evidence from Nicholson directly on 22 March 2005 when he made number of observations about this issue, including remarking:

> "I would be surprised if many licensed premises in Scotland – with the possible exception of 24-hour supermarkets, for example – sought longer hours than they currently have for selling alcohol, although I am gazing into the crystal ball."

When asked if a provision banning 24-hour licences would result in applications for 23 hours and 59 minutes, he said:

> "That was really a point about drafting rather than policy. I have not had a response from the Executive. It might persuade me that I have misunderstood or got it wrong, but it seems to me that although the idea is, as I understand it, to create a kind of presumption against 24-hour opening – with which I would not quarrel – the bill will not achieve that."

The 24-hour licensing "myth" was also referred to oral evidence at the same session on 22 March 2005, by Peter Daniels,[30] who said:

> ". . . we supported the basic principle of Nicholson that decisions on opening hours should be left to the boards. The decision that is taken by each board will depend on the circumstances in its area. What might be applicable in East Renfrewshire might not be applicable in Glasgow, just a few miles across the border. There has been a popular myth that the Nicholson report would mean having 24-hour opening, but the boards could decide to reduce the licensing hours from their present level."

Notwithstanding all of these submissions to remove fear surrounding the mistaken idea that any new licensing system would create 24-hour drinking, in the Stage 1 Report, the Committee said:

> "The Committee considers that this provision in the Bill will have an impact in tackling the problems associated with drinking only if it is used in conjunction with other measures in the Bill such as banning irresponsible drinks promotions and the use of Licensing Standards Officers . . . The Committee gave some thought as to whether a cut-off point of 24-hours was appropriate. Inevitably, any time limit selected will be somewhat arbitrary in nature. However, in relation to the 24-hour limit, the Committee had concerns that allowing licensed premises to advertise '24-hour drinking', even in exceptional circumstances, might send out a signal that drinking for very long periods of time is an acceptable reason for visiting a particular licensed premises. The Committee also noted that the provision in the Bill could have the consequence that certain licensed premises may never close – or close only for very short periods."

These considerations suggest a continued misdirection as to whether 24-hour drinking would in any practical sense be a reality, and instead the fear of 24-hour drinking meant that something had to be done to make sure this could not be achieved, notwithstanding that it was not a culture which existed within the licensed trade,[31] nor was it proposed to exist. The 24-hour licensing hobgoblin continued to be a discussed as a genuine threat and this is visible in the full Parliamentary debate on Stage 1 of the Licensing Bill which occurred on 22 June 2005. During that session, the then Deputy Minister for Finance and Public Reform posed the question of whether Government should "*endorse 24-hour drinking*", suggesting perhaps that the optics of a deregulated system would of itself lead to irresponsibility. Later in that debate, Green MSP Patrick Harvie said:

> "In the minister's policy document – and, I think, in his opening speech – he quite rightly dismissed the myth of 24-hour drinking. I have received e-mails and one or two letters from people who are concerned that there will be 24-hour drinking – that perception is still out there, and we need to challenge it. The presumption against 24-hour drinking is absolutely the right approach, but there is no reason why we should not welcome a premises-by-premises approach, with determination made locally."

30 Peter Daniels, the then Chief Executive of East Renfrewshire Council, was the Chair of a Working Group called "Off-sales in the Community" which produced the secondary report in the run up to the 2005 Act.

31 It has been remarked that if one really wanted to drink for 24 hours, this could be achieved by attending different premises, or being resident in a hotel, although in these examples this implies that the customer has been able to be served and that the management themselves have been happy to serve. It has also been remarked that one can drink for a straight 24 hours at home.

Extraordinary, fevered reaction to the 24-hour drinking red herring was even more visceral at Stage 3 of the Bill debate on 16 November 2005, a session deplored by Ministers during and afterwards, as well as by political commentators and indeed licensing practitioners. The upshot of all the hullabaloo appeared to me to be that the Parliamentary desire to create a special rule to prevent 24-hour *licensing* was in fact an artifice on which Parliament could send a message that it did not support 24-hour *drinking*. The eventual result of the caterwauling on 16 November 2005 was section 64 as we have it now, replete with the "exceptional circumstances" test.

So, when might this provision be adopted back in the real world? The Explanatory Notes to the 2005 Act on section 64 say:

> "This is a test which will have to be applied on a case by case basis. Guidance will set out national guidelines on the policy that should be adopted by Licensing Boards in relation to circumstances that might merit 24-hour opening. Boards are required to set out their policy on licensing hours for their area in their policy statements."[32]

This passes the buck somewhat! The Regulatory Impact Assessment to the Licensing Bill references this provision only once, to say that "exemptions to 24-hour opening" would be agreed by the National Licensing Forum, which of course never happened.[33] The original Guidance for Licensing Boards did not provide significant illumination, merely stating:

> "Ministers are of the view that Licensing Boards should consider 'exceptional circumstances' to cover special events such as one-off local or national festivals. It is unlikely that 'exceptional circumstances' would be constituted in the case of premises where there were routine requests to sell alcohol for 24-hours."[34]

The Policy Memorandum for the Licensing Bill does not provide much beyond the rationale for clearing away the old 1976 "regular extension" system:

> "The original intention was that extensions to standard opening hours would be granted infrequently, for example in certain holiday resorts and at peak holiday periods. The reality today, however, is that regular and lengthy extensions to statutory permitted hours are so widespread that the whole concept of permitted hours has very largely been eroded. 10,000 of the current 17,000 licensed premises in Scotland operate with regular extensions to the standard permitted hours. The Bill introduces a more modern approach and gets rid of the practice of giving extensions in favour of clarity up front about acceptable hours. There is a presumption in the Bill against 24-hour licensing hours. A holder of a licence would be required to specify their hours in their operating plans submitted to the Licensing Board for approval and drawn up with regard to the Board's published policy statement, which would set out the Board's general approach to policy on licensing hours for their area".[35]

This again only take us so far as the thinking behind the need to create a general presumption against 24-hour licensing as a specific provision within the Bill, noting that each licensing board would always determine a local policy and assess all applications on their merits or demerits in any event.

Reviewing all of this background, it seems correct to suggest that the section 64 provision was inserted in order to satiate significant hyperbole both within

32 2005 Act, Explanatory Notes, para 135.
33 Licensing (Scotland) Bill, Regulatory Impact Assessment, para 109.
34 Guidance to Licensing Boards (Scottish Government, April 2007) para 21.
35 Policy Memorandum, Licensing Bill (SP Bill 37-PM), 28 February 2005, para 97.

and outwith Parliament surrounding the erroneous hysteria that the Licensing Bill would result in "24-hour" drinking, with resultant misery.

With no examples of what might constitute "exceptional circumstances" other than the somewhat paltry suggestion of "local or national festivals", it has been left to local licensing boards to decide what events in their jurisdiction, if any, they are prepared to allow a 24-hour licence, and it is open to any person to object to applications seeking any hours of any kind. As far as I am aware no licensing board in Scotland has ever issued a permanent 24-hour licence to any sort of operator be it retail or leisure. There are some (a very few) examples of boards granting one-off extensions which do allow a period of 24 hours or longer but the only ones I have been able to confirm were to allow continuous trade over Hogmanay and New Year's Day for certain club premises.

This, ironically, is what the original Nicholson style-system would have achieved in any event. Any suggestion that licensing boards might issue 24-hour licences like confetti can only have been made by someone unfamiliar with appearing before licensing boards in Scotland.

2.4 Grounds for refusal: an application seeking off-sale hours outwith 10am to 10pm

Section 65 of the 2005 Act is in the following terms:

> **"65 Licensed hours: off-sales**
> (1) This section applies where an application specified in subsection (2) is made to a Licensing Board in relation to any premises, but only so far as the application is for—
> (a) a licence authorising the sale of alcohol for consumption off the premises, or
> (b) an extension of off-sales hours in relation to the premises.
> (2) That application is—
> (a) a premises licence application,
> (b) a premises licence variation application,
> (c) an occasional licence application, or
> (d) an extended hours application.
> (3) If the off-sales hours proposed in the application are such that alcohol would be sold for consumption off the premises—
> (a) before 10am,
> (b) after 10pm, or
> (c) both,
> on any day, the Board must refuse the application."

So, to make that clear, under the 2005 Act the maximum licensing hours for off-sales are 10am to 10pm, 7 days a week. This can be contrasted to the 1976 provisions, which allowed 8am to 10pm Monday to Saturday, and 12.30pm to 10pm on Sundays. It can also be contrasted to the Licensing Act 2003, which has no restrictions at all and it is possible to have a 24-hour off-sale licence.

The off-sale hours apply to all off-sale sales, and not just those that occur on traditional off-sale premises like a shop or supermarket. Many other on-sales licensed premises also have an off-sale facility, such as pubs and hotels. The 10am to 10pm rule applies to all of those licences as well. A pub, restaurant or hotel type premises might have, for example, on-sales hours of 11am to 1am, but, even so, the maximum off-sales hours would still be 10am to 10pm, despite what the on-sales hours are. As for the exact nature of the off-sale facility, some pubs or hotels might have a designated "off-sale" area, perhaps on the gantry behind the bar, or even in a specific "shop" area within the premises. Another example might be simply that a restaurant owner wishes the ability to offer his customer a bottle of the wine he has enjoyed with a meal, to take home.

It is common in many licensing board areas to see the commencement hour for off-sales mirror that of the on-sales – in other words, that if the premises have an 11am start for on-sales, this is also the start time for off-sales. It is thought sensible by many licensing boards that both types of purchase should commence contemporaneously as this would remove confusion for staff as well as customers.[36]

In the preceding paragraphs on the 24-hour licensing question, I began to analyse why Parliament took the step of creating the presumption against a 24-hour licence. A similar question might be asked as to why the hours of 10am to 10pm were agreed given the original proposal was to have no set times other than the presumption against 24-hours. Examining Parliament's record on the issue of off-sale times is depressing reading, as I alluded to above, but it bears scrutiny so one understands the law and understands the policy intent.

The Bill, as originally introduced, contained no restriction on off-sale hours (or on-sale hours) whatsoever, adopting as it did the Nicholson approach. At Stage 2 of the Bill, a clause was inserted,[37] which created a maximum off-sale period of 8am to 11pm seven days a week.[38]

Bruce Crawford MSP, who introduced the amendment, cited a number of reasons for seeking to propose this limit on off-sale hours: (1) the general issue of alcohol misuse, (2) concerns about 24-hour licences, (3) a concern that allowing off-sales to open later would lead to people buying off-sales on the way home from clubs and pubs, and (4) concerns raised by the Scottish Grocers' Federation that later hours would only be given to out-of-town supermarkets, thus having a deleterious effect on local convenience stores. These appear, to my reading of the Parliamentary record, to be the central reasons and it is perhaps as a result of lobbying from several groups, concerned at the Nicholson open-ended approach to licensed hours, that the Government saw fit to amend this.

Reaction on the Holyrood debating floor was varied, with a number of interjections made by ministers perhaps unhelpfully putting themselves in the place of the local licensing boards, such as one suggestion that certain off-sales in some housing schemes in Glasgow should close even earlier than 9pm because "some licence holders clearly are not responsible"[39] and even comments like "I am concerned by the fact that boards across Scotland have made decisions that have not been consistent and have not always been in the best interests of their communities."[40] George Lyon MSP, the Minister who had the licensing brief at the time of the debate, ventilated the key issue thus: "should we trust local boards to respond to the needs of their communities or should we impose decisions from the centre?". In the result, the 8am to 11pm amendment passed 4 votes to 3, with 2 abstentions.

36 It should be noted that there may be a legitimate reason for an on-sales premises to seek an earlier commencement for off-sales, such as where the facility is used to fulfil remote orders which may be placed online.

37 Clause 60A.

38 This was introduced by way of Amendment 5 at the Stage 2 debate on 27 September 2005.

39 Paul Martin MSP (Labour).

40 Bristow Muldoon MSP (Labour).

The Stage 3 and final debate took place on 16 November 2005, now infamous as one of the poorest examples of Scottish parliamentary democracy. The front cover of the contemporaneous edition of *Scottish Licensing and Law Practice* carried the headline: "Off-sales hours slashed as last-minute amendments tarnish final Bill debate".[41]

It was clear that the topic of licensing hours was one creating significant stress levels for Parliamentarians and many were informed by the media furore over the English position.[42]

At the outset of the debate that morning in Holyrood, members were grasping with a number of competing motions and amendments, some in handwritten form lodged that same day. This was the author of significant confusion for members on the floor of the debating chamber. At the start of the proceedings, Bruce Crawford called for a point of order on the amendments, saying:

> "It will be interesting to see what further twists and turns will arise on this day of chaos".

The Deputy Presiding Officer Murray Tosh took considerable flak from John Swinney and Fergus Ewing in allowing a handwritten amendment from Andrew Arbuckle proposing to delete the 8am to 11pm provision, leaving it open-ended, as many members had not seen it, to which the DPO said it was available to view "at the back of the chamber".

Tommy Sheridan then said:

> "In the Parliament's six years, this is the most shambolic meeting that we have had on a very important piece of legislation."

There then followed acrimony from other MSPs who had not bothered to lodge their own amendments because they did not believe they would be accepted past the customary deadline, only to find three further and separate amendments which were accepted past said deadline.

Temperatures at Holyrood were clearly rising. A short recess was called to allow the piece of paper at the back of the chamber to be circulated but clearly the debate on the Licensing Bill was a dog's dinner. Alasdair Morgan said, after recess:

> "Members will agree that in view of the bill's importance to the people of Scotland and the Parliament, what has gone on so far today does a disservice to the people of Scotland. It has not been a good advertisement for the way in which we conduct our business. I ask that the Presiding Officers and the Executive reflect maturely on how we got to this state of affairs, so that we are never in this situation again."

After a number of amendments and debates on other aspects of the Bill, an amendment by Bristow Muldoon was presented to further amend the off-sales hours to prevent off-sales between 10pm and 3am, alongside the amendment by Andrew Arbuckle to pass the bill as it was originally introduced. A further

41 [2005] 32 SLLP 1.

42 It is important to note that the Licensing Act 2003, applicable to England and Wales, was commenced on 24 November 2005. All of the mainstream newspapers were therefore full of colourful stories about the English "24-hour licensing" at the same time as this debate was taking place. There is no doubt that Scottish Parliamentarians were influenced by this rhetoric and there can be no doubt that stakeholders and concerned local constituents were raising concerns over liberalising of licensing laws to their local MSP, having read continuously about "Binge Britain" and "24-hour licensing".

amendment, by Frank McAveety, proposed 10am to 10pm. These competing proposals then resulted in a terse and unedifying exchange.[43]

The general tenor of the debate appears to encircle the issue of prescription versus local decision-making. Andrew Arbuckle says:

> "Scotland is a diverse country and a one-size-fits-all policy on licensing is not appropriate. Issues about alcohol sales in Glasgow are not the same as those, for example, in Newburgh in Fife or in Aberdeenshire. I say to Frank McAveety that it is not correct to impose the Glasgow solution on the rest of the country."

He goes on to add: "It is perverse to say that although local people appear to know best for on-sales, they need to be told what to do for off-sales." The debate continued for some time in what were described as "near chaotic scenes". The *Scottish Licensing Law and Practice* commentary described it thus: "As MSPs filed into the chamber for the final vote, amendments on loose sheets of paper were, according to one commentator, 'flying like tickertape'", with licensing Minister George Lyon "clearly exasperated".

In the result, Mr McAveety's amendment was the one which gained most support, and the 10am to 10pm rule was inserted and became law.[44] This Bismarckian[45] approach to law-making resulted in a reduction in the maximum off-sale hours by 9.5 hours across the week, with shops and off-sales premises losing 8am to 10am six days a week, and gaining 10am to 12.30pm on Sundays.

43 Bruce Crawford said: "entertainment like this cannot be bought. I was thinking more of ferrets and sacks". He goes on to describe the debate thus:

> "As far as the shenanigans of earlier today are concerned, I cannot understand why the Executive has allowed itself to get into such a situation at this late juncture – it is chaos. To people outside, it must look like panic and that can only be embarrassing for the Executive. Unfortunately, it is also embarrassing for Parliament, which the Executive has brought into disrepute because of how it has handled proceedings this afternoon. It has been a boorach. Parliament is built on a former brewery site and there is an expression about organising a proverbial something or other in a brewery; the Executive has not managed to do that on this occasion and should hang its head in shame."

44 I have been asked on countless occasions why Scotland's off-sales are restricted from 10am to 10pm by clients in the retail sector, both independent and national operators, by licensing practitioners, and by family and friends. In my view it is instructive to note that the reasoning for the 10am to 10pm restriction clearly emanates from Mr McAveety's experiences in representing the Glasgow Shettleston area. He discusses, for example, attending AA meetings in the Saltmarket area of Glasgow and alcohol harm he sees in his area. In response to Mike Rumbles MSP proposing that hours should be left to local licensing boards to decide, he says: "We can get too caught up in the debate over local and national decision making. My principal objective is to find an approach that best reflects the consensus in the wider public. We, as parliamentarians, are asked to make such decisions". It appears to me that Mr McAveety wilfully ignored his "principal objective", and succeeded not in finding a wider consensus but in imposing his own, no doubt well-intentioned, view based purely on reaction to alcohol issues in his local area. The irony for me, as someone who appears regularly before the City of Glasgow Licensing Board, is that Parliament imposed a national restriction proposed by a Glasgow MSP on the basis that local boards could not be trusted with off-sale timings, as if the Glasgow board notoriously hands out off-sale licences with no regard to local alcohol harm – the reality, of course, is that such applications come under significant scrutiny.

45 Although the quote about sausages and law-making was, as I understood it, attributed to Otto von Bismarck, an article by Fred Shapiro in the *New York Times* on 21 July 2008 states: "When a [political] candidate refers to Otto von Bismarck's famous maxim about 'laws and sausages,' grin knowingly, point out that the Iron Chancellor was not associated with that quip until the 1930s and cite *The Daily Cleveland Herald*, Mar. 29, 1869, quoting the lawyer-poet John Godfrey Saxe that 'Laws, like sausages, cease to inspire respect in proportion as we know how they are made'."

This brings us on to the (often overlooked) second part of this ground of refusal, namely where:

> "in considering whether the granting of the application would be inconsistent with any of the licensing objectives, the Board must, in particular, consider the effect (if any) which the off-sales hours proposed in the application would have on the occurrence of antisocial behaviour".[46]

This might be shortly termed a "belt and braces" provision in that it requires licensing boards to pay particular attention to antisocial behaviour in relation to considering the ground of refusal based on the licensing objectives (which is explored below). This requirement might most obviously fall under the Public Nuisance objective, but the other objectives may also have some relevance. This special provision is linked to the *hours of the operation*, as opposed to the overall proposed licence. The implication is that certain off-sale licensed hours may have an association with antisocial behaviour, and that such behaviour may be a more relevant factor at certain times of the day as opposed to others. That, of course, is a fairly broad proposition. It may be too obvious to link the later hours to the concept of concern, and it is not always true that antisocial behaviour only occurs after dark. For example, there are cases where retailers have faced issues such as a ten o'clock "rush" of customers with harmful patterns of drinking, queuing before 10am to attempt to buy their alcohol for the day.

That brings us to the end of analysis apropos the technical grounds of refusal.

3 GROUNDS OF REFUSAL: THE "MERIT-BASED" GROUNDS

Unlike the technical grounds of refusal, the four merit-based grounds of refusal are where the real balance of success for any application is debated, and thus lives or dies, because very few, if any, applications where the technical grounds apply ever reach a hearing. The merit-based grounds of refusal are the "subjective" grounds where, unlike the competency or technical grounds, there is room for interpretation, there are grey areas, and the ultimate decision sits with the view of the board, whose approach will be with an open mind; in contrast with the competency grounds, where there is no wiggle room and the board's hands are tied to make a refusal determination if the relevant context exists. Let us examine the four merit-based grounds of refusal.

3.1 Refusal on the ground that the applicant is not a fit and proper person

The first ground is the so-called "fit and proper" test and this is the most recent ground to be introduced to the 2005 Act. There are and have been a number of similar "fitness" style tests in licensing laws over the years and whilst the 2005 Act version is the most modern iteration, it is not identical to its forebears. Section 17(1)(a) of the Licensing (Scotland) Act 1976 said a board shall refuse an application if it finds:

46 2005 Act, s 65(5).

> "that the applicant, or the person on whose behalf or for whose benefit the applicant will manage the premises or, in the case of an application to which section 11 of this Act applies, the applicant or the employee or agent named in the application is not a fit and proper person to be the holder of a licence".

The Civic Government (Scotland) Act 1982 has a similar ground of refusal:[47]

> "A licensing authority shall refuse an application to grant or renew a licence if, in their opinion—
> (a) the applicant or, where the applicant is not a natural person, any director of it or partner in it or any other person responsible for its management, is either—
> (i) for the time being disqualified under section 7(6) of this Act, or
> (ii) not a fit and proper person to be the holder of the licence".

So, the concept of fitness is not a new one for the world of licensing law in Scotland. However, when the 2005 Act was first passed, this ground of refusal did not exist and in fact had been specifically resisted owing to the belief that the wider principles which underpinned the Act, *viz* the licensing objectives and the separation of premises and personal licences, would satisfy all ills; that there should be a move away from focusing on the errancy of individuals to a more objectified approach, or to put this another way:

> "The new system moves away from the moral judgement of who is a 'fit and proper person' as required under the Licensing (Scotland) Act 1976".[48]

This attracted concern from constabularies across the country at the time of the original Bill, but as matters moved forward and the 2005 Act began to live and breathe the lament was joined by other stakeholders including representatives of the licensed trade, keen to see irresponsibility addressed for fear of being tarnished by association.

Re-introducing a "fit and proper" test to the alcohol licensing regime finally came about following lobbying from Police Scotland and other parties and was included in the Air Weapons and Licensing (Scotland) Act 2015. The re-introduction of a test was part of the original Bill. The Explanatory Notes to the Bill as introduced confirm:

> "The Bill introduces a 'fit and proper person test' into the processes for obtaining, reviewing and revoking licenses [sic] under the 2005 Act by virtue of sections 45 to 53. In each of these sections, the fit and proper test is considered with regard to the licensing objectives."[49]

The Policy Memorandum provides further background and explanation:

> "Since the 2005 Act came into force there has been considerable debate and serious concern expressed regarding the impact of removing the 'fit and proper test' from the alcohol licensing regime in Scotland, and the lack of a 'fit and proper person' test has been much criticised by the police, Licensing Boards and those within the alcohol trade . . . The introduction of the 'fit and proper' test in this Bill will provide greater scope to present information to Boards, and give them the ability to consider a greater breadth of relevant information when making decisions about applicants, licence holders and connected persons. It will also provide Licensing Boards with greater powers to tackle crime, particularly serious organised crime, by allowing the

47 Schedule 1 para 5(3)(a).
48 Policy Memorandum to the Licensing (Scotland) Bill, para 90, p 21.
49 Paragraph 138, Explanatory Notes, Air Weapons and Licensing Bill (as introduced) 15 May 2014.

consideration of a wider range of information including police intelligence and any associations with those deemed to be unsuitable."[50]

The "fit and proper" ground of refusal, properly narrated immediately below, was inserted by way of section 43(3)(a)(i) of the 2015 Act and was commenced on 15 May 2017.[51]

Section 23(5)(ba) of the 2005 Act now narrates the "fit and proper" test as follows:

> "that the Licensing Board consider, having regard to the licensing objectives, that the applicant is not a fit and proper person to be the holder of a premises licence".

The eagle-eyed reader will instantly recognise a crucial difference between the 1976 Act fitness test, the 1982 Act fitness test, and this, the 2005 Act test – they key section being the language "having regard to the licensing objectives". This brings us on to explore what may be meant by "fit and proper" under the 2005 Act.

During the Stage 1 debate on the Bill, MSP Gil Paterson welcomed the (re) introduction of the test saying it:

> "will offer some comfort to families across Scotland that those who hold an alcohol licence have been through a vigorous process, that they can be trusted and that their character is 'fit and proper' to sell alcohol".[52]

However, the 2005 Act test should not be confused with some direct character assessment, as this ignores the requirement for there to be some link to the licensing objectives, and, perhaps without knowing it, Gil Paterson's reference to fitness "to sell alcohol" strikes very closely at what the jurisprudence says the licensing objectives are, and therefore what the "fit and proper" test is. At the same debate, MSP Willie Coffey said:

> "Although there was agreement on that from some of those who gave evidence to the committee, there were also some reservations expressed, mainly with regard to linking the test to the broader licensing objectives and the possibility that that would give rise to further litigation. I hope that consideration of that issue at stage 2 will help us to resolve it one way or the other."

There was no further amendment to the wording, however, leaving us to ponder the "fit and proper" test through the prism of the five licensing objectives.

The Policy Memorandum to the Bill had this to say, neatly side-swerving any attempt to provide proper guidance:

> "A definition of 'fit and proper' is not necessary as Licensing Boards are familiar with the 'fit and proper' determination from other licensing regimes and there is sufficient experience and case law to guide decision making. This is in accordance with various other Acts that use the test. Furthermore, a definition of 'fit and proper' could limit the range of information local authorities can consider and fetter their discretion. Each application should be considered on its own merits."[53]

50 Paragraphs 134–136, Policy Memorandum, Air Weapons and Licensing Bill (as introduced), 14 May 2014.

51 Air Weapons and Licensing (Scotland) Act 2015 (Commencement No. 6 and Saving Provisions) Order 2017 (SSI 2017/119) art 2 and Sch.

52 23 April 2015.

53 Paragraph 137, Policy Memorandum, Air Weapons and Licensing Bill (as introduced), 14 May 2014.

This very much leaves licensing boards to decide for themselves what may or may not constitute "fit and proper", and the absence of any definition was raised as an issue by a number of stakeholders.[54] If the licensing board does refuse on this ground, they must also be specific which licensing objective they had regard to in reaching the decision.[55]

As discussed at length elsewhere in this book, one must always remember that the licensing objectives are alcohol licensing objectives and not general public interest objectives. This provides a remit within which the objectives can be viewed and utilised. To put it another way, under the 2005 Act there are limitations as to what material is relevant for the purposes of the licensing objectives under our fit and proper test, and that material must have some connection to the sale or consumption of alcohol, or the operation of alcohol licensed premises.

A useful comparison here is with the 1976 Act provisions, as this clearly delineates the difference between the old and new "fit and proper" test. Section 17(3) of the 1976 Act states:

> "the licensing board may have regard to any misconduct on the part of any person mentioned in that paragraph, whether or not constituting a breach of this Act or any byelaw made thereunder, which in the opinion of the board has a bearing on his fitness to hold a licence".

Clearly, then, Parliament made provision for an extremely wide definition of fit and proper under the 1976 Act, allowing the licensing board to take into account non-licensing matters. Under the 2005 Act, Parliament has not taken this approach and has specifically curtailed the fit and proper test so that it must have regard to the licensing objectives. This creates an obvious difficulty for those who would seek to point the finger at an applicant in relation to behaviours or activities they disapprove of, should those behaviours or activities not have a licensing link. This link, necessarily, can only ever be a subjective test of connectedness – a test conducted in the first instance by the licensing board, and ultimately the courts.

It is worth noting at this stage that the "finger pointing exercise", as I term it, is a reminder of the burden of proof in the quasi-judicial licensing hearing. It is not for the applicant to prove that he is fit and proper as regards the licensing objectives. It is for the board to take the view that he is not fit and proper. It is for other parties such as the police to submit evidence that he is not fit and proper, should that be their view. The onus is therefore on the third party to make a case in the first instance. There is, of course, a "practical onus" for the applicant to respond, that is, to rebut any allegations of unfitness. But he should not be tasked with proving he is fit and proper absent any evidence or material to the contrary.

54 See, for example, "Clarity is needed on fit and proper", from *Scottish Licensed Trade News* on 11 May 2017. In this article the then SLTA Chief Executive Paul Waterson said: "Everyone supports fit and proper for various reasons but no one knows what it means." Chair of the National Licensed Trade Partnership, Donald McLeod, added: "There has to be a definition of fit and proper; everyone needs to be clear on what it means."

55 This requirement exists at s 23(8)(b) of the 2005 Act and was introduced by s 43(3)(c) of the Air Weapons and Licensing (Scotland) Act 2015, commenced as of 15 May 2017 by the Air Weapons and Licensing (Scotland) Act 2015 (Commencement No. 6 and Saving Provisions) Order 2017.

So, what types of unfitness or impropriety are sufficiently closely connected to the licensing objectives? There is no 2005 Act jurisprudence on the extent of what can be considered appropriate material for the "fit and proper" test, although that will surely come over time. This is a complicated area with no small amount of clairvoyance and imagination required from the budding legal author. I have broken down a series of proposed behaviour types for further exploration:

- Fit and proper: general mismanagement of licensed premises
- Fit and proper: technical breach of the 2005 Act itself
- Fit and proper: personal relationship with alcohol
- Fit and proper: the presence of criminal convictions
- Fit and proper: unacceptable or improper conduct with no link to alcohol or to licensed premises.

3.1.1 Fit and proper: mismanagement of licensed premises

Behaviours which are causally related to the person's operation or management of a licensed premises would surely meet the criteria. For example, if a licensing board had previously taken action in respect of a premises licence review where an individual had mismanaged their premises, then one can see an obvious connection between failure to meet the terms of the Act and the fit and proper test in a new application by the same person or entity. In that light, it is worth noting that the Act does of course provide that a personal licence may be subject to a separate review hearing at the instance of the licensing board, following upon materials being brought to their attention in the course of a premises licence review. The test, in that circumstance, is that the individual was acting in a manner "inconsistent" with the licensing objectives, whilst working in the licensed premises.[56] So again, there is some clear logic in that the behaviours must be linked to the person working on the premises.

In this example, it might not necessarily be the case that action was taken against the premises licence holder or indeed that the board decided to take action instigating a review against a personal licence holder, in order for a future finding of unfitness to be considered or imposed. It could be that an individual involved bore no action or sanction under the Act at that time, but is later involved in some other malfeasance, and that subsequently a party such as the police has regard to the earlier behaviours in order to fortify an argument of a pattern of unfitness, with regard to more recent nefarious activities.

To give a more direct example, if a person ran premises with no regard to the law, then it may seem obvious that the connection to the licensing objectives is direct and unarguable. If someone allows drunkenness, if they serve to under-age persons, if they encourage violence or recklessness, if they sell drink outside their licensed hours, if they serve drunks, if they do not address antisocial behaviour, then these behaviours surely demonstrate a mis-management of licensed premises, and that has caused harm to the licensing objectives.

Another strand to this area might be lack of experience. A person's tender years in their licensed trade career may have resulted in mis-management, or perhaps the applicant has no experience at all, and is applying for a licence for

56 2005 Act, s 84(2).

the first time with no tangible background or link to the licensed trade. Would inexperience constitute a difficulty in passing the "fit and proper" threshold? It certainly was a factor which was capable of assessment under the old 1976 Act "fit and proper" test. In *Din v City of Glasgow District Licensing Board*,[57] the Court of Session said that: "the board was entitled to consider material bearing upon the applicant's experience as being relevant to the issue which it had to determine [that the applicant was fit and proper]",[58] but that in this case there was "no material upon which the board was entitled to hold that, by reason of some unspecified lack of experience, the applicant was not a fit and proper person . . . it is not possible for us to discover from the proceedings or the s 18(2) letter, in what way, and by what standard of reference, his experience or lack of it disqualified him."[59]

Plainly then, lack of experience has been a ground which points to unfitness but in order to reach that view the board must have some transparency as to what "standard of reference" they believe is appropriate to hold the applicant to account to. Considering this decision in light of the 2005 Act "fit and proper" test, a board would of course have to link the lack of experience to the licensing objectives and narrate how it was linked, but also navigate (if they were so inclined) around the fact that an application can be made competently by someone who has reached the age of 18.

If a board were to look beyond the essential competency of an application in this way, I would venture that the licensing objectives should not of themselves be considered the "standard of reference" but more the underlying structure against which a standard must be set. Achieving this may be problematic. A board could, in the statement of licensing policy, outline what it might consider to be relevant to the "fit and proper" test, but it could not fetter its discretion by having a policy set in stone with unyielding parameters, regarding experience. A policy which said, for example, an applicant with less than one year's experience would not be sufficiently experienced to qualify as fit and proper would likely be subject to challenge as an example of the board fettering its own discretion, as well as appearing to contradict the fact that a lawful applicant can be aged 18.

This also opens up another curiosity, as to whether there is any different standard as regards personal and premises licence applicants. There is certainly no statutory difference in relation to the language used *prima facie*. Interestingly, however, if a person is applying for a personal licence, then the structure of the 2005 Act appears to indicate that the presence of their statutory qualification, that is, the personal licence training certificate, is designed to send the signal to the board that the person has been suitably trained, ergo has received enough licensing wisdom to be granted a licence. That appears to suggest, then, it would be improper to refuse a personal licence on the fitness ground due to inexperience where, say, an 18-year-old applicant has never worked a day in the trade.

On the other hand, there is no statutory qualification required for an applicant for a premises licence so no similar signal to be sent in that application process. An individual applicant for a premises licence need not be a personal

57 1996 SLT 363.
58 Ibid para 365.
59 Ibid para 366.

licence holder, and similarly the connected persons to a non-natural applicant such as company directors do not need to possess a personal licence to apply for a premises licence.

In the absence of a statutory training requirement, it may well be argued that it is open to a licensing board to interrogate a premises licence applicant as to their experience in not simply their understanding of the licensing laws, but in running a licensed premises. This does happen in practice. It is not uncommon for boards to ask company directors, for example, if they have put themselves through the personal licence course, and it is not uncommon for agents to put that information forward as part of their submission. There is, of course, no legal requirement for the director of an applicant company to hold a relevant certificate or personal licence, but again it sends a signal to the board that the said director is taking the process seriously and is therefore of relevance to the wider consideration of the application.

In addition to the structural differences in what is needed to competently apply for a premises licence in contrast to a personal licence, there a number of different considerations for a premises licence holder as opposed to a personal licence holder, such as duties placed upon the premises licence holder *viz* observance of mandatory conditions.

Whilst there is no direct case law on this point yet, I would venture that concerns over the ability to manage a licensed premises due to inexperience could be capable of activating the fitness test where a premises licence were sought by someone who is so inexperienced that the objectives are clearly going to be undermined – with the caveat that the board would have to found this view on something more than mere speculation, by interrogation, and thereafter placing weight on answers given or materials provided as they believe appropriate.

The idea of protecting the objectives from someone so inexperienced that they (the objectives that is) would come to harm, in some ways, sits well with the separate judicial idea of "future proofing" the licensing objectives so as to avoid injury being done to them in the context of making a decision during a review hearing.[60]

3.1.2 Fit and proper: breach of the 2005 Act itself

What should be clear is that any behaviour which results in a licensing offence, or behaviour which is a breach of a personal or premises licence, can clearly be deemed to have the necessary link to the licensing objectives. I have noted above general mismanagement of premises but I think this separate category is needed to highlight more specific examples of technical breaches. This might include breach of licence conditions, or failure to observe or deal with other requirements of the Act such as, for example, knowingly allowing a manager to be named on two licences at once (although the prevalence of this scenario

60 *Lidl UK GmbH v City of Glasgow Licensing Board* [2013] CSIH 25:

> "the process of review is essentially forward looking. It involves examining whether the continuance of the particular premises licence in issue, without taking any of the steps listed in section 39(2) [that is, the sanctions open to a Board, e.g. suspension, revocation, etc], would be inconsistent with endeavouring to achieve the licensing objective in question. The process of review is therefore not directed to imposing a penalty in respect of some past event which is not likely to recur to an extent liable to jeopardise the licensing objective."

should become ever more unlikely with the advent of the internal police IT system "Innkeeper" as details can be shared across licensing board jurisdictions); allowing trade to occur having missed the deadline(s) for a change of day-to-day manager; not observing technical requirements such as updating names and address details, and various other matters which a licence holder is required to adhere to. These examples relate to offences or breaches of the Act in relation to the specific requirements placed upon a person as a licence holder but some of them can also relate to behaviours for someone seeking a licence, who has not been a licence holder, as it is possible they may have worked in the licensed trade and therefore as an employee caused an offence or breach of a condition of a licence.

3.1.3 Fit and proper: personal relationship with alcohol

That brings us to consider personal actions or behaviours which link to alcohol, as opposed to the operation of licensed premises. Does the individual relationship a person has with alcohol have any connectedness to the licensing objectives and therefore the "fit and proper" test? If a person abuses alcohol, are they fit to serve it to others, and supervise their consumption sensibly? It may be more difficult for a licensing board to be presented with incontrovertible evidence that a person is an alcoholic, compared with a black and white breach of a licence condition. If the person is drunk and incapable whilst supposed to be managing the premises, few would argue that there is no link to the licensing objectives there.

However, what if a problematic relationship with alcohol is demonstrated outside working on licensed premises, or even if the person does work in the trade but is not "on shift" when those behaviours are demonstrated? In *Kennedy v Angus Licensing Board*,[61] a personal licence holder was convicted of drink driving in February 2012. It should be noted that she reported the conviction to the licensing board as required. Separately, the police reported the matter to the licensing board under the auspices of section 83 of the Act and recommended that the personal licence be revoked having regard to the licensing objective of Preventing Crime and Disorder. The facts of the case were that the personal licence holder had been witnessed leaving the pub she herself operated in the small hours of the morning, entering her vehicle and driving into a parked car twice. She was later found to be over the legal limit and claimed that after clearing up the pub for the night after hours she had consumed two or three glasses of wine.

The Board suspended her licence for 6 months and in their statement of reasons suggested that the following matters were relevant:

- The licence holder had a previous conviction for drink driving
- The alcohol had been consumed in licensed premises
- The offence was a "serious disregard for the law"
- If she was unfit to drive, she would not have been able to attend to her responsibilities as a personal licence holder
- On any view she should not have been consuming alcohol on the actual premises even though shut.

61 Forfar Sheriff Court (Sheriff Veal), 22 August 2012, unreported.

Sheriff Veal disagreed with the board's approach, however; and, perhaps surprisingly, found that her personal actions and personal consumption of alcohol was remote from her duties as a personal licence holder, even where the incident had occurred after consumption of alcohol on the premises she managed, immediately outside that premises.

Finally on this point, it does seem doubtful that the "fit" in "fit and proper" refers to a person's individual health more generally. Looking at the approach to this under the 1976 Act, Cummins seems to be dismissive[62] that an individual's health was of relevance in the practical application of the test at that time, notwithstanding and noting as he does that Clayson did refer to "health" in his report as well as an English case from 1912 which refers to fitness as embracing "health, temper and disposition". I struggle to recall a 2005 Act case in which a licensing board has interrogated the physical fitness of an applicant. This, however, can be directly contrasted to the position under the Civic Government (Scotland) Act 1982, where the health of the individual is a common aspect of fit and proper deliberation, particularly in relation to private hire and taxi driver applicants, where it can clearly be seen that there is a real public safety consideration in knowing that the person driving your taxi is not likely to expire at the wheel, leaving you also exposed to injury or death, with the concomitant insurance implications this may bring. I do not envisage licensing boards sending publicans for medical exams.

3.1.4 Fit and proper: the presence of criminal convictions

The role of the police in confirming and narrating criminal convictions as part of the licence application process is narrated in detail in the previous chapter. The Act has a statutory list of "relevant offences" (on which, see Chapter 19 at Section 2.1 and Appendix G). Clearly, then, these convictions are of some import in the scheme of the 2005 Act and it is at all times a requirement of the board to have regard to the police conviction report. What weight they attach to the presence of convictions is a matter for them, but the presence of the fit and proper test does mean the licensing board has a further ground of possible refusal where convictions are present. Prior to the introduction of the fitness test in the 2005 Act, a board would have to found on the licensing objectives directly, notably the objective of Preventing Crime and Disorder, to refuse an application. Now, the presence of the fitness test gives the board this alternative route to go down (see my further comments below on a comparison of the use of the licensing objectives in the fit and proper refusal versus the inconsistency ground of refusal).

Factors which will be taken into account are the severity of the offence, the circumstances under which the offence occurred, the penalty, the vintage of the conviction, as well as, of course, whatever the police and the applicant has to say about it. The presence of a criminal conviction does not mean the police will always object, and the presence of a conviction or convictions does not necessarily mean a licence will not be granted. Each case on its own merits, of course.

The first ever personal licence appeal case under the 2005 Act was *Arora*

62 J C Cummins, *Licensing Law in Scotland* (2nd edn, Butterworths, 2000) p 77.

v City of Glasgow Licensing Board.[63] In this case, Mr Arora had applied for a personal licence. He had a conviction for drink driving, and the board refused his application with regard to the licensing objectives. The police had not recommended refusal but merely noted the presence of the conviction in their report. On appeal it was argued that the existence of the conviction did not of itself amount to inconsistency with the licensing objectives and that the board had applied "the old 1976 Act fit and proper test". In upholding the appeal, Sheriff Powrie makes a number of points of interest to this issue:

> ". . . were licensing boards to do no more than equate the existence of such an error of judgment with a necessity to refuse an application under section 74(6) then very few, if any, licences would be granted. Accordingly, in my opinion, in order to apply the section 74(6) test correctly, a licensing board, in refusing an application, requires to identify a separate, discernible factor pointing to necessity for the purposes of the crime prevention objective . . . The mere existence of the offence under section 5 of the 1988 Act did not justify the conclusion that it was necessary to refuse the application. There required to be a discrete reason for the board's conclusion that it was so necessary and that reason required to be properly explained . . . I would also add that, where a chief constable has decided not to recommend that the application be refused, in my judgment, a licensing board must, at the very least, provide an explanation as to why it has decided to take a view contrary to that of the chief constable. Section 74(6) makes it clear that the board is required to have 'regard to the chief constable's notice'. To my mind, that process involves a reflection upon the significance of the notice and the need for a licensing board to render explicit its own approach to the matter."[64]

This is a clear statement that the mere presence of a conviction is not enough to satisfy a refusal and I would argue that this is true regardless of whether the ground was the fit and proper test or inconsistency with the licensing objectives (as was the case in *Arora*).[65] Note also that the appeal was upheld even though the conviction was alcohol related, and therefore had some "nexus" with the licensing objectives.

Consider also the decision in *Shafiq v North Lanarkshire Licensing Board*,[66] again one of the earliest appeals under the 2005 Act, and relating to refusal of a conversion application as a result of a conviction. On the point of the absence of a police recommendation to refuse notwithstanding the presence of a criminal conviction, Sheriff Powrie said:

> "no sufficient reasons are given by the Respondents as to why they did not consider such an absence of a recommendation to refuse the Application was not material to the reasoning of the Licensing Board. I accept that the Respondents were entitled to make their own assessment and were not bound by any lack of objection by the Chief Constable, but I consider it material that they did not set out any reasons why they did not consider such a lack of objection to be material."[67]

In this case, as with *Arora*, the conviction was also alcohol related. Here, the nexus with the licensing objectives was even stronger, as the conviction was in

63 2010 SLT (Sh Ct) 212.

64 Ibid paras 13–17.

65 The requirement to "go beyond" the mere presence of a conviction is not a 2005 Act creation: see *Hussain v Motherwell Licensing Board*, Hamilton Sheriff Court, 9 September 1982, unreported; and *Anwar v Clydesdale District Licensing Board*, Lanark Sheriff Court, 17 June 1991, unreported.

66 [2009] ScotSC 64.

67 Ibid para 141.

fact of selling alcohol to persons under-age, and again, notwithstanding that clear link to the licensing objectives, the appeal was upheld.

Fundamentally, the approach taken by a licensing board where considering refusal as a result of the presence of convictions must demonstrate their own discrete analysis of the convictions, must not have a mere passing regard or acknowledgement of the view of the police, and provide some reasoning where their decision either supports or departs from the police view. And lastly, this exercise must be applied, as noted above, no matter how closely the conviction is connected to the licensing objectives.

Finally, on this matter, although perhaps somewhat contrarily, it is perhaps useful to explore how licensing law deals with *sub judice* matters, that is allegations where there may be a pending trial and for which there is no conviction. In general terms, it is open to a party to present *sub judice* information to a licensing board, although of course this will in almost all cases be the police. There is nothing per se to prevent a licensing board from considering sub *judice* matters but it is open to the "accused" to submit to the board that they should either ignore those matters, or allow the justice system to reach a conclusion before a decision is reached on a licence.

Police letters will often entreat a board to consider *sub judice* matters on the basis that they argue there is no prejudice to the case in doing so. That may be as well, as regards the contrast between civil and criminal proceedings, but there is certainly the potential for personal prejudice to the licence holder or applicant, when members of the press can be and are present at licensing hearings, and may report on *sub judice* allegations.

I have certainly represented parties where *sub judice* matters have been led, and the board has agreed with my request to continue the case to allow for the criminal trial to reach a resolution, but that is at the board's discretion; I have also represented parties where the reverse is true. I have also represented licence holders who want the licensing matter done or dusted one way or the other, to deal with it and move on; and not have delay waiting on the criminal matter to reach a conclusion. Drawing from my own experience, the board will take into account the severity of the allegation as well as the surrounding context as to whether there is any immediate harm to the wider public, as well as harm to the personal reputation of the person before them.

It should also be remembered that whilst it is a matter for the applicant or licence holder to choose not to rebut whatever the *sub judice* matters are, the absence of that rebuttal is something the board members can have regard to, and add such weight to it as they see fit. This is the operation of the practical onus which exists in licensing law: whilst it is accepted there may be no legal onus in respect of the burden of proof, it is certainly the case that it is for the applicant or licence holder to rebut objections or adverse information presented as part of the licensing case,[68] as the licensing board can only be expected to make decisions based on the material before it.[69]

On a practical note, if an agent is instructed to make a *sub judice* submission, this in most cases would be raised as a preliminary matter and would be a matter of professional courtesy to ensure the clerk is aware of this ahead of the hearing. This would allow for a discussion as to the merits of a continuation

68 *Glasgow District Licensing Board v Din* 1995 SC 244; 1995 SCLR 290.
69 *Strathclyde Police v North Lanarkshire Licensing Board* 2003 SLT 1268.

submission on *sub judice* grounds as a preliminary matter. An agent could, for example, request that the board have sight of the *sub judice* matter without the detail being narrated publicly, so that if a decision to continue the matter is to be entertained, this might be achieved without the details ending up in the press.

3.1.5 Fit and proper: unacceptable or improper conduct with no link to alcohol or to licensed premises

This brings us back to a central theme of the licensing nexus; viewed through the primary prism of *Brightcrew* and associated jurisprudence, and the specific limitation of this particular 2005 Act ground of refusal requiring to "have regard" to the licensing objectives. It may be instructive to consider what the courts had to say about the wider interpretation of the fitness test in the previous licensing regime, as a barometer. A key case on the definition of "fit and proper" from the 1976 era is *J & J Inns Ltd v Angus District Licensing Board*,[70] which confirmed that unfitness could be established through association with other third parties who may be of questionable character. Contrast that example with the 2005 Act decision in *Ask Entertainment Pub Ltd and Ask Entertainment Nightclubs Ltd v Aberdeen Licensing Board*.[71] In this case the issue of alleged nefarious associations was also axiomatic to a licensing board decision, here to revoke two licences. In seeking reviews of these licences, the police provided information to the effect that a director of the companies was "in cahoots" with known drug dealers and allowed them to use his licensed premises to further that activity. Sheriff Principal Pyle said:

> "In my opinion, the defenders have been unable to identify a proper basis in fact for their conclusion that the licensed premises were being used for purposes likely to cause crime and disorder. The difficulty for the defenders is that while they had ample evidence upon which they could find, as they did, that Harrison associated with known drug criminals they had very little to find a nexus (*Kennedy v Angus Licensing Board*, unreported, Forfar, Sheriff Veal, 22 August 2012) between that association and the licensing of the premises for the sale of alcohol. It seems to me that on that crucial point the only evidence is mere assertion by Grampian Police which has been repeated by the defenders. Even if it had been proved to the satisfaction of the defenders (which on the evidence it could not be) that Harrison was concerned in the supply of controlled drugs in Aberdeen contrary to the Misuse of Drugs Act, in order to establish the necessary link to the premises there would have had to have been evidence of the premises being used in furtherance of that criminal activity. As it was, the only evidence before the defenders was of known drug dealers being in the company of Harrison within the premises. There was no evidence of any conversations among them or some other interaction which might be about drug dealing or the like."

As with the *Arora* requirement for the licensing board to have conducted a discrete analysis of convictions, that requirement is mirrored here, as regards police evidence of nefarious "associations" with the licence holder, Sheriff Principal Pyle saying:

> "While it might be unfair to say that the defenders merely accepted what the police said, it was nevertheless their role critically to analyse the conclusion which the

70 1992 SLT 930.
71 [2013] ScotSC 9.

> police had reached. If they had done so, they would have found that there was in fact no evidence, other than of a most superficial kind, which created the necessary nexus between Harrison's associations and the sale of alcohol in the premises."

The *Ask* case, then, indicates that even what in general terms might be viewed as a significantly detrimental association, with known drug dealers, and even though they were found to be in the licence holder's company on his own licensed premises, that fact alone was still insufficient to forge a nexus with the licensing objectives. On this basis, unacceptable conduct or improper behaviour with even less of a connection, such as connections with criminals entirely outside the licensed business, may then struggle to be a proper footing for a refusal on the grounds of the "fit and proper" test.

In relation to that wider assessment of material from the police, on 11 May 2017, Inspector Stuart Cameron of Police Scotland's National Liquor and Civic Licensing Policy Unit said:

> "officers and staff should identify all information available and thereafter take into account factors such as the relevancy, gravity and the time elapsed when considering disclosure. Any information disclosed should only be for the purpose of determining the applicant's fitness to hold a particular licence. For that reason, I consider that the reasoning process employed by officers and staff must demonstrate that they have considered *only the person's fitness for the material licence.*"[72]

I add emphasis to the last few words of this quote as it again points to the underlying concept that 2005 Act fitness is a narrower test than that under the 1976 Act, and a narrower test than that under the 1982 Act.

A final point of relevance to the *Ask* case is the use of "police intelligence", linking back to the reference in the original Policy Memorandum that the ability to refer to police intelligence was part of the reason for re-introducing the "fit and proper" test. The central issue with the use of intelligence is that the detail of the intelligence must be known; it cannot be correct for the police to point a finger and say that a licence holder is a villain, but withhold the evidence confirming so. The intelligence must be stated. It must be capable of being assessed by the licence holder who has the right to refute it, and it must be capable of being assessed by the licensing board. In *Anderson v Security Industry Authority*,[73] the court said, in a wide-ranging judgment which looked at police evidence, the following:

> "one would expect to see a clear threat to public safety normally arising from a serious offence allegedly having taken place where the licensee has been charged but bailed and/or some other circumstance which indicates it is in the public interest to suspend the licence. In general the letter of 11 August 2009 contains a number of bald allegations which are unspecific as to time and place . . . One assumes that if there was any information linking Mr Ronney to any of the activities set out in these letters, that would have been stated. Therefore, in so far as Mr Ronney is concerned, applying the currently applicable criteria for revocation, there is nothing pled against him which would meet the terms of this criteria ...There are no convictions for offences that can amount to compelling evidence of criminal activity. Therefore what is left is a series of allegations which are unspecific in nature. Throughout the letter of 11 August there is mention of 'criminal associates', 'criminal contacts',

72 In relation to unfitness to hold a particular licence or any licence, see also *Chief Constable of Strathclyde v City of Glasgow District Licensing Board and Anr* [1995] 2 SLLP 11.

73 Dumbarton Sheriff Court, 8 March 2011, unreported.

> 'associations with Strathclyde based criminals' and 'criminal links in London'. As has previously been observed, none of these 'associates' or 'contacts' is named. There are simply bald assertions by the police regarding alleged criminal associates. In my view that does not amount to compelling evidence of criminal association."

This judgment, which relates to suspension and revocation of multiple SIA licences, brings out the fundamental issue of police intelligence being nothing more than a whisper, unless it is detailed and probative.

What then, of other behaviours of the individual him- or herself, as opposed to the company they keep? Might there be a difference between what I shall postulate as a wider interpretation of the "fit and proper" test so as to include whether the applicant should be allowed to deal with the public in controlled, regulated circumstances, especially where that environment can be abused and members of the public can be vulnerable and subject to harm arising from alcohol? My approach here might be better phrased simply as – can they be trusted? There is no doubt that this wider lens approach of entrusting the applicant to sensibly run a licensed premises is one which would befit the 1982 Act definition – issues of general public safety being axiomatic to that Act. For example, being in an enclosed space such as a private hire car might be a factor when the driver of that car has a criminal record for assault or sexual violence. This trust theorem is often described by leading English lawyer James Button as a "safe and suitable" test; perhaps a more modern iteration of what is mean by "fit and proper".

Another example of this from the 1976 Act is *Kelly v City of Glasgow Licensing Board and Chief Constable of Strathclyde Police*,[74] in which a finding of unfitness was upheld and where the court said:

> "the Board was entitled to take into account convictions which were unconnected with the actual operation of licensed premises but which, in nature, might serve to vouch past misconduct on the part of the applicant and, consequentially, a lack of fitness to hold a licence."

But would a refusal on these types of behaviours, which would be fairly robust and difficult to challenge under the civic regime or the 1976 regime, enjoy the same robustness under the 2005 Act? No doubt further jurisprudence will enlighten.

A final element I wish to explore in this complicated area is the difference, if any, in a refusal on the grounds of the "fit and proper" test *with regard* to the licensing objectives, or separately a refusal on the discrete ground of the application being *inconsistent* with the licensing objectives.

The distinction between the two approaches, for me, lies in understanding that the fitness test is surely concerned with the personal characteristics of the *applicant* as opposed to the characteristics of the *application*. What I mean by that is that the fit and proper test is surely a test only aimed at the individual applicant whether they be a natural individual person or non-natural legal entity. The fitness test is not aimed at geographical or other aspects of the application, the premises, the location and so on. An application might be refused, therefore, on the grounds of inconsistency with licensing objectives because of issues in the local area, perhaps such as evidence of health harms, or evidence of antisocial behaviour which would be exacerbated by the grant of a licence.

74 Glasgow Sheriff Court, October 2003, unreported.

Prior to the fitness test being re-introduced, adverse characteristics attaching to the applicant would likely lead the board to refuse on inconsistency with the objectives. It is of course open to a board to refuse on more than one ground.

Interestingly, it seems to me that the fitness test is a more "extreme" ground of refusal – a position I suggest while noting that Parliament has decreed that unfitness in an existing licence must result in a revocation; whereas other lesser sanctions are available if a board upholds a review based on the licensing objectives. If that logic holds, and can be applied to the concepts of unfitness versus inconsistency in the context of grounds of refusal, then it *may* be argued that it is open to a board to refuse based on inconsistency with the licensing objectives where the applicant's behaviours or characteristics may not be so extreme as to activate the "fit and proper" test, but may be of some lesser colour which does activate the inconsistency with the licensing objectives ground of refusal. This position appears fortified by the insertion of the word "otherwise" in relation to the inconsistency ground, to which we now turn.

3.2 Refusal on inconsistency with the licensing objectives

Having reflected on this ground immediately above, we now turn to examine it in more detail. The starting point is to re-examine the wording of the statute. Section 23(5)(c) confirms that a ground of refusal for a premises licence is:

> "that the Licensing Board considers that the granting of the application would otherwise be inconsistent with one or more of the licensing objectives".

A licensing board can refuse the application with reference to one, some, or all of the licensing objectives, but it must specify which of the objectives it is referring to.[75] A bland refusal based "on the licensing objectives" without further clarity would constitute an error of law. Similarly, a refusal based on, and specified as being based on, all five of the licensing objectives without any narrative as to why each objective is engaged, is likely to attract judicial ire for being a cosmetic exercise and an improper application of the law. The objectives should not be used as a "broad brush" ground of refusal – there must be probative evidence with a causal link to demonstrate that the grant of the application would be inconsistent with that specific objective or objectives.

In my own experience, I would suggest that this is the ground most commonly used by boards to refuse applications, which is perhaps as a result of the fact that the five objectives do cover a fairly wide patch (notwithstanding that they must relate to alcohol licensing).

When might an application be inconsistent with the licensing objectives? The definition of "inconsistency" in the context of the 2005 Act does, of course, have to relate to the judicially understood definition of "licensing". As Lord Eassie says in *Brightcrew*:

> "inconsistency with a licensing objective is inconsistency flowing from the permitting of the sale of alcohol on the premises in question".[76]

The *Cambridge Dictionary* defines "inconsistent" as being something where "different parts of it do not agree, or it does not agree with something else", or

75 2005 Act, s 23(8)(b).

76 *Brightcrew Ltd v City of Glasgow Licensing Board* [2011] CSIH 46 at para 26.

"not staying the same in behaviour or quality". The *Collins Dictionary* provides a number of other explanations: "not behaving in the same way every time a similar situation occurs"; "Someone or something that is inconsistent does not stay the same, being sometimes good and sometimes bad"; and "if something is inconsistent with a set of ideas or values, it does not fit in well with them or match them".

On this basis, inconsistency with the licensing objectives is not therefore an extreme prejudice to the objectives, but some lower threshold. If the Act were to say that the grant of the licence would "undermine" the licensing objectives, for example, that would have created a higher threshold as to undermine something is certainly more adverse than mere inconsistency. However, it should not be read that inconsistency can be tipped with the slightest of adverse detail. Balancing this is the use of the phrase "*would* otherwise be" as opposed to "*may* otherwise be" in the ground of refusal. I discuss the general nature of the objectives at length in Chapter 3 but it is worth repeating here a key extract from the decision in *Martin McColl Ltd v Aberdeen City Licensing Board*:[77]

> "It is very clear that [the Board] require, when applying such factors as are relevant, to come to a view that these would be inconsistent with one or more of the licensing objectives (Section 23(5(c)) and in that event that the board must refuse the application. That is, however, a completely different test from a set of circumstances which may be so inconsistent. This is the difference between possibility and probability."

In other words, a licensing board must be satisfied to a level of probability, in comparison to mere possibility, that the application would be inconsistent.

The word "otherwise" was inserted by section 43(3)(a)(ii) of the Air Weapons and Licensing (Scotland) Act 2015 and commenced on 15 May 2017.[78] Neither the explanatory notes to the Bill, nor the Act itself, provide an explanation for the insertion of this word. Looking at it in the context of the provision, its purpose appears to be to link the reference to the licensing objectives in section 23(5)(c) to the reference to the licensing objectives in the predecessor provision at section 23(5)(b). In other words, it forges a connection between the objectives as regards the general inconsistency test, and the fit and proper test. It appears to create a differential, perhaps in context, in rank, or in both, as regards the objectives, namely that the use of the objectives in the fit and proper test has either a higher threshold or a separate legal meaning than its use in the inconsistency test. Put in long form, this might all be read to say something like "It is a ground of refusal that the board considers that the grant of the application would be inconsistent with the licensing objectives, even if they find that the applicant is fit and proper having regard to those objectives".

My view here is that the insertion of the word "otherwise" confirms that the fit and proper test always relates to the applicant, whilst the inconsistency test relates to the application; but that might not be the end of the matter. The identity of the applicant is a feature of the application, so there is also a case to say that the inconsistency test may also may relate to the identity of applicant as a sort of "fall-back" position, where the "fit and proper" ground cannot be

77 30 November 2016, unreported.

78 Air Weapons and Licensing (Scotland) Act 2015 (Commencement No. 6 and Saving Provisions) Order 2017 (SSI 2017/119), art 2 and Sch.

made out, as the inconsistency ground of refusal appears to be a test with a lower threshold or burden of proof.

In relation to how much adverse material there needs to be to trigger "inconsistency", this is very much a question of fact and degree for the individual circumstances, but it is worth highlighting cases such as *Arora* and *Shafiq* mentioned above, where the presence of an alcohol-related conviction was not sufficient material of its own accord to prove to be "inconsistent" with the objective of Preventing Crime and Disorder. Similarly, perhaps evidence of a single failed test purchase on the record of an applicant would not be sufficient to create an inconsistency, noting the outcomes in *Lidl UK GmbH v City of Glasgow Licensing Board*,[79] and the earlier *Co-operative Group Ltd v Inverclyde Licensing Board*.[80] The broad thread here appears to suggest that minimal or single instance events might not be enough material to amount to an inconsistency.

A wider, and separate, approach to the dogma of inconsistency, is upon adoption by the board of the parameters of its own statement of licensing policy in refusing the application. A licensing board policy may, for example, feature "standard" hours for access by children and young people on certain types of premises. An applicant seeking hours outwith this "standard" approach might face a refusal on the grounds of inconsistency with the licensing objective of Protecting Children and Young Persons from Harm, because what is proposed is inconsistent with the licensing board policy on access by children and young persons. The "strength of material" in such a refusal is in the policy itself, having been consulted on, formulated and adopted. One might be able to challenge the policy if it is unlawful or is not evidence-based, of course, but if the policy is lawful and has proceeded on probative evidence, in order to reach a policy position which is designed to support the licensing objectives, then an application outside that policy position could clearly be rejected as being inconsistent with the licensing objectives.

There is a special rule which relates to inconsistency with the licensing objectives for off-sale applications under section 65(5):

> "Where subsection (3) does not apply, in considering whether the granting of the application would be inconsistent with any of the licensing objectives, the Board must, in particular, consider the effect (if any) which the off-sales hours proposed in the application would have on the occurrence of antisocial behaviour."

This provision was inserted as something of a reactionary position to the heated debates in Parliament at the time of discussing the statutory off-sale hours but emanates from the wider deliberations of the Daniels Committee and pays homage to the work of that committee. Its existence suggests that there is something intrinsically antisocial about off-sales licensed hours, which in my view is not a position that was made out when the matter was debated in Parliament. It strikes me as a somewhat cosmetic or even redundant provision, given that the foul play it intends to identify is something which licensing boards can and do have regard to in respect of the principal grounds of refusal under the Act in any event, without having to be led towards one key message

79 [2013] CSIH 25.

80 Greenock Sheriff Court, 8 October 2010, unreported – but see commentary at [2010] 46 SLLP 6.

as this section appears to do. Notwithstanding my reluctance to be positive about the need for the provision, a number of elements in it provide the flexibility boards need in order not to be hamstrung by it – in that they "must consider the effect" but there is no determination as to what the outcome of that consideration must be; plus the use of the words "if any" in parentheses confirms that this is not a black and white issue.

Material which might be considered relevant in relation to each of the individual objectives, and therefore to whether such material is inconsistent with those objectives, is explored in great detail in Chapter 3 and should be referred to in conjunction with the text above for a fuller understanding of this ground of refusal.

3.3 Refusal on "suitability" grounds

Whilst the "fit and proper" test relates to the suitability of the applicant, this separate ground of refusal is an analysis not of the person or persons making the application, but of the application premises and environs. The full wording of this ground of refusal is at section 23(5)(d) and is as follows:

> "that, having regard to—
> (i) the nature of the activities proposed to be carried on in the subject premises,
> (ii) the location, character and condition of the premises, and
> (iii) the persons likely to frequent the premises,
> the Board considers that the premises are unsuitable for use for the sale of alcohol".

At first glimpse, the suitability ground appears to be made up three separate types of analysis: the activities part; the location, character and condition part; and the persons likely to frequent part. Certainly, I would suggest that general application of this ground of refusal in practice would appear to suggest that any one of these three tests is sufficient, of its own accord, to allow a board to find that the premises are unsuitable. There is, however, something of a gremlin lurking in this section of the Act.

The use of "and" in statutory interpretation tends to infer that there has to be a link between the part before and the part after the use of the "and"; that there is a connection. This is referred to as the "conjunctive", in that the word "and" conjoins the tests, as opposed to if the word "or" was used instead, which would be described as "disjunctive", because it disjoins the tests. Even the use of a comma, as opposed to a semi-colon, at the end of parts (i), (ii) and (iii) indicates a form of cumulation and increasing connection. Looking at the 1976 Act wording by comparison it is a very close forebear to the wording in the 2005 Act, but instead of the three tests being separated out in subparagraphs, they are run together as follows:

> "that the premises to which an application relates are not suitable or convenient for the sale of alcoholic liquor, having regard to their location, their character and condition, the nature and extent of the proposed use of the premises, and the persons likely to resort to the premises".

Perhaps bizarrely, separating the three elements out, but with the use of the conjunctive "and", strengthens the view that all three elements must be present for the ground of refusal to be made out. The matter would be sufficiently clear if Parliament had used the word "or" at the end of subparagraph (ii) instead of "and".

Having said all of that, I am going to examine each element in turn.

First, the **nature of the activities proposed to be carried out** is one of the parts of the Act which on a first reading might entice us out of the shadow of *Brightcrew*. Here, a licensing board might be able to take account of activities other than the sale and consumption of alcohol. As I discuss at length above, the operating plan element to the premises licence application contains a large number of activities, such as restaurant meals, gaming, adult entertainment, and so on. The application can also propose activities outside those pre-specified on the application form. Whilst this ground does allow the board to examine the activities of the premises in the round, the central test of suitability remains that of the sale of alcohol. It may be helpful to read this element broken down without the statutory disruptions, which would be as follows:

> "that having regard to the nature of the activities proposed to be carried on in the subject premises the Board considers that the premises are unsuitable for use for the sale of alcohol".

So, a board might query the activities. It may ask about the restaurant facilities. It may ask about the film, theatre or indoor sports. But these activities *of themselves* are not for the board to assess – the job of the board is to assess them in the context that they occur where alcohol is sold. So, whilst cage fighting or a "bucking bronco" apparatus might be a form of indoor sport which some board members have an issue with of themselves, that wider query as to the safety of such an activity is not the key test; the key test is *the proposed introduction* of the sale of alcohol to that environment, which might be unsuitable. This distinction might be difficult to draw at a hearing when a board member raises what they view as legitimate concerns about the activity itself. Clerks would therefore do well to steer the member back to how the introduction of alcohol may impact upon the activity.

Secondly, the **location, character and condition** of the premises is a sweeping comment. The **location** element of this appears to cross over with considerations of locality in respect of overprovision but, given that overprovision is a separate ground of refusal, this suggests that location in this regard is not referable to the number of other licensed premises in the location, but is about some other way in which the location is unsuitable for the sale of alcohol. Might it be deemed unsuitable, for example, to grant an off-sale licence immediately adjacent to an alcohol treatment centre or homeless shelter? Perhaps. What may be more difficult to interrogate is whether suitability of location might include how the use of the premises for the sale of alcohol might impinge on "amenity". This has no small interaction with the requirement to produce a certificate of suitability under section 50 of the Act as regards planning consent. The existence of the planning certificate indicates that the premises have been adjudged to be suitable in that location. This is why, when some objectors discuss amenity-related issues such as property values, they are typically given short (but polite) shrift from the licensing board. In *Leisure Inns (UK) Ltd v Perth and Kinross District Licensing Board*[81] the issue of planning

81 1993 SLT 796.

permission, amenity, and how that factored into a decision to grant a licence, was examined albeit under the old 1976 regime. In that case the Lord Justice Clerk observed:

> "I am satisfied that the appellants were entitled to consider the matter of amenity, although since planning permission had been received for this application for a provisional grant of a licence, the appellants should, in my opinion, have been slow to hold that any detrimental effect on amenity was to be apprehended. In any event, if they were to hold such, they would require to have material before them to justify such a conclusion. Having considered all the material which was before the appellants I am satisfied that they had no sound basis for concluding that there was a strong possibility that the use of the premises would have a detrimental effect on the amenity of the objectors' premises. Other than assertions from the objectors that their amenity would be affected, there appears to be no basis for any such conclusion."[82]

Whilst this is another expression of the general rule that decisions must be made on evidential material, and not mere speculation, it is also useful in linking the position that a board could take general amenity factors into account under the equivalent ground of refusal (i.e. location) under the 1976 Act, but should be slow to believe there would be detriment based on conjecture. Thinking of how this case would apply under the 2005 Act regime, it seems to me that the scope to consider wider "planning" style amenity issues under the ground has narrowed, noting the "essential remit" of the board focusing on alcohol, the ambit of the licensing objectives and general framework of the Act, albeit that, of course, the objectives have their own stand-alone ground of refusal.

In relation to **character and condition**, Cummins, in his examination of the equivalent 1976 Act provision, says: "Very little consideration has required to be given to the meaning of 'character'. It has been suggested that 'character' and 'condition' are of equivalent meaning and 'can connote more than a physical state'."[83] It seems difficult to suggest that character and condition might link to the physical safety of the building given that this is dealt with under other legislation and that certificates of suitability are required as regards both building standards and food hygiene. It is also helpful to remember that a board should not seek to adopt some other, unknown standard in relation to these matters,[84] nor fall foul of straying outside their essential remit.

One should remember that just because premises are technically safe for the public to enter under building or fire regulations, does not necessarily mean that their character or condition is suitable for the sale of alcohol. Suppose the operator of a soft play facility with a small café area decides to sell alcohol to mom and pop as they watch little Jimmy run about with little Josie. Might the "child rich" environment of a soft play premises mean that its character is unsuitable for the sale of alcohol? Perhaps. Similarly, if one seeks to license a swimming pool area, do the wet floors mean that the condition of the premises

82 Ibid para 799.

83 J C Cummins, *Licensing Law in Scotland* (2nd edn, Butterworths, 2000) p 87; with regard to the decision he points to in *Mount Charlotte Investments plc v City of Glasgow District Licensing Board* 1992 SCLR 311.

84 *Northset Ltd v City of Glasgow Licensing Board*, Glasgow Sheriff Court, 22 March 2012, unreported.

is unsuitable in case someone slips whilst under the influence carrying a glass of Pimms? Perhaps.

Thirdly, there are the **persons likely to frequent**[85] **the premises**. Just what sort of vagabond might this be aimed squarely at?

A good example of this under the 1976 Act approach might have been to suggest that the premises would be likely to attract that much-pilloried element of the local demographic – "youths". But the stereotype of the troublesome teen also has some crossover with location, if it is to be proposed that a nearby school (or perhaps even a young offenders institution) is of relevance; and also crosses over with the requirement to assess possible antisocial behaviour in respect of off-sale applications, as well as with the licensing objectives of Protecting Children and Young Persons from harm as well as Preventing Public Nuisance. Similarly, if it is to be argued that persons likely to frequent the premises are persons with alcohol harm issues because of a nearby treatment centre, then that also crosses with the location point.

When one steps back and examines the "suitability" grounds as a whole, it appears that they have been uplifted from the 1976 Act and in fact a large swathe of the mischiefs they are designed to address are captured by the wider infiltration of the licensing objectives, across so many areas of possible harm.

3.4 Refusal on the ground of overprovision

The legal concept of overprovision is explored in relation to licensing board policy in Chapter 4 at Section 7 and readers should read the commentary here with that wider context in mind. The specific ground of refusal is located at section 23(5)(e) and is as follows:

> "that the Board considers that, if the application were to be granted, there would, as a result, be overprovision of licensed premises, or licensed premises of the same or similar description as the subject premises, in the locality."

This must be read in conjunction, of course, with what the Act has to say about how overprovision must be assessed by the licensing board in respect of their statement of licensing policy. Section 7 of the Act creates this duty as follows:

> **"7 Duty to assess overprovision**
>
> (1) Each licensing policy statement published by a Licensing Board must, in particular, include a statement as to the extent to which the Board considers there to be overprovision of—
>
> (a) licensed premises, or
>
> (b) licensed premises of a particular description,
>
> in any locality within the Board's area.
>
> (2) It is for the Licensing Board to determine the 'localities' within the Board's area for the purposes of this Act and in doing so the Board may determine that the whole of the Board's area is a locality.

85 What does "frequent" mean in this context? If one frequents premises, one attends at or visits the premises. The implication is that the attendance is not a one-off. The *Cambridge Dictionary* gives us: "to be in or visit a particular place often"; whilst the *Collins Dictionary* suggests: "If someone frequents a particular place, they regularly go there."

(3) In considering whether there is overprovision for the purposes of subsection (1) in any locality, the Board …

(a) must have regard to the number and capacity of licensed premises in the locality,

(aa) may have regard to such other matters as the Board thinks fit including, in particular, the licensed hours of licensed premises in the locality, and

(b) must consult the persons specified in subsection (4).

(4) Those persons are—

(a) the chief constable,

(aa) the relevant health board,

(b) such persons as appear to the Board to be representative of the interests of—

(i) holders of premises licences in respect of premises within the locality,

(ii) persons resident in the locality, and

(c) such other persons as the Board thinks fit.

(5) In this section, references to 'licensed premises' do not include references to any premises in respect of which an occasional licence has effect."

Where an application has been made in a locality where the licensing board has adopted an overprovision policy, the effect is that there is a rebuttable presumption against the grant of a new licence in that area. This is the one scenario where the Act does "take a view" by creating a default position to refuse the application, by inverting the onus of the burden of proof. In an overprovision zone application, it is up to the applicant to seek to justify grant by creating an argument that the licence should be granted as an exception to the policy, or perhaps by arguing that the policy is unlawful in some way. What this means practically is that an applicant seeking a licence in an overprovision zone is up against it: the application is extremely likely to attract objections from the NHS and possibly other persons; and the board stance is that the application should be refused as there is a presumption against grant. An applicant therefore needs to put significant work into any presentation in order to "rebut" the presumption.

It should be made clear that a finding of overprovision is capable even where the licensing board has not adopted the relevant locality as an area of overprovision within its statement of licensing policy. Each application is considered on its own merits and that includes the ability to refuse based on overprovision on a case-by-case basis, notwithstanding any policy, and notwithstanding any previous decisions to grant or refuse even in the same locality.[86]

That being said, the absence of an overprovision policy in a particular locality remains a relevant consideration and it is open to an applicant to point to the policy as evidence that the board should not find that overprovision applies to the present application on the basis that the board has done the hard yards and reached a view that overprovision does not apply in that locality. The Guidance to Licensing Boards talks of exceptional cases as follows:

> "in which an applicant is able to demonstrate that grant of the application would not undermine the licensing objectives, or those objectives would not be undermined if the applicant's operating plan were to be modified or the grant of the licence made subject to appropriate conditions".[87]

This statement is not the full story, as the relationship between overprovi-

86 *Tesco Stores Ltd v City of Glasgow Licensing Board* 2013 SLT (Sh Ct) 75 – see paras 42–47.

87 Guidance to Licensing Boards (April 2007) para 56.

sion and the licensing objectives is a complex and nuanced one, and this is discussed in some detail below.

Deconstructing the principle of overprovision is a complex ask. I am going to look at what is meant by "same or similar description"; and what is meant by "locality", before turning to elaborate on the wider existential concept itself.

3.4.1 Overprovision: defining "same or similar description"

There are a few parts to the wording of this ground of refusal, and indeed the related assessment provisions in section 7, which require to be unpicked. The first element is to consider what is meant by "licensed premises of the same or similar description as the subject premises". Note that there appears to be consideration in the wording of the section for overprovision of licensed premises generally, capturing all types, and then separately overprovision of licensed premises of a similar description. This allows a board to reach a view that there is overprovision looking at all types of premises within an area, or separately to take a view that there is overprovision of a particular class of premises. So, whilst a board might have concern about the number of off-sales in a locality, where the application is for an on-sales restaurant, it would be open to them to consider that the ground of refusal does not apply owing to the class of premises being sought.

It might be thought that the reference to "description" in this section links back to the requirement to provide a "general description" of the application premises as part of the new licence process. The environment of the language used to provide a description is, however, fluid and open, to say the least. There is no "tick box" approach allowing for an obvious categorisation – to do so would of course renege on the Nicholson ethos of the single premises licence. So, when the ground of refusal here talks of premises of the same or similar description, the practical implications of that appear to arise in generalities as opposed to a forensic dissection of the particular wording used in the application at hand, by comparison to the language used in general descriptions on licences for existing premises.

In the context of a hearing, one might have no regard whatsoever to the general description and instead the debate may focus on a discussion of classifications such as "pubs" versus "shops" versus "supermarkets", and so on. It is open to the applicant to propose what premises in the locality might be deemed to be of the same or similar description. The Guidance to Licensing Boards makes a number of suggestions on this point, in what might be described as a valiant attempt to assist boards, as follows:

- "'vertical drinking establishments' are distinguishable from those catering predominantly or exclusively for persons taking meals;
- nightclubs are likely to have a more significant impact on town centres, city centres and communities than concert halls and theatres, although all may have a large capacity and provide entertainment;
- the Licensing Board would be entitled to decide that premises specialising in adult entertainment such as lap-dancing and pole-dancing were entirely distinct from other entertainment venues;
- in recent years, 'chameleon' premises have developed in which the facilities offered during the day are markedly different from those provided in the evening,

with, for example, a switch from a food-led operation to a nightclub style of operation;

- a town or city centre hotel may have little or no impact on the licensing objectives and produce benefits for tourism and the local economy, while a hotel in a residential area with few letting bedrooms and extensive bar facilities may have a negative impact on the amenity of local residents;
- in rural areas a hotel whose trade is mainly derived from bar sales may provide a valuable local function;
- large supermarkets serving catchment areas larger than the localities in which they are situated and delicatessens selling speciality foods with a limited range of wines and spirits for consumption off the premises can be distinguished from shops devoted to off-sales and local convenience stores selling a general range of groceries. Convenience stores may provide an essential local service in some communities, particularly those with an elderly population where transport considerations make it difficult for residents to take advantage of more extensive shopping facilities available at large supermarkets in adjoining localities."[88]

These comparisons are helpful in that they do explore different types of business models but the application of the guidance at the coal face of licensing hearings is scant, with boards often taking a more severe or blunt approach, for example to focus on whether the premises are offering on-sales only, off-sales only, or both. That might take the analysis so far and it is a matter for boards to decide on. A slightly more nuanced approach might see a discussion as to whether different types of off-sale premises should be counted as part of the analysis – for example, should a small, dedicated off-sale wine shop be treated as premises of the same or similar description to a large national supermarket? Should hotel premises be counted the same as a pub? Should nightclub premises be counted the same as a bowling alley? Different boards have different approaches on this, as one might expect.

Whilst it can be argued that the 1976 Act approach had ultimately resulted in a (supposedly) straightforward assessment of pure numbers,[89] with any requirement to consider individuality of operation or facilities becoming a "perfunctory exercise,"[90] earlier case law from the 1976 Act era appears to suggest that the courts were previously prepared to entertain the idea of differing "facilities" within this analysis. Cummins says on these earlier 1976 Act decisions:

> ". . . it was considered that an assessment of 'facilities' required a qualitative examination of the proposals. Thus, an applicant for a new off-sale licence could pray in aid the superior choice of wine which he would offer,[91] and in *Mohammed v Docherty*[92] it was held that the board required to consider not only the licensed facilities which could be provided but also 'what present facilities are actually being provided or could be provided in the future'."[93]

The reference to non-licensed facilities here is quite interesting to reflect on in the 2005 Act context, given the premises licence and operating plan

88 Guidance to Licensing Boards (2007) para 52.

89 *Chung v Wigtown Divisional Licensing Board* 1993 SLT 1118; but see also *Caledonian Nightclubs Ltd v City of Glasgow District Licensing Board* 1996 SLT 451.

90 J C Cummins, *Licensing Law in Scotland* (2nd edn, Butterworths, 2000) p 99.

91 *Augustus Barnett v Bute and Cowal Divisional Licensing Board* 1989 SLT 572.

92 1992 SLT 230.

93 J C Cummins, *Licensing Law in Scotland* (2nd edn, Butterworths, 2000) p 95.

place controls on activities other than the sale of alcohol, and the intended aim of the 2005 Act to move away from what Nicholson called a "largely arithmetical" comparison. The Guidance to Licensing Boards is clear that the ethos of the new approach to overprovision was to move away from the 1976 Act strictures and allow boards to take into account a much more targeted or specific approach to distinguish differing types of business model, calling the old approach "undesirable" and saying the "Licensing Board is disabled from drawing distinctions between different proposals".[94]

The issue of "same and similar description" was explored, to some effect, in the case of *Tesco Stores Ltd v City of Glasgow Licensing Board*.[95] Following refusal of an off-sale licence for a Tesco store, one of the pleadings was that the Glasgow board had failed to distinguish between dedicated off-sales premises and supermarkets. Whilst there is no definitive judicial expression given, as the pleading was not ultimately relied on during the appeal, the Sheriff indicates that he would have adopted the reasoning of the board and said he would not have upheld an appeal on this particular ground. The reasoning proposed by the board was as follows:

> "the board were permitted to make a wider comparison than simply with those premises where an identical retail operation was undertaken. The pursuer's submission had made reference to the Licensing Policy Statement on overprovision, but senior counsel pointed out that paragraph 7.7 thereof permitted comparison not only with the same or similar business, but additionally with licensed premises which carried on 'readily distinguishable' activities. It was a widening, not a narrowing, provision. A court could only interfere with a board's decision if no reasonable board could have reached such a decision on overprovision. Senior counsel referred to *Chung v Wigtown District Licensing Board* 1993 SC 166, in which the Inner House had declined to interfere with such a decision. The court was concerned with understanding the recent effects of an amendment to the licensing legislation. Having done so, the court identified that the board had, in deciding to make comparison with a variety of differing business, acted within the discretion afforded to them. The board appeared to have carried out a similar exercise in the present case, and they could not be faulted for exercising their discretion so as to make comparison with other licensed premises operating business which were not identical."[96]

Whilst these expressions are *obiter*, it is useful to draw down the point about whether premises need to be "identical" in order to be treated as "same or similar" in the wider context of the overprovision ground of refusal, and to note that this wording suggests the boards would enjoy a wide discretion. It seems, then, that the result is that it is a matter for boards to decide what premises might be of a "same or similar description" both in relation to any overprovision policy, and on a case-by-case basis – meaning some of the older 1976 Act "facilities" cases could have renewed relevance, where a board deems it appropriate to go into that level of detail. There is no judicial imposition, then, of an analysis of the categorisation as proposed by the Guidance to Licensing Boards, but those types of distinctions may remain valid, if a licensing board considers them to be so in the present context of the case or policy being considered.

94 Guidance to Licensing Boards (April 2007) paras 29–34.
95 2013 SLT (Sh Ct) 75.
96 Ibid para 20.

However, clearly, where the licensing board is making any sort of comparison with other premises, it must be clear on the information it is taking into account in considering those other premises, and that information must itself be clear. For example, if a board wishes to refuse an off-sale licence, taking into account the off-sale capacity of other premises, it must be clear on what those other capacities are and whether it is taking into account premises which have an off-sale capacity only, or also those premises which have both on- and off-sale capacities, and specify what these other capacities are.[97]

A final point on this issue is that the board, must, of course, get its sums right. If there is a factual error such as in relying on the wrong number of premises in the locality, having miscounted, this would be a ground for appeal. An interesting example of this comes from the early days of the 2005 Act in the form of *G101 Off Sales Ltd v South Lanarkshire Licensing Board*.[98] In this case, the board had "double counted" an Aldi premises. Due to the vagaries of the since abandoned "stated case" process for appeals which was originally in place when the Act came into force,[99] the Sheriff dismissed the case as the "mistake" had been capable of being airbrushed during the "stated case" process; but such a result would surely not occur in a summary application, and indeed this case was one of the examples cited to Parliament as to why the stated case process was flawed as it allowed a licensing board the ability to have a "second go" at providing reasons, leaving the ability to appeal almost a worthless exercise.

3.4.2 Overprovision: defining "locality"

We then need to examine what might be meant by "locality" in the context of this refusal. Again, licensing boards take differing views on this. For the purpose of the overprovision assessment within any policy, we now have clarity that the board can identify its whole jurisdiction as a locality and it need not be smaller areas within that entire jurisdiction. However, there is also a separate discussion to be had about how a board goes about identifying locality on a "case-by-case" basis. This is an interesting point. Is there any difference between the legal status of overprovision in terms of policy, and the legal status of overprovision in terms of individual applications where overprovision might be salient, but there is no policy that covers that locality?

Here are some examples of contrasting approaches of how licensing boards deal with this conundrum, by identifying localities in relation to individual applications:

- The premises are located within a pre-ordained overprovision locality under the terms of the statement of licensing policy. That locality is considered in relation to the application. One would hope that the applicant or agent is aware of this prior to even lodging the application. In a case like this, there can be no question as to the locality because it should be perfectly clear upon a reading of the policy.

97 See *Nasir v North Lanarkshire Licensing Board*, Hamilton Sheriff Court, 17 November 2011, unreported.

98 Glasgow Sheriff Court, 10 July 2009, unreported. See Robert Skinner, "Appeals: Reasons for Change" [2009] 43 SLLP 21 for a short commentary on this case (albeit note that the respondent is erroneously listed as North Lanarkshire Licensing Board).

99 See Chapter 20 at Section 1, footnote 3.

- The locality is pre-ordained prior to a hearing and is not within an overprovision zone, so is based on whether the premises are within a defined city or town centre area. If within the city centre, a small radius will be used of, say, 200 metres; if outwith the city, a larger radius of, say, 500 metres is used.
- The locality is pre-ordained prior to a hearing but is not within an overprovision zone. The applicant is sent a locality map showing the area which has been chosen and this will take into account the special geography and demography of the particular area, and would not necessarily be a blunt radial approach like the one immediately above.[100] If, for example, the premises are located on the cusp of a forested area, the locality might be delineated to cover the residential area to one side of the premises, and not include the forest.
- The locality is defined with direct reference to intermediate data zones provided by the Scottish Index of Multiple Deprivation.
- The locality is defined with reference to council ward areas.
- Two or three proposed localities of increasing size are discussed at the start of a hearing, with views from the applicant and other interested parties as to which of the localities they believe to be appropriate; a decision is then taken by the board to adopt one of the options.

Leaving aside the efficacy or merits of these differing approaches, the key thing is that the locality must be defined. If it is not, that would constitute an error in law.[101] It should be possible, at least in theory, to challenge the area agreed upon by the board as the relevant locality at the time of the hearing. An objector, for example, could argue that the locality should have been a larger area than the one adopted. It is difficult to see how successful this might be or even how a licensing board would deal with it, in the cut and thrust of a hearing. Many boards have adopted practices such as those above and it is simply accepted that this is how locality is defined. I suspect that if a party to an application chose to challenge the locality, the response would be to note the challenge, dismiss it, and move on to hear the case. An applicant with one eye on appeal may make the point and have it noted; but as there is no statutory rule as to how a board agrees on what a locality is, on a case-by-case basis, a challenge absent technical grounds might be difficult to run on appeal.

However, if the locality is pre-determined as a result of the statement of licensing policy, and if it can be shown that the policy is flawed either in relation to establishment of the relevant locality, or some wider error in law, then the adoption of that locality may be grounds for a lawful challenge on the basis that if the policy is unlawful, the policy should not apply and should be set aside. In relation to flaw in the policy consultation process, I examine this in detail below, but for the concurrent purpose of exploring "locality", it is worth visiting the outcome of the decision in *Martin McColl Ltd v Aberdeen City Licensing Board*.[102] In this case the Board took what the Sheriff describes as the "cosmetic" step of creating an overprovision policy for its whole jurisdiction save two particular areas (Anguston and Kirkhill) where there was little of

100 This approach is one which found favour in the courts in *Loosefoot Entertainment Ltd v City of Glasgow District Licensing Board* 1991 SLT 843.

101 See, for example, *Ross v Moray District Licensing Board* 1995 SLT 447; and *Botterills of Blantyre v Hamilton District Licensing Board* 1986 SLT 14.

102 Aberdeen Sheriff Court, 26 August 2015, unreported.

anything, instead of a proper analysis of localities, the numbers of licences and capacities in terms of the Act. The context of this "cosmetic" decision is that, at that time, section 7(2) did not contain the wording "and in doing so the Board may determine that the whole of the Board's area is a locality", which was only added by an amendment under section 55(2)(a) of the Air Weapons and Licensing (Scotland) Act 2015 and commenced as of 30 September 2016.[103] There was some debate in licensing circles prior to this amendment about whether a board could indeed select its whole jurisdiction. Aberdeen, mindful of this debate, clearly took the view that a "whole jurisdiction" locality might be challenged but this is what led them down the path of error, in that their focus was on avoiding this hypothetical hobgoblin rather than on following what the Act required.

In the context of our discussion here about the selection of locality, this case is a reminder that the selection of locality as part of an overprovision policy must not be a cosmetic exercise but must be based on the evidence arising from a lawfully conducted consultation following the statutory requirements.

Now that we have made some effort to explore two key elements of overprovision, namely what is meant by locality and what premises of the "same or similar description" are, it is high time I made an effort to explain what is meant by "overprovision" at all. Wish me luck.

3.4.3 Overprovision: what is it? Part 1: an overview

Whilst trying to avoid irony, I would propose that the concept of overprovision is about provision. That is, provision of licensed premises, but also provision of factors which are corollary to the existence of the premises themselves – in terms of the Act, those factors are capacities of those premises, the licensed hours of those premises, and "such other matters the licensing board thinks fit"[104] in relation to those premises. But that understanding only takes us so far, and is still a very cold and technical analysis. What we actually need to do is lift the lid on *why* the concept of overprovision exists at all.

Scott Blair, the leading licensing Advocate, describes an early appeal decision thus:

> "The view that the Board has a wide discretion to determine the question of overprovision is a long established principle of Scottish Licensing law. In *Walsh v. Magistrates of Pollokshaws*,[105] the renewal of a licence was refused on the ground that the 'district was congested'. In the opinion of Lord Davey, the licensing court had been "entitled to form the opinion, based on their local knowledge and enquiries . . . and that a number of licensed houses in the town was in excess of the reasonable requirements of the inhabitants".[106]

The vintage exploration in *Walsh* is a good start even if it only takes us so far, given that "need", "demand" or what is described as the "reasonable requirements of the inhabitants", is not a 2005 Act test. The use of the word

103 Air Weapons and Licensing (Scotland) Act 2015 (Commencement No. 4, Transitional and Saving Provisions) Order 2016 (SSI 2016/132), art 2(b).

104 2005 Act, s 7(3)(aa).

105 1907 SC (HL) 1.

106 Scott Blair, "*Buzzworks v South Ayrshire and Tesco v Glasgow* – the implications for overprovision" (September 2013) p 22.

"congestion", on the other hand, remains salient. The Explanatory Notes to the Licensing Bill describe overprovision as:

> "identifying whether there are some areas within a Board's control which have reached saturation point in terms of the numbers and concentration of on-sales or off-sales or both".[107]

The Policy Memorandum to the Bill says:

> "Overprovision is the root of problems being experienced by many communities where there has been no coherent overall policy in place."[108]

It goes on to offer further colour as follows:

> "Overprovision in a 'locality', whether this is a street, several streets or a Council ward, can lead to an increased level of problems associated with misuse of alcohol. This may take the form of nuisance issues such as noise and broken glass in the street, intimidation by those entering or exiting licensed premises or increased violence and crime."[109]

Adding all of this together, it seems clear to me at least that the inherent origin of overprovision is that of detriment. The whole concept exists because of a widely held and widely understood philosophical concept that overprovision of licensed premises in a locality can lead to detriment for that locality.

When overprovision was introduced as a ground of refusal under the 1976 Act, there is no doubt that it was couched in terms relatable to issues of antisocial behaviour and crime and disorder arising in a locality as a result of that locality having an oversupply of licensed premises – a concentration or congestion of premises in a locality which, when added together, has led to exacerbation or indeed creation of public nuisance. But the concept attracted detractors. Nicholson had this to say:

> "the 'overprovision' ground has been criticised, largely on the basis that it is unworkable in practice. Inevitably, perhaps, the provision has given rise to difficulty over the years in relation to what constitutes 'the locality'. Moreover, the concept of overprovision itself may be far from clear. As was said to us by a very experienced board chairman: 'If there are already 12 licensed premises in a given area, how can you say that there will be overprovision when there are 13; or will there only be overprovision when the number rises to 14?'. To that there might be added the further complexity that, by concentrating only on the number of licensed premises, no account can be taken of the size, type and capacity of such premises. We should add that the 'overprovision' ground has also been criticised on the basis that, since it is not qualified by any reference to amenity or public order, it is capable of being used in restraint of trade whereas, at least according to some of our consultees, the number of licensed premises in a given locality should be determined solely by market forces and the process of competition."[110]

It is interesting to note the challenge identified above as overprovision not having a specific link to amenity or public order. We will come back later to the related issue of the interaction between overprovision and the licensing objectives. Focusing on overprovision and detriment, I again look back to Nicholson who proffers an excellent analysis thus:

107 Explanatory Notes, Licensing Bill as introduced on 28 February 2005, para 329.
108 Policy Memorandum, Licensing Bill as introduced on 28 February 2005, para 23.
109 Ibid para 47.
110 Nicholson Report, para 6.30, p 90.

"we are firmly of the view that an over-abundance of licensed premises in close proximity to each other can have wholly unacceptable consequences of various kinds. The view of the police, based on their experience around the country, is that density of licensed premises in a particular area is likely to lead to a disproportionate amount of disorder near to those premises and in a substantial surrounding area. Local residents who live close to such concentrations of licensed premises have told us that, although they may be unable to fault the way in which individual premises are operated, the cumulative effect of having so many more or less in the one place is that levels of disturbance and public nuisance regularly reach unacceptable levels, particularly very late at night. The foregoing problems are, of course, likely to be exacerbated when one has regard to the fact that many of the premises which are to be found in densely licensed areas are of a size which enables many hundreds of patrons to be inside a single pub or club at the same time. When such places close, probably at around 3 or 4 a.m., the consequence is that several thousand patrons may emerge onto the streets at about the same time. A further consequence of having a very large concentration of licensed premises in the same area is that, for the very reason that is founded on by those who support the 'market forces' argument, many, or indeed all, such premises will engage in a range of promotional activities in order to attract customers at the expense of their commercial competitors."[111]

The very last element of this analysis is now redundant, with the advent of the minimum pricing laws as well as the plethora of mandatory conditions which apply to all premises licences and attack the concept of irresponsible promotions. But his Committee's earlier comments here in relation to disorder and disturbance are axiomatic to the philosophy of overprovision then, and now. There is one final passage in Nicholson to which we must turn:

"the difficulty with the 'overprovision' ground as it presently stands is that it directs attention to questions of density in an unfocused way which is likely to result in no more than a somewhat arid and uncertain arithmetical exercise. In our view the number of licensed premises in a given area should be considered not simply as a matter of arithmetic but by reference to the implications which that may have in the context of the 'licensing principles'. Moreover, it is also our view that, when consideration is being given to such matters, account should be taken not only of the number of licensed premises in a particular area but also of their type, size and capacity."[112]

Again, note his proposal that overprovision should not be merely a "numbers game" but have some deeper meaning – in his suggestion, with reference to the licensing objectives (as they became known), to which we will return shortly.

It may be slightly mischievous to propose that a licensing board knows overprovision when it sees it. If it looks like a duck, and quacks like a duck, then it is a duck.[113] So, in this sense, if a board has evidence that the preponderance of licensed premises in a locality is of itself leading to public nuisance, crime and disorder, then a state of overprovision may be said to exist. However, properly understood, this state does not arise purely because there is concentration of premises in a locality, but arises where there is evidence of detriment

111 Nicholson Report, para 6.34, pp 90 and 91.

112 Ibid para 6.35, p 92.

113 Unless, of course, it is a duck-billed platypus, which makes a low-pitched growling sound. I imagine the sound to be like the harrumphery of a certain peer (who whilst in practice was especially well-known in the Kingdom of Fife), as he reviewed earlier versions of this text and corrected many blemishes.

as a result of that concentration of premises. Overprovision is not a numbers game, but should be an evidence-led and evidence-rich finding that additional premises would bring harm.

The need for a balanced view on numbers of licences is one which was narrated by the Local Government and Transport Committee in their Stage 2 Report when the Licensing Bill was passing through the Scottish Parliament. Amongst other comments, the Committee said:

> "The Committee had concerns over whether numbers of licences would be used as a crude measure of overprovision, perhaps with the result that, for example, an application for a licence for a restaurant could be refused, on the basis that there was a general overprovision of licences within a locality . . . it is not in the interests of Scotland's tourism and hospitality industry to allow no future growth in on-sales licensed premises . . . the Committee would wish [the views of the community] to be balanced with a need to safeguard the existence of a vibrant retail sector, and in particular the viability of small grocery shops and foodstores which might not achieve sufficient turnover to ensure the survival of the business were they not to be granted a licence."[114]

Overprovision should not, therefore, be held to exist based purely on the fact that a number of premises exist in a locality. And one must not merely draw an inference that the existence of these premises is a negative – one must only reach that view on judicious consideration of probative, empirical evidence.

This brings us to take a modest side-step into the issue of what that probative evidence may be. The first answer to that is, of course, the overprovision assessment within the licensing board policy. If it is to be assumed that the policy was consulted upon properly and lawfully, and the results and decisions were based on that evidence wherever it led, then the policy itself can be taken to be the necessary evidence needed. This only holds where the policy is lawful, but let us assume that it is.

The second string as to what may constitute probative evidence is material which might be presented to the board by any party in the course of an application (see the quote from the *Tesco* case above). This may be the views or objections from the NHS or local residents, or indeed any person. The third string is commonly referred to as "local knowledge"; namely, knowledge which the members of the licensing board bring to the table themselves.

The licensing board may make use of its own local knowledge in the formulation of an overprovision policy, but it may also make use of its own local knowledge in finding overprovision on a case-by-case basis. It should be remembered that licensing board members all have their own lived experience and background to bring to any hearing, but, on top of that, as elected councillors representing a local ward area, it can be assumed that a board member who is also an elected councillor for the locality where a licensed premises is proposed to operate, will have relevant knowledge of that area in terms of its socio-economic make-up as well as local geographical features or sociological trends or behaviours which may be of relevance. There are a number of well-known cases on the principle of local knowledge in licensing law in Scotland.

In *Pagliocca v Glasgow District Licensing Board*,[115] the issue was considered

114 Licensing (Scotland) Bill, Stage 2 Report, Local Government and Transport Committee, paras 60–2.

115 1994 SC 561.

as a key reason behind the refusal of an entertainment licence under the 1976 Act. What *Pagliocca* appears to confirm is that the courts expect licensing board members (and officials for that matter) to bring their own local experience to bear in relation to consideration of such applications, but where a decision is made with reliance on that knowledge, it must be transparent. The court said:

> "We think that there is force in the argument of counsel for the board that a licensing board, unlike a court, is entitled, and indeed expected, to bring to bear on applications made before it its own local knowledge and licensing experience. This knowledge and experience subsists in the members of the board, whoever they may be, and in the board's officials who advise. It appears to us, however, that this element can be brought to bear upon a board's decision in two rather different ways. The first is where a board is able to draw upon specific information within its own knowledge of matters relevant to an application and that knowledge is material to the decision which they are to take. In the case of such specific knowledge, or where the board has private information which is not available to the parties, the rules of natural justice require its disclosure to the parties for comment before a decision is reached."[116]

This was also explored in *Mirza v City of Glasgow Licensing Board.*[117] In this case an off-sale licence was refused on the grounds of overprovision and in doing so the board said that they had regard to local knowledge. The court was satisfied that the board had made clear what that local knowledge was, referencing an exchange at the hearing concerning the local geography of the area and in particular the location of a nearby pedestrian crossing, albeit that appears scant. This was in contrast to a number of other 1976 Act decisions where it had been clear that attempts to use ill-defined local knowledge as a magic wand absent any probative evidence would not be upheld by the courts. So it appeared that ultimately there were two forms of "local knowledge" under the 1976 Act: properly defined and evidenced local knowledge as regards most other aspects of the licensing law; and a special "local knowledge-lite", where a more opaque approach was allowable in reference to refusal on the ground of overprovision.

To bring matters up to date, and considering this in the context of the 2005 Act, we have the following as stated by Sheriff Ross in *Tesco Stores Ltd v City of Glasgow Licensing Board*:[118]

> "It is not obliged, for example, to limit itself to the submissions made or evidence presented, but may draw upon its own knowledge of an area, whereas a court could not. It may rely on local knowledge in drawing inferences from the material before it. Imprecision is, accordingly, acceptable, provided the decision is reasonable in the overall circumstances."[119]

So a licensing board has a fair amount of leeway in considering local knowledge – but if a board does wish to rely on this, it must state what that knowledge is.[120] This is a matter of natural justice. The applicant, or indeed other parties, must have the local knowledge disclosed to them so that they can attempt to rebut it. To put it another way: "It seems elementary justice to us that the

116 Ibid at 566.
117 1996 SC 450.
118 2013 SLT (Sh Ct) 75.
119 Ibid at para 58.
120 *Freeland v Glasgow District Licensing Board* 1980 SC 101.

applicant or objector should be told about it so that he may have the opportunity of meeting it or commenting upon it"[121]; or "if a board has relied upon any specific, material information, it must not rely upon undisclosed material but must give the applicant an opportunity to make submissions upon that material".[122] This does not just apply to a case-by-case decision. In relation to a policy case, if a policy were founded on some undeclared "local knowledge", then that would be capable of challenge on the above footing.[123]

3.4.4 Overprovision: what is it? Part 2: a focus on alcohol display and off-sale capacity

Turning back to explore the central mischief of overprovision, I now examine how this is determined with regard to off-sale capacity, as this is a new concept under the 2005 Act. Under the 1976 Act, overprovision was clearly referable to wider issues of antisocial behaviour and nuisance. Under the 2005 Act, whilst that remains of some import as we have just explored above, a new line of interrogation arises – which flows from the consideration of capacities and, in particular, off-sale display capacities. A board can decide that overprovision exists purely in relation to off-sale display capacity; as a distinct form of overprovision to off-sale licences. The distinction may be difficult to process, but such a policy might be devised where the board takes no issue with off-sale premises where there is no public display of alcohol. For example, a brewery or distillery operation may be licensed purely to allow for online despatch sales to be processed and shipped out from the premises. In such a case, the premises may have no public access and no alcohol on display in that sense.

Off-sale display capacity is about how much alcohol is "on show" to the public. This is often conflated with "availability". Importantly, "availability" is not a legal concept but an academic one. There may be some difficulties in reconciling availability with off-sale display capacity as a concept, given that the amount of alcohol on display is not, in reality, the amount of alcohol which is available. The amount of alcohol available is actually a far higher number. The amount on display is merely that, an amount of alcohol which happens to be on display at a particular time, located in a restricted display area. The availability theorem, as it links to a licensing consideration of overprovision, does not and cannot take account of all the alcohol which is available for sale, but simply not on display.

This creates an anachronism not just in terms of what the true amount of alcohol "available" for sale might be, but also in that the legal test is not one of availability, but is instead about locality. Thus, when an argument is made that a greater degree of availability of alcohol of itself will create a state of overprovision, that proposition is not in my view sustainable in law unless it is fortified with dependable, causal evidence as to how that availability is negatively impacting on the locality. One may point by way of example to the presence of

121 Ibid at 104.

122 *Tesco Stores Ltd v City of Glasgow Licensing Board* 2013 SLT (Sh Ct) 75.

123 *Marini v South Lanarkshire Licensing Board (Hamilton Division)*, unreported. Appeal resulted in a remit agreed on a joint motion at Hamilton Sheriff Court and licence granted at remitted hearing on 20 May 2019.

large depot or warehouse facilities which may be located in a certain area, but make no deliveries (or at least very few deliveries) to that local area.

Another way of approaching this dilemma is to understand that simple availability is akin to thinking, improperly in my view, that overprovision of on-sales premises is purely a numbers game. The same deeper philosophy about understanding what mischief the concept of overprovision is designed to tackle is as relevant to off-sale display capacity as it is to overall numbers of on-sales premises. Overprovision should be more than a "numbers game", whether it is numbers of on-sales premises, or numbers of bottles on a shelf. This position is strengthened when you consider the ability of a licensing board to take into account "such other matters as it thinks fit". It should not be sufficient for a board to determine that the presence of one additional licence, or say 30m^2 of new display capacity, creates a status of overprovision without dependable material and causal evidence as to why that additional provision poses a detriment.

Another way of putting this would be to say that the legal test is not one of "sufficiency" – it is not for a licensing board to determine that they believe the current numbers of licences or capacity and so on is sufficient; it is not about demand, and it is not about need.[124] The true test is evidence of detriment.

3.4.5 Overprovision: what is it? Part 3: the relationship between overprovision and the licensing objectives

I say above that the true test is evidence of detriment. Given that detriment in the world of the 2005 Act is viewed through the prism of the licensing objectives, a central mission for us is to explore the link between overprovision and the licensing objectives.

A number of appeal decisions explore refusals on the ground of overprovision, allowing us to consider any link between overprovision and the licensing objectives, including *Tesco Stores Ltd v City of Glasgow Licensing Board*[125] which had adopted the jurisprudence on this issue from the earlier *Buzzworks Leisure Ltd v South Ayrshire Licensing Board and JD Wetherspoon plc*[126] and *Tesco Stores Ltd v Aberdeen City Licensing Board.*[127] It is worth unpicking the tapestry of these three appeals together as they are interlinked.

In the *Aberdeen* case, which was the first licensing appeal under the Act to focus on the issue of overprovision, the refusal of a new off-sale licence on the grounds of overprovision was overturned on appeal because the Sheriff took the view that the board had erred by not "having regard" to the licensing objectives in finding that overprovision applied. The relevant passage is:

> "What the Board then had to do was to consider whether, if the application were to be granted, there would as a result be overprovision of licensed premises of that description in the locality. In so doing it had to have regard to the licensing objectives set out in section 4 of the Act. So far as I can judge, it did not do this. On the contrary, it does not appear from either the statement of reasons or the elaboration

124 On "sufficiency" as an incorrect test, see also *Din v City of Glasgow District Licensing Board* 1996 SLT 363.

125 2013 SLT (Sh Ct) 75.

126 2012 SLT 442.

127 [2010] 46 SLLP 15.

> of these in the stated case that the Board had any regard at all to the licensing objectives as it ought to have done. Instead it simply concluded, without reference to these objectives, that the addition of the 27.94 square metres attributable to the appellants' premises, equating as it did to a 21% increase in the capacity of off consumption premises in the locality, would constitute a significant increase in the overall capacity of premises of this type in the locality and hence that the addition of the appellants' premises would lead to overprovision. It might have been a different matter if it had been explained, for example, that to have granted the present application would have resulted in a number and capacity of off consumption premises in the locality of Cults which would in turn have created a risk of public nuisance or harm to children."[128]

It is now generally accepted that this approach is flawed and certainly the other cases take a different approach, however there is still some merit in at least one element of the decision, which is the requirement for a board to explain why a state of overprovision is found to be held in a particular case as opposed to declaring a refusal on overprovision without elaboration. We will return to this point later.

The next big overprovision case is *Buzzworks*. Here the South Ayrshire licensing board had followed the *dicta* of the *Aberdeen* case by not refusing an application by J D Wetherspoon on the ground of overprovision because they could not make out a link between it and any inconsistency with the licensing objectives. The decision to grant was subject to judicial review by Buzzworks Leisure Ltd, a local operator of licensed premises who had objected and been a party to proceedings.[129]

In this case, Temporary Judge Morag Wise QC said:

> "It seems to me to be clear, having regard to the way in which the statutory provisions are expressed, that the correct approach for the Board to take in considering an application is to consider each of the grounds for refusal in turn and decide whether any one of them applies."[130]

This is a clear statement as to the "stand alone" nature of the separate grounds of refusal under the Act. She goes on to examine the possible overlap of the licensing objectives and says:

> "Against the backdrop of the interplay between the legislation, the Guidance, and the formulation of policy by each licensing board, there is no doubt that the licensing objectives are at the heart of decision-making. However, as a simple matter of statutory construction, sub-sections (4) and (5) of section 23 enunciate five discrete statutory grounds for refusal, any one of which is sufficient to require the Board to refuse the application. Thus, for example, if the Board were satisfied in any given case that the subject premises in question were excluded premises then there could be no question of the application being granted even where it was wholly consistent with all of the licensing objectives. Of course there will be overlap between some of the factors pertinent to ground for refusal 23(5)(c) and those involved in some of the

128 Ibid at 24 (para 16).

129 The decision was subject to judicial review due to the anomaly in the Act which does not allow an objector to an application for a new premises licence to make an appeal by way of summary application to the sheriff court. For a contemporary analysis of the decision of the licensing board, see "Overprovision objection sparks Ayrshire trade war" [2011] 47 SLLP 3; and for a contemporary analysis after the appeal outcome, see "Buzzworks ruling leaves new licences in danger zone" [2011] 49 SLLP 1.

130 [2011] 49 SLLP 24 at para 39.

other grounds such as unsuitability and overprovision. The way in which the provision is framed, however, clearly lends itself to situations where, notwithstanding that an application would not be inconsistent with one or more of the licensing objectives, it may well still be refused."[131]

On the point that South Ayrshire Licensing Board had slavishly followed the *Aberdeen* appeal, and considered itself bound to substantiate a link between the objectives in order to make out a refusal on overprovision, she said:

"In essence, the Board considered that it had no power to refuse the application on grounds of overprovision because it had found that the application was not inconsistent with any of the licensing objectives. In my view, this constituted a clear error in approach in that overprovision ought to have been considered as a distinct ground regardless of the decision on consistency with the licensing objectives."[132]

She also addresses the *Aberdeen* case so:

"insofar as the decision of the Sheriff Principal suggests that consideration of overprovision and the licensing objectives are part of a single exercise when making a determination under section 23(5) I am of the view that such an approach is incorrect. As indicated, I am of the view that a Board requires to consider separately and decide upon each relevant ground for refusal. This will invariably require consideration of whether an application is consistent or inconsistent with the licensing objectives."[133]

Finally, on the interplay between the licensing objectives and overprovision she says:

"There is no question of overprovision, unsuitability of premises or any of the other grounds being subsets of some over-arching ground for refusal of inconsistency with the licensing objectives. Were it so, the legislation would have been differently drafted and would have included overprovision and unsuitability within the factors to be taken into account in considering inconsistency with the licensing objectives. I have no difficulty with the submission made by senior counsel for the first respondent that, were the grounds for refusal to be imagined in the form of a Venn diagram, there would necessarily be an overlap between the circle representing the licensing objectives and that representing overprovision. However, by definition, an overlap in that context requires there to be an area within each of the circles representing each of the grounds that is quite separate from the overlapping factors. It is the factors peculiar to overprovision and separate from the issue of the licensing objectives that the Board have failed to make a substantive decision on in this case."[134]

The *Buzzworks* case is therefore immensely helpful in trying to tease out what relationship there is, if any, between overprovision and the licensing objectives. In my reading of the above, it is clear that the two grounds of refusal are distinct. A board need not establish inconsistency with the licensing objectives in order to make out the ground of overprovision – but there *is* a relationship at work here, which a board should not ignore and which *Buzzworks* labels an "overlap". By definition, therefore, at least part of what constitutes overprovision is some aspect of a form of detriment to the licensing objectives. Separately, there may be some factors unrelated to the licensing objectives

131 Ibid para 39.
132 Ibid para 40.
133 Ibid para 40.
134 Ibid para 40.

which might also lead to a finding of overprovision. In either case, those issues need to be made out.

That brings us all back to the *Tesco* appeal in Glasgow. Here, the separation of these two grounds of refusal is described by the Sheriff as "the alleged necessity of applying the licensing objectives". Having had regard to the *Buzzworks* decision, he agrees with the dismissal of the previous *Aberdeen* case, saying:

> "It was not correct to say that there can only be overprovision if the application is also inconsistent with the licensing objectives."[135]

But he also goes on to confirm that there is some relationship between overprovision and the licensing objectives. What the *Buzzworks* case refers to as "an overlap", he describes as an "indirect link", as follows:

> "I can agree with the pursuer's submission to the extent that overprovision must be seen in the context of the 2005 Act objectives. However, this is not a direct process but an indirect one. The defender's duties are expressly provided for: if it has had 'regard to the licensing policy statement' (section 6(4)), it has done all that is required of it in this respect. It is not claimed that the defender failed to do this. It will be noted that, in consulting its own Licensing Policy Statement under section 6(4), a board is already, indirectly, ensuring that the criteria considered are consistent with the licensing objectives (see section 6(3)(a)). In the present case, the defender has expressly included this check in their drafting of the Licensing Policy Statement (production 5/3), at paragraph 7.5. It is plain that they had the licensing objectives in mind. I therefore reject the pursuer's submission to the effect that the assessment of overprovision under section 23(e) must expressly incorporate an assessment of the licensing objectives. The licensing objectives are only directly relevant under section 23(c)."[136]

So, here we have a statement that overprovision "must be seen" in the context of the licensing objectives, but only by way of an indirect link which appears to be satisfied where the board, in considering overprovision in the instant case before it, also has regard to its policy statement (which of course it is required to do anyway). If, then, the policy itself has not properly or lawfully explored how the licensing objectives interlink with overprovision within that policy, this could be subject to possible challenge.

In *Shafiq v Dundee City Licensing Board*[137] the board's reasoning to refuse on overprovision was influenced by:

> "problems in the past in this locality with underage drinking which seemed to have been eradicated. The Board felt that increasing the number and capacity of off-sales outlets in the locality could, at some point in the future, lead to the return of these types of problems, albeit there was nothing to suggest at the moment that granting this particular application would be inconsistent with any of the licensing objectives."

It was conceded in the appeal that there was no factual evidence before the Board other than the potential relevance of a past history of under-age drinking which had now been eradicated. Sheriff Principal Dunlop QC said:

135 2013 SLT (Sh Ct) 75 at 81.
136 Ibid at 81–2.
137 Dundee Sheriff Court, 28 November 2013, unreported.

"there is no explanation to be found in the board's statement as to how that past history can be linked to the undermining of the licensing objectives over time by the grant of this application. More importantly, there is no evidential basis for that view since it was conceded that there was no evidence that any of the prior problems were related to premises in the locality".

He goes on to use the phrase: "pure speculation". He also discusses the interplay between the licensing objectives and the overprovision ground of refusal as follows:

"It seems to me that that consequence [undermining the licensing objectives] still needs to be linked to the overall number and capacity of licensed premises which will exist in the locality if this particular application is granted. Lacking any suggestion that the previous problems were linked to the provision of alcohol within the locality in my view it is impossible to see how it can be said that the grant of this application would undermine the licensing objectives in issue on the hypothesis that the previous problems would re-emerge. In my opinion there is simply no evidence to warrant that link."

On the face of it this decision was another reminder that a licensing board must base its decisions on probative evidence and not on clairvoyance or speculation. Here, the board did make an effort to link the licensing objectives to overprovision, albeit that they did so without any evidence. Their statement of reasons even defined overprovision in these terms: "Overprovision is a means by which Licensing Boards can try to see that the licensing objectives contained in section 4 of the Act are not compromised over time."[138]

Shafiq is of interest but must now be read in the context of the *Buzzworks* and Glasgow *Tesco* cases. The Sheriff Principal in *Shafiq* does not refer to those cases so it is unclear if those cases were in his mind. In *Shafiq*, the Dundee Board appears, it may be argued, to have fallen into the same trap as Aberdeen in the earlier *Tesco* appeal and conflated the two separate grounds of refusal from the very beginning. Overprovision appears to be analysed not of its own accord (as it should have been) but solely with regard to the licensing objectives, and on an "ad hoc" basis with regard to the limited evidence of past difficulties.

But there is, in my submission, more clarity to divine in this morass. First, the *Shafiq* idea of a board analysing overprovision with regard to issues "over time" appears to sit well with the *Buzzworks* approach, which has regard to what I might refer to as "cumulative impact".[139] In other words, that future issues could be contemplated as part of a board's view on overprovision. That view is also endorsed in the Glasgow *Tesco* case. One of the reasons I think the ground of overprovision is separated from the ground of the objectives is to allow the board breathing room to consider cumulative impact, that is, that overprovision might capture a wider view of detriment which may occur over a

138 As an aside, it also interests me that the "future proofing" of the licensing objectives is swirling around here somewhere, a concept which has had judicial analysis in cases unrelated to overprovision such as *Lidl UK GmbH v City of Glasgow Licensing Board* [2013] CSIH 25 and *Trust Inns Ltd v City of Glasgow Licensing Board* [2015] CSIH 5.

139 The phrase "cumulative impact zones" is used under the Licensing Act 2003 in England and Wales as a broad equivalent to Scottish overprovision zones, and is descendent of what were known as "alcohol disorder zones": on which, see Stephen McGowan, "Polluter Pays and Alcohol Disorder Zones" [2009] 40 SLLP 21. See also "Polluter pays policing plan ditched" [2005] 32 SLLP 7; and "ADZ's stumble as fresh objections are raised" (2008) (70) LR 1.

period of time and lead to a deterioration of the maintenance of the objectives. The Guidance to Licensing Boards says that overprovision:

> "recognises that halting the growth of licensed premises in localities is not intended to restrict trade but may be required to preserve public order, protect the amenity of local communities, and mitigate the adverse health effects of increased alcohol consumption resulting from growing outlet density."

In *Buzzworks*, the Board had not analysed the issue of overprovision as a separate concept (which of course they should have done). They had not looked at numbers, types of licences, or localities. So a common thread one may discern comes back to the quality of analysis by the Board of the overprovision question: on what evidence is there a concern, how and why does that evidence suggest that the grant would lead to overprovision. Further, that evidence may be that overprovision has a link to the licensing objectives, or it may be that overprovision applies for non-licensing objectives reasoning. Overprovision cannot be viewed wholly as uninformed by the objectives. Overprovision cannot be viewed in a vacuum. There is an indirect process at work. There must be context, and it seems to me that a large part of the context is the licensing objectives. Licensing board members plainly must have the licensing objectives in mind when considering a policy approach to overprovision and must do the same when considering overprovision as a distinct ground of refusal, albeit that they may also decide that overprovision applies for non-licensing objective reasons.

This brings me back to ponder what type of material might be relevant to form a view of overprovision, which is not related to the licensing objectives? In *Buzzworks* the Judge offered a tantalising glimpse:

> "It is the factors peculiar to overprovision and separate from the issue of the licensing objectives that the Board have failed to make a substantive decision on in this case. There were examples under the previous legislation of the sheer scale of a proposal being a relevant factor in consideration of overprovision."[140]

It may be some time before we have further judicial wisdom on what might constitute "factors peculiar to overprovision and separate from the issue of the licensing objectives". Readers will have noted that a very large part of the content in these pages, and in the sources I have had regard to, discusses overprovision almost singularly from the standpoint of detriment, and in particular detriment to the licensing objectives.

140 [2011] 49 SLLP 24 at 29.

Chapter 11

Premises Licences – Part 5 Special Cases

1 SPECIAL CASES

Having looked extensively at origin, effect, duration, determination, and so on, I now want to examine a number of special provisions in the Act, which cater for particular types of premises and certain situations. These are:

- club premises;
- provisional premises licences;
- temporary premises licences;
- excluded premises;
- exempt premises;
- vehicles and vessels;
- selling to trade and wholesale premises; and
- remote sales.

2 SPECIAL CASES: CLUB PREMISES

The phrase "club premises", previously known in licensing law as "registered" clubs, is the general expression used in the Act and in practice to refer to not-for-profit club style premises such as members' clubs, miners' welfare institutes, bowling clubs, masonic and Orange lodges, golf clubs, tennis clubs, and a myriad of other club style premises. The phrase "club premises" should not be confused with the common reference to club as a short-hand for nightclub.

Club premises were only licensed, in the sense we understand it, as of 1 September 2009. Prior to the onset of the 2005 Act, clubs were treated very differently and for generations were regulated not through the licensing boards, but through a form of registration with the local sheriff court which can be traced to the Licensing (Scotland) Act 1903. This registration was a permission which allowed the entitlement to provide alcohol, but it would not be quite correct to say that it allowed the "sale" of alcohol, on the basis that part of the whole ethos of separating out such premises was their private, not-for-profit status where they were run not for commercial benefit but for the members themselves. These club premises were (and are) effectively and ultimately owned by the members themselves and therefore the members also owned all of the property of the club, including the drink, the provision of which was controlled by the elected officials or office bearers. So, under law, there was no licensable sale of alcohol because no sale took place when both parties to the transaction were one and the same.[1] The members already owned the alcohol so there was no contractual sale in the traditional sense. This "special status" was the primary reason which led to clubs being treated differently.

A key element to this special status, which remains in some aspects of the 2005 Act provisions, is that the club is seen to be a *bona fide* club and not a commercial operation masquerading as something it is not. To that extent the 1976 Act laid down a plethora of rules which would have to be met in order to successfully register a club[2] (noted at Appendix E for comparative purposes), but the principal rule was, as with the 2005 Act, that the club had to be *bona fide*.

One of the earliest expressions of this, such as it is, in the licensing context is *McWilliams v Main*,[3] which related to premises known as the Tolbooth Club in Leith. Here, a conviction arising from what purported to be a club which benefited one individual, namely Mr McWilliams, was unsound because of evidence presented on appeal that the above rules were observed and in place, and that there was no proof he made any personal profit. The club itself was, as far as I can make out, a drinking club which offered the facility to its members especially on a Sunday when the pubs were closed, but as Lord Pearson says in the case: "The magistrate describes it as an attempt to evade the licensing laws. But in my opinion the attempt is successful"[4]. So here, although the club appears to be designed so as to allow the consumption of alcohol in a social setting where the licensing laws prohibited it otherwise, the club was still found to be *bona fide* because it met the 1976 rules; and was not-for-profit.

The "evasion" referred to by Lord Pearson might have had some influence on the Nicholson approach in looking to bring clubs within the licensing mainframe. Although 1976 Act licensing boards did have a modicum of insight into club premises, in that they regulated the annual regular extension applications allowing certain later hours to be traded, the reality was that they had no influence over how alcohol was sold or consumed in club premises. In fact, this hands-off approach even extended into rights of entry, with police not entitled to enter a registered club without a warrant.[5]

Nicholson did not consider the Clayson arrangement of clubs being registered with the sheriff to be of any practical use in the early stages of the twenty-first century and saw his report as an opportunity to strike through it, going so far as to say that the 1976 Act approach was "anomalous and indefensible".[6] Axiomatic to the change in tone on clubs was, as I understand Nicholson, a move away from esoteric debate on the legal nature of a sale, to view clubs with regard to the proposed licensing objectives. In other words, it

1 *Humphrey v Tudgay* [1915] 1 KB 119, as approved in the Scottish licensing case *Crossgates British Legion Club v Davidson* 1954 SLT 124. In *Crossgates*, the Lord Justice General Cooper said: "when a member of a members club is served with liquor by a servant of that club no sale takes place" (at 125).

2 A general exception annexed to this provision was that these rules did not require to be evidenced where the club was "any lodge of Freemasons duly constituted under a charter from the Grand Lodge of Scotland".

3 (1902) 9 SLT 503.

4 Ibid at 507.

5 1976 Act, s 114.

6 Nicholson Report, para 9.2, p 111.

became more important for policy reasons that the supply and consumption of alcohol was subject to the same public safety scrutiny, checks and balances that application of the licensing laws would allow, over some principled stance aligned to a guarded independence of private clubs.

Much of the argument on this particular point seems to spring from the debatable proposition that people were simply better-behaved in a club environment in comparison to a traditional public house style setting, because of the unwritten "social" rules which applied in condoning decent behaviours in a private club, fortified by the written club constitution and rules which might see a member's rights removed, resulting in embarrassment amongst one's fellows. Nicholson said:

> "Given that we are recommending an enhanced supervisory role for licensing boards, and given that it would not be practicable to set up a separate supervisory system solely for clubs, it appears to us that there is an overwhelming case for bringing clubs within the general licensing system which we are proposing, and thus within the supervisory system to be operated by licensing boards."[7]

The 2005 Act sweeps away the debate over whether the sale of alcohol by a club is a sale. Section 3(1) and (2) of the Act say:

> "(1) A supply of alcohol which is not otherwise a sale of the alcohol is, in the circumstances described in subsection (2) [...], to be treated for the purposes of this Act as if it were a sale of the alcohol.
> (2) The first set of circumstances is where the supply is by or on behalf of a club to, or to the order of, a member of the club."

In addition to this, the position is fortified by an amendment/interpretation which was added to section 147(2). As enacted, section 147(2) reads:

> "In this Act, references to selling alcohol or other goods to trade are references to selling the alcohol or goods to a person for the purposes of the person's trade; and related expressions are to be construed accordingly."

Regulation 4 of the Licensing (Clubs) (Scotland) Regulations 2007[8] adds the following:

> "In relation to a club which falls within the description prescribed in regulation 2(1), section 147(2) of the Act is to apply as if the expression 'selling alcohol or other goods to trade' included selling alcohol or goods to a person for the purposes of the business of the club."

The purpose of the section 147 clarification is again to recognise that whilst a club might not "trade" in the commercial sense, it has a place within the licensing system and in particular that it links to the ability of wholesale operators to sell alcohol to a club, noting that there may not be "trade" in the conventional sense.

So, notwithstanding that the general Scots law of contract may yet harbour a view on whether the sale is not in fact a sale for those general purposes, as far as licensing law is concerned it *is* to be treated as a sale. This provision ensures that clubs are caught by the licensing system by confirming that the transaction is a licensable transaction, meaning that all club premises which

7 Nicholson Report, para 9.4, p 112.
8 SSI 2007/76.

provide alcohol need to hold a premises licence.[9] Whilst clubs were brought into the licensing mainstream in 2009, their special status was also recognised – perhaps along with their "important traditions".[10]

In relation to the "special status", when Parliament was debating the Licensing Bill the language used in the Policy Memorandum was that "Scottish Ministers would be provided with a regulatory power to exempt very small clubs should they meet certain conditions set out in the Bill".[11] Of course, the "exemption" referred to here could only go so far, and in the same document a number of suggestions were made:

> "In the majority of cases, the premises manager would be a member of staff employed by the club to run its bar. However, we recognise that for a number of small clubs, bar facilities and the supply of alcohol is a minor part of their activities and it would not be feasible for them to undergo the cost of training attached to appointing a premises manager. Ministers would, therefore, have a power by regulation to exempt clubs from having to have a premises manager. The decision to exempt would be subject to further detailed discussion with clubs but could be based, for example, on bar turnover or the number of club members."[12]

The notion that exemptions from certain provisions of the Act would be based on turnover, either of drink or of members, appears fanciful when viewed from afar, although no doubt well intentioned at the time. The finalised approach, which is the one we now have and which is examined below, is more legalistic but certainly not without detractors. However, it is fair to say that Sheriff Principal Nicholson appeared satisfied with the Bill's treatment of clubs. Whilst giving evidence during Parliamentary debates on the Bill, he said:

> "We thought that there was no particularly sound argument for allowing clubs to retain that special, almost privileged, position. However, at the same time, we acknowledged that clubs have a character that is very different from that of ordinary commercial licensed premises and we were anxious that that difference should be recognised as appropriate in the bill. As far as I can tell, the bill seems to do that."[13]

It is also fair to say that member club representatives were pretty defensive of their special status and certainly made a number of valid points about how the application of the Act might not marry the practical reality of club operation, albeit that the general sense one gets is that the club representatives knew that

9 It may appear unsurprising that club representatives were consulted on as part of the Licensing Bill and many opposed being brought into the licensing system. The Scottish Executive met with a number of representatives of members' clubs on 18 August and 26 November 2004 and responses to the white paper consultation bear out that opposition. However, there must have been pragmatism on the part of some correspondent clubs. During Parliamentary debate on 22 March 2005, Scottish Government civil servant Jacqueline Conlan, who was overseeing the Bill, said: "We have had much discussion with clubs. We have developed the position with their full co-operation and, as far as I know, they are happy with it".

10 A phrase used in the Licensing (Scotland) Bill Regulatory Impact Assessment, p 3. For an overview of the clubs' "dilemma" at the time of conversion, see Caroline Brown (Loudon!) "Members' Clubs: constitutions, conditions, and the scope for challenge" [2009] 43 SLLP 17); and further Sean Hoath, "The Clubs Conundrum" [2011] 49 SLLP 11.

11 Policy Memorandum to the Licensing Bill, 22 February 2005, para 72, p 16.

12 Ibid para 88, p 20.

13 Local Government and Transport Committee, 22 March 2005.

the writing was very much on the clubhouse wall. During debates, a representative of the National Union of Students (NUS) said:

> "We welcome the publication of the bill and we support the five key licensing objectives that it outlines . . . We take this opportunity to highlight the unique nature of student associations and to point out that providing bars and licensed premises is only a small part of what they do – it is not their main function and it is not their sole reason for existence."[14]

The Coal Industry Social Welfare Organisation (Scotland) (CISWO) also appeared and offered this testimony:

> ". . . we sincerely request that the Scottish Parliament and Scottish Executive protect the special status of registered clubs under the new licensing system . . . I stress the special nature of members clubs and emphasise that they are not open to the general public for the sale of alcohol. That needs to be properly highlighted in the bill to avoid confusion and to prevent opposition from people in the licensed trade and elsewhere who consider that registered clubs compete unfairly with ordinary licensed premises."[15]

In the same debates, the NUS made good points about training requirements being enforced where the bar staff were transient volunteers in many cases, and that this would create a negative consequence in terms of practical delivery, and CISWO made good points about why clubs should have a special status in terms of the licensing fee structure. A wider point about competition by clubs with the licensed trade, that is, commercial pubs and bars and so on, is also well observed here. There is no doubt that pub operators were greatly concerned about clubs operating akin to a pub or bar "under the radar", and no doubt that they had concerns that clubs were in reality operating on a commercial or quasi-commercial basis and thus providing them with uneven competition.[16]

2.1 What is a "club" for the purposes of the 2005 Act?

Club premises are sometimes referred to in licensing circles as "Section 125 clubs". As noted above, section 125 creates "special provision for certain clubs". The "certain clubs" aspect is laid out under the Licensing (Clubs) (Scotland) Regulations 2007.[17] There are two key tests: first, that the club is not conducted for the purposes of making a profit; and, secondly, that the club must have a written constitution which includes the following provisions:

- the business of the club is to be under the management of a committee or other governing body elected by the members of the club,
- no person under 18 is to be admitted as a member of the club (unless the club is devoted primarily to some sporting purpose or is a students' union),

14 Melanie Ward, NUS, Local Government and Transport Committee, 12 April 2005.

15 Ian McAlpine, CISWO Scotland, Local Government and Transport Committee, 12 April 2005.

16 These issues were raised with the Scottish Government on numerous occasions by trade as well as clerks and licensing board members, but any suggestion that there would be moves to curtail so-called exploitation of the system by clubs was roundly dismissed and the Government view was that abuses be dealt with by local licensing boards (see "Scottish Government: club abuses 'a matter for licensing boards'" [2012] 51 SLLP 1).

17 SSI 2007/76.

- no member of the committee or other governing body and no person employed by the club is to have any personal interest in the sale of alcohol on the club premises or in the profits arising from such sale,
- other than when an occasional licence is in effect, no person is to be supplied with alcohol on the club premises unless that person is a member, or a guest of a member and in the company of the member, or a member of another club,
- where guests of members are supplied with alcohol on occasions when an occasional licence is not in force, a book must be kept detailing the date, the name and address of the guest, and the name of the member accompanying the guest,
- correct accounts and books must be kept showing the financial affairs and intromissions of the club,
- there must be at least twenty-five members, and
- no person is to be allowed honorary or temporary membership of the club or to be relieved of any payment of the regular entrance fee or subscription except to allow temporary participation in the activity which is the primary purpose of the club, and except in accordance with specific provision set out in the club rules.

It may be instructive to look at the most troublesome of these in a bit more detail.

2.1.1 Club rules: management of the club by committee

This rule is present to fortify the position that the club is not a commercial enterprise by ensuring that it is run by elected committee and not a sole individual. Note that the regulations do not go so far as to prescribe how the committee must be elected, how it must run, or how it must vote. That is all left to the club members to decide for themselves.[18]

2.1.2 Club rules: persons aged under 18

This rule states that "no person under 18 is to be admitted as a member of the club (unless the club is devoted primarily to some sporting purpose or is a students' union)". In the case of a students' union, it must be a union of a Scottish university, or a further education college under the management of an education authority recognised and certified as such.[19] Junior members are acceptable for sporting clubs such as rugby, tennis and golf clubs. There is no further prescription under these regulations; so as long as the club is a *bona fide* sporting club they can admit junior members of whatever age they see appropriate, although it is of course sensible that the approach they take is adopted as part of the constitution.

It is important to recognise the distinction between admittance as a member, and admittance to the premises, as these are not necessarily the same. The old

18 This is in contrast to the equivalent rule under the 1976 Act which imposed a maximum one-year term per committee, certain rules on having non-elected members on the committee, as well as requiring "periodic meetings" (1976 Act, s 107(1)(c)). See *Baillieston Miners' Welfare Society and Social Club v Chief Constable of Lanarkshire* 1966 SLT (Sh Ct) 31.

19 Regulation 2(3).

1976 Act approach required a blanket ban on alcohol sales to all persons aged under 18 (except in relation to student unions). That is not the case under the 2005 Act and the general rules of sale and consumption to persons aged under 18 apply. In addition, this rule has no special bearing on access by children and young persons under the terms of the premises licence. The premises licence will cater for such access based on whatever the licensing board has approved.

2.1.3 Club rules: personal interest in the sale of alcohol

The rule here states: "no member of the committee or other governing body and no person employed by the club is to have any personal interest in the sale of alcohol on the club premises or in the profits arising from such sale". This provision makes it clear that not only should the club itself not be a commercial enterprise, but that no individual involved in the club or employed by the club should have a personal interest in the sale of alcohol or profits. This does not, of course, mean a person cannot be employed without some form of remuneration,[20] but it does prohibit a person making a personal profit from the alcohol sale. Any profit from the sale of alcohol must go to club funds and in that sense is not treated as commercial profit.[21]

2.1.4 Club rules: the rule around alcohol and "bona fide guests"

There are a couple of rules which relate to ensuring that persons other than members, namely only *bona fide* guests of members, can consume alcohol. These rules are not in play where an occasional licence is in effect (see below). The first element of this is that "no person is to be supplied with alcohol on the club premises unless that person is a member, or a guest of a member and in the company of the member, or a member of another club". The second element is about record-keeping to ensure the *bona fide* guest element is observed, thus: "a book must be kept detailing the date, the name and address of the guest, and the name of the member accompanying the guest".

Note, first, that there is no limit on the number of *bona fide* guests that a member can sign in, although the guests do need to be "in the company" of the member. As there is no definition provided, "in the company of" might mean sitting at a cosy table for two, or in a room with three hundred revellers.

That brings us on to another vexed question, namely whether the guest can buy alcohol directly. The reality is that this does of course happen. It happens all the time in most if not all clubs across the country. It does not appear to make any practical sense that a guest should be prohibited from buying a drink for the member at whose invitation he has attended the club, perhaps sitting in the club lounge after a round of golf. Cummins took the view that, under the old provision in the 1976 Act, the guest was not entitled to purchase directly,[22] however, that view was not shared by all practitioners at the time, and must

20 In the case of *Drongan and District Working Men's Social Club, Petitioners* 1966 SLT (Sh Ct) 73, the existence of an "honorarium" to officers was not held to defeat the equivalent provision of the time.

21 *Graff v Evans* (1882) 8 QBD 373.

22 J C Cummins, *Licensing Law in Scotland* (2nd edn, Butterworths, 2000) pp 380–1.

now be seen against what was a much broader and complex arrangement for registration for clubs and where, in times past, sale to a non-member was more clearly an unlawful act.[23]

Trying to unpick this with reference to the 2005 Act provisions brings forward a few avenues.

First, the fact that there is no specific provision preventing the guest buying alcohol themselves provided they are in the company of the member, can be compared with the wording which does exist in relation to residents of licensed premises obtaining alcohol outwith licensed hours. The 2005 Act creates an exemption to the general offence of selling outside licensed hours where alcohol is "sold to a person who resides on the premises".[24] This comparison is perhaps useful. In the case of residents, it is made clear that the resident must be the one to purchase alcohol. There is no provision preventing the resident from purchasing on behalf of a non-resident in their company. Comparing that to the case of club members and *bona fide* guests, *expressic unius, exclusio alterius*, there is no express requirement that the alcohol must be sold only to the member, only that it cannot be "supplied" to a guest unless they are in a member's company. In the context of the 2005 Act, the phrase "supply" is to be treated as a sale under section 3 as including "by or on behalf of a club to, or to the order of, a member of the club". If a guest buys a round of drinks having been signed in by the member, it might be suggested that this is covered by the phrase "to the order of", which appears to present some form of general authorisation.

However, I do believe the matter is much clearer than that. The 2005 Act swept away the statutory soil in which the 1976 principles took root. The scheme of the Act has moved away from many of the older principles that may have been at play. First, club premises are now licensed premises, whereas they were not under the 1976 Act, and there is no longer any offence of "trafficking". The scheme of the 2005 Act is very clearly a move away from a focus on antiquarian rules about alcohol provision under a myriad of byzantine circumstances, instead focusing very clearly on alcohol provision being seen through the lens of the licensing objectives. Secondly, the supply of alcohol is now treated as a sale like in any other licensed premises and does not attract some ethereal and legally separate quality; and, thirdly, and perhaps principally, there is no licensing interaction between the club rules and the premises licence (on which, see more below at Section 2.3) and therefore even if sale direct to a guest was a breach of this rule (which I suggest is not the case), there is no licensing penalty and no criminal offence has been committed, *ergo* the matter is neither here nor there.

Finally, the provision for allowing members of other clubs to obtain alcohol without having to sign in or be in the company of a member is designed to reflect the common practice of visiting clubs, especially for the likes of bowling clubs where there is a match between one club and the other.

23 *Newman v Jones* (1886) 17 QBD 132.
24 2005 Act, s 63(2)(d).

2.1.5 Club rules: temporary or honorary memberships

The rule here states: "no person is to be allowed honorary or temporary membership of the club or to be relieved of any payment of the regular entrance fee or subscription except to allow temporary participation in the activity which is the primary purpose of the club, and except in accordance with specific provision set out in the club rules". There is no further provision made under the licensing laws as to the nature of these honorary or temporary memberships so that is a matter which is left to the club itself to confirm and affirm by way of its constitution or governing document.

What is important to note, however, is that the wording is very precise in relation to the *purpose* of the temporary or honorary membership, and that is to take part in the primary activity of the club; in other words, that these memberships are not to be created as a fiction to allow a non-member into the bar! The reference to an "entrance fee or subscription" is a direct lift from the 1976 Act provisions and to me finds little logic in the 2005 Act system – there is no reference to any wider requirement for an entrance fee or subscription elsewhere in the rules noted above, whereas this was a stated 1976 Act requirement.[25] In fact, an additional entrance fee was frowned upon as it created an impression that the club was being run as a commercial enterprise.[26]

2.2 Club premises: disapplication of certain provisions

The whole purpose of agreeing to all of the above rules is to take advantage of certain exemptions which are offered under the Act to clubs which comply. It should be stated first that club premises may take advantage of a much lower licensing application and annual fee than commercial licensed premises but that is not a "disapplication" *per se*, rather more of a benefit. Section 125 of the Act disapplies a series of provisions of the Act in respect of where premises are used "wholly or mainly for the purposes of any club". These are:

- the overprovision assessment[27]
- the requirement for a premises manager to be nominated on the operating plan[28]
- overprovision as a ground of refusal for a premises licence[29]
- details of the premises manager on the premises licence[30]
- overprovision as a ground of refusal for a variation[31]
- the mandatory condition for premises licences that there has to be a premises manager in order for alcohol to be sold[32]
- the mandatory condition for premises licences that sales of alcohol have to be authorised by a personal licence holder[33]

25 1976 Act, s 107(1)(i).
26 *Chief Constable of Glasgow v Piccadilly Club* 1968 SLT (Sh Ct) 33.
27 2005 Act, s 7.
28 2005 Act, s 20(4)(g).
29 2005 Act, s 23(5)(e).
30 2005 Act, s 26(2)(a)(ii).
31 2005 Act, s 30(5)(d).
32 2005 Act, Sch 3 para 4(1)(a).
33 2005 Act, Sch 3 para 5.

- the mandatory condition for occasional licences that sales of alcohol have to be authorised by a personal licence holder[34]
- the requirement to provide baby changing facilities.[35]

In short, these exemptions can be filtered down to two key areas: (1) clubs are not involved in any aspect of overprovision; and (2) clubs need not have a designated premises manager and need not observe related rules about personal licence holders and authorisation of alcohol sales. Let us examine these a little more closely.

2.2.1 Clubs and overprovision

Under the 1976 Act registered clubs were not included in any assessment of overprovision, such as it was under the old regime. To include club premises within an assessment was an error in law: clubs were not licensed premises under the 1976 Act, as we have noted above.[36] Whilst club premises are now licensed premises for the purposes of the 2005 Act, it is not altogether clear from section 125 that they are to be discounted for the purposes of the overprovision *assessment* under section 7 as well as the ground of refusal relating to overprovision under section 23(5)(e).[37] I think it is clear that an application for a section 125 qualifying club cannot be refused on the grounds of overprovision, but I think the generally held view that clubs can be considered within an overprovision policy assessment, or even considered in a bespoke assessment of a locality against a particular application, is one worthy of further scrutiny.

The Explanatory Notes say: "The general effect [of s 125] is that such clubs would not need to have a premises manager and the overprovision ground of refusal would not apply". The focus here is on the overprovision ground being discluded where the application qualifies under section 125. There is no overt

34 2005 Act, Sch 4 para 4.

35 2005 Act, Sch 3 para 12.

36 One of the last overprovision appeals under the 1976 Act was *Barracuda Pubs Ltd v Midlothian Licensing Board* 2006, which related to a "Smith & Jones" public house in Dalkeith. The case is unreported as a joint motion for remit was approved by the court following agreement between the agent for the applicant, the then R & JM Hill Brown & Co, and Midlothian Licensing Board, the Board having included a local member's club within its list of premises in refusing the new public house licence on the grounds of overprovision. The application was granted at the remitted hearing.

37 Divining the policy reason behind removing clubs from the ambit of overprovision refusal must, necessarily, relate to the "special status" point which is explored above, although the parliamentary process on this point is opaque. I have been unable to locate any "smoking gun" which provides a targeted answer on this particular issue, save the generalised acceptance that as clubs are somehow different, they should not be treated as having any impact on overprovision. With the amount of focus on the topic of overprovision and the public health objective subsequent to the commencement of the 2005 Act, I do wonder if this provision will be lobbied against at some time in the future. There can be no real evidential basis for the proposition that alcohol is somehow consumed more responsibly in a club premises or that the totems which underpin the public health approach such as concepts of "availability" magically disappear where the alcohol provision is in a club. A key aspect of the separation of treatment between clubs and other licensed premises is, of course, the commercial aspect (or lack thereof) to a club. Might the public health approach be more lenient where the premises are not governed by a commercial desire to sell alcohol and accept that it is merely a facility for members? I doubt it. Given how sophisticated the public health voice is in licensing circles now, it seems to me that had that voice been as clear back in 2005, Parliament would have been asked to revisit this approach.

statement either in the Act or in the Notes that clubs should not be included within the assessment of overprovision in an area. One might go further and observe that the Act *does* make specific provision for types of licence which are not to be treated as licensed premises for the purposes of the ground of refusal on overprovision:

> "In subsection (5)(e), references to 'licensed premises' do not include licensed premises in respect of which an occasional licence has effect."[38]

It can be argued, therefore, that in taking a positive step to actively remove a type of licensed premises, in this case occasional licensed premises, but not also include a reference to section 125 club premises, then by omission said club premises can in fact, perhaps counterintuitively, be counted for the purposes of considering overprovision where the applicant is not a club premises.

A final point of interest here is to acknowledge that some existing "club" premises might be referred to in the context of a refusal under the ground of overprovision either on a policy basis or on a case-by-case basis, where the "club" has shed its section 125 status, on which see Section 2.4 below.

2.2.2 Clubs and the premises manager/personal licence holders

There is no doubt that the reasoning behind the disapplication of the need to have a designated premises manager, or to have alcohol sales authorised by a personal licence holder, emanates from a concern that many clubs did not have people in such positions and that they also experience a high turnover of office bearers or other officials who might have had, from time to time, the overall management brief of dealing with alcohol sales. But it is also clear that, at the start at least, this was only going to apply to certain smaller clubs, and not all club premises. During Parliamentary debates on the Licensing Bill, a senior civil servant dealing with the Bill said:

> ". . . we intend to exempt very small clubs from the requirement to have a personal licence holder. That has been a concern, particularly of bowling clubs that have very few members and are very small but have the capacity for members to have a drink. We have said that we will examine that."[39]

This was backed up in the Justice Committee Stage 1 Report, which said:

> "we intend to prescribe a further category of members club that may be exempted from the requirement to have a premises manager who is a personal licence holder. This exemption would be applied only to very small clubs for whom the financial burden of employing a personal licence holder would be too great."[40]

The Regulatory Impact Assessment of the Licensing Bill also said:

> ". . . very small clubs with limited resources would not be required to have a designated personal licence holder. The level of exemption to the personal licence will be set out in later regulations following the fee review but could, for example, be based on bar turnover."[41]

38 2005 Act, s 23(9).
39 Jacqueline Conlan, Local Government and Transport Committee, 22 March 2005.
40 As noted in the Local Government and Transport Committee Stage 1 Report at Annex A, p 117.
41 Regulatory Impact Assessment to the Licensing (Scotland) Bill, para 58, p 20.

Taking all this together we have what appears to have been some best Parliamentary intentions to create a sub-category of club premises where the disapplication of the need for a premises manager would solely reside. The proposition in the course of the Bill that this would be dealt with either through the club regulations themselves, or the separate fee regulations, appears to have been overlooked or purposefully left behind as perhaps too complex to deliver. The result is, as noted above, that the disapplication of the need for the premises manager and indeed any authorisation of alcohol sales by a personal licence holder applies to all club premises and there is no other smaller or sub-category recognised by the Act.

2.3 Interplay between licensing law and a club's constitution

It is fairly common for misunderstanding and mystery to pervade the relationship between a club's premises licence and its constitution. Fundamentally, it must be accepted that it is not the job of the licensing board to regulate the operation of a private club other than how it supplies alcohol and how alcohol is consumed there, barring any bespoke conditions (although I suggest that any condition which interferes with the constitution beyond the scope of the 2005 Act is likely to be *ultra vires*). There is also no longer any other underlying special law of club constitutions, save the common law and criminal law.

The sole purpose of the club regulations is to ensure that a club's constitution has a minimum number of rules in order to qualify under section 125. That is the single interaction between licensing authority and club. The wider constitution is not the business of the Licensing Standards Officer, not the business of the licensing police, and not the business of the Licensing Board. It is akin to a constitution of an unlicensed club – the licensing authorities have no remit. To put it another way, observing the constitution is not a condition of the premises licence.

What this means is that clubs can be seen to "flout" the section 125 status as there is no mechanism save a potential review of the premises licence (on which see later in this chapter) if an argument can be made that this relates to the licensing objectives in some way. But even this is a difficulty. To illustrate this, take the scenario where a club lets in the public to drink without regard to rules over signing-in and *bona fide* guests. If the result of that is violence or disorder, then a licensing objective may be engaged. But if there is no adverse incident and it is all very respectable, how is the licensing objective engaged? There is no doubt that the constitution has been broken, but, as it is not a condition of the licence to observe the constitution, it is difficult to see what a licensing board would make of this.

Taking this away from the key issue of public access, a condition which purported to give licensing boards some remit in the terms of a club constitution would fly in the face of the purpose of the 2005 Act and the licensing objectives which underpin it because alcohol is just one element to a club constitution.

Having said that, one must also recognise that the constitution of the club cannot interfere with the premises licence save that it is open for a club to impose more restrictive policies upon itself which go further than those imposed by the licence. An example of that might be that the club imposes a more restrictive access for under 18s which goes beyond whatever is imposed in the licence. There is an argument that as a matter of public confidence, whatever rules there may be in the constitution should mirror the terms of the licence, but even so, that is not a legal requirement and the relationship is not prescriptive – the licence is directory, not mandatory.

In other words, the club's constitution – as it relates to licensing matters – cannot seek to widen or relax the terms of the licence but it can restrict the terms of the licence on a unilateral, self-imposed basis as it is the club's licence to operate up to such maximum within the absolute maximums that the licence allows, just as a commercial business may choose to do so on a policy or *ad hoc* basis.

In some cases, club constitutions "go further" than the licensing laws not through active choice but because there is still some confusion over what is and is not allowed. It is not uncommon to find club constitutions with archaic treatment of children and young person's access which does not mirror the terms of the premises licence. I have certainly dealt with a number of club clients whose rulebooks have all manner of anachronisms, such as references to "excisable liquors", bans on children aged under 14 being able to see a bar, or even provisions preventing the sale of spirits, none of which are based in current law.

2.4 Bona fide clubs operating with "full" or unrestricted licences

One of the trends which licensing lawyers have noted across the decade or so of practice under the 2005 Act has been the move by some clubs away from the section 125 status. This is sometimes referred to as going for a "full" licence, an "open" licence or an "unrestricted licence". The vast majority of licensing boards allow this process to be conducted by way of a major variation application, although at least one insists on a new licence application.

The Act itself is silent on this type of process, although noting that the activation of section 125 is by way of ticking a box on the application form, and that in some cases the general description of the premises licence will refer to the club status, I have always taken the view that given a variation can be to vary "any other information contained or referred to within the licence, and includes an addition, deletion, or other modification", a club that wishes to lose the section 125 status can achieve this by way of a major variation.

The reason why this might be of interest to clubs is that it allows them to operate selling directly to the public without worrying about special rules for access or worrying about whether they can or can't do certain things having regard to the minimum constitutional requirements which are laid out above. The fear of the "mainstream" licensed trade I referred to earlier, as regards clubs competing with them on some form of commercial basis, finds a full-throated voice here. Many clubs have found that, in order to survive, they have had to lessen their grip on the objects or purposes of the club and try to attract a wider demographic. There are plenty of anecdotal stories about clubs operating like a full access pub without having regard to their licence or their constitution, that is for sure, but what is also true is that there has been a marked rise in applications by clubs seeking to rid themselves of the section 125 shackles as they evolve and change to survive.

The effect of removing the section 125 status on an existing, licensed club is not altogether well understood, which I put down to a very long hangover in separating the 1976 Act approach to clubs, and the 2005 Act approach; as well as the absence of any clear process in the 2005 Act.

It is wholly open to club premises to get rid of their section 125 status and, if successful in doing so, they do not have to have regard to the minimum constitution requirements noted above in licensing terms. The principal practical impact is that they can admit the public on an unrestricted basis, that is, without regard to any rules over *bona fide* guests, and all the rest of it. The wider impact is that as far as licensing law is concerned it means they can do what they like with that constitution. The club may convert to a full-blown commercial enterprise. The club may still be a members' club. It may still have a constitution and may still observe some of the licensing club regulations as noted above. It is just that it is no longer a club for the purposes of licensing law, which is entirely the point of the application to remove the section 125 status in the first place.

It is accepted that "mainstream" licensed premises like pubs and bars will feel aggrieved club premises can let in the public and trade like any other pub or bar, but that is neither here nor there as regards the law, albeit it may be seen by some as a betrayal. It is to be remembered that there is no lawful interaction between the licence and the constitution of the club beyond the minimum requirements laid out in the requirements noted above, which is purely designed to achieve section 125 status. To make matters abundantly clear, if a club separates itself from the section 125 status, then the constitution becomes irrelevant as regards licensing, as noted in the paragraphs above.

It also entirely open to a club to continue to operate as a not-for-profit club, and to continue to adhere to some of the conditions as regards the regulations noted above, whilst also having a full or public access licence. It then becomes a matter for the club to self-police its own constitution; and this perhaps is where it can be difficult to separate the two in the mind.

Under the 1976 Act, this would never have been the case, because the Sheriff court system regulated the constitution beyond the sale of alcohol. That is no longer the reality. That scrutiny has been removed. It is not the job of the licensing board to ensure standards of clubs in relation to constitutional matters – that is clearly outwith the essential remit of the licensing board, being the governance of the sale and consumption of alcohol. The other side of that coin is, of course, that any sale or supply or consumption of alcohol which is a breach of the premises licence or offends the licensing objectives is very much a matter for the licensing board.

What all of this means is that whether by intention or more likely omission, the very nature of licensed private members' clubs has altered to some degree since the onset of the 2005 Act in 2009; principally, that the governance of all matters of the club other than that which is alcohol related has no regulator, no watchdog, no ombudsman. At the same time, many traditional clubs have faced a membership crisis as society has changed and people have moved away from these types of social clubs. I also believe that it is correct to observe, from my own experience of appearing at licensing boards up and down the country, that there has been a rise in concerns over the behaviour of clubs, notwithstanding the various submissions to Nicholson and the Scottish Parliament to the effect that clubs were not as liable to alcohol-related disorder because members were better behaved than the general public in pubs, and that alcohol was an ancillary offer to the main objects of the club.

It should be noted that, in shedding the section 125 status, there could be other non-licensing implications for club premises in relation to how this affects rateable value and taxation, so advice should be sought.

2.4.1 Removal of the section 125 status and impact on gambling permissions

A further area for confusion for those who remove the special status that section 125 affords is the relationship between that status and gaming permissions. Club gaming permits and permissions are discussed in more detail in Chapter 21 at Section 11, but the issue is worth some comment here as the topic is poorly understood not least because amendments were required to the relevant regulations.

The first question is whether there is a prerequisite to hold a premises licence under the 2005 Act in order to obtain a club gaming or club machine permit at all. There are two basic tests for an applicant to be eligible to apply for a club machine or club gaming permit. The first is indeed that the premises must have a premises licence under the 2005 Act, and such licence must be one subject to section 125 of that Act. The second is that the premises must also meet the relevant definitions of club types under the Gambling Act 2005.

It should always be remembered by the clubs, therefore, that if they shed the section 125 status as a result of a more fundamental change, such as a move to a commercial operation, then that impacts on the existing gambling permissions under the Gambling Act 2005 and in my view has the practical effect of cancellation of a club permit as the holder is no longer a competent holder of such a permit.

These specialist gaming permissions are all discussed in detail in Chapter 21.

2.5 Club premises and occasional licences

The club regulations make specific provision for occasional licences on club premises and, as touched upon above, the process has the sole purpose of lifting the general prohibition on allowing members of the public to attend club premises unfettered. The wording is: "other than when an occasional licence is in effect, no person is to be supplied with alcohol on the club premises unless that person is a member, or a guest of a member and in the company of the member, or a member of another club". The regulations deal with the issue of "double licensing" as follows:

> "The fact that a premises licence is in effect in respect of premises used wholly or mainly for the purposes of a club which falls within the description prescribed in regulation 2(1) is not (despite the exclusion of licensed premises in section 56(1) of the Act) to prevent an occasional licence being issued in respect of those premises."[42]

Perhaps most interestingly conditions attaching to the principal premises licence are "not to have effect" in respect of club premises during the time an occasional licence is also in force. It is difficult to penetrate how the legislature felt this provision would be well-met across the licensing community. There was no debate of the regulations at all, when they passed through the Local Government and Transport Committee in February 2007.[43]

42 Licensing (Clubs) (Scotland) Regulations 2007 (SSI 2007/76) reg 3.

43 Jack Cummins points out to me, in his peer review of the text, that there was a Scottish Parliamentary election on the horizon!

Whilst the occasional licence for clubs may have its origins in allowing public access, the effect of this particular provision is that the mandatory conditions attached to the premises licence are disapplied; however, of course, the vast majority of those exact conditions are "re-applied" under Schedule 4 as "mandatory" conditions which attach to the occasional licence. The operation of this is important in appreciating that the requirement to observe those occasional licence conditions sits with the holder of that occasional licence, and that person is not necessarily the same person who holds the premises licence for the club.

The regulations do restrict the number of occasional licences that may be used in this fashion. The licensing board may issue, in any 12-month period, no more than four occasional licences with a duration of four days or more and no more than twelve occasional licences with a duration of less than four days. In either event, the total number of days covered by occasional licences may not exceed 56, so it is up to the club premises and applicant for the occasional licence to decide how to manipulate these rules to their advantage.

The issues percolating around clubs and occasional licences are examined in more detail in Chapter 18 at Section 7.

3 SPECIAL CASES: PROVISIONAL PREMISES LICENCES

It is quite common to want to apply for a licence for premises that are still under construction, conversion, or even where there is nothing more than an empty plot of land. From an applicant's perspective, obtaining the licence can be important to secure funding, to secure a buyer or tenant, or to otherwise have commercial certainty that a licence is in place for a project which may be months or even years from being traded. Under these types of circumstances, a prospective applicant can seek to secure a "provisional licence".

3.1 What is a provisional licence?

Under the 1976 Act, there were two types of provisional grant to cover these circumstances: a "site only" provisional grant under section 26(2) of that Act, and a "detailed" provisional grant under section 26(1). These two options were most useful to the potential applicant – the section 26(2) application could be lodged without detailed licensing plans, only a "location plan" being required. In addition, the certificate of suitability process under the 1976 Act did not insist on the planning certificate being lodged with the application (although some boards did ask for this), instead allowing applicants to present the certificate further down the line and even in some cases up to the day of the hearing.[44] Nicholson was very clear that the 1976 treatment of such cases should simply be replicated under the new system.[45]

The 2005 Act makes provision for just one type of provisional licence under the general heading "Premises under construction or conversion", which is the headline text preceding section 45 of the Act. Section 45(1) says:

44 On the loss of the 1976 Act s 26(2) "outline grant", see further, "Provisional Grant Investment Dangers" [2009] 42 SLLP 6.

45 Nicholson Report, para 6.12, p 81.

"A premises licence application may be made in relation to any premises despite the fact that, at the time the application is made, the premises are yet to be, or are in the course of being, constructed or converted for use as licensed premises."

The Guidance to Licensing Boards offers nothing of merit in relation to provisional licences,[46] and the Explanatory Notes to the Act have little to say beyond repetition of the statute. The Policy Memorandum does not mention provisional licences at all. There is no reference to why Parliament decided to go forward with a single provisional licence (as opposed to the two types available under the 1976 Act[47]) at any stage of the Bill from any Committee or full Parliamentary debate, and certainly nothing which assists in appreciating the binary approach within that system.[48] Yet, for practitioners, the provisional licence is well understood, and I would suggest that most new licences are in fact provisional licences. There may be benefit in seeking a provisional licence even where premises are not under construction and indeed may be fully trading such as our old friend the unlicensed restaurant – first, the applicant is reducing initial overheads by only paying out for the provisional licence fee as well as any fee for just one certificate of suitability, namely in relation to planning. There may also be a strategic element in applying for the provisional as opposed to a full licence where there is some concern about the likelihood of grant. The proprietor may wish to secure provisional licensing permission in order to support placing his property on the market, and the presence of the provisional licence may add value as well as comfort.

There has been some debate over the reference to "premises under construction or conversion" in that it has been suggested by some that the provisional licence option is only open where there are building works occurring, or proposed to occur. This approach would prevent an existing, built premises from applying for a provisional licence. There are many reasons why an established business might want to go down the provisional route, such as savings on cost as noted above, or that they do not have a proposed premises manager

46 Guidance to Licensing Boards (April 2007) para 100.

47 The loss of a "site only" option is, for me at least, to be lamented. Advising on a number of developer projects across Scotland, it is an option which would be of some use to seek early certainty, and would avoid the need in many cases to create layout plans which are no more than fiction and fable. The key ability to go forward with a location plan only might now seem anathema to licensing board members unfamiliar with the 1976 Act system, and it remains to be seen how such an option could navigate the 2005 Act framework with regard to the much more detailed application form: a "location plan only" approach would struggle with providing details on capacity, access by children and young persons, as well as activities, if the layout is not known. During the passage of the Air Weapons and Licensing Bill, I gave evidence at the Scottish Parliament on behalf of the Institute of Licensing to support the reintroduction of a site-only provisional licence (a position which was supported by the Law Society of Scotland) but this was rejected by the Local Government and Regeneration Committee. The Scottish Government Bill team gave a written response to the proposal, with the somewhat opaque belief that it "has the potential to undermine facets of the licensing regime and would not be widely supported by other licensing stakeholders". (See the Stage 1 Report to the Air Weapons and Licensing Bill, 23 March 2015, para 254; and the SPICe Briefing, Air Weapons and Licensing (Scotland) Bill – Stage 3, 15/36, 18 June 2005, p 13.) It appears therefore that the site-only provisional licence is now no more than a licensing footnote.

48 At the Local Government and Transport Committee evidential session on 19 April 2005, the then clerk to the Edinburgh licensing board Robert Millar raised the issue of "finalising" provisional licences where there may be wider aspects to a development still under construction but his remarks were not debated.

with a valid personal licence at the time the application is being considered. In practice, there are plenty of examples across Scotland of provisional licences being sought for established, built premises. Cummins argues that "conversion" can be read sensibly so as to include conversion from a non-licensed premises to a licensed premises.[49]

A provisional premises licence is not a licence "in effect" unless it has been confirmed by the licensing board (see below) so it may not be relied upon to allow the sale of alcohol until such time as the confirmation procedure has been completed.

3.2 Duration of a provisional premises licence

A provisional licence under the 2005 Act has a four-year currency,[50] which is referred to as "the provisional period", and if it has not been confirmed within this period, the licence is treated as revoked. Note that the provisional premises licence must be confirmed; in other words, the confirmation application must be granted. It will not be sufficient that the confirmation application is simply lodged prior to the expiry of the provisional premises licence.[51]

3.2.1 Renewal of a provisional premises licence

The holder of the provisional licence can apply to the licensing board to have the provisional period extended if he can show that the completion, construction or conversion of the premises has been delayed, and that delay has been caused by factors outwith the licence holder's control.

If the board is satisfied as to the reasons for the delay, it may extend the provisional period as it considers appropriate. In practice, the applicant will no doubt advise the board of how matters are progressing on site and be in a position to suggest a date that the premises will be nearing completion, should the board be minded to allow the extension.

There is no formal application process for renewal of a provisional licence. The provisional licence holder need merely to write and request the renewal, however the timing of the request is important to consider.

3.3 The provisional premises licence application

The application form is the same as for a full premises licence and the requirements are also the same, save that only a section 50 certificate from planning is required, and that no information regarding the premises manager need be given. Whilst a solitary reading of section 46(2) would seem to indicate that the layout plan and operating plan are to be submitted at the time the confirmation application is lodged (see below), section 45(10) states that the requirements for "full" premises licence applications under

49 J C Cummins, *Licensing (Scotland) Act 2005*, Annotated Statute (3rd edn, W Green, 2013) para 45-03, p 92.

50 This was originally a 2-year period, and subsequently amended to 4 years by s 185 of the Criminal Justice and Licensing (Scotland) Act 2010, commenced as of 13 December 2010 via the Criminal Justice and Licensing (Scotland) Act 2010 (Commencement No. 6, Transitional and Savings Provisions) Order 2010 (SSI 2010/413).

51 2005 Act, s 45(4).

section 20 apply equally to provisional premises licence applications, save for the section 50 certificates and premises manager information. In the result, it is clear from section 46(5) that the provisional premises licence *is* to be lodged with the same level of detail and following the same process as for a full premises licence. In other words, all the processes for a new premises licence outlined in Chapter 8, and the determination of such an application discussed in Chapter 10, are virtually identical to that of a provisional premises licence.

3.4 Confirmation of the provisional premises licence

"Confirmation" relates to a separate, administrative process which requires to be followed in order to convert a provisional licence to a full licence. Confirmation is dealt with under section 46 of the Act. The confirmation application may be lodged any time before the expiry of the provisional period, but it should be lodged in enough time that the application can be granted prior to the expiry of the provisional period. Section 46(2) requires the confirmation application to be lodged with the layout plan, the operating plan, and the outstanding section 50 certificates in relation to building standards and food hygiene. The layout plan and operating plan may have been varied since the time of the original grant of the provisional premises licence and the confirmation process is also used to make sure that any changes of this nature have been verified and approved by the licensing board in the proper way. The premises manager details must be given and of course that person must hold a valid personal licence. The confirmation application must also be accompanied by the appropriate fee (see below).

Typically, the process is that, following grant of the provisional licence, the holder will begin works. These works may take some time but should be carried out in relation to the approved building warrant. It may be that some works will change as a result of matters which crop up during the fit out, and this perhaps necessitates an amendment to the building warrant. That might also necessitate a variation to the layout plan of the premises. All these matters will have to be dealt with on an ongoing basis.

Eventually the licence holder reaches a stage where an end to the works is in sight and the glorious opening day is on the horizon. In order to lodge the confirmation application, the remaining certificates of suitability will be required. It is imperative therefore that correspondence with the relevant officers in building standards and food hygiene is on a continuing basis, to ensure that these certificates have been requested and are ready to be issued as soon as works complete and matters have been signed off. To that end, where advising a provisional licence holder it is sensible to have the paperwork lodged for the remaining certificates of suitability at an early stage in the final parts of the process.

In respect of the section 50 certificate from building standards, before it is issued and therefore before the confirmation can be lodged there will have to be a certificate of completion or temporary occupation in place, in relation to the building warrant. The section 50 certificate follows on from the completion certificate. It is not unheard of for there to be confusion between these two certificates and it is up to the provisional licence holder or his agent to make sure all of this is ticking along. Separately, one must not forget the issue of the food hygiene certificate and this might also require a different approach depending on the local authority and the individual officer. In many cases the officer will want to have personally visited the premises to make sure the requisite number of sinks are in place, or that the ventilation in the kitchen is satisfactory, and so on.[52]

The distinction between acceptance of a completion certificate (or temporary occupation permission) and the release of the section 50 certificate can and does create a waiting period between the "practical completion" of the building, and the granting of the confirmation of the licence; meaning the premises has been completed and is ready to trade but cannot sell alcohol until the confirmation has been granted. It is not always the same building standards officer dealing with these two separate processes, which can add to administrative delay. To add to this, in some licensing board areas a further special licensing site visit is required, causing further time and delay between completion of the works, and the formal confirmation of the licence. In such circumstances, it is common practice to utilise occasional licences to bridge any gap between completion and sign-off of the works, and the formal grant of the confirmation.

That being necessary, the provisional licence holder needs to be mindful of a couple of matters: (1) notwithstanding my comments above that a provisional premises licence is nevertheless a premises licence, some licensing boards take the view that the holder of a provisional licence cannot apply for occasional licences, and in those jurisdictions the occasional licence applications would need to be made by either a full premises licence holder (which may be the same person as the provisional licence holder if they also hold other "full" licences), or a personal licence holder; and (2) the timing of the occasional licences needs to be thought of well in advance. In some areas licensing boards will require as much as 6 weeks' notice of an application.

The board must confirm the provisional premises licence if it is satisfied that since the provisional premises licence was issued there have been no variations, or, if there have been variations, that these have been approved by way of application to the board. These are, of course, variations to either the layout plan or operating plan. It is possible therefore that a provisional licence might be subject to a major variation, and that this variation has not yet been approved prior to the proposed confirmation of the licence. Such matters need to be very carefully considered and properly timed. It is possible that a variation which includes a layout change as well as a change to the operating plan could be separated in order to ensure the confirmation can proceed: for example, if an increase in capacity is sought as a result of a layout change, then in order to allow confirmation the provisional licence holder could lodge a minor variation to deal with the layout change, with a separate major variation application dealing with the increase to capacity. This approach would allow the provisional licence to be confirmed based on the corrected layout, albeit with the original occupancy capacity, and the licence holder would have to

52 Food hygiene officers will also use such visits to remind operators to comply with the Food Premises (Registration) Regulations 1991 (SI 1991/2825) and complete registration details, where this has not been dealt with previously. Operators should be mindful that the registration should be completed at least 28 days prior to the proposed opening of the premises.

observe such capacity until his major variation can be approved to deliver the increase.[53]

3.5 Fees for provisional premises licence and confirmation

The fee for a provisional premises licence will ultimately be the same as a full premises licence dependent on rateable value, but the initial fee, that is the fee payable when lodging the provisional premises licence application, is the fee under category 1, namely £200 (or sometimes a bit less, depending on the licensing board). The remainder of the fee is paid at the time the holder of the provisional premises licence lodges the confirmation application.[54] If the rateable value is not known, then the confirmation can be lodged without a fee being paid, however the fee must then be paid at the point that the rateable value has been set.

3.6 Provisional licences and other applications

One of the more interesting dynamics of the 2005 Act is the comparison between the legal status of a "full" premises licence, and a provisional licence. Can a provisional licence be subject to the same processes that a full licence can, such as transfers or variation? This is a matter which has attracted some debate amongst licensing practitioners. The origin appears to be the definition in section 17 that a premises licence is "a licence issued by a Licensing Board under section 26(1) or 47(2) authorising the sale of alcohol on the premises". The reference to "authorising the sale of alcohol" appears to some to exclude the provisional licence on the basis that alcohol may not be sold from a provisional licence until it has been confirmed.

That approach perhaps overlooks the earlier reference in the same sentence to section 26(1). Both "full" and "provisional" licences are issued under section 26(1) and the "authorising the sale of alcohol" should be read not as an explicit (technical) carving out of provisional licences, but instead should be read for its true purpose, which is that the wording is merely a definition as to the central purpose of the premises licence in the first place.

Whilst I accept the issue could be clearer in the statute (as many things could be under the 2005 Act), the policy intention was actually raised in Parliament at the Local Government and Transport Committee on 22 September 2005 during the Stage 2 debates. David Davidson MSP lodged an amendment[55] to allow provisional licences to be subject to transfer and variation, arguing that the Act did not allow for this. In response to this, George Lyon said:

> "[The Amendment] is unnecessary. A provisional premises licence is a type of premises licence. Accordingly, references in sections 27 to 33 to a premises licence already cover a provisional premises licence. That means that a provisional premises licence may be varied or transferred if required."

53 It should be noted, however, that this "hiving off" of the layout changes in order to seek approval under the minor variation procedure might not work in every licensing board area.

54 Licensing (Fees) (Scotland) Regulations 2007 (SSI 2007/553), reg 10.

55 Amendment 167.

This intent is displayed in legislative form under section 46(5) where there is direct reference to the ability to seek a minor or major variation in respect of a provisional licence prior to the licence being confirmed (as I discuss above). Whilst there is no specific reference to provisional licences in the transfer provisions under section 33 and section 34, it is to be accepted that a provisional licence is a type of premises licence; the holder of such a licence is therefore a "premises licence holder", so the provisions of section 33 are open to that holder. Similarly, the variation provisions under section 27 can also be activated by a "premises licence holder". The matter is put beyond doubt with an examination of section 45(5), which makes clear that a provisional licence is a type of premises licence, thus putting into statute the intent George Lyon MSP referred to.

3.7 Provisional licences and "double licensing"

A separate, more tantalising question is whether a single premises can be subject to more than one provisional licence, or whether premises which hold a full licence may also be subject to a provisional licence application. It seems to be generally accepted that one cannot hold two "full" premises licences for the same premises, although there is no explicit rule stated in the Act to that effect.[56]

However, it is accepted in practice that premises which hold a full premises licence may be subject to an *application* for a provisional licence. A typical example of where this would occur is when premises are to be separated internally, perhaps because one part is being sold off. I was instructed in a case where premises with a single licence were set over two floors: a basement and ground level. New owners of the property decided to split the premises, aiming to operate the ground floor bar, and lease out the basement to a tenant seeking to run a separate nightclub offer. The correct approach to achieve this, in my view, is to seek a provisional licence for one half of the premises, say the basement, with an application to vary the existing licence to shrink it back to cover the ground floor.

The timing of all of this is crucial of course. A minor variation to reduce the licensed area and capacity should not be lodged until it is known what the outcome of the provisional application will be, or, at least, be lodged with the clerk but with instructions to treat it as undelivered and not to be granted until the provisional licence is also granted. The provisional licence may therefore be granted on the basis of an undertaking at the licensing board hearing that the minor variation can also be granted administratively, thus resulting in two licences where before there was only one.[57] In addition, section 139(1) of the 1976 Act defined a "new licence" as:

> "a licence granted in respect of premises for which, at the time of the application for such grant, either no licence was in force or a licence in a form different from the form of licence so granted was in force".

56 This is in contrast to the Gambling Act 2005 – see Chapter 21 at Section 3 and related footnote 8.

57 Under the 1976 Act, it was competent to have a provisional licence in place "beneath" an existing and active licence. However, it must be remembered that the 1976 Act world had distinct categories of licence, meaning that someone who wished to move from the "Refreshment" licence to the "Public House" licence would always have to lodge a new licence; whereas in the 2005 Act world, changes in operational matters would always be achieved by way of a variation application.

Thus, opening the door for an alternative licence in "different form". That different form was held to include the general layout of the premises, in *Docherty v Leitch*,[58] noting that the 1976 Act had provision for "alterations" to a layout only to a certain point, and if the alterations were significant a new licence would have to be sought.

In practice as well as theoretically, then, it is possible for premises to have more than one licence, where one of those licences is a provisional licence, and where it is intended that the other licence is to be surrendered or varied in some way prior to the confirmation of the provisional licence. It is doubtful that a board would be prepared to entertain two provisional licences (or full licences for that matter) applying to the same set of premises.[59]

3.8 Provisional licences and overprovision

There are some mixed views in the licensing community on whether provisional licences should be captured as part of an overprovision assessment. Where a board has listed provisional licences in an overprovision assessment it may be open to an applicant to ask the board to carve out any provisional licences on a "merits" basis that (a) the premises are not trading, and (b) capacities are only theoretical until such times as the licence is confirmed, but this is fortified with the reference to the definition of "licensed premises" meaning premises where a premises licence *has effect*; and a provisional licence does not have effect until confirmed. A contrary view is that a provisional licence is also a premises licence, so it might be suggested that provisional licences should be part of any overprovision assessment in terms of policy, and should also form part of any analysis to a refusal of a licence on the grounds of overprovision. A provisional premises licence will have a stated occupancy capacity and/or alcohol display capacity, so even though the licence is not yet activated, these numbers can be taken and used as a part of the analysis. On the basis that the language in section 7, which sets the stall for overprovision assessments, is "licensed premises", and not "premises licences", this may suggest that the correct view would be to carve out provisional licences from any assessment.

58 1998 SLT 374.

59 This can be contrasted to the position under the Licensing Act 2003 in England and Wales, where so-called "shadow licences" (or "mirror licences") can be sought and granted. These are typically sought by landlords as a sort of safety net or fall-back position where the tenant holds the licence, so that the landlord has comfort that, should the tenant lose the licence for some reason, they can rely on the shadow licence to move on with the premises under their own stewardship or with a new tenant. The 2003 Act makes no specific provision for this form of double licensing, but the practice was homologated in the case of *Extreme Oyster and Star Oyster Ltd v Guildford Borough Council* [2013] EWHC 2174 (Admin). It would be interesting to see what the Scottish courts might make of a "shadow" licence, given that the Act does not explicitly prohibit more than one licence for one premises, nor does the Guidance to Licensing Boards – both of which were key points in the case above.

4 SPECIAL CASES: TEMPORARY PREMISES LICENCES

The temporary premises licence is provided for under section 47 of the Act, and is a licence issued to the holder of a premises licence in respect of premises other than those to which the "principal" premises licence applies. Nicholson made no reference to temporary licences. Temporary licences are not referred to in the Guidance to Licensing Boards. The Explanatory Notes to the 2005 Act do offer a modest drop of insight:

> "This section caters for the circumstances where premises which already have a premises licence are undergoing reconstruction or conversion work. The licence holder may want to move into temporary premises pending completion of the work. This section allows the licence holder to apply to the Licensing Board for a premises licence covering the temporary premises. Such a licence is referred to as a 'temporary premises licence'."

The purpose of the temporary licence is therefore to allow a trader to use temporary premises to continue his business whilst his main premises are undergoing, or are to undergo, reconstruction or conversion. The fee for a temporary licence application is set by the board.[60]

The licensing board may only grant a temporary premises licence if satisfied that the temporary premises are:[61]

- suitable for the sale of alcohol; and
- that it is necessary to grant the application to enable the licence holder to carry on his business whilst the principal premises are being reconstructed or converted.

If a temporary licence is granted under these circumstances, it will automatically have the same conditions that are attached to the principal premises licence, unless the board sees fit to except them or vary them as required,[62] thus allowing the board a considerable degree of flexibility.

A temporary licence has a maximum life span of two years, although the Act allows for the holder of the temporary licence to apply to extend this period by up to a further twelve months. The Act is not especially clear on whether this additional twelve months can continue on a rolling basis with subsequent renewal requests and I would take the view that this provision could be read widely.[63] If the "principal" premises have not yet been reconstructed then a board could allow further extensions; or, alternatively, the applicant could seek a fresh temporary licence application.

The temporary licence process does not mirror the premises licence process. There is no statutory requirement for section 50 certificates, nor is there any statutory application form. There is also no process in place to deal with consultation and objections or representations. All of this, therefore, is left to the board and the applicant to reach a view on. I have dealt with two such applications, both of which arose following the destruction of the principle premises following a fire. In the absence of all of the procedure as noted above, it seems to me to be sensible to procure reports from officials,

60 Licensing (Fees) (Scotland) Regulations 2007 (SSI 2007/553), reg 11(3)(e).
61 2005 Act, s 47(3).
62 2005 Act, s 47(5)(b).
63 2005 Act, s 47(6).

if not full section 50 certificates, to give the board assurance that the temporary premises are safe for the public to use, that is "suitable for the sale of alcohol", and a premises licence and operating plan application form which mirror the detail of the premises licence. The board might deem it prudent to have the application considered at a hearing of the board, given how rare the temporary licence process is.

Where a temporary licence is granted, a copy must be sent to the police.[64]

5 SPECIAL CASES: EXCLUDED PREMISES

A full explanation of the law surrounding excluded premises is provided in Chapter 10 at Section 2.1.

6 SPECIAL CASES: EXEMPT PREMISES

Section 1(1) of the Act says that alcohol is not to be sold on any premises except where a premises (or occasional) licence is in force, with two exceptions: where the premises are "exempt premises", and selling to trade (dealt with below). Exempt premises are defined in section 124 as:

- an examination station at specially designated airports,
- approved wharves at ports and hoverports,
- an aircraft, hovercraft or railway vehicle while engaged on a journey,
- a vessel whilst engaged on an international journey or a journey (other than an international journey) forming part of a ferry service, or
- premises occupied for the purposes of the armed forces of the Crown.

Interestingly, there was some debate prior to the onset of the 2005 Act over the possible inclusion of distilleries within the definition of "exempt premises" in order to safeguard the customary "tastings" which occur on such premises. In a parliamentary question on 18 November 2008, Justice Minister Kenny MacAskill said:

> "[The 2005 Act] does not exempt distillery visitor centre and whisky shops . . . but we are clear that we do not propose to ban promotions that explain the method of production, history and heritage of Scotland's quality products. We have already given the Scotch Whisky Association an assurance that we will discuss these matters with them before proposing any regulatory action to end the irresponsible promotion of alcohol. I also gave an assurance, when I met the Scotch Whisky Association and toured Dewar's World of Whisky on 21 July 2008, that our proposals will not prevent drams being provided as part of distillery tours."

Distillery visitor centres are not, in the result, exempt premises. As to the suggestion that "tastings" would have some special status within the licensing system, this was a false flag. There is no specific provision for tastings in this sense. In some areas, having "tastings" as part of an off-sale licence premises like a shop in a distillery may require the applicant to seek full on-sales and in turn having to agree occupancy and sanitary capacities. The 2005 Act

64 2005 Act, s 47(4A).

treatment of "tastings" is discussed in detail in Chapter 5 at Section 3.1. In addition, tastings which are part of a paid-for tour or ticket price are, of course, a licensable supply of alcohol (see Chapter 2 at Section 3).

6.1 Exempt premises: airports

The first class of exempt premises are "examination stations" at designated airports. An examination station is defined in the Customs and Excise Management Act 1979 as the area for the loading and unloading of goods, and the embarkation and disembarkation of passengers – in other words, the areas of the airport after security controls to which only travellers and staff have access. The distinction is commonly referred to as "landside" and "airside".

The effect of this is that any bar, pub, restaurant or other premises selling alcohol, located after the security checkpoints and to which only passengers have access, that is, "airside" premises, does not require a licence. The 2005 Act's treatment of airports is novel in comparison to the old 1976 Act regime. Under the 1976 Act, a licence was required for such facilities; however, the "permitted hours" did not apply,[65] meaning that the premises could function 24 hours a day, 7 days a week. This provision was, no doubt, used to allow for the fact that passengers were arriving and departing from various time zones. The 2005 Act, rather than using an exemption on the hours of trade, simply provides that no licence is required at all.

The airports to which these provisions apply are laid down in the Licensing (Designated Airports) (Scotland) Order 2007[66] and are: Aberdeen, Edinburgh, Glasgow, Glasgow Prestwick, Inverness and Sumburgh.[67] It appears that, notwithstanding Nicholson referred to these provisions applying to "international airports",[68] and the fact that the Act restricted the anticipated Order to including an airport "only if it appears to [Scottish Ministers] to be one at which there is a substantial amount of international passenger traffic",[69] the exemption applies regardless of whether the premises offering alcohol are used by domestic or international departures travellers, given the absence of any distinction being made in the statute and regulations.

6.2 Exempt premises: approved wharves at ports or hoverports

The next class of exempt premises is "an approved wharf at a port or hoverport so designated".[70] The definition of "approved wharf" is taken from

65 1976 Act, s 63.

66 SSI 2007/97.

67 In 2016, the separation of airside premises in England and Wales came under formal post-legislative scrutiny following concern about behaviours in such unlicensed premises attracting adverse media attention. This resulted in a Call to Evidence which was released on 1 November 2018 with a clear proposal to bring airside premises back within the ambit of the 2003 Act. This has yet to be taken forward. There have also been calls north of the border to consider removing the exemption, from airlines who have been subject to malign press over customer behaviour mid-flight, as well as other third parties. See, for example, "Airport alcohol ban call after Scottish arrest figure released", *The Scotsman*, 20 September 2017. There has been no clear position stated on this from the Scottish Government.

68 Nicholson Report, para 14.32, p 154.

69 2005 Act, s 124(2).

70 2005 Act, s 124(1)(b).

section 20A of the Customs and Excise Management Act 1979 which in turn borrows from section 20 of that Act. The definition amounts to wharves which have been approved by Excise Commissioners, or a place specified or approved under certain EEC regulations[71] other than an examination station. This exemption is on all fours with the airport class of exemption, in that there is a distinction between areas of the premises which are restricted except to travellers. The Guidance to Licensing Boards states that the exemption of "wharfside" premises is designed to cover:

> "areas to which the non-travelling public do not have access and are subject to stringent by-laws. The exemption is to enable the provision of refreshment of travellers at any time."

Unlike the equivalent provisions for airports, there is no Order specifying certain wharves to which the exemption applies so it is to be assumed all Scottish wharves which meet the customs definition as noted above are exempt from the 2005 Act.[72]

6.3 Exempt premises: aircraft, hovercraft or railway vehicles

Section 124(1)(c) says that "an aircraft, a hovercraft or a railway vehicle[73] while engaged on a journey" is exempt from the licence requirement. The reference to "while engaged on a journey" carves out the scenario where one of those forms of transport, which is stationary, decommissioned and no longer in use, might conceivably be licensed such as where it has become a form of tourist attraction. The Act goes so far as to prescribe what is meant by "engaged on a journey" as follows:

> "(a) any period ending with its departure when preparations are being made for the journey, and
> (b) any period after its arrival at its destination when it continues to be occupied by those (or any of those) who made the journey (or any part of it)."

So, alcohol may be served prior to departure, and after arrival whilst those who made the journey are still on board. The Policy Memorandum to the Bill said:

> "A train would not require a licence every time it stops at a station when it is engaged in a journey even if this was a lengthy delay due to adverse conditions."[74]

The serving of alcohol on such modes of travel, whilst being exempt from the 2005 Act, is often subject to the travel operator's own policy on alcohol provision. In many cases, alcohol will not be served until the journey is properly commenced, and may only be served during certain times of the day.

71 Article 46 of Council Regulation (EEC) No. 2913/92.

72 According to www.marine.gov.scot there are a number of wharves across Scotland which from north to south include: Sullom Voe (Shetland), Orkney, Cromarty Firth, Peterhead, Aberdeen, Glensanda, Dundee, Forth, Clyde, Loch Ryan, and Cairnryan.

73 "Railway vehicle" is defined at section 147(1) of the Act as follows: "'railway vehicle' means a railway vehicle within the meaning of section 83 of the Railways Act 1993 (c. 43) that is used in the provision of a railway service within the meaning of section 82 of that Act (excluding the wider meaning of 'railway' given by section 81(2) of that Act)".

74 Policy Memorandum to the Licensing (Scotland) Bill, 22 February 2005, para 72, p 17.

6.4 Exempt premises: vessels and ferry services

The 1976 Act made particular provision to have alcohol restricted on vessels and ferries on certain times on a Sunday.[75] Nicholson said of this:

> "In our opinion any social or religious rationale which may at one time have underpinned this provision is now unlikely to attract much, if any, support."[76]

The Scottish Parliament went one step further, exempting any need for a licence at all. The 2005 Act exempts vessels and ferry services under one of the following categories:

(a) an international journey, or
(b) a journey (other than an international journey) forming part of a ferry service.

The comments above at Section 6.3 concerning the definition of being "engaged on a journey" apply equally to ferry services. The use of a vessel which is not engaged in a ferry service or an international journey is therefore not exempt; and where alcohol is to be sold on such a vessel, perhaps used as part of a leisure cruise service on one of Scotland's fine lochs, the vessel would require a premises licence (see below). "Vessel" is defined at section 147(1) of the Act as follows:

> "'vessel' includes a ship, boat, raft or other apparatus constructed or adapted for floating on water".

6.5 Exempt premises: armed forces

The full definition of what constitutes this type of exempt premises is:

> "premises which are occupied (whether indefinitely or temporarily) for the purposes of the armed forces of the Crown, except while being used for other purposes".

Section 124(1)(e) might be seen as the 2005 Act continuation of the provisions of section 138 of the 1976 Act, which exempted the sale of alcohol from the unlicensed offence of "trafficking" under that Act from "service canteens" under the "authority of the Secretary of State"; which meant no licence was required, and also that sale could occur at any time from one of these canteens, or "authorised mess".[77] This, historically, was a provision designed to reflect the fact that such premises were located on defence territory and therefore outwith the normal scope of civil regulation, subject to military byelaws and under military police jurisdiction, and in respect of hours, to reflect the comings and goings at unusual hours of armed forces personnel.

Examples of locations where armed forces are in occupation include armed forces bases such as at Kinloss or Lossiemouth, and other areas referred to as the "Defence Training Estate". My understanding is that the day-to-day

75 1976 Act, s 93.

76 Nicholson Report, para 14.40, p 156.

77 I have sometimes heard shop or bar facilities on armed forces premises being called "NAAFI" premises. This refers to "Navy, Army and Airforce Institutes" which for many years was the collective that organised canteens and other amenities. NAAFI now only operates furth of UK shores.

provision of alcohol and bar premises is now controlled through Ministry of Defence standing orders, which are localised to each location throughout the United Kingdom. Comparison can be made to locations where there are facilities and residential accommodation for the families of armed forces personnel, as in my experience these can be located near to, but outwith, armed forces premises, or "on the other side of the wire". Whilst such facilities might be predominantly used by the family of armed forces personnel, and such personnel themselves, they may not be exempt premises for the purposes of the Act and I have certainly represented licence holders who fall into this scenario.

6.6 Exempt premises and offences

Part 8 of the Act deals with offences and these are looked at in more detail in Chapter 19 but it should be noted that section 122 of the Act operates to include exempt premises in the scope of offences by defining "relevant premises" in connection with some offences as any licensed premises, exempt premises, and any premises for the selling of alcohol to trade. Thus, whilst certain premises may operate with no licence, licensing offences may still occur there.

7 SPECIAL CASES: VEHICLES AND VESSELS

"Premises" is defined in section 147(1) as "any place and includes a vehicle, vessel or moveable structure", and section 1(1) requires a premises licence in order for alcohol to be sold from "premises". Sections 126, 127 and 128 make specific provisions under the Act for vehicles, vessels, and moveable structures as "premises" in this regard. The 2005 Act distinguishes these situations in two main ways: first, it provides for multiple licences for one vehicle, vessel or moveable structure; and, secondly, it disapplies a number of key requirements for typical premises. It is to be hoped that these provisions are somewhat more transparent than the equivalent 1976 Act measures, which Nicholson described as "almost incapable of sensible comprehension".[78]

There is further provision in relation to vessels under the Licensing (Vessels etc) (Scotland) Regulations 2007.[79] Regulation 4, for example, allows a single individual to be the named premises manager for more than one set of premises if each of those premises is a vessel that is not permanently moored or berthed, and regulation 2 actually removes vessels from the licence requirement altogether if (a) the vessel is not moored or berthed in any place; and (b) there are no more than fifty persons on board the vessel.

Note that there are specific provisions and offences in relation to the control of alcohol sales in relation to trains and ferries. These are discussed in Chapter 19 at Sections 11.6 and 11.7.

7.1 Vehicles and vessels: the multiple licence requirement

Section 126(1) and (2) make provision for premises that are not always in the same place. In the case of ships or vessels that are not permanently moored

78 Nicholson Report, para 14.54, p 160.
79 SSI 2007/545.

or berthed, they are to be treated as "premises" in the place where they are usually moored or berthed. Vehicles and moveable structures which are not permanently located in one spot are to be treated as "premises" in the place where they are situated, and each other such place at which they are, or are to be, used. The effect of this is that multiple premises licences may be required for a single vehicle, vessel or moveable structure, depending on the locations of the spots where they are situated – this could mean premises licences for the same vehicle, vessel or moveable structure from different licensing boards depending on the geographical location of each spot used to situate it. The Policy Memorandum to the Bill explained it thus:

> "A vehicle or moveable structure – e.g. tent or inflatable building – which is not permanently located in the same place, would be treated as a premises located at any place where it is parked or set. So if licensable activities are carried out on or from the vehicle when it is parked, a premises licence would be required, and where such activities take place when it is parked in more than one place, the vehicle or moveable structure would be treated as if it were separate premises at each location and, therefore, separate premises licences would be required."[80]

7.2 Vehicles and vessels: provisions which do not apply

In relation to an application for a premises licence for a vessel, the provisions which require the production of certificates of suitability and the notification to neighbours and the fire authority do not apply.[81]

In relation to an application for a premises licence for a vehicle or other moveable structure, a number of exemptions and variations from the provisions of the Act are in place. These are:

- "Appropriate licensing board" means either the licensing board in whose area the premises are used or, where the premises are used in more than one area, the board in whose area the premises are used to the greater or greatest extent; and, if this does not apply, such other board nominated as appropriate.
- The requirements to produce certificates of suitability do not apply.
- The requirements to notify neighbours, the fire authority and community councils do not apply.
- Notification of the application must be made to the "relevant council".[82]
- "Locality" in the context of moving vehicles and vessels is taken to mean simply the whole area of the appropriate licensing board.

8 TRADE SALES/SELLING TO TRADE

Section 1(1) of the 2005 Act says that alcohol may not be sold on any premises unless a premises or occasional licence is in force. However, section 1(2)(b) says that this does not apply in relation to "the selling of alcohol to trade". Section 147(2) defines selling to trade as "selling the alcohol or goods to a

80 Policy Memorandum to the Licensing (Scotland) Bill, 22 February 2005, para 72, p 17.

81 *Viz*, s 50, s 20(2)(b)(iii), s 45(10)(a) and s 46(2)(d) in relation to certificates of suitability; and s 21(1)(a), (e) and s 29(4) in relation to notification.

82 As opposed to the council in whose area the premises are situated.

person for the purposes of the person's trade". The Policy Memorandum to the Bill said:

> "Wholesalers would be exempt from the licensing system for trade only sales but would be included in the system for all sales by retail. This means that where a wholesaler sells to the public the wholesaler must obtain a premises licence. It would be an offence for a wholesaler to sell alcohol from any premises other than that which is used wholly for the purposes of wholesales."[83]

Here the rule is simply that no licence is required when selling alcohol to a person who is buying the alcohol for the purposes of his trade. The "sale" of the alcohol to a trader is not a "sale" for the purposes of licensing law. Note that there is no rule in relation to the quantity or type of alcohol being sold. This is in contrast to the 1976 Act provisions, which relied on the definition of "wholesale" in the Alcoholic Liquor Duties Act 1979 as:

> "the sale at any one time to any person of quantities not less than the following, viz (a) in the case of spirits, wine or made-wine two gallons or one case; or (b) in the case of beer, four and a half gallons or two cases".[84]

If the business plan of wholesale premises therefore includes making sales to the general public (even if only occasionally), then a premises licence will be required.

The Act also recognises that there may be two types of wholesaler, namely one who sells alcohol from premises which are licensed premises,[85] and one who sells alcohol from premises which are used exclusively for the purpose of the selling of goods, whether solely alcohol or not. Under section 117 it is an offence to sell alcohol to trade otherwise than from premises which are exclusively used for the purpose of the selling of goods (whether solely alcohol or not). A wholesaler may act strictly as a wholesaler, or may operate a dual system of selling to trade as well as to public. That may be the general public, or it could be sales to staff, who are also "the public" as far as licensing law is concerned, as they are not buying the alcohol for the purposes of their trade but for their own personal consumption or other reason (e.g. as a gift).

It should be noted that section 122 of the Act provides that, for the purposes of certain offences under the Act, premises used for the selling of alcohol to trade are classed as "relevant premises", meaning that unlicensed wholesalers may still be subject to certain licensing offences under the Act. So, for

83 Policy Memorandum to the Licensing (Scotland) Bill, 22 February 2005, para 72, p 17.

84 Section 138(2) of the 1976 Act states: "save as expressly provided for in this Act, nothing shall prohibit the sale of alcoholic liquor by a wholesaler". Those provisions are found in s 90A (added by the Law Reform (Miscellaneous Provisions) (Scotland) Act 1990, s 52), which states that the wholesaler must sell from premises used exclusively for wholesale trading, but with the restriction on the quantity, not to whom the alcohol is sold (see also *Wood v Mackenzie* 1925 JC 13).

85 This distinction is important because it captures the activity of a normal retailer such as a supermarket from which a trader might buy goods for his trade, as well as "specialist" wholesale premises which might also sell to the public. This clarity was lacking in the Act as passed, and so the reference to "licensed premises" was inserted into s 117 via the Criminal Justice and Licensing (Scotland) Act 2010 and commenced as of 13 December 2010 by virtue of the Criminal Justice and Licensing (Scotland) Act 2010 (Commencement No. 6, Transitional and Savings Provisions) Order 2010 (SSI 2010/413). On the background to this amendment, see "Trade sales problem to be corrected" [2009] 41 SLLP 6.

example, the requirement under section 110 to display a notice applies to unlicensed wholesalers as well as licensed premises.

8.1 Licensed wholesalers and trade sales

Following the introduction of minimum pricing, a significant issue arose around the application of the condition to wholesalers whose premises were also subject to a premises licence. A divergence arose in the licensing community as to whether trade sales would have to comply with the minimum price requirement where a licence was in place.

It is clear that business premises which only sell to trade and which are not also licensed premises have no concerns in this regard, as with no licence in place there are no licence conditions or requirements to worry about. It is also clear that the intention of the legislation was to reflect the everyday scenario whereupon licensed businesses need to buy stock without the general regulation of the 2005 Act applying to that transaction, primarily because the entire policy of the Act is public facing and does not concern itself with a business-to-business sale. The trader is not purchasing the alcohol for their own consumption but to re-sell it, at a profit no doubt, to the public.

Where business premises that deal in sales to trade also have a premises licence, the question then is whether the conditions which attach to that licence affect *all* alcohol sales that occur on the premises – that is, both the sales to trade, and the sales to the public. The idea that the minimum price did not apply to trade sales from a licensed premises created considerable difficulty for some licensing practitioners who took the alternative view; and indeed the extension of the idea that any of the licence conditions which related to the sale of alcohol ought not to apply to trade sales was a wider issue which had not necessarily been promulgated across the licensing community prior to the minimum price bringing it to the fore.

The sudden spectre of conditions relating to irresponsible promotions and other matters being inert on licensed wholesale premises resulted in concern from some public commentators, suggesting that such operators would purposefully evade responsible operating practices, undermining the system. It was argued that this would leave the wholesaler open to chicanery and some suggested a "dual pricing" system would also lead to enforcement difficulties in ensuring that the minimum price was being applied correctly.

It is to be made clear that there is a notable divergence of opinions on this wider matter, and there are those in the licensing community who hold strongly to the view that all premises are subject to the mandatory conditions in relation to all sales, whether "to trade" or otherwise. For my own part, I have no difficulty with the proposition that the *relevant* mandatory premises licence conditions do not apply to sales to trade.[86] I contend that sales to trade are not a licensable sale of alcohol under the 2005 Act, as it made clear by the relationship between the definition of "selling to trade" at section 147 and the exemption under section 1(2)(b). Sales to trade are, in essence,

86 The alternative view might be summarised as saying that if you have a licence, then MUP applies as it is a condition of that licence, and that if Parliament had wished it, it could have removed MUP from trade sales at the time; and, of course, the subsequent regulations noted below did have that effect.

outside the scope of the Act whether from licensed premises or from unlicensed premises.

This is why the licensed hours do not apply to sales to trade, as is made clear at section 63(2)(f)(i). This is also why the rules and offences in relation to the delivery of alcohol from vehicles are disapplied where the alcohol is being delivered to a trader for the purposes of that person's trade, as is specified under section 119(7). A sale to trade is not a sale made "under and in accordance with" the premises licence as a normal public sale must be. Properly understood, one must carve out the notion of trade sales having any link to the premises licence framework even where the sale occurs from premises which happen to be subject to a licence.

In relation to minimum pricing, this means it is perfectly acceptable for a licensed wholesaler to have two prices for the same product: (i) a trade price for sale to a trader, and (ii) the public price. The trade price can be whatever the licensed wholesaler wants it to be. The public price must not be below the minimum price. There are a number of business models beyond that of the traditional wholesale warehouse style operator for whom all of this is also relevant. Take, for example, brewery premises which produce their own product on site. The brewery despatches kegs of fine ales to various pubs. The brewery also has a shop which the public can access, and they also have an online offering, so the premises is used as a despatch point for remote public sales. The brewery has a premises licence which covers the entire premises to authorise the sale of beer to the public online, despatched from the goods entrance, and face-to-face in the shop. The kegs of beer which are sold to the trade are effectively invisible as far as the licence is concerned. The brewery can sell its beer to the trade below the minimum price, it can sell two kegs for the price of one: in short, it can do what it wants because the beer sold to the trade *is not sold under the licence.*

We can explore this in relation to the language used in the mandatory conditions other than minimum pricing. The condition relating to irresponsible promotions, for example, does not apply to trade sales because "drinks promotion" is defined as an activity which promotes the buying of alcohol, and a trade sale is not a sale. The condition relating to staff training requires staff to undertake the training where they work in a capacity which "involves the person making sales of alcohol"; but sale to trade is not a sale of alcohol; and so on. However, whilst this sort of targeted analysis might be helpful in making the point, it comes down to the fact that trade sales are essentially invisible to the licensing framework, even where such sales occur on licensed premises.

To be clear, however, a licensed wholesaler must observe the mandatory licence conditions in relation to public sales. It is therefore a matter for the wholesaler who does allow public sales as well as trade sales to ensure that the conditions are met when there is a public sale. I do concur that, operationally, this could make life complicated for some licensed wholesalers, but while representing a number of such businesses I have observed the sophistication of their diligence and practices, and it is a matter for them to ensure that they have processes in place to ensure that trade sales are genuine.

The Scottish Government proposed that, notwithstanding their stated view that minimum pricing did not apply to trade sales, the matter should be clarified and put beyond doubt for trade and consumer clarity. A proposed amendment under the Alcohol (Minimum Price per Unit) (Scotland) Amendment

Order 2020[87] was consulted on and introduced a new provision to the previous Alcohol (Minimum Price per Unit) (Scotland) Order 2018,[88] stating "The minimum price per unit specified in article 2 does not apply for the purpose of sales to trade." This was commenced on 3 April 2020.

9 REMOTE SALES

The 2005 Act makes provision for "remote sales", or

> "where, in connection with any sale of alcohol, the premises from which the alcohol is despatched for delivery in pursuance of the sale is not the same as those where the order for the alcohol is taken".[89]

The rule is very simple: if the despatching premises are located in Scotland, then the sale is treated as having taken place on those premises, thereby activating the premises licence requirement under section 1(1). Contrarily, yet obviously, if the despatching premises are outside Scotland, then the 2005 Act does not apply.

Types of businesses which offer remote sales are varied. In many cases the licensed premises might simply be a warehouse full of refreshing beers, and orders which are placed on a brewery website are filled and despatched from the warehouse, possibly in vans or by mail. It may also be that the remote sale is part of a premises licence which also features on sales or where the principal sales are on sales. Specialist Italian restaurant premises might also have an off-sale facility allowing a related business to offer *aperitifs* or *digestifs* to be ordered and delivered separately. The premises might be a high street retailer with a home delivery option online so that when ordering your weekly shop you might also order some wine. The premises might be a pub or bar which is capitalising on the home delivery services offered by Deliveroo, Uber Eats or the like, and customers can call in to order pizza and beer.[90] The premises might be a small unit on an industrial estate where wine is stored and uplifted for delivery as part of a wine club. The example given in the Explanatory Notes to the Licensing Bill, which was then replicated in the Notes to the Act, was:

> ". . . when alcohol is bought via mail order or a telephone call centre and sent out for delivery from a separate warehouse, the sale would, for the purposes of this Bill, be treated as having taken place at the warehouse and not the call centre. The requirement for a premises licence would, therefore, apply to the warehouse rather than the call centre."[91]

Under the heading of "Internet and mail order sales", the Guidance to the Licensing Boards has this wisdom to offer:

87 SSI 2020/81.
88 SSI 2018/135. This order set the minimum price at 50p per unit.
89 2005 Act, s 139(1).
90 The addition of home deliveries of food or drink is thought by some licensing boards to be required on the basis that it should be noted as an additional activity in Q5(f) of the operating plan. This appears largely to ensure that the board is satisfied that appropriate checks are in place in relation to age verification and so on. The inclusion of home delivery of food and drink within an operating plan is also referred to in Chapter 8 at Section 3.8 and footnote 41.
91 Explanatory Notes to the Licensing (Scotland) Bill, 22 February 2005, para 257, p 34.

"A premises licence will not be required for a location, e.g. a call centre at which an order is taken or placed. A premises licence would however be required for the premises from which alcohol is specifically selected for and despatched to the purchaser, e.g. a warehouse."[92]

Taking all of these examples, what is clear is that remote sales are a form of off-sales. Alcohol is ordered remotely and delivered from one premises to another premises and the consumption is off the premises from which it was despatched. Nicholson, when giving evidence during the progress of the Licensing (Scotland) Bill, offered a further example of alcohol delivery which was not caught by the provisions dealing with "despatch":

"One of the problems is that some people who operate as alcohol salesmen – wine reps, in particular – might not have premises at all. They might import directly from France, Germany, Spain or Italy, and any premises that they have might be no more than transitory storage premises from which the boxes are put on the back of a lorry and driven to Edinburgh, Glasgow, Aberdeen or wherever. Such businesses might be difficult to regulate within a framework that provides for premises licences, personal licence holders and so on. That is why it is important to include that on-going provision, under which ministers will be able to react as appropriate if it appears that there is an increase in one or other style of business and to make appropriate regulations."[93]

It remains to be seen how many examples of the travelling wine salesman have been examined since 2009 but it is of course possible to license a vehicle, as is noted above.

9.1 Remote sales – when does the sale occur?

Readers will be well aware, of course, that the maximum hours for off-sale sales are 10am to 10pm. A key question, then, is whether I can make an order for remote delivery outside these licensed hours. I discuss the definition of a "sale" in Chapter 2 at Section 3, but for ease of reference we should note that section 147 of the Act defines "sale" as including exposing to sale; or offering for sale. A reading of that provision alone would seem to imply that simply offering off-sales after 10pm is treated as a sale and therefore would be illegal. However, section 63(6) says:

"Nothing in this section prevents or restricts—
(a) the ordering of alcohol for consumption off licensed premises, or
(b) the despatch of alcohol so ordered by the person selling it."

The key words for me are "ordering" and "despatch". Section 63(6) allows the order to be placed outside licensed hours. The order should not be paid for until the start of the next period of licensed hours – 10am the next morning, or that morning. The order having been paid for at 10am (by automatic deduction of funds from the purchaser's account), the alcohol can be despatched by the seller at any time from 10am – but not delivered between 12 midnight and 6am.

The time that the order is placed is not the time of the sale, nor is the time of delivery of the goods the time that the sale occurs.[94] The sale crystallises

92 Guidance to Licensing Boards (2007) para 71, p 25.
93 Local Government and Transport Committee, 22 March 2005.
94 In *Valentine v Bell* 1930 SLT 685, the court held that delivery was not a relevant consideration as to whether a sale had taken place.

at the time payment is made. An order can therefore be placed by a person at any time, be received by another at any time, but only paid for during the licensed hours.

I am aware that retailers take different approaches on this. Some retailers will simply prevent any alcohol being ordered outside 10am to 10pm and if you happen to have a bottle of Loch Lomond Brewery Silkie Stout in your online basket when you place the order at 10.10pm the website will block the order and tell you to remove the alcoholic product. Other retailers will allow the order to be placed at any time, but if made after 10pm the order will not be processed until 10am the following morning at the earliest, which is when funds would be lifted from your bank account.

9.2 Remote sales: "click and collect" services

Click and collect is a popular form of consumer transaction whereupon the purchaser of goods which have been ordered online can choose to collect the item in local premises, as opposed to delivery of the item. The first question is whether "click and collect" is an activity which needs to be specified on a premises licence. In my view this is a sensible approach and there is no doubt that licensing boards have paid much more attention to this type of facility following the onset of the Coronavirus pandemic. Licensing boards now reflect this type of activity in policy and ask for licence applicants to include reference to this as well as wording in relation to home deliveries. This is necessary not simply to reflect the collection of alcoholic goods, but of general retail and food items and in some cases a premises may offer collection facilities which they are providing for third parties, such as Amazon collection points.

Where a customer is ordering alcohol and this is to be uplifted from certain premises, a question arises as to whether the premises where the product is collected require to be licensed. In my view that is not necessary. If the alcohol has been despatched to the collection point, then it is the premises from which it has despatched that require to be licensed. The 2005 Act makes no reference to any "collection" of the goods having to occur in or from licensed premises. If the alcohol has been sold and despatched from licensed premises, then that should be the end of the matter and the fact that it might be collected from a shop is no different to it being delivered by mail at home.[95]

It may be argued that the shop which hands over the alcohol is supplying said alcohol, however the shop worker is no different to the postman; and the position can be repelled noting that the provisions which relate to supply of alcohol pursuant to a contract under section 3 are designed to cover supplies where there has been no direct sale. This is not the case with a "click and collect" sale, and, further, there is no contract between the customer and the dispensary: the contract is between the customer and the seller.

The Scottish Government recognised the legality of "click and collect" services in their Guidance on Minimum Pricing:

95 This also means that the checks such as age verification which would apply to alcohol being delivered at home (see 9.3.2 in this Chapter), also apply to alcohol which is being collected. In other words, the usual rules around "Challenge 25" and not giving alcohol to persons who are drunk, and so on, still apply.

"12. In relation to 'click and collect' facilities, these facilities are acting as a post box/collection point rather than a despatch point. The point of despatch would be where the goods have been despatched from to the 'click and collect' facilities."

9.3 Remote sales and delivery of alcohol

There are two key elements to be aware of in relation to the delivery of alcohol, namely (a) knowing when alcohol can be delivered; and (b) what rules must be observed.

9.3.1 When can alcohol be delivered?

It is illegal to deliver alcohol between 12midnight and 6am. If your weekly supermarket shop contains alcohol, it can legally arrive anytime between 6am and midnight; but if the driver is delayed he will have to wait till 6am the following morning. This provision, under section 120 of the Act, might shortly be referred to as the "dial-a-swally" condition. During the progress of the Licensing (Scotland) Bill, Michael McMahon MSP said:

"I have spoken to senior police officers in Lanarkshire who are concerned that, since the publication of the [Nicholson] report, they have been dealing with a new development that is addressed neither in the report nor in the bill. I am referring to the new way of delivering drink to people's homes, which is commonly known as dial-a-drink or, in Lanarkshire – dial-a-swally."[96]

The Stage 1 Report to the Licensing (Scotland) Bill said:

"The Committee welcomes the proposal in the Bill to prevent alcohol being delivered between midnight and 6am, but is agreed that more may need to be done to ensure that adequate age checks are made by delivery workers. The Committee acknowledges that it may be difficult to find a workable solution to this problem but nevertheless calls on the Executive to consider, following discussions with the police, whether there are workable ways in which the Bill can be amended to ensure that under-age people are not able to use dial-a-drink services."[97]

The "rules for delivery" noted at 9.3.2 below were already a part of the Bill as introduced so they should not be read as answering the above in some way, as was the offence of delivering alcohol to a child or young person. No further provision was made to fortify against delivery to children or young people so it must have been thought, ultimately, that the criminal offence was sufficient. A further shock for those concerned about lack of regulation for deliveries is the wording in relation to the mandatory condition for staff training:[98] the two-hour course required for all staff relates to persons who "work in the premises".[99] It must be conceded that delivery drivers do not work "in" the licensed premises and therefore the staff training provision does not cover them. In addition to that gremlin, the staff training provision also

96 Local Government and Transport Committee, 22 March 2005.

97 Stage 1 Report by the Local Government and Transport Committee, Licensing (Scotland) Bill, para 71, p 14. Sadly, references to "swally" had been replaced by the more supine "drink".

98 The staff training condition is explored in detail in Chapter 15 at Section 4.5

99 2005 Act, Sch 3 para 6(1).

only applies to staff who are involved in "making sales of alcohol" or serving alcohol for consumption on licensed premises.[100] Delivery drivers are not "making sales of alcohol" (see Section 9.1 above as to when the sale occurs), nor serving the alcohol in an on-sales licensed premises.

Notwithstanding all of this, it is of course open to a premises licence holder to deliver the staff training to delivery drivers as a matter of best practice, and many do.

9.3.2 The rules for delivery of alcohol

Section 119 of the Act is headed "Delivery of alcohol from vehicles etc". This section creates a series of offences in relation to matters which must be observed when alcohol is to be delivered from a "vehicle or receptacle".[101] The Explanatory Notes state the purpose of these rules is to ensure: "all such deliveries and carrying of alcohol in vehicles is properly and clearly recorded".[102] The rules might be summarised as follows:

- Before the alcohol is despatched certain details must be entered into a day book kept on the premises from where the despatch occurs.
- Before the alcohol is despatched certain details must be entered into a delivery book or invoice which is carried by the person delivering the alcohol.
- The information to be entered into the day book and the delivery book/invoice is:
  - The quantity of the alcohol
  - The description of the alcohol
  - The price of the alcohol
  - The name and address of the person to whom it is to be delivered.
- It is an offence to carry any alcohol other than what is stated on the books; and an offence to deliver anywhere other than the address stated on the books.

Readers should also note that it is an offence to deliver alcohol to a child or young person[103] such as "circumstances where a child takes delivery of a consignment of alcohol ordered by an adult by telephone".[104] It is also an offence to send a child or young person to collect alcohol.[105] These offences are explored in more detail in Chapter 19 at Section 4. In general, it should be noted that the principle of age verification is identical to that when endeavouring to assess age in an on-sales or off-sales shop environment. In other words, alcohol cannot be delivered to a person under the age of 18 and the usual checks in relation to "Challenge 25" and age verification apply just as if the person receiving the alcohol was a customer at the bar or at the till.

Some licensing boards have introduced a local condition which requires age

100 Ibid para 6(2)(a) and (b).
101 2005 Act, s 119(1).
102 Explanatory Notes to the 2005 Act, para 244.
103 2005 Act, s 108(3).
104 Guidance to Licensing Boards (2007), para 258, p 58.
105 2005 Act, s 108(2).

verification at the point of delivery, owing to a possible lacuna in that paragraph 9A(3) of Schedule 3 is deemed only to apply to face-to-face transactions "on the premises". Notwithstanding this potential gap, advice to operators should of course be to follow age verification processes.

Chapter 12

Premises Licences – Part 6 Transfers

1 TRANSFER OF A PREMISES LICENCE

The provisions for transfer of a premises licence are found in section 33 and section 34. The application attracts a fee to be determined by the board.[1] The purpose of a transfer application is to permanently move the licence into the hands of a separate party. At the point of transfer, the old premises licence holder ceases to be such, and the transferee becomes the new premises licence holder. Under the 1976 Act this was commonly a two-stage process: a "temporary" transfer, which was granted under delegated powers, and then a "permanent" transfer, which was considered at the next quarterly licensing although such applications were a procession and usually a formality.[2] The 2005 Act process is one application which is more than likely to be granted under delegated powers but can also be put to a hearing if necessary (on which, see below). Explaining the 2005 Act rationale, the Regulatory Impact Assessment says:

> "Where a business changes hands due to death, bankruptcy, incapacity or sale, an application for transfer would be required to the Licensing Board, with a set fee."[3]

As we will discover below, Parliament missed a trick in properly identifying the number of ways in which a licence may require to be transferred. It is often said by licensing practitioners that the transfer provisions in the 2005 Act are the single most woeful element of the statute.

2 TYPES OF TRANSFER AND WHO MAY APPLY

The following table is presented to assist in summarising who can apply and under what circumstances. The rules surrounding who can apply under certain circumstances are found in the Licence Transfer (Prescribed Persons) (Scotland) Regulations 2007[4] ("the Transfer Regulations", see Table 12.1).

In the case of an application under section 33, this can be made at any time. In the case of an application under section 34, the application must be made within 28 days of the date of the occurrence of the stated event otherwise the

1 Licensing (Fees) (Scotland) Regulations 2007 (SSI 2007/553), reg 11.

2 It was also possible to go straight for the permanent transfer but this was not popular as the incoming party could not trade ahead of the grant – meaning a long wait until the next quarterly hearing – see Section 11.5 of this chapter.

3 Licensing (Scotland) Bill, Regulatory Impact Assessment (22 February 2005) para 53, p 19.

4 SSI 2007/34.

Table 12.1 Who may apply for transfers

Type of Transfer	*Event/Reason*	*Who may apply*
Section 33	Any/Unspecified	Current premises licence holder
Section 34	Death of the licence holder	The executor of the estate, or a personal representative
Section 34	Licence holder becomes incapable	A person appointed under the Adults with Incapacity (Scotland) Act 2000; or a person appointed under a power of attorney
Section 34	Licence holder becomes insolvent	The appointed insolvency practitioner
Section 34	Dissolution	The administrator responsible for dissolution
Section 34	Transfer of the business	Any person to whom the business in question is transferred

licence ceases to have effect,[5] save that this cessation does not apply where the transfer is as a result of the "transfer of the business" (see below). Let us examine in more detail how these arrangements work.

2.1 Transfers under section 33

Section 33(1) provides:

> "A premises licence holder may apply to the appropriate licensing board for the transfer of the licence to such person as is specified in the application".

The only restriction on the identity of the transferee, as with the grant of a full premises licence, is that they cannot be an individual aged under 18.[6] When the 2005 Act came into being it seemed strange to licensing solicitors that the applicant would not be the transferee, as this was not possible for so long under the 1976 Act system. In fact, the utility of section 33 is now enjoyed by many practitioners as it allows a degree of flexibility as well as protection for the existing licence holder. With a section 33 application, it can be lodged at any time and under any circumstances, with the existing licence holder controlling the process as they are the applicant. In other words, the applicant is the transferor, not the transferee. Having this element of control has proven attractive to sellers of licensed premises keen to ensure that they have the whip-hand in relation to the transfer of the associated licence. Section 33 can also be used in situations which do not neatly fit into the section 34 arrangements, presuming the existing licence holder is available and able to authorise or consent to the transfer in some way.

There is a separate question about what happens where a section 33 transfer application is pending, and one of the section 34 events occurs. This is discussed below at Section 5.

5 2005 Act, s 28(2). There is a question over the meaning of "ceases to have effect". There are divergent views on this. Some believe that ceases to have effect means that the licence is irretrievably lost. On the other hand, the Act does appear to distinguish the loss of a licence through revocation or surrender. It may take a judicial review to settle the matter, but most licensing experts believe that the licence is lost. See also Chapter 7, Section 2.1.2.

6 2005 Act, s 33(2).

2.2 Transfers under section 34

Section 34 permits the transfer facility to be used by persons other than the premises licence holder in the following circumstances:

- the licence holder dies,
- the licence holder becomes incapable,
- the licence holder becomes insolvent,
- the licence holder is dissolved, or
- the business is transferred by sale or otherwise to another person.

These are sometimes referred to as the section 34 "events". Let us look at each one in turn.

2.2.1 Death of the licence holder

In the case of death, the applicant may be any executor or personal representative of the licence holder. The difference between "any executor" or a "personal representative" may relate to whether the deceased is intestate although the Act is not particularly helpful in this area. If there is no will, then there is no executor(s) to take up the application for transfer. The phrase "personal representative" is given no further definition in either the Transfer Regulations or the Act but it is a term which is used and widely accepted as *including* a person appointed under the Scots law of intestacy through what is known as the "confirmation" process when a person's estate is wound up, so the administrator appointed to that process would fit this category. Similarly, if the licence holder has died and the executor has predeceased them, or is unwilling to take up the role, then other parties can apply to the Sheriff to become what is known as the *executor-dative* and I would submit that this person, properly appointed, would qualify under section 34. As the phrase "personal representative" is not defined, it is open to boards to take a wide view on what that may mean.

Noting that there is a 28-day deadline to lodge the section 34 application, it may not be lost on readers that in some cases the person who may be in a position to make the application might not know of this requirement, or may not even have been legally able to make the application, within those 28 days. It may also be the case that the person is or was aware of the section 34 requirements but is not in a position to make good on the requirements of licensing law when in the full throes of grief. It is possible for a licensing board to exercise the "slip-rule" power under section 135 of the Act which does allow non-compliance with certain procedural aspects to be excused. The Act says:

> "(1) A Licensing Board may relieve any applicant or other party to proceedings before the Board of any failure to comply with any procedural provision if—
> (a) the failure is due to mistake, oversight or other excusable cause, and
> (b) the Board considers it appropriate in all the circumstance to relieve the failure."

The reference to "procedural provision" includes "any other requirement imposed by virtue of this Act as respects the procedure to be followed in connection with applications made to, or other proceedings before, a Licensing Board", and it is accepted by a good number of licensing boards that section

135 can be employed by the board in circumstances where a death has occurred and the 28-day deadline has been missed. The section 135 slip rule can in fact be deployed where any of the section 34 events has occurred and the 28 days has been missed, but that is a matter entirely for the licensing board to agree or not agree on a case-by-case basis.

2.2.2 Licence holder is made legally incapable

Where the licence holder has become *incapax* (legally incompetent), the applicant may be any person who has been granted power of attorney or is authorised to act by virtue of the Adults with Incapacity (Scotland) Act 2000. The exact definition of "incapable" is found in section 1(6) of the 2000 Act:

> "(6) For the purposes of this Act, and unless the context otherwise requires—
> 'adult' means a person who has attained the age of 16 years;
> 'incapable' means incapable of—
> (a) acting; or
> (b) making decisions; or
> (c) communicating decisions; or
> (d) understanding decisions; or
> (e) retaining the memory of decisions,
> as mentioned in any provision of this Act, by reason of mental disorder or of inability to communicate because of physical disability; but a person shall not fall within this definition by reason only of a lack or deficiency in a faculty of communication if that lack or deficiency can be made good by human or mechanical aid (whether of an interpretative nature or otherwise); and
> 'incapacity' shall be construed accordingly."

Note that the definition of "adult" for these specific purposes is to a person aged 16 or over, whereas under licensing law an adult is someone aged 18 or over. The difference is of no consequence in the context of the licence transfer arrangements as no one under the age of 18 can hold a licence in any event.

Advice on having a power of attorney should be taken from someone other than a licensing solicitor of course, but I imagine that confirming authority under the 2000 Act could take some time. My observations above concerning the use of section 135 are pertinent here.[7]

2.2.3 Licence holder becomes insolvent

In respect of insolvency, the applicant is any person acting as an insolvency practitioner (within the meaning of the Insolvency Act 1986, s 388) in relation to the licence holder; where the licence holder has been dissolved, the applicant may be the person in charge of the administration. Section 28(7) provides a list of what circumstances are to be taken as the licence holder "becoming insolvent", as follows:

> "(a) an individual or partnership becomes insolvent on—
> (i) the approval of a voluntary arrangement proposed by the individual or partnership,
> (ii) being adjudged bankrupt,

7 Some of the issues surrounding the issue of incapacity are explored in a Question and Answer at [2011] 49 SLLP 10.

(iii) the individual's or partnership's estate being sequestrated,
(iv) entering into a deed of arrangement made for the benefit of creditors, or
(v) granting a trust deed for creditors, and

(b) a company becomes insolvent on—
(i) the approval of a voluntary arrangement proposed by its creditors,
(ii) the appointment of an administrator or administrative receiver in respect of it, or
(iii) going into liquidation."

As is the case with any of the section 34 events, the purpose of the prescribed persons provisions is to allow an escape route, to avoid the finality of a section 28 declaration that the licence has ceased to have effect as a result of one of the events occurring. However, whilst this escape route is only open to certain prescribed persons, the aim of all of this is merely to allow that person to drag the licence away from the precipice of cessation – having done so, it is not always intended that the same person will retain the licence going forward. This is especially true in relation to insolvency where the insolvency practitioner will, in most cases, look to save the licence as there is some value in it, but then aim to divest themselves of that licence as quickly as they can. This has resulted in a practice of lodging two transfers following a section 34 insolvency, as follows:

- Application One: a section 34 transfer from the insolvent licence holder to the appointed insolvency practitioner
- Application Two: a section 33 transfer from the appointed insolvency practitioner to a third party.

This practice is often referred to as "back-to-back" transfers and licensing boards will allow both applications to be processed simultaneously to the point of grant and, assuming all is well with police reports and so on, will grant the applications "back-to-back" on the same day in most cases.[8] This process secures the licence but also reduces the liability which the insolvency practitioner may be (even if only theoretically) exposed to because the period of time that they actually hold the licence is reduced to a matter of seconds. In many cases the second transfer is to a purchaser or "end user" which the insolvency practitioner has identified. In other cases, a purchase is not forthcoming, and the second transfer may be to a management company who will parachute in and run the premises until such time as a purchaser is located. There would then be a third transfer from the management company to the purchaser. In such circumstances various agreements would need to be signed including the provision of "back letters" or multiple signed letters of consent to ensure that parties are protected. Specialist advice should certainly be sought in these cases.

In relation to the potential of liability, the insolvency practitioner will be less concerned when dealing with premises which are closed, for with no trading the vast majority of offences under the Act cannot occur. However, some

8 I have come across occasions when licensing boards do not allow the applications to be lodged simultaneously on the basis that the first application has not yet been granted and, therefore, the second application is incompetent as the applicant is not yet the licence holder, but in the main our old friend "the pragmatic view" of the clerk will come to bear and the applications can be processed in tandem.

technical offences may still be activated such as non-payment of the annual fee, or in relation to changes in personal circumstances such as a change in name or home address, which must be notified to the licensing board within one month.

Where, on the other hand, the premises are trading, in the majority of cases the insolvency practitioner will take advice to appoint a *pro tem* management company. However, that is not always the case. In some cases, the insolvency practitioner will go in and run the business for a period of time but that is now rare.

In my experience of dealing with a large number of such scenarios, criminal liability attaching to an insolvency practitioner is a remote possibility, albeit, of course, always there. Having spoken with police representatives on innumerable occasions about this, it is my experience that if a licensing offence were to occur, such as a sale to a child for example, the police would be unlikely to charge an insolvency practitioner who has had to take a licence in terms of the operation of section 34 unless that person is directly responsible for the offence. It is more likely the police, if charging anyone, would charge the member of staff who made the sale and possibly the premises manager/ responsible person. That notwithstanding, the hypothetical liability always remains and therefore the back-to-back transfers are attractive and almost always the way through. In each case, the insolvency practitioner would do well to take the advice of a specialist licensing solicitor.

Where the licence holder enters an administration or some form of voluntary arrangement, and re-emerges, then the licence can be transferred from the insolvency practitioner back to that same entity now that it is no longer insolvent.

2.2.4 Licence holder is dissolved

This section 34 event is activated where "the premises licence holder, being a person other than an individual, a partnership or a company, is dissolved"[9] and the person who may make the section 34 transfer application is "any person responsible for administering the dissolution of the licence holder".[10] This provision, excluding as it does most legal entities including individuals, partnerships and companies, is very narrow. It really only relates in practice to licences held by unincorporated associations such as members clubs and voluntary organisations.

In such a case, there is no appointed person or regulator to deal with and the dissolution will be effected by the mode outlined in the articles or other governing document of the club. If there is no such document, or no such clause, then the process for dissolution should be agreed by a vote of the members. If the organisation is a registered charity, there may be other steps to follow to achieve dissolution, such as ensuring any remaining assets are divested to an organisation with similar aims. In the context of the 2005 Act, if we assume that an office bearer of some description is appointed to oversee the dissolution, then that person must decide what to do with the licence. It may be that they simply allow the licence to lapse and cease to have effect on

9 2005 Act, s 28(5)(e) and s 34(3)(c).
10 The Transfer Regulations (SSI 2007/34) reg 6.

day 29. However, it may be that the licence relates to premises which the club or other body owns and is selling off, in which case the administrator of the dissolution may wish to apply to take the licence in their name in order to save it, and then subsequently transfer it to a third party. In such circumstances the licence itself will have an intrinsic value.

What this section 34 event does not capture is the dissolution of a limited company. In fact, the 2005 Act does not deal with this at all. This means that there is no prescribed escape route for a licence which is held by a company that has been dissolved (unless by reason of insolvency) and therefore the licence held by such a company has no formal status under the Act. A number of practices have arisen in which this situation might be remedied, so that the licence is "restored".

- **Dissolution of a limited company**: *dealing with the Crown*. On one interpretation, the licence is an asset of the dissolved company and this means that it becomes Crown property in the same way that other company assets do. The entity which deals with *bona vacantia* is the QLTR – the Queen's and Lord Treasurer's Remembrancer, the body which deals with ownerless property. If one deals with the QLTR, one can request it to consent to the transfer of the licence back to a third party. However, this is an expensive process as the QLTR will require a considerable sum in order to agree, and, due to the complexity of dealing with this, there are likely to be additional legal fees incurred.
- **Dissolution of a limited company**: *restoring the company to the register*. Under the Companies Act 2006, a party may petition to the sheriff court to have a company restored to the company register following a dissolution. This could be for any number of legitimate reasons and in our case would be to allow the company to then consent to the transfer of the licence to a third party (before presumably being dissolved again). This process is also costly, with fees involved in a summary application to appear before the sheriff (who may or may not agree); and of course restoring the company is not to be undertaken lightly as bringing it back to life may restore not just the company but other matters which may or may not be controversial.
- **Dissolution of a limited company**: *transfer minus consent*. In some areas a licensing board might be willing to overlook all of this technical grief and simply grant a transfer, perhaps a section 33 or even a section 34, based on proof of right to occupy.
- **Dissolution of a limited company**: *apply for a new licence*. If all else fails, one can have the clerk confirm that the dissolution of the company means that the licence has ceased to have effect as the premises have ceased to be used for the sale of alcohol, or otherwise lost in some licensing ether somewhere; and therefore a new licence could be sought. This means procuring section 50 certificates and lodging a new application. This way through the mess of the 2005 Act is not easy either; as it means the premises will have to meet current building regulations (which may involve exorbitant cost or be impossible) and food hygiene requirements, as well as the cost and delay of getting a new licence granted when there is no guarantee of grant. There are no "grandfather rights" in this circumstance.

2.2.5 Where the business is being transferred "by sale or otherwise"

Where the business is being transferred, the person who may apply is any person to whom the business in question is transferred. The Explanatory Notes to s 34 say:

> "Where a sale or transfer is being made the transferee and transferor may therefore choose whether it is to be the transferor who makes the application (under section 33) or the transferee (section 34)."

This explanation sounds very simple! I imagine that when section 34 was drafted the "transfer of the business" route was taken to be the most common route and is of course supposed to capture where there is a "transfer of the business" from party A to party B as in most conveyancing transactions resulting in a transfer of the licence, such as a sale of premises or a new lease or assignation of a lease to a new tenant.

The provision leaves a lot to be desired however, as not every conveyance is as a result of the "*transfer of the business*". What if there is no business? What if it is simply the bricks and mortar which is being sold or leased? What if the premises are closed? What if there is no "transfer" in the legal sense of the business and it is just that the existing operator for their own reasons wants to move the licence from one company to another? One example would include where the premises are owned by a landlord pub company but traded by a tenant. The licence is held by the tenant, but the parties agree that the pub company should hold the licence going forward. There is no transfer of the business in this scenario as the tenant is running the business and they are staying in place. Another example is where a UK-wide operator decides to hold its Scottish premises in a separate limited company for any number of reasons, perhaps to avoid the necessity to report convictions to Scottish licensing boards which relate to English incidents. Again, there is no transfer of the business in this scenario, it is just that the licence is being moved from one company to another company within the same organisation. It could also be that a multi-premises operator is looking to sell a portfolio of premises and in advance of this puts those premises into a separate company for the purposes of the sale. Again, there is no transfer of the business in that ordinary scenario. The narrowness of the wording in section 34 excludes these perfectly normal and legitimate occurrences. It could be that some of these events can be dealt with by way of the section 33 transfer route but that is not available for every instance and, even where it might be theoretically available, it might not be practically available.

Some licensing boards are prepared to effectively ignore all of this technical wrangling and allow a section 34 where it is obvious that a new operator is to take over the premises or where the operator may not be new but there is a letter of consent, and will not look beyond that. On the other hand, some licensing boards do look to observe the eccentricities of section 34 and will ask applicants to demonstrate what the "transfer of the business" is, which can be difficult when the transactional documentation is sometimes unavailable or commercially sensitive; and is even more difficult where there is no transfer of the business occurring, such as where premises are not trading or where it is an internal transfer within the same owner.

3 TRANSFERS: APPLICATION AND DETERMINATION

The procedure for an application by either the premises licence holder, or another person if one of the above circumstances arises, is the same.[11] The application form must be completed noting the transferee and any connected persons and whether any of these persons have convictions. The appropriate fee must be paid (which is set locally by the licensing board) and the principal premises licence must be returned with the application, or where it cannot be so returned, with an explanation as to why.[12] An additional fee might be levied where the original licence is not returned with the application. Broadly speaking, an application for transfer would take at least a month as an absolute minimum, assuming all is well, but can take several months to process in certain areas.

Once the application is lodged, the licensing board must give notice of the application, along with a copy, to the police. Thereafter, the police have 21 days from the date they receive the notice to report back to the licensing board with one of two notices in relation to relevant offences; in other words, whether the applicant has been convicted of any or not, and, if he has, detailing those convictions.[13] The police can also choose to object to the application in relation to the fit and proper test or in relation to any of the licensing objectives, whether based on the presence of convictions or not and therefore regardless of the two notices supplied to the board. Section 33(7A)[14] of the Act allows the police *carte blanche* in offering any other information about the transferee which they think the board would consider relevant, including reference to prospective connected persons and interested parties.[15] So, the police may submit a report under section 33(6) confirming there are no relevant convictions but go on to recommend refusal based on other information which is supplied by them.

After the board has received correspondence from the police, it has two courses of action. If the police say there are no relevant convictions and do not recommend refusal, and do not supply other information suggesting there is an issue, the board must grant the application. If, on the other hand, the police report indicates that there are relevant convictions, or if additional information has been supplied, the board must hold a hearing in order to determine the application.[16]

The hearing must take place within 42 days of the date the board receives the relevant correspondence from the police.[17] Note that there is no provision for objections or representations for any other party including the LSO, and strangely there is no provision to give the applicant notice of the hearing

11 The procedure is found in s 33(4)–(10), which is applied to applications made by persons other than the licence holder by s 34(4).

12 2005 Act, s 33(3)(b).

13 Remember that "spent" convictions may not be referred to: s 129(4).

14 This provision was inserted by s 44(2)(a) of the Air Weapons and Licensing (Scotland) Act 2015 and commenced as of 15 May 2017 via the Air Weapons and Licensing (Scotland) Act 2015 (Commencement No. 6 and Saving Provisions) Order 2017 (SSI 2017/119) and effectively homologated the practice already occurring where the police would provide information beyond that of the presence of convictions in order to object to the applicant for a transfer.

15 See Chapter 7, Section 3.1.1 in relation to the concept and definition of "interested party".

16 2005 Act, s 33(9).

17 Licensing (Procedure) (Scotland) Regulations 2007, reg 13(2)(a).

although in practice one would expect at least 7 days' notice in accordance with the period prescribed for other applications.

The licensing board will hear from the police and the licence holder and make a decision.[18] The grounds of refusal for a transfer application are:

(a) that, having regard to the licensing objectives, the transferee is not a fit and proper person to be the holder of a premises licence,
(b) that it is otherwise necessary to refuse the application for the purposes of any of the licensing objectives.

These grounds are explored in detail as they relate to new licence applications in Chapter 10 (at Section 3.1 in relation to the fit and proper test; and at Section 3.2 in relation to the licensing objectives) and those general principles apply here too; although note that the ground of refusal in relation to the licensing objectives as regards a new licence or major variation is "inconsistency" with the licensing objectives; whereas with a transfer application the test is that it "necessary for the purposes" of the licensing objectives. The use of "inconsistency" and "necessary" in these separate processes may have been intentional, noting that the application is essential about the transferee as opposed to the premises; so that, for example, behaviours which might not quite activate the fit and proper test could otherwise be considered under the wider objectives; but also noting that in my view the threshold for "necessary" is higher than that of "inconsistency".

4 TRANSFER APPLICATIONS AND PROOF OF RIGHT TO OCCUPY OR LETTERS OF CONSENT

It is common for licensing boards to request a "letter of consent" from the current licence holder to the transfer, though there is no statutory footing for this under the 2005 Act. The practice is, however, well established.[19] In those cases where a letter of consent cannot be produced from the current licence holder, such as where the licence holder has absconded or simply refuses to sign the consent for their own reasons, the board might seek proof of right to occupy by the incoming party. This practice likely originates from *Budge v Goudie*,[20] in which it was held that the applicant for a transfer of a licence must be in possession of the premises and thus able to carry on the business.

5 PENDING APPLICATIONS AND "RIVAL" TRANSFERS

There is a question as to how to deal with competing or rival applications for transfer. This comes up most frequently in relation to insolvency situations where some third party has lodged an application under section 34 or where the licence holder had lodged an application under section 33 just prior to

18 If the board proposes to refuse a transfer notwithstanding no recommendation to do so from the police, it would do well to explain why: see *Kelly v Renfrewshire Licensing Board*, Paisley Sheriff Court, 1 November 2011 (as digested at [2012] 51 SLLP 23).

19 See *Hawick Heritable Investment Bank Ltd v Huggan* (1902) 5 F 75 for an early example of a transfer where a letter of consent was not forthcoming.

20 (1895) 2 SLT 406.

becoming insolvent. A key issue is whether the application that was lodged first is the one which takes precedence. In my view the timeline is irrelevant where one of the section 34 events has occurred, as the only application which can lawfully be taken forward after a section 34 event is the one lodged by the prescribed person. Section 28(1)(b) makes it clear that if no application is lodged by a prescribed person within 28 days, then the licence ceases to have effect. There is no provision to circumvent this where a rival or competing application is lodged. Using the insolvency example, if a section 33 or even a section 34 "transfer of the business" application were lodged by the director of a company or some other person a few days before the insolvency of that company occurred, that application would become irrelevant because of the operation of section 28(1)(b).[21] In my view an application made by someone other than a prescribed person would have to be returned by the clerk regardless of when it was lodged. The operation of section 28(1)(b) does not even allow for a situation where a licence transfer had been effected to a party other than the section 34 prescribed person, meaning, even if the third party had the licence granted to them after a section 34 event, it would still cease to have effect upon the expiration of the 28 days.

If no section 34 event has occurred, and the licensing board is dealing with two competing applications under section 33 or possibly under the *lacunae* of section 34, this becomes a more difficult matter to wade through as it is not the job of the licensing board to become an arbiter or to take a stand on some real estate related dispute. The board might, in such circumstances, look to take matters forward in relation to which of the competing parties can evidence right of lawful occupation.

6 VARIATIONS LINKED TO TRANSFER, OR VICE VERSA

One of the more flexible, yet under-used, features of the 2005 Act is the ability for a person seeking a transfer of the licence to "attach" the application to an application for a variation. This covers the scenario where an incoming party wishes to operate the premises in a way dissimilar to the existing licence holder and wishes to know that the licensing board will approve of the proposed new operation before committing to the transfer.

If an applicant has lodged both a transfer and a variation, they can intimate under section 35(3) to the licensing board that the transfer is contingent on the success of the variation. On that basis, the board must determine the variation first and, if successful, then consider the transfer. If the variation is refused, the application for transfer falls.[22] Consideration might have to be given as to when the "effect" of the variation might be, so that the variation is approved at a hearing but not given effect until the transfer is granted subsequently.

If the applicant does not make an intimation under section 35(3), then the licensing board must determine the application for transfer first, and then the application for variation. In these circumstances, if the transfer is refused,

21 There is a separate argument about whether, in an insolvency context, a purported attempt to transfer a licence might constitute a gratuitous alienation.
22 2005 Act, s 35(4).

the variation falls. It is of course perfectly acceptable for a person to lodge both a transfer and a variation which are not "combined" under section 35.

7 "PRE-TRANSFER TRADING" AND LIABILITY

Under the 1976 Act, it was an offence for someone to trade from another person's licence. This was a form of "trafficking". The offence of trafficking does not exist under the 2005 Act and this means that it is lawful for one person to trade from another person's licence. This may happen for any number of reasons, such as where an area of a licensed premises is given over as a formal concession or franchise to a "pop-up" business. It may also happen where, for example, there are a number of stalls selling different alcohol products such as craft beer or gin, within premises which hold a permanent premises licence, and each stall holder is taking cash or card payments directly. In the context of a transfer application, this can and does often occur where the incoming party commences trading the premises prior to the grant of the transfer of the premises licence. Consideration should be given to adopting a form of legal agreement between the parties in order to deal with duties and liabilities.

The first thing to be made clear is that no offence is committed under such an arrangement of itself. The 2005 Act is not especially concerned with where the profits go (save any concerns over organised crime) and instead is focused on the alcohol being sold and consumed responsibly and the operation of the licensing objectives. It is a matter for the licence holder to decide whether they are comfortable in allowing a third party to sell alcohol from their licence, knowing that ultimately the buck stops with them as the premises licence holder, and no doubt the sensible premises licence holder will have due diligence, authorisations, training and so forth, in place. This is a very common scenario where a landlord or heritable proprietor holds the premises licence, but a tenant runs the business day to day.

However, whilst the 2005 Act does not prevent "pre-transfer trading", this does not mean it is without peril and the two parties need to be very clear upon the terms whereby this might be allowed. This might be by way of indemnification under the terms of any sale or lease documentation although one can never truly indemnify against a criminal conviction. If we assume the premises will trade sensibly and no mischief occurs, then there should be no issue. But if licence conditions are breached, or offences occur, then theoretically the premises licence holder is liable as the licence is still in their name even though they no longer own the premises and are not involved in the day-to-day operation. The prudent adviser would ensure that any commercial property related paperwork covers all of these matters, from observing the conditions and ensuring no harm comes to the licence, to making it clear who is going to pay the annual fee if the transfer has not crystallised by 1 October.

In some cases the sale or lease documentation is completely silent on the licence, perhaps because those advising have no experience of the matter. If the incoming party does not wish to make use of the licence then it is incumbent upon the premises licence holder to ensure the licence is surrendered timeously. Perhaps the parties agree to a quick deal involving little if any involvement with solicitors. It is not unheard of for a deal to have no mention of the licence and the incoming party is left to pick up the pieces after the sale has concluded.

8 PROPOSED AMENDMENTS TO THE TRANSFER REGIME UNDER SECTION 33A

Even before the 2005 Act commenced, licensing solicitors were bemoaning the transfer provisions. Persistent wailing over several years was finally rewarded with a proposed new transfer approach under a new section 33A, which was legislated for at section 59 of the Air Weapons and Licensing (Scotland) Act 2015. However, despite best intentions, the proposed section 33A would likely create more difficulties than it would solve. At the time of writing there was no active proposal to commence section 33A,[23] and it may be that an alternative process is eventually legislated for.

23 Section 33A contains many gremlins: requiring a transfer application to be accompanied at the point of lodging by a letter of consent, when these may not be forthcoming until a later stage for various reasons, thus creating additional delay to the completion of commercial transactions; proposing an ability to specify a date the application would be granted, when such a demand can barely be credible; and a transfer absent consent could only proceed where the applicant has failed to contact the current licence holder, leaving the process exposed to ridicule by the licence holder who wilfully withholds consent.

Chapter 13

Premises Licences – Part 7 Variations

1 VARIATION OF A PREMISES LICENCE

Once a premises licence has been granted, alcohol may not be sold and activities may not occur unless under and in accordance with that licence. But that does not mean the licence is carved in tablets of stone (save the mandatory conditions) and it is open to the licence holder to seek approval to change its terms. A permanent change to the licence is catered for under section 29 of the 2005 Act by a process known as "variation". The Regulatory Impact Assessment for the Bill stated most enthusiastically that:

> "[t]he premises licence would cover any premises for the sale of alcohol. No renewals would be involved and if an operating plan was well prepared, only very rare variations should be necessary".[1]

Variations are far from rare. Licensed premises change hands every day, and new operators will often need the licence to do something differently than what was done before. Variations may also arise from investment in a premises adding new features or facilities. Variations also include changing the designated premises manager (see below) and hundreds of such applications are processed by licensing boards all over Scotland every year. In addition to examples of what one might call "proactive" variations, where the licence holder is seeking to do something new, there are also innumerable examples of "reactive" variations because the licence holder was doing something they did not have permission for.

The reference to the operating plan being "well prepared" in the quote above, whilst well-meaning, did not reflect the reality at transition where thousands of applications were processed in haste under a new system which was not fully comprehended, and the process was error-strewn. It is a regular occurrence to come across a licence which was poorly converted and contains deficiencies. Sometimes these issues are identified by the licence holder or by their agent as part of a health-check; but they might also be spotted by a LSO or police officer.[2]

The changes which may constitute a variation are defined in section 29(5) of the Act as follows:

> "(a) any of the conditions to which the licence is subject (other than mandatory conditions[3])

1 Regulatory Impact Assessment, Licensing (Scotland) Bill, March 2005, para 53.
2 How the officer deals with the issue is on a case-by-case basis.
3 The full list of all the mandatory conditions is explored in detail in Chapter 15.

> (b) any of the information contained in the operating plan contained in the licence,
> (c) the layout plan contained in the licence, or
> (d) any other information contained or referred to in the licence,
> and includes an addition, deletion or other modification."

Theoretically, there is no detail within the four corners of the licence that cannot be covered by one of the above forms of variation.[4] Nicholson proposed that variations would be:

> "variation of the operations described in the original operating plan or schedule. Such a variation might involve, for example, no more than a change in the name of the designated personal licence holder in charge of the premises, or it might involve a change in the operating plan itself such as a change in the layout and use of the premises or a change in opening hours."[5]

There are two types of variation application: a "variation", which is referred to throughout the licensing community as a "major variation"; and a minor variation. Which type will be required depends on the type of change the operator wishes to make, and although one might assume that simple, uncontentious changes with little impact would follow the minor variation route, whereas more "material" changes would follow the "full" or "major" variation route, this is not always the case. Nicholson's plan to separate the minor from the major was as follows:

> "To cater for such changing circumstances it will be necessary to have a procedure whereby a premises licensee can apply to a licensing board for a variation of terms and conditions. In a simple case, such as a change of ownership, all that is likely to be required is a simple application to the licensing board. Where the application is not objected to by those entitled to do so, we consider that the variation should simply be granted as a largely administrative matter, and without the necessity of a formal hearing. Indeed, subject to a board's declared policies, this may well be something which could properly be delegated to the clerk of a licensing board. In the case of a more major variation in the nature of the operation being carried on in the premises we consider that the applicant should be required, among other things, to satisfy the board that the application has the approval of planning, building control, the fire authority and so on. Some national guidance as to what will constitute a major or a minor variation of the terms and conditions of a premises licence is likely to be helpful. That could be provided in primary legislation, but we tend to think that it would be better if guidelines were to be set out in licensing boards' declared policies ..."[6]

The idea that the definition of what might constitute a minor variation should be left to local board policy was not carried forward and Parliament prescribed what forms of variation should be treated as "minor". Viewing Nicholson's proposal from over a decade of practice under the 2005 Act system, it seems to me that leaving the definition of what would be accepted as "minor" to individual licensing boards would have created an almost unworkable approach

4 One example is the licence reference number. It ought not to be possible to change this number even though it is a detail of the licence. In at least one licensing board area, the practice was to change the reference number any time a variation was authorised. This led to significant confusion with various reference numbers floating around for one set of premises. At least one licensing board takes the view that a s 125 club cannot remove that status by way of variation because the s 125 status is not a detail of the licence but is a statutory class of premises licence which sits "above" the four corners of the document.

5 Nicholson Report, para 4.5, p 58.

6 Nicholson Report, para 4.24, p 68.

where what is minor in one jurisdiction is not in another, especially from the perspective of operators who hold multiple licences across jurisdictions.

2 MINOR VARIATIONS

The Act provides for a number of specific types of variation which are to be treated as "minor variations". The Guidance to Licensing Boards says:

> "The Act provides a simple procedure for licensees to make minor variations to their premises layout which could be approved in a simple and straightforward way. Such changes are those that do not have any impact on the licensing objectives."[7]

The reference to the impact on the licensing objectives is helpful in that it underlines that the point of the minor variation process is that it is designed to catch uncontentious, administrative changes, or simple changes to the licence which are so innocuous that they would need no consultation or consideration. The following paragraphs are an examination of the different types of minor variation. It should be noted that items at subheadings 2.1 and 2.3 were provided for on the face of the Act as passed. Items at 2.4 to 2.9 were all added at a later stage via the Licensing (Minor Variations) (Scotland) Regulations 2011,[8] which were commenced as of 28 March 2011. The Executive Note to the 2011 Regulations says:

> "The aim [of introducing these new types of minor variation] is to further ensure consistency and give greater clarification of what can be processed as a minor variation. This will, in turn, reduce costs for the Board as they will no longer require to undertake the full consultation and hearing process required for a normal variation. It also reduces costs for the applicants as there is a substantially lower fee level for processing a minor variation."

A regulatory impact assessment for the new minor variations adds:

> "The revised process expands the circumstances where a variation is considered minor and is designed to allow licensees to make small changes to their licences in a quicker and cheaper way."

2.1 Minor variations: change to the layout plan

A change to the layout plan which does not result in an inconsistency with the operating plan is a minor variation.[9] Changes to the layout plan may result in a minor or a major variation, depending on the exact nature of the changes and how these interact with the licence and operating plan. Examples of a change in layout which would necessitate a major variation may include:

- the addition of a beer garden when the operating plan does not cater for external drinking;
- the creation of a games room when gaming is not provided for in the operating plan; or
- the creation of a dance floor when dance facilities are not provided for in the operating plan.

7 Guidance to Licensing Boards (Scottish Government, April 2007) para 85, p 27.
8 SSI 2011/151.
9 2005 Act, s 29(6)(a).

In each of these examples the reader should note that the layout change also necessitates a change to the operating plan, which is a determinant factor in gauging whether the proposal is minor or major.

These matters are not always straightforward. An early parliamentary exchange highlights the type of issue which may arise:

> "The Convener: Will you also clarify for Mr Crawford whether premises will be required to submit a variation to their licences for the installation of facilities such as a juke-box or pool table?
> George Lyon: Our intention is that such changes to the layout of premises would be deemed to be a minor variation."[10]

Notwithstanding the best intentions of Mr Lyon, who at the time of this exchange was the Government minister in charge of licensing, the addition of a jukebox may require a major variation, if the premises do not currently have permission for "recorded music" as an activity on the operating plan, and the addition of a pool table may also require a major variation where the premises do not currently have permission for "indoor sports" as an activity on the operating plan.

Another key consideration is a layout change which will result in a higher capacity. That would fall within the ambit of a major variation. We know (see below) that a decrease in capacity is a minor variation so an increase in capacity is therefore certainly a major variation. An example might be premises which install a mezzanine level, creating room for 60 new diners. The layout change is, on the face of it, not particularly controversial, but the capacity of the licence would need to be increased from say 120 to 180 in order to reflect the new dining area (see Section 2.7 below for further comments on this particular issue).

If a layout change is proposed which does not result in a higher capacity and does not need any other activity added to or amended within the operating plan, then this is most likely to be a minor variation. Changes like moving the bar, or reconfiguring the layout of fixed seating, and other changes to the layout are all most likely to fall under the minor variation procedure.

2.2 Minor variations: restriction of terms of entry by children or young persons

Section 29(6)(b) says that a minor variation is:

> "any variation reflecting any restriction or proposed restriction of the terms on which they are allowed entry to the premises".

Note that a minor variation in relation to children and young persons is only where terms of entry are to be restricted. If, therefore, the operator seeks to liberalise access in any way, then by definition a major variation application will be required. Whilst uncommon, it is not unheard of for a licence holder to pursue this type of minor variation. A good example would be where a new operator takes on a bar and wishes to operate it as a nightclub, or perhaps wishes still to run the premises as a bar but as one where no children or young persons are allowed for operational or management reasons. There are further

10 Local Government and Transport Committee, 20 September 2005.

specific terms on which children and young persons' access restrictions might fall under the minor variation procedure and these are noted at Section 2.6 below.

2.3 Minor variations: change of premises manager

This is one of the most common applications in the licensing system and there are a number of strands to this. These are discussed fully at Section 3.3 below.

2.4 Minor variations: change of premises name

Most licensing boards in Scotland issue a premises licence which bears the name of the premises. The notable exception to that is Edinburgh, which has never carried that information on its licences. The changing of a premises name is clearly an inoffensive matter[11] and correctly this is seen as purely an administrative function to be followed. The enforcement of this is not, I would suggest, on the top of the agenda and there are countless examples of premises licences bearing the previous name of a former operator or trading incarnation. It is a matter which should be resolved and might most commonly be fixed at the same time as other matters are being attended to.

2.5 Minor variations: a temporary or permanent reduction in the licensed hours

The temporary reduction in licensed hours element of this is, for me, a red herring. This links to the hobgoblin that is the so-called "duty to trade" and this is discussed in full detail in Chapter 16 at Section 9. The reality is that the licence is discretionary, not mandatory – that is, the licence can be used up to the extent that it permits and does not need to be slavishly followed to the red line of that extent. It is perfectly acceptable for a premises licence holder not to trade all of the hours that the licence allows. There is therefore no need for a licence holder to seek to vary his licence for a temporary reduction in hours as this can be achieved unilaterally when the licence holder decides to do so. A permanent reduction in hours may be a different beast although such applications are rarely proposed by licence holders themselves. Even where the licence holder does not consistently use the hours, there is simply no need to reduce them. The licence, and the hours that it permits, may have some commercial value and it may therefore be prudent to ensure that the licence is as flexible as possible.

11 In one case I am aware of, a board member sought to clarify whether a change of name could be denied because the proposed new name was political. The process does not allow the board to take any view on the new name and the application cannot be refused. If a name was used which breached advertising standards, then that would be a matter for the ASA, not the licensing board. Similarly, if there was an intellectual property dispute over the name, that is irrelevant for alcohol licensing purposes and the application would have to be granted anyway. Parties would have to take up such a conflict separately and the premises might be renamed depending on the outcome.

2.6 Minor variations: further restrictions in relation to children and young persons

Regulation 2(c) of the 2011 Regulations provides for the following class of minor variation:

> "(c) in relation to the access of children or young persons onto the premises any variation to the operating plan so as to—
> (i) increase the minimum age at which children or young persons may be allowed onto the premises;
> (ii) reduce the times at which children or young persons are allowed onto the premises;
> (iii) restrict the access of children or young persons to certain parts of the premises;".

It is open to an on-sale premises to ask for permission to allow children from birth. However, one of the mandatory conditions which attach to an on-sale premises licence is that, where children under the age of five are to be admitted, there must be baby-changing facilities "accessible to persons of either gender". In some cases, a pub finds it cannot accommodate baby-changing facilities and will amend the licence to avoid the condition to increase the minimum age to five. A licensee might also do this for their own operational reasons.

A premises licence holder might also, again for operational or management reasons, decide that they want to restrict the times children and young persons can access the premises – perhaps where the style of premises becomes more adult in a later part of the night; and the same logic applies to restricting children and young persons to certain parts of the premises, such as wanting to prevent them being in an area where there are pool tables or some other reason relating to layout.

It is unusual, in my experience, to see a licence holder self-impose minor variations of this nature, but it can originate where the licence holder wishes to put the matter beyond doubt in order to have clarity with staff as well as with the general public as to what is and is not allowed.

2.7 Minor variations: reduction in capacity

A reduction in capacity may occur where an area which was formerly given over to standing or seated patrons is reassigned for some other use – for example, the creation of a dedicated dance floor, or where a bar is to be extended. A reduction may also occur where a premises is itself reduced in size – perhaps where single premises are to be carved into two distinct licensed premises, or where one portion of premises is converted into a non-licensing use. A question which may be raised is how best to deal with an application where there are aspects which are both major variations and minor variations. If the layout is changed to incorporate a dance floor, but the licence does not permit dance facilities, and the licence holder wants permission to be approved for other layout changes as part of the same scheme, then one option is to separate out the variations. So, for example, the minor layout changes and a reduction in capacity might be dealt with under a minor, whilst at the same time a major variation is processed to add dance facilities to the operating plan. The licence holder should take advice on these matters.

A reduction in capacity might be thought sensible for operational reasons. Perhaps a nightclub operator has inherited a licence with a capacity that is substantially above what is appropriate. For staff training purposes, and to ensure a clear message is given to staff, security, and to customers, the licence holder might seek to reduce the capacity. The reduction in capacity might be forced upon the licence holder, perhaps as a result of a fire audit, and whilst any fire risk assessment does not automatically engage with a licence, the licence holder may decide that it is prudent to ensure the number on the licence matches the number on the fire risk assessment.

2.8 Minor variations: cessation of the provision of live or recorded music at a decibel level exceeding 85 decibels

Regulation 2(e) of the 2011 Regulations states: "any variation resulting in the cessation of the provision of live or recorded music at a decibel level exceeding 85 decibels" is a minor variation. The reference to 85 decibels strikes to the core of what this provision is designed to achieve, and this relates to whether premises might be classed as "late opening premises" and thereby activating a number of additional mandatory conditions which only apply to such a premises. The purpose of this appears to be to allow premises to "re-classify" as premises which do not activate the late opening conditions. However, that being so, then the process is potentially flawed. There is no specific process that by activating this minor variation additional conditions fall away, and it might be argued that this can only be achieved by way of a major variation. On the other hand, it could be said that the late-opening conditions only apply where the licence meets the criteria for such conditions to apply, perhaps in the same way that there are off-sale only conditions which, whilst they may be stated on a premises licence, are inert if that licence is an on-sale only licence.

2.9 Minor variations: when the premises are fully occupied, more customers are likely to be seated than standing

Regulation 2(f) of the 2011 Regulations says "any variation to provide that, when the premises are fully occupied, more customers are likely to be seated than standing" is a minor variation. This variant is kindred to that immediately above and must relate to the premises being classified as late-opening premises. When making a premises licence application the applicant can "tick a box" to say that more people will be standing than seated, to indicate that it is a "late opening" premises such as a nightclub and therefore the licensing board will be on notice that the additional mandatory conditions which apply to such premises should be activated. This provision appears to be about reversing that where the style of premises may change, say from a nightclub to a bar, but again the process is flawed because there is no accompanying provision to make the late night conditions fall away if such a variation is approved. Only a major variation can achieve that. The role of late opening premises and the corollary conditions are discussed in full in Chapter 15 at Section 8.

3 APPLICATION AND DETERMINATION OF A MINOR VARIATION

Application for minor variation is made to the relevant licensing board using the statutory application form and must be submitted along with the principal licence and appropriate fee. If the principal licence cannot be located, an explanation can be given,[12] and an additional fee might be payable for a duplicate in some board areas. The procedure for a minor variation is incredibly simple: the board must grant the application. The only process required, therefore, is the determination of whether the application lodged falls into one of the categories above: that is, to check that what is requested is certainly a minor variation. The application fee for a minor variation is set in regulations at £20 (save a premises manager change, which is £31).[13]

3.1 Determination of a minor variation: is the application a minor variation at all?

Whilst an experienced agent can be pretty confident in most circumstances that an application is a minor variation, it is worthwhile reflecting on the fact that there is a difference between the competent lodging of the application, and the application being granted by the licensing board. What I mean by that is, with the exception of the application pertaining to a change in the designated premises manager, the minor variation is not subject to an interim, deemed or automatic grant. The application must be checked and verified. It must then be granted. If the licensing board takes the view the application is not a minor variation, then it is incompetent and should be returned to the applicant. The decision to reject an application on this basis is not a prescribed process but would be a decision typically taken by the clerk, meaning a challenge to that decision would have to proceed by way of judicial review.

3.2 Determination of a minor variation: certificates of suitability?

The Act creates no requirement for the submission of certificates of suitability under section 50 in respect of a minor variation. So, whilst proposed works may indeed require a building warrant and so on, that makes no difference to the prescribed licensing process. Notwithstanding this, I have known at least one board to insist on the presentation of section 50 certificates to "support" a minor variation. Such a request is clearly unlawful, but in many instances in the world of licensing one must take a cool-headed approach and consider that in seeking to achieve the desired outcome for the licence holder it may be better to adhere to the request as the alternative may result in delay or rejection which can only be repelled, under these circumstances, by way of judicial review.

12 Where the licence has been lost or stolen, some licensing boards insist on the licence holder providing a police reference number to confirm they have reported the loss. This can be achieved using the 101 service, if necessary.

13 Licensing (Fees) (Scotland) Regulations 2007 (SSI 2007/553), reg 12(1)(b).

3.3 Minor variation to substitute a new premises manager

The Act makes specific provision for when the variation sought is to put a new designated premises manager on the licence. The Act refers to such an individual as a "premises manager". However, the phrase "designated premises manager" or "DPM" has become the most commonly used term to describe this person, maybe as a result of cross-pollination with the 2003 Act, which refers to the equivalent role as the "designated premises supervisor" or DPS. The fee for this specific type of application is set in regulations at £31.[14] The proposed premises manager must hold a valid personal licence and cannot be named on another premises licence.[15]

3.3.1 The immediate effect provision for variation of premises manager

Under section 31, if the minor variation application seeks to substitute another individual as premises manager, and if the applicant requests that the variation should have immediate effect, the premises licence is treated during the period of application as if it was already granted. The purpose of this is to ensure that there continues to be a premises manager. It is a mandatory condition of any premises licence that alcohol cannot be sold when there is no premises manager in respect of the premises,[16] and under certain circumstances the premises may indeed not be selling alcohol at that time – so the immediate effect provision means alcohol sales can recommence.

There is a question as to just how immediate this effect might be. The Act says that the immediate effect is during the "application period", and the "application period" runs from when the licensing board "receives" the application.[17] If an application is lodged by mail or by hand, and one has receipt or proof of delivery, it is reasonable to take that as the application having been "received". Such instances are very often rushed jobs in trying to get premises trading again after it has been noted that the old manager has left and a temporary cessation of alcohol sales is in force.

3.3.2 Variation of a premises manager: the "7 days and 6 weeks rule"

There is a "grace period" provision in relation to naming a new premises manager following the departure of the former. Section 54 describes itself as

14 Licensing (Fees) (Scotland) Regulations 2007, reg 12(1)(a).

15 There is often a "managerial merry-go-round" with DPMs moving around from one premises to another, which is a perfectly normal and everyday aspect of some businesses. The question as to when a premises manager is removed from one licence so as to be able to be named on another often crops up. The legal position is that as of the moment that the 7-day notice has been intimated, that personal licence holder is free to be named on another premises licence. The 7-day notice could therefore be intimated, and an "immediate effect" DPM change variation lodged on the same day. If the 7-day notice has not been given, and the proposed premises manager for one premises is still named on another, then the effect of this is that the variation application for the proposed premises is incompetent. In practice, what might happen is that a board will become aware of the manager being named elsewhere and flag this up to the applicant or agent. Thereafter, on production of evidence that the 7-day notice has been given, the application is processed.

16 2005 Act, Sch 3 para 4(1)(a). See Chapter 15 at Section 4.3.

17 2005 Act, s 31(3)(a).

a provision for the "dismissal, resignation or death of the premises manager". The exact details of events which might activate the grace period are at section 54(2) as follows:

> "(a) the premises manager ceases to work at the premises,
> (b) the premises manager becomes incapable for any reason of acting as premises manager,
> (c) the premises manager dies, or
> (d) the personal licence held by the premises manager is revoked or suspended."

If any of these situations apply,[18] then certain actions must be taken by the premises licence holder in order to ensure alcohol sales can continue. If these actions are not taken then the licensing board must vary the licence so that no premises manager is specified, requiring the sale of alcohol to cease immediately. The actual premises licence is not affected by this process other than that it is (hopefully) temporarily incapable of allowing the sale of alcohol. There is no restriction on other activities or uses of the premises such as accommodation, providing meals, soft drinks, and so on. In some cases, an operator might find a police officer instructing the "closure" of the premises but that is not correct. Only alcohol sales must cease.

The actions needed to prevent this scenario are:

- First, the premises licence holder must, within *7 days* of the date that the former premises manager ceased to work on the premises, give notice of this to the licensing board[19].
- Secondly, the premises licence holder must lodge a variation to substitute a new manager no later than *6 weeks* after the date the manager ceased to work.[20]

I find it useful to think of these actions combined as the "7 Days and 6 Weeks Rule". It is critical to note that there is no "pick and choose" element to this rule. Both the 7 days' notice and the new premises manager variation 6-week deadline must be complied with. If either of these processes is missed, then the sale of alcohol must immediately cease until a new premises manager can be named. If a random inspection of premises by a LSO or police officer discovers that the manager left some time ago, then the reaction to that must be stop alcohol sales immediately until a new manager is named.

If premises are closed (for example, undergoing a refurbishment), then there is no need to name a new premises manager during any period of closure if the old one has moved on. Where there is no trading, the premises licence holder can allow the 6 weeks to pass but must then remember to name a new manager prior to the re-commencement of alcohol sales after the refurbishment is complete.

18 The drafting of the key events under s 54(2) is most unhelpful. By specifying certain key circumstances as opposed to a more general wording it creates an argument about what happens when a manager is no longer the manager for some other, unprescribed reason. What of the manager who remains working on the premises but has been promoted or demoted and has not "ceased to work" at the premises but works in a new capacity? What of the manager who is a tenant of the premises licence holder and for whom authority to sell alcohol has been withdrawn under the terms of a lease? The solution may be that it is open to the licence holder to name a new manager without giving notice under s 54 first, but that does not detract from the inelegance of s 54(2).

19 2005 Act, s 54(3).

20 2005 Act, s 54(4)(b).

3.3.3 Changing premises managers and missed deadlines

Some parties have criticised the 7-day rule in the event of the death of the nominated premises manager; grieving families or colleagues would have only 7 days after the date of death to ensure a letter is sent to the board, and at a time of high stress this may be missed. However, section 135 of the Act – that is, the dispensing power of the board – could be used in such a case. Section 135 allows the board to relieve an applicant of "any failure to comply with any procedural provision" if the failure is due to mistake, oversight, or other excusable cause.

The applicability of section 135 to "missed deadlines" such as the 7 days or 6 weeks is not normally invoked formally. It is more likely that an approach will be taken that the premises should cease the sale of alcohol until such time as a new manager is named. The application to name a new manager can be given immediate effect, so in the majority of cases this does not prove too disruptive to trading premises.

This depends, of course, on having the luxury of another personal licence holder who is able and willing to have him- or herself named as the premises manager on the licence in question. In one case I was involved with, on a random visit on Christmas Eve the authorities spotted premises trading where the premises manager had left many months ago. The premises licence holder did not have another personal licence holder on the books, and the local authority office closed at lunchtime, reopening on 4 January the following year. No application could be lodged and no one from the board's office could be reached: this resulted in the closure of the premises over the busiest two weeks of the year.

3.3.4 Reversing a premises manager change?

A question which arises from time to time is whether the invocation of the 7-day notice can be reversed or ignored, and, if neither applies, can the same person be reinstated after the notice is given? This situation could arise where a premises manager changes their mind about leaving the premises, or where a prospective new employee backs out at the last minute. A separate question arises as to whether a variation to name the new manager can be withdrawn if the immediate effect provision has been activated.

There is no specific provision to allow a 7-day notice to be recalled or rescinded once given. Some licensing boards have, in my experience, been willing to overlook the absence of such a provision as a matter of common sense. In such a case, it is treated as if the notice was never given and the same premises manager remains the premises manager. In other cases, a question arises as to whether the same person can be "re-named" having given intimation that they are to leave. The specific wording of section 54 suggests that "another individual" should be named and some boards take this to mean that a person cannot be re-named on the licence by way of a minor variation application if the notice has been triggered.

This means some other third party, who requires to hold a valid personal licence and not be named on another licence, must be found out there in the licensing phantom zone and named instead. In such circumstances, that application cannot be a fiction[21] and, thus, this can create real headache for

21 There is no specific criminal offence or provision under the Act which covers the scenario

operators trying to find someone who can be named on a temporary basis to keep premises trading.

Since the onset of the use of the Police Scotland internal system known as "Innkeeper", the central licensing database the police operate, the prevalence of people being named on more than one licence by accident or oversight has fallen dramatically. However, it still appears to be an unwritten rule of the Act that the discovery of a "DPM drama" is always after 3pm on a Friday when there is precious little time to fix it!

In relation to whether an "immediate effect" variation can then be withdrawn, the answer is – yes. Section 31(3)(b)(ii) makes it clear that such an application can be withdrawn prior to the formal grant of the variation by the licensing board, which could occur some days or weeks after the application was lodged.

4 MAJOR (NON-MINOR) VARIATIONS

As a quick reminder, section 29(5) defines a "variation" as a variation (including addition, deletion or other modification) of:

- any of the conditions to which the licence is subject,[22]
- any of the information contained in the operating plan,
- the layout plan, or
- any other information contained or referred to in the licence.

It may be noted that if a variation is not a minor variation, then it is a major variation. Major variation applications (actually referred to in the Act as "non-minor" variations) are therefore applications which relate to adding new activities, amending existing conditions, extending the operating hours on a permanent basis, amending existing activities, relaxing access by children and young persons, increasing capacity, and a plethora of other possible changes.

4.1 Application and determination of a major variation

The procedure for a major variation is in stark contrast to a minor variation; the level of work required is effectively equal to a new premises licence application. The fee for a variation is set independently by the board, so applicants should check in advance.[23] Fees generally range from the order of £130 to £160. However, South Lanarkshire divisional boards charge a significant percentage of the maximum new licence fee, which in some cases means the fee for a major variation is £1333.33.

In terms of process, section 29(4) states that section 21(1) and (2) and

where application to name a new manager is made without that person's consent or knowledge, or even where the person knowingly allows it but has no intention of working at the premises. It is, however, theoretically open to the licensing board to consider treating the application as being invalid or not made if such a situation is evidenced. It may be interesting to note that, under the 2003 Act, the incoming DPS must sign a statutory form confirming they consent to being named as the DPS on the relevant premises.

22 Except "mandatory" conditions, which may not be varied: see Chapter 15 for a full discussion of mandatory conditions.

23 Licensing (Fees) (Scotland) Regulations 2007 (SSI 2007/553), reg 12(2).

section 22 apply "in relation to a premises licence variation application as they apply to a premises licence application". Section 21, it will be recalled, relates to the notification of the application by the licensing board to the parties identified in section 21(1) and section 22 provides for objections and representations to the application. To put it shortly, all of the processes outlined in Chapter 8 in relation to the lodging of a new licence application by the applicant, and the processing of the application by the licensing board, apply equally where the application is a major variation, save that of course the application is to vary the terms of an existing licence and therefore the focus of the process is on the *variation sought*, not the licence itself, and that no section 50 certificates need be pursued (see Section 4.3 below).

After all the preliminary matters, public consultation and so on have all been taken care of, the board must hold a hearing to determine the variation application.[24]

4.2 Grounds for refusal of a major variation application

The approach to determining a major variation is a replication of the approach to a new licence application in that the Act can be said not to be either a granting or a refusing Act by way of default. Each application is taken on its own merits, and the board must refuse the application if one or more of the grounds of refusal apply and must grant the application if none of the grounds of refusal applies.

The grounds of refusal for a variation application are found in section 30(5) and are in similar terms to the grounds of a refusal for a premises licence application:

- a previous application seeking the same variation has been considered and refused within the previous year, or it seeks 24-hour licensing without exceptional circumstances, or it seeks off-sale hours outwith 10am to 10pm,
- inconsistency with one or more of the licensing objectives,
- unsuitability having regard to activities, location, character, condition and persons likely to frequent the premises (taking into account the variation sought),
- overprovision (taking into account the variation sought).

Note that the "fit and proper" ground of refusal does not apply to a major variation application. The remaining grounds of refusal are examined in considerable detail in Chapter 10 and the majority of that commentary can be read to apply to major variations with one key distinction: the refusal must of course relate *to the proposed variation sought*. In practice, it is not uncommon for third parties to view the major variation process as an "in" to raise any number of issues about the wider operation of the application premises and whilst these may otherwise be salient and pertinent, if they have no relevance to the major variation sought then they are irrelevant to the application and irrelevant to the determination of the application.

For example, if a licence holder applies to open at 11am on a Sunday morning instead of 12.30pm, and local residents lodge objections which complain about karaoke on Friday nights, then those considerations are of no import to the application. Another example would be where the premises are seeking to

24 2005 Act, s 30(3).

add an activity and objections are made on the grounds of overprovision. It is difficult to see how a request to add recorded music for the playing of background music in an off-sale premises could result in refusal on overprovision grounds. Notwithstanding this, as an agent you can find yourself in a position where the board wishes to look into other parts of the licence and will use the variation hearing to do so; for example, if the board has "updated" conditions relating to children and young persons, it might ask you to accept the updated conditions at the same time as granting the variation. These "requests" may or may not be acceptable to the applicant!

The board has the power to amend the conditions on the licence following grant of the variation, should it think it appropriate.[25] The variation sought might, for example, relate to a new activity and it may be that existing local conditions are no longer appropriate or need tweaked. A board cannot amend the mandatory conditions or the late-night conditions, nor can it add a condition which relates to a matter that is regulated under another enactment.[26]

If the application for variation is refused, the board must specify which ground(s) of refusal apply, and if the ground is inconsistency with the licensing objectives, which objective(s) is relevant. Under the terms of section 32, if an application is refused, no further application can be made for the same variation in respect of the same premises within one year after the decision unless the board gives a direction otherwise at the time of the first refusal.[27] This means "piping up" at the time.

4.3 Major variations and certificates of suitability

There is no requirement to produce certificates of suitability in order to support a major variation even where the changes do require a building warrant or updated clearance from the food hygiene officer such as where a kitchen is being installed to commence bar meals. See my comments above. The local authority is of course a consultee to the application and in most cases it is convention for building standards and even food hygiene to present a report or representation to an application. It would not be competent, in my view, for a licensing board to refuse a major variation application because of an issue with building warrant or food hygiene. Those matters should be resolved directly with building standards and with food hygiene.

That being said, back in the real world of practising licensing law it is sensible to try and accommodate any concern and, from an agent's perspective, one can sometimes end up being a project manager and general "near-legal" strategist as well as a licensing lawyer. One must recognise that a building control issue might impact on the application in that the capacity may require to be amended, or perhaps the layout plans changed. There are numerous cases where an application is continued to allow issues with building standards to be resolved and the sensible applicant or agent will work constructively with all the officials to find a way through.

25 2005 Act, s 30(6).

26 Duplication with other statutory regimes is discussed in detail in Chapter 15 at Section 6.1.3 but remember also the "essential remit" of the licensing board in relation to alcohol, per *Brightcrew* et al.

27 2005 Act, s 32(3).

4.4 Major variations and modifications prior to determination

Section 23(7) of the Act allows a board to propose modifications to a new licence application. This is discussed in Chapter 10 towards the end of Section 10.1 where I describe the "horse-trading" which might occur at a hearing: the applicant, sensing the mood of the board or reacting to objections, might propose a modification to the application such as an earlier terminal hour for an outside area, and so on. Section 23(7) is couched in terms that indicate that the modification is proposed by the board, rather than the applicant, and structurally that is accurate when it comes to the board making a decision, but is of course not the entire picture during the submissions themselves when modifications can be proposed in the heat of the hearing by any party. Now contrast this to the major variation process. Unlike section 21 and section 22, section 23 does not apply to major variations. The "modification" provision at section 23(7) does not therefore apply to major variations, and section 30 provides no equivalent ability.

In other words, perhaps surprisingly, an application for a major variation cannot in law be "modified" in same way a new licence can at a hearing. This *lacuna* does not stop that very thing from happening time and time again at hearings. It is a part of normal practice that the "horse-trading" which might occur in a new licence will also occur in a major variation hearing. It is not uncommon to see a case where, for example, additional hours are sought to 3am but at the hearing the lesser hour of 2am is proposed by some party, and accepted and granted on that basis, *in ex omne majus continet in se minus.*

4.5 Variations and layout changes: when should they be carried out?

A variation to the layout of the premises might be contained within either a minor or a major variation. In both cases, there is a question as to when the works might be able to commence. It seems sensible to suggest that the position ought to be that works should not commence until after the licensing board has given approval to the variation, but regrettably it is not that straightforward. Our old friend the pragmatic view is required here, given the potential for criminal sanction.

The issue is that, whilst it is clear that premises cannot operate in breach of the licence, which includes the layout plan and therefore includes changing that layout without permission, at the point a variation for the new layout is granted, the premises are also in breach of the same offence, for at that point the licence now bears the new layout plan, even though the old layout is the one which exists in the real world. This *Janus-faced* dilemma means that the licence holder is going to be in breach of his licence either way. This can be contrasted to the 1976 Act position whereby the licence holder proposing "alterations" under section 35 of that Act certainly had to obtain approval prior to works being carried out, and if the works were not carried out, a further application would be required to lodge a plan with the old (current) layout;[28] and there was even provision for licensing boards to force works to be

28 Jack Cummins tells me he cannot recall the practice of sending a new ("old") layout plan in these circumstances and instead the convention was to simply write to the clerk to say the authorised works were not proceeding.

carried out during the renewal process, and also to require unauthorised works to be restored to the previous layout by application to the sheriff.

My view is that if I am satisfied that the works can proceed by way of a minor variation, then it is safe to tell the client to start the works, knowing that a minor variation cannot be refused. In such a case, the commencement of the works becomes academic because the licence holder knows the board must grant the application. If the works are covered under a major variation, that decision becomes trickier, but I have certainly stood in front of licensing boards where a variation is being sought and works are in progress or have even been completed. I have also been brought to task by some boards about the works being done; and in other cases, the boards have been relaxed and even commented on the dilemma in the course of the hearing. It is a matter for the individual licence holder to take a view on and in doing so it would be sensible to seek advice.

Whilst, as I have noted above, there is no process for certificates of suitability under the Act for variations, operators who do crack on with works under either a minor or a major variation must also remember that licensing approval does not absolve the requirement for approval under other legislation such as the need to get planning permission, building warrant, and so on.

Chapter 14

Premises Licences – Part 8 Reviews

1 REVIEW OF A PREMISES LICENCE

Sections 36 and 37 of the Act contain the procedures for what is known as a "review" of a premises licence. A review proposal is, in short, where a third party (or sometimes the licensing board) requests that the board conduct a review into the licence on the basis of some purported mischief or devilment and is designed to allow the board members to take steps they consider necessary or appropriate for the purposes of any of the licensing objectives. The review provisions therefore provide a possible "sanctions structure".[1] The origin of the review process can be found in concerns over the limitations of the equivalent procedure under the 1976 Act which, in effect, only allowed the suspension of a licence upon application by the police. Nicholson said:

> "we consider that licensing boards should have available to them a range of sanctions which they can apply when they are satisfied, on the basis of a complaint made by a Liquor Licensing Standards Officer or any other person entitled to do so, that a premises licensee has failed to comply with the terms and conditions which are attached to the licence."[2]

The 2005 Act review framework is therefore an agile, flexible beast in comparison to the strictures of the 1976 Act. The grounds on which a licence can be reviewed are varied, and the steps which are open to a licensing board leave them empowered to take very specific, bespoke action on a case-by-case basis, which can demonstrate leniency or, at the other end of the spectrum, mean that a licence is permanently revoked. Prior to turning to the process of the review hearing and possible outcomes, I want to explore in more detail the underlying purpose of a premises licence review.

2 THE "PURPOSE" OF A PREMISES LICENCE REVIEW

In a general sense, the review process is of course designed to make sure that a licence is not set in stone and granted for life, so that if it is abused it can be restricted or removed. There are, however, two particular themes I would like to explore in this section: (a) that the review process is fundamentally not about punishment; and (b) the question of "fault" and whether strict liability operates in licensing reviews.

1 Licensing (Scotland) Bill, Regulatory Impact Assessment, para 102, p 30.
2 Nicholson Report, para 7.12, p 100.

2.1 Purpose of premises licence reviews: should they be punitive?

The leading case in this regard is *Lidl UK GmbH v City of Glasgow Licensing Board*.[3] This was a long-awaited landmark case from the Court of Session concerning test purchase failure and suspension. A Lidl store in Glasgow failed a single test purchase. They passed a follow-up test. There were no other issues before the Board. The board suspended the licence for 5 days. Sheriff Mitchell had, at first instance, rejected the appeal and said that the Board was entitled to impose a sanction such as a suspension as a "deterrent" to ward off other licence holders from acting unlawfully. This decision was at odds with decisions from other courts, for example *Co-operative Group Ltd v Inverclyde Licensing Board*,[4] in which a suspension was over-turned on appeal as "disproportionate" following a single test purchase failure, the sheriff taking the view that a written warning was the correct disposal.

The decision from the Court of Session affirms the view that sanctions open to a board should be considered based on the individual merits of the case "for and against" and submissions and evidence presented, and not as some wider tool of deterrence, and therefore chimes with *Kennedy v Angus Licensing Board*.[5]

Of wider jurisprudential significance were the interesting things the judgment had to say about the "review" process itself:

> "the process of review is essentially forward looking. It involves examining whether the continuance of the particular premises licence in issue, without taking any of the steps listed in section 39(2) [that is, the sanctions open to a Board, e.g. suspension, revocation, etc], would be inconsistent with endeavouring to achieve the licensing objective in question. The process of review is therefore not directed to imposing a penalty in respect of some past event which is not likely to recur to an extent liable to jeopardise the licensing objective."

There is a clear statement here that the sanctions open to a Board at review should not be used to penalise for retrospective detriment, but rather should be imposed where it is necessary in order to protect the licensing objectives going forward. This has become referred to by some commentators as a process of "future proofing" the licensing objectives.

There are further pearls of wisdom to be had from this decision. It affirms the importance of having robust and demonstrable due diligence:

> "Further, it is clear, not only from the Statement of Reasons issued by the respondents, but also from the terms of the transcript of the proceedings before the respondents, that the respondents accepted the existence of the appellants' policies and procedures and that those policies and procedures were adequate, and should, if applied, have prevented sales of alcoholic drinks to a child or young person . . . In our opinion Sheriff Mitchell erred in not noting the absence of such criticism during the hearing before the respondents and in purporting to identify criticisms of the appellants' practices and procedures as having been open to the respondents, notwithstanding that the respondents had made no mention on them in their Statement of Reasons."

3 [2013] CSIH 25.

4 Greenock Sheriff Court, 8 October 2010, unreported. See [2010] 46 SLLP 6 for some commentary on the case.

5 22 August 2012, unreported. This case is discussed in Chapter 10 at Section 3.1.3.

Analysis of the risk profile of a possible breach, and evidence that measures have been put in place to prevent or minimise those risks, are key elements likely to be scrutinised in a review hearing. If the licence holder can demonstrate that the likelihood of the mischief (whatever it may be) reoccurring is minimal as a result of steps they themselves have taken in terms of responsible management of their premises or such other steps as may be sensible pertaining to the particulars of the individual case, then this might allow a licensing board the flexibility to discard some of the more severe possible steps. This assumes that the board is persuaded that the objectives have been protected against future harm. The *Lidl* decision later links the issue of due diligence to the question of deterrence:

> "Plainly the appellants were not in any need of deterrence, since they had acted responsibly before Mr Singleton's lapse and also in response to it. Imposing a penalty upon a premises licence holder who is not at fault can hardly be seen as justified by any proper notion of the deterrence of others."

The decision in *Nelson v Renfrewshire Licensing Board*[6] is another case in which the courts have determined a licensing board has acted incorrectly in punishing a licence holder by suspending his licence for past misdeeds, following the *Lidl* case above, albeit the lawfulness of the case is itself under an unfortunate cloud.[7] In *Nelson*, the licence holder had appointed a manager and that manager had allowed an illegal lock-in to occur. Mr Nelson was unaware of the lock-in occuring and had later sacked both the manager and another employee who was present. The Board suspended the licence with immediate effect for two weeks as a result of this sole incident. The *Nelson* judgment is of note as the court said that it was clear from the *Lidl* decision that the general philosophy of the review process was about "future proofing" the licensing objectives, was not restricted to test-purchasing cases but of general application to the law in relation to reviews under the 2005 Act.

The court said that suspension should only be used as a corrective measure to allow steps to be taken whilst the suspension was in effect, to adopt actions which would remedy whatever the problem had been. The Board did not identify what those steps should have been and it therefore appeared that the decision was one of a penalty rather than a measure intended to protect the licensing objectives going forward, and this was wrong in law.

The issue of punishment was also explored in *Tesco Stores Ltd v Midlothian Licensing Board*.[8] In this case, Sheriff Principal Stephen said:

> "it is difficult to avoid the conclusion that suspension was also disproportionate in the whole circumstances for the reasons I have already given. Suspension was indeed punitive and if that is the purpose of the licensing legislation then no doubt Parliament should have made that clear."[9]

6 Paisley Sheriff Court, 22 October 2013, unreported.

7 This case was heard and decided by Sheriff Pender. It transpired, sometime after the decision had been made, that the Sheriff Principal had not, as a matter of procedure, authorised the case to be heard by a Sheriff as was required. This was through oversight as opposed to an overt decision by the Sheriff Principal, but it does mean that the validity of the decision can be questioned on this technical point.

8 [2012] ScotSC 48.

9 Ibid at para 73.

In *Trust Inns Ltd v City of Glasgow Licensing Board*[10] a revocation of a licence was upheld (amongst other reasons) where the sheriff was satisfied that:

> "the defender's decision in the present case to revoke the premises licence did not constitute a punishment, but rather a necessary and appropriate step to further the licensing objectives".[11]

This case can be separated from the *Lidl*, *Tesco* and *Nelson* cases discussed above, and is therefore a useful comparator where the courts were satisfied that a revocation was not a punishment. *Trusts Inns* concerned a Glasgow public house known as the Scotch. In June 2013, Police Scotland called for a review of the licence and it was revoked principally in relation to evidence that the premises had become associated with drug dealing and drug taking.

The licence holder endeavoured to defend their position by taking a series of steps to mitigate the issues, and in addition, as a landlord licence holder, they had also replaced the tenant. The premises licence holder had not themselves operated the premises and therefore were not directly responsible for allowing the culture of drug taking which had developed at the premises. A key part of the judgment from Sheriff Reid is as follows:

> ". . . the [licensing board] had made an assessment of the nature of the perceived drug problem within the premises; it had made an assessment of the value and efficacy of the pursuer's remedial actions; and it also considered whether (and when) the situation was likely to improve. The defender concluded that the situation was not likely significantly to improve within a reasonable time. Its reasoning can be discerned from the statement. The culture of drug misuse was so embedded, and the steps taken to date had been so ineffective, that the belated recent introduction of a new tenant, drug wipes and torches would not resolve matters 'in the near future'. In other words, the defender was having to contemplate the unattractive prospect of allowing the premises to continue to operate in a manner that envisaged ongoing drug misuse while the pursuer's efforts (which had singularly failed to eliminate the pattern and culture of drug misuse) hopefully worked through. In that context, the defender was indeed having proper regard to how the licensing objectives would be achieved in the future."[12]

This case can therefore be distinguished from "single instance" review hearing outcomes for which there was no previous history or repetition or in which there was a significant level of "due diligence" and prompt action. In *Trust Inns*, by comparison, the Sheriff takes the view that there had been a long history of issues which had not been properly addressed or resolved and one is very much left with the impression that the Sheriff agrees with the Board that the actions taken by the licence holder (including removal of the tenant) could be categorised as "too little, too late":

> "[Trust Inns] submitted that the [licensing board] failed to take due account of the fact that there had been no further recorded incidents of drug misuse since the change of tenancy. It is correct that the statement of reasons makes no explicit reference to this issue. That is not surprising. It did not feature significantly in the submissions at the review hearing. Nevertheless, the [licensing board] was entitled to proceed on the basis of the substantial material then available to it. There was no undue passage of time between the allegations contained within the review

10 [2014] ScotSC 15.
11 Ibid at para 60.
12 Ibid at para 59.

application and the consideration of those allegations at the review hearing such as to render the allegations historic or stale. Besides, the [licensing board] had before it a sufficiently recent, detailed and extensive body of evidence bearing upon the operation of the premises, drawn over a sufficiently lengthy period of time, to enable it to reach an informed decision on the extent to which a 'pattern and culture of drug misuse' had become embedded within the premises, and the likely effect upon that culture of the recent introduction of the new tenant."[13]

Each case will of course turn on its own facts and merits, but it is helpful to see how there is again a spectrum of sorts as to when a sanction or step should be deployed.

2.2 Purpose of licence reviews: the question of "fault"

A separate general theme arising from the law of reviews is that of fault, and whether there is a form of "strict liability" in operation. Part of the wider context to this is to note that Parliament did specifically remove virtually all references to "knowingly allowing" offences under the Act so that there is certainly a form of vicarious liability in action, and that being the case it is also fair to suggest that the buck stops with the premises licence holder. The existence of *vicarious liability* does not mean that the Act also imposes *strict liability*. In fact, it means the opposite – the actions of the premises licence holder in terms of due diligence are certainly of relevance to the consideration of outcomes in a review context, as would evidence of knowledge or connivance, inaction or disinterest as regards whatever the mischief may be. Legal defences are provided for in relation to some of the criminal offences which are typically centred around due diligence. In addition to that, as we have just been discussing in relation to *Lidl*, the courts do and have recognised that human error can occur notwithstanding "gold standard" due diligence, and that therefore licensing boards should be cognisant of that, for example in *A M Landsburgh (St Andrews) Ltd v Fife Licensing Board*,[14] where a suspension of a licence was overturned:

"In coming to their decision [the licensing board] appear to have ignored or placed little weight on the successful tests or on the training and other measures taken by the Pursuers . . . There are also worrying indications in the decision that the Board seem to exclude the possibility of both human error or possible deliberate misconduct on the part of serving staff."[15]

The concept of fault in licensing review was perhaps first examined in *Nelson*, in which the court said that the Board had erred in law in finding that the grounds of review had been established because there was no act or omission on the part of the licence holder which had compromised the licensing objectives. In that case the court said it was not correct to consider that the licence holder had failed to discharge their responsibility by leaving the premises to be run by the manager because the licence holder had, up until the illegal lock-in which occurred in that case, no evidence or information that the manager would be anything but a responsible manager. The licence holder had not allowed a serious incident to occur.

13 Ibid.
14 [2009] 42 SLLP 23.
15 Ibid.

So, the issue of "fault" was important in the context of the facts of the *Nelson* case which provides some clarity that the licence holder should not automatically be held to account by operation of a form of strict liability because of the actions of another such as an appointed manager, and in my view that logic holds notwithstanding the technical issue over the case itself (see page 356 at footnote 7). A licensing board has various options open to it where the actions or conduct in relation to the premises is by a person who holds a personal licence and where it is clear that the alleged detriment has arisen by the action/inaction of that person, and where it is clear that the alleged detriment has not arisen by the action/inaction of the premises licence holder. In such circumstances steps could be taken in relation to the personal licence.

But even though there is no strict liability per se, it is important to state that the premises licence holder is not somehow entirely protected in a case where another party is at direct fault. There is or should be a proportionate assessment of the fault, as well as the actions, of the premises licence holder and in extreme cases, even if there is no fault at the feet of the licence holder, the most extreme of sanctions may still be lawful. Whilst the complicity or otherwise of the premises licence holder is of import, *Trust Inns* confirms that fault may ultimately be an irrelevancy, in certain circumstances. The sheriff said:

> ". . . even if it could have been argued that the pursuer had timeously taken all practicable steps available to it (which, clearly, the defender concluded was not the case here) it would have been open to the defender to conclude, on the material available to it, that, through no fault of the pursuer, the premises had become blighted by criminal or nuisance behaviour, thereby jeopardising compliance with the licensing objectives, and justifying revocation of the licence . . . That is because the licensing objectives are not fault-based. They seek to protect and promote a wider range of public interests, quite distinct from issues of fault, blame or culpability."[16]

It is not clear from this passage how the reference to a "wider range of public interests" sits with the *Brightcrew*-related jurisprudence concerning whether the licensing objectives are about protecting and promoting "wider public interests". It moves the debate away from the fact that the objectives are licensing objectives (and not public interest objectives) to a separate question about whether the responsibility or otherwise of a licence holder can become an irrelevancy in having their licence revoked. This passage suggests, therefore, that even if the licence holder has acted impeccably, the licence could still be revoked because of prevailing features attributable to the premises such as was the case in *Trust Inns* where a culture of drug dealing and drug taking had become "embedded" in the premises. This again can be distinguished from *Lidl*, where the Court of Session thought poorly of the blameless licensee having had their licence suspended in order to send a message to others; but that was not the case in *Trust Inns*.

The *Trust Inns* approach, applied proportionately, must be correct, otherwise the most extreme sanctions available to the licensing board would never be available where a premises licence holder is not the one operating the business. However, even *Trust Inns* does not impose strict liability, otherwise what would be the point in the hearing at all? The sanctions are not laid out so as to apply to certain occurences, such as "five days' suspension for under-age sales,

16 [2014] ScotSC 15.

to retrain staff". To put it another way, there is no reality in which unassailable, gold-plated compliance exists. That ignores the basic truth of the human condition. Mistakes can be made. But there is a stark difference between an operator who does so knowingly or glibly without recourse to the law or the detriment it may bring, compared with the operator with an incredibly robust management and system who takes their duties very seriously.

The key is that the board must not discount the complicity or culpability of the premises licence holder; neither should they ignore the endeavours to prevent and respond to whatever the mischief has been by the licence holder. In certain extreme cases, like *Trust Inns*, the ultimate sanction might still be the right sanction *despite* the best intentions and actions of the premises licence holder. It would be open in such circumstances to not make a finding that the licence holder was not fit and proper, having acknowledged that the premises licence holder could do no more, but, for the purposes of the licensing objectives, to find the licence still required to be varied, suspended or revoked.

If, however, a licensing board discounted the positive actions of the premises licence holder in a different type of case where there was no prevailing damage to the objectives, which was almost insurmountable, that might lead the board down the path of error.

3 THE GROUNDS FOR REVIEW

"Any person" may apply for a premises licence review, on one of the following grounds:

- that, having regard to the licensing objectives, the licence holder is not a fit and proper person to be the holder of a premises licence;[17]
- that one or more of the conditions to which the premises licence is subject has been breached;[18] or
- any other ground in relation to the licensing objectives.[19]

The application for review must specify the alleged ground of review; in the case of a breach of condition(s), which condition(s) have been breached; and in the case of the licensing objectives, which objective the ground relates to. These requirements are sometimes treated with a modest amount of flexibility where the review proposal is made by someone who is not familiar with the specific form of wording used in the licensing objectives or is unaware of the exact text of a mandatory condition. It does seem odd or perhaps unfair that a member of the public, who may wish to complain about the conduct of premises by calling for a review, would have to be familiar with section 36(3) and (5), and matters such as specific conditions and licensing objectives, in order for the application for review to be competent.

In addition to specifying the ground of review, section 36(5A) allows the review proposer to include "any information that the applicant considers may

17 The 2005 Act concept of what is meant by "fit and proper" is discussed in detail in Chapter 10 at Section 3.1.
18 The conditions to which a premises licence is subject are explored in Chapter 15.
19 The 2005 Act concept of what is meant by the "licensing objectives" is discussed in Chapter 3.

be relevant to consideration by the Licensing Board of the alleged ground for review" in relation not just to the premises licence holder, but also connected persons and interested parties (on which, see Chapter 7, Section 3.1.1).

In some cases, licensing boards have gone to the trouble of providing pro-forma documents in order to allow the review proposer to "tick a box" to indicate which objective is relevant. Additional materials have been made available online by alcohol health charities. I have encountered a number of cases where clerks have taken the decision to treat generic complaints about licensed premises as review requests notwithstanding the absence of any specific reference to the Act, licensing objectives or licence conditions. Where a generic complaint has been received of this type of unspecified nature, it may be appropriate to ask the LSO to contact the complainant in the first instance.

The review proposal will of course be brought before a hearing of the licensing board (see Section 4 below). If the licensing board finds that the grounds of review are not established, then the matter ends there. This is important because it requires the licensing board to make a discrete decision as to whether the grounds are established before making any decision as to what steps it may have to take. Yet, how and when the board makes this decision varies from board to board. In some areas, a decision will be taken on the grounds, before then inviting further comment from the parties as to what the next steps should be. In some cases, the licensing board will hear everything up front, go away to debate the matter in private, and then come back to announce that the grounds are established, and if they are, immediately announcing what steps they wish to take.

Which approach is to be preferred is perhaps up for debate, but certainly a board that does not actively and clearly make a decision as to whether the grounds have been established, would err in law. The precise order of how a board reaches these outcomes is not prescribed, but it is clear that there must be a distinct and separate decision as to whether the grounds are established, and the parties must be given the opportunity to address the board, on that specific point.

For example, if a licensing board makes a "double announcement" of finding that the grounds of review are established, and then announces the steps they are going to take, where the licence holder has been given no opportunity to address the board on the steps, that in my view that would (barring the point I make below about the "fit and proper" ground) constitute a breach of natural justice. My own view is to prefer the practice of having a separate series of submissions as to what the appropriate steps are, the grounds of review having been established. It may well be that my position is that the grounds should not be established, and therefore I do not wish to have to make submissions on steps and sanctions until I know if the board is with me or not.

Secondly, having to make submissions on steps and sanctions as part of a single global submission can lead to the impression that there is some concession on the part of the licence holder that the grounds should be established. One might find oneself acting in a most solemn case, perhaps involving a death, where for various reasons the grounds are not established and therefore it is not appropriate to debate the steps until that primary decision has been made. It is a matter for the applicant or agent to make sure that they reserve their position to make further submissions depending on how the licensing board deals with business.

However, the matter is a touch more complicated if the fit and proper ground of review is established, as upon establishing this ground it is mandatory under section 39(2A) to revoke the licence; so the licence holder or their agent can have no submissions to make as to sanctions or steps. In these circumstances, then, where the fitness ground is invoked or in play, it may be necessary to have a fuller submission to take into account the wider steps which are available to a licensing board.

A licensing board can decide that one of the grounds has been established even if that was not the ground which had been referred to in the original review proposal. There is no prescription in the Act which "ties" the licensing board into only being able to examine the ground which is relied upon, and in fact the Act makes provision for the opposite. Section 38(6)(b) states that a board can:

> "take into account any information relevant to any ground for review even though it is not relevant to any circumstances alleged in the review proposal or application under consideration".

And, at section 39(1), it is stated that a board can take steps having established a ground:

> "whether or not on the basis of any circumstances alleged in the premises licence review proposal or application considered at the hearing".

So, for example, if a review applicant suggests that the licence holder is not fit and proper but does not rely on any of the other grounds, the licensing board can still choose to not find that the "fit and proper" ground applies but that perhaps the licensing objectives ground does apply, and take steps accordingly. Or, for example, a board might receive a review proposal from a resident based purely on a single breach of a condition of the licence but during the review process other information comes to light, perhaps from the LSO or during the hearing, that indicates that the licence holder has not just breached one condition, but many. In such a case, the board can rely on the "fit and proper" ground even though it was not proposed in the original review proposal, as it is entitled to consider material before it other than that presented in the original review proposal, and the additional material may for example demonstrate a cumulative impact of incidents or events which means it is necessary to deploy the fit and proper ground.[20]

In other words, a licensing board is entitled to find that one or any of the grounds of review are established based on the material before it. There is a particular passage in *Melville v City of Glasgow Licensing Board*[21] which, whilst long, is instructive in this context and so is repeated in full:

> "The position advanced by the pursuer's agent was unashamedly stark. He argued that, faced with a dispute on a material factual issue, a Licensing Board could never properly prefer one version over the other, unless evidence was heard from witnesses; and, therefore, it followed, if evidence was not heard from witnesses, a Licensing Board could never properly be satisfied that the ground for review was established . . . I am not persuaded that the pursuer's agent's submission is

20 On the consideration of cumulative incidents, see *McKay v Banff and Buchan Western Division Licensing Board* 1991 SLT 20.

21 [2012] ScotSC 77.

> correct as stated. The logical consequence of the pursuer's submission would be that Licensing Boards would routinely find themselves disabled from reaching a decision on a review application by virtue merely of a denial of the applicant's material factual allegations, unless the Board then exercises its discretion to hear evidence to resolve the conflict. Although the present case turned on the issue of onus, it seems to me that there may well be other cases where, depending upon the circumstances, notwithstanding the emergence of a dispute upon a material issue of fact, that dispute may well be capable of being resolved by a Licensing Board, without the necessity of hearing evidence from witnesses. To explain, a Licensing Board is entitled to reach a decision on a review application on the basis of the material before it. In this context, such material means all information (which may include documents, or submissions or objections, written or oral . . . which tends logically to show the existence or non-existence of facts relevant to the issue to be determined. The Board can take account of any material which, as a matter of reason, has some 'probative value' in the sense so described. In other words, the Board must not spin a coin, or consult an astrologer, or proceed on a whim, prejudice, or assumption. If the material is capable of having any probative value, the weight to be attached to it is a matter for the Licensing Board as decision-maker. The mere fact that material is disputed, or that the Board is faced with conflicting versions of events, does not necessarily disable the Board from reaching a decision to find the grounds for review established. Rather, if there is a dispute between the parties on a material issue of fact, and rebuttal material is presented, the value to be attached to those conflicting pieces of material remains a matter for the Board to assess, as the decision-maker."[22]

It is of interest to consider what may happen where the material before the board includes material which did not form part of the original review application or associated paperwork which has been served on parties in advance. For example, if the review proposer, during the course of the hearing, seeks to make new submissions about materials and allegations which did not form part of the original review proposal, then it might be said that the licensing board should intervene and make it clear that such "new" material should not be led before them, as fair notice has not been given. It is extremely common for licensing boards to issue "guidance" from the bench when party objectors such as residents are in attendance and warn them not to stray from the terms of their objection or indeed review application.

On the other hand, if the new material being offered by the review proposer is in order to rebut submissions made by the licence holder, then there should be some leeway. This was the case in *Coyle v Glasgow City Council*,[23] a House in Multiple Occupation (HMO) licence appeal, where "new" material introduced by the police in objecting to the renewal of the licence was held not to breach natural justice on the basis that the material was offered in response to submissions made by the agent for Mr Coyle. *Coyle* should not be viewed, however, as *carte blanche* to introduce any new material simply because the licence holder has made submissions, but new material which would, for example, directly contradict a point being made. It is then a matter for the licensing board to place such weight on that "new" material as it thinks appropriate.

This links to the reliance on "local knowledge" by the members of the board,

22 Ibid paras 95–100.
23 [2012] CSIH 33.

who may wish to raise "new material" themselves in terms of any awareness they may have of a particular issue, during the course of a hearing.[24]

Not all review proposals may make it to a hearing at all. In a similar fashion to the provisions for objections and representations, the board has the power to reject an application to review a premises licence if it thinks the application is frivolous or vexatious, but also if it does not disclose any matter relevant to any ground for review. If the board rejects an application for a review, it must give notice of this decision, with reasons, to the person seeking the review.[25]

Where, for example, a resident calls for a review hearing with a complaint that does not relate to a licensing matter, a board might reject the proposal and perhaps the resident would be advised in the notice that the complaint is not a matter for the board but should be taken up with an alternate regulatory body.

4 DETERMINATION OF A REVIEW PROPOSAL

If the board makes a review proposal, or has received an application for review that it has accepted, it must hold a hearing in order to discuss the terms of the review and make determinations as required, within 42 days of the receipt or date of the proposal.[26] If a review hearing is to be held, the licensing board must give notice to the applicant and the licence holder with at least 7 days' notice, as well as the appropriate LSO (see below on the role of LSOs in review hearings).

The requirement to hold the review hearing within 42 days means that these hearings are not always held within the agenda of a "typical" licensing board meeting where applications such as new licences and variations may be dealt with. It may be that a review proposal will be heard at the end of the agenda of a pre-scheduled hearing, but if there is no hearing then a special hearing may have to be set. There is nothing in the Act which prevents a review hearing from being continued and heard substantively outside the 42-day window, on the basis that there has been a first calling of the case within the 42 days – the exact requirement being that a hearing is "held", not "determined". This scenario may arise where, for example, an agent has been given very short notice and asks the licensing board to delay the case for a month in order to properly prepare.[27]

What of a review which is assigned to a hearing, but does not go ahead on the day, perhaps because the board is inquorate? One can certainly argue that

24 The principle of "local knowledge" as a licensing construct is examined in detail in Chapter 10 at Section 3.4.3.

25 2005 Act, s 36(7)(a). The board may also recover expenses from persons submitting frivolous or vexatious applications for review: see s 36(7)(b).

26 Licensing (Procedure) (Scotland) Regulations 2007 (SSI 2007/453), reg 13(2)(b).

27 A decision to take one of the "39 steps" (i.e., a decision under the 2005 Act, s 39) with the licence holder in absentia might be subject to challenge where efforts to contact the licence holder have been relaxed. In *Lanvend Ltd v Cunninghame District Licensing Board*, Kilmarnock Sheriff Court, 10 August 1987, unreported, the court held "due notice" had not been given (as required under the 1976 Act) where a closure order was approved knowing that the citation had gone to the wrong address. In *Dolan v City of Glasgow District Council* [1990] SCLR 553 the court held that the board had met the obligation to "notify" through recorded delivery letters even though these had been returned.

the 42-day rule is a mandatory requirement, otherwise what is the point in the provision? It is not guidance. It is an essential step in the proceedings of a statutory process and there is no dispensation provision. Section 135 affords a board the power to relieve procedural failings by parties before the board, but not by the board itself. There is also some wider case law on this point, emanating from the darkest recesses of tax law, in *Petch v Gurney (HM Inspector of Taxes); Gurney (HM Inspector of Taxes) v Petch*.[28]

The relevant paragraph is:

> "Where statute requires an act to be done in a particular manner, it may be possible to regard the requirement that the act be done as mandatory but the requirement that it be done in a particular manner as merely directory. In such a case the statutory requirement can be treated as substantially complied with if the act is done in a manner which is not less satisfactory having regard to the purpose of the legislature in imposing the requirement. But that is not the case with a stipulation as to time. If the only time limit which is prescribed is not obligatory, there is no time limit at all. Doing an act late is not the equivalent of doing it in time. That is why Grove J said in *Barker v Palmer* (1881) 8 QBD 9 at p. 10: '. . . provisions with respect to time are always obligatory, unless a power of extending the time is given to the Court . . .' This probably cannot be laid down as a universal rule, but in my judgment it must be the normal one. Unless the court is given a power to extend the time, or some other and final mandatory time limit can be spelled out of the statute, a time limit cannot be relaxed without being dispensed with altogether; and it cannot be dispensed with altogether unless the substantive requirement itself can be dispensed with."

The Inner House of the Court of Session in Edinburgh was persuaded by this in the case of *WY v Law Society of Scotland*;[29] and in that holiest of holies, a gambling law appeal, *Freddie Williams Bookmakers v East Ayrshire Licensing Board*[30] the general requirement that deadlines must be met was underlined, in this case that an appeal had to be lodged within the prescribed timeframe (here being 21 days). We await a judicial examination of all of this as regards the 2005 Act.

For the purposes of the review hearing, the board may request further information from any person and in any manner as the board thinks fit and take this information into account.[31] This is, however, merely a request and there is no legal authority to compel the production of information. The board may think poorly of any active rebuttal to provide information, however there may well be lawful or legitimate reasons for the withholding of information, such as where the information might relate to a matter which is *sub judice* and the party decides not to provide information on the advice of a solicitor. The board may also request attendance at the hearing of any person in order to provide information and production of documentation. The board may request such attendance, but again has no force of law to compel it. If the request is made to a personal licence holder to attend, where no separate request has been made concerning a potential review into the personal licence, the purpose of that may be to speak to an incident or give witness to a version of events and may be of real consequence to that personal licence holder. It should always be borne in mind that the personal licence holder might thereafter be cited to

28 [1994] BTC 274. My thanks to Scott Blair for directing me to this gem.
29 2009 SC 430.
30 [2012] CSIH 89.
31 2005 Act, s 38(6).

a review of their own, and so any party, but especially a licence holder, should take legal advice before appearing in this context.

4.1 The board's powers on review

The board has wide powers at a premises licence review hearing. It should be noted first that where there is a finding that the premises licence holder is not a fit and proper person the board *must* revoke the licence. During the Air Weapons and Licensing Bill Stage 2 debate, Michael Matheson MSP, the then Minister for Justice said:

> "The bill provides for immediate revocation of a premises licence on the grounds that, having regard to the licensing objectives, the licence holder is not a fit-and-proper person to be the holder of a premises licence. However, concerns have been raised that without alternative disposals available to it, the board might be reluctant to find that a person is not fit and proper to hold a premises licence. I remain of the view that revocation is the correct option when a person is deemed not to be fit and proper to hold a premises licence."

This provides the blunt policy background as to why Parliament decided that a finding of unfitness must lead to revocation, although there are a number of possible responses to this outcome, noted at Section 7.2 below. In all other cases, however, if the licensing board is satisfied that a ground for review has been established, it *may* take any of the steps noted below "for the purposes of any of the licensing objectives", but in doing so note that a board must look at the objectives individually and provide an explanation as to how any or each of the objectives has been breached: that is, they must identify the nexus between the "failures" and which of the objectives is engaged. The emphasis of the word *may* is of some import – it is entirely competent for a board to find that the grounds for review are established, but take no action.

The steps are provided for under section 39 of the Act and I am therefore emboldened to playfully refer to them as the "39 steps". Not all the steps are mutually exclusive and it is open to a licensing board to impose one or more of them, save of course where the licence is to be revoked as there would be little point in imposing one of the lesser steps.

4.1.1 Powers on review: issue a written warning

This is the lowest of the sanctions other than where no action is proposed, notwithstanding the grounds have been established. A written warning is exactly that, a formal letter issuing a warning as to future conduct. The format of the warning letter is not prescribed so it is a matter for the licensing board to decide how detailed this letter needs to be. Noting the separate provisions to issue a "notice" (see below), which will confirm the outcome of the review in basic terms, and noting that the written warning is not a full statement of reasons, I would suggest that most examples are relatively short, but will at least identify the conduct which led to the grounds being established and the action/inaction which created concern. It should be noted that there is no specific "totting up" process as regards the issue of written warnings, which can be contrasted to the system of endorsements applicable to personal licences, although of course any series of reviews relating to the same set of premises which have resulted in multiple warning letters might eventually lead a board to consider a more severe sanction.

4.1.2 Powers on review: make a variation of the licence

This is perhaps the most interesting of possible outcomes as it could be used to change virtually any aspect of the licence save the identity of the licence holder and the licence reference number. A variation could change the general description, it could remove the designated premises manager, it could remove the ability to conduct certain activities such as live and recorded music, it could restrict the hours of operation or prevent children and young persons from entering the premises. The variation might also relate to the layout plan: for example, the variation could de-license an outdoor area. In addition, the Act also allows the board to impose any such variation permanently, or on a time-limited basis.[32] Variation also includes the ability to impose new local conditions.

4.1.3 Powers on review: suspend the licence

If the board decides to make an order for suspension, this can be for such period as it may determine. The immediacy of a suspension is an issue which has been considered by the courts. In *Nelson*, Sheriff Pender criticised the Board for making the suspension take immediate effect as this robbed the licence holder of the opportunity to seek an interim recall without suffering the consequences of the suspension and described this as "draconian" in circumstances where it may take four or five days to get an application for interim recall heard, and in doing so followed the judgment in *Tesco Stores Ltd v Midlothian Licensing Board*.[33] In that case, an immediate 48-hour suspension was imposed at a hearing on 15 December 2011. This was recalled on an interim basis and the full appeal subsequently upheld. Sheriff Principal Stephen said:

> "It is indeed difficult to see how a short period of suspension would prevent a recurrence other than for that very short period. Accordingly, it is difficult to see how a short period of suspension would prevent a recurrence. A short period of suspension will undoubtedly be a penalty for the pursuers. They are involved in a significant number of alcohol transactions on a daily and weekly basis. The loss of trading in alcohol over the weekend prior to Christmas would enhance the penalty. It would also inconvenience and in effect penalise the customers of the pursuers who would be denied an opportunity of buying all their requirements in respect of both food and alcohol on the same premises. The steps available to any Licensing Board in terms of section 39 of the Act do not include the power to impose a financial penalty however the suspension of a premises licence would clearly restrict the ability of the pursuers to trade over the period of the suspension. This would, in effect, be a significant financial penalty."

Interestingly, the idea of allowing boards the ability to impose fines was actually debated during the Nicholson committee researches, but discounted. Nicholson said:

32 2005 Act, s 39(3).
33 2012 ScotSC 48.

> "Some of our consultees proposed that in future licensing boards should be empowered to impose financial penalties – in effect fines – on errant licensees. However, we do not support that proposal. In the first place, we consider that the imposition of fines is properly a function of a court and not of a body which is largely administrative, and only partly judicial, in character. In the second place, the imposition of fines inevitably gives rise to a problem as to what enforcement procedures should be in place in the event that a fine is not paid. The courts can deal with that problem by the threat, and ultimately the imposition, of imprisonment in default of payment, but we do not consider that that would be appropriate in the case of licensing boards. Accordingly, for the foregoing reasons we reject the suggestion that licensing boards should be empowered to impose purely financial penalties."[34]

The effect of a suspension is a matter which has caused the writer some concern. There can be no doubt that the purpose of the suspension provision is to provide that, during the period of suspension, the licence has no force and cannot be relied upon, albeit we do know it can still be subject to any of the typical application processes such as transfer or variation. But does the suspension relate to the sale of alcohol only, or suspension of all other activities which may occur under the terms of the licence?

For example, if a hotel has its licence suspended, does this mean it cannot provide accommodation or serve its guests breakfast, with recorded music gently straining in the background? Unlike the 1976 Act, the 2005 Act is silent as to the exact effect of the suspension, albeit it is implicit. Under the 1976 Act, a period of suspension meant only that alcohol sales had to cease – but the 1976 Act did not control the wider activities in the way the 2005 Act does.[35]

Take the *Tesco* case mentioned above. When that licence was suspended just prior to Christmas, there is no question that, whilst the alcohol sales ceased until the interim recall was granted, the general retail operation continued. That general retail operation would be a feature of the operating plan. There are no doubt many other real-life examples where supermarkets or convenience stores have continued to trade in general retail whilst the licence was suspended.[36]

Whilst it is clear that Parliament certainly envisaged that alcohol sales should cease during a period of suspension, it also seems to me that the status of the cessation exists in a different ethereal state to that of, for example, the cessation of alcohol sales which operates when the 6-week deadline for a change of manager has passed, where the Act does provide that the effect there is that "alcohol is not to be sold on the premises".[37] Similarly, we also know that activities other than the sale of alcohol may not occur unless they are featured in the operating plan, meaning that the licence does have import to the occurrence of the activities, otherwise there would be no point in the

34 Nicholson Report, para 7.11, p 100.

35 1976 Act, s 31(7).

36 It might be argued that suspension means only suspension of alcohol sales, on the basis (1) that one should have regard to the *Brightcrew* dictum about the "essential remit" of the board being about the regulation of alcohol, and, possibly, (2) that the variation power under s 39 can in some sense "suspend" the provision of an activity on a time-limited basis and therefore the suspension step should be read as only pertaining to alcohol sales.

37 2005 Act, Sch 3 para 4(1)(a).

mandatory condition at Schedule 3 paragraph 3. It might be said that the mandatory conditions do not apply when a licence is suspended but that is by operation of the absence of alcohol sales occurring or by operation of law – for example, it cannot be argued that the annual fee is not payable if the period of suspension happens to catch 1 October when it falls due. This is made clear by the Licensing (Fees) (Scotland) Regulations 2007[38], which confirm that an annual fee is due even where a premises licence is suspended, but in doing so appears to separate the "status" of a licence under suspension from the wider provisions of "ceasing to have effect", just in the same way that section 28(4) is carved out from the events under section 28(5).

This therefore creates a dilemma. If the licence were revoked, then in our hotel example the premises could simply operate as an unlicensed hotel and could provide accommodation, meals and activities and so on, as the licensing laws would no longer apply. In our supermarket example it would simply trade as an unlicensed supermarket. If one accepts a licence under suspension has phantasmic properties, it may be possible to posit that other activities narrated on the licence should cease. But perhaps that would be a shibboleth, in light of recent jurisprudence on the essential function of the licensing board being the regulation of the sale and supply of alcohol.

A solution, if one chooses to accept it, would appear to be in the definition of "premises licence" in section 17, where the suspension means there is *pro tem* no licence *authorising the sale of alcohol*, and the other activities are unaffected – although there may be implications for permissions under other enactments such as gaming permissions or civic licences.

4.1.4 Powers on review: revoke the licence

The revocation of a licence means the licence is kaput. It is dead. It has ceased to exist. It is an ex-licence. There are particular provisions which apply where the revocation occurs as a mandatory step following a finding under the "fit and proper" ground (see below) that allow the licence to be brought back to life, but those remedies only exist because the effect of the revocation has been stayed by 28 days. In a case where the revocation arises from a finding in relation to one of the other grounds of review, *viz* a breach of conditions or the licence objectives, then that revocation is imminent and final (albeit the decision can be subject to an interim recall and full appeal: see below and Chapter 20).[39]

4.1.5 Powers on review: take no action

Although this is not specifically mentioned as a power, the presence of the word "may" indicates that the imposition of one or some of "39 steps" is not mandatory once the grounds of review are established. In other words, it is open to a licensing board to find that the grounds of review are established, but then take no action. It is worth reminding ourselves that one of the aims of the Act was that:

38 SSI 2007/553.

39 The first ever revocation of a premises licence under the 2005 Act is thought to have been by the East Dunbartonshire Licensing Board in December 2009 for a premises known as "Liquor Store" in Kirkintilloch: see "Boards get tough as sanctions bite" [2009] 43 SLLP 14.

> "it would require Boards to follow procedures which should give licence holders the opportunity to remedy an emerging problem before suspension or revocation became an option".[40]

For example, it might be that a review proposal has been brought forward with no attempt to resolve the problem prior to this, and it may be that the premises licence holder is not even aware that there is a problem to fix. It may also be that, factually, a ground of review has been established, but that the issue has been dealt with satisfactorily or is of such minor consequence that the board feels no action is necessary. It could be that the board takes no action but gives an informal steer "from the bench" to take certain actions such as asking parties to meet and liaise over an issue, or ask that the LSO monitors the situation and brings the matter back to a review hearing if necessary.

In relation to any of the powers of review, it should be noted that the general law in relation causality, connectedness, and probative evidence which I discuss in detail in relation to grounds of refusal of a premises licence[41] also apply here. The *Lidl* case is of some merit in reminding boards to base their decisions on evidence, and on evidence which is referable to the set of premises subject to the review proposal:

> "insofar as the Chief Constable had informed the respondents of concerns respecting the prevalence of under-age drinking in the locality, there was nothing offered to show, or even to suggest, that the appellant's shop premises had been the source of supply to the under-age drinkers in question".

The issue of evidence also comes through very plainly in the decision in *Ask Entertainment Pub Ltd and Ask Entertainment Nightclubs Ltd v Aberdeen Licensing Board*,[42] which of course arises from a revocation of the licence(s) involved following a review hearing, and reminds us very plainly that a board must carry out its own independent assessment of the evidence placed before it, attaching such weight to that evidence as it thinks appropriate, and in doing so must forge a nexus between the conduct complained of and the licensing objectives. Similar breadcrumbs are laid down for us to pick up in *Melville v City of Glasgow Licensing Board*[43] as regards conflicting or disputed evidence, with a clear message that reasoning must be provided as to why one version of events is preferred over another:

> "The fatal flaw in the Statement of Reasons is that the Statement gives no insight whatsoever into why the information provided by the Chief Constable was preferred. The Statement offers no explanation of, or discussion upon, the nature or quality or merits of the conflicting evidence presented to the defender. The Statement offers no comment upon the source, form, content or substance, or credibility or reliability, of the conflicting material presented to it. In particular, the Statement sheds no light on why the police evidence was preferred to the pursuer's evidence. The result is that an informed reader is left in real and substantial doubt as to why the defender chose to accept the police evidence over the pursuer's evidence. Absent any such explanation, an informed reader might assume that the defender had simply flipped a coin. No doubt, that would be an incorrect assumption in this case. But no better explanation is offered. It is precisely to avoid opaque, arbitrary or irrational

40 Licensing (Scotland) Bill, Regulatory Impact Assessment, para 103, p 30.
41 On which see Chapter 10 at Sections 3.1, 3.1.3 and 3.2 (for example).
42 [2013] ScotSC 9. I discuss this case in Chapter 10 at Section 3.1.5.
43 [2012] ScotSC 77.

decision-making (or the appearance of such) that adequate reasons are required – to explain what was decided, and how and why."[44]

Finally, it should be noted that it is possible for a licensing board to impose a step but delay the effect of this for some reason. It could be that the licence holder specifically asks the board to start a suspension or revocation from a date sometime after the hearing, and that could be to allow the licence holder to take legal advice with a view to pursuing an interim recall. It could be that the delay is for some other operational reason or where the immediacy of the step might be, in the eyes of the licence holder, disproportionate, or having an effect beyond the "future proofing". This, of course, was precisely the position in *Tesco Stores Ltd v Midlothian Licensing Board*, discussed above in relation to the power of suspension, where the immediacy of a suspension was criticised by the Sheriff Principal for coming immediately prior to the Christmas season, and would therefore have the greatest deleterious financial impact, and because it may have prevented the licence holder from seeking an immediate legal recourse.

Any delay to the effect of one of the "39 steps" is a matter for the licensing board to decide on a case-by-case basis, save where there is a revocation on the grounds of the fit and proper test, as that decision is automatically "stayed" for 28 days (see Section 7.2 below).

5 REVIEW PROPOSALS AND THE ROLE OF LICENSING STANDARDS OFFICERS

Licensing Standards Officers are generally involved in the review process in one of two ways: (1) where some other party has called for the review, and the LSO is asked to comment and offer views; or (2) where the LSO is the proposer of the premises licence review.

5.1 LSOs and involvement with third-party review proposals

The LSO is given notice of any third-party review proposal by the licensing board, under section 38(3)(b)(ii). The LSO must then prepare a report on their view of the circumstances, and the board must take this report into account at the hearing under section 38(4)(b). What weight the board members give to the report is a matter for them. The LSO's report will, of course, be based on information gleaned prior to the hearing and it may well be the case that the report divulges information in relation to how the problem has arisen, and what steps the licence holder has taken to remedy the situation, or it may indicate that the problems raised by the person seeking the review are not substantiated as far as the LSO interaction with the premises is concerned, such as where there are allegations of breaches of conditions, but the LSO has found this not to be the case during visits.

The LSO report may also have little to say about the review, if anything. It may be that the review is based on an issue that is a police matter, for example, and therefore it is not for the LSO to "step into the shoes" of the police or any

44 Ibid paras 72–5.

other proposer of a review. In some areas the board relies very heavily on the view of the LSO, asking for personal opinions to be put forward. This could be just as much in favour of the licence holder (for example, where the LSO may state that they believe them to be a responsible operator), as it could be negative towards the licence holder. In either event, a loud note of caution should be heralded. Offering testimony of this nature at a licensing hearing is best reserved to what the LSO sees is the factual position, as opposed to personal opinion or value judgement. It is not the role of the LSO to take one side or another and reporting should instead be kept within the bounds of offering a factual status as to their involvement, if any. It may be that the report says nothing at all other than to confirm the dates of any recent compliance visit and what the results of that were.

There is no specific provision under the Act that requires the LSO report to be served on either the review proposer or the licence holder. However, natural justice would suggest that the report should be circulated to the parties, otherwise they are not in possession of the same information that is before the licensing board and certainly cannot be expected to answer to any information which they have not seen. In the unsuccessful appeal to the Court of Session in *Trust Inns Ltd v City of Glasgow Licensing Board*,[45] the issue of an absent LSO report was examined. It was suggested that the board had erred in law by not having regard to a report from the LSO, nor serving a copy of it on the licence holder. The court had this to say:

> "While the 2005 Act makes no explicit provision for the disclosure of the LSO report to the premises licence holder, nevertheless, in compliance with principles of natural justice, the content of the report would require to be divulged to the premises licence holder, if requested. However, in the present case, neither the pursuer nor its agent requested disclosure (by the LSO or by the Board) of the content of the LSO report. The pursuer (in this case represented by an experienced solicitor) knew or ought to have known that the LSO was obliged, under statute, to submit a report on the review application; that such a report would, in all likelihood, have been submitted; and that the LSO was present at the reviewing hearing. It is artificial to suggest (as was stated by the pursuer's counsel) that, in some sense, the report was withheld from the pursuer. The content of the LSO report was freely available to the pursuer and its agents, if they had requested it. They did not avail themselves of that opportunity. Accordingly, no breach of principles of natural justice arises in the present case. In any event, given the neutral and uninformative terms of the LSO report, if there had been such a breach, it would, in my judgment, have been technical at best, with no material bearing upon the outcome of the defender's deliberations."[46]

Whilst it seems to me that section 38 should ideally import a duty on the board to serve a copy of any report or material produced in relation to the licence review which it may take into account at the hearing on the licence holder (just as under section 22 the board is required to serve copy objections on a licence applicant), *Trust Inns* suggests that the onus on obtaining any LSO report in the context of a review hearing lies at the feet of the licence holder, or at least it does so when that person is represented by an experienced licensing solicitor. Therefore, where instructed on a review hearing, as a matter of good practice an agent should write to the licensing board asking for a copy of any related

45 [2015] CSIH 5.
46 Ibid at para 12.

papers, including the LSO report, as soon as possible. On the other hand, it might be argued that it is also a matter of professional courtesy for an LSO to ensure that a copy of their report is emailed, where they are aware of any agent being appointed.

5.2 LSOs as the review proposer

The LSO role in a third-party review is very much as a neutral observer, who may offer certain facts as they see them and may indeed offer no view at all as to the details of the review proposal. That approach is not the case, of course, where LSOs are themselves review proposers. If we think back to the three key grounds of review, these relate to the fit and proper test, breach of conditions, and the licensing objectives. There is a special rule where the review is to be brought by an LSO, and relates to a breach of conditions: he or she should only do so where other opportunities to remedy the breach have failed. Nicholson said:

> "it should be borne in mind that, if our earlier recommendations in this chapter relative to Liquor Licensing Standards Officers are accepted, many transgressions by a licensee will not come to the notice of a licensing board until after informal attempts to secure compliance have been tried and failed. Accordingly, it is to be assumed that cases brought before a board will often have some sort of background of noncompliance, and for that reason will not be entirely trivial."[47]

The Act provides a statutory framework to allow the licence holder to fall back into compliance and gives the LSO a step to issue a notice, under section 14, in order to raise and ameliorate concerns in this regard. If these processes are not followed, then the review proposal should be challenged in advance or at the hearing. A decision flowing from a review where these earlier steps have not been followed is unlawful as the Act has put this matter beyond doubt at section 36(4):

> "(4) A Licensing Standards Officer may make a premises licence review application on the ground specified in subsection (3)(a) only if—
> (a) in relation to the alleged ground for review, the Officer or any other Licensing Standards Officer has issued to the licence holder a notice under section 14(2)(a)(i), and
> (b) the licence holder has failed to take the action specified in the notice to the satisfaction of the Officer."

It should of course be noted that this special provision only relates to a breach of conditions, and it is therefore competent for the LSO to go straight to review whether the ground of review relates to the fit and proper test or the licensing objectives. In addition, there is no other special provision made for LSOs in relation to review applications, meaning they are simply treated as "any person" for the purposes of the review process, save that where they themselves are the review proposer, section 38(3)(b)(ii) indicates that the requirement to produce a report does not apply. This means that a LSO-driven review proposal should not be treated any differently to a review proposal made by any other party.

47 Nicolson Report, para 7.12, p 101.

6 REVIEW PROPOSALS BY THE LICENSING BOARD

The licensing board has a separate power to call for a review hearing on its own initiative, under section 37. The grounds for review under section 37 are the same as those under section 36. It has been said by mulitple commentators that there may be an inherent human rights issue here, as the board is effectively a party to its own proceedings. There is no equivalent provision under the English 2003 Act. It will be interesting to note whether any challenge to a decision of a board under a review of its own initiative on this ground would meet with success on appeal, but we await such a judgment. There have, however, been some examples of review hearings being abandonded as a result of this issue.

There was one reported hearing from Fife Licensing Board in 2010 in which a review hearing was abandoned by a vote of four to three on this basis. It captured the front page of the *Scottish Licensing Law and Practice* journal under the headline "Human rights submissions halt premises licence review" in which solicitor Tom Johnston said: "It is utterly inconceivable that the same person who called for a review would then be the person making the decision."

In North Ayrshire attempts were made in early 2014 to impose a new policy condition in relation to "breakfast hours" which would impose an 11am commencement hour on a number of premises that enjoyed earlier hours. These attempts were abandoned at the hearing following submissions the author had made on behalf of a client which included reference to the natural justice issue, that the proposal was a disproportionate interference with Article 1 to Protocol 1 of ECHR, and that the proposal was not targeted to specific issues at specific premises but instead was an attempt to apply more restrictive hours to existing licensed premises on a blanket basis.

Whilst these types of "substantive" section 37 review proposals are relatively uncommon, review proposals brought by the licensing board itself for technical matters are common. The most ubiquitous is in relation to the payment of annual fees, or to be precise – the non-payment of annual fees.[48] But it is also used by some licensing boards in circumstances such as to declare that a premises licence has ceased to have effect by operation of the Act and therefore revoke the licence, albeit that I am not sure that the revocation of the licence under the review process has a proper link to the relevant provision under section 28.

The Glasgow board has indicated it will use this power to review the licences of those premises that were granted a 4am licence as part of a pilot project in 2019, in order to either make the 4am permanent or move the premises back to 3am.

7 POST REVIEW HEARING – WHAT NEXT?

There is a reporting provision contained within section 39A of the Act, which requires the licensing board to issue a notice following a review hearing, or, to be more precise, where it decides to take one of the "39 steps", or where

48 For more on non-payment of the annual fee, see Chapter 5 at Section 4, Chapter 7 at Section 2.1.2, and Chapter 15 at Section 4.12.

it decides to take no action (i.e. not take one of the "39 steps"), or where the mandatory revocation step is invoked following a finding that the fit and proper ground for review is established. The notice is a "notice of decision" and, whilst the format is not prescribed, it is typically in the format of a simple letter confirming the outcome and which provisions of the Act were relied upon. The letter will not go into any great level of detail. The notice should be issued to the licence holder and to the party who made the review proposal. If a statement of reasons is requested, it must be given to the licence holder and the party who made the review proposal.[49]

Note that, with the exception of a revocation in relation to the fit and proper test (see below) and unless otherwise directed by the licensing board, a decision made by it at a review hearing will have immediate effect notwithstanding and despite any appeal.[50]

There is provision for the sheriff principal to recall a suspension or revocation order pending determination of the appeal on application by the appellant, and if satisfied "on the balance of convenience" that it is appropriate to do so. The role of this process, known as "interim recall", is discussed in Chapter 20 at Section 6, but it should be noted here that the interim recall is only open in cases of suspension or revocation, and therefore cannot be used where a variation is imposed or a letter of warning issued.

In relation to a licence under suspension, it is worthwhile noting that applications can be made which relate to the licence notwithstanding that the licence does not have effect during the period of suspension.[51] The Act does, as is noted below, make provision for applications such as variations and transfers to try to reverse the impact of one of a suspension or revocation, but it is also competent for a licence holder to make applications as a matter of generality, where the aim is not to reverse the suspension *per se* but perhaps some wider goal or proposal as to how they wish to move the licence or business forward after the period of suspension has been served. For example, the business may be sold, and a transfer application is lodged, or an application to change the designated premises manager might be made during a period of suspension following a review hearing, in anticipation of the premises re-opening under a new manager once the suspension concludes.

One of the interesting developments yet to come from the law of revocation and the fit and proper test is: what, if anything, might or should happen to other licences held by a person who has been declared unfit and had a particular licence revoked? As matters stand, the Act provides no automatic process or indeed any sort of process to deal with this conundrum. If a person holds two licences, and one is revoked on the basis that he is not fit and proper to hold a licence, the other licence is unaffected by that process. This begs the question as to how a person can be unfit to hold one licence and remain fit to hold another.

Further, what should happen to a new licence application made by a party who has been previously declared unfit? Does a separate new application, whether for the same or different premises, allow the applicant to shed that status and be treated anew? Under the 1976 Act, suspension of a licence was

49 2005 Act, s 39A.
50 2005 Act, s 132(7). See Chapter 20 on appeals generally.
51 *Datelock Ltd and another v Bain and another* 1998 SLT 381.

possible following a finding of unfitness, and once the suspension period had been served, it seems accepted that the licence holder "reverted" to being a fit and proper person. But that approach must be seen through the prism of the 1976 process where suspension was and could be viewed as a punishment[52] and therefore the punishment had been served; and such an approach does not sit well with the 2005 Act or its jurisprudence.[53]

Of course, a large number of "multiple" operators in some cases hold hundreds of licences across Scotland, so the idea that a revocation for one premises would impact on the rest seems fanciful. One might argue that the unfitness relates to their ability to hold that particular licence, at that particular set of premises, as opposed to any licence, but that remains to be seen when the wording in the Act says that unfitness relates to "a premises licence" as opposed to "this premises licence" or "the premises licence to which the review proposal relates". It will be interesting to see if a review proposal is ever brought on the basis of a finding of unfitness being imposed in relation to a separate premises, either within the same licensing jurisdiction, or outwith, and what a licensing board might make of that.[54]

7.1 Application to "review" a suspension or variation

If a licence has been varied or suspended following a review hearing, the licence holder may make an application to the board to reverse the variation or lift the suspension. Most unhelpfully, section 40 refers to this proposed reversal process as a "review" of the licensing board's decision, that is, a review of the outcome of the review. There is no prescribed format for this request; however, it is to be assumed the "application" should be in writing and a simple letter of request should suffice. The board may grant such a request if satisfied that the variation or suspension is no longer necessary by reason of "a change of circumstances", and the exact power is that the board may "revoke the suspension or variation". If a board revokes a suspension, the suspension is lifted and no longer has effect. If a board revokes the variation, then that variation no longer has effect and the licence is returned to its state prior to the variation being imposed (for example, if the variation was to reduce the trading hours, then the revocation of that variation would be to restore the original trading hours to the licence).

Whilst the Act makes no special provision for what constitutes the "change of circumstances" under which the section 40 power may be deployed, examples may include a change in the licence holder, or a change in management practices or procedures which have remedied or propose to remedy whatever ailed the board in the first place. There is no provision for how a licensing board should determine the section 40 request, so in practice it is a matter for the licensing board to decide whether it should go to a hearing or be granted under delegated powers.

52 *McKenzie v Renfrew District Licensing Board* 1991 SCLR (Notes) 859.

53 See J C Cummins, *Licensing Law in Scotland* (2nd edn, Butterworths, 2000) p 193 on the 1976 Act approach to this.

54 There is no requirement for a licence holder to notify other licensing boards that a finding of unfitness has been found in a certain area, nor is there any requirement on the board to notify other boards where that licence holder may also hold licences.

7.2 Recall of a "fit and proper" revocation within 28 days

Where a licensing board has found that the "fit and proper" ground of review applies, they must revoke the licence. However, the effect of the revocation is stayed for 28 days during which the licence remains in force.[55] This is a grace period which was inserted by Parliament in response to concerns during the passage of the Air Weapons and Licensing (Scotland) Act 2015 that the immediate revocation was overly draconian. The grace period is to cater for the possibility that an application might be made to either transfer or vary the licence, but these provisions bring forth a number of practical issues.

First, a board must recall the revocation if a transfer of the licence is granted. That, of course, implies that all is well with the transfer application and it is open to the board to refuse that application if a ground of refusal applies. Take the example where the transferee is a "clean skin" or a front for the party who had held the licence which was revoked. The licensing board may or may not be aware that the application for transfer is a fiction and the controller of the licence remains the same. That would be a matter for the police to comment on as part of the transfer application. Interestingly, the board may only countenance a recall of a revocation where the application for transfer of the licence has been made under section 33 but not section 34. In other words, only the licence holder may make the application. It is not clear to me from a review of the Parliamentary passage of the Air Weapons and Licensing (Scotland) Act 2015 why this should be restricted to section 33 transfers. One can envisage a case, for example, where upon impending revocation of the licence, or perhaps for unconnected reasons, the licence holder is made insolvent. In such circumstances, the appointed insolvency practitioner would have no recourse as section 33 is not open to them, save a "pragmatic approach" from the clerk. Another scenario might be where a licence is held by a tenant, who has since absconded having landed the premises in sufficient trouble to get the licence revoked. Here, we would have a landlord who has identified a third-party operator who wishes to take the licence on, or perhaps wants to take it on themselves, but cannot, because only the existing licence holder can make an application under section 33, and he or she has disappeared. It might even leave the person whose actions have resulted in the revocation of the licence being in a position to bargain for quantum in return for authorising the section 33 application.

Secondly, a board must recall the revocation if a variation of the licence is granted:

> "that the Board considers would remove the ground on which the licence was revoked under section 39(2A)."

This is a complex provision to unpick. On the basis that the reason for the revocation is the identity of the licence holder, it is difficult to see at first blush how a variation of the licence might remedy the issues, when the licence holder remains the same. Being unaware of any such cases occurring to date, one might speculate that the unfitness could have related to a particular activity occurring on the premises, and perhaps a variation removing that activity would then lead a board to the view that the fitness of the licence holder to

55 2005 Act, s 39(2B).

conduct the remaining activities is of less concern. Perhaps the variation is to run the premises as a completely different offer, such as converting a nightclub to a bistro or restaurant, and the unfitness related to the licence holder's ability to properly manage a late-night premises. A third hypothetical scenario might be the unfitness related to the licence holder's ability to properly safeguard children and young persons on the premises, and the variation is to remove access by under 18s. This is of course speculation, and it remains to be seen whether, in such cases, a board might not have simply varied the licence themselves.

Interestingly, in some of these cases it is curious to consider that the variation application might be a minor variation, which of course cannot be refused and therefore might give a licence holder argument that his revocation should be lifted upon making a minor variation. But, the recall of the revocation is a separate process, so that where the variation does fall to be granted as a minor variation, that does not mean the recall of the revocation would be automatic because there is a discrete question for the board to decide: whether that variation removes the ground on which the licence was revoked. If the board does not take that view, then the variation is for nought because the revocation will crystallise at the 28-day point.

There is provision for the 28 days to be extended where a transfer or variation has been lodged within that 28-day period but has not yet been determined.[56]

8 THE REVIEW "TRAP": APPEAL DEADLINES

Practitioners should be most wary of what has become known as the "review trap", which relates to the timing of appeals following a decision taken in the context of a review hearing. In an appeal arising from a new licence or major variation application, an appeal may be made within 21 days following the issue of the statement of reasons. That is not the case with a decision in a review hearing. The appeal must be lodged within 21 days of the date of that decision, regardless of whether any statement of reasons has been requested or issued. Similarly, one should not be confused with the issue of the decision notice under section 39A and how that may affect any appeal timeline – it doesn't. The appeal deadline runs from the date of the decision, regardless of when the decision notice has been issued or received. For more on this and on appeals, see Chapter 20.

56 2005 Act, s 39B(4)(b).

Chapter 15

Licence Conditions under the Licensing (Scotland) Act 2005

1 OVERVIEW

One of the surprising aspects for those unacquainted with the old 1976 regime is that there was no obvious provision for conditions to be attached to the grant of a licence in the way that we now accept it as the 2005 Act norm. The 1976 Act did provide for conditions to be attached to occasional and regular extensions under section 64 of that Act, occasional licences and children's certificates, but there were no "mandatory conditions" as we understand them now.[1] The four exceptions to this were: conditions introduced through byelaws;[2] a condition restricting the sale of spirits;[3] conditions regarding the sale of alcohol on entertainment licensed premises (in order to ensure that sales were "ancillary" to the entertainment);[4] and conditions regarding health and safety for certain events,[5] which also gave the board power to add its own conditions.[6]

The 2005 Act took a markedly different approach, allowing for a substantial and complex framework for conditions so that now every single premises licence is subject to an array of conditions, some mandatory to all licences in Scotland, and some which may apply to that single set of premises alone.

2 THE GENERAL NATURE OF LICENCE CONDITIONS

Section 27(9) of the Act states conditions are designed to require or prohibit an action in connection with the sale of alcohol or any other activity carried

1 There were some attempts to introduce 2005 Act concepts to 1976 Act licences "ahead of time". In November 2008, the South Ayrshire Licensing Board issued a draft "Code of Conduct" for "Off-sale licences" which contained provisions similar to many mandatory 2005 Act conditions.

2 Perhaps the most famous case concerning conditions attached in this way is *Applegate Inns Ltd v North Lanarkshire Licensing Board* [1997] 6 SLLP 6.

3 1976 Act, s 29.

4 1976 Act, s 101(2).

5 1976 Act, ss 18A, 18B (added by the Licensing (Amendment) (Scotland) Act 1996). This amendment was brought about to try to control "rave" events, popular in the early 1990s, but, after implementation, began to be used as a matter of course for entertainment and public house licences covering premises at which music is played or relayed, and at which persons could engage in dancing. In the main, the s 18 conditions were applied to nightclub premises. See further "Rave rules miss mark?" [1996] 3 SLLP 3.

6 This did not give the board *carte blanche*; the conditions had to be *intra vires* and relate to health and safety matters (see *British Airports Authority v Secretary of State for Scotland* 1979 SC 200 on *vires*; and [1997] 6 SLLP 10 for a commentary on the health and safety conditions envisaged, for a flavour of life under the 1976 Act).

on in the premises. The general nature of a condition is therefore to enforce something to be done in connection with the sale of alcohol or other activities, or to prevent something being done relating to those matters. It should be noted therefore that the Act does allow interference with activities which appear on the operating plan other than the sale of alcohol, notwithstanding the voluminous discussion of the *Brightcrew* "essential remit" elsewhere in the book. Here, there is a clear statement that an activity which is provided for in the licence can be regulated by way of a condition (but see Section **4.1** below in relation to restrictions, as the position is not necessarily irreconcilable). Thinking of the purpose of licence conditions generally brings us back to understanding what a licence is, at its most basic level.

Where the rule of law recognises that a certain activity may be lawful and desirable, but could have deleterious effects, controls can be placed in order to ensure that the provision of that activity is regulated and therefore it is to be accepted that public safety of some hue is a key consideration for the allowance of that activity. What is a licence, if not itself a "condition"? It is a permission to do a thing, within certain bounds. That is also, therefore, what a licence condition is, albeit on a more targeted basis. It is a permission to do a thing, under certain rules or requirements, with regard to whatever the wider public policy might be.

It may also be an imposition to prevent one thing, whilst the other (for our purposes the sale of alcohol) is occurring. Simply put, the wider purpose of a condition is to provide further regulation concerning a particular matter. This is often described as a limitation or imposition of an additional rule which relates to how the licence may be operated. A condition is not necessarily a limitation, and may in fact allow an activity to occur so long as certain requirements are met.

Thinking about the lawful framework on which conditions rest, it is instructive to reflect back to what is a leading Scots law licensing case decision, namely *Stewart v Perth and Kinross Council*.[7] A 1982 Act case concerning a second-hand dealer licence, this auspicious decision is of import as to the wider role of licensing conditions. In short, the decision affirms the general principle of "proper purpose" as regards conditions. In a licensing context, a condition must relate to the purpose of the licensing legislation that Parliament intended. In *Stewart*, it was held that conditions which required information to be given to buyers of second-hand cars, whilst commendable, were unlawful as they were outwith the scope of the 1982 Act. This was perhaps most recently affirmed in the "burger van" case of *McCluskey and others v North Lanarkshire Council*,[8] where an attempted ban on allowing snack vans to be located near primary schools was thwarted because the aim of the ban was focused on allegations concerning the nutritional value of the foods sold from the vans, as well as a desire that the ban would help the local authority achieve targets in relation to separate legislative requirements for school meals. Again, whilst the court held that both nutrition and school meal take-up were desirable matters, these were not matters the 1982 Act was designed to address. There is in fact a substantial swathe of jurisprudence on this wider point, including *Spook*

7 [2004] UKHL 16.
8 [2016] SC HAM 3.

Erection Ltd v City of Edinburgh District Council,[9] *Gerry Cottle's Circus Ltd v City of Edinburgh District Council*[10] and *Dunsmore v Lindsay*.[11] We will examine how the 2005 Act attempts to deal with this, later in this chapter.

The Act provides for four "classes" of condition which can attach to a premises licence under section 27 of the 2005 Act. These are:

- mandatory conditions,
- discretionary conditions,
- local conditions, and
- late night conditions.

We will now look at each of these in turn, in more detail, with the exception of the "discretionary conditions" (sometimes referred to as "pool conditions"), which were envisaged to be drafted by the Scottish Government and "dipped into" by boards as and when they felt it appropriate, but which never formally materialised and may end up being a legislative ghost.

3 MANDATORY CONDITIONS

Section 27(1) provides that the list of conditions specified in Schedule 3 to the 2005 Act shall attach to all premises (save where the condition excludes otherwise: for example some conditions only relate to "off-sales only" licences, and so on). The Explanatory Notes to section 27 say that the mandatory conditions regime was:

> "intended to ensure national consistency on those matters specified in schedule 3".

The Policy Memorandum underscores this, saying:

> "It is crucial that standards in the licensed trade should be maintained at a high level and should not be undermined by an increase in competition under the new system. To ensure consistency of standards and on key issues identified as requiring a national approach, schedule 3 to the Bill sets out those standard licence conditions that would be a mandatory requirement under this Bill."[12]

This reasoning is explored further in the Guidance to the Licensing Boards, which states:

> "Flexibility to deal with local circumstances is a vital component of the new licensing regime. However, local discretion must be balanced with a clear and effective national framework within which Boards must operate. This is reflected in the requirement that all premises licences issued under the Act will be subject to a range of mandatory licence conditions set out in schedule 3 of the Act."[13]

The presence of the mandatory conditions under Schedule 3 to the Act delivers upon that national consistency, or national framework – up to a point, as there can of course be local differences in interpretation of some aspects of these conditions.

9 1995 SLT 107.
10 1990 SLT 235.
11 (1903) 11 SLT 545.
12 Policy Memorandum to the Licensing (Scotland) Bill, para 85, p 19.
13 Guidance to Licensing Boards (April 2007) para 111, p 31.

The conditions under Schedule 3 may be added to by regulation as Scottish Ministers see fit for the purposes of any of the licensing objectives, or to extend the application of an existing condition, so it should be noted that the smorgasbord of mandatory conditions is a moveable feast and, of course, the list of conditions has been added to and amended on a few occasions since 2009. Note that the mandatory conditions may apply to on-sale premises only, off-sale premises only, or to both; and also, that specific classes of premises licence may be exempt from particular conditions.

For ease of reference I have listed all of the mandatory conditions with the relevant paragraph number in this initial list and will discuss each condition in detail later on.

- Alcohol is to be sold on the premises only in accordance with the operating plan contained in the licence (paragraph 2(1)).
- Any other activity to be carried on in the premises is to be carried on only in accordance with the operating plan contained in the licence (paragraph 2(2)).
- Alcohol is not to be sold on the premises at any time when there is no premises manager in respect of the premises, the premises manager does not hold a personal licence, the personal licence held by the premises manager has been suspended, or the licensing qualification held by the manager is not appropriate to the premises (paragraph 4).
- Every sale of alcohol made on the premises must be authorised (whether generally or specifically) by the premises manager or another person who holds a personal licence (paragraph 5).
- Any person who works on the premises (whether paid or unpaid) making sales of alcohol or serving alcohol may not work in such capacity unless he has complied with staff training requirements (paragraph 6); and a record of such training must be kept on the premises (paragraph 6(2A).[14]
- Alcohol must not be sold on the premises at a price below its minimum price (paragraph 6A).[15]
- A package containing two or more alcoholic products (whether of the same or different kinds) may only be sold on the premises at a price equal to or greater than the sum of the prices at which each alcoholic product is for sale on the premises (paragraph 6B).[16]
- Where the price at which any alcohol sold on the premises *for consumption on the premises*[17] is varied, (a) the variation (referred to in this paragraph as "the earlier price variation") may be brought into effect only at the beginning of a period of licensed hours, and (b) no further variation of the price at which that or any other alcohol is sold on the premises *for consumption on the premises*[18] may be brought into effect before the expiry of the period of

14 The additional requirement concerning keeping staff training records on the premises was added by the Licensing (Mandatory Conditions No. 2) (Scotland) Regulations 2007 (SSI 2007/546) reg 2.

15 This modest looking provision was introduced by the Alcohol (Minimum Pricing) (Scotland) Act 2012, s 1(2).

16 This condition was added by virtue of s 2 of the Alcohol etc (Scotland) Act 2010.

17 The italicised text was added by virtue of s 3 of the Alcohol etc (Scotland) Act 2010.

18 Ibid.

72 hours beginning with the coming into effect of the earlier price variation (paragraph 7).

- Where the price at which any alcohol sold on the premises for consumption off the premises is varied, (a) the variation (referred to in this paragraph as "the earlier price variation") may be brought into effect only at the beginning of a period of licensed hours, and (b) no further variation in the price at which that alcohol is sold on the premises may be brought into effect before the expiry of the period of 72 hours beginning with the coming into effect of the earlier price variation (paragraph 7A).
- No irresponsible promotions may be carried on in or in connection with the premises (paragraph 8).
- If the premises licence authorises on-sales, tap water fit for drinking must be provided free of charge and other non-alcoholic drinks must be made available for purchase "at a reasonable price" (paragraph 9).
- There must be an age verification policy in relation to the sale of alcohol on the premises (paragraph 9A).[19]
- The annual fee must be paid (paragraph 10).
- Where alcohol is to be sold for consumption on the premises, a sign of at least A4 size must be displayed so that it is "reasonably visible to customers" and which states either that persons under the age of 18 are not permitted on the premises or, where they are, to which parts of the premises they are allowed access (paragraph 11).[20]
- Baby changing facilities accessible to persons of either gender must be installed in the premises (paragraph 12).
- Where alcohol is for sale solely for consumption off the premises, alcohol may be displayed only in one or both of the following: a single area of the premises agreed by the board and holder of the licence; or a single area of the premises which is inaccessible to the public (paragraph 13). [21]
- Any drinks promotions on the premises may only take place within one of these two areas or a separate tasting room (paragraph 13(1B))[22] and a drinks promotion in connection with the premises may not take place in the vicinity of the premises (paragraph 13(1C)).[23]

4 MANDATORY CONDITIONS: A CLOSER LOOK

Each of the mandatory conditions requires further explanation. Many of them did not exist at the point the Act became an Act. Some of them were added later by regulations, some added by later primary legislation, and some amended by later primary legislation. It is not unreasonable to see why there is criticism of the Scottish Parliament in relation to the clarity of licensing law when one examines the MC Escher-like approach to drafting, volume and transparency of the conditions framework, especially when one remembers

19 This was added by virtue of s 6 of the Alcohol etc (Scotland) Act 2010.

20 Added by the Licensing (Mandatory Conditions) (Scotland) Regulations 2007 (SSI 2007/457) reg 2.

21 This was added by the Licensing (Mandatory Conditions No. 2) (Scotland) Regulations 2007 (SSI 2007/546).

22 This was added by s 5(3) of the Alcohol etc (Scotland) Act 2010.

23 Ibid.

that to breach a condition is a criminal offence which can lead to 6 months' imprisonment. Yet a humble publican or shopkeeper is expected to undertake the studious approach of a legal author, and delve through the various laws, regulations, amendments and so on to reach a true view of what the law states: which is not, of course, the same as understanding what it means either in theory or in practice. I am going to look at all fifteen conditions in turn in an effort to make sense of it all.

4.1 Alcohol is not to be sold unless in accordance with the operating plan (paragraph 2(1))

The operating plan is axiomatic to the legitimate operation of licensed premises in Scotland and is discussed in some detail in Chapter 8 at Section 3 in relation to the application process, and completion of the form. Although often described as if it is a separate document, it is in fact a part of the premises licence itself. The "premises licence" is actually four documents: the premises licence, the operating plan, the licence summary, and the layout plan. The operating plan is a schedule that outlines a variety of ways in which the premises are authorised to trade. It features, for example, the licensed hours, the activities which are permitted, the rules over children and young persons' access, the capacity, the premises manager details, and so on. In relation to this first condition, of course, we are focusing on the sale of alcohol in accordance with the operating plan.

A key part of this relates to the licensed hours. Alcohol cannot be sold outside the hours that appear on the operating plan. These are referred to, on the statutory operating plan itself, as "core" hours, although the terminology of "core hours" does not appear in the Act and is not itself defined. Despite that *lacuna*, it is to be taken that *core* hours simply means *licensed* hours (other hours are available). So, although there is a specific offence of selling alcohol outside licensed hours, it is also suggested that, as the sale was not in accordance with the licence, the separate offence under section 1 of the 2005 Act is in play.

There are other possible ways in which some suggest the consideration under this condition is more than a control over the licensed hours, such as in relation to the location of where the alcohol is sold. For example, if alcohol were to be sold in an area of the premises which is not covered by the licence, it might be said the alcohol was not sold in accordance with the demise of the licence, but I am not convinced that this is the correct approach. The "general description" of the premises, which might outline the physical layout, is not a part of the operating plan; nor is the layout plan which may show unlicensed areas as well as the areas covered by the licence. The offence there would be a straightforward section 1 offence of an unlicensed sale, as opposed to a breach of this condition. There might be specific conditions added to a licence which directly relate to the sale of alcohol, such as that alcohol sales must cease in the beer garden by 10pm; but, again, that is a separate local licence condition and so breach would be a breach of that specific condition.

4.2 Any other activity to be carried on in the premises is to be carried on only in accordance with the operating plan contained in the licence (paragraph 2(2))

Activities in the operating plan are legion, and may be specifically prescribed in the statutory form, or perhaps added on an individual basis by the applicant or licence holder at the time of the original grant of the licence or by subsequent major variation. In each case, the operating plan will confirm whether the activity is permissible, and whether it is permissible both inside and/or outside the licensed hours. In many cases premises may trade outwith the licensed hours by providing activities or selling food or drink other than, of course, alcohol. Examples of this are the provision of general grocery sales in a shop before the off-sale commencement hour of 10am, or a bar or hotel offering breakfasts or teas/coffees, and so on.

The list of prescribed activities is briefly listed here, for ease of reference. Each of these activities is explored in detail in Chapter 8 at Section 3.6 and readers should have regard to those examinations in considering the context of breach of this condition.

- Accommodation
- Conference facilities
- Restaurant facilities
- Bar meals
- Club/group meetings
- Receptions
- Recorded music
- Live performances
- Dance facilities
- Theatre
- Films
- Indoor/outdoor sports
- Gaming
- Adult entertainment.

These, of course, are merely the pre-prescribed activities and in most cases an operating plan will have additional activities specified. The key part is that if one provides an activity not catered for, it is a breach of this condition.

4.3 The premises manager (paragraph 4)

Alcohol is not to be sold on the premises at any time when there is no premises manager in respect of the premises, or the premises manager does not hold a personal licence, or the personal licence held by the premises manager has been suspended, or the licensing qualification held by the manager is not appropriate to the premises. Let us take each of these situations in turn.

First, no alcohol should be sold at any time when there is "no premises manager": remembering that the phrase most used in practice to refer to this person is "designated premises manager" (DPM), what is being struck at here is not the absence of someone who as a matter of employment *but not law* is a manager of the premises (in whatever capacity that might state on his or her employment contract), but instead the provision focuses on the person who is *designated on the premises licence* as the premises manager. A person can be a manager of a premises without being the premises manager.

Secondly, where the manager does not hold a personal licence. This element refers to when a designated premises manager has either surrendered their licence, or had the licence revoked. The review processes for personal licences are discussed in detail in Chapter 17 at Section 5.

Thirdly, where the manager's personal licence has been suspended. This again can only have arisen as a result of a personal licence review hearing and the suspension has been imposed by the licensing board.

Fourthly, and finally, is the probable historical oddity of "appropriate qualifications": the "appropriateness" of a licensing qualification in this context really comes down to whether the personal licence holder sat a course that was specifically for on- or off-sales. He would not have been issued with a personal licence unless the course itself was approved, so a breach of this condition would only arise if the person has, for example, gained a qualification for off-sale premises, and is now working on on-sale premises (or vice versa). However, this was very much overlooked in the early life of the 2005 Act and I am not aware of many instances where a licensing board questioned a personal licence application where the supporting training certificate was for solely on- or off-sales. This would require the board to interrogate the applicant's current or prospective employment, which the application process is not designed to facilitate. And one cannot tell from looking at a personal licence whether the underlying training certificate was for purely on- or off-sales and not both.

I was consulted on a small handful of cases where the police queried persons who had moved from a shop job to working in a pub, where the underlying certificate was for off-sales only, but in the round this type of query was, in my experience, rare indeed, and actually occasioned because of wider issues with the individual.

When the personal licence training was first launched, only ServeWise, the training arm of Alcohol Focus Scotland, offered a separate on- and off-sale course. Most awarding bodies, like BIIAB, conjoined the training into one course so the certificate holder would have no issues working in either on- or off-sale premises. As of 2021, my understanding is that all training providers have now moved to providing a single course which is "appropriate" for both off- and on-sales.

The question in all of these cases is, what effect does the condition have if one of the situations arises? The condition states that "alcohol is not to be sold". In other words, if one of these events transpires, sales of alcohol must cease. This does not mean the premises licence is lost or that it ceases to have effect. It also does not mean that other activities which are authorised on the operating plan must cease: for example, if hotel premises were in one of these situations, this would not prevent the provision of meals, accommodation, or entertainment. It simply prevents the sale of alcohol.

A further emphasis must be explored on the operative word "sold". "Alcohol is not to be sold": that does not mean it cannot be given for free; and it also does not prevent customers bringing their own.[24] It is not uncommon for an agent to advise their client that "BYOB" can be a fall-back whilst the issue with the premises manager is resolved: but that must be with the appropriate advice

24 For more discussion on when alcohol is or is not "sold", see Chapter 2.

about the continuance of the licensing rules and regulations underpinning the Act and on the face of the individual licence. In other words, just because the alcohol is not sold by the premises, does not mean a licensing offence cannot occur. As I state above, the licence is still in force.

In each case, the solution to the problem is to name a new premises manager who holds a valid personal licence and is not named on another premises licence. That is achieved by way of an application for minor variation to name the new manager, which can be given immediate effect if requested. In such a case, the lodgement of the application can be deemed to cure the defect and alcohol sales can recommence. The gravity of alcohol sale cessation can therefore be remedied in short order, assuming the licence holder can identify another valid personal licence holder, perhaps from existing staff or by an external hire.

For more detail on rules surrounding the premises manager and variations, see Chapter 13 at Section 3.3.

4.4 Alcohol sales authorisation (paragraph 5)

As noted above, paragraph 4(1) of Schedule 3 to the 2005 Act states:

> "Alcohol is not to be sold on the premises at any time when—
> (a) there is no premises manager in respect of the premises".

Paragraph 5 states:

> "Every sale of alcohol made on the premises must be authorised (whether generally or specifically) by—
> (a) the premises manager, or
> (b) another person who holds a personal licence."

Paragraph 4(3) states:

> "Nothing in sub-paragraph (1) or paragraph 5 is to be read as requiring the premises manager to be present on the premises at the time any sale of alcohol is made."

Let us pull all of this together.

One of the early controversies of the 2005 Act was the question of whether the above provisions meant that the premises manager, or another personal licence holder, always had to be physically present in order for alcohol sales to occur. In England and Wales, the provisions of the 2003 Act regarding authorisation are couched in similar terms. The DCMS guidance on the matter states: "Authorisation does not imply direct supervision of each sale of alcohol by a personal licence holder", but goes on to add: "[w]hether or not an authorisation has been given [by an absent personal licence holder] ... would, ultimately, be a matter for a court to determine".[25]

Some commentators argued for the so-called "permanent presence" doctrine – if every sale requires to be authorised by a personal licence holder and the premises manager need not be present, then the inference is that another personal licence holder would be required to be on the premises. This side of the debate was also given weight by the potential difficulty in prosecuting absentee management in relation to what, at that time, were a

25 See also "Sales authorisations: The DCMS Guidance" [2006] 35 SLLP 10.

number of "knowingly allowing" offences that could occur under the Act as originally enacted: for example, the offence of "knowingly allowing" alcohol to be sold without a premises licence, or not in accordance with a premises licence (s 1(3), as originally enacted); the offence of knowingly allowing alcohol to be sold to a child or young person (s 103, as originally enacted); and so on. As discussed in Chapter 19 at Section 2.3.3, as a result of the Criminal Justice and Licensing (Scotland) Act 2010 the words "knowingly allowed" have been virtually stricken from the Act, delivering a fatal blow to this old argument.[26]

The debate rests, then, not on "permanent presence" but on the absence of specific regard to the premises manager being physically present, bolstered by the authorisation being allowed "generally or specifically"; that is, the "general authorisation" could be by way of a sign behind the bar or at a checkout area stating something like:

> "The premises manager authorises staff to sell alcohol in his absence", or
> "All alcohol sales on these premises are authorised by the premises manager"

thereby avoiding the need for personal presence by use of generalisation, whereas the "specific authorisation" might be read as the authorisation the premises manager gives to his staff when physically present.

An alternative to the one-line sign behind the bar as suggested above is deployed at many premises, in the form of a "staff authorisation sheet" or similarly titled document that lists all staff including their employment start date, and is signed by the premises manager to confirm he or she has authorised those members to make alcohol sales. Such documents are para-statutory responses to evidence compliance with the condition: not legally required, but good practice.

It should be apparent by the correct reading of section 54 that this condition is not breached where there is an absence of a personal licence holder following the departure of the premises manager. There is no doctrine of "permanent presence", so even when a business only has one personal licence holder on the books, and that person leaves, there is no difficulty. As section 54(5) states:

> "Any breach of the conditions specified in paragraphs 4 and 5 of schedule 3 in the period beginning with the occurrence of the event and ending with the receipt by the Licensing Board of the application referred to in subsection (4)(b) is, so far as it is attributable to the occurrence of the event, to be disregarded."

In other words, the "authorisation" condition we are focusing on here is to be disregarded during the 6-week period after a notification has been intimated to the licensing board that the premises manager has ceased to hold that position for whatever reason.

26 Prior to the Criminal Justice and Licensing (Scotland) Act 2010, in order for a person to be proved to have knowingly allowed an action, they must have had direct, personal knowledge of the action, as decided in *Noble v Heatly* 1967 JC 5, 1967 SLT 26. This is a well-established principle in Scots law and differs from England, where the so-called "doctrine of delegation" means that an absent personal or premises licence holder can be convicted of an offence of this sort that takes place when he is not physically there. As was the case in, e.g., *Howker v Robinson* [1973] QB 178, [1972] 3 WLR 234. For a substantial consideration on the contrast between *Noble* and the doctrine of delegation, see J C Cummins, *Licensing (Scotland) Act 2005*, Annotated Statute (3rd edn, W Green, 2013) pp 146–8 (notes to s 103) and p 204 (notes to Sch 3 paras 4 and 5). In the 2005 Act context, see Chapter 12 Section 3.

An additional provision fortifying this is that the Licensing Conditions (Late Opening Premises) (Scotland) Regulations 2007[27] make specific provision for a personal licence holder to be on the premises after 1am, which can be read to indicate that permanent presence is not otherwise required.

As an interesting vignette, the matter was (almost) brought to a head when the Scottish Beer and Pub Association sought a judicial review of the City of Glasgow Licensing Board's licensing policy statement (2010–2013). The relevant section of the policy statement was in the following terms:

> "Licence holders should ensure that the premises manager or other responsible personal licence holder is present on the premises at all times when alcohol is sold."[28]

But this statement was in relation to matters which the board *suggests* could be covered by a risk assessment, on which the statement says:

> "The board will not be seeking to approve risk assessments and will not take them into account in considering applications."[29]

The effect was that the review had sought to clarify the legality of a stance that the policy statement did not in fact take and was therefore a nullity. The SBPA, whilst no doubt well-intentioned, probably selected the wrong target in terms of seeking legal clarity. It certainly generated stories in the trade press,[30] some of them ill-informed, noting that the policy remained in its original terms, and therefore drew attention to the wider issue of the problem at that time, but the matter may have been better raised against a board with a more specific statement in its policy.[31]

In the result, both sides claimed victory (the SBPA were awarded expenses, but the policy remained in its original terms) but the real losers were those hoping for a judicial analysis of the problem as the petition was withdrawn.[32]

4.5 Staff training (paragraph 6 and (2A))

Staff training is required for all persons[33] who either make sales of alcohol or serve it for consumption on the premises:[34] full-time, part-time, casual, paid or unpaid, except personal licence holders (who are deemed not to need the staff training because they have been subject to the full personal licence training course), and the training requirements themselves are prescribed in the

27 SSI 2007/336.

28 Glasgow Licensing Board Statement of Licensing Policy (2010–2013) para 3.4, p 23.

29 Ibid para 3.2, p 22.

30 "Glasgow Licensing Board forced to pay out £12,000", *The Caterer*, 24 November 2008; see also "Personal Licence Row Deadlock" [2008] 39 SLLP 1.

31 For an insight into the acrimony of this issue from the time, see the exchange of public letters between the then clerk to the Glasgow Licensing Board, Stewart Ferguson, "Smoke and Mirrors" [2008] 39 SLLP 10; and the response from the then Chief of the SPBA, Patrick Browne: "Smoke and Mirrors: SBPA response" [2009] 40 SLLP 7.

32 The debate is analysed at length at [2008] 39 SLLP 1.

33 Although there was an early dalliance with exempting casual staff: the Regulatory Impact Assessment to the Licensing (Scotland) Bill, which was published in March 2005, says: "Exemptions will be allowed for casual staff who have worked in the trade for less than 4 months" (para 59).

34 See my comments in relation to how the provision affects delivery staff at Chapter 11, Section 9.3.1.

Licensing (Training of Staff) (Scotland) Regulations 2007.[35] The regulations require that staff receive "relevant training", which must be provided by either a person holding a personal licence, or a qualification allowing him to provide such training.

On the question of who can deliver the training, the holder of a personal licence is rather more easy to identify than the second group of authorised persons to deliver the training: those with some other form of qualification. The Regulations state that the training can be delivered by a person who holds a personal licence or "a qualification accredited for the purposes of this regulation by the Scottish Qualifications Authority". The existence of these other qualifications has for many proven to be a cypher and they have not been widely publicised.

There are in fact around one hundred such qualifications and the relevant details of each qualification could at one time be found on the licensing page of the SQA website. Strangely, the vast majority of these have no link to licensing or the hospitality trade *per se* and are more akin to general "train the trainer" style qualifications. It seems odd to me that there is no requirement of a decent working knowledge of the licensing laws before being able to train licensed premises staff. Conversely, there is also the point that there is a difference between understanding the licensing laws and being an effective trainer.

The quality of delivery of staff training remains an issue I come across regularly. LSOs frequently report issues of poor staff training (or none at all), missing or incorrect training records, and so on. If staff training is not done, then that is a matter for the licence holder – not the member of staff – to atone for. The member of staff personally breaches no rule by not being trained (that does not excuse them from prosecution in the commission of an offence). The duty is entirely with the premises licence holder. Staff training is, however, transferable, so staff need not go through the training if they move to work in different premises or for a different employer. That being said, I would always recommend that a diligent licence holder ensure that the staff training is carried out on a regular basis and I believe it good practice to have any new member of staff retrained even if the training has been received at a previous place of employment and the staff member has proper records. Many operators will retrain staff on a regular basis in any event.

There is no requirement for the staff training to be refreshed but having an ongoing training regime is a fundamental part of "due diligence", as well as being common sense. The training itself has to be at least two hours long and must cover the following matters:

- the legal basis for the training of staff,
- the licensing objectives,
- the definition of "alcohol",
- what constitutes an unlicensed sale,
- functions of LSOs, including powers of entry,
- nature of the operating plan and its place in the licensing system,
- different types of premises licence conditions,
- special provisions for clubs under section 125,
- licensed hours,
- offences under the Act, specifically in relation to children and young persons,

35 SSI 2007/397.

- proof of age requirements,
- test purchasing,
- best practice as regards standards of service and refusals,
- units of alcohol and the relationship between units and the strengths of different alcohol drinks,
- sensible drinking limits, and
- good practice in conflict management.

Although the SQA provides a template for the delivery of this staff training, which they call "Safe Sale and Service of Alcohol", there is no mandatory format or assessment requirement here. The personal licence holder or qualification holder merely needs to discuss these topics with the staff member and ensure that discussion lasts for at least two hours in order to meet the basic requirement. The absence of any more regimented form of training assessment means the strength of the staff training can be questioned. I have witnessed many hearings where LSOs will question whether the staff training condition has actually been met and submit that staff have just signed the form. In some cases, LSOs have been known to quiz members of staff on fundamental concepts like the licensing objectives in order to follow a hunch that no training has really been provided. Whether it is for a LSO to "look behind" the signed form is a matter of debate but in my view it is the role of LSOs to ensure compliance with licence conditions, one of which is staff training. I do not think it unreasonable that LSOs should seek to make sure staff are trained properly so that, in turn, premises are managed correctly.

There is sometimes a question raised about remote delivery of the staff training provisions. I see no prohibition in the Act to completion of the course online or remotely so long as the subjects are properly covered, and that there is some interface which allows a personal licence holder to validate the learning and to satisfy themselves that the person has spent at least two hours in digesting the detail.

The mandatory condition in relation to the keeping of training records is an amendment of the original condition regarding staff training and the specific form of the training record itself is provided for under the schedule to the Licensing (Mandatory Conditions No. 2) (Scotland) Regulations 2007[36] and requires a signed declaration from the staff member and trainer. The declarations are as follows:

> "I [insert name of member of staff] confirm that I have received the training required by the Licensing (Training of Staff) (Scotland) Regulations 2007"; and
> "I [insert name] confirm that I have provided the above named member of staff with the training required under the Licensing (Training of Staff) (Scotland) Regulations 2007 on [please insert date or dates]."

The trainer is then required to give details of his or her personal licence, or the details of the "appropriate qualification" they hold and the name of their employer if any.

Note that the wording of the declaration says: "date or dates". This implies that the two hours' training could be spread over more than one day either face

36 SSI 2007/546.

to face, or in the e-learning environment. Whilst that is no doubt true, what is important to remember is that no member of staff should be making sales of alcohol until the training has been delivered in full.

4.6 Minimum pricing (paragraph 6A)

The minimum unit pricing condition ("MUP") is one of the longest running licensing law sagas but also one of the longest running legal sagas involving the Scottish Parliament. Interestingly, it was considered as a part of the original Licensing Bill back in 2005, as an alternative to the proposed mandatory condition on irresponsible promotions. The Policy Memorandum to the Bill explains that proposal thus:

> "The use of price schemes is favoured by many, including some sectors of the licensed trade. Under this option each Licensing Board would be required to initiate a scheme which set the minimum price that could be charged for various kinds of alcoholic drink. Two Licensing Boards had already set up such a scheme which applied to on-sales only. The advantages are that it is a simple and effective means to control promotions without relying on a vague definition and is a means to avoid inconsistency between Boards. However, it does not rule out happy hours and it would be a difficult task for Boards to set appropriate prices. Aberdeen Board recently attempted to set higher minimum prices than others and this decision was successfully challenged by two pub and nightclub operators. This has led to the withdrawal of other minimum price schemes."[37]

The Stage 1 Report to the Bill provides some further explanation as to why minimum pricing was not taken forward at the time of the onset of the 2005 Act:

> "Executive officials offered further explanation of why the minimum pricing routed had been rejected— 'It is felt that minimum pricing is a fairly invasive approach, as it requires individual licensing boards to set prices for a tariff of drinks, which would lead to a lot of variation throughout the country. It was felt that non-differential pricing avoided that, was less invasive and could be applied across the board. It would be difficult to impose minimum pricing in members clubs, for example. Because they traditionally impose lower prices, we would almost have to allow separate tariffs for each club or for clubs in general, whereas non-differential pricing can be imposed across the board without running into some of those difficulties.'"[38]

There can scarcely be a more famous (or infamous) licensing law than minimum unit pricing. The legal challenge surrounding the adoption of MUP led to significant media coverage over many years and the existential concept of the measure has been challenged on a continual basis and debated amongst academics and commentators. Minimum pricing was legislated for under the Alcohol (Minimum Pricing) (Scotland) Act 2012. The purpose of the Act was to insert a new mandatory condition under Schedule 3. After the 2012 Act was passed, various members of the alcohol industry challenged its legality. It would not be true, however, to suppose (as has been suggested in various press

37 Policy Memorandum, Licensing Bill, 22 February 2005, para 136, p 31. For further background on further failed efforts to introduce minimum pricing before the 2012 Act, see "Opposition attacks minimum pricing" [2009] 43 SLLP 4.

38 Local Government and Transport Committee, Stage 1 Report to the Licensing (Scotland) Bill, para 402, p 86.

reports) that the case was brought by the alcohol industry at large; the policy was publicly supported by, *inter alia*, the Scottish Licensed Trade Association, Tennent Caledonian Breweries, and Greene King.

The case went through the various levels of the UK courts and the European Court of Justice. The Court of Session in Edinburgh referred consideration as regards compliance with EU law to the Supreme Court, and it was ultimately decided in *Scotch Whisky Association and others v Lord Advocate and another*.[39]

The practical dimension is that the MUP is a mandatory condition like all the others and the effect of the condition is that alcohol may not be sold below the minimum price. Paragraph 6A(3) of the amended Schedule 3 says:

> "(3) The minimum price of alcohol is to be calculated according to the following formula—
>
> MPU × S × V × 100
>
> where—
>
> MPU is the minimum price per unit,
> S is the strength of the alcohol, and
> V is the volume of the alcohol in litres."

The minimum price unit was set at 50p under the Alcohol (Minimum Price per Unit) (Scotland) Order 2018[40] and the condition came into effect as of 1 May 2018. It may be useful to illustrate this with some basic examples.

> 1 litre bottle of Vodka at 37.5% ABV = £18.75
> 300ml can of stout at 5% ABV = £1.50
> 750ml bottle of tonic wine at 15% ABV = £5.63
> 1.5 litre bottle of malt whisky at 40% ABV = £30.

The 2012 Act also made some provision to deal with the scenario where alcohol is part of a package. Paragraph 6A(2) says:

> "(2) Where alcohol is supplied together with other products or services for a single price, sub-paragraph (1) applies as if the alcohol were supplied on its own for that price."

The effect of this is that the overall price of the wider package or services to which the alcohol is also a part may not fall below the minimum price. The Scottish Government published guidance as to the practical effect of minimum pricing on 20 April 2018. This sought to provide assistance and clarity in a number of areas of conjecture but with considerable caveats:

> "6. Whilst this guidance deals with many of the more common issues arising, it cannot cover every scenario. Where there is a situation where a retailer is in doubt about whether minimum pricing has been complied with, the safest option would be to err on the side of caution. It may be that legal advice would need to be sought. It is ultimately the retailer's responsibility to be able to demonstrate that minimum pricing has been complied with.
>
> 7. The views expressed in this guidance do not bind Licensing Boards or the courts. The correct interpretation of legislation is, ultimately, a matter for the courts."

The guidance introduces a number of provisions. I have focused on a selection of these for further elaboration as to practical impact of the condition. In

39 [2017] UKSC 76.
40 SSI 2018/135.

Table 15.1 Ingredients of a Long Island Iced Tea

Product	*%ABV*	*Units (approx)*	*MUP*
15 ml Bacardi Carta Blanca light rum	37.5%	0.4	20p
15 ml Rutte Dry Gin	43%	0.35	17.5p
15 ml Ketel One Vodka	40%	0.375	18.75p
15 ml Patrón Silver blanco tequila	40%	0.375	18.75p
15 ml De Kuyper Triple Sec	40%	0.375	18.75p
15 ml Monin Pure Cane Sugar Syrup	N/A	N/A	N/A
15 ml Freshly squeezed lemon juice	N/A	N/A	N/A
15 ml Freshly squeezed lime juice	N/A	N/A	N/A
Top up with Coca-Cola	N/A	N/A	N/A
Total		1.5	94p

relation to cocktails and mixed drinks, for example, the guidance mirrors the Explanatory Notes to the 2012 Act, which say:

> "Where different alcohol drinks are mixed, for example in a cocktail, the declared ABV must be used for any alcohol to which relevant labelling provisions apply and the ABV for any other alcohol. The minimum price for each alcoholic component of the drink will need to be calculated and then added together to provide a minimum price for the whole drink. Any non-alcoholic drink added to the alcoholic products does not require to be included in the calculation as a minimum price does not apply to non-alcoholic drinks."[41]

If one takes a standard recipe for a Long Island Iced Tea then the calculation would look something like Table 15.1.

This means that a Long Island Iced Tea to the specifications listed in Table 15.1 cannot be charged for any less than 94 pence. Good luck, reader, in finding a Long Island Iced Tea at this price.

In relation to the use of vouchers and coupons, the guidance says:

> "Generally, vouchers and discounts that are clearly linked to a reward scheme or a refund are classed as cash equivalents so may be used as part (or full) payment for the alcoholic product. Vouchers and discounts which are not clearly linked to a reward scheme or a refund may not be used where the voucher or discount would take the cost of the alcoholic product below the minimum price."

The lawfulness of the use of vouchers to reduce the cost of drink depends on whether the voucher has been obtained through some transaction of a cash equivalent value. So, for example, if a customer uses loyalty points to reduce the cost of a bottle of spirits to an amount which is below the minimum price, this is allowed because the loyalty points equate to a "cash equivalent". Cash equivalency also applies where a loyalty scheme or reward card type offer is in place.

On the other hand, a promotional scheme which would discount the cost of drink below MUP without the customer having had to pay cash equivalency to access that promotion, would be unlawful (such as a £5 off voucher in a local newspaper). Such a scheme would be lawful if the discount did not take the price below MUP. There is, of course, a separate question as to whether such a scheme would comply with the 72-hour rule and the law on irresponsible promotions.

Where a voucher or coupon has been obtained for nothing, such as where a

41 Explanatory Notes to the 2012 Act, Section 1, Note 12.

customer has cut it out of a newspaper (e.g. a "£5 off voucher"), this could not be used to reduce the cost of alcohol below the minimum price but could of course go towards reduction of the wider basket of goods so long as the value of those goods is £5 or greater.

In relation to promotions which include the offer of a free alcoholic drink, such as a meal for two with a "free" bottle of prosecco, there are two key points: (1) if the "free" drink is tied to the supply of some other product or service such as a meal, the cost of that other product or service cannot be below the MUP; and (2) if the free drink is simply a free drink and not tied to the supply of some other product or service, then MUP does not apply because the drink has not been sold. Unhelpfully, the Scottish Government guidance contradicts the 2005 Act as regards the provision of "free" tasting samples in distillery tours. The guidance states:

> "Distillery tours tend to operate on the basis of a charge for the tour itself with free samples offered. In this case, minimum pricing will not apply as there is no sale of alcohol."[42]

That, of course, is wrong. Section 3 of the Act confirms that a supply of alcohol pursuant to a contract, such as a ticket for a distillery tour, is treated as a sale of alcohol. However, it is doubtful that minimum pricing is imperilled due to the likely cost of the ticket (as noted above in relation to alcohol being supplied with other products).

Minimum pricing has been described as a "grand experiment". The 2012 Act contains what is referred to as a "sunset clause", which is a legislative device to reverse the effect of the provisions. This was inserted on the basis that it was recognised by Parliament that the provision was novel and that if it did not have the desired effect, this would allow the measure to fall away. The presence of the sunset clause was a key reason why the courts ultimately upheld the lawfulness of the provision and it means that minimum pricing is, in effect, running under a pilot scheme[43]. Section 2 of the 2012 Act says "the minimum pricing provisions expire at the end of the 6 year period, unless an order is made".

The Order referred to is, of course, an Order making MUP permanent. This provision means that, absent such an Order, the grand experiment will be over, and the minimum pricing condition will fall off the statute books and cease to apply as a "live" condition attached to premises licences. The Order must be made sometime between the 5-year anniversary and 6-year anniversary of the adoption of MUP, meaning sometime between 1 May 2024 and 1 May 2025.

The Order will be subject to the affirmative procedure, meaning it will be debated in Parliament. In order to assist with that debate, the 2012 Act has also created a reporting obligation:

> **"3 Report on operation and effect of minimum pricing provisions**
> (1) The Scottish Ministers must, as soon as practicable after the end of the 5 year period, lay before the Scottish Parliament a report on the operation and effect of the minimum pricing provisions during that period."

42 Guidance on the Implementation of Minimum Pricing for Alcohol (Scottish Government, April 2018) p 24.

43 The author has opposed calls to change the terms of the pilot by increasing the minimum price: see Stephen McGowan, "MUP: the Grand Experiment must run its course" (*Scottish Local Retailer*, 11 March 2021).

This report is designed to provide Parliament with the information it needs to assess whether MUP has been effective and therefore should be placed on the statute books permanently.

The research for this wider report was entrusted to the NHS and the University of Sheffield, which had of course designed the model on which MUP was sold to the Scottish Parliament in the first place. Various strands and mini projects of research were underway almost as soon as MUP came into effect, and a number of reports are expected to be published piecemeal over the course of the 5-year experiment. The 2012 Act sets out the basic framework of the 5-year report as follows:

> "(2) The report must, in particular, contain information about the effect that the operation of the minimum pricing provisions has had on—
> (a) the licensing objectives specified in section 4 of the Licensing (Scotland) Act 2005 ("the 2005 Act"),
> (b) such categories of person as the Scottish Ministers consider appropriate, and
> (c) the businesses of—
> (i) holders of premises licenses granted under the 2005 Act, and
> (ii) producers of alcohol.
> (3) The categories mentioned in subsection (2)(b) may be determined by reference to characteristics including—
> (a) age,
> (b) gender,
> (c) social and economic deprivation,
> (d) alcohol consumption, and
> (e) such other characteristics as the Scottish Ministers consider appropriate.
> (4) In preparing the report, the Scottish Ministers must consult—
> (a) such persons as appear to them to be representative of the interests of—
> (i) holders of premises licenses granted under the 2005 Act,
> (ii) producers of alcohol,
> (b) such persons as they consider appropriate having functions in relation to—
> (i) health,
> (ii) prevention of crime,
> (iii) education,
> (iv) social work,
> (v) children and young people, and
> (c) such other persons (if any) as they consider appropriate."

Although by 2020 a number of reports had already been published about the "first year" of the condition, there is little benefit in speculating without significant further research. In the Policy Note to the Order introducing the 50p minimum price, the Scottish Government said:

> "The (Sheffield University) model estimates that a 50p minimum price per unit will lead to a reduction in consumption and consequent harms, with the reduction in consumption seen disproportionately in those who drink the most."

It is against these three key presumptions – *viz* (a) a reduction in consumption generally, (b) a reduction in "consequent harms", and (c) a positive disproportionate reduction in consumption by those who drink the most – that the grand experiment will stand or fall.

Multiple/"multi-buy" package restrictions (paragraph 6B)

This condition relates to multiple product packages such as a four-pack of beer. The condition was inserted into the Act by the Alcohol etc (Scotland) Act 2010 and came into force on 1 October 2011. It resulted from concerns that the existing "irresponsible promotions" conditions did not go far enough in tackling "supermarket deals",[44] focusing on on-sales premises. It bans discounts on multiples so that, for example, a pack of four cans of beer cannot be sold for any less than four times the cost of a single can. In order words, if a bottle of Harviestoun's Engineer's Reserve costs £4, then a pre-packaged four-pack must be sold for at least £16. This, however, only applies if the premises stocks the product as a single, so can be ignored by simply choosing to stock the multi-pack option only or stocking a different size (i.e. volume) of the single item.

The Guidance to Licensing Boards, issued by the Scottish Government in June 2013 following the Alcohol etc (Scotland) Act 2010, says:

> "The licence condition prevents retailers from selling alcoholic products packaged together at a lower price than the customer could buy the same products individually. The intention behind this is to ensure that customers are not encouraged to purchase alcoholic products packaged together because it is cheaper than purchasing the products individually."

Whilst the introduction of the condition did result in the end of "3 bottles of wine for £10" style deals, common in supermarkets, what replaced it at that time was the same bottles being retailed at £3.33. The retail sector has since moved on and now offers other deals which are compliant with the licence conditions but still offer customer choice.

Further illogicality arises when one considers that the condition does not apply to *multiples of multi-packs* so there is nothing to stop a licence holder from selling four multi-packs of beer for the price of three (assuming this remains compliant with minimum pricing), thereby driving a coach and horses through the legislation and actually creating an inverse incentive to sell more alcohol. The drafting of this condition is another example of the poor quality of licensing law in Scotland, which in several instances has proven ill-thought through and reactionary.

In relation to packages that contain an alcoholic product and a non-alcoholic product, the provision does not apply. The 2013 Guidance, which erroneously repeats itself on this point at paragraphs 2.3 and 2.4, says:

> "The provision also only applies to a package containing more than one alcoholic product. So if an alcoholic drink is packaged with a non-alcoholic product, cheese for instance, then this provision does not apply. For example, the provision does not apply to a bottle of wine packaged with cheese."

It would, on the other hand, apply to a package with two bottles of wine and a lump of cheese. It would also apply to a festive hamper with a variety of food, drink and products if at least two of these were alcoholic.

44 See, for example, "MacAskill ignites multi-buy row" [2009] 43 SLLP 5.

4.8 Price variations/"the 72-hour rule" (paragraphs 7 and 7A)

The 72-hour rule was originally devised to put an end to "happy hours" but has resulted in many premises running "happy days" instead. The ban on "happy hours" pre-dates the 2005 Act with both South Ayrshire and Glasgow Licensing Boards, to name but two, introducing local policies banning happy hour promotions in the twilight years of the 1976 Act, with such policies having a clear influence on the existence of this condition. The original policy was in fact for a "48-hour rule" and the intent behind this measure was explained thus:

> "We believe that one of the most effective ways to tackle promotions is to tackle price. Such policies, based on minimum pricing and non-differential pricing, have already been trialled successfully in Scotland. The Bill sets out in the form of a national licence condition for premises licences a 'non-differential' pricing policy which requires licence holders to maintain their price list for a minimum of 48 hours. Prices may only be decreased or increased on a 48 hour frequency."[45]

It must be immediately remarked that there are two versions of this condition: paragraph 7, which relates to on-sales; and paragraph 7A, which relates to off-sales. The reason for the distinction is detailed below.

The specific wording for on-sales is:

> "7 Where the price at which any alcohol sold on the premises for consumption on the premises[46] is varied—
> (a) the variation (referred to in this paragraph as 'the earlier price variation') may be brought into effect only at the beginning of a period of licensed hours, and
> (b) no further variation of the price at which that or any other alcohol is sold on the premises for consumption on the premises may be brought into effect before the expiry of the period of 72 hours beginning with the coming into effect of the earlier price variation."

The 72-hour rule as far as on-sales is concerned is therefore that the price of *all alcohol* sold must be fixed at the commencement of licensed hours on a given day, and must then stay at those prices for 72 hours thereafter, before it can be varied again (either up or down), but such variation can only then be at the commencement of the next period of licensed hours and again the new price must be fixed for the following 72 hours, and so on.

In other words, simply by wishing to change the price of one product, I tie myself into all other products being fixed within the 72-hour window. To give an example, if I sell a pint of Fallen Chew Chew Caramel Stout at £4 on Monday, I must also sell it at £4 on Tuesday and Wednesday and all other products must stay at the same price across those three days. If I find that I would like to increase the price of Chew Chew to £5 on Thursday I can if I wish, but, if I do, that results in another 72-hour "price lock" for all products. This means different products cannot go up or down. Everything must change at the same time, if there is to be a change.

The specific wording for off-sales is worth introducing at this point, which under paragraph 7A is as follows:

45 Policy Memorandum to the Licensing (Scotland) Bill, para 131, p 29.
46 The words "for consumption on the premises" were added by way of s 3(2) of the Alcohol etc Scotland Act 2010, and commenced as of 1 October 2011 via the Alcohol etc (Scotland) Act 2010 (Commencement) Order 2011 (SSI 2011/149).

"7A Where the price at which any alcohol sold on the premises for consumption off the premises is varied—

(a) the variation (referred to in this paragraph as 'the earlier price variation') may be brought into effect only at the beginning of a period of licensed hours, and
(b) no further variation in the price at which that alcohol is sold on the premises may be brought into effect before the expiry of the period of 72 hours beginning with the coming into effect of the earlier price variation."

The eagle-eyed reader will spot the subtle but crucial difference. With on-sales, the key element to paraphrase is: "Where the price at which *any* alcohol sold on the premises is varied . . . no variation for that *or any other alcohol* may be brought into effect." This wording originally applied to both on- and off-sale purchases. This led to confusion in the retail trade as it meant price changes across all products would have to occur simultaneously, meaning considerable restriction given the sheer number of various products that one might find on a typical supermarket shelf. In order to clarify this, Parliament introduced paragraph 7A and amended paragraph 7 to create the on-sales/off-sales distinction.

The net effect of this for off-sale premises is that it confirms that each individual alcoholic product has its own wee 72-hour period to observe and can do so snugly in a bubble, without regard to any variations to the price of other products on the shelf. This applies, then, not just to different brands of alcohol or different products by the same supplier, but different sizes too: in other words, an operator can vary the price of a bottle of Pinotage on Monday, but is free to vary the price of the Own-Brand Malbec or Cloudy Bay Chardonnay (etc) on Tuesday (assuming the Malbec has not itself been subject to a variation within the last 72 hours); and an operator who varies the price of a 330ml can of Brewdog's Dead Pony Club on a Thursday is free to vary the price of the bottled version of Dead Pony Club on a Friday or Saturday (again assuming the bottles have not been subject to a price variation themselves within the last 72 hours). On the other hand, as noted above, this flexibility does not apply with on-sales.

Can a product be subject to simultaneous price differential (a) if it is sold from two separate parts of the same premises, or (b) if offered to two different classes of customer, who meet certain requirements? The answer to both is yes.

In the case of the same product being sold at two different prices in two different locations under the same licence, this is a long-standing arrangement which pre-dates even the 1976 Act, where in many traditional pubs across the land a separate price list exists for the public bar, compared with the lounge. The 72-hour rule does not affect this sort of price differential. What it does mean is that the separate prices need to observe their own 72-hour rules (as described above) but in addition to that there is a wider obligation to make sure customers are informed as to the price of the product they are purchasing, although this sits with obligations under the Consumer Protection from Unfair Trading Regulations 2008,[47] not the 2005 Act.

Price differentials can also be offered depending on the customer, again even if purchases are made simultaneously. If I and my associate attend a public house together and both request a pint of Old Jock by Broughton Brewery, and if I meet certain requirements that my associate does not, I

47 SI 2008/1277.

might access a different price than he. This may occur where, for example, the premises offer a customer loyalty card scheme. If I am a member of the scheme, I can access a different price list. In my case, my pint of Old Jock turns out to be £1 cheaper than that of my colleague, because I am the holder of the loyalty card. This type of price variation is also unaffected by the 72-hour rule but, again, each price must observe its own 72-hour rule: the "normal" price must be fixed for 72 hours, and the "loyalty card" price must be fixed for 72 hours.

This arrangement may apply to different classes of customer in a variety of circumstances and need not be based on membership of a loyalty scheme. In each case, however, there must be a discernible class of person, and in each case the customer who meets those requirements and the customer who does not must be able to understand the price differential, in most cases by being able to observe the price list. In the case of the loyalty card example, the customer might be able to view the normal price list, but at the same time see a note that loyalty card customers enjoy a 15 per cent discount on all purchases.

These arrangements were homologated following scrutiny in the case of *Mitchells & Butlers Retail Ltd v Dundee City Licensing Board*,[48] which concerned the use of a customer discount card, primarily aimed at the local student population, at the city's Nether Inn public house.[49] The appeal arose following the issue of a section 14 notice to the premises licence holder from a LSO who claimed that the use of a discount card was in breach of the 72-hour rule. As the licence holder disagreed, and refused to withdraw the use of the card, this resulted in a premises licence review hearing at which the licensing board upheld the grounds of review and imposed a written warning.[50] Mitchells & Butlers appealed the warning. In a brief but important decision, Sheriff Principal Dunlop QC says:

> "The starting point in the application of paragraph 7 is 'the price at which any alcohol is sold'. In itself that phrase says nothing about whether individual alcoholic products must be sold at a uniform price and the lounge bar/public bar distinction referred to by counsel is an example of circumstances in which one might readily expect such a differential pricing structure to exist within the same licensed premises. Nor in my opinion is there anything in the wider provisions of paragraph 7 which precludes differential pricing of individual products. Rather the focus of attention is the variation of an existing price within a prescribed period of time. Thus at the beginning of a period of licensed hours the question is what are the prices prevailing or set at that time and it is nothing to the point that there may be different prices for the same product. But once the prices have been set, even if different prices for the same product, it is those prices which may not be varied within a period of 72 hours thereafter. In my view that construction reflects the natural meaning of the words used in paragraph 7 but in any event is consistent with what I consider to be the underlying purpose of this provision as reflected in the various parliamentary

48 2011 SLT (Sh Ct) 53.

49 The Nether Inn premises are of some distinction as it was here, whilst I was drumming with the Blues Buddahs at the Dundee Blues Festival in 2003, that I met a certain Niall Hassard for the first time, as he was tending bar – although it was not until years later that we realised the connection!

50 See "Discount dispute goes to appeal" [2010] 45 SLLP 1 for an analysis in the immediate aftermath of the board decision; and "Landmark 'promotions' judgement clears discount card" [2010] 47 SLLP 3 for analysis post appeal.

> comments and explanatory notes to which counsel referred, namely the avoidance of circumstances in which people are encouraged to consume in a shorter period of time a larger amount of alcohol than they would otherwise consume. In other words it is a measure aimed at discouraging 'binge drinking' . . . the price differential between card holders and non card holders is fixed so that the two categories of prices remain the same over any 72 hour period. It follows that in my opinion there has been no unlawful variation of prices in breach of the provisions of paragraph 7 of schedule 3."[51]

Finally, the condition makes it clear that the price variation can only take effect at the commencement of a period of licensed hours – stopping the prices going up at some point during the day or night. This is a not unknown phenomenon in the UK trade generally. The idea that the prices are increased say after 9pm on a Saturday night is sometimes referred to as "event pricing". Whilst it is clear that the price of alcohol cannot be changed during the course of the licensed hours, if there is some form of surcharge which is levied on any purchase made, whether alcohol, non-alcoholic beverages or food, and this is made clear to the customer, then such a tactic may evade the 72-hour provision. An operator who pays special overheads for live entertainment or DJs on certain nights can point to the fact that these are additional costs and the "event pricing" is not an increase of the cost of the alcohol but is a levy to reflect the additional provision of the entertainment and is akin to a ticket price. This would need to be clearly demonstrated and itemised on the receipt and should be clearly messaged to the customers as a separate charge.

4.9 Irresponsible promotions (paragraph 8)

The ban on "irresponsible promotions" has been one of the most lauded elements of the 2005 Act regime, but is also one of the most poorly understood; as it is unnecessarily complex and is an area ripe with drafting errors and unintended gaps or grey areas. The notion of creating a "banned list" of types of promotion can be traced back to the general concerns of alcohol abuse and binge drinking which were pervasive in the later stages of the 1990s when consumption was at extremely high levels and this was seen as inevitably linked to the competitive promotional activity of the trade. These trends had been identified in the latter stages of the 1976 Act already, with a number of boards seeking to adopt their own policies such as the Glasgow and South Ayrshire happy hours ban and the (failed) Aberdeen dalliance with a local minimum pricing. Nicholson said:

> "we deal with the problems associated with intensive promotional activities, and there we suggest the inclusion in all premises licences of a standard condition aimed at curbing promotional activity which is of an irresponsible kind".[52]

The 2005 Act deals with the idea of promotions generally by creating a wider provision for what constitutes, first, a "drinks promotion": in relation to any premises, being "any activity which promotes, or seeks to promote, the buying or consumption of any alcohol on the premises". The Guidance to Licensing Boards states, unashamedly:

51 2011 SLT (Sh Ct) 53 at para 8.
52 Nicholson Report, para 4.13, p 62.

Table 15.2 Summary of promotions

Provision	*Summary of promotion*	*Applicability to licence*
Paragraph 8(2)(a)	Persons under 18	On- and Off-sales
Paragraph 8(2)(b)	Supply free of alcohol on purchase of alcohol	On- and Off-sales
Paragraph 8(2)(c)	Supply of additional alcohol at a reduced price on purchase of alcohol	On-sales only
Paragraph 8(2)(d)	Unlimited alcohol for fixed fee	On-sales only
Paragraph 8(2)(e)	Encouragement to buy or consume larger measure	On-sales only
Paragraph 8(2)(f)	Strength of alcohol	On- and Off-sales
Paragraph 8(2)(g)	Rewarding drinking quickly	On- and Off-sales
Paragraph 8(2)(h)	Alcohol as a reward or prize	On- and Off-sales

> "It is expected that the mandatory conditions set out in the schedule 3 to the Act provide a clear statement of what would be considered an irresponsible promotion, and should not lead to ambiguity in many cases."[53]

It is imperative to comprehend that a "drinks promotion" is not of itself irresponsible – to be irresponsible it must be one of the promotions defined in paragraph 8(2) of Schedule 3. It is often assumed that promotional activity by licensed premises may breach the Act but in fact the opposite is true: by legislating for *certain types* of promotion to be deemed as irresponsible, the general position is that a drinks promotion is simply that – a lawful drinks promotion. Note further that a "drinks promotion" in this context is not the same thing as a "drinks promotion" under paragraph 13A (discussed below), which most unhelpfully uses the exact same term to mean something completely different.

As some of the banned promotions apply to on-sales, and some to both on- and off-sales, the introductory table above (Table 15.2) may be of use.

Let us now explore each of these types of banned promotion in turn.

Paragraph 8(2)(a): a promotion that relates to a drink likely to appeal to persons aged under 18

This applies to both on- and off-sales. There is an interesting if glib differentiation here between a product that may intrinsically be likely to appeal to persons aged under 18, and a promotion of that drink, being likely to appeal to persons under 18. Note that the condition says the promotion which "relates to a drink likely to appeal to persons under 18". So, my reading of this is that the irresponsibility is derived not from the style or format of the promotion, but the drink itself.[54] There are a number of examples of certain products being classed as irresponsible in terms of their own branding/appearance or name, as decided by the drinks industry watchdog The Portman Group.[55]

Another issue with this provision is the inference that alcohol products

53 Guidance to Licensing Boards (2007) para 135, p 36.

54 This rouses the curious gremlin about whether a drink which is not of itself going to be attractive to young people would fall foul of this promotion if subject to "trendy" marketing which is going to pique the interest of a younger crowd.

55 Products such as Running with Sceptres (March 2020), Juicebox (January 2020), Sweet

should be made to be unappealing to persons aged under 18 as if the consumption is itself irresponsible, when the Act itself makes provision for the sale of alcohol which can be given to a young person aged 16 or 17, when consuming a meal.

Paragraph 8(2)(b): a promotion that involves the supply of an alcoholic drink free of charge or at a reduced price on the purchase of one or more drinks (whether or not alcoholic drinks)

This applies to both on- and off-sales. This would catch, for example, "buy two pints of ale and get one free", or "buy two large glasses of wine and get the rest of the bottle". It would also catch "buy three Irn Brus and get a free pint of Tennents" but would not catch "buy a pint of Tennents and get three Irn Brus for free". The provision was originally only applicable to on-sales purchases but was then "extended" to catch off-sales by virtue of section 4(2) of the Alcohol etc (Scotland) Act 2010, which came into effect on 1 October 2011.[56] The Guidance to Licensing Boards issued following the Alcohol Act provides the following list of examples of off-trade promotions which would be caught by this condition:

- buy one, get one free
- three for the price of two
- five for the price of four, cheapest free
- 3 bottles of wine for £10, and/or
- buy six, get 20% off.

Paragraph 8(2)(c): a promotion that involves the supply free of charge or at a reduced price of one or more measures of an alcoholic drink on the purchase of one or more measures of an alcoholic drink

This applies to on-sales only. It is remarkably similar to the previous provision, but the use of the word "measure" seems for most to strike at the practice commonly referred to in sales terminology as "upselling". The practice had been well established in Scotland, and usually takes place when a patron buys a measure of spirits, perhaps with a mixer. The server will advise the patron that he may "double up" for an extra fee of, say, 50p where the initial drink may have cost £3. Another example might be the server offering a "large" glass of Merlot instead of the "small" glass where the small is £3.50 and the large, which is twice the size, is £5.

There is no doubt that "Go large" or "doubling up" promotions are liable to be caught out by this but suggestions that offering a double for any less than twice the price of a single are in clear breach of the law are, in my view, misplaced.

It remains legal to have a double measure at a price which is less than twice the value of a single. What is illegal is where a premises tries to "upsell" the larger measure. So, if I ask for a Banditti rum and coke and the barman asks

Little Glitter Bomb Bubblegum Gin Liqueur (May 2019) and Unicorn Tears Raspberry Gin Liqueur (April 2019) are recent examples.

56 Alcohol etc (Scotland) Act 2010 (Commencement) Order 2011 (SSI 2011/149).

"Do you want to make that a double for an extra £1?", then that would be in breach of the Act because it is an attempt to supply the larger measure. But simply having a price list and allowing the customer to make his or her own choice about whether they wish a single or a double is not, in my view, illegal.

It must be clear that the 2005 Act has not imposed "linear pricing" (that is, a double must cost twice the amount of a single, and so on). On 20 September 2005 George Lyon MSP said that the then Scottish Executive had taken legal advice on whether Schedule 3 imposed linear pricing, and that advice was that it did not. The purpose was not to introduce linear pricing, but deal with certain promotional activity instead. The Scottish Beer and Pub Association (SBPA) argued that it did introduce linear pricing, which the Executive rejected. An Office of Fair Trading (OFT) complaint was pursued by the SBPA at this time, but it was also rejected on the basis that the OFT did not believe challenging the then Licensing (Scotland) Bill was within their remit. Licensing boards across Scotland have local policies which confirm that linear pricing in this context is a misnomer. The Perth and Kinross Licensing Board, for example, states in its 2013–2016 statement of licensing policy: "For the avoidance of doubt, the Board does not consider that there must be linear pricing of alcohol according to the size of measure."

Having a double measure for less than the cost of two singles does not offend this provision: the larger measure is merely available at a certain price; it is not conditional on the purchase of one or more measures of the drink. It therefore only becomes irresponsible, in my view, if the barman tries to upsell the larger measure, which offends the separate provision under paragraph 8(2)(e) discussed below.

There is a difference, then, in my mind between an advert or promotion that merely confirms the price of certain measures and one that "pushes" the larger measure in some way.

On the applicability of this condition to on-sales only, the policy thinking was:

> "We do not believe that this policy can presently be extended to off-sales promotions in the absence of any concrete evidence to suggest that purchasing a large quantity of alcohol in an off-licence is linked to immediate consumption and to binge drinking. However, we accept that there is anecdotal evidence, particularly in relation to drinking by young people, to suggest that large quantities of alcohol purchased in an off-sales may be taken home to drink as a precursor to a night out and may encourage binge drinking."[57]

There was some concern about this provision only applying to on-sales premises on the basis that it was said that the use of the word "measure" should be read widely to include alcohol in a sealed container such as a can or bottle. The Guidance to Licensing Boards had the following to say:

> "The reasoning behind this is that the use of the word 'measure' was causing some confusion in an off-sales context as it is more associated with an on-sales environment."

This was, to some extent, addressed when the Alcohol etc (Scotland) Act 2010 introduced partial linear pricing for multi-pack deals (see above at Section 4.7).

57 Policy Memorandum to the Licensing (Scotland) Bill, para 133, p 30.

Paragraph 8(2)(d): a promotion provides for unlimited amounts of alcohol for a fixed charge (including charge for entry)

This type of promotion was common and popular around the time of conversion to the 2005 Act, although perhaps not in the form envisaged by those seeking to address a mischief here. The provision was directed at the practice which had cropped up in some areas of paying, say, £10 to enter a nightclub, and the drink would be free all night. These types of events were, however, rare and the provision ended up affecting more promotions like festive season or similar "package deals". Many hotels, for example, offered fixed Christmas party "deals" which included your three-course meal with all the trimmings (cranberry sauce optional), entertainment, and an open bar. That is no longer possible and such deals now should enforce a limit of alcoholic beverages which may be obtained as part of the deal, as well as taking into account other considerations such as management discretion not to serve and offering non-alcoholic alternatives. Advice should, of course, be sought.

Paragraph 8(2)(e): a promotion that encourages, or seeks to encourage, a person to buy or consume a larger measure of alcohol than the person had otherwise intended to buy or consume

This provision has similarities in ethos to the ones above in relation to "buy one get one free", and "upselling". The core offence in all three is the "pushing" of additional alcohol. Given this provision sits separately, it does not relate to "buy one get one free" or "upselling" but instead to other, multifarious practices which may occur. A degree of common sense should be applied here. I do not think that, for example, upon approaching a bar having finished my half pint of Brewed Awakening by Cromarty Brewery, the barman is committing an offence by asking me if I wish the "same again", as some licensed trade trainers reportedly taught in the early days of the 2005 Act. That scenario appears to me to fall into the simple parameters of the server ascertaining what the next order will be, in a colloquial manner. If, on the other hand, I had been drinking a half pint, and upon arrival at the bar I am told "Go on, just have a full pint this time", then this would be a problem. The difference is, of course, intent. In the second scenario, the intent is to push me into buying a larger measure. There is an entirely separate question about whether such an exchange can even be treated as a "drinks promotion" in the wider sense but it does appear to offend the spirit of what is intended.

This provision is also relied upon by those seeking to strike at the practice of a "free drink" such as a "free drink" on arrival at an event, or a "free drink" to mum with her Mother's Day meal, and so on. I doubt that it can be read to capture such activity. The provision of the free drink is not a larger measure than intended; it is just a free drink (but also see below on whether it can be treated as a "prize or reward") and there is no connectedness between what is offered and some smaller measure which had originally been hoped for, which is what the provision requires. Similarly, if a free drink is given on the occurrence of an event such as a sporting outcome, then again this provision would not trigger as the supply of the drink is not linked to any request for a smaller measure (but also see below on whether this might be a "reward"). The supply of a free alcoholic drink is also not, in my view, caught by the separate condition relating to price variations. The fact the alcohol is given free means that it has not been sold, and therefore the price variation condition does not apply.

Paragraph 8(2)(f): a promotion that is based on the strength of alcohol

This applies to on-sales only. This banned promotion is, for me at least, probably the most difficult to offer examples of. It is especially troublesome when one considers the variety of beers which are now available, and in particular beers that have a higher alcohol content than typical lagers or ales. This category of product, sometimes referred to as "amplified beers", could include beers such as imperial stouts, barley-wine products, or double or triple IPAs. I struggle with the concept that the strength of these types of products is of itself inherently irresponsible. I doubt that this provision makes that the case, especially when a stronger beer such as a 10% stout is clearly to be drunk sensibly and appreciated over a longer period. In one case I was involved with, a particular ale product with a high ABV was advertised by a pub under a banner along the lines of "Are you man enough to handle this beer?". The local LSO took issue with this as it appeared to breach the condition on the basis that the consumption of a high-strength beer was being associated with manliness when it might have been better to promote it based on quality or provenance.

Paragraph 8(2)(g): a promotion that rewards or encourages, or seeks to reward or encourage, drinking alcohol quickly

This applies to both on- and off-sales. There have been a few examples of this type of irresponsible promotion which have come across my desk over the years. In one case I was instructed on, a pub had instigated a "prize night" scenario where guests would proceed through to the next round based on downing a drink in one go. I think that would squarely offend this provision. In other cases, there have been plenty of sporting clubs which have a "yard of ale" style event where an individual is encouraged to drink the full yard in one go, although whether this is a true "drinks promotion" is perhaps for debate.

Other "drinking games" which encourage quick consumption might also fall foul of this provision. In 2014, for example, a phenomenon known as "neknomination", where a person was to drink a large amount of strong alcohol in one go and then "nominate" friends to do the same, cropped up in some licensed premises. In these cases it was most likely customers were adopting this pattern of behaviour without encouragement by staff or by management, but it is not unforeseeable that the practice would be struck at as an irresponsible occurrence with regard to this provision because of the element of haste.

Paragraph 8(2)(h): a promotion that offers alcohol as a reward or prize, unless the alcohol is in a sealed container and consumed off the premises

This applies to both on- and off-sales. This provision makes it clear that only alcohol in a sealed container to take away can be given as a prize. Note that it would be perfectly acceptable to have, for example, a crate of beer or a bottle of spirits as a prize in a pub quiz competition, so long as it is unopened and taken away for consumption off the premises. It would not, however, be acceptable to give the winning team a round of drinks for immediate consumption. By extension, if the prize were a voucher then the voucher could only be redeemed against food, non-alcoholic drinks, or alcoholic drinks for off-sale consumption.

I have had some queries over the years asking just how sealed a container needs to be. I think the answer to that is that the container cannot be open! There are a number of receptacles in use these days such as growlers and tetra-pak style cartons. These can keep products like freshly poured beer fresher for longer. The fact that a container can be opened and sealed again is not, in my view, relevant, as long as it is sealed at the appropriate time, that is whilst on the premises and whilst leaving the premises (and of course, should remain sealed if public bye-laws prohibiting street drinking apply).

A separate consideration arises over the use of the word "reward". In some cases, the provision of an alcoholic product following the conclusion of a process, or the realisation of a possible event, has led to complaint and investigation by LSOs. A common example might be where a pub has an offer of a free pint if Scotland win a game of football. Leaving aside the infrequency of such an event, does the supply of the pint to punters at the end of the game constitute a "reward"? My position is that the purpose of the provision is to strike at rewarding someone who themselves has engaged in a process which they have manipulated or had some control over, and a favourable outcome leads to the supply of the drink.

In these types of cases, the customer is simply in attendance at the premises and is provided a free beer because Scotland has won. That is no different to providing a free beer for no reason at all, which again has no restriction. The matter would be different if the customer had to engage in some sort of process, the successful completion of which entitled them to "claim" the "free" beer. In that case, it might be said that the drink is in fact a proper reward – meaning not that it could not be supplied, but that it would have to be supplied in a sealed container for consumption off the premises.

The Parliamentary intention must also be remembered. What was the purpose of the banning of certain promotions? The Explanatory Notes remind us that "These conditions are aimed at reducing the problems of binge drinking and under-age drinking."[58]

That completes our review of the irresponsible promotions and brings us back to explore the remaining mandatory conditions.

4.10 Tap water and non-alcoholic drinks (paragraph 9)

Paragraph 9 states:

> "(1) The conditions specified in this paragraph apply only to the extent that the premises licence authorises the sale of alcohol for consumption on the premises.
> (2) Tap water fit for drinking must be provided free of charge on request.
> (3) Other non-alcoholic drinks must be available for purchase at a reasonable price."

58 Explanatory Notes to the 2005 Act, para 319.

The first part of this, of course, confirms that the condition does not apply to off-sale licensed premises. This is especially important in relation to the reference to other drinks being sold at reasonable prices. What may or may not be deemed to be a "reasonable price" is surely a matter of some dubiety. This small provision, if it were to be challenged, might create as much fuss as the proposal to introduce minimum pricing did. Attempts to control pricing under the old 1976 Act were found to be *ultra vires* following the decision in *Mitchells & Butlers Retail Ltd v Aberdeen City Licensing Board*[59] and I do retain reservations over the lawfulness of this seemingly modest price control measure. How does one assess what is deemed to be reasonable? Does *Wednesbury* reasonableness apply to the price of a bottle of Ginger Beer[60] in a city nightclub or village pub? If the LSO were to issue a section 14 notice and go on to apply for a premises licence review on the ground he or she felt the price of a can of Coke was too expensive, how is the board to deal with that? Comparisons with rival premises?

The obligation to provide tap water fit for drinking is also one which causes the licensed trade some concern. It does not sit well with their common law right to refuse service. On the face of it, as the licence holder "must" provide tap water free of charge, there is an implication that the discretion as to whom a licence holder chooses to serve is fettered.

The obligation to provide tap water free of charge can irk members of the licensed trade. The water is not free to them. They pay for water like any other business. But they also pay for the glass, the ice, the slice of lemon, the wages of the person serving the water, the electricity used to clean the glass or freeze the ice, the PRS fees to allow the person drinking the water to listen to background music, and so on.

It has been put to me that the obligation to provide tap water means that the common law right to refuse service can be evaded. On one view, it might be said that the directory element is not that the tap water must be provided, but that if it is to be provided, it is provided free of charge. It is couched in terms which appear to me to aim towards customer choice; choice beyond a product which is alcoholic. The condition does not, then, to my mind, mean that ne'er-do-wells and vagabonds can side-swerve a denial of service or a request to leave by asking for tap water.

4.11 Age verification policy/"Challenge 25" (paragraph 9A)

One of the newer mandatory conditions, the requirement to have an "age verification policy" was introduced via section 6 of the Alcohol etc (Scotland) Act 2010 and came into force at midnight on Saturday 1 October 2011.[61] The specific condition is as follows:

> "(1) There must be an age verification policy in relation to the sale of alcohol on the premises.
> (2) An 'age verification policy' is a policy that steps are to be taken to establish the age of a person attempting to buy alcohol on the premises ('the customer') if it appears to the person selling the alcohol that the customer may be less than 25 years of age (or such older age as may be specified in the policy).

59 [2005] 30 SLLP 24.
60 With or without snail.
61 Alcohol etc (Scotland) Act 2010 (Commencement) Order 2011 (SSI 2011/149).

> (3) The condition specified in this paragraph does not apply in relation to any sale of alcohol which takes place on the premises merely by virtue of being treated, by section 139, as taking place on the premises."

The condition is shortly referred to as the "Challenge 25" condition, although note that the reference to 25 is the *youngest* age to which the policy can have regard. I am not aware of any Challenge 30, 40, or even Challenge 75 schemes in practice in the trade. However, every now and again a news headline surfaces concerning a person in more advancing years being refused alcohol, with tongue firmly in cheek.

Some trade commentators continue to express concern over systemic mixed messages on alcohol sales to under 18s and argue that the condition confused matters. For a considerable number of years, "18" has been the magic age at which alcohol can be purchased legally and that remains the case. It is common public knowledge and hardly an arcane licensing edict. But I do have some sympathy on contradictions here, as the 2005 Act gives out mixed messages on this both in terms of statutory notices and the prescribed legal defences open to those charged with selling to under-agers; and how this sits with the "Challenge 25" age verification condition.

The statutory notice which is required to be displayed on every licensed premises in Scotland, under section 110 of the 2005 Act, is imaginatively known as the "section 110 notice". It requires the following wording to be displayed:

> "It is an offence for a person under the age of 18 to buy or attempt to buy alcohol on these premises. It is also an offence for any other person to buy or attempt to buy alcohol on these premises for a person under the age of 18. Where there is doubt as to whether a person attempting to buy alcohol on these premises is aged 18 or over, alcohol will not be sold to the person except on production of evidence showing the person to be 18 or over."

The notice is in fact wrong. It ignores the exception to the offence of someone buying certain types of alcohol for a 16- or 17-year-old where the alcohol is to be consumed along with a meal. That is perfectly legal.

Now consider the legal defence open to someone charged with selling alcohol to someone under 18:

> "(2) It is a defence for a person charged with [selling alcohol to a child or young person] to show that—
> (a) the accused believed the child or young person to be aged 18 or over, and
> (b) either—
> (i) the accused had taken reasonable steps to establish the child's or young person's age, or
> (ii) no reasonable person could have suspected from the child's or young person's appearance that the child or young person was aged under 18.
> (3) For the purposes of subsection (2)(b)(i), the accused is to be treated as having taken reasonable steps to establish the child's or young person's age if and only if—
> (a) the accused was shown any of the documents mentioned in subsection (4), and
> (b) that document would have convinced a reasonable person."[62]

There are two defences open to the accused here. Both require the accused to "believe" the person was aged 18 or over. The first defence is that the accused

62 2005 Act, s 102(2).

asked the person for ID and the ID would have convinced a "reasonable person" that it was genuine. The second defence is that no reasonable person would have suspected from the appearance of the child or young person that they looked under 18. So, if the person trying to buy the drink looks 18 or over to a reasonable person then the defence is met and it matters not whether ID was asked for or not.

Now consider the wording of the "Challenge 25" age verification policy. The actual wording does not appear to require the licence holder to enforce the policy; only to have such a policy. In other words, the only breach of the condition is if there is no policy; it is not a breach if the policy is not followed, which is an absurdity. The wording is that there "must be an age verification policy"; not that "the licence holder must adhere to the terms of an age verification policy". It is yet another example of bad drafting in our licensing laws and surely this was not the intention of Parliament. The intention must have been to penalise licence holders who do not follow the terms of the policy. Worse, the condition does not require such a policy to be in writing, which makes compliance with the condition difficult to enforce when a licence holder need only state such a policy exists in some ethereal form to meet the test.

Even more confusingly, it is common to see a "Challenge 25" A4 poster in licensed premises, yet the display of such a notice is not a legal requirement and the poster is not of itself a policy. In the Guidance to Licensing Boards following the Alcohol etc (Scotland) Act 2010, the paragraph concerning this condition includes the following gem: "A premises licence holder may wish to adopt a written document stating what the policy is. An example of a policy is attached as annex B". Yet, no Annex B exists!

My advice to clients is always: (a) to have a written age verification policy; (b) to have all members of staff sign a form to confirm they have been trained in the policy; and (c) to display a "Challenge 25" notice. Whilst none of these points is a legal requirement, it all adds up to due diligence, best practice, and responsible management.

There is an interesting question to consider about the "test purchasing" of the age verification policy. There has been an example of a local authority (not a licensing board, which is of itself questionable), instructing licensing standards officers to "test purchase" the "Challenge 25" condition by employing (whether for gratuity or not) an 18-year-old to enter the premises and attempt to buy alcohol; and then advising licence holders they were in breach of the condition if they had not asked that person for ID, on the subjective view that, as far as the officer was concerned, the 18-year-old appeared to be aged under 25.

The 2005 Act makes no provision for this sort of action and in my view such a "test purchase" is subject to challenge as *ultra vires*. Secondly, based on my points above, there was no breach of the condition because it only requires that such a policy exists; not that it be implemented. If the business has a policy, then that is the end of the matter. This exposes the problem with there being no requirement for the policy to be in writing. How, then, do you evidence that the policy actually exists? And finally, where or what is the evidential burden regarding what age a "reasonable person" thinks the 18-year-old is?

The licensing standards officer must think the person looks under 25. But that is a subjective view. The Licensing Board will not have access to an image of the person for data protection reasons. I would suggest it is not appropriate for a Board to proceed to place sanctions on a licence holder who is deemed to have breached the condition with this lack of evidential burden; and instead based purely on the licensing officer saying the test purchaser looked under 25.

Now try to tie all of that in with the legal defence to the actual offence of selling alcohol to a child or young person – that no reasonable person would have believed the person was aged under 18 – there is no mention of the person having to look under 25. This means that the "Challenge 25" "message" – that, if the person looks aged under 25, they should be asked for ID, sits uncomfortably with the fact that the legal defence to the criminal offence is simply that the person looks aged 18.

To put it another way, there is clear contradiction at play here. If I think the person before me is aged 19 and I sell her drink then I have a statutory defence to prosecution for the offence of under-age selling; but simultaneously I may be in breach of a licence condition (leaving aside my comments above on what may constitute a breach of the "Challenge 25" condition) which is a separate offence and to which there is no statutory defence. And, the breach of the licence condition sits with the premises licence holder, not the member of staff. Even worse, the age verification policy condition is not referable to the section 110 notice – which only advises customers that the "test" for getting served is that they appear to be aged 18; not that they look under 25. As I say above, there is no legal requirement to display "Challenge 25" literature, posters or wording.

In summary, the age verification condition, and how it sits with the wider Act, is a guddle.

A final possible anomaly with this condition is that paragraph 6(3) restricts the ambit of the condition to premises licences other than those which are licensed because they are premises from which alcohol is despatched. What this means is that "Challenge 25" does not apply to a sale made remotely, sensibly on the basis that, at least for now, the person making the order on their smart device is not subject to facial recognition technology or a live stream of them placing the order being viewed by a member of staff. Yet, the principal provision of age verification regarding not selling alcohol to someone under 18 does, of course, apply. In the online world, this is verified through the use of the payment card to purchase the goods as well as data entry requesting self-certification of the purchaser's age. It does seem unsatisfactory that these provisions appear to clash in an increasingly digital age.

4.12 Annual licence fee (paragraph 10)

The annual licence fee falls due on 1 October of each year[63] and is set based on the rateable value. There is a sliding scale for the level of fee, which is the maximum a licensing board can charge. The majority of boards simply charge the maximum, but some have conducted assessments and offer reduced fees based on their understanding of how much they need to have the system wash its face.

The licensing board is obliged under the Licensing (Fees) (Scotland) Regulations 2007[64] to issue a reminder to premises licence holders concerning payment of the annual fee. The notification "is to be given no later than 30

63 Or, 30 days after the date the licence takes effect. In practice, most boards ignore this and simply look for the fee to be paid on 1 October each year.

64 SSI 2007/553, reg 9(1).

Table 15.3 Annual fees

Category	*Rateable value*	*Premises licence application fee max*	*Premises licence annual fee max*
1	Nil or no rateable value. Visitor attractions (alcohol not consumed on premises) Accommodation (guests only) etc	£200	**£180**
2	£1–£11,500	£800	**£220**
3	£11,501–£35,000	£1,100	**£280**
4	£35,001–£70,000	£1,300	**£500**
5	£70,001–£140,000	£1,700	**£700**
6	Over £140,000	£2,000	**£900**

days before the date on which the fee is due and is to specify the amount of the fee payable." Whilst this obligation on the licensing board exists, there is no provision to excuse non-payment if the notification has not been received or even, through a failure of the board, has not been issued at all. The existence of the reminder notification is welcome, of course, but premises licence holders should not rely or wait on it to spur them into payment. As the fee falls on 1 October each year, and payment of it is a mandatory condition, the requirement to pay the annual fee should be well known and adhered to.

A reminder of maximum annual fees (with application fee for context) is shown in Table 15.3.

Non-payment of the fee is of course a breach of the mandatory licence condition, but each licensing board responds to non-payment in different ways. Does the fee sit with the premises or the licensee? In my view the annual fee sits with the tenure of the licence holder who held the licence at the time the fee fell due. However, at least one licensing board will check if annual fees are outstanding upon receipt of a transfer application, with the implication the application decision will not be reached unless the fees are paid off. There is no mechanism for annual fees to be settled pro rata following a transfer, so, in my view, whoever is the premises licence holder as at 1 October is the party required to pay the fee in full, regardless of the date the licence was transferred. In my view, outstanding annual licence fees should be treated like any other civil debt owed to the local authority, such as business rates, and be pursued through the civil courts.

Non-payment of the annual fee and links to review hearings under section 37 are discussed in Chapter 7 at Section 12.5 and more generally in Chapter 5 at Section 4.

4.13 Under 18s access notice (paragraph 11)

This is a requirement to display a special notice concerning access to the premises by children and young persons. This is not to be confused with the notice required under section 110. In this case, the notice requirement only applies to on-sales premises[65] and must be displayed "so that it is reasonably visible to customers entering the premises". The notice is an A4 sign which

65 Licensing (Mandatory Conditions) (Scotland) Regulations 2007 (SSI 2007/457), reg 2.

either (a) states that persons aged under 18 are not allowed on the premises; or (b) states that under 18s are permitted on the premises or on such parts of the premises as are specified on the sign. The form of the notice is not prescribed in the same way as the separate notice under section 110 of the 2005 Act, but it must be A4 in size. Examples (not to scale) of such a sign are set out in Figure 15.1.

The Licensing (Scotland) Act 2005

Notice Concerning Admission of Under 18s

The Bull and Bush, Union Street, Aberdeen

No Persons Under 18 are allowed on these premises under any circumstances

Figure 15.1 Notice concerning admission of under 18s: example 1

Another example might be as shown in Figure 15.2.

The Licensing (Scotland) Act 2005

Notice Concerning Admission of Under 18s

The Regal Hotel, English Street, Dumfries

Under 18s are permitted in the lounge and restaurant, but not the public bar

Figure 15.2 Notice concerning admission of under 18s: example 2

Noting that, in some cases, certain premises licences will have very specific rules about admission of under 18s, the notice may be much more precise, such as in Figure 15.3 (see overleaf).

The location where this notice is to be displayed is effectively at the entrance to the premises. This is different from the section 110 notice, which must be displayed where sales of alcohol are made such as at the bar or a checkout till. It is good practice to have a few laminated copies of the notice and to make sure they are checked by staff every now and again; and if one is becoming a bit worn, to replace it with a fresh copy.

The Licensing (Scotland) Act 2005
Notice Concerning Admission of Under 18s
The Happy-Go-Lucky-Local, Bath Street, Glasgow
Under 18s are permitted access to the premises as follows:
In the restaurant area at the rear of the premises: when accompanied by an adult up to 11pm or, when attending a private function, to the end of that function
In the snug bar: young persons aged 16 or 17 when accompanied by an adult for the purposes of taking a meal; but no access allowed for persons aged 15 and under

Figure 15.3 Notice concerning admission of under 18s: example 3

4.14 Baby changing facilities (paragraph 12)

This mandatory condition, which specifies that there must be baby changing facilities accessible by persons of either gender, does not apply to off-sale premises, vehicles, vessels, moveable structures, section 125 club premises, and to premises where children under the age of five are not admitted.

It is not uncommon to come across a licence which specifies ages of children and young person's admissible to the premises as "5 to 17", which in most cases will be a hangover from the conversion process where there were no baby changing facilities at the time and the applicant was forced to accept these terms.

The facility has to be available to both men and women. It is acceptable that the facility may be located in a unisex toilet, and that may be a unisex accessible toilet. In cases where premises do not have space or funds to install permanent facilities, portable facilities can be considered.

An operator who introduced facilities, but who has a licence allowing over 5s only, would require to lodge a major variation application to allow under 5s on the premises.

4.15 The single display area (paragraph 13)

The conditions relating to the single display area are complex and I have broken them down into two parts. In this paragraph, we will focus on the condition as it relates to controlling the location and display of alcoholic products. In Section 4.16, we will look at how the condition affects "advertisements" or promotions of alcohol, as well as the location of other non-alcoholic products.

There are those who take the view that the display of alcohol should be controlled in order to affect the amount that is consumed by Scotland as a nation; alcohol is not just another commodity and should not be treated as such. This view may be shortly termed as the "tattie scone" doctrine: then Minister for Justice, SNP MSP Kenny MacAskill famously said that shoppers should not be able to buy alcohol "like a pint of milk or packet of tattie scones". In an interview with *The Guardian*, he said: "It seems every aisle you turn to has alcohol in your face . . . alcohol is not just another commodity, it is a licensed drug." Of course, this terminology is directly influenced by the seminal work *Alcohol: No Ordinary Commodity*,[66] which underpins much of the current health debate on alcohol, proposing as it does a "whole population approach" to the perceived harms of alcohol sale and consumption.

The 2005 Act creates a restriction not just on where alcohol may be displayed, but later added restrictions where adverts or "promotions" of alcohol may be located (these are discussed below). The position was not always as rigid as appears to have been proposed in the earlier stages of the Bill:

> "Boards would have specific power to impose a discretionary condition requiring the provision of separate display areas for alcohol for those premises where that would be appropriate. To avoid placing a heavy burden on small corner shops, this would be a voluntary condition."[67]

Early suggestions such as this, which hinted at some relaxed approach for smaller convenience stores and grocers, fell by the wayside. The SNP administration was firmly of the view that display had to be controlled without exception. The Executive Note to the regulations that adopted the single display area provision is worth repeating in full here as it clearly demonstrates the policy objectives and links to the MacAskill "tattie scone" position:

> "The Government's policy is that displays of alcohol for consumption off the premises should in general be confined to a single area of premises. Many stores have an obvious 'wines, beers and spirits' section, aisle, or shelves. These are sometimes in one corner of the premises, with décor and floor coverings that distinguish the area from the rest of the store. Other premises will have one area of shelving given over exclusively to the display of alcohol. However, it is now common for alcohol to be displayed at various other points around a store. Larger stores can accommodate a number of separate alcohol displays including displays directly inside a shop doorway, at checkouts, or on numerous 'end of aisle' displays. 'Cross merchandising' or 'food-matching' also enables alcohol to be displayed alongside other items to encourage purchasing – for example, wine located in a cheese section or beer located beside barbeques and garden furniture.
>
> The Government is concerned that these omnipresent alcohol displays encourage us to think of alcohol as an ordinary commodity. The policy intention behind these Regulations is that by requiring all alcohol to be displayed together, in a particular part of a store, the customer will need to make a conscious decision to go to that area if they intend to browse or select an alcohol product. They would no longer encounter numerous alcohol displays as they select their everyday groceries which may help to emphasise that alcohol is not an ordinary commodity, should not be seen as such, and should not be sold as such."

66 Thomas Babor, *Alcohol: No Ordinary Commodity: Research and Public Policy* (2nd edn, Oxford University Press, 2010).

67 Policy Memorandum to the Licensing (Scotland) Bill, para 86, p 20.

This then, is the background to the "single display area" condition, the exact terms of which are as follows:

> "alcohol which is for sale solely for consumption off the premises may be displayed only in one or both of the following—
> (a) a single area of the premises agreed by the board and holder of the licence; or
> (b) a single area of the premises which is inaccessible to the public."

This first aspect of the regulations is the interpretation of what area(s) may consist or constitute a single display area; this has varied from board to board and discrepancies have arisen. Some boards are content to treat the general area of an aisle or aisles as a single area; others take the view that a single "facing" is a single display area, to the extent that two shelves facing each other on the same aisle would be separate display areas. Some applications have been lodged with layout plans showing quite disparate areas as a "single display area". Advice should be sought.

Other issues arise when one considers the commonplace techniques some supermarkets and stores use to display alcohol, such as separate stalls and conical shaped stand-alone display shelving. If these are in the aisle where alcohol is displayed, do they constitute a separate area?

Typically, the "inaccessible area" will be the display shelving behind the till, where perhaps higher-value items such as malt whisky might be stored.

The Scottish Parliament amended this provision to create special rules for distillery and brewery premises. In the Licensing (Mandatory Conditions) (Scotland) Regulations 2009,[68] provision was made to "ignore" the single display rules under the following circumstances:

> "This paragraph does not apply in respect of premises—
> (a) whose main function is to provide a visitor attraction, and
> (b) where—
> (i) the premises form part of a larger site which is used principally for the production of alcoholic drinks, or
> (ii) the visitor attraction is used principally to provide information about and promote the history and attributes of a particular alcoholic drink or a particular category of alcoholic drink."

This follows concern from alcohol manufacturers that the provisions had been written purely with retail premises such as supermarkets in mind, thus ignoring the very different circumstances under which alcohol would be "displayed" in, for example, a working distillery and visitor centre, which would, in essence, be one big alcohol display area and a very different environment to a retail shop.[69]

The Executive Note to the Regulations provides further policy context, confirming the position:

> "The policy objective is primarily to exempt distillery visitor centres from the requirements of the 2007 Regulations. Distillery visitor centres are part of distillery sites, many of which are open for distillery tours. They seek to explain the method of production, history and heritage of whisky and showcase the best of Scottish products. Although alcohol is available for purchase, the main function of the visitor centre is to provide a high-quality visitor experience. Operators of such visitor centres have explained that the effect of the 2007 Regulations would mean that such

68 SSI 2009/270.
69 See "Display areas reprieve for distilleries" [2009] 40 SLLP 4.

> facilities would need to alter their layout to one that resembled a grocery store, rather than allowing them to enhance the visitor experience and develop their facilities. The Scottish Government accepts that view.
>
> The Scottish Government does not wish to restrict the exemption to distillery visitor centres. Some breweries also operate visitor centres on a similar basis (or may choose to do so in the future) therefore the regulations refer to premises used principally for the production of alcoholic drinks, rather than specifically to distilleries. Furthermore, the Scottish Government notes that there are other visitor attractions (such as the Scotch Whisky Heritage Centre) which are not part of a production site but which carry out a similar function. They provide information about, and promote, the history and attributes of Scotch Whisky. Again, the Scottish Government does not want to diminish the visitor experience at these premises which are designed to showcase Scotch Whisky."

It should also be remembered that the single display area provisions only apply to alcohol which is for off-sale consumption. So, for example, a bistro or deli which may enjoy both on- and off-sales could have a bespoke display for products it is selling to take away like gift hampers or wine; but separately can have other alcohol displayed anywhere so long as that other alcohol is only available for consumption on the premises.

4.16 Promotion (advertising) of alcohol within and outwith off-sale premises (paragraph 13(1), (1B) and (1C))

Another exasperating fiddle with the licensing laws of Scotland is this boorach, the result of lobbying from anti-alcohol charities and health groups. The whole enterprise kicks off with an immediate false start by using the word "promotion" as this creates confusion with the separate condition relating to irresponsible promotions. In this context, the word promotion should be read as a form of "advertising" to make life that little bit simpler, but the legal definition is at paragraph 13(4):

> "'drinks promotion' means any activity which promotes, or seeks to promote, the buying of any alcohol sold on the premises for consumption off the premises".

Dealing first with the issue of cross-over goods and the placement of non-alcoholic goods within the designated alcohol display area, the appropriate provision is found at paragraph 13(2) and is as follows:

> "(2) In an area agreed in terms of sub-paragraph (1)(a), a product other than alcohol may be displayed only if it is—
>
> (a) a non-alcoholic drink;
> (b) packaged with, and may be purchased only along with, alcohol
> (c) a branded non-alcoholic product, or
> (d) a newspaper, magazine or other publication."

The items at (c) and (d) were added by way of s 5(4)(b) of the Alcohol etc (Scotland) Act 2010 and commenced from 1 October 2011.[70] This provision means that only these four categories of products may be displayed, in addition to the alcohol, in a designated alcohol display area. Non-alcoholic drinks are typically "mixer" options, such as having tonics next to the gin and so on. Pre-packaged goods would include examples such as gift packages of cheese and wine or port.

70 Alcohol etc (Scotland) Act 2010 (Commencement) Order 2011 (SSI 2011/149).

Branded non-alcoholic products include glassware, t-shirts or any other goods which carry an alcoholic brand but which are not themselves alcoholic, as defined here:

> "'branded non-alcoholic product' means a product which does not consist of or contain alcohol and which—
> (a) bears a name or image of, or
> (b) is an image of,
> an alcoholic product (namely, a product consisting of or containing alcohol)".

However, these goods are not treated as "drinks promotions" and may therefore be located anywhere at all, if they are for sale. If they are not for sale, they must be located in the designated alcohol display area. So, for example, if a Guinness branded T-shirt is for sale then it can be displayed anywhere. If that T-shirt is part of a promotional display, on the other hand, and therefore not for sale, it must be located in the alcohol display area.

In relation to "newspaper, magazine or other publications", the complexity continues apace. Paragraph 13(4) says that "drinks promotion" does not include newspapers, magazines or other publications which are for sale, or where they are not for sale, where it "does not relate only or primarily to alcohol". This last element is designed to allow the provision of supermarket own-brand literature that you might find at the cash desk or elsewhere, which may have images or details of alcoholic products for sale. The interplay between paragraph 13(2)(d) and 13(4) on the point of newspapers etc is practically unfathomable but the effect is that, if the newspaper etc relates only to or primarily to alcohol, then it can only be located in the designated display area.

One area of further confusion is the status of posters. A poster, advertising alcohol, would fall under the general definition of "promotion" in this condition; but it might also in turn be exempt, if it can be treated as falling under the definition of "other publication". The Guidance to Licensing Boards provides no further wisdom save to say that it talks about "publications which are not for sale",[71] which appears to suggest that "publication" is designed to capture pamphlets as opposed to wall-mounted posters. Further, the test also includes the reference to whether the publication relates solely or primarily to alcohol. If a supermarket brochure, free to lift and peruse, contains some element of alcohol advertising, this would surely fall under the exemption. What then of the poster that displays a number of retail items of which alcohol is only one and in the minority? In an appendix to the Guidance noted above, the Government stated that where the surface area was "50% or more" this would be "likely not to comply". This appendix, a form of "Q&A", was widely criticised at the time of issue and has now disappeared from the guidance document, leaving us to ponder whether any clear 50% rule is a mere figment – but the "primarily" test remains, at paragraph 13(4) in relation to the definition of "drinks promotion". This means it is lawful to have a poster where the alcohol is ancillary or secondary to other products.

This bring us on to look at a final element of this most obtuse of licence conditions, namely the concept that promotions may occur within premises, but not within the vicinity of a premises. Paragraph 13(1C) says:

71 This is the Guidance to Licensing Boards issued in respect of the Alcohol etc Scotland Act 2010, dated 25 June 2013: para 3.6, p 6.

> "A drinks promotion in connection with the premises may not take place in the vicinity of the premises."

It is to be assumed that the policy purpose behind this is somewhat similar to the approach taken under the gaming legislation of the 1960s, that is, to construct an inability to advertise a product outside as it might "entice" someone in to purchase said product. Paragraph 13(1D) takes matters further:

> "For the purposes of sub-paragraph (1C), the 'vicinity' means the area extending 200 metres from the boundary of the premises (as shown on the layout plan)."

In short, a business cannot advertise the sale of alcohol from that premises other than no less than 200 metres away. Guidance to Licensing Boards under the Alcohol etc Scotland Act 2010, which introduced the provision, has the following wisdom to offer, which I have repeated here in full:

> "Section 5(3) also amends paragraph 13 to prohibit drinks promotions in the vicinity of the premises if such promotions are 'in connection with the premises'. This means that a licence-holder will not breach the licence condition if there is a drinks promotion in the vicinity of the premises that is not in connection with the premises, for example, an advertisement for an alcoholic product over which the licensee had no control on a bus shelter outside the premises. The reasoning behind this is a recognition that not all drinks promotions within the vicinity of the licensed premises will be within the control of the premises licence-holder. The 'vicinity' means the area extending 200 metres from the boundary of the premises as shown on the layout plan."

A question arises as to advertising that is part of the actual premises. Does this provision catch, for example, the name above the door, or outward posters on display in the window? The intent of the condition is, in my view, not relatable to the four walls of the premises. A business with the name "Buckets of Booze" above the door does not offend the provision. If a sign were erected across the road, with an arrow pointing to the shop under the name "Buckets of Booze", that would be different. In relation to posters in the window, these in my view do not offend this provision either, although caution should be deployed noting that the poster, being a promotion of alcohol, would only be capable of being located on that window if that area of the shop were included within the designated alcohol display area.

5 DISCRETIONARY CONDITIONS

Section 27(5) gives the Scottish Ministers the power to prescribe conditions which licensing boards may, at their own discretion, impose on the grant of a premises licence. Despite the onslaught of licensing laws since the 2005 Act, somewhat amazingly there have been no regulations providing for any discretionary conditions. The Policy Memorandum to the Licensing (Scotland) Bill indicated, amongst other things, that baby changing facilities and single display areas were examples of future "discretionary" conditions, although in fact these ended up being enacted as mandatory conditions, as noted above. The Guidance to Licensing Boards also contains a list of "sample" conditions, particularly in relation to late night premises, but these are not section 27(5) discretionary conditions. It may be said that the concept of a "pool" of conditions which licensing boards could dip in and out of may have been viewed as fettering discretion, or perhaps argued that boards who may have blithely adopted such conditions might have been subject to challenge on the grounds of connectedness. As it is, no discretionary conditions exist so the point is moot.

6 LOCAL CONDITIONS

Although the Act imposes a large number of mandatory conditions on premises licences, it rightly also empowers licensing boards to go beyond these and look to impose their own conditions, based on the merits and circumstances of the individual case. The background to this requirement was discussed by Nicholson as follows:

> "there may be a question as to whether, in the absence of formal objections or representations, a licensing board should be entitled at its own hand to modify the terms of a premises licence by varying, or by adding to, the terms set out in an applicant's operating plan or schedule. As we understand it, the Licensing Bill for England and Wales requires that a premises licence should be granted in precisely the terms sought if no representations to a contrary effect have been advanced by any of those entitled to put forward such representations. Our general scheme, on the other hand, would entitle licensing boards to take a much more pro-active role than is contemplated for licensing authorities in England and Wales; and it would, we believe, be consistent with such a role that boards should be entitled, even in the absence of objections, to require modification of proposed terms and conditions before agreeing to the grant of a premises licence. Any such requirement would be made by reference to the declared statements of policy issued by the board in question and by reference to what is necessary for the promotion of the "licensing principles".

The Act therefore does provide the board with a power to create and frame conditions of its own volition ("at its own hand"), as it considers "necessary or expedient for the purposes of any of the licensing objectives."[72]

6.1 Restrictions on the extent of local conditions

Throughout this book I have sought to emphasise the concept of "purpose". Licensing law has a purpose, which is the regulation of the particular activity. It should not be put to an improper purpose. This general totem extends to the *vires* of a board in relation to the types of conditions which they might seek to impose. Nicholson said:

> "There is, no doubt, a theoretical risk that, by allowing licensing boards to modify the terms of a premises licence, even in the absence of objections, it would be possible for a licensing board to pursue a policy which would be entirely at odds with the relatively relaxed licensing regime which we are proposing in this report . . . However, all licensing boards will be required to conduct their business consistently with declared policies (which will themselves have to comply with the 'licensing principles'): and all decisions taken by licensing boards would, under our proposals, be subject to an appeal. Moreover, under our proposals licensing boards would be required to have regard to national guidance offered by Ministers (possibly on the basis of advice given by the National Licensing Forum). In our view all of that is

72 2005 Act, s 27(6).

likely to provide a sufficient safeguard against any decisions in relation to the terms of a premises licence which are merely capricious and which are inconsistent with the general thrust of any new legislation. In our view any small risk that licensing boards might misuse a power to modify the terms of a licence, even in the absence of objections, will be outweighed by the desirability of allowing boards, on their own initiative, to take such steps as appear to be appropriate in the interests of promoting the 'licensing principles'."[73]

By opening out the licensing system, and opening out the "licence" itself, Nicholson recognised that this could leave the process exposed to arbitrary decision-making or would too easily leave the door ajar to a board falling into error by straying from the true path of the licensing purpose. These general concerns are explored in the Explanatory Notes to section 27, which say:

> "this power could be used in circumstances where additional conditions were needed for the purposes of any of the five licensing objectives established by the Act and where some other form of activity not covered by schedule 3 was being undertaken on the premises. However, under subsection (7) a Board may only impose additional licence conditions which do not run counter to the effect of national conditions, and which do not attempt to alter or add to those conditions to make them more onerous or restrictive . . . These can cover both the sale of alcohol <u>and any other activity carried out on the premises</u>."

The underlined text is as it appears in Explanatory Notes themselves and is not my emphasis. This bring us back to a core juxtaposition within the Act. A licensing board may attach conditions which relate to activities other than the sale of alcohol but may only do so where necessary or expedient for the purposes of the licensing objectives. So, in order to conditionalise an activity, a board must be able to find that nexus between the activity and one of the objectives, and therefore, must find a link between that activity and alcohol. It may be obvious to infer that because the activity occurs on a licensed premises, that itself is the link, but I do not think that takes the connection far enough. The condition must strike at a mischief which has its roots in one of the objectives and manifests itself as a result of the provision of that activity. This, to put it another way, is a form of limitation on the general power to attach conditions. The Act lays out a number of ways in which the limitation is expressed, in particular circumstances.

6.1.1 A local condition may not be inconsistent with a mandatory or discretionary condition[74]

This principle ensures that licensing boards do no alter the mandatory conditions themselves by adding their own variant, and is designed to ensure that the national framework of mandatory licence conditions is not fettered on a local basis. A condition which sought to relax or otherwise amend a mandatory condition so that the effect was contrary or at least different to the mandatory condition would be unlawful. Inconsistency, as we have seen elsewhere, is a relatively low threshold so any tinkering with the format of the mandatory conditions is best avoided.

73 Nicholson Report, para 4.15, p 63.
74 2005 Act, s 27(7)(a).

6.1.2 A local condition may not purport to make a mandatory or discretionary condition more restrictive[75]

This rule is a further expression of that above but again makes it very clear that mandatory conditions cannot be interfered with. The idea that a board might wish to make a mandatory condition more restrictive is ruled out. An example of this might be imposing a condition requiring "permanent presence" of a personal licence holder or extending the price variation condition for a period longer than 72 hours.

6.1.3 A local condition may not relate to a matter which is regulated under another enactment

This rule gives voice to the wider ethos, imported by *Brightcrew* and a number of other appeal decisions, that the essential remit of the licensing board is the regulation of alcohol and strikes at the core of licensing purpose. The Act lists as examples the planning, building control and food hygiene regulatory regimes[76] but of course the principle applies to any other area of law such as immigration, competition, nutritional standards, equalities, and so on.

This restriction on local conditions is often described as being a way of avoiding duplication of regulations with other regimes. It may not be lost on some readers that whilst this rule specifically applies to local conditions, one or two of the mandatory conditions are at odds with the general principle. An example of this is baby changing facilities. These are quite adequately provided for in the regulations under the Building (Scotland) Act 2003 but, notwithstanding this, are now prescribed as a mandatory condition for premises licences. The difficulty is that it leaves no room for manoeuvre to take account of individual premises and situations; had it been a discretionary condition then at least the applicant could make a submission as to why the baby changing condition should not apply to them.

Take, for example, a small restaurant with, say, twenty covers, of which there are many in Scotland. These premises will struggle to find room to fit in baby changing facilities accessible by persons of either gender and are now faced with the dilemma of having to undertake not to allow children under five on the premises in order to avoid the condition. It does seem to me to be an invidious position that, whenever a telephone booking is made, potential customers must be asked if they intend bringing children under five in order to avoid not just a service issue but the prospect of committing a criminal offence by breaching a licence condition.

If this duplication did not exist, then the control of such facilities would rest with the building regulations, a fundamental principle of which is that they are not to be retrospectively enforced, and which even take account of the fact

75 2005 Act, s 27(7)(b). Strangely, this restriction does not seem to apply to late night conditions, implying that a board could place a local condition in conflict with, or more restrictive than, those conditions. Back in November 2008, the South Ayrshire Licensing Board issued a draft "Code of Conduct" for "Off-sale licences". Many of the provisions it sought to introduce would fall foul of this "restriction" rule under the 2005 Act, and it is doubtful that retailers would sign up to it on an informal basis.

76 2005 Act, s 27(7)(c).

that some existing premises may simply not be able to comply with modern regulations.

An example of duplication in relation to local conditions is those conditions attached by some boards relating to the location of gaming machines. Such matters are definitively regulated by the Gambling Act 2005, yet some boards have decided to implement more restrictive conditions regarding the machines.

Another example of this cross-over is in relation to noise nuisance and audibility. Whilst it is clear that public nuisance arising from licensed premises may take many forms such as raised voices from revellers as well nuisance from entertainment such as live music, this type of condition transgresses the terms of section 27(7) when there is clear legislative provision to deal with noise nuisance under the Environmental Protection Act 1990. The interplay between noise nuisance and licensing law is explored in relation to the licensing objective of public nuisance in Chapter 3, Section 4.2. This friction may yet be explored in the courts.

7 VARIATION OF EXISTING CONDITIONS?

Section 27A of the Act is one of the more anomalous elements of the statute. On the face of it, the provision purports to confer a power to licensing boards to unilaterally vary the terms of conditions on current licences, and there is no exclusion to carve out the mandatory conditions as beyond the scope of that power. The board may make the variation "where it is satisfied that the variation is necessary or expedient for the purposes of any of the licensing objectives"[77] and the variation may be imposed on all premises, particular premises, premises of a particular description, or premises in a particular area within a board's jurisdiction.[78] There is provision for a hearing, yet no provision for appeal.

This power is in stark contradiction to the generality of the conditions framework and means that the mandatory conditions are no longer mandatory, or, at least, are only mandatory at the point a new licence is granted, and may then be altered by the board at some later date. The power also grates with the general provision of section 27(7) which prevents boards from interfering with the mandatory conditions as noted above.[79]

The origin of this provision was in attempts to have licensing boards raise the general age of purchase in off-sale premises to 21, and a framework was needed to allow that power to be applied across multiple premises. This was debated during the Criminal Justice and Licensing (Scotland) Act 2010 but was met with derision[80] to the extent that when section 27A was inserted in the Act, Parliament did so only with a provision at section 27A(2) to specifically prevent the age of sale from being increased.

Thus, we were left with a provision which might fundamentally change the

77 2005 Act, s 27A(5).
78 2005 Act, s 27A(3).
79 See "Variations could prove fatal" [2009] 43 SLLP 9 for a contemporary analysis of the power when it was first proposed.
80 See "Raising the minimum off-sale age" [2008] 39 SLLP 4.

whole scope of the Act and which had been originally designed to allow the age of purchase to be increased, only now to simultaneously carve out the very reason the framework had been proposed in the first place!

The practical application of section 27A is nil, for the power only applies to matters which are to be prescribed, and no matters have been prescribed, leaving the provision toothless. The presence of section 27A is one of a number of examples that underline how poor law emanates from reactionary politics.

8 LATE NIGHT CONDITIONS

Section 27(3) and (4) states that the board must impose conditions prescribed in regulations to those premises where the operating plan specifies that the premises will, on any occasion, be open for a continuous period beginning on one day and ending after 1am on the following day. The purpose behind this separate approach is described in the Guidance thus:

> "To support the objectives of the Act, Ministers intend that certain premises should have further mandatory conditions attached to their premises licence if they list in their operating plan that they wish to operate after 1 am. Such conditions are appropriate and proportionate in meeting the needs of public safety and tackling crime. For example a small restaurant has a very different effect on the night-time economy when compared to a large nightclub or 'super pub'."[81]

The relevant instrument is the Licensing Conditions (Late Opening Premises) (Scotland) Regulations 2007.[82] The regulations operate by providing a schedule of conditions to attach to late-night premises, and then by making provision about which of these conditions should apply to particular premises. The Guidance to Licensing Boards (2007) says:

> "The intention of this definition is to differentiate those premises which will attract large amounts of customers and where the consumption of alcohol is a major component of the premises operation. Such additional mandatory conditions are not necessarily appropriate for other late opening premises, e.g. hotels and restaurants and so they are excluded from the definition."[83]

The first condition applies to any and all premises that open after 1:00 am, and is:

- A person suitably trained in first aid must be present on the premises from 1am until closing time or 5am, whichever is the earlier.

The remaining conditions will only apply to premises which meet the description in regulation 3: first, that the premises must have a capacity of 250 or more;[84] and, secondly, must regularly provide at any time between 1am and 5am:

81 Guidance to Licensing Boards (2007), para 116, pp 31–2.
82 SSI 2007/336.
83 Guidance to Licensing Boards (2007), para 118, p 32.
84 If the premises have a capacity of less than 250, these "extra" conditions will not apply.

- live or recorded music exceeding 85dB;[85]
- facilities for dancing;
- adult entertainment;[86]

or, when fully occupied, are likely to have more customers standing than seated.

The remaining additional conditions are:

- A personal licence holder must be on the premises from 1am until 5am or closing time, whichever is the earlier.
- The premises must have written policies regarding evacuation and prevention of drug misuse.
- CCTV must be installed to the satisfaction of the police and be in good working order.
- There must be a responsible person in charge of monitoring the "safety and wellbeing" of persons using toilet facilities on the premises.
- A door steward registered under the Private Security Industry Act 2001 must be positioned at every entrance to the premises from 1am until 5am or closing time, whichever is the earlier.

We will look at all of these conditions in turn.

8.1 Late night conditions: first aid trainer

As noted above, this condition applies to all premises which are open after 1am. There is no specificity as to the nature of the training required to fulfil this condition and it is to be assumed that general certificated first aid training courses will suffice.

8.2 Late night conditions: permanent presence of a personal licence holder

As is explored in Section 4.4 of this chapter, this condition is the exception to the general rule that there is no requirement for permanent presence of a personal licence. It is made clear here that this *does* apply where premises are open after 1am, and meet one of the various tests laid out above. Note that the condition relates to a personal licence holder and not the premises manager. In other words, the condition is satisfied if any person who is the holder of a valid personal licence is physically present in the premises, whether he or she be the designated premises manager or not.

85 This provision is particularly interesting. The aim is, of course, to catch premises such as nightclubs where live and recorded music are played for people to dance along to. Conversational speech is usually 60dB; a vacuum cleaner is 70dB; and standing next to a speaker at a disco can reach 100dB; but the problem is that this is all relative to the point of origin of the sound and the distance between that and the point where the sound is being measured. Is the 85dB rule to be taken as a measurement of the noise from next to a speaker; from the dance floor; or from out in the street?

86 See Section 8.8 below.

8.3 Late night conditions: written policies on evacuation and prevention of drug misuse

The presence of the word "written" is most useful when one contrasts this to the provisions for the "Challenge 25" condition where a similar requirement is absent. These documents are a legal condition, so they must be kept on the premises in a location where they can be viewed by a LSO or police officer. Evacuation will necessarily deal with matters such as escape protocol, safeguarding of staff and customers, and external gathering zones. The drug policy will deal with matters such as how to spot drug dealing and drug use, what to do with confiscated paraphernalia, and reporting obligations.

8.4 Late night conditions: CCTV should be installed to the satisfaction of the police and be in good working order

In my experience the police will, in most areas, not seek to prescribe any particular make or model of CCTV and are more concerned with having a system that can be accessed and footage downloaded as possible evidence, but there are areas where there are very detailed lists of what is considered acceptable.[87] In some systems the footage is written over after a certain period such as a month, which seems to be acceptable. The biggest concern I experience from the police is not the quality of the system, but that staff are not trained in how to access the footage and in many cases this can impede criminal investigations. It is sometimes said that licence holders will not train staff on accessing CCTV as the knowledge could be used to ill-effect, but in my view it is sensible to have at least one person on the premises who has access to and can manipulate the CCTV system in case of emergency or police need. The other element to consider is the coverage the system provides, that is, to avoid blind spots and so on. The police might also like to see the system cover the external areas of the premises as well as internal areas. Licence holders using CCTV are "data controllers" under the Data Protection Act 2018 so would do well also to consider implications under that regime in terms of signage and sharing of images and footage.

8.5 Late night conditions: monitoring of toilet facilities

This condition supplements the policy on drug use and is clearly geared at preventing the use of toilet facilities for illegal activities as well as public safety in relation to persons who may be ill due to consumption of legal or illegal substances and may need medical attention urgently. The provision is not met, in my view, by the presence of a person who is there to provide cosmetics or beauty products hoping for tips, but should relate to a trained and sensible member of staff whose job it is to check the toilets on a regular basis and be aware of how to respond to a medical emergency. The condition does not impose permanent presence, so having someone in charge of inspecting the facilities on a rota basis would be sufficient.

87 Police Scotland produced a guidance document relating to this condition in August 2013, which breaks down the techical requirements into "required" and "advised" groupings, and deals with items such as positioning, lighting, image retrieval and so on, although as this predates GDPR it may no longer be in use.

8.6 Late night conditions: door supervisors

This condition creates a minimum number of licensed door stewards who must be present at appropriate premises, namely, at least one per entrance. The practical reality is that nightclubs and other late night venues will risk assess the need for stewarding and this often means more than one or in fact multiple stewards on the premises and not just at the door, but inside and perhaps on a roaming basis.

8.7 Additional conditions for late night premises?

The Guidance to Licensing Boards provides the following list of "suggested" additional local conditions which might be attached to late-opening premises:[88]

- Active membership of any Radiolink or Pubwatch-type scheme: where a local scheme based on radio link to the Police or Pubwatch or a scheme with similar principles exists, the premises should be a member. In considering this option Licensing Boards should consider whether any scheme has the resources to support an influx of members.
- Participation in the "Best Bar None" schemes which aim to promote safer premises.
- Closure Policy, e.g. the last 30 minutes of music must be slow and considerably quieter.
- Last entry policy/curfew on entrance.
- Staff present who have undertaken Advanced First Aid training: Boards should take into consideration local arrangements on busy nights and link to the city centre triage may be a more appropriate option.
- Premises to have a glass collection policy.
- The use of plastic or toughened glass where non-glass or toughened glass receptacles are required to be used throughout the premises.
- Agreed times for the disposal of glassware: disposal of glassware should be made at a reasonable time as agreed by the Licensing Board.
- Noise control: steps should be in place to minimise noise leakage from the premises.
- Staffing policy: a personal licence holder must be nominated as being in charge at all times and to be on the premises, each bar must be supervised by a personal licence holder.
- Register of staff: a register must be maintained by the nominated person in charge each day and or at shift handover times.
- Door control policy: consideration should be given to best practice used throughout the industry and again to which premises such measures are applied. Options could include
  - Door supervisors wearing yellow reflective tabards
  - How door stewards are able to communicate with each other
  - Door steward minimum numbers or ratio to clientele.
- Ensuring no bottles or glasses are removed by customers leaving the venue.

88 Guidance to Licensing Boards (2007), para 123, pp 33–4.

- Search policy: rather than having a blanket search policy, to use a search policy which is appropriate to trading conditions perhaps in conjunction to discussions with the police.
- Policies to ensure patrons are not put in vulnerable situations after leaving e.g. allowing the phoning of a taxi and waiting in a specific area.

These "suggested" conditions were formulated in 2007 prior to the commencement of the Act and, whilst well intentioned, some of them are more robust than others. Many premises do take advantage of a Radiolink or Pubwatch, and many have search policies. A condition controlling the disposal of glassware is less likely to feature as it is not a licensing condition. The presence of these sample conditions is purely for information, as the Guidance itself says: "This is not an exhaustive list and does not restrict Licensing Boards in any way".

8.8 The definition of adult entertainment

The regulations provide a specific definition of what constitutes "adult entertainment" for the purposes of the application of the late-night conditions. It is any form of entertainment which:

> "(a) involves a person performing an act of an erotic or sexually explicit nature; and (b) is provided wholly or mainly for the sexual gratification or titillation of the audience".[89]

This definition and how it sits within the scheme of the 2005 Act is discussed in detail in Chapter 8 at Section 3.6.16.

89 SSI 2007/336, reg 1(2).

Chapter 16

The Licensed Hours

1 OVERVIEW

Understanding the 2005 Act approach to licensed hours is aided by a grasp of the previous system. The 1976 Act operated on the basis of established "permitted hours" during which alcohol could be sold for consumption on the premises, and "trading hours" during which alcohol could be sold for consumption off the premises.[1] The permitted hours could be extended by way of a "regular extension" application, which could increase the terminal hour on an annual basis, plug the archaic "gap" in Sunday afternoon trading, or allow the premises to open earlier, all for one year before another regular extension application would be required. The hours could also be extended by way of an application for an occasional extension in order to have extra hours for special events.

The 2005 Act takes a completely different approach in respect of on-sales premises. The Explanatory Notes to section 62 say:

> "The Act introduces a more modern approach and gets rid of the practice of giving extensions to hours in favour of clarity up front about acceptable hours."

The complexity of standard permitted hours, and a separate permission for the annual extension of hours, was therefore seen as unwieldy. Indeed, as we discussed in Chapter 7 and the origin of the premises licence itself, the 2005 Act was predicated on abandoning the idea of set hours altogether. There are therefore no set "permitted hours" for on-sales, nor is there any need to seek permanent additional hours through a "regular extension" process – instead there is a presumption that any hour of the day could be a licensed hour (although there is a general statement against 24-hour opening, discussed at Section 8 below).

Off-sales hours are a rather different matter – instead of the liberal, broad-brush approach to on-sales, off-sales hours are in fact more restrictive under the 2005 Act than they were under the 1976 Act and the concept is discussed at Section 3 below.

The phrase "licensed hours" is defined in section 62 of the Act as follows:

> "(1) In this Act, 'licensed hours' means, in relation to licensed premises—
> (a) in the case of licensed premises in respect of which a premises licence has effect, the period or periods of time specified for the time being in the operating plan

1 For the avoidance of doubt, the 1976 Act permitted hours were: 11am to 11pm Monday to Saturday and 12.30pm to 2.30pm and 6.30pm to 11pm on Sundays. The 1976 "trading hours" were 8am to 10pm Monday to Saturday and 12.30pm to 10pm on Sundays.

contained in the premises licence as those during which alcohol is to be sold on the premises, and

(b) in the case of licensed premises in respect of which an occasional licence has effect, the period or periods of time specified in the licence as those during which alcohol may be sold on the premises,

and a reference to a period of licensed hours is a reference to any of those periods of time."

In short, the "licensed hours" are the hours during which alcohol may be sold. This may seem an obvious point but licensed premises will open outside the licensed hours on a frequent basis to provide other services or goods – a 24-hour supermarket, for example, or a pub which opens at 9am to provide breakfasts, or a hotel which is open around the clock to provide a number of guest services.

It is useful to note that, unlike the separation in law of on-sales and off-sales hours in the 1976 Act, the "licensed hours" as far as the 2005 Act goes, equates to both variants. The artifice of the licensed hours as a legal construct and the "categorisation" of premises is discussed in relation to the general scheme of the Act in Chapter 7 at Section 2.

2 THE LICENSED HOURS: ON-SALES

Aside from the provisions of section 64, which states that 24-hour licences may be granted only in "exceptional circumstances", it is entirely in the hands of the applicant for a premises licence to seek whichever hours he or she wishes, and it is entirely within the power of the licensing board to grant those hours, or such other hours that they are happy with. The on-sales hours are therefore those hours specified in the operating plan attached to the premises licence as granted by the board and such hours can vary on a premises-to-premises basis. Of course, it is not quite as simple as that. The board will have a view on the hours it considers appropriate for the area in which the application premises are situated and the style of operation, and this information should be in the policy statement. Applicants should review the policy statement for an idea of the sort of hours they are likely to be allowed. It is still for the applicant to decide whichever hours he wishes to seek, and each application before the board should be considered on its own merits. Exceptions can be, and have been, made. The likelihood is, however, that the standard hours will be awarded. The completion of the application form requesting on-sales hours is discussed in Chapter 8 at Section 3.2.

3 THE LICENSED HOURS: OFF-SALES

The maximum licensed hours for off-sales are found buried in section 65(3) and are, rather simply, 10am to 10pm. No alcohol may be sold for consumption off the premises before 10am, nor after 10pm. This represents a full seven-and-a-half hours fewer than those available under the 1976 Act. Remember that "off-sales hours" is not simply a term for off-sale premises; it also applies to on-sale premises which also provide an off-sale facility, such as the "cairry-oot"[2]

2 Aka "kerry-oot", or "carry-out".

from public house style premises or the ability to take home a bottle of wine from a restaurant. Off-sales hours may also be used for despatch premises such as warehouses, store-rooms, or production facilities like breweries and distilleries, where there may equally be a proper customer-facing shop as well as a despatch facility to satisfy orders made remotely.[3]

Section 65(3) does not provide that any applicant seeking off-sales hours will automatically be awarded the hours of 10am to 10pm. These are simply the maximum that may be granted – it remains for the licensing board to determine the actual hours granted. A common example of this is in relation to traditional public house style premises which provide an off-sale facility where many boards have taken the view that the off-sales hours must commence at that same time as the on-sales hours, typically 11am. Since transition, it remains the case that most licensing boards prefer to see the commencement of both on- and off-sales in conformity, although of course there will be some exceptions to that such as a genuine hybrid premises (like a visitor attraction) with, for example, a dedicated shop area as well as a restaurant facility. The completion of the application form requesting off-sales hours is discussed in Chapter 8 at Section 3.3.

4 EXCEPTIONS TO THE LICENSED HOURS

Section 63, which makes it an offence for alcohol to be sold[4] or consumed outwith the licensed hours,[5] makes provision for a number of exceptions, where it might be possible to sell alcohol outside the licensed hours, or consume alcohol outside the licensed hours, which are as follows.

4.1 Exceptions: alcohol may be consumed within 15 minutes of the end of the licensed hours[6]

This is commonly referred to as "drinking-up time". The crucial part is that the 15 minutes are to allow the completion of consumption of alcohol which has been bought prior to the end of the licensed hours in an on-sales setting where there is no food being consumed. If a bar has a licence till 1am, then alcohol may only be sold up until 1am at the latest. Consumption may occur until 1.15am.

It is a curious anomaly in the Act that the operating plan must detail activities which occur outside the licensed hours, yet this does not as a matter of practice include the drinking-up time even though it is an activity (the consumption of alcohol) which is occurring outside the licensed hours. That 15-minute period might see other activities occurring like background music

3 See Chapter 11 at Section 9 for a wider discussion on remote sales under the 2005 Act.

4 A sale outwith the licensed hours but subsequently refunded is still a completed sale transaction: *Major v Normand* [1995] 2 SLLP 6.

5 Of course, this means both before the start of the licensed hours and after the end of the licensed hours. Sales before the lawful start hour are usually associated with early kick-off times for certain football matches; however, in one case the police entered licensed premises prior to opening to find seven men hiding in a cupboard, each holding a drink and dressed like Santa Claus: [1999] 14 SLLP 44.

6 2005 Act, s 63(2)(a).

and so on and it might be argued that this should be narrated as an activity outwith the licensed hours. It is possibly considered *de minimis* for this short-time period to be narrated in this way; or is simply overlooked. If premises were licensed till 1am, but then wished to run an "after hours" facility till say 2am or later, that is likely to be a different matter and would require a major variation. Such facilities are not unheard of and some late opening premises can be used as safe spaces providing food and shelter and a "cool down" space for revellers in order to reduce public disorder on the streets, after the "nightclub" element of the premises has ceased.

4.2 Exceptions: alcohol may be taken from licensed premises within 15 minutes of the end of the licensed hours[7]

The exact provision here is that it is not an offence to:

> "allow alcohol to be taken from licensed premises at any time within 15 minutes of the end of any period of licensed hours if the alcohol—
> (i) was sold during that period, and
> (ii) is not taken from the premises in an open container".

This is far from clear, in my view. On the face of it, it appears to be directed at off-sale purchases given the alcohol is being taken away from the premises. As we know, off-sales can only occur up till 10pm at the latest. This means that the removal of alcohol which has been purchased during "that period" can only occur up until 10.15pm. This is a most curious provision when one considers that a person may be in on-sales premises until 11pm or later, yet have to leave prior to 10.15pm in order to avoid the commission of the offence, should they have purchased alcohol to take home. Take the example of a couple having a meal in a restaurant. They have enjoyed a particular wine and ask to add a bottle to the bill for them to take home. Under this provision, they would not be allowed to take the bottle home with them unless they are leaving by 10.15pm. In an off-trade example, if I am in a 24-hour supermarket and have bought alcohol just prior to the 10pm cut off, I need to be out the front door by 10.15pm. If I am half-way through a shop, therefore, I would need to buy the alcohol, remove it and place it in the car, and then return to complete my shop.

The provision finds its roots in section 54(3)(b) of the 1976 Act and I think this is where the disconnect lies. That provision related only to "permitted hours", meaning on-sales hours. The provision did not apply to off-sale purchases. It must also be recognised that this was in the context that the permitted hours did not include certain portions of the day on a Sunday so the aim of the original offence was to stop people usurping the old Sunday afternoon prohibition. When this has been translated through to the 2005 Act, the historical context, and differentiation between on- and off-sales, has been lost, leaving a provision which is wholly unsatisfactory.

7 2005 Act, s 63(2)(b).

4.3 Exceptions: alcohol may be consumed on or taken from the licensed premises outwith the licensed hours by residents and guests of residents[8]

This is a well-trodden provision and is linked to that under Section 4.4 immediately below. This provision means that alcohol may be consumed by residents and their guests at any time. The provision does not mean that the resident can insist on being served. This remains very much a discretionary activity which is in the hands of the licence holder. There is no definition provided as to what constitutes a resident. The ordinarily understood meaning of the term would be to imply that the person is residing on the premises at least for the period on which the alcohol is consumed, typically meaning an overnight stay. Under the 1976 Act, further guidance was provided as to what constituted a resident as follows:

> "a person shall be treated as residing in any premises, notwithstanding that he occupies sleeping accommodation in a separate building, if he is provided with that accommodation in the course of a business of providing board and lodging for reward at those premises and the building is habitually used for the purpose by way of annex or overflow in connection with those premises and is occupied and managed with those premises."[9]

The 2005 Act contains no such equivalent widening of the understanding of "premises" in this context. It is common for "licensed premises" to cover more than one building such as an annex or overflow as described here. Interestingly, section 63 talks of the exception of consuming alcohol on licensed premises where the person "resides on the premises" when it could just as easily have said "resides on the licensed premises" given the phrase "licensed premises" is used elsewhere in the same provision. It might be said, therefore, that there is a difference between the licensed premises, and the premises. As a matter of fact, that is certainly the case. The licence may not cover the whole premises. The question then becomes, does one have to be a resident "within the red line" of the licensed premises in order to meet the term? Notwithstanding the absence of a particular definition, I would tend to the view that a wider understanding of premises is implicit, meaning facilities like rooms within a neighbouring building would count towards the exception.

4.4 Exceptions: alcohol may be sold outwith the licensed hours to a person who resides on the premises[10]

This sister provision to that above confirms that, in the scenario where a resident at, for example, a hotel, is being served alcohol, the actual sale of the alcohol must be to that resident. This means that the guest may consume the alcohol outside the usual licensed hours, but it must be bought for them by a resident. This explains a common strategy in hotels where, after a certain point, alcohol orders can only be placed on the tab for a room and not be bought by cash or card at the bar.

8 2005 Act, s 63(2)(c).
9 1976 Act, s 139(3).
10 2005 Act, s 63(2)(d).

4.5 Exceptions: alcohol may be consumed within 30 minutes of the end of the licensed hours when it is consumed as ancillary to a meal[11]

This is the corollary provision to that examined under Section 4.1 above. The exact wording of the provision is that is not an offence to:

> "allow alcohol to be consumed on licensed premises at a meal at any time within 30 minutes of the end of any period of licensed hours if the alcohol was sold—
> (i) during that period,
> (ii) at the same time as the meal, and
> (iii) for consumption at the meal".

The philosophy behind the 30 minutes drinking-up time when the alcohol is consumed with a meal presumably emanates from the belief that one quaffs that drink at a more leisurely place whilst also dining. Note the qualifications that the alcohol must be sold during the principal licensed hours, but also that it must have been sold "at the same time as the meal" and for "consumption at the meal". The legal concept of a meal is discussed at Chapter 8 at Section 3.6.3 on restaurant facilities/bar meals as regards the "substance" of the edibles provided, but here we have another element to the concept, namely time. At what point is alcohol sold "at the same time" as the meal? Whilst it may seem this is to be taken literally, there is case law which indicates that the meal is a wider experience than the arrival of the plate of food to the moment you, satiated, put down your cutlery and draw breath. In *Heatly v McIntyre*,[12] the question of when drinks ceased to be "ancillary to a meal" under the Licensing (Scotland) Act 1962 was considered. Here, a group of friends out for a meal at the Kontiki restaurant on Lothian Road in Edinburgh had been served drinks some 30 minutes after completion of their meal. The court looked at whether drinks could be served both pre and post the actual meal. Lord Justice Clerk Grant said:

> ". . . a person may have an aperitif before his meal; he may have brandy or liqueurs or some other drink after his meal, but so long as these drinks are ancillary to the meal no breach . . . occurs. There must, I think, come to a point of time when drinks served considerably after the end of the meal cease to be ancillary thereto. As I have said, however, each case must be judged on its own facts and it is only in light of those facts that one can decide whether a particular service of drinks had lost, by lapse of time, its ancillary character."[13]

In general terms, there is no absolute requirement on alcohol being sold as ancillary to a meal under the 2005 Act in the way that there was under a restaurant licence under the 1976 Act, but the rule above is the nearest thing to it. On the basis that the law does recognise "the meal" to be some existential concept beyond the mechanics of the consumption of food, and that enforcement of such matters is therefore problematic, I think it is fair to say that most restaurant style premises might observe the 30-minute rule without too much difficulty.

11 2005 Act, s 63(2)(e).
12 1965 SLT 81.
13 Ibid at para 82.

4.6 Exceptions: alcohol may be sold outwith the licensed hours, if sold to a trader for the purposes of the person's trade

The notion of trade sales is well understood in that people who sell alcohol to the public must be able to purchase their stock from somewhere. It is accepted that, as the purpose of the purchase is not for consumption but for onward sale, there is no need to restrict the hours. The wider legal concept of trade sales and wholesales is discussed at length in Chapter 11 at Section 8.

4.7 Exceptions: are staff drinks after hours lawful?

Finally, on the topic of exceptions to the licensed hours, it is worth a moment to reflect on the issue of "lock-ins". Section 54 of the 1976 Act, which catered for the equivalent exceptions, also provided for an exception in the case of:

> "the supply of alcoholic liquor for consumption on licensed premises to any private friends of the holder of the licence bona fide entertained by him at his own expense".

There is no equivalent provision in the 2005 Act, meaning a licence holder cannot serve his own friends (or anyone else for that matter) after-hours; thus 2009 signalled the death knell of the after-hours staff drink, the legality of which had in any event been a matter of some dubiety.[14] Any consumption after hours whether paid for or free is therefore a criminal offence.

5 GENERAL EXTENSIONS (ON-SALES)

The idea of a "general extension" was a new philosophy in Scottish licensing law when introduced in 2009, and a welcome one. The purpose of a general extension is, in short, to allow a licensing board to issue a decree that later hours will be available without application under certain circumstances. The power was not a feature in the original Bill, and first appeared as a proposed paragraph 61A to the Bill at Stage 2. In the Stage 1 Report, the Committee had said:

> "The Committee recommends that the Executive brings forward amendments at Stage 2 of the Bill to provide for a system of occasional extensions in certain tightly-defined circumstances."[15]

When the issue was debated in Parliament during Stage 2, George Lyon said that the purpose of the "general extension" provisions was:

> "to introduce a power for boards to make general dispensations on licensed hours in relation to special events of national or local significance, including Christmas and new year. The power is drafted to provide flexibility for boards in deciding how it should be applied."[16]

The use of the language "special events of local or national significance" appears to have been an effort to assuage concerns raised by Alcohol Focus Scotland which had suggested that allowing for extensions of this nature "might in practice become routine", which was a comment related to the

14 See *Jack v Thom* 1952 JC 41; also "Staff drinks: a grey area" [2002] 21 SLLP 8.
15 Stage 1 Report to the Licensing (Scotland) Bill, para 48, p 10.
16 Stage 2 debate, Local Government and Transport Committee, 27 September 2005.

wider issue of 24-hour licensing. In the result, the proposed clause 61A was passed on these terms and became section 67 of the 2005 Act.

Section 67 permits a licensing board to authorise a blanket extension for all premises, or certain type of premises, within its area (or defined localities in its area), without any need for the premises to make an application, in order to cater for a special event of "local or national significance". Whilst it is noted above that the Parliamentarians nodded very clearly towards the festive season, it is worth remarking that it is clear the intent was beyond this sole time period.[17] In practice, there are a large number of examples of general extensions applying in various parts of the country. These are issued for recurring events of both national and international significance such as the Edinburgh Festival, as well as one-off events such as sporting occasions (e.g. Glasgow hosting the Commonwealth Games in 2014).

A general extension may apply to specific parts of a board area, to specific types of premises, to specific types of licensed hours, and can be for such a period as the board sees fit to determine.[18] Once a board has determined that a general extension shall apply, there are three key notification steps to follow:

> "Where a Licensing Board makes a determination under subsection (1), the Board must—
> (a) give notice of the determination to—
>   (i) the chief constable, and
>   (ii) the holders of premises licences and occasional licences in respect of premises to which the determination applies, and
> (b) publicise it in such manner as the Board sees fit."[19]

In short, the board must advise the police, the trade, and the wider public. There is no provision for objections in relation to this power, or for hearings. There is no application process. In reality, the licensing board will take views on proposed general extensions before reaching a decision. Some boards, such as Aberdeen City, will conduct annual consultations on what the general extension for the festive season should be. The details of general extensions are now usually issued on the council's website.

A key element of the general extension is that it is optional. It is up to the licence holder to decide whether to trade those extra hours or not; although, for those who do, it is frequently the case that a board will require the licence to have appropriate wording in the "seasonal variations" element of the licence, such as:

> "Such additional licensed hours as may be approved by the licensing board from time to time by way of general extension such as the festive season, local holidays, or other events."

6 EXTENDED HOURS APPLICATIONS (ON-SALES)

The licensed hours provided for in the operating plan of a premises licence may be extended to cater for special occasions or events by way of an application to the licensing board called an "extended hours application" (otherwise referred to as an "occasional extension"). This process is not to be confused

17 An example given during the debate was the "Tall Ships" festival in Glasgow.
18 2005 Act, s 67(2) and (3).
19 2005 Act, s 67(4).

with the extra hours offered under a general extension as discussed above. This application process is targeted at single premises looking for an extension for a particular scenario. The Act allows such "one-off" extensions to be considered where it is for:

> "(i) a special event or occasion to be catered for on the premises, or
> (ii) a special event of local or national significance".[20]

Typical examples of when these applications are likely to be used include the festive season, weddings, birthday parties, funerals, sporting events, local holidays, Halloween, local festivals, and so on. The fee for an extended hours application is £10.[21]

An extended hours application may not be made in respect of an occasional licence.[22] The extension applied for may last for up to one month. If the licensed hours are extended in this way, they may not be further extended by a subsequent application,[23] preventing an "extension of the extension".

The application process requires the submission of a form detailing the premises to which the extension is sought, what extra hours are sought, and details as to why the extension is sought. Whilst section 69(5) and (6) allow applications to be made with as little as 24 hours' notice (where the application "requires to be dealt with quickly"[24]), accepting an application at such short notice is entirely at the discretion of the licensing board and all boards have an expected notice period which in some areas is as much as 6 weeks ahead of the date of the proposed extension.

6.1 Determination of an extended hours application

If a board receives an extended hours application, it must give notice of it along with a copy of the application to the police and the relevant LSO. The police have 10 days within which to submit a report as to whether they think the application should be refused on the basis that it is necessary to do so for the purposes of any of the licensing objectives. The LSO also has 10 days from receipt of the application but may[25] lodge a general report with his comments on the application.

Once these reports are in, the board may consider the application at a hearing within 42 days of the date the application was received,[26] or by delegated powers. If no hearing is to be convened, the board must ensure that the applicant has the opportunity to comment on any report from the police or LSO before taking a decision. Once a decision has been made, the board must give notice of this to the applicant, the police and the LSO, and there is provision

20 2005 Act, s 68(1)(b).
21 Licensing (Fees) (Scotland) Regulations 2007 (SSI 2007/553), reg 16. The fee under the 1976 Act was £17.
22 2005 Act, s 68(6).
23 2005 Act, s 68(4).
24 2005 Act, s 69(4).
25 Section 69(3) says that the LSO "must" lodge the report. However, s 69(6), which was inserted by s 190(2) of the Criminal Justice and Licensing (Scotland) Act 2010 and commenced as of 1 October 2011 via the Criminal Justice and Licensing (Scotland) Act 2010 (Commencement No. 8, Transitional and Savings Provisions) Order 2011 (SSI 2011/178), says that the word "must" should be read as "may". Why s 69(3) was not simply amended to say may instead of must is yet another licensing enigma.
26 Licensing (Procedure) (Scotland) Regulations 2007 (SSI 2007/453) reg 13(2)(d).

for any of these parties to request a statement of reasons.[27] The request must be made within 14 days; the statement must be issued within a further 14 days, and in the form set out in Schedule 4 to the Procedural Regulations.[28]

In practice, these extensions will often engender a dialogue between the applicant and the authorities unless there is some considerable opposition. It is highly likely that the police, for example, might propose conditions which would be applied to the grant of the extended hours and it might be that the applicant is more than happy to accept them. This dialogue would be ratified by communication with the clerk's office allowing the delegated councillor or clerk to observe agreement as to conditions, thus allowing an application to be granted on those terms.

Section 70A confers a very special power to licensing boards when granting an extended hours application, which is that they:

> "may make such variation of the conditions to which the licence is subject as the Board considers necessary or expedient for the purposes of any of the licensing objectives."

This, on the face of it, allows modification of conditions to tailor the licence to the unique nature of the event or occasion for which the extended hours are sought. However, perhaps confusingly, the power relates to not just the "extended hours", but also the "period of licensed hours that the extension applies to";[29] in other words, conditions can be varied during the whole portion of the licensed hours on the day the extension is due to have effect, *not just during the extension itself*.

Unfortunately this is another example of poor law, as it is unclear whether this power can be applied to the mandatory conditions under Schedule 3 noting the separate provisions under section 27 of the Act, which prevent a board from interfering with those mandatory conditions when considering a new licence application. It might be argued that, in addition to the statutory constructs of new licence applications and extended hours applications having separate locations within the Act (and can therefore be distinguished), a more esoteric approach is to consider that this power interferes with the whole period of licensed hours and not just the extension. The Act does not explicitly say that the mandatory conditions are not to be interfered with via section 70A, leaving us to postulate as above.[30] I tend to the view that this was not the intention, but the drafting leaves the door ajar.

7 EFFECT OF BRITISH SUMMERTIME

The 2005 Act takes a remarkably polished stance in relation to dealing with changes to the clocks at the start and end of BST – it is to be treated as if it

27 2005 Act, s 70(5). There is no equivalent provision in the 1976 regime.

28 Licensing (Procedure) (Scotland) Regulations 2007, reg 15.

29 Explanatory Notes to s 191 of the Criminal Justice and Licensing (Scotland) Act 2010, which inserted the s 70A provision.

30 This dilemma is somewhat similar to the theoretical impact of s 27A of the Act, which allows boards to unilaterally make "a variation of the conditions to which a premises licence . . . is subject" even though that flies in the face of s 27(7) and the role of the mandatory conditions. The s 27A power, however, only applies to "prescribed matters", and no matters have been prescribed, so it is a zombie provision. See Chapter 8 Section 4.2.

never happened.[31] In other words, on the night that the clocks go forward or back, the licensed hours are to stay the same as if BST had not begun or ended. This breath of fresh air removed the scattergun approaches to dealing with this under the 1976 regime, which included forcing premises to shut an hour early, having to apply for occasional extensions to stay open an hour later, or ignoring the changes completely.

8 PRESUMPTION AGAINST 24-HOUR LICENSING

Nicholson suggested that there should be no set "permitted hours" as in the 1976 Act and that it should be open to an applicant to seek a licence for any hours. Nicholson believed that licensing boards had the appropriate local knowledge and experience to take a view on the hours proposed. Nonetheless, the Scottish Executive (as it was then) was wary of entrusting this function to licensing boards and, no doubt influenced by colourful media attention on the matter, inserted a presumptive provision against 24-hour licensing.

Section 64 effectively provides that a board must refuse any application before it that, if granted, would have the effect of allowing alcohol to be sold on the application premises for a continuous period of 24 hours, unless the board is satisfied that there are "exceptional circumstances" which would justify such hours. This provision, the wider social context of the 24-hour licensing spectre, and the specific debates in Parliament, are examined at length in Chapter 10 at Section 2.3.

9 THE "DUTY TO TRADE"

Of all the licensing hobgoblins, this is a particularly difficult imp to banish. In order to properly comment on the concept, one must understand the historical context. Section 54(5) of the 1976 Act states:

> "Nothing in this Act shall be taken to require any premises to be open for the sale or supply of alcoholic liquor during the permitted hours".[32]

There is no similar provision in the 2005 Act. Parties from some quarters have, in turn, treated this silence as an overt indication that the reverse is true for licensed premises under the 2005 Act: that premises are required to always be open during their licensed hours.

This was in fact the Scottish Government policy position in the run up to transition. The then head of the Government's licensing team, Gary Cox, said:

> "There have been some further discussions among licensing solicitors about whether premises have to be open for the hours set out on their operating plan, the so-called

31 2005 Act, s 66. Yay.

32 But one which was of great import to the trade, who were assured that incidental closures regardless of the reason would not affect their licence. For balance it is worth noting that under the 1976 Act a more substantial period of closure could have led to the refusal of a renewal application: see *Mount Charlotte Investments plc v City of Glasgow District Licensing Board* 1992 SCLR 311.

'duty to trade'. I'd like to take this opportunity to reiterate the Scottish Government's position on this issue. Paragraph 2(1) of Schedule 3 to the Licensing (Scotland) Act 2005 provides a mandatory licence condition that requires licensees to operate only in accordance with the operating plan contained in the licence. Premises are expected to remain open for the hours granted."[33]

Although he also pointed to a "common sense" approach, that position was in my view a misstep. When the Act came into force, a number of licensing boards and police forces flirted with the idea of supporting the notion of a duty to trade but in the end only a handful of licensing boards took it with any degree of seriousness, with one or two indicating licences could be reviewed if it was found they were not trading the full hours. The Guidance to Licensing Boards has the following wisdom to offer:

"Boards must recognise that there may be circumstances which would reasonably cause a temporary deviation from the trading hours given in the operating plan, for example a bereavement, illness, holidays, or where the weather makes a premises inaccessible. This is not an exhaustive list but one which simply illustrates certain difficulties which licence holders may encounter. Such circumstance should not ordinarily be considered a breach of the operating plan. Boards are expected to adopt a common sense approach with regard to such cases. Ministers also expect a common sense approach by Licensing Boards where licensed premises, when faced with no demand for customers, wish to close early and therefore not trade for their full complement of licensed trading hours. In considering such issues Licensing Boards should given particular attention to whether these "un-used" hours are preventing new entrants into the market. If so, consideration should be given to changing the operating plan of the premises concerned."[34]

Although the "duty to trade" appears to not dare speak its name in the guidance, the undercurrent of the above paragraphs is very much that there is some implicit duty. Section 1(1) of the Act says that:

"Alcohol is not to be sold except under and in accordance with [a premises licence]".

Schedule 3 paragraph 2 imposes a mandatory condition as follows:

"Alcohol is to be sold on the premises only in accordance with the operating plan contained in the licence."

Within these two provisions lies the supposed "duty to trade". The argument is that as the licensed hours are a part of the licence and a part of the operating plan, not trading to those exact hours is not selling alcohol "in accordance" with the operating plan.

I demur.[35] It is my considered opinion that the phrase "only in accordance with" must mean that the operator must stay within the terms of the maximum leeway allowed within the licence; not that he must adhere to the full allowance at all times. In other words, the phrase "only in accordance with" is permissive, not compulsive – it is not mandatory. A licence is not a diktat. It is a permission allowing a thing to occur within and not outwith the limits of that permission. This can be borne out by looking at the Act's sister

33 See "'Open all hours' warning to trade" (40 SLLP 4).

34 Guidance to Licensing Boards, paras 69 and 70.

35 I am not alone in my demurral: see Jack Cummins' excellent article "Is there a Duty to Trade?" [2009] 41 SLLP 14, and Tom Johnston "Duty to Trade Revisited", *Journal of the Law Society of Scotland*, 19 July 2010

provision in relation to activities. Whilst Schedule 3 paragraph 2 discusses the sale of alcohol in accordance with the licence, paragraph 3 says:

> "Any other activity to be carried on in the premises is to be carried on only in accordance with the operating plan contained in the licence."

If you believe that there is a duty to trade the full hours in selling alcohol, then by the same logic you must also believe the Act creates a statutory duty to provide all of the activities allowable under the licence at all times of the day and night.[36] That view can only be repugnant to reasonableness. Clearly Parliament could not have intended that a premises must have all activities all taking place during the whole duration of the licensed hours.

In addition, the argument ignores the very many premises that do not trade in the typical sense on a daily basis. The duty to trade presupposes that all licensed premises are like pubs. They are not! Think of the number of art centres, theatres, distilleries, visitor attractions and other similar premises all over Scotland which trade erratically, opening on some days but not others, only for certain portions of certain days; and this may change on a week-to-week basis depending on business and events. The idea of having fixed hours which one must trade simply cannot apply to them.

The argument in the Guidance that the "unused" currency of a licence would in some way prejudice other entrants to the market who would be quite willing to use those hours is, in my view, a difficult one to square with the reality of practice. I am not aware of any clamour in the trade over sitting licence holders "hoarding" an allocation of unused hours; however, it is worth noting that licensing hours are now a part of the overprovision assessment.[37]

Finally, to me it must be illogical and absurd that a licensing Act (especially one that contains an objective of protecting and improving public health) should penalise licence holders for not selling alcohol. For that is what the duty to trade does. There are, as I understand it, only two licensing boards that now still fixate on some form of the duty to trade; in respect of at least one of these, the approach taken is not forcing premises to open, but instead to ask applicants only to apply for the hours they will genuinely trade. Thus, for example, a supermarket that might normally apply for 10am to 10pm in any other licensing board area, might be encouraged to seek a licence of say 10am to 8pm in an area where those are the anticipated trading hours. This approach is taken on the view that licensed hours are a matter of public record and having licensed hours which are longer than the trading reality might undermine public confidence or create issues for people turning up at premises thinking they would be open when they are not.

Regrettably we may need case law before the matter is put out of doubt. The nearest we have had to judicial scrutiny of the matter was in *Wm Morrison Supermarkets plc v South Aberdeenshire Licensing Board*[38] in which Morrisons had sought judicial review of the Board's policy stance on the "duty to trade".

36 This would be an absurdity: a licence authorising live performances outwith the core licensed hours (for example), would be under a legal obligation to have live performances occurring 24 hours a day, 7 days a week, 365 days a year, under penalty of committing a criminal offence should the performer, gasping, seek a modest respite.

37 See Chapter 4 at Section 7 on overprovision assessments, and Chapter 10 at Section 3.4.3 on overprovision as a ground of refusal.

38 [2010] CSOH 66.

Unfortunately, presiding judge Lord Brailsford[39] took the view that judicial review should not be used to challenge a policy stance; that the issue was hypothetical. He was pressed by both parties to give an *obiter* view but refused to do so.[40]

This "duty to trade" requirement could be used, it is argued, against a licence holder who may not be using his late hours on a Thursday night, for example, as he is holding back another entrant to the market who would use the hours, and that these unused portions would affect the board's ability to calculate overprovision. There are then those who point to section 67(5) and suggest that if Parliament had intended an exemption from a requirement to trade under all the licensed hours it would have provided for it.

This, in my view, is one of the most frustrating aspects of the new regime. It is inequitable that non-operation of portions of licensed hours would lead to enforcement mechanisms to have those unused hours taken away, or that premises found to be closed on several Mondays in a row should forfeit the opportunity to trade on Mondays ever again, and that premises are forced to remain open on a particularly quiet Wednesday night for fear of losing their right to stay open at all on Wednesday nights.

The original version of the 2005 Act did in fact have a provision in the same terms as the 1976 Act, section 54(5) but it was later removed, and an amendment to reinstate it was, regrettably, rejected. The reasons for this remain unfathomable. Is the Act in fact silent on this matter? On one view, no. Section 20(4)(b) states that the operating plan must contain:

> "a statement of the times during which it is proposed that alcohol be sold on the premises".

The crucial word is, of course, "proposed". The Act does not say that the operating plan must contain "a statement of the times during which alcohol *must* be sold".

39 Lord Brailsford once bought a drum kit from me to raise funds for charity. This is of no consequence to the licensing laws, but nevertheless an interest I ought to declare.

40 See Andrew Hunter "The 'duty to trade' judicial review: a disappointing outcome" [2010] 45 SLLP 12.

Chapter 17

Personal Licences

1 OVERVIEW

Personal licences are the second part of the principally two-tiered structure of licensing regulation under the 2005 Act and are dealt with in Part 6 and the Personal Licence (Scotland) Regulations 2007.[1] The desire to create a specific licence which would apply to an individual person as opposed to the premises licence clearly emanates from the equivalent provisions in the Licensing Act 2003. Nicholson pointed to this and suggested that, having regard to the 2003 Act system:

> "A personal licence should authorise the holder of such a licence to manage and operate licensed premises, to sell or supply alcohol without supervision, and to supervise others."[2]

The role of the personal licence within the scheme of the Act is, in the first instance, inextricably linked to the role of the premises manager, the person who is named on a premises licence, albeit:

> "[o]ne designated personal licence holder per premises would be required but some premises may decide to employ more than one personal licence holder".[3]

The function of the personal licence was also described as a permission which would:

> "allow holders to sell alcohol in the same way that a driving licence permits the driving of any car".[4]

It is clear that the role, at its most basic, is to ensure responsible management of licensed premises. Nicholson said:

> "under our proposals the designated personal licence holder in any licensed premises will be responsible for ensuring that the business of those premises is conducted in a manner which is consistent with the terms of the premises licence, with the law, and with the promotion of the licensing principles. It will in our view be for that person to ensure that unqualified transient staff are given an adequate amount of inhouse training and are at all times under the supervision of a fully trained member of staff."[5]

1 SSI 2007/77. On the introduction of personal licences in the run up to the 2005 Act, see Mairi Millar, "Spare a thought for personal licences" [2007] 37 SLLP 27.
2 Nicholson Report, para 4.10(d), p 61.
3 Ibid para 52, p 19.
4 Regulatory Impact Assessment to the Licensing (Scotland) Bill, para 8, p 2.
5 Nicholson Report, para 4.23, p 67.

This was underscored further in the initial Licensing Bill as follows:

> "The emphasis [of the personal licence] is on ensuring appropriate training, both in the applicable law and in how to deal with customers. For this reason, we expect the personal licence to become a recognised qualification held by those pursuing a career in the licensed trade."[6]

However, as we will see, the personal licence has a wider place beyond the managerial duties of a premises manager and the Guidance to Licensing Boards chides us to remember that:

> "It should be stressed that a personal licence is not a qualification that is associated with business competency."[7]

A personal licence is defined in the Act at section 71 in fairly blunt terms:

> "In this Act, 'personal licence', in relation to an individual, means a licence—
> (a) issued to the individual by a Licensing Board under section 76(1) of this Act, and
> (b) authorising the individual to supervise or authorise the sale of alcohol."

There are, however four key functions that a person holding a personal licence may perform:

- they may be a premises manager on a premises licence;
- they may 'generally or specifically' authorise the sale of alcohol in premises holding a premises licence (whether they are the premises manager or not); and
- they may apply for an occasional licence in their own name in order to authorise the sale of alcohol at unlicensed premises;
- they may conduct staff training (i.e. compliance with the mandatory 2-hour staff training provision[8]).

The "portability" of a personal licence is countrywide. A personal licence issued to an individual by the Orkney Licensing Board may be used by that person in order to authorise the sale of alcohol in premises within the area of the Clackmannanshire board; a person holding a personal licence issued by the East Lothian board may make an application for an occasional licence for premises within the jurisdiction of the West Dunbartonshire board, and so on. The "portability" stops at the border, however: – an English personal licence is of no assistance in Scotland (and the converse is also true) as the statute requires a personal licence to be a licence issued under the 2005 Act in order to enjoy the benefits, as you will note from the terms of section 71 above.

The numbers of personal licences in force has varied across the lifespan of the 2005 Act, as can be seen in Table 17.1.[9]

The significant drop in 2014/15 relates to the five-year "refresher" issue which is discussed below. The figures to be issued for 2019/20 will likely show a similar drop which relates to the ten-year renewal point.

6 Policy Memorandum to the Licensing (Scotland) Bill, para 89, p 20.
7 Guidance to Licensing Boards (2007) para 159.
8 See Chapter 8 Section 2.1.5 on the mandatory condition for staff training.
9 These numbers are extracted from the Scottish Government Liquor Licensing Statistics.

Table 17.1 Numbers of personal licences

Year	*Number of personal licences in force*
2010/11	40,286
2011/12	47,681
2012/13	52,848
2013/14	57,968
2014/15	50,263
2015/16	54,557
2016/17	56,236
2017/18	58,262
2018/19	56,944

2 APPLICATION PROCESS

In order to apply for a personal licence, there are four simple requirements: the applicant must be an individual aged 18 or over; hold an approved training certificate; lodge certified passport photos; and pay the £50 fee. There is no requirement to indicate any level of experience[10] but see my comments in relation to the interaction of the fit and proper test and experience in Chapter 10 at Section 3.1.1.

An application for a personal licence should properly be made by an individual to the licensing board within whose area they are ordinarily resident, or, in any other case, to any licensing board.[11] For example, if the applicant lives in Milngavie, in the outskirts of Glasgow, but works in a pub on Byres Road in the west end of Glasgow, then he should be applying to East Dunbartonshire for his personal licence as that is the local authority in which Milngavie is to be found, even though he works in the Glasgow City area. Where this rule would not apply could be in circumstances where the applicant is an area manager perhaps based in England and will stay in various temporary accommodations, or where the application is made by someone from outside Scotland who plans to move there in the future to work in the licensed trade. Once the licence is issued by a particular board, it:

> "remains the 'relevant Licensing Board' for it and its holder, even though the individual may move out of the area or take employment elsewhere within the period for which the licence is valid".[12]

The application form itself is laid down in Schedule 2 to the Personal Licence (Scotland) Regulations 2007[13] and requires such personal information as name, address, date of birth, national insurance number and contact

10 Under the 1976 Act, there was no lower limit at which an individual could hold a licence or be nominated on a licence as a day-to-day manager, but most boards across Scotland had some sort of policy regarding a minimum level of experience which could only be achieved by someone of more advanced years – Glasgow introduced its "fitness" policy as far back as June 1995: see [1995] 1 SLLP 5. In one infamous case, a board member from one area when considering an application by a woman in her early twenties, pronounced that he would not issue a licence to "that wee lassie". Of course, being a wee lassie was not a ground of refusal under the 1976 Act.

11 2005 Act, s 72.

12 Guidance to Licensing Boards (2007), para 177.

13 SSI 2007/77.

details. The form also requires applicants to confirm whether they already hold a personal licence; whether they have any other applications pending; and if a previous application has been refused or if they have had a licence revoked. Applicants must disclose any relevant or foreign convictions. There is provision for the form to be submitted electronically[14] although this appears to be non-existent in practice. The fee for a personal licence is set at £50,[15] but the fee for a replacement duplicate of the licence is determined by the board.[16]

An application for a personal licence must be signed by the individual to whom the application relates. An agent may not sign the application. Back in 2007, when there was some debate over the matter, the Law Society of Scotland took the unusual step of writing to each board to indicate that the forms should be accepted where signed by an agent on behalf of the applicant,[17] but the matter was put out of doubt with an amendment to law requiring the form to be signed by the applicant. The policy position appears to be that the personal signature adds some "weight" to the declaration made in terms of criminal offences, although why that remains true for personal licences and not premises licences or other applications, which may be signed by an agent, remains unexplained.

The application must be accompanied by evidence of the approved training, usually a copy of the appropriate training certificate, two passport-sized photographs and the fee. The Licensing Qualification (Scotland) Regulations 2007[18] provide that a "licensing qualification" means a qualification that has been accredited by the Scottish Ministers. A number of personal licence holder courses have been "accredited" for this purpose including those of the BIIAB, ServeWise, Highfield and others. The training courses typically exist of an element of home study, a day of face-to-face tuition and a multiple choice exam under formal exam conditions, and there are online versions available too.

The photographs must measure 45mm by 35mm, be taken against a light background, show the full face of the applicant (no sunglasses or non-religious headgear), and one of the photographs must be signed by a "person of standing in the community", as in the following example:

"I certify that this is a true likeness of Michael McDougall".

Below this statement should be the name of the person certifying the photograph. Although it is not a requirement to do so, many people also add a signature and/or date.

Interestingly, the Procedural Regulations make a special provision for where a personal licence application has been lodged together with a premises licence application, and the applicant for the personal licence is named as the premises manager on the premises licence application. In that case, the personal licence is to be determined no later than the date that the premises licence application is determined.[19]

14 Personal Licence (Scotland) Regulations 2007, reg 4 (incorrectly numbered as another reg 2).
15 Licensing (Fees) (Scotland) Regulations 2007 (SSI 2007/553), reg 17.
16 Ibid reg 11(3)(f).
17 "Law society intervenes in personal licence applications dispute" [2007] 38 SLLP 20.
18 SSI 2007/98.
19 Licensing (Procedure) (Scotland) Regulations 2007 (SSI 2007/453), reg 19.

Once the application is competently lodged, it is over to the licensing board to process and determine the application.

2.1 Notification requirements for a personal licence application

A personal licence application is not consulted on as widely as a premises licence is. In fact, there are only two parties who can interact with the application, namely the police, and the LSO. There is no public consultation and no provision for objections from any party save those two.

2.1.1 Personal licence applications: police reports

The police, upon receiving notice from the board of the application (along with a copy of the form), have a period of 21 days within which to produce one of two reports (or notices), in much the same fashion as in connection with a premises licence.[20] The first notice is to state that there are no relevant or foreign convictions (so far as the police have been able to ascertain), and the second notice is to state that there are such convictions, and will detail them. Of course, the application form obliges the applicant to declare unspent convicitions and failure to do so is itself an offence. At present, spent convictions do not need to be declared nor can they be taken into account by the licensing board. This is set to change as a result of section 52 of the Air Weapons and Licensing (Scotland) Act 2015 which reverses the position by repealing section 129(4), although at the time of writing the provision which will enable this has not yet been commenced.

In addition to the provision of one of the two notices discussed above, where the chief constable:

> "considers that it is necessary for the purposes of any of the licensing objectives that the personal licence application be refused, the chief constable may include in the notice a recommendation to that effect."[21]

To be clear, the police can object to the application whether there are convictions or not. They may object to the application on the basis of the convictions, or on other material. It may be that they seek only to object on other material notwithstanding the presence of convictions. What is of note is the absence of the fit and proper test as a part of the police reporting function. This jars with the equivalent right of the police to object to a premises licence with regard to the fit and proper test, and of course a licensing board may refuse a personal licence with regard to the fit and proper test (see below) so it seems odd that the police are restricted in their submissions to the "necessary for the purposes of the licensing objectives" test alone.

The absence of convictions is generally an indication that an application for a personal licence will be successful; however, due to the series of amendments to the 2005 Act with regard to the police power of objection described above, this is not the full story. Contrarily, the presence of a criminal conviction does not mean an application will be refused *per se* as it depends on whether the

20 2005 Act, s 73(1).

21 2005 Act, s 73(4), as amended by s 206(1) and Sch 6 para 12 of the Criminal Justice and Licensing (Scotland) Act 2010.

police wish to object because of the offence, and separately the view of the licensing board in considering the presence of the offence and the view of the police.

The wider issues of convictions, police reports on same, and their relevance to the considerations of the licensing board are discussed in detail in Chapter 9 at Section 3.2; and in relation to the fit and proper test in Chapter 10 at Section 3.1.4. The applicability of the wider licensing law on convictions as to premises licences is equivalent to personal licences, so not repeated here.

2.1.2 Personal licence applications: LSO reports

When the 2005 Act was commenced, there was no official role for a LSO in relation to personal licence applications, the only party competent for comment being the police. Over time, this led to some concern from LSOs that their inability to have a say in relation to personal licence applications meant that their knowledge of the trade and of individuals working in the trade gained through experience in the front line was being lost. Efforts were made to remedy that, which resulted in section 46(3) of the Air Weapons and Licensing (Scotland) Act 2015 creating a new section 73A to the 2005 Act that allows the LSO a formal role in the personal licence process.[22]

Now, a personal licence application must be notified to the appropriate LSO. The LSO then has 21 days to respond "by giving the Licensing Board any information in relation to the applicant that the Officer considers may be relevant to consideration by the Board of the application".[23] This power is discretionary so it may be that the LSO provides no report. In some cases, depending on local practice, there may be a report issued which simply says "no comment". It is interesting to note that the power is not a right to make a recommendation to refuse akin to the equivalent power the police have in respect of personal licences. Instead, it is a much wider provision in some ways because it allows the LSO *carte blanche* to offer "any information" the officer considers relevant. The language used suggests that the LSO should be providing information on a factual basis, as opposed to presenting a subjective view on whether the ground of refusal applies. This links back to wider points I have made about the role of the LSO as an impartial agent within the licensing system, see Chapter 6 at Section 3.1.

2.2 Determination and issue of licence

Section 74 covers the process of determination. It is a fairly messy provision, having been amended on a number of occasions, and taking account of how the police report and LSO report might impact on determination.

The provision is set up to be a "must grant" as long as certain factors apply or do not apply, namely, if the application competencies have been met and there is no adverse police or LSO report, then the board must grant the appli-

22 Section 73A was commenced as of 15 May 2017 under the Air Weapons and Licensing (Scotland) Act 2015 (Commencement No. 6 and Saving Provisions) Order 2017 (SSI 2017/119).

23 2005 Act, s 73A(2).

cation. If the "competency" grounds are not met, the board must refuse the application. These are:

- the applicant must be 18,
- the applicant must possess an appropriate licensing qualification,
- the applicant does not already hold a personal licence,
- the applicant has not had a licence revoked in the last five years, save where the revocation resulted from failure to deal with refresher training provisions.[24]

Assuming these are met, and assuming that there is some notice from either the police or LSO to deal with, then the next step is to consider whether a hearing must be called. This depends on the nature of the reports:

- If the police recommend refusal, a hearing *must* be called.
- If the police do not recommend refusal, a hearing *may* be called.
- If the police have not recommended refusal but the LSO has provided a report, a hearing *may* be called.

In the case of the latter two, an application cannot be refused without the hearing occurring.[25] If a hearing is to occur, then the format of that will be along the same lines as I have discussed generally in Chapter 4 at Section 5.1 as well as Chapter 10 at Section 1; but, in short compass, the police and/or LSO will be able to speak to their report, and the applicant will be able to respond to that as well as put any wider comments about their desire to obtain the licence. The Guidance to Licensing Boards, in examining hearings for personal licence applications, goes so far as to say:

> "These hearings are not courts of law. Anyone asked to provide the Boards with evidence does not do so under oath. They are an opportunity for Boards to hear all the circumstances relating to a particular case to aid them in making a judgement, and also an opportunity for a licence holder's case to be heard. Any hearing should not be intimidating for the licence holder, and hearings should be conducted in an open and fair manner. However, Boards will be acting in a quasi-judicial manner and an appropriate degree of formality will be necessary."[26]

2.2.1 Grounds of refusal for a personal licence

Noting my comments above, we have established that a personal licence can only be refused on merit-based grounds following a hearing. There is a separate provision dealing with a surrendered licence or non-renewed licence which might have been subject to scrutiny had it not been surrendered or not renewed, so as to "catch" a supposedly fresh applicant whose purpose in that previous surrender or non-renewal was clandestine.[27] Leaving that set of circumstances aside, we know that an application may be not considered without a hearing where it is not competent. Where the application is competent, but a hearing is required, then the grounds of refusal of a personal licence for consideration are:

24 2005 Act, s 74(3)(c).
25 2005 Act, s 74(5B).
26 Guidance to Licensing Boards (2007), para 180.
27 2005 Act, s 74(7) and (8).

"(a) that, having regard to the licensing objectives, the applicant is not a fit and proper person to be the holder of a personal licence,
(b) that it is otherwise necessary to refuse the application for the purposes of any of the licensing objectives".[28]

The "fit and proper" test, and the reference to the licensing objectives as grounds of refusal, are discussed at length in Chapter 10 at Section 3.1 and 3.2 respectively, and the wider philosophy of the objectives is of course the sole focus of Chapter 3.

Once the board has made the decision to grant or refuse the application (inclusive of a renewal application), it must give notice of its decision in writing to the applicant and the police.[29] A statement of reasons may be requested, but this request must be received by the board within 14 days of the receipt by the applicant of the board's decision notice. If the statement is requested, it must be given to both the applicant and the police within a further 14 days, in the form set out in Schedule 4 to the Procedural Regulations.[30]

The form of the licence itself is in Schedule 1 to the regulations and features the personal details of the applicant, a reference number and the board logo. It also has appendices for training records; convictions and endorsements (or "black marks" – see below) and requires a photo to be attached. The Guidance to Licensing Boards set down a "unique local authority identifier" in order to assist with the process of creating a reference number for licences, so, for example, the first ever personal licence issued by Glasgow Licensing Board has the reference GC0001.[31] The full list of identifier codes is provided at Appendix F.

3 DURATION, RENEWAL AND TRAINING

Section 77 of the Act provides that a personal licence has a currency of 10 years and may be renewed for further periods of 10 years at a time thereafter. A personal licence will not have force during any suspension and the period of suspension served may not be "added on" to the currency of the licence that remains for 10 years regardless of any duration of suspension.[32] The licence will not have effect if revoked, surrendered or allowed to lapse. If the licence is to be surrendered, this must be done in writing and the licence itself sent along with the letter. If the holder of the personal licence changes name or address, they must advise the licensing board within one month of that change,[33] by returning the principal licence so it can be updated with the correct information and re-issued. If the original is not available, the licence holder would have to report the licence as lost by calling 101 and obtaining a police incident reference number, and, when writing to the board, provide this number along with any payment needed for a duplicate licence.

28 2005 Act, s 74(6A).
29 2005 Act, s 79.
30 Licensing (Procedure) (Scotland) Regulations 2007, reg 15.
31 The author is the proud holder of this very licence!
32 2005 Act, s 77(4).
33 2005 Act, s 88(3).

3.1 Renewal of a personal licence

A personal licence lasts for 10 years and the holder must apply to renew it if they wish it to continue. The licensing board that issued the licence has a duty to write to the licence holder not later than 9 months before the expiry of the licence, in order to remind the holder that the licence will cease to have effect unless renewed.[34] It is of course incumbent upon the licence holder to make the application regardless of whether a reminder is received or not.

Noting the portability of the licence, it should always be remembered that the licence vests with the licensing board which issued it, so if the holder is working in or has moved to some area other than that of the issuing licensing board, this is irrelevant. The issuing licensing board is the one to which the renewal application must be made.[35]

The renewal application, if required, must be lodged by the holder of the personal licence in a special and horribly worded "renewal window" which is "the period of 9 months beginning 12 months before the expiry date of the licence"[36]. In other words, the renewal application must be lodged no earlier than twelve months but no later than three months prior to its expiry, creating a 9-month window of opportunity for the renewal application to be lodged.[37] The renewal application is the same form as a grant of a personal licence, attracts the same fee, and follows the same procedure.[38] It must be accompanied by the original licence or a statement of reasons as to why it could not be produced, and, although not particularly specified by the Act, updated photographs are expected to make sure the licence reflects the holder's appearance, however youthful their looks may be.

Whilst the procedure for a renewal follows that of the initial application, it is worth noting the particular requirement for training. Following considerable ignominy over what the training requirements would be for a renewal application (as the Act is unclear on this), the accepted route put forward by the Scottish Government in a guidance note is for the applicant to undergo a refresher course (see below). This issue has been vastly misunderstood and, in the run up to the first clutch of renewals falling due in 2019, many licence holders did not undergo the training or lodge their renewal application correctly. The lifecycle of the personal licence, as far as training is concerned, should be as follows:

34 2005 Act, s 77(8).

35 Interestingly, Nicholson proposed that a licensing board where the person was working should be notified of the renewal application, but this was never carried through: "We suggest that an application for renewal of a personal licence should be made to the licensing board which granted the licence in the first instance but, if the licence holder is working at the relevant time in the area of a different licensing board, that application should also be intimated to that other licensing board" (Nicholson Report, para 6.11, p 80).

36 2005 Act, s 78(2). This "renewal window" was originally 3 months and 1 month, and amended to 12 and 9 by ss 60(4)(a)(i) and (ii) of the Air Weapons and Licensing (Scotland) Act 2015, the amendment taking effect from 15 May 2017 via the Air Weapons and Licensing (Scotland) Act 2015 (Commencement No. 6 and Saving Provisions) Order 2017 (SSI 2017/119).

37 This process almost defies rational comprehension. It would have been so much simpler to allow the application to be made at any point up until the date of expiry and allow the licence to continue until such time as it has been renewed or refused. This is how licences such as taxi driver licences are renewed under the 1982 Act.

38 2005 Act, s 78(5).

- Full day course passed, then first application made.
- A half-day refresher course sat and passed prior to the 5-year anniversary of the grant of the licence and evidence (i.e. updated training certificate) sent to the board no later than 3 months after the 5-year anniversary (see below).
- Another half-day refresher course must be sat and passed prior to the 10-year renewal point. This has to be a "new" half-day course and not the certificate obtained at the 5-year point. It is suggested that evidence of the training (i.e. updated training certificate) is submitted with the renewal application within the window specified as above; however, the actual position is that the renewal must be lodged in the window specified and the updated training can be sent within 3 months of the 10-year anniversary.

It has been observed that all of this is unnecessarily complex and it has also been observed that thousands of personal licences were lost at the first 5-year point in 2014, and at the first renewal point in 2019, because of failure to adhere to these processes.[39]

3.2 Requirement to produce refresher training at five years

The 2005 Act requires a personal licence holder to undertake "refresher" training every 5 years after the issue of the licence. The refresher training is not to be confused with the "renewal" of the licence as discussed at Section 3.1 above. It might be helpful to think of the refresher training requirement as a condition of the licence: the training must be done; or else the licence lapses at the relevant point.

The exact requirement is as noted above, namely that the holder of a personal licence must sit and pass a half-day refresher training course prior to the 5-year anniversary of the grant of their licence. That training certificate must be sent to the licensing board no later than 3 months after the 5-year anniversary. If either of these dates is missed, then the licensing board must revoke the licence and there is no leeway or appeal.

In 2014 when this process was required for those who had obtained the first personal licences back in 2009, the form of training which was supposed to be undertaken was not properly accredited: when the issue was finally realised, there was a rush-job to organise updated training and accreditations. This resulted in chaos as tens of thousands of people tried to get themselves on courses which were not yet available, and even those who were successful did not always then properly notify the licensing board that they had passed the course: the result was that several thousand personal licences were revoked for failure to follow the process correctly.[40] Even worse, the Act contained a 5-year ban on re-application for persons who had lost their licence in this sce-

39 The Licensing Act 2003 was amended to abolish personal licence renewals, which now have unlimited currency and no ongoing training requirements. The licences can be subject to review and be suspended and revoked under similar processes to those under the 2005 Act.

40 For some coverage of the issues at the time, see my articles: "Don't forget refresher training", *Scottish Local Retailer*, 11 March 2013; "Is this the end of the road for Personal Licences?", *Scottish Local Retailer*, 6 November 2013; and "Thousands of licences at risk in Scotland under training rule", *Bar Magazine*, 1 August 2014. Lessons might have been learned following the Gadarene rush of premises manager nominations during the conversion process, the deadline for which had to be extended back in 2009 due to an equivalent issue, on which see "Pressure mounts on application processing" [2009] 40 SLLP 3.

nario, although that was later amended and, if a licence does lapse following failure to produce evidence of refresher training, the remedy is to apply for a brand new personal licence.

If the personal licence holder is a designated premises manager then there is a knock-on effect on the premises licence. At the point the licence lapses, that person can no longer hold the position of premises manager and the "7 days and 6 weeks" rule should apply.[41]

4 CONDUCT OF A PERSONAL LICENCE HOLDER

Duties and conduct of a personal licence holder are discussed separately in Chapter 19.

5 REVIEWS OF PERSONAL LICENCES

Although a personal licence lasts for 10 years and can be renewed for periods of 10 years thereafter, a personal licence may also be subject to certain constraints imposed by a licensing board as a result of a "review" process. The review process for personal licences is scattered across a number of different provisions and has become fairly complicated as a result of various amendments to the Act over the years.

There are in fact four ways in which a review hearing may be called in relation to a personal licence:

- where it is found that there has been "conduct inconsistent" with the licensing objectives in the course of a premises licence review;
- where a relevant offence has been reported;
- where the police request a review directly; and
- where a review is requested directly by a Licensing Standards Officer.

Let us have a look at these separate processes in turn before turning to sanctions.

5.1 Personal licence reviews: conduct inconsistent with the licensing objectives arising from a premises licence review

We have looked in Chapter 14 at the processes surrounding the review of a premises licence. As was noted, one of the outcomes of a premises review hearing is that the licensing board can make a finding that any personal licence holder whose actions have been analysed in the course of the premises licence review has acted in a manner which is "inconsistent" with any of the five licensing objectives and this is dealt with in section 84 of the Act. A key element to this personal licence review route is that the person is or was working in the premises to which the premises licence review relates.[42]

This finding may be made by a licensing board regardless of which licensing board issued the personal licence. In other words, the Midlothian Licensing

41 See Chapter 13, Section 3.3.2.
42 2005 Act, s 84(1).

Board could make a finding against an individual whose licence was issued by West Lothian Licensing Board or indeed any board. The Act also empowers that board to take steps or sanctions in respect of the personal licence even if it was issued by another board.

In circumstances where the conduct of a personal licence holder is referred to in the review proposal, that individual is normally cited to attend the premises licence review hearing. If, during the course of that hearing, the board hears evidence that suggests to them that the person has acted in a manner which is inconsistent with the licensing objectives, then the board can make a finding to that end.

The impact of such a finding is, in short, that a separate review hearing into that person's personal licence must occur. If the person is still working within that licensing board area, then it may hold the hearing. If, on the other hand, the issuing board is aware that the person is working in another jurisdiction, they must write to that licensing board and give notice of their finding together with a recommendation as to whether the licence should be revoked, suspended or endorsed.[43] If the board which has made a finding under section 84 following a premises licence review is unsure as to where the person is now working, then it can issue the notice to the licensing board that issued the personal licence in the first place. In all three of these eventualities, a hearing must occur.

At the hearing the licensing board must give the licence holder as well as "such other persons as they consider to be appropriate" an opportunity to be heard. This allows submissions to be made by not just the police or LSO, but perhaps other individuals who may have something to say about the conduct (whether for good or ill) of the personal licence holder.

If the board is satisfied that it is necessary to do so for the purposes of any of the licensing objectives, it may make an order imposing one of the sanctions which are discussed below. The use of the phrase "if satisfied" means, of course, that it is possible that the board may not in fact be satisfied that it is necessary to make an order and therefore no action would be taken against the personal licence holder.

5.2 Personal licence reviews: declaration of a relevant offence

Section 82 of the Act imposes a duty on the holder of a personal licence to declare criminal convictions to the licensing board that issued the personal licence as well as any licensing board in whose jurisdiction they are working, within a period of one month from the date of conviction. Failure to comply with this is a criminal offence. In addition to reporting the matter to relevant licensing boards, the personal licence holder also has to return the principal personal licence, or a statement for failure to produce it if it is not "practicable". There is no specific provision for how to deal with a situation where the person has to submit the principal licence to more than one board, if such a report is necessary. It is to be assumed that the correct course of action therefore would be to send the principal licence to the board that issued the licence, and provide any other board with a statement confirming that this is where the licence has been sent.

43 2005 Act, s 84(3)(b) and (4).

Where a personal licence holder notifies the licensing board of a conviction, this activates a process which the board must follow under section 83, which will result in a personal licence review hearing. The first stage is that the board must give notice of the conviction details they have received to the police. The police then have 21 days from the receipt of the notice to respond, and are required to give one of two possible notices in return:

- a notice saying that the police cannot confirm the existence of the conviction, or that it does not relate to a relevant or foreign offence; or
- a notice confirming the existence of the reported conviction and that it does relate to a relevant or foreign offence.

If the police return the first notice, then that is the end of the matter and the board "may not take any further action".[44]

If the police return the second notice, they may also make a recommendation that the licence be endorsed, suspended or revoked having regard to any of the five licensing objectives. It is therefore conceivable that the second notice may not contain such a recommendation; however, if the second notice is received then the licensing board has discretion as to whether they wish to hold a hearing where such a recommendation is made or not.[45]

The procedure for a hearing under these circumstances is also found under section 83 and broadly mirrors the review hearing processes elsewhere in that the licence holder is given an opportunity to be heard, as are the police, and the licensing board may then take steps or not. The steps and sanctions are discussed below.

5.3 Personal licence reviews: police section 84A review

Section 84A of the 2005 Act was introduced by the Criminal Justice and Licensing (Scotland) Act 2010[46] and allows the police to directly request a personal licence review where they believe the personal licence holder has acted inconsistently with any of the five licensing objectives. Where such a request is received, the processes outlined above are followed.

5.4 Personal licence reviews: licensing standards officer section 84B review

This provision is the newest in the canon of reviews and came to life as a result of the Air Weapons and Licensing (Scotland) Act 2015.[47] It effectively mirrors the provision above, thus allowing a LSO to directly request a review

44 2005 Act, s 83(6).

45 When the Act was originally passed, the board had to hold a hearing regardless of whether the police included a recommendation to take steps against the personal licence or not. This was amended to remove that restrictive practice under s 51(a) of the Air Weapons and Licensing (Scotland) Act 2015 as of 15 May 2017 via the Air Weapons and Licensing (Scotland) Act 2015 (Commencement No. 6 and Saving Provisions) Order 2017 (SSI 2017/119).

46 Section 206(1) of the 2010 Act, and commenced as of 13 December 2010 under the Criminal Justice and Licensing (Scotland) Act 2010 (Commencement No. 6, Transitional and Savings Provisions) Order 2010 (SSI 2010/413).

47 Section 58 of the 2015 Act, and commenced as of 15 May 2017 under the Air Weapons and Licensing (Scotland) Act 2015 (Commencement No. 6 and Saving Provisions) Order 2017 (SSI 2017/119).

of a personal licence where the person has acted in a manner inconsistent with the licensing objectives, save a caveat that the power applies only where the person is or was working in that officer's area (thus preventing a LSO from a particular area seeking a review of a personal licence relating to a person outwith their jurisdiction). Again, the review process and steps open to a licensing board simply replicate those narrated above.

5.5 Personal licence reviews: sanctions available

In each of the four routes to review of a personal licence noted above, there is a series of steps or sanctions open to the licensing board in relation to a finding that such steps are necessary for the purposes of the licensing objectives, which are that they *may* make an order:

- to endorse the licence;
- to suspend the licence; and
- to revoke the licence.

It is of course open to the board to find that the grounds are established and take no action, just as it is open to the board to find (where appropriate) that the grounds for review are not established, and there the matter ends.

Finally, it is also open to the board in each review process to find that the personal licence holder is not a fit and proper person to hold a licence having regard to the licensing objectives. In that case, the licensing board must revoke the licence.

The "endorsement" of a personal licence is first mentioned in the Act at section 83(9)(c), in relation to convictions subsequent to the issue of the licence, but of course is an outcome open in all four of the potential review processes. The origin of this sanction is found in the following text from Nicholson:

> "we consider that provision should be made for a much less severe sanction such as an admonition, or what might be described as an 'endorsement' of the licence. We are not suggesting that there should be a system, such as that under the Road Traffic Acts, where a specified number of endorsements, or penalty points, will lead to an automatic disqualification in the event of further offending. On the other hand, we think that there may be circumstances where a breach of duty will properly call for some recognition, albeit of a minor kind, but with the realisation that even minor offending, if repeated, could result in a much more serious sanction at a future stage. We suggest, however, that any admonition or endorsement should no longer be capable of being taken into account after the expiry of a period of 10 years."[48]

An endorsement may be shortly viewed as a "black mark" on the personal licence. Endorsements will sit on the personal licence for a period of 5 years from the date the endorsement was made, at which point the holder of the licence may apply to the board to have it removed from his licence, an administrative process which the board must comply with. There is no real penalty for not making this request as an endorsement that has expired is to be disregarded.[49]

If a personal licence attracts three endorsements, this triggers a requirement

48 Nicholson Report, para 7.21, p 105.
49 2005 Act, s 85.

for the board that issued the licence to hold a hearing.[50] The board has the power to suspend (for a period not greater than 6 months) or revoke the personal licence at this hearing so long as it has first given the personal licence holder (and other such persons as the board thinks appropriate) an opportunity to be heard, and it considers it necessary to do so for the purposes of any of the licensing objectives. If an order to revoke or suspend is carried, the board must notify the holder and specify the reasons for the order.

If the principal order is to go directly to a suspension, then the maximum period is 6 months. It is to be considered that the suspension of a licence must be to achieve some goal in relation to the licensing objectives, as opposed to a punishment. This concept is touched on in Chapter 10 at Section 3.1.1 as regards the "fit and proper" test and "future proofing" the licensing objectives, as well as in relation to premises licence reviews in Chapter 14 at Section 2.1. The effect of a suspension on the personal licence is that the person may not carry out any of the prescribed duties that a personal licence holder is able to do: this means that person cannot be a designated premises manager, they cannot conduct staff training, or authorise alcohol sales. There is also an argument that a personal licence holder under suspension cannot be the applicant for an occasional licence. It is to be noted that there is nothing to stop a personal licence holder whose licence is under suspension to carry on their job as a "manager" of a licensed premises, they just cannot be the premises manager named on the premises licence.

There is no separate provision linking the existence of an endorsement to the renewal process and it appears that the intent of the legislation is to treat the two processes as separate: in other words, that there should be no double punishment for the issue which led to the endorsement.[51]

6 PERSONAL LICENCES AND AUTHORISATION

See Chapter 15 at Section 4.4 in relation to personal licences and the concept of "authorisation" of alcohol sales.

50 2005 Act, s 86(1).

51 The Policy Memorandum to the Licensing (Scotland) Bill says, "On their own, endorsements would not prevent the renewal of a personal licence": para 119, p 27.

Chapter 18

Occasional Licences[1]

1 OVERVIEW

Occasional licences are dealt with in Part 4 of the Act. Unhappily, there is no immediate definition as to what an occasional licence actually is, save that section 56(1) says such licences may be issued to:

> "any premises (other than licensed premises) within the Board's area".

Nicholson described occasional licences under the 1976 Act as being something to obtain:

> "in the course of catering for an event taking place outwith the licensed premises in respect of which he is the holder of a licence. A typical example of that would be the provision of catering, including the sale of alcohol, at a wedding reception or other social event held on private property."[2]

As originally envisaged, therefore, the point of an occasional licence was to cater for short one-off events where alcohol would be sold other than from licensed premises, such as hosting a local gala day or fête, or:

> "for the temporary sale or supply of alcohol which is not authorised by a premises licence".[3]

In other words, an occasional licence is a short-life licence (sometimes only lasting a few hours) that affixes to unlicensed premises, but cannot be applied for in respect of licensed premises.[4] These licences have, however, developed into an indispensable tool for the licensed trade and should not be viewed simply as a permission for an existing publican to cater for a wedding reception in a local hall.

Occasional licences are now used for myriad events, pop-up bars, local markets, large-scale festivals, fund-raising activities for "charities, schools and local community groups",[5] and, in some cases, to provide a temporary option to allow trading whilst awaiting the grant of a full licence (on which, see Section 9 below). The apparent rise of occasional licence use is inextricably linked to the popularity and increase of short-life events, street food markets, craft beer and spirit tastings, and so on.

1 Co-authored by Niall JN Hassard
2 Nicholson Report, para 14.24, p 150.
3 Guidance to Licensing Boards (April 2007) para 137.
4 Note, however, that s 125 members' club premises can be subject to an occasional licence application to permit non-member events.
5 Regulatory Impact Assessment to the Licensing (Scotland) Bill, para 32.

So-called "pop-up" facilities will often have an alcohol offer, and these regularly feature in disused industrial or outdoor public spaces perhaps not suitable for the more rigorous premises licence application process. These markets can run at regular intervals and/or for prolonged periods. Many pub and restaurant operators will also use occasional licences to license external pavement café areas (in conjunction with other permits), running them consecutively across the summer months to allow customers to sit and enjoy the fine Scottish sun. A small cadre supports the view that an occasional licence can only be sought for a designated "event", but the 2005 Act does not require that, whereas the 1976 Act equivalent did.[6]

The occasional licence process is a relatively "light touch" application procedure in comparison to other processes under the 2005 Act, no doubt due to the fact that it is designed to authorise alcohol sales on a temporary basis.

2 APPLYING FOR AN OCCASIONAL LICENCE

Arguably the 2005 Act provisions are (frustratingly) limber on the one hand, and prescriptive on the other. Section 56(2) sets out who can apply for an occasional licence, *viz*:

- a premises licence holder,
- a personal licence holder, and
- a representative of a voluntary organisation.

A premises licence holder in this context does of course mean the holder of any premises licence (in contrast to the old rules under the 1976 Act)[7] under the 2005 Act, but a question arises as to whether this extends to the holder of a provisional premises licence. Some licensing boards take the view that "premises licence holder" does not include a provisional premises licence, notwithstanding that the Act does appear to confirm that a provisional premises licence is a premises licence, and processes under the Act which attach to premises licences also attach to provisional premises licences such as variation and transfer. I discuss this conundrum further in Chapter 11 at Section 3.6.

With respect to a personal licence applicant, I take the view that the personal licence must be in force and valid. In other words, a personal licence which has expired, or is under suspension, or has been revoked, is not *terra firma* on which a competent occasional licence application can be made.

The most elusive of applicant identities is, however, the "voluntary organisation". In practice, the lack of definition as to what constitutes a "voluntary

6 The only reference to the need for an event is in relation to applications by voluntary organisations where the sale of alcohol should be at "an event" in connection with the activities of the organisation. It is also worth noting that, as Scotland looked to remove itself from Coronavirus "lockdown" in June 2020, the Scottish Government unexpectedly issued statutory guidance to licensing boards in respect of the use of occasional licences, encouraging them to think positively about concurrent occasional licence applications for outdoor spaces in order to support business and economic recovery from the virus.

7 The 2005 Act removed the irksome difficulty for those who had operated under entertainment or refreshment licences under the 1976 Act, who were prohibited from making application for the equivalent licence. This caused particular problems for such premises with external areas, with many forced to apply for a full new licence to cover the outside area.

Table 18.1 Numbers of occasional licences

Year	*Occasional licences (Scotland)*
2018/19	25,726
2017/18	24,299
2016/17	23,619
2015/16	24,430

organisation" rears its head at the most inopportune moments, normally as the event to which the application pertains looms large. Nicholson warned of this, saying:

> "We think, however, that there might be some advantage if there were to be a statutory definition of 'voluntary organisation'. No such definition is given in the 1976 Act, and we are of the view that in the absence of a definition there may be room for dispute as to the types of organisation which are entitled to seek a permission of this kind."[8]

In light of the fact that a definition is not contained in the 2005 Act, or the Regulations,[9] it remains open to interpretation. The Scottish Council for Voluntary Organisations (SCVO) defines a voluntary organisation as follows:

> ". . . a group of people who have decided to work together to accomplish a common agreed non-commercial purpose, such as a club, society, local group or community association. A voluntary association is the simplest form of legal structure and is often appropriate for small scale activities which do not involve leasing premises or employing staff."

Licensing boards concerned about possible exploitation under the auspices of being a voluntary association would be advised to set out their criteria as to who qualifies in their statement of licensing policy.

The broadening of the prescribed applicant, as well as the increasingly popularity of pop-up style businesses, creates a general suggestion that there has been an upturn in the number of applications. Table 18.1 gives the details that we have available to us. Prior to 2015/16, the Scottish Government did not collate a record of occasional licences granted under the 2005 Act, and there are no equivalent statistics in any Government publication as to numbers of occasional licences or permissions issued under the 1976 Act.[10]

Those concerned about the liberal use of occasional licences should pause and take some comfort as there are checks in place to ensure that any such applications are considered appropriately.

2.1 Notification of an occasional licence application

The licensing board is required to give notice of the application, along with a copy of it, to the Chief Constable (the police) and Licensing Standards

8 Nicholson Report, para 14.25, p 151. This echoed the remarks of his predecessor Clayson (para 15.04). The only other legislative guidance available was in the English Licensing (Occasional Permissions) Act 1983, in which "voluntary organisation" was determined as being an organisation carried on not for "purposes of private gain". This Act was repealed by the Licensing Act 2003.

9 Namely, the Occasional Licence (Scotland) Regulations 2007 (SSI 2007/96).

10 Scottish Government Liquor Licensing Statistics.

Officer (LSO). The Procedural Regulations also require the licensing board to publish details of the application on the board's website for a continuous period of 7 days[11] to coincide with the notification to the police and LSO. The pool of consultees is notably smaller than for a premises licence application under section 21. It does not, for example, include community councils or the health board. It is perhaps useful to note that a number of licensing boards will, through local convention, give notice of occasional licence applications to local elected members and the relevant community council.

The LSO has a 21-day period within which to lodge a report with the board setting out their comments, which may be as benign or adverse as they see fit. The 21-day timeframe can be modified by the licensing board under section 57(5) to fast track the process down to 24 hours, on cause shown. [12]

Perhaps oddly, no similar provision exists for the police. This is as a result of the repeal of the original section 57(2) which had afforded the police a power to make a recommendation to refuse the application on "the crime prevention" objective, that is, on the licensing objective of Preventing Crime and Disorder. This was repealed[13] on the basis that the police wanted the power to recommend refusal on any of the five licensing objectives, but the repeal did not replace the provision with a formal "recommendation to refuse" process, instead leaving the matter open – and therefore leaving the police to make such comment as they may, not as party with special status, but as "any person" under section 58 (see below).

2.2 Objections and representations to an occasional licence

Section 58 provides for objections and representations to an application for an occasional licence. "Any person" may not only object to such an application, but may make representations, including representations in support of the application or suggesting conditions that the person considers should be imposed.

Conditions could be suggested with regard to upholding the licensing objectives. Whilst, in theory, any person may comment or object (if they saw the advert on the board's website), in practice, objections and representations routinely only come from the police and LSO. The grounds of objection to an occasional licence are linked to the grounds of refusal under section 59(6) and this is discussed in Section 5 below.

A common issue that arises with occasional licences is a request for a local condition to be added which strays into the mandatory conditions and is more onerous than same. For example, a condition often requested is, "a personal licence holder must be present at all times alcohol is being sold". Occasional licences are granted under s 60 and they are subject to the mandatory conditions set out in Schedule 4 to the 2005 Act,[14] which I discuss in

11 Licensing (Procedure) (Scotland) Regulations 2007 (SSI 2007/453), reg 18.

12 This may, for example, be to license a church hall at short notice for a funeral purvey. The "fast track" process was not part of the original 2005 Act and was only added later via the Criminal Justice and Licensing (Scotland) Act 2010 – on which see "Fast track for occasional licences" [2008] 41 SLLP 5.

13 See Sch 6 para 9 of the Criminal Justice and Licensing (Scotland) Act 2010 – as commenced on 1 November 2011 by the Criminal Justice and Licensing (Scotland) Act 2010 (Commencement No. 9, Transitional and Savings Provisions) Order 2011 (SSI 2011/354).

14 2005 Act, s 60(1).

detail at Section 5.1 below. Section 60(5) states that a Licensing Board may not impose a local condition which is inconsistent with a mandatory condition, or would have the effect of making any such condition more onerous or more restrictive.

If the licensing board receives an objection or representation, it must be copied to the applicant within 7 days[15] and the board must have regard to it in determining the application. The board may, however, reject the objection or representation on the grounds that it is frivolous or vexatious.[16] The board should also consider any response from the applicant.

3 DURATION AND NUMBER OF OCCASIONAL LICENCES

Section 56(5) provides that an occasional licence may not exceed a period of 14 days. At the time of writing there is no restriction on the number of occasional licence applications which may be lodged by a premises licence holder or personal licence holder, but section 56(6) restricts the number which may be applied for by a voluntary organisation to not more than four occasional licences which seek to cover a period greater than four days, and not more than twelve occasional licences for a period of three days or less, and between the two there can be no more than 56 days in total covered by the occasional licences sought.

The "maximums" for voluntary organisations are higher than the old equivalent permissions under the 1976 Act, which placed a restriction of no more than four permissions in any one year (although this was in all likelihood abused).[17] A clear policy position is promulgated that this increase was designed to greater support island and rural communities:

> "Rural communities in general can also be expected to benefit from our proposals to increase the number of occasional licences that may be granted to voluntary bodies in a year. This would include, for example, village hall committees."[18]

There is specific provision for club premises, on which see Section 7 below.

4 FORM OF APPLICATION AND LICENCE

Section 56(7) and (8) require an occasional licence to show the following information:

- name and address of the holder of the licence,
- description of the premises in respect of which the licence is issued,
- description of the activities to be carried on in the premises,
- statement of the period during which the licence has effect,
- statement of the times during which alcohol may be sold on the premises,

15 Licensing (Procedure) (Scotland) Regulations 2007, reg 11(2).

16 2005 Act, s 58(3). If the objection or representation is rejected on this basis, the board may recover any expenses incurred in considering it (s 58(4)), a provision designed no doubt to try to ward off serial complainers.

17 Licensing (Scotland) Act 1976, s 34(2).

18 Policy Memorandum to the Licensing (Scotland) Bill, para 166.

- statement as to whether alcohol is to be sold for consumption on or off the premises, or both,
- statement of the times at which any other activities in addition to the sale of alcohol are to be carried on in the premises,
- where alcohol is to be sold for consumption on the premises, a statement as to whether children or young persons are to be allowed entry and, if they are, a statement of the terms on which they are allowed entry including ages, times at which entry is allowed, and parts of the premises to which they are allowed, and
- conditions of the licence.

The form of the application and licence itself are laid down in Schedules 1 and 2 to the Occasional Licence (Scotland) Regulations 2007.[19]

5 DETERMINATION OF AN OCCASIONAL LICENCE APPLICATION

The good news for those intending to apply for occasional licences is that if there is no notice from the police and LSO, and no notice of objection or representation, then the board must grant the application.

If any of those notices applies, then a hearing may take place within 42 days of the date the application was received,[20] at which the board must consider whether any of the grounds of refusal apply. The grounds of refusal (s 59(6)) are that:

- the premises to which the application relates are excluded premises,
- the application seeks a 24-hour licence and there are no exceptional circumstances,
- the application seeks off-sales hours outwith 10am to 10pm,
- the granting of the application would be inconsistent with one of the licensing objectives, and
- having regard to the proposed activities, location, character and condition of the premises, or the persons likely to frequent the premises, the board considers that the premises are unsuitable for use for the sale of alcohol.

Occasional licence hearings are relatively infrequent in practice, with the vast majority of licensing boards having a scheme of delegation in place to allow determination by a board member based on written submissions.

The board must give notice of its decision to the applicant, police, LSO and parties to the application.[21] Those persons may request a statement of reasons from the board as to how it reached the decision; the request must be lodged within 14 days of the date the notice is received and thereafter the board has a further 14 days to issue the statement, which is to be in the form in Schedule 4 to the Licensing (Procedure) (Scotland) Regulations 2007.[22] Note that any appeal by summary application must be lodged no later than 21 days after

19 SSI 2007/96.
20 Licensing (Procedure) (Scotland) Regulations 2007, reg 13(2)(c).
21 2005 Act, s 61(1).
22 SSI 2007/453; reg 15.

the date of the decision regardless of whether a statement of reasons has been requested and is awaited.

5.1 Occasional licences and mandatory conditions

Where an occasional licence is granted, it is subject to a series of mandatory conditions which are contained in Schedule 4 to the Act. The occasional licence mandatory conditions are similar to the premises licence mandatory conditions which are discussed in detail in Chapter 15, save that some have some technical variances which I have noted here, and some do not apply at all:

- **Compliance with the licence:** where the Schedule 3 conditions discuss features of an "operating plan", the Schedule 4 conditions discuss the licence, meaning the occasional licence.
- **Authorisation of sales of alcohol:** as with a premises licence, sales must be authorised generally or specifically by a person who holds a personal licence, save that this condition does not apply where the holder of the occasional licence is a voluntary organisation.
- **Voluntary organisations:** where the licence is held by a voluntary organisation, alcohol can only be sold at an event in connection with that organisation's activities.
- **Minimum pricing:** applies as per a premises licence.
- **Multi-pack ban:** applies as per a premises licence.
- **72-hour rule:** applies as per a premises licence.
- **Irresponsible drinks promotions:** applies as per a premises licence.
- **Provision of non-alcoholic drinks and tap water**: applies as per a premises licence.
- **Age verification policy ("Challenge 25"):** applies as per a premises licence.
- **Premises manager**: no condition.
- **Training of staff**: no condition.
- **Notices**: no condition.
- **Baby changing facilities**: no condition.
- **Off-sales display restrictions**: no condition.

In relation to staff training, it is often considered an oversight that staff who are serving alcohol at an "occasional" event need not be subject to the same scrutiny as staff working in permanent premises. The original policy position here was that temporary staff should not be subject to the same level of scrutiny given occasional licences were often used by small bodies and charities in a low-level capacity and might have someone like a volunteer committee member pouring Chardonnay into plastic cups. In relation to voluntary organisations, the Local Government and Transport Committee said during the passing of the Bill:

> "The Committee considers that it would not be appropriate for detailed training to be given to representatives of voluntary organisations who sell alcohol at events held using occasional licences. However, the Committee considers that there may be scope for a basic form of training to be given to representatives of voluntary organisations so that they are aware of their responsibilities in selling alcohol. The Committee would not want this training requirement to be onerous – it could, for

> example, take the form of a package of information which all applicants for occasional licences are required to read and understand. But the Committee considers that even a basic level of instruction and training would be beneficial and would address some of the concerns which were highlighted in evidence at Stage 1."[23]

The absence of staff training as a condition of occasional licences was not universally well received. In evidence during the passing of the Bill, Councillor Attridge of Edinburgh Licensing Board expressed concerns over the lack of training, as did Alcohol Focus Scotland, who said:

> ". . . there is a risk that, if people at such events are not involved in the educational process and dispense or sell alcohol without understanding what they are doing, all the other provisions on licensing will be undermined".[24]

Whilst the staff training condition does not apply to occasional licences, my advice to clients seeking such licences is that it is a matter of best practice to require staff to have undergone the training. Similarly, whilst there is no requirement to have a named premises manager, and no requirement for a personal licence holder to be physically present at all times when alcohol is sold from an occasional licence, it is a matter of best practice to have a personal licence holder present. Along the same lines, whilst there is no requirement to have a Schedule 3 notice concerning the access to the premises by children and young persons, it is worth remembering that the section 110 notice requirement does apply to occasional licences, and there is no harm in displaying your own notice to confirm access arrangements and other non-statutory notices such as a "Challenge 25" poster.

6 OCCASIONAL LICENCES FOR MOVING PREMISES

Section 126 makes various provisions for applications in respect of vehicles, vessels and other moveable structures. Under section 126(9), in an application for an occasional licence for moving premises, the premises are to be treated as premises situated within the area of the "appropriate licensing board", meaning either the board in whose area the premises are to be used, or, where the premises are to be used in more than one board area, the board in whose area the premises are used to a greater or greatest extent, and if neither of those provisions apply, such other appropriate licensing board nominated as such. For more detail on the licensing of moving vehicles, see Chapter 11 at Section 7.

7 OCCASIONAL LICENCES AND CLUBS

One of the novel aspects of the 2005 Act regime is to be found in the Licensing (Clubs) (Scotland) Regulations 2007.[25] Regulation 3 provides for occasional licences to be applied for in respect of club premises – a rare example of

23 Stage 1 Report to the Licensing (Scotland) Bill, Local Government and Transport Committee, para 34.

24 Ibid para 236.

25 SSI 2007/76.

"double licensing" – the principal effect of which is to allow full public access to club premises but also that, when the occasional licence has force, the conditions attaching to the principal premises licence are "not to have effect".

This provision has been controversial, and has attracted negative comment from the "mainstream" licensed trade, unhappy that they could have to compete with club premises on an uneven playing field when the occasional licences are in force, especially in relation to the exclusion of the restrictive conditions on allowing members and guests only – in other words, when an occasional licence is in force over club premises, members of the public can freely use the facilities, including consuming alcohol at the bar.[26]

The regulation, however, does restrict the number of occasional licences that may be used in this fashion. The licensing board may issue, in any 12-month period, no more than four occasional licences with a duration of four days or more and no more than twelve occasional licences with a duration of less than four days. In either event, the total number of days covered by occasional licences may not exceed 56, so it is up to the club premises and applicant for the occasional licence to decide how to manipulate these rules to their advantage.

The special nature of club premises is explored in significant detail in Chapter 11 at Section 2. The interplay between Schedule 3 and Schedule 4 conditions where an occasional licence has effect "superseding" the premises licence is discussed in Chapter 11 at Section 2.5.

8 INTERPLAY BETWEEN OCCASIONAL LICENCES AND PUBLIC ENTERTAINMENT LICENSING

Occasional licences have many uses including the fêtes and galas referenced above but additionally are vital to the outdoor music and festival scene. Interestingly, the music festival and large-scale event use of occasional licences was one of the first battlegrounds around these temporary permissions.

The occasional licence regime was criticised due to the interplay between it and the handling of public entertainment licensing under the Civic Government (Scotland) Act 1982. As originally implemented, the 2005 Act provided an exemption from the need for an organiser to seek a Public Entertainment Licence (PEL) under section 41(2)(f) of the Civic Government (Scotland) Act 1982. It stated that a PEL was not needed for:

> "Licensed premises within the meaning of the Licensing (Scotland) Act 2005 (asp 16) in which public entertainment is being provided during licensed hours ..."

This definition of "licensed premises" included premises licensed by way of occasional licence. Critics pointed out that large-scale events and festivals could, in theory, take place under the authority of a simple occasional licence with little statutory notification required and for a fee of just £10. Such criticism was redoubled in the wake of the *Brightcrew* case, with licensing boards suggesting it was problematic for partner agencies and council officials concerned with wider issues than the sale and supply of alcohol.

26 For early expressions of these concerns, see for example "Club occasional licences 'outrage'" [2006] 35 SLLP 3.

As a result of these concerns, the 1982 Act was amended by section 75 of the Air Weapons and Licensing (Scotland) Act 2015 to apply only to:

> "premises in respect of which a premises licence within the meaning of section 17 of the Licensing (Scotland) Act 2005 has effect in which public entertainment is being provided during licensed hours …"

This removed the PEL exemption for occasional licences, the change coming into effect as of 1 November 2016.[27] Since that time, whilst it is clear to sophisticated operators of large-scale events that they will need to obtain both a temporary public entertainment licence and an occasional licence, there has been a slew of news stories about small community groups "caught out" by the need to obtain both for smaller events, although that is also partly to do with the removal of the exemption from a licensing requirement for attendance at such events where they were free to attend.[28]

As an aside it should be noted that Public Entertainment Licensing is an optional form of licence and subject to the terms of each Local Authority's relevant Resolution. This means that in some local authority areas an event may need a temporary PEL in addition to an occasional licence, whereas in a neighbouring local authority it may not.[29]

Licensing boards have long asked the Scottish Government to revisit the application fee level and limits on the number and duration of occasional licences. The Scottish Government completed a long-promised public consultation around these issues in July 2019. It is thought that proposals emanating from the consultation would see an increase in the fees for occasional licences on a form of sliding scale, based perhaps on the identity of the applicant or the nature of the event, as well as giving licensing boards greater powers to "block" occasional licence use where it was felt this was abusing the system, by circumventing the full premises licence process. Legislation by way of an amendment to the relevant regulations was expected in the latter part of 2020 but the impact of Covid-19 on licensing and society as a whole has meant that this has been delayed; and the thrust of opposition to concurrent licences has perhaps had the sting removed with the issue of further statutory guidance effectively tasking boards with allowing back-to-back occasional licences especially for outdoor areas, to support business recovery from the virus.[30]

9 INTERPLAY BETWEEN OCCASIONAL LICENCES AND PROVISIONAL LICENCES

As noted in the introduction to this chapter, an occasional licence can only be sought for premises other than licensed premises. Differing interpretations

27 Air Weapons and Licensing (Scotland) Act 2015 (Commencement No. 5 and Saving Provisions) Order 2016 (SSI 2016/307).

28 This change was brought in by s 176 of the Criminal Justice and Licensing (Scotland) Act 2010, and then commenced on 1 April 2012 by the Criminal Justice and Licensing (Scotland) Act 2010 (Commencement No. 8, Transitional and Savings Provisions) Order 2011 (SSI 2011/178).

29 For more detail on the operation of public entertainment licensing, see Stephen McGowan, *Local Government Licensing Law in Scotland* (Institute of Licensing, 2012) ch12.

30 Guidance to Licensing Boards (18 June 2020): "Update on occasional licence use for licensed premises affected by closure due to the coronavirus pandemic".

have sparked debate about the use of occasional licences as a "stopgap" between the date of the grant of a provisional premises licence under section 45 and confirmation of same under section 46.

"Licensed premises" is a defined term under section 147(1) and means premises in respect of which a premises licence or occasional licence has effect. Many practitioners and licensing boards take the view that premises benefiting from a provisional premises licence under section 45 fall outwith the scope of the definition of licensed premises by virtue of section 45(3), which states that a premises licence issued in respect of any such premises does not take effect unless and until it is confirmed by the Licensing Board which issued it in accordance with section 46. As a result of taking this view, it is generally accepted by licensing boards that one is not barred from applying for an occasional licence for premises that have been granted a provisional premises licence pending confirmation. This interpretation is a pragmatic one given the alternative view, that the provisional premises licence is simply a premises licence, is also taken by those same boards when it comes to allowing other application processes to obtemper to provisional licences such as variation and transfer.

The desire to use occasional licences pending confirmation can arise due to the local arrangements in place which govern the confirmation process and are ultimately pursued to ensure that premises can trade as soon as possible. The local approaches to the confirmation process vary wildly across Scotland and can result in delays in formalising the paperwork post practical completion. I explore the confirmation of provisional licences in more detail in Chapter 11 at section 3.4.

The approach taken by different licensing boards will vary according to the practice of officials in building standards or in food safety, all of whom are part of the process. In some cases, for example, certificates of suitability might be issued subject to reviewing layout plans and checking the appropriate certification is in place to allow a confirmation application to be lodged – but the application itself might not be granted until a further physical inspection has been conducted by the relevant officers, and "clear" reports received back at the licensing section.

In other areas, on the other hand, the relevant officers will *not* routinely issue the Section 50 unless and until an inspection has been undertaken. Thereafter, the confirmation is granted as a desk top exercise.

Inevitably there can be delays in arranging the required inspections and this could result in the delayed opening of new premises. Having the certainty that a licence to sell alcohol will be in place, for example, for the opening day of a new supermarket is the reason practitioners, whenever possible, utilise occasional licences as a stopgap.

It should be further noted that there is no consistent approach taken by licensing boards in allowing occasionals to bridge the gap pending confirmation. Some licensing boards will issue an occasional licence in such circumstances, but only on receipt of certificates of suitability. On the other hand, some licensing boards will not consider occasional licence applications pending confirmation at all.

Chapter 19

Offences, Conduct and Liability

1 OVERVIEW

This chapter deals with offences created by the 2005 Act, provisions for order, control, and the general conduct required of persons working in licensed premises and those who frequent such premises. Many of the 2005 Act provisions are not dissimilar to those which have existed in the licensing law for some time, but new offences have been created, old ones amended, and wider concepts introduced. The control of order is dealt with generally in Part 7 of the 2005 Act, and offences provided for generally in Part 8, but both aspects filter through to the other portions of the Act. For the purposes of this book all the offences have been collated into this one chapter, for ease of reference. In addition, this chapter also deals with the question of liability, vicarious liability, and due diligence.

2 OFFENCES

As a broad brush introduction to the notion of licensing offences, and other forms of offence under the Act, it is worth exploring the idea that there are different categories or types of offence which are "linked" to the 2005 Act in some way. There are, first, what we might call "licensing offences", and by that I mean any offence created by the 2005 Act itself. There are also "relevant offences", which is a term explored below, relating to both licensing and non-licensing offences, that is, offences under other enactments and under the common law, which Parliament has declared as being of sufficient relevance to the licensing process that they need to be declared when they occur and relate to a licence holder or an applicant. There is also a wider point to be made about the relevance of offences that might be committed by persons frequenting licensed premises, which might be neither "licensing offences" nor "relevant offences", in relation to the control of order in licensed premises.

2.1 Offences: the "relevant" offences

The 2005 Act creates a statutory list of offences which are described as "relevant offences" for the purposes of ascertaining relevancy in applications or other processes under the Act. The point of this list is that the presence of a conviction on it might have some bearing on an application or other process outcome. The "relevant" offences may be committed by an applicant whether individual or otherwise, or by a licence holder, responsible person, connected person, or even just any person – these defined terms are explained below – in relation to the provisions of the 2005 Act. The term "relevant offence" is defined in section 129 of the Act as those offences provided for in regulations and they are listed below, but it should be noted that the Act does in fact make reference to relevant *and foreign* offences. "Foreign offences", in this context, simply means offences from foreign legal jurisdictions that equate to the relevant offences in Scots or UK law.

As matters stand, an offence is not "relevant" if it is considered "spent" under the terms of the Rehabilitation of Offenders Act 1974 and therefore does not require to be declared,[1] and it cannot be taken into account by a licensing board. That position is to be reversed as a result of section 52 of the Air Weapons and Licensing (Scotland) Act 2015, which repeals section 129(4) of the 2005 Act, the effect of which will be that spent convictions will have to be declared and *could* be capable of interrogation by a licensing board. The ability to consider spent convictions was the position under the 1976 Act and remains the case under the Civic Government (Scotland) Act 1982. The Scottish Government has, at the time of writing, delayed the commencement of section 52 of the 2015 Act, which in the first instance was to prevent any deleterious impact to the wider issues being experienced at the 10-year personal licence renewal point in 2019, but subsequently as a result of separate, wider changes which are proposed to be made in relation to the scheme of the Rehabilitation of Offenders Act 1974.

It is to be assumed that section 129(4) will at some point be repealed. Once that occurs, licensing boards will, it is expected, be required to follow the old 1976 Act approach to the consideration of spent convictions which is that a two-step procedure is required: the board must first make a conscious decision to admit the offences prior to hearing them and taking them into account, and then can only do so if satisfied at any stage that justice cannot otherwise be done, following the dicta in *Adamson v Waveney District Council*,[2] *O'Doherty v Renfrewshire Council*[3] and *Kelly v City of Glasgow Licensing Board*.[4] What this means in practice is that the licensing board should not have sight of the details of the spent conviction until after a separate initial decision to admit it has been agreed. It would be a matter for the police to make submissions as to why the spent convictions should be considered, and for the applicant or licence holder to say why they should not be (if that is their view). It is difficult to engage in this type of argument without spilling into the details of what the spent conviction is, but factors which might be proposed as relevant would include the vintage of the offence, the nature or gravity of the offence, the penalty imposed, and so on.

Note also that the fact that a conviction is under appeal does not prevent any action by a licensing board that it is entitled to take in connection with the conviction.[5]

The relevant offences are prescribed in the Licensing (Relevant Offences)

1 It is not always easy to ascertain whether an offence has become spent or not. An applicant may wish to seek legal advice on this matter.
2 [1997] 8 SLLP 17.
3 1998 SLT 327; [1997] 7 SLLP 6.
4 [2004] 27 SLLP 43.
5 2005 Act, s 130.

(Scotland) Regulations 2007[6] and are split into three parts, covering violent and sexual offences, a large number of statutory offences, and various common law offences. The full list of relevant offences is found at Appendix G.[7]

One must acknowledge that the existence and role of the concept of "relevant offences" is an uncomfortable bedfellow to the concept of "principal purpose" in the licensing regime. Note that some of the offences are only relevant if alcohol is involved: for example, those relating to trade descriptions and trade marks – thus creating the necessary nexus referred to in other parts of the book. What of the multitude of other offences noted here where there is no limitation as to the involvement or role of alcohol? It is clear that these offences are not to be ignored, but the friction exists, and may not be capable of reconciliation without wisdom from the courts.

2.2 Offences: the role of bodies corporate

In relation to any of the offences provided for by the 2005 Act, section 141 is relevant if the offence is committed by a body corporate (e.g. a limited company), a Scottish partnership, or an unincorporated association other than a Scottish partnership. The broad thrust is that such an entity can be found guilty in respect of the actions of a "relevant person". If it is proved that the offence was committed with the consent, connivance or neglect of a "relevant person" (or a person purporting to be a relevant person), then that person may also be found guilty of the offence. "Relevant person" is defined in section 141(2) as:

> "(a) in relation to a body corporate other than a council, a director, manager, secretary, member or other similar officer of the body,
> (b) in relation to a council, an officer or member of the council,
> (c) in relation to a Scottish partnership, a partner, and
> (d) in relation to an unincorporated association other than a Scottish partnership, a person who is concerned in the management and control of the association."

I will deal with the issue of vicarious liability for connected persons and others at Section 3 below.

2.3 Offences: a word on scope and key definitions

There are a number of key phrases used by the Act which require explanation before going into the details of particular offences. Offences may be committed by a "responsible person"; they may occur on "relevant premises"; and the offence may be where someone "knowingly allows" or "allows" something to happen. All of these require elaboration.

6 SSI 2007/513.

7 There are one or two particular items of note in relation to the relevant offences. First, readers will see at Appendix G that there are offences in relation to the Gaming Act 1968, the Betting, Gaming and Lotteries Act 1963 and the Lotteries and Amusements Act 1976. Those Acts have now been repealed and the relevant statute is the Gambling Act 2005. The list of offences was compiled in the transitional period leading up to full implementation of the new gambling legislation, and the 2007 Regulations have not been updated even as of 2021, so these now arcane references remain. Although the "catch-all" provisions noted at reg 2(b)(i) and (ii) provide some comfort, it is to be hoped that Parliament can get round to amending and updating the regulations so that the correct law, and correct criminal offences, are adequately catered for.

2.3.1 Definitions: "relevant premises"

"Relevant premises" is defined in section 122 of the Act as any licensed premises, any exempt premises on which alcohol is sold, and any premises used for the selling of alcohol to trade. This definition is very important: it confirms that, although exempt premises and premises selling to trade do not require a premises licence, the actions which take place on such premises may still be caught by offences under the Act.

2.3.2 Definitions: "responsible person"

"Responsible person" is also defined in section 122 and means, in relation to "relevant premises":

- where a premises licence has effect, the premises manager,
- where an occasional licence has effect, the licence holder,
- in other relevant premises, the person having control and management of the premises, and
- in any of the above cases, a person aged 18 or over who works on the premises in a capacity (whether paid or unpaid) which either authorises him to sell alcohol, or, in relation to any offence of "allowing" something to be done, authorises him to prevent the doing of the thing.

2.3.3 Definitions: "knowingly allows"

The legal concept of "knowingly allows" is one which has caused much debate throughout Scots law, not simply in licensing. A number of licensing offences started life as offences which required the person charged to have actual knowledge of the offence occurring, hence "knowingly". However, section 195 of the Criminal Justice and Licensing (Scotland) Act 2010 deleted the word "knowingly" from the vast majority of licensing offences as of 13 December 2010.[8] This change was brought about following submissions from Police Scotland concerned at the paucity of convictions arising against licence holders who did not have actual knowledge of an offence. The list of offences which were altered to remove the knowledge requirement is as follows:

(a) section 1(3)(b) – allowing the sale of alcohol not in accordance with a premises or occasional licence;
(b) section 103(1) – allowing the sale of alcohol to a child or young person;
(c) section 106(2) – allowing consumption of alcohol by a child or young person;
(d) section 107(1) – unsupervised sale of alcohol by a child or young person;
(e) section 118(1) – selling alcohol from an unlicensed vehicle;
(f) section 120(2) and (3) – delivering alcohol outside 6am to 12midnight, or allowing it to be delivered (by another person);
(g) section 121(1) – keeping smuggled goods on licensed premises;
(h) section 127(4) – selling alcohol or allowing alcohol to be sold on a train in breach of a prohibition order; and

8 The changes were commenced under the Criminal Justice and Licensing (Scotland) Act 2010 (Commencement No. 6, Transitional and Savings Provisions) Order 2010 (SSI 2010/413).

(i) section 128(5) – selling alcohol or allowing alcohol to be sold on a ferry in breach of a prohibition order.

The offences where the word "knowingly" remains, are:

(a) section 104B – knowingly buying or attempting to buy alcohol for a child or young person;
(b) section 106 – a child or young person knowingly consuming alcohol on licensed premises;
(c) section 109 – knowingly sending a child or young person to obtain alcohol;
(d) section 134A – knowingly making a false statement in a licensing application;
(e) Schedule 1 paragraph 3(2) – a councillor knowingly acting as a board member whilst disqualified.

There is a therefore a different approach to what might be referred to as the *mens rea* of the commission of an offence in relation to actual knowledge of an offence. Where a "knowingly allowing/allows" offence is in play, the person must have had actual knowledge.[9] That is not necessary where the offence is one which does not require to be committed "knowingly". What this means, therefore, is that in all offences save the ones noted immediately above, the doctrine of vicarious liability applies, to which we now turn.

3 VICARIOUS LIABILITY AND DUE DILIGENCE

Having examined offences, a similar high-level analysis is required for the connected licensing principles of "vicarious liability" and "due diligence", both of which appear in a number of places in the Act with special reference to certain offences.

3.1 Vicarious liability: what is it?

In short, vicarious liability means that certain persons can be found guilty of an offence they did not themselves commit. There is now, as noted above, a two-tier approach to this in respect of whether the "knowingly" element is present or not.

The deletion of the word "knowingly" from the affected licensing offences[10] brings to an end the historical position concerning actual knowledge, or the absence of it, being a bar to prosecution, and brings Scotland more into line with the English licensing law concept sometimes referred to as the "doctrine of delegation" under *Howker v Robinson*.[11] This applies for those offences where there is no "knowingly" element.

The position now, therefore, is that persons other than the individual who committed the offence (other than a "knowingly" offence – see the list above) may be found guilty even without actual knowledge. This may apply to a

9 *Noble v Heatly* 1967 JC 5; 1967 SLT 26.

10 For a contemporary analysis of the deletion of "knowingly" from the 2005 Act, see "Vicarious responsibility makes a comeback" [2009] 44 SLLP 5; and Audrey Junner (as Audrey Young) "Vicarious Liability Comeback: A tangled web" [2010] 46 SLLP 6.

11 [1973] QB 178.

licence holder who is not an individual person such as a company or partnership, and to a "connected person" associated with that entity such as a director or partner, as well as to an individual who may be the licence holder. In terms of criminal liability, the persons who can be convicted of one of these licensing offences are therefore:

(a) the person who actually committed the offence
(b) the premises manager
(c) the premises licence holder
(d) connected persons: e.g. directors of a limited company if that company is the premises licence holder.

If we take the example of a member of bar staff who sells to a person underage, that staff member can be convicted of the offence, but so can the designated premises manager, the premises licence holder (where an individual or non-individual), and so can the connected persons such as directors of the company which holds the licence – even where none of these other people were present when the sale occurred and indeed in some cases (such as directors) may never have set foot in the premises.

I would suggest that, through my own observations in practice, it is common for Police Scotland to charge any of (a) to (c) above but less common for them to charge persons under category (d) where they are satisfied that the connected person is not involved in the day-to-day running of the premises. This is not a hard and fast rule, merely a practitioner's observation. For example, a limited company which is a small business and whose directors also have operational control of a premises on a day-to-day basis, would appear to be more likely to attract a charge than a director of a large national retailer or pub company who may have limited knowledge of the goings on in particular premises out of the many thousands that company may own. Of course, whilst charging such a person may be rare, that is not to say that it could not and has not occurred.

A separate consideration is whether or not such a charge would result in a conviction. The unpredictability of the Procurator Fiscal is relevant here. Whilst someone may be charged with a licensing offence as described above, whether or not that person is going to be prosecuted is at the hand of the Fiscal. There are numerous examples of alleged licensing offences reported to the Fiscal which have resulted in "no proceedings"; perhaps due to lack of evidence, perhaps because it would not be in the public interest to pursue the conviction, or perhaps for cost reasons. The Fiscal may also elect to deal with the matter by way of a warning letter, or other alternatives to prosecution such as the acceptance of fines.

This brings us on to revisit the position concerning the small number of remaining offences where the "knowingly" test still applies. In these cases, personal knowledge of the commission of the offence is necessary and the leading case here remains the famous *Noble v Heatly*.[12] This case is the bedrock on which sits the Scottish licensing jurisprudence on the phrase "knowingly allows" and, in short, it confirms that actual knowledge is required; implied knowledge or awareness is not sufficient.

Taking a step back from the issue of who might be liable by operation of law, it is important to remember that, where a fiscal wishes to proceed with

12 1967 JC 5; 1967 SLT 26.

a prosecution, there are statutory defences open to someone who may be vicariously liable, and this can generally be referred to as the legal defence of "due diligence".

3.2 Due diligence: what is it?

In short compass, a due diligence defence is where the person who is charged with an offence they did not directly commit themselves can demonstrate that they have taken "all reasonable steps" to prevent or avoid the offence from happening in the first place. In doing so they create a legal defence to escape conviction. These steps need be in place and to be "living and breathing" actions which the person and the business is taking in order to prevent occurrence of an offence.

It is not a 2005 Act invention, of course,[13] but the importance of due diligence under the Act has been demonstrated in a number of appeals, perhaps most significantly in the licensing appeal of *Lidl UK GmbH v City of Glasgow Licensing Board.*[14] The *Lidl* case demonstrates the importance of a robust due diligence system in the context of a licensing review hearing and is discussed in detail in Chapter 14 at Section 2.1. In short, whilst an offence had occurred – in this case a failure to ascertain a person's age in a "test purchase" – the court took the view that the board had fallen into error in suspending the licence by not giving adequate weight to the fact that, by the board's own acceptance, due diligence was in place:

> "it was accepted by the [licensing board] that, on receipt of the information that the sale had been made, the appellants had promptly investigated matters; they had viewed their internal CCTV footage; and they had readily concluded that the employee concerned, Mr Singleton, had breached the policies and procedures which they had established and in which he had been fully trained. The appellants' response had been unequivocal. Mr Singleton had instantly been dismissed. Accordingly, whatever the reason, if any, for Mr Singleton's lapse, he no longer remained in the appellants' employment. In addition to dismissing Mr Singleton, the appellants had immediately put all their employees through an additional training programme to enforce yet further the employees' awareness of the need to adhere to the procedures and policies the appellants had laid down to ensure that alcoholic drinks are not sold to those of insufficient age to lawfully purchase such drinks. Further, it is clear, not only from the Statement of Reasons issued by the respondents, but also from the terms of the transcript of the proceedings before the respondents, that the respondents accepted the existence of the appellants' policies and procedures and that those policies and procedures were adequate, and should, if applied, have prevented sales of alcoholic drinks to a child or young person."[15]

In other words, the board were too quick to dispense with the position that this was a human error and was not a failure of the operator or its due diligence, having put substantial steps in place to endeavour to ensure such an eventuality would be avoided.

13 See *Baxter v Central Fife Divisional Licensing Board and Chief Constable of Fife Constabulary* [1999] 14 SLLP 32 for a discussion on whether a licence holder could have "absolute liability", and see Alan Barron, "Due diligence: boards on the wrong track?" [2008] 39 SLLP 21 for an account from the dog days of the 1976 Act.

14 [2013] CSIH 25.

15 Ibid paras 37 and 38.

What I say we should take from this is that no due diligence, however "gold plated", can guarantee the absence of an offence entirely. Mistakes can always be made. The focus for a licensing board should be not on the occurrence of the event *per se*, but (a) on what steps and measures the licence holder had in place to prevent issues arising, how these were observed and adopted in practice; and (b) how the licence holder responded to the occurrence of the event – what did they learn and what changes occurred? Of course, in relation to the potential criminal offence, the focus will only be on (a).

There are two criminal law cases which give further insight to the issue of due diligence under the 2005 Act. The first of these is *Epic Group (Scotland) Ltd v Shanks*.[16] The Epic Group case is a rare example of a criminal appeal, where the operator of the Aberdeen nightclub "Prohibition" was convicted of selling alcohol to two young persons, and then had the conviction quashed on appeal.

In this case, the original conviction had been based on the view that, notwithstanding the due diligence processes in place, clearly these processes had failed because the two young persons had, as a matter of fact, been sold alcohol. This was where the sheriff fell into error: the fact that a sale occurred is not the "limbo pole" under which one must waver. The test is whether steps were in place and how robust those steps were; there is no hard and fast rule here but the threshold is that of "reasonableness".

Has the operator taken "all reasonable steps" to prevent the offence from occurring? Any system can fail, even the most robust. In the *Epic Group* case the operator had been convicted of selling alcohol to two 17-year-old women. The operator provided detail of the age verification checks, staff training, "Challenge 25" and other steps that they had in place but the court decided to convict on the basis that these policies had been ineffective, as demonstrated by the under-age sale. On appeal, the court agreed that the test is not whether the policies (those documents and processes which would amount to due diligence) were effective, but whether all due diligence had been exercised.[17] The case demonstrates the fundamental importance of strong due diligence but that that success in avoiding the thing prepared for is not necessarily the correct test; and should also serve as a reminder that in a case where the licence holder is tricked on purpose, perhaps some consideration should be given to those doing the deceiving. In this case, the two young persons had actually been used as prosecution witnesses against the operator. The following extract is of note:

> "No doubt some other step can always, in retrospect, be identified. That does not, of itself, however, show that the statutory test of due diligence has not been met."[18]

Underlying any system is human error, and the law recognises that mistakes can be made because the people tasked with carrying out procedures and processes are human beings. Another way of expressing this might be to say that vicarious liability is not strict liability.

Hot on the heels of the *Epic Group* case was a case involving my client,

16 [2014] HCJAC 20; [2015] LLR 1.

17 On what is meant by "all due diligence", see the English case of *Cambridgeshire County Council v Kama* [2008] 39 SLLP 26.

18 *Epic Group* at para 9.

Terence Feeney v Procurator Fiscal Paisley.[19] In this case Mr Feeney, who is the holder of a premises licence for an off-sales, was convicted following an underage sale by a member of his staff when he was not present. He appealed and the conviction was quashed. He had provided the staff member with training on refusal of sales and on asking for ID. There were till prompts in place. The staff member confirmed that all of this training had been received by her but that she had processed the sale anyway because there was a queue forming. There was no evidence of any other issues. This information was presented to the justice but he took the view a more "robust" practice should have been in place and Mr Feeney was convicted. However, on appeal, the court confirmed that the justice had not been made aware of the defence of due diligence under the Licensing (Scotland) Act 2005. The appellate court "extends sympathy" to the justice for not being aware of this and having to contend with "the complexity of the legislation and its amendments".

The court took the view that the evidence led by Mr Feeney did establish that due diligence was in place and that therefore the conviction should not stand. The appellate court was advised of the decision in the *Epic Group* case. The advocate for the fiscal appears to have tried to distinguish the *Epic Group* case on the basis that the failure in Mr Feeney's premises had been "systemic". The court did not agree with this and said:

> "In our view, in relation to an off-licence shop such as the appellants, it has not been established that there was some failure in training or in supervision."

The *Feeney* case, on the back of the *Epic Group* case, is yet further confirmation that a premises licence holder would do well to ensure that they have taken reasonable steps to avoid offences occurring by way of demonstrable training practices and other management or supervision policies, as in doing so the legal defence is fortified.

4 OFFENCES RELATING TO CHILDREN AND YOUNG PERSONS

The 2005 Act makes provision for two general areas of offence under Part 8. The first of these are offences relating to children and young persons, to which we now turn. The following offences can be found in this section of the text: sale of alcohol to a child or young person; allowing the sale of alcohol to a child or young person; sale of liqueur confectionery to children; purchase of alcohol by or for a child or young person; consumption of alcohol by a child or young person; unsupervised sale of alcohol by a child or young person; delivery of alcohol by or to a child or young person; sending a child or young person to obtain alcohol; the duty to display a notice in relation to children and young people; and, finally, the offence of supplying alcohol to a child or young person.

4.1 Definitions: children and young persons and acceptable ID

The definitions of "child" and "young person" are found in section 147 of the Act. A child is a person aged 15 or younger, and a young person is a person

19 2014 SCCR 504.

aged either 16 or 17. When the 2005 Act was first introduced, the relevant licensing objective was the "protection of children from harm". This was amended to "protection of children *and young persons* from harm" as a result of section 41 of the Air Weapons and Licensing (Scotland) Act 2015, as of 15 May 2017.[20]

It is also instructive to look here at the definitions in relation to age verification and acceptable forms of ID. The forms of ID which are acceptable are a valid passport, EU or UK[21] photo card driver's licence, ID accredited by the PASS scheme,[22] a biometric immigration document, an EU national ID card or a national ID card from Norway, Iceland, Switzerland and Liechtenstein, or a military ID document (known as a "Form 90").[23]

There are a couple of points of note here. First, PASS cards were added to reflect the practice of organisations other than PASS becoming accredited by them, to bear their hologram and the relevant instrument also removed the original reference to the British Retail Consortium. It is not uncommon to find some higher education cards or bodies like "Young Scot" with a PASS hologram.

Secondly, I would remind licensees that the effect of a list of acceptable forms of identification is not an instruction that these forms of identification *must* be accepted. It is still entirely up to the licensee to decide whether or not to allow service. Just because the customer can produce a valid form of ID does not mean they are entitled to be served. It is entirely discretionary. What the specification of identification documents does do, is introduce the right to rely on production of these forms of ID as evidence of "due diligence" in terms of the defence to offences under the Act, as well as compliance with "Challenge 25".

4.1.1 Sale of alcohol to a child or young person

Section 102 of the 2005 Act creates the offence of selling alcohol to a child or young person.[24] Perhaps somewhat unusually, when the Act was passed this was a new offence in Scots law. The previous equivalent had been the offence of selling alcohol to persons aged under 18 *in licensed premises*.[25] This is a much more generic offence, removing the requirement for the offence to occur on licensed premises in order for it to be borne out. This offence is extremely well understood, though it is nuanced.

In 2009, the Scottish Parliament debated increasing the age at which a person could purchase alcohol from off-sale premises from 18 to 21. This was met with considerable opposition. The proposals were formulated following

20 Air Weapons and Licensing (Scotland) Act 2015 (Commencement No. 6 and Saving Provisions) Order 2017 (SSI 2017/119).

21 The ability to use a UK driver's licence was introduced as of 31 January 2020 via the Licensing (Amendment) (EU Exit) (Scotland) Regulations 2019 (SSI 2019/6).

22 Proof of Age Standards Scheme cards were added via the Sale of Alcohol to Children and Young Persons (Scotland) Regulations 2007 (SSI 2007/93), reg 2(2) and commenced on 1 September 2009 when the Act went live.

23 The ability to accept a biometric immigration document, EU national ID card (or equivalent as noted) and military ID came into force on 1 October 2013 as a result of Sale of Alcohol to Children and Young Persons (Scotland) Amendment Regulations 2013 (SSI 2013/199).

24 Conviction may lead to a fine not exceeding level 5, imprisonment not exceeding 3 months, or both: 2005 Act, s 102(5).

25 1976 Act, s 68(1).

"pilot" schemes in Armadale, Stenhousemuir, Larbert and Cupar. The use of these pilots was controversial: the SNP government hailed a dramatic decrease of antisocial behaviour when the age of purchase had been increased to 21, but failed to also point out that the age increase was only one of a number of measures taken as part of a holistic action plan on the problems of youth disorder, including a more visible police presence. When the matter was debated in Parliament on 2 October 2008, the proposal was voted against by 72 to 47,[26] and although the SNP administration at that time stated they would not disregard the measure entirely, it came to nought.

A proposal of this nature subsequently resurfaced as part of the consultation into the Criminal Justice and Licensing (Scotland) Act 2010. This was aborted, and I discuss this in Chapter 15 at Section 7. Commentators in the 2008 debate and the 2010 Act proposals always point to the apparent absurdity in the increase when a member of the armed forces, 18 years of age, returning from a tour of duty, and who might also be a premises and personal licence holder, on becoming engaged to be married cannot buy a bottle of celebratory wine on their way back from the polling station having voted in a general election.

There is a "due diligence" defence open to a person charged with this offence (see above on the generalities of due diligence). The defence is that: (a) the accused believed the person to be aged 18 or over and either (i) had taken reasonable steps to establish the person's age, or (ii) no reasonable person could have suspected from the person's appearance that he was aged under 18.

"Reasonable steps" in this context means having requested one of the forms of acceptable photographic ID, being shown the ID as requested, and that the ID shown would have convinced a reasonable person. This means that the person charged has a defence if the ID was fake, where it was a pretty good fake. The reality is that fake ID can be obtained with alacrity and the quality is excellent in most cases. It also means that a person charged has a defence if the ID is genuine but does not relate to the person bearing it (otherwise known as the "wee brother" test). If the person is a close family relation and the photo is very like that person, then it is possible that the ID may be accepted.

Also of note here is that this offence is markedly changed from the equivalent under the 1976 legislation. Section 68(4) of that Act allowed persons aged 16 or 17 to purchase alcohol[27] for themselves to consume, when ancillary to a meal in a part of the premises set aside for the provision of meals. Under the 2005 Act, there is no circumstance when anyone aged under 18 may legally purchase alcohol (see 4.1.4 below).

It has been interesting from a practitioner perspective to see how this part of the law had responded or interacted with the mandatory age verification condition requiring premises licence holders to observe what is commonly known as a "Challenge 25" policy (see Chapter 15 at Section 4.11). There is an inherent friction between adherence to that condition, which requires a judgement call of a person's appearance with a threshold of 25 years of age,

26 The value of the results as a basis for legislation has also been criticised: see further, "'Success' of under-21 alcohol ban is mere SNP spin, says professor", *The Scotsman*, 12 September 2008.

27 The 1976 Act restricted the forms of alcohol a 16- or 17-year-old may purchase to beer, wine, made-wine, porter, cider or perry.

in comparison to the offence and due diligence defence described here, which requires a judgement call of a person's appearance with a lower threshold of 18 years of age. The point is that non-adherence to the condition does not necessarily invoke this separate criminal offence. If a person adjudges a customer to be aged 20 and serves them based on appearance, they (assuming a reasonable person would believe the person to be aged over 18) have the legal defence open to them under section 102 even though they have breached the mandatory age verification condition. I think the guidance to operators must be to first of all observe the condition, as in doing so this surely fortifies the ability to invoke the section 102 defence.

4.1.2 Allowing the sale of alcohol to a child or young person

Any responsible person who allows alcohol to be sold to a child or young person on any relevant premises commits an offence.[28] This offence is the sister provision to the one above, and is focused not on the person who made the actual sale, but on the other persons (as described earlier in this chapter) who might be found guilty by operation of the doctrine of vicarious responsibility. Note the absence of a requirement for actual knowledge.

4.1.3 Sale of liqueur confectionery to children

In my view one of the curiosities of the 2005 Act is section 104, which makes specific provision for an offence where liqueur confectionery is sold to a child.[29] The offending person can be "any person" and does not need to be a "responsible person", which is a marked difference to the remainder of these offences. Liqueur confectionery is defined in section 147(1) as:

> "confectionery which—
> (a) contains alcohol in a proportion not greater than 0.2 litres of alcohol (of a strength not exceeding 57%) per kilogramme of the confectionery, and
> (b) either consists of separate pieces weighing not more than 50 grammes or is designed to be broken into such pieces for the purposes of consumption".

This terminology has been lifted directly[30] from section 123 of the 1976 Act, but the operation of section 123 was to remove liqueur confectionery from the entire ambit of that Act, so that there was no control of such sales – confectioners, chocolatiers and sweet[31] shops were able to safely sell liqueur confectionery to

28 2005 Act, s 103.

29 Conviction will result in a fine not exceeding level 2 on the standard scale.

30 Although the original definition also included a reference to the temperature (20°C) of the potentially offensive sweeties!

31 The budding licensing law historian would do well not to be confused by the reference to "sweets" littered throughout the historical legislation: the Licensing Amendment (Scotland) Act 1897, for example, altered the grocer's certificate first introduced by the Forbes Mackenzie Act of 1853 so that a certificate could be granted for the "sale of sweets by retail". Prior to the commencement of the 1976 legislation, there were four types of certificate (either public house, hotel or grocer's): a certificate allowing the sale of porter and ale; a certificate allowing the sale of wines, porter and ale; a certificate allowing the sale of sweets; and a "full certificate" allowing the sale of porter, ale, wine and sweets. An enlightening definition of the expression, however, is hidden away in the Finance Act 1910, s 52 and is in the following terms: "any liquor made from fruit or sugar mixed with any other material which has undergone a process

children aged 15 or less until 1 September 2009. I examine the operation of this provision under the 2005 Act further in Chapter 2 at Section 2.3.

4.1.4 Supply of alcohol to a child or supply of alcohol to a young person

Sections 104A and 104B create identical provisions concerning supply of alcohol to children and young persons, and these offences were inserted into the 2005 Act by section 53(1) of the Air Weapons and Licensing (Scotland) Act 2015 and commenced as of 15 May 2017.[32] These offences were designed to close a "gap" identified by the police concerning adults providing under-age persons with alcohol in public places. The policy position was explained thus:

> "Under the current licensing regime, adults can legally supply alcohol to someone under the age of 18 outwith a licensed premises [sic]. This facilitates outdoor drinking dens of young people where those in the group who are over 18 buy alcohol for younger members. The measures within the Bill will close this loophole and give the police the powers they need to disrupt these drinking dens."[33]

Originally, section 105 (discussed immediately below) had contained an offence of purchase of alcohol by an adult for a child or young person – what we might call an "agency" or "proxy" purchase. That offence was deleted and replaced with these wider, convoluted provisions and they contain a number of exceptions. The section 104A offence is:

> "A person, other than a child or young person, who—
> (a) buys or attempts to buy alcohol—
> (i) on behalf of a child, or
> (ii) for a child, or
> (b) gives alcohol (or otherwise makes it available) to a child,
> commits an offence.

The section 104B offence is identical save it refers to young persons instead of children and the "with a meal" provision is present.[34]

The offence(s) does not apply to consumption other than in a public place, meaning an adult who supplies alcohol in a domestic setting such as a parent allowing their child to have a glass of wine with dinner is not caught. This also means an 18-year-old hosting a house party for their 16- and 17-year-old companions is not caught by the offence. The offence does not apply where the supply is for the purposes of religious worship – the so-called "communion wine" exemption. A special definition is provided for public place:

> " 'public place' includes—
> (a) relevant premises,
> (b) any place to which the public have access for the time being (whether on payment of a fee or otherwise), and

of fermentation in the manufacture thereof, and includes British wines, made wines, mead, and metheglin". Metheglin is a type of spiced mead.

32 Air Weapons and Licensing (Scotland) Act 2015 (Commencement No. 6 and Saving Provisions) Order 2017 (SSI 2017/119). See also "Crack down on 'party flats'" [2011] 47 SLLP 4.

33 Policy Memorandum to the Air Weapons and Licensing (Scotland) Bill (as introduced), para 125.

34 Conviction will lead to a fine not exceeding level 5, imprisonment not exceeding 3 months, or both.

(c) any place to which the public do not have access but to which the child unlawfully gains access."

"Relevant premises" in this context does, of course, mean licensed premises.

4.1.5 Purchase of alcohol by a child or young person and consumption of alcohol by a child or young person

Section 105 relates to the purchase of alcohol by a child or young person,[35] which is a criminal offence. Section 106 relates to consumption of alcohol by a child or young person. I am discussing these together due to obvious link between the two. The section 105 offence applies whether the purchase is for that child or young person, or for someone else. The only exception catered for is that it is legal for a young person to purchase alcohol if doing so in connection with a "test purchase", that is, where authorised to do so by the police to determine whether an offence is being committed under section 102 (discussed further below).

Noting the link to the corollary offence above pertaining to the person who made the sale, I am often asked if it is an offence for a child or young person not just to try to buy alcohol, but to use ID fraudulently to obtain alcohol. This might be either that the ID is fake, or that they are seeking to rely on legitimate ID which belongs to someone else (such as the "wee brother" test mentioned above). Section 6 of the Identity Documents Act 2010 makes it a criminal offence for a person to be in possession of an identity document without reasonable excuse which is fake, improperly obtained, or which relates to someone else.[36]

The exception for agency sales is where the sale takes place on licensed premises and is for a young person to consume along with a meal, so long as the drink bought is "beer, wine, cider or perry". The 2005 Act retains the term "perry" but has dropped "porter" when compared with the equivalent provision of the old 1976 Act. Some parties suggested that the terms "porter" and "perry" had become anachronistic; porter, of course, referring to a dark beer of which stout is a variant, and being the author's favourite alcoholic beverage, and perry meaning pear cider.[37] Perry experienced a resurgence of popularity in recent years, perhaps indicating why the term has been retained, but the absence of "porter" from section 106 does not mean that a young person may not drink a pint of porter as the Alcoholic Liquor Duties Act 1979, s 1(3) defines "beer" as including "ale, porter and stout".

Section 106 contains two offences, providing that a child or young person who *knowingly* consumes alcohol on relevant premises commits an offence,[38] and that any responsible person who allows this to happen commits an offence.[39] However, following from the special provisions for young persons

35 Conviction will lead to a fine not exceeding level 1.

36 This applies across the United Kingdom and was enacted on 21 December 2010. A conviction in Scotland can result in imprisonment up to 12 months.

37 Made, of course, from perry pears. Pear cider made from other pear varieties is not perry but pear cider, as any respectable perry pear grower will tell you. These, my friends, are the finer points of detail which make the job of a legal author fun.

38 Leading to a level 3 fine.

39 Leading to a level 5 fine, 3 months' imprisonment, or both.

under section 105, an exception to these offences is where the alcohol is consumed by a young person along with a meal.

The key aspect of the interplay between section 105 and section 106 is to note that it is legal for an adult to purchase alcohol for consumption along with a meal by a 16- or 17-year-old but it is not legal for the young person to buy the alcohol for themselves (as was the case under the 1976 provisions).

What is meant by "along with", and what is meant by "a meal", is discussed in some detail in Chapter 8 at Section 3.6.3 discussing "restaurant facilities" and "bar meals" as activities on the premises licence operating plan.

An interesting side-consideration here relates to educational facilities and tastings. A client once asked me whether it was lawful to allow 16- and 17-year-olds to be involved in tastings as part of a hospitality training cook school, which was also licensed with a public restaurant where student chefs and waiters would cut their teeth. The alcohol was wine which was to be paired with certain foods and would be "swilled and spat" to help the budding chefs understand the interplay of flavours and educate their palates. The offence relates to "consumption", which is a term not explicitly defined in the Act. If the alcohol is not swallowed, but merely swilled for training purposes and spat out, one might argue that a common-sense interpretation would allow for tastings in an educational environment.

4.1.6 Test purchasing

The offence of sending a child or young person to obtain alcohol does not apply where the person is sent by the police for the purposes of facilitating a "test purchase": that is, a check as to whether the licence holder is complying with the law in relation to under-age sales. The history of test purchasing is fraught with some difficulty and indeed the reality is that, due to the changing legislative framework under which the police operate changing over a period of time, and in particular ongoing amendments to the Regulation of Investigatory Powers Act 2000, my understanding is that these activities are not currently pursued.[40]

4.1.7 Unsupervised sale of alcohol by a child or young person

Section 107 introduces a general rule that it is an offence for a responsible person to allow alcohol to be sold, supplied or served by a child or young person on any relevant premises.[41] This covers the use of under-18 staff on licensed premises.[42] Operators will be pleased to note that there are exceptions to this where:

- the sale of alcohol is for consumption off the premises, or
- the sale of alcohol is for consumption on the premises, but along with a meal supplied on the premises.

40 See Appendix H for a brief history of test purchasing.

41 Leading to a level 1 fine.

42 It should be noted that, whilst the Act creates provision for under 18s working in licensed premises, some local authorities have byelaws in operation concerning the employment of children, such as Highland Council. These byelaws should be checked where appropriate. See "Employing children" [2008] 39 SLLP 11.

In these two exceptions, the sale itself still has to be specifically authorised by a responsible person or any person aged over 18 who is authorised by a responsible person in relation to this exemption.

The first exception, in practical terms, means that it is quite legal for a person aged under 18 to supply alcohol for consumption off the premises, for example at a supermarket checkout, so long as the sale is specifically authorised by a relevant person at the time of the sale. Supermarket shoppers will be familiar with the young checkout assistant calling a supervisor to "clear" the alcohol element of their groceries.

The second exemption operates to cover, in the main, restaurant style premises or premises where the alcohol is sold together with a meal. It does not operate so as to allow persons aged under 18 to work behind a bar per se, as the exemption only relates to supply or service and not the sale. It also does not permit a "drinks only" table service of alcohol by a person aged under 18 – only table service of alcohol if the patrons are consuming a meal and the alcohol is to be consumed along with that meal. In this example, it may be best practice to have a written statement signed and dated between the responsible person and the staff that person wishes to "authorise" in something like the following terms:

> "I [name of responsible person], hereby authorise the undernoted individuals for the purposes of s 107 of the Licensing (Scotland) Act 2005."

An interesting query may arise in relation to the provisions of a given operating plan and access by children and young persons. It is accepted by some licensing boards that there is no need to narrate wording capturing the ability of under 18s to work on premises beyond those hours laid down in the operating plan on the basis that the Act envisages this, as long as section 107 is adhered to. It is thought that the terms of the operating plan are intended to be directed towards customers only and that the rules do not apply to staff, so that the operating plan does not control access of anyone aged under 18 if they are a member of staff. However, some boards have looked for wording on operating plans to cover staff, so this should be considered on a case-by-case basis.

What, then, of young persons employed and working on the premises (not necessarily employed by the premises) not connected to the sale, supply or service of alcohol, and therefore not captured within the ambit of section 107? One example of this might be a 17-year-old playing in a live band. If the operating plan allows access for under 18s until 10pm only, does this preclude that performer being on the premises after that time? I am aware of some operating plans which do have special reference to performers. It is difficult to fathom whether the logic which appears to apply to staff involved with alcohol also applies to other types of "staff" such as in this example. It seems to me the provisions were not intended to prevent our 17-year-old prodigy from playing in a licensed music venue or concert hall, or even in a local pub, but local approaches to this will vary.

4.1.8 Delivery of alcohol by or to a child or young person

In relation to an off-sale, it is an offence for any responsible person to allow delivery of the alcohol by a child or young person, and any responsible person who delivers the alcohol or allows it to be delivered to a child or young person commits an offence.[43] Both offences are found in section 108.

Deliveries are permitted to a child or young person if the child or young person is receiving the alcohol for the purposes of their employment in which part of their job is to facilitate the delivery of alcohol (e.g. a supermarket storeperson).[44]

There is a defence available to a person charged with an offence under this section, and that is to show that the accused believed the child or young person to be aged 18 or over and either:

- had taken reasonable steps to establish the child or young person's age; or
- no reasonable person could have suspected from the child's or young person's appearance that the child or young person was aged under 18.

"Reasonable steps" in this context are defined in section 108(6) as being where the accused has been shown an acceptable form of identification (as narrated at Section 4.1), and the document would have convinced a reasonable person.

There is a further special defence for a responsible person charged with allowing alcohol to be delivered to a child or young person, and that is that they took "all reasonable precautions and exercised due diligence" not to commit the offence.[45] This defence is no doubt provided as the responsible person will not be present at the time the alcohol is handed over.

4.1.9 Sending a child or young person to obtain alcohol

Section 109 provides that it is an offence to send a child or young person to obtain alcohol from relevant premises for consumption off the premises,[46] and it is immaterial where the child or young person goes to obtain the alcohol.

4.1.10 Duty to display a notice concerning children and young persons

Under the 2005 Act, as has been seen, licences have to be displayed and produced upon request. This provision, under section 110, introduces yet another notice requirement, this time in relation to offences concerning children and young persons.[47]

The notice itself must be in the following terms:[48]

> "It is an offence for a person under the age of 18 to buy or attempt to buy alcohol on these premises.
> It is also an offence for any other person to buy or attempt to buy alcohol on these premises for a person under the age of 18.

43 Both offences, if proved, lead to a fine not exceeding level 3.

44 It matters not whether the position is paid or unpaid: 2005 Act, s 108(4)).

45 See my comments in Chapter 11 at Section 9.3.1 on the issue of staff training and delivery staff.

46 Leading to a level 5 fine, 3 months' imprisonment, or both.

47 One of the interesting differences between the 1976 Act and the 2005 Act is the need to display notices and licence documentation. Under the 1976 Act, the only legal requirement for a notice was if a children's certificate was in force, and even then the certificate itself did not need to be displayed but merely a sign saying that there was a certificate and to which parts of the premises it applied.

48 Sale of Alcohol to Children and Young Persons (Scotland) Regulations 2007 (SSI 2007/93).

Where there is doubt as to whether a person attempting to buy alcohol on these premises is aged 18 or over, alcohol will not be sold to the person except on production of evidence showing the person to be 18 or over."

The notice is, in part, erroneous. It is not an offence for a person to purchase alcohol for a person aged 16 or 17 if that person is consuming the drink with a meal, if it is either beer, cider, wine or perry.[49]

The notice must be displayed at all times, at each point of sale, in a position where it is "readily visible" to any person seeking to buy alcohol.[50] Failure to adhere to these requirements is an offence.[51] In an on-sales environment, one might expect to see the notice at the bar, whereas in a shop or supermarket one might expect to see it at the till point.

5 OFFENCES RELATING TO DRUNKENNESS AND DISORDERLY CONDUCT

This section deals with the following offences: drunk persons entering or in premises on which alcohol is sold; obtaining of alcohol by or for a drunk person; sale of alcohol to a drunk person; drunkenness of premises manager or responsible persons; disorderly conduct; and refusal to leave premises. The levels of convictions arising from these offences is extremely low – see Appendix K.

5.1 Definitions: "drunk" and "drunk and incapable"

The legal definitions of "drunk" and "drunk and incapable" have been the subject of some debate. One of the key Scottish cases is *Dunning v Cardle*[52] in which the phrase "sufficiently inebriated as to justify the description of drunk" was used, but it was held that it was also "a matter of degree". In *Lanham v Rickwood*,[53] an English case, "drunk" was held to have a "natural and ordinary" meaning of being deprived of self-control through intoxicating liquor. Certainly, there is separation in severity between "drunk" and "drunk and incapable". Other examples of what may legally constitute "drunk" are: having a Blood Alcohol Content (BAC) of 50mg of alcohol in 100ml of blood (the level the statutory offence of drink-driving is activated); "having taken intoxicating liquor to an extent which affected steady self-control";[54] and in *Keith v Bell*,[55] the definition of "state of intoxication" was held to connote a graver disposition than that of "drunk" or "under the influence of drink".

My understanding on this issue is that there has purposefully been no attempt by the legislators to enshrine a definition of "drunk" due to the physiological, environmental and temporal factors which all must be taken into account when assessing drunkenness (or lack thereof). Alcohol consumption

49 This discrepancy was brought to the attention of the Scottish Parliament, but it was believed that the notice was already prolix, and to add this exemption would lead to confusion and dilute the primary message.
50 2005 Act, s 110(2).
51 Liable to a fine not exceeding level 3.
52 1981 SLT (Notes) 107.
53 (1984) 148 JP 737; (1984) 148 JPN 733; (1984) 81 LSG 1915.
54 *Neale v RMJE (a minor)* (1984) 80 Cr App R 20.
55 1943 SC (J) 65; 1944 SLT 31.

affects individuals in an individual way and for that reason it is almost impossible to create a single definition. What the Act does, however, is recognise that there is a spectrum of drunkenness. Certainly, there is a difference in law between "drunk" and "drunk and incapable", and the case law underlines that subjective approach.

5.2 Drunk persons entering or in premises on which alcohol is sold

Section 111 of the 2005 Act creates two separate offences: first, it is an offence to attempt to enter licensed premises whilst drunk; and it is an offence to be in licensed premises whilst drunk and incapable of taking care of oneself.[56] There is an exemption to the former offence where the person is resident on the premises, such as a hotel. Note that there is no specification for the attempt to enter to be successful or otherwise; the mere attempt itself is enough to trigger the offence. Also note that the difference between being merely drunk, and drunk and incapable, is in stark relief with these two offences. It is an offence to attempt to enter licensed premises whilst being drunk, but it is not an offence to be drunk in licensed premises. The offence is to be drunk *and incapable*. Thus, the law recognises that it is not an offence to be drunk in licensed premises. Note that a police constable can arrest a person committing an offence under this section without warrant,[57] but prosecutions of these offences remain extremely low, and historically that has always been the case.

5.3 Obtaining alcohol by or for a drunk person

Section 112 creates the offence of obtaining or attempting to obtain alcohol for consumption on the premises by a person who is drunk; and in another example of an "agency" or "proxy" offence, the offence of helping a person who is drunk to obtain or consume alcohol.[58] When taken into account with the preceding comment about the lawfulness of being in a premises whilst merely drunk, this offence clarifies that that drunk person cannot attempt to purchase or obtain more drink, nor can someone else make similar attempts on their behalf.

5.4 Sale of alcohol to a drunk person

The flip side to the previous paragraph is, of course, the corollary offence of selling alcohol to a drunk person, found in section 113. Any responsible person who sells alcohol to a drunk person on relevant premises commits such an offence.[59] Prosecutions following from such offences are remarkably low in number – between 2002 and 2008 only two licence holders were prosecuted for selling alcohol to a drunk person[60], and since 2009 only two further convictions have arisen from section 113 (with 55 non-court disposals).[61]

56 Both of which may lead to a fine not exceeding level 1.
57 2005 Act, s 111(3).
58 Both of these offences lead to a fine not exceeding level 3.
59 Liable to a fine not exceeding level 3.
60 Source: data received 1 April 2021 from the Scottish Government Safer Communities Directorate, in response to a FOI request by the author.
61 This statistic was brought to the attention of the SNP administration in December 2008 by

5.5 Premises manager and responsible person not to be drunk

Section 114 provides that it is an offence for any responsible person in relation to any relevant premises to be drunk while on the premises. This offence requires further elaboration. First, one must note that it does not say that it is an offence to consume alcohol, but to be drunk.

The purpose of this offence is clearly to strike at drunkenness amongst those in charge of licensed premises. It is interesting to note that the exact definitions used, with the reference to "any", means that (theoretically at least) anyone who works in the trade who satisfies the definition of "responsible person", may fall foul of the offence even on premises to which their employment is unconnected. That, of course would be an absurdity and is perhaps an unintended error in the drafting. From a policy standpoint, the matter is clearly directed at someone who is "on shift". This opens further lines of enquiry, however.

First of all, there is nothing here or in law generally to prevent a bartender having a drink in the premises where they are employed at the end of a shift, presuming that is still within the licensed hours of course. As discussed in Chapter 16 at Section 4.6, there is no longer any exemption for bar staff to enjoy a pint after the licensed hours have ended (if indeed there ever was). But does the section 114 offence activate where the consumption takes place during the licensed hours whilst the individual is off duty?

It is not uncommon to find that an employee of a bar may frequent the premises socially. This is especially so in more rural parts of Scotland where the particular premises may be the only local pub in the area, for example. I do not believe that section 114 prevents consumption per se for the "off duty" responsible person. The test is that of "drunk", however, not "drunk and incapable", and as the offence is not restricted in the terms of the statute to "whilst on duty", in theory the off-duty employee may have a drink, but may not go on to consume so much alcohol that he becomes drunk.[62] A common-sense approach would appear to have some use in these situations.

In discussing the equivalent 1976 offence, Cummins points out that:

> "[i]t is of no consequence that the premises are closed to the public or that the consumption of alcohol leading to drunkenness took place elsewhere".[63]

It is also of no consequence that the drunkenness takes place outwith the licensed hours.[64] These observations remain salient.

An operator may wish to question himself whether, as a matter of best practice (as opposed to any legal requirement), it is appropriate for staff to consume alcohol on the premises where they are also (albeit at a different time) entrusted to observe licensing laws and monitor the consumption of others. It can be argued that such a person's authority to deal with an adverse

Liberal Democrat MSP Robert Brown, who argued that the government was more interested in "fiddling about" with alcohol laws rather than having the existing law enforced. See "'Use existing laws to curb alcohol abuse', Lib Dem urges", *The Herald*, 2 December 2008.

62 A wider point is whether the person, whilst not working, falls to meet the description of premises manager or responsible person if they are not on the premises in that capacity. See Chapter 10, Section 3.1.3.

63 J C Cummins, *Licensing Law in Scotland* (2nd edn, Butterworths, 2000) p 158 (notes to s 114).

64 *Kessack v Smith* (1905) 7 F 75.

incident may be eroded if that person has themselves acted in a similar way on the same premises at another time.

5.6 Disorderly conduct

Conflict and disorder are, regrettably, an undeniable part of life for staff in licensed premises to contend with. The good people of the licensed trade in Scotland are sometimes faced with violence, intimidation, and aggression between patrons and also directed towards themselves. There are specific offences laid out in section 115 of the Act dealing with disorder in licensed premises.

The first of these is the offence of a person on relevant premises who, *whilst drunk*, behaves in a disorderly manner *or* uses obscene or indecent language to the annoyance of any person. This offence has a number of aspects worthy of exploration. The first part is that the offence only applies if the person is drunk. Thus, a tee-totaller who indulges in frothy invective with his evening companion at the bar is shielded from the activation of this particular offence, although common law offences may be committed such as an old-fashioned breach of the peace.

The next element of the offence is that there are two types of activity which engage it: first, behaving in a disorderly manner; or, secondly, using obscene or indecent language to the annoyance of any person. This may be a controversial provision to enforce, as the "annoyance of any person" is such a broad phrase. [65]

The law considers not just the person causing the stooshie but whether it has been allowed to happen, as it is also an offence for any responsible person in relation to any relevant premises to allow a breach of the peace, drunkenness or other disorderly conduct.[66] As this is not a "knowingly allows" offence, the legal defence of due diligence applies and is framed under section 115 as follows:

> "(3) It is a defence for a person charged with an offence under subsection (2) ('the accused') to prove—
> (a) that the accused, or an employee or agent of the accused, took all reasonable precautions and exercised due diligence not to commit the offence, or
> (b) that there were no lawful and reasonably practicable means by which the accused could prevent the conduct giving rise to the offence."

Note this directly strikes at my earlier point that licensing law is not necessarily aimed at the occurrence of the event itself, recognising that incidents can happen, but to examine what steps were in place prior to the incident to evidence that the premises were well managed, or, also in this case, that there was nothing that the responsible person could reasonably have done to stop the incident from occurring. This is worth restating. If a random person walks into a public bar and stabs a patron perhaps for some reason or for none, then the terms of section 115(3)(b) protect the licence holder and any responsible person.

65 Behaving in a disorderly manner will lead to a fine not exceeding level 3, imprisonment not exceeding 60 days, or both; using obscene or indecent language will lead to a fine not exceeding level 3.

66 2005 Act, s 115(2). This offence can lead to a fine not exceeding level 3.

5.7 Refusal to leave premises, the "right to refuse", and "reasonable force"

A licensee's "right of refusal" has been enshrined in common law for over 100 years. In *R v Armagh Justices*,[67] Holmes J stated that a licence holder could "pick and choose" his customers, and in *R v Rymer*[68] it was held that a member of the public could not insist on being served in a public house. In this case a patron entering a public house had brought with him a "large and undesirable" dog.[69]

There is sometimes confusion on this point in considering whether premises are "public" premises simply because the public may attend there. A "public house" (or any other licensed premises for that matter) is not a "public place" in as much as it is not true to say that a member of the public can insist on being there.[70] The public are on the licensed premises at the implicit invitation of the licensee and under their permission only, and that invitation can be withdrawn at their whim. My request for a pint is an offer to buy that pint; it can therefore be refused. The offeror cannot insist on being served.

Being refused entry to premises, as opposed to service within it, is a simple extension of the right of refusal to serve. A door steward is acting on behalf of, or under instructions by, the licence holder and therefore can exercise the right of refusal on the licence holder's behalf. The same applies to bar staff who refuse entry or service; they are acting as an agent of the licence holder and are entitled to refuse.

This broad-brush right of refusal has been somewhat curtailed in more modern times in that there are now some statutory provisions preventing a licence holder from refusing service on certain grounds. These statutory grounds have been brought together under the ambit of the Equality Act 2010 and are now referred to as "protected characteristics" under section 4 of that Act. The protected characteristics are as follows:

- age;
- disability;
- gender reassignment;
- marriage and civil partnership;
- pregnancy and maternity;
- race;
- religion or belief;
- sex;
- sexual orientation.

The 2010 Act also creates protections where you are discriminated against because a family member has one of these characteristics. One of the examples given in Citizens Advice literature on this topic is refusal to a club premises because your partner is transsexual. Licence holders need to be aware of the

67 (1897) 2 LR Ir 57

68 (1877) 2 QBD 136. It is unclear if the publican had refused to serve the dog or his owner.

69 There is no detail given on the breed, though it is surely fair to assume it was not a Border Terrier, as they are all good boys.

70 See further Peter Coulson, "Come what may, a licensee is still master of his own house", *Morning Advertiser*, 5 September 2008, for an English view on the right to refuse.

impact of the 2010 Act on the common law right of refusal and remember that, although the right exists, it is not an invitation to exercise prejudice and does not cure illegality by way of discrimination.

To put it another way, a licence holder can refuse entry or service so long as the reason for that refusal is not based on one of the above protected characteristics. I cannot refuse service to someone who is gay, straight, or of a particular religious view because of that characteristic. If a person happens to fall into one of the protected characteristics that does not excuse them from undesirable behaviours, so where such behaviours are demonstrated and it is those behaviours which lead to the refusal, that is a lawful refusal.[71]

An interesting question arises concerning the "barring" of customers relying upon the right of refusal, and the use of Pubwatch schemes. What happens if the refusal is not implemented by a single operator but is a "blanket" refusal by an organisation such as a Pubwatch? This was exactly the case in *R (on the application of Boyle) v Haverhill Pubwatch*.[72] Here Mr Boyle was barred from all premises under the Haverhill Pubwatch scheme. He sought judicial review of this decision. The Pubwatch scheme was run by the operators although it had input from the local council and police. There was a question as to whether the Pubwatch was an "arm" of the authorities, but the court held that those authorities were merely "interested parties", not part of the decision-making process, and that the Pubwatch was not a "sock puppet" organisation.

Importantly, the court held that the blanket decision of all publicans in the Pubwatch to bar Mr Boyle was an extension of their individual right as licensees to refuse service. In other words, that the Pubwatch blanket ban was simply a more organised and efficient demonstration of the individual right of refusal and therefore perfectly legal.

The *Haverhill* case confirms that the extension of the right of refusal through a Pubwatch or similar scheme should be lawful, but it is also a warning shot to police and licensing authorities not to get too involved in this type of scheme, otherwise the banning decisions could be subject to succesful judicial review. This could, for example, arise if a licensing board is in the habit of attaching a condition to a premises licence requiring the holder to join the local Pubwatch. By compelling membership, there could be an argument that the authority is going beyond a sort of "advisory" relationship with the Pubwatch and this may undermine the decisions the Pubwatch makes. It is important, therefore, that such organisations remain independent from Police Scotland and local licensing boards whilst remaining important for those bodies to have an active participation.

Section 116 complements the presumptive right of refusal by creating an offence of refusing to leave licensed premises when asked to do so by a responsible person or the police, due to behaving in a disorderly manner.[73] There is a separate offence of refusing to leave premises after the end of a period of licensed hours.[74]

71 See Niall Hassard, "Equalities for all: the new framework" [2011] 47 SLLP 9.

72 [2009] All ER (D) 105 (Oct).

73 In *Campbell v Adair* 1945 JC 29, "disorderly" was held to be something just short of an action that would constitute a breach of the peace. Any offence under s 116 may lead to a fine not exceeding level 3.

74 2005 Act, s 116(2).

5.7.1 The use of "reasonable force"

There is provision for the use of "reasonable force" by an "authorised person" if a person fails to remove themselves from the premises after being asked to do so by a responsible person or police constable. Authorised person, in this context, is defined at section 116(6) as a responsible person or any other person who works on the premises and is authorised for the purposes of this section. There is no definition as to the form of authorisation and it should be taken that there is implicit authority granted to most if not all staff working in licensed premises. It may be helpful to have some sort of written authorisation system in place, perhaps linked to the wider "authorisation" of alcohol sales (see Chapter 15 at Section 4.4) to allow certain staff to step in if there is an incident requiring ejection by force.

Unhelpfully, the phrase "reasonable force" is not defined in the Act. My own view would be that reasonable force in such circumstances is the minimum amount of force required to keep the person refusing to leave, other people, and oneself, safe. Using your arms to control a person from raising their fist and striking at you or others as you frog-march the person from the building might be considered reasonable; whereas kicking the miscreant as you do so might not.

A brief side-step into Scots criminal law may be instructive here, to consider the Scots law legal defence of self-defence. The leading case remains *HM Advocate v Docherty*.[75] There are three main aspects to a lawful use of force in the context of self-defence, which are:

- Imminent danger to life or limb, to you or another person.
- The amount of force used must be necessary for your own or the other person's safety.
- If you have some means of escape or retreat from the threat, you are bound to use it.

The last point in particular is of interest to us in the licensing context. Whilst the licensing provision of reasonable force exists, one must never put oneself in harm's way.

Part of the difficulty for the trade in such circumstances is the fine line between authorised expulsion and use of force and committing an offence. In *Duncan v Lockhart*,[76] a licence holder was convicted of assault and breach of the peace in connection with his removal of a customer from the premises.

5.7.2 Detention of customers who have committed offences

Can the licence holder or his staff detain a customer, presumably after said customer has committed offences, and in anticipation of the imminent arrival of the police? The answer to this riddle is found not in the 2005 Act but, perhaps a little surprisingly, in the Civic Government (Scotland) Act 1982, and requires a bit of explanation.

We'll start with section 50 of the 1982 Act, which says:

75 1954 JC 1.
76 1995 GWD 1-15.

> "Any person who, while not in the care or protection of a suitable person, is, in a public place, drunk and incapable of taking care of himself shall be guilty of an offence".

The definition of "public place" is interesting here. The 1982 Act actually creates a special definition of "public place" for the purposes of this specific offence. The general definition under the 1982 Act would not, in my view, include a pub, because it says (at section 133): "any place . . . to which the public have unrestricted access".

The general public does not have unrestricted access to licensed premises: members of the public are there at the invitation of the licensee, and that invitation can be withdrawn (see my comments above on the "right of refusal"). However, section 50 of the 1982 Act relaxes that definition specifically in relation to this offence as follows:

> " 'public place' has the same meaning as in section 133 of this Act but includes—
> (a) any place to which at the material time the public are permitted to have access, whether on payment or otherwise".

That broadening of the definition would, in my view, capture a pub or licensed premises. That brings me on to section 59 of the 1982 Act, which says:

> "The owner, tenant, or occupier of any property in, upon, or in respect of, which an offence to which this section applies is being committed or any person authorised by him may apprehend any person whom the owner or, as the case may be, the tenant, occupier or authorised person finds committing that offence and detain the apprehended person until the arrival of a constable."

Section 59 applies to section 50, so it appears to me that a licence holder or his authorised agent such as a member of staff *is entitled* to apprehend and detain a customer where that customer is drunk and incapable.

A separate, but crucial consideration is whether this power should in fact be used. Responding to a violent incident in licensed premises is something that must be properly risk assessed and requires special training delivered to staff. Serious thought must be given to the matter when there is a risk of physical danger; so, although the power exists, this should not be treated lightly, and links back to my earlier comment about not putting oneself in harm's way.

6 SECURITY LAW AND LICENSED PREMISES

It is worth considering at this stage the law concerning security staff and how this might apply to licensed premises. Private security law in the United Kingdom is regulated by the Private Security Industry Act 2001[77] which has had effect in Scotland since 1 November 2007.

The broad aim of the 2001 Act is to provide a regulatory platform for the provision of security services in a multitude of formats. Previously, the licensing of security personnel had been carried out by the local authority,[78] and it was felt that there was no national harmonisation, leading to a scattergun

77 The Act originally had effect in England and Wales only, but was later extended to Scotland by the Serious Organised Crime and Police Act 2005 via Sch 15 para 12.

78 See, e.g., "Aberdeen City introduces steward registration scheme" [1999] 12 SLLP 4.

approach. The Act was also enacted for policy reasons – it was felt that much of the security industry was completely unregulated and as a result had become populated with undesirables.

The function of the Act is to require a licence for certain activities (known as "licensable activities"), which include a number of roles such as manned guarding; immobilisation; restriction and removal of vehicles; and key holding. The manned guarding activity itself contains a number of distinct types of role, including cash and valuables in transit; close protection (bodyguarding); door supervision; public space supervision; and security guards. It should be stated at the outset that the onus for securing a door supervisor's licence lies squarely on the shoulders of the individual seeking to work in that area.[79]

The Act is chiefly regulated by the Security Industry Authority (SIA). The SIA is an independent body created by the 2001 Act and has two basic regulatory remits: to license individuals working in the security industry (where applicable); and to run the "Approved Contractor Scheme". The Approved Contractor Scheme is used to afford special status to organisations providing security services. A series of hurdles must be cleared before the status can be awarded, but it does have benefits: for example, a company providing door supervisors is allowed to deploy staff whilst their application is pending, as long as 85 per cent of its staff hold the relevant licence.[80]

The SIA has powers, under section 19 of the 2001 Act, to enter and inspect premises owned or occupied by a person who appears to be conducting licensable activities.[81]

6.1 Application of security law to non-SIA premises staff

One of the chief concerns about SIA licensing for the licensed trade is: "Who, other than specifically hired door stewards, requires an SIA licence?" It is well established that persons employed in the licensed trade are working in an industry that, from time to time, requires those within it to deal with difficult and potentially violent situations. Prior to the new security regime, many licensed premises would not have specific door stewards but simply expect their own bar staff to deal with any trouble and physically remove any persons requiring some fresh air.

Are there any SIA licensing implications in the instance where a person employed to tend the bar suddenly has to become involved in a drunken fight between two customers, requiring him to come from behind the bar and intervene, perhaps to the extent of using force to remove the troublemaker? We have, of course, discussed above the relevant law under the 2005 Act concerning reasonable force.

Whilst this right exists, if a person finds himself in such a situation on an

79 Working without the licence is an offence and could lead to 6 months' imprisonment and/or a fine of up to £5,000.

80 An "ACS" company can issue an applicant with what is known as a "Licence Dispensation Notice". Each LDN is valid for 8 weeks and can be renewed by the ACS company for a further 8 weeks. At the end of this second period the ACS company must have approval from the SIA to issue further LDNs.

81 As well as a number of other classes of person known as a "regulated person", which is widely defined in s 8 so as to allow inspection of unlicensed persons and persons holding themselves out to be licensed.

infrequent basis, could he avoid the requirement for an SIA licence? The SIA has provided guidance, which states:

> "The manned guarding activities which require a licence do not apply to the activities of a person who, incidental to the carrying out of activities which are not wholly or mainly the activities of a security operative, responds to a sudden or unexpected occurrence."[82]

So, it would seem that as long as such responses are indeed incidental, bar staff who are employed specifically without any supervision duties, will escape the need for an SIA licence. If, on the other hand, the employee has within his remit a general supervision element, perhaps involving "walk-rounds" of the premises and ensuring the safety of customers, or stepping in to help at the door from time to time, then that individual will almost certainly require an SIA licence.

6.2 Actions of security staff, delict and vicarious liability

Is the premises licence holder delictually liable for the actions of the door staff or security personnel on his premises? What happens if the door supervisor is heavy-handed in removing a patron and an assault occurs? It is established that the case of *Lister v Hesley Hall Ltd*[83] provides the modern test for when an employer becomes liable for the actions of his employee. A form of vicarious responsibility applies here. Pre-*Lister*, the doctrine was that any liability could only arise from activities in the course of an employee's employment – but *Lister* widened this definition to add any activities "sufficiently closely connected", and with it removed the necessity for those activities to be actively authorised.

It may be agreed that the safety of persons frequenting licensed premises lies in the hands of the licence holder, or persons to whom he has delegated the task. This would, of course, include door supervisors, whether in-house or out-sourced. The *Lister* test was considered in *Mattis v Pollock*.[84] In this case a door supervisor was involved in a scuffle after he prevented a man from accessing the club he was guarding, was then chased from the club and sought refuge in his nearby flat. The door supervisor returned to the club later that night armed with a knife and stabbed a man who had been in the party of the person with whom he had previously fought. The victim, who was rendered paraplegic as a result of the attack, brought a claim of damages against the club owner on the grounds that he was vicariously liable and, on appeal, won his case, the court applying the *Lister* test. It is of note that, in *Mattis*, the landlord encouraged the door supervisor to carry out his duties in an aggressive and intimidating manner, and this helped establish a duty of care from the landlord to the victim in the eyes of the court.

82 https://www.sia.homeoffice.gov.uk/Pages/licensing-manned-guarding.aspx
83 [2002] 1 AC 215.
84 [2003] EWCA Civ 887; [2003] 1 WLR 2158.

Table 19.1 Criminal offences, part 1

Provision (2005 Act)	*Offence*
s 8(1)[1]	Attempting to influence a board member
s 15(5)[2]	Obstruction of a licensing standards officer in the exercise of his powers relating to entry and inspection of premises or refusal to give assistance when asked
Sch 1 para 3(2)[3]	Acting as member of the licensing board whilst disqualified from holding such a role

1 See Chapter 4, Section 2.1.
2 See Chapter 6, Section 4.2.1.
3 See Chapter 4, Section 4.1.

7 OFFENCES RELATING TO LICENSING BOARDS, FORUMS AND STANDARDS OFFICERS

There are three specific offences here, which are discussed in terms at the relevant chapter elsewhere in this book, but listed in Table 19.1 for ease of reference.

8 OFFENCES RELATING TO PREMISES AND OCCASIONAL LICENCES

Table 19.2 is the list of offences which relate to premises and occasional licences, which have been referred to in the relevant chapter.

Table 19.2 Criminal offences, part 2

Provision (2005 Act)	*Offence*
s 1(1)[1]	Alcohol may not be sold unless under and in accordance with a premises licence or occasional licence granted under the 2005 Act[2]
s 24(11)[3]	Failure of an applicant for a premises licence to provide the licensing board with details of a conviction within one month of the date of conviction whilst the application is processing
s 41(3)[4]	Failure of a premises licence holder charged with a relevant offence to produce to the court his premises licence at the first relevant appearance
s 43(5)[5]	Failure of a premises licence holder to provide the licensing board with details of a conviction within one month of the date of conviction
s 48(3)[6]	Failure of a premises licence holder to advise the board of a change of personal details within one month of the date of the occurrence of the change
s 49(4)[7]	Failure of a premises licence holder to produce the licence for updating when asked to do so by the board
s 52(3)[8]	Failure to keep the premises licence, or a certified copy of it, on the premises and to display a summary, or certified copy, prominently so it can be read by anyone frequenting the premises
s 52(6)[9]	Failure to produce the premises licence when asked to do so by a constable or LSO

1 See, in general terms, Chapter 2 on the licence requirement itself, and Chapter 8, Section 3 on the issue of activities other than the sale and consumption of alcohol in the operating plan, and Chapter 15, Section 4.1 on the interplay between s 1(1) and the related mandatory condition.
2 An interesting example of this from the 1976 era occurred in *Graves or Crocket v Lees* [1997] 8 SLLP 23 in which alcohol was being sold from a taxi office. The accused argued, unsuccessfully, that the transactions were not of a "commercial nature".
3 See Chapter 8, Section 2.4.
4 See Chapter 7, Section 3.2.
5 See Chapter 7, Section 3.3.
6 See Chapter 7, Section 3.4.
7 See Chapter 7, Section 3.5.
8 Ibid.
9 Ibid.

9 OFFENCES RELATING TO PERSONAL LICENCES

The particular offences relating to personal licences, most of which are referred to in Chapter 17, are laid out in Table 19.3.

Table 19.3 Criminal offences, part 3

Provision (2005 Act)	*Offence*
s 75(10)	Failure of an applicant for a personal licence to provide the licensing board with details of a conviction within one month of the date of conviction whilst the application is being processed
s 80(3)	Failure of a personal licence holder charged with a relevant offence to produce to the court his premises licence at the first relevant appearance
s 82(5)	Failure of a personal licence holder to provide the licensing board with details of a conviction within one month of the date of conviction
s 88(3)	Failure of a personal licence holder to advise the board of change of name or address within one month of the date of the occurrence of the change
s 89(9)	Failure of a personal licence holder to produce the licence for updating when asked to do so by the board
s 93(3)	Failure to produce the personal licence when asked to do so by a constable or LSO

10 OFFENCES RELATING TO THE LICENSED HOURS

Offences provided for in the 2005 Act in relation to the licensed hours, as mentioned in Chapter 16 of this book, are as listed in Table 19.4.

Table 19.4 Criminal offences, part 4

Provision (2005 Act)	*Offence*
s 63(1)	Selling, allowing to sell, allowing to consume, allowing to be taken away alcohol outside the licensed hours
s 63(4)	Consuming alcohol on, or taking alcohol away from licensed premises outside the licensed hours, if requested not to do so by a responsible person

11 MISCELLANEOUS OFFENCES

The Act provides for a specific list of "miscellaneous" offences in Part 8, but in fact there are a number of other offences throughout the Act which might shortly be termed as "miscellaneous" and so they are all considered here.

11.1 Offences relating to sale of alcohol to trade

"Selling to trade" is defined in section 147(2) as:

> "selling the alcohol or goods to a person for the purposes of the person's trade".

Section 117 provides that it is an offence to sell alcohol to trade unless from licensed premises or premises which are used exclusively for the purpose of selling goods (whether alcohol or not) to trade.[85] Section 1(2) states that no premises licence is required for the sale of alcohol if it is "to trade". Putting all this together, if the premises from which alcohol is sold are being used solely to sell products to traders for the purposes of their trade, then no premises licence is required. If, on the other hand, the premises sell articles to the public, or to traders but for their own consumption or use, then the trade exemption will not apply, and a premises licence requirement will be activated. Trade sales are discussed in more detail in Chapter 11 at Section 8.

11.2 Prohibition of unauthorised sale of alcohol on moving vehicles

A person who sells alcohol from a moving vehicle which is not covered by a premises or occasional licence commits an offence.[86] This provision relates not to vehicles used for delivery of alcohol but where the sale is actually occurring from that vehicle in real time. The licensing of vehicles in this fashion is perhaps uncommon but a number of businesses which hire out vehicles for special occasions, during which alcohol would be supplied to passengers, could be caught by this depending on the contractual nature of the agreement. Offers such as the hire of limousines which include bottles of champagne, for example, would be caught by this offence by virtue of the section 3 provision concerning supply of alcohol pursuant to a contract. The licensing of vehicles and vessels is discussed in Chapter 11 at Section 7.

11.3 Delivery of alcohol from vehicles etc

It is, of course, quite legal for off-sale purchases to be delivered to a private home by a vehicle. There are numerous examples of this from supermarkets and wine clubs to craft breweries and indeed a large number of other premises, especially in the lockdown period of Covid-19, as businesses valiantly carried on in some form whilst closed. There are, however, rules to be observed in relation to the keeping of records for such deliveries. Section 119 makes it an offence for deliveries of this order to occur unless certain information is

85 Leading to a fine not exceeding level 5.

86 2005 Act, s 118. A person guilty of an offence under this section is liable on summary conviction to a fine not exceeding £20,000, imprisonment for a term not exceeding 3 months, or both.

entered into a "day book", delivery book and customer invoice prior to the commencement of the journey to deliver the alcohol, namely the quantity, description and price of the alcohol and the name and address of the person to whom it is to be delivered.[87] It is also an offence not to deliver the alcohol to the address as stated in the records, or to be carrying more alcohol than is noted.

There is specific provision for a constable or LSO to check the records, vehicle and receptacles used for the delivery of the alcohol, and to refuse either party access in that regard is an offence.[88]

This offence does not apply where the delivery is in connection with a contract between the supplier of the alcohol and a trader, and the alcohol has been purchased for the purposes of that person's trade.

11.4 Prohibition of late-night deliveries of alcohol

Deliveries of alcohol may only take place between 6am and midnight. Any delivery outside those times is illegal and an offence under section 120. Any responsible person who delivers alcohol between midnight and 6am, or a responsible person who allows the alcohol to be delivered, commits an offence.[89]

Anecdotal evidence from the period pre-commencement of the 2005 Act suggested that there were businesses or individuals offering what might colloquially be termed as a "dial-a-drink" service for home delivery during the wee small hours or beyond. Any delivery of alcohol to a domestic residence is illegal under the terms of section 120 if it occurs between midnight and 6am. The offence applies where the sale has occurred "on relevant premises". For the purposes of remote sales, the licensed premises are those from which the alcohol is despatched. This is discussed in more detail in Chapter 11 at Section 9.

The offence does not apply where the delivery is to licensed premises.[90] Some licensed premises may have local conditions concerning deliveries. In the earlier days of the 2005 Act I recall some cases where licensing boards had imposed local conditions requiring deliveries to be made within agreed hours, where there had perhaps been noise issues or some local difficulty. Persons making deliveries to such premises would need to be made aware of licence conditions and what any local planning restrictions might be.

Although this provision prevents the delivery of alcohol between midnight and 6am, this does not affect the order or despatch of the alcohol if that occurs during this period. Section 63(6) allows an order to be placed for an off-sale purchase outwith the licensed hours. This would capture, for example, an internet shopping order containing alcoholic products during that time. The same subsection also authorises despatch of alcohol outside the licensed hours – such as the supermarket lorry leaving the warehouse at 3am.

There remains a question mark over order fulfilment, however, and this brings us back to the issue on when the sale occurs. In *Valentine v Bell*[91] the

87 Such an offence can lead to a fine not exceeding level 3.
88 2005 Act, s 119(5).
89 Leading to a fine not exceeding level 4.
90 2005 Act, s 120(2).
91 1930 SLT 685. See also *Sinclair v Beattie* 1934 SLT 40.

court held that delivery was not a relevant consideration as to whether a sale has taken place, so we can remove that element from our query. We also know that it would be unlawful for alcohol to be sold outwith the licensed hours. This does not mean that an order cannot be *placed*. Ordering online, then, a customer may be allowed to request his bottles of finest stout at 1am, say, but the sale should not be fulfilled, that is, payment should not be taken, until 10am the following morning, at which point it may be dispatched. It is worth remembering that if the alcohol is despatched furth of Scotland none of this is relevant.

11.5 Keeping of smuggled goods

Section 121 provides that any responsible person who knowingly keeps or allows to be kept on licensed premises any goods which have been imported without any duty having been paid, or otherwise unlawfully imported, commits an offence.[92]

11.6 Prohibition of sale of alcohol on trains

Section 127 makes provision for a sheriff to make an order banning alcohol sales on trains, at train stations, and in respect of travelling between stations, where asked to do so by a police officer and if satisfied that it is necessary to prevent disorder. A typical example of the use of this power will be in connection with football-related traffic; for example, when Scotland plays at Hampden. It is an offence to sell, or knowingly allow the sale of alcohol whilst such a ban is in place.[93] See Chapter 11 at Section 6.3 for further detail on alcohol and train journeys.

11.7 Prohibition of sale of alcohol on ferries

In the same terms as above, the 2005 Act creates a power to ban alcohol on ferries. A breach of such a ban is an offence under section 128(5).[94] See Chapter 11 at Section 6.4 on alcohol and vessels or ferries.

11.8 Obstruction of inspections

The 2005 Act recognises that, when premises are subject to a licensing application,[95] it may be sensible to inspect the premises in order to determine whether the terms of the application are suitable. Section 137 makes specific provision for inspections by the police and a LSO in order to assess applications: this includes using "reasonable force", but note that the inspection should take place "at any reasonable time before the determination of a relevant proposal or application". It is an offence for any person to intentionally obstruct a

92 A conviction under this section may lead to a fine not exceeding level 3. There is also provision for the goods to be forfeited or destroyed (s 121(3)).

93 Leading to a fine not exceeding £20,000, 3 months' imprisonment, or both.

94 Leading to a fine not exceeding £20,000, 3 months' imprisonment, or both.

95 A premises licence application, a variation, a review, a temporary licence application, an occasional licence application, or an extended hours application.

constable or LSO exercising this power.[96] See Chapter 6 at Section 4.1 for a detailed examination of LSO powers of entry, inspection and seizure.

11.9 Obstruction of a police constable

A police constable may enter and inspect any licensed premises *at any time*. This includes club premises. A constable may also enter and inspect unlicensed premises from which food or drink is sold at any time if he has reasonable grounds for believing that an offence under the 2005 Act is being committed; however, in this case, if the officer is below the rank of inspector he must first have written authority from a justice of the peace or officer of or above the rank of inspector.

A number of councillors who sit on a licensing board are also justices of the peace, so this route could be used if the licensing board had concerns about particular premises. In the case of entering and inspecting unlicensed premises, the police have 8 days from the date the authority is given to carry out the inspection.

Any person who intentionally obstructs a police officer exercising a power under this section commits an offence.[97] It is commonplace for police officers to attend at or inspect licensed premises on a random basis or for an informal discussion. There need not be any complaint for the police to wish to visit particular premises. They may simply be "doing the rounds". It is prudent for licence holders and their staff to deal courteously with police officers and offer any assistance or answers to their queries, especially in light of this offence. On the other hand, it is incumbent upon Police Scotland to ensure that their officers are properly trained in the conduct of licensed premises inspections and that officers do not create issues where there are none: for example, by advising a licence holder during a visit that the premises may have to close as the premises manager or another personal licence is not there at the time, as well as adopting a common-sense approach to inspections, such as not taking management away from their duties to perform basic document inspections at 11pm on a busy Friday night. I understand that internal Police Scotland guidance on the issue of inspections or visits of this nature reminds officers that such events should be "proportionate".

12 EXCLUSION ORDERS

Section 94 of the 2005 Act creates a new power, that of the "exclusion order", a consolidation of the provisions of the preceding Licensing Premises (Exclusion of Certain Persons) Act 1980, which allowed a violent offender to be excluded from the licensed premises on which the offence occurred for a period of between three months and two years. Many licensees will be familiar with barring patrons who make nuisances of themselves, but now the courts

96 2005 Act, s 137(5); conviction under this section may lead to a fine not exceeding level 3.

97 2005 Act, s 138(5); leading to a fine not exceeding level 3. Under the Licensing (Scotland) Act 1903, if a constable was called upon to assist with the ejection of a patron whilst not in uniform, he was permitted to produce his baton to demand assistance from bystanders (as reported at [2002] 22 SLLP 20).

have the power to lawfully bar a person by order from particular licensed premises if a violent offence has been committed on or in the vicinity of any licensed premises.[98] Section 94 also allows the holder of a premises licence to make a summary application to seek such an order.

If an authorised person suspects a patron entering licensed premises to be in breach of an exclusion order, he may by virtue of section 95(4) remove the person from the premises, and, if necessary, use reasonable force.

Exclusion orders are rare. Most members of the licensed trade are unaware of their rights in this context. However, they are not non-existent, and there are a handful of examples of exclusion orders in various parts of Scotland. Some individuals have been given orders barring them from certain pubs, from pubs in a certain area, and (anecdotally) from all pubs in Scotland.

13 CLOSURE ORDERS

Under section 97 of the 2005 Act a senior police officer (inspector and above) has power to request that licensed premises be closed in the interests of public safety. Application must be made to the relevant licensing board and it will be up to the board to determine the length of the closure. The form of closure orders and emergency closure orders is laid down in the Licensing (Closure Orders) (Scotland) Regulations 2007.[99]

A closure order (or emergency closure order) must be terminated under section 98 when the police are satisfied that it is no longer necessary in the interest of public safety. The use of closure orders has, historically, been incredibly rare to the point that they have been a licensing footnote. However, since the onset of the 2005 Act and more particularly with the national licensing approach under Police Scotland, this unused "tool" began to appear here and there as the 2005 Act bedded in. To the best of my knowledge there were no formal closure orders anywhere in Scotland between 2009 and 2013. In 2014, however, four closure orders were sought by Police Scotland, all of which were successful. These related to premises in East Lothian, Midlothian, Aberdeen and Glasgow, with Aberdeen nightclub "Chaplins" having the honour of being the first under the 2005 Act.

Under section 26 of the Antisocial Behaviour etc (Scotland) Act 2004 a senior police officer may serve a closure notice that prohibits access to anyone other than someone normally resident on the premises, although this is another power rarely, if ever, referred to, let alone utilised.

13.1 Emergency closure orders

A senior police officer (which means an officer of the rank of superintendent or above[100]) may make an "emergency closure order" of their own volition if they believe that there is, or is likely to be, an imminent threat of disorder such that closure is necessary in the interests of public safety and there is no time to apply for a normal closure order. The maximum duration for an emergency

98 See my comments above at Section 5.7.1 on "reasonable force".

99 SSI 2007/35.

100 2005 Act, s 147(1).

closure order is 24 hours; however, section 99 makes provision for the extension of such an order for a further period not exceeding 24 hours. In the case where an extension for a further 24 hours is sought, this can only be pursued by an officer of the rank of inspector or above. The extension would be where there continues to be a risk to public safety to the extent that the closure should remain in force. An extension to an emergency closure order cannot, however, be enforced until the police have given notice of it to a "responsible person". As stated above, the notice itself is prescribed under the 2007 Regulations but, in addition to this, regulation 5 also requires a "senior police officer" to give notice "as soon as practicable" when an emergency closure order is made, extended, or terminated, to the appropriate licensing board.

In practice, the police will often ask the licence holder to close informally, in order to allow dispersal of any trouble, perhaps even for a few hours. In 2009, when I was writing *Licensing and Gambling Law in Scotland*, I stated "there are as yet no recorded instances of a formal emergency closure order being put in place". In 2020, as I complete the text for this part of the book, I do so during the period of Covid-19 "lockdown", and emergency closure orders have become front page news after the Government enforced closure of all licensed premises. A small number of licensed premises remained open, and Police Scotland confirmed at that time that emergency closure orders were instigated to make premises immediately shut up shop in light of the countrywide pandemic, perhaps most notably for a Greenock premises known as "Cheers".[101] In one case I am aware of during the Covid-19 lockdown, a client was served with an emergency closure order although the premises was open only to allow takeaway facilities,[102] and the following day an apology was issued.

101 This licence was subsequently revoked at a hearing of the Inverclyde Licensing Board in June 2020.

102 The Coronavirus (Scotland) Act 2020 had, of course, created an implied term in all on-sales premises licences that "home deliveries" was a permissible activity. See Appendix I on the 2020 Act temporary amendments.

Chapter 20

Appeals under the Licensing (Scotland) Act 2005

1 OVERVIEW

The appeals process is dealt with under sections 131 and 132 of the 2005 Act, implementing Schedule 5 to the Act, and augmented by further provision for procedure under section 132(9) by the Act of Sederunt (Summary Applications, Statutory Applications and Appeals etc Rules) 1999[1] as amended by the Act of Sederunt (Sheriff Court Rules) (Miscellaneous Amendments) (No. 2) 2010.[2] The appeal procedures are themselves subject to the general Scots law of civil procedure, so for the purposes of this book I have attempted to provide a basic introductory overview and illustrate the process with a "light touch".

It is worth noting that when the 2005 Act came into force the appeal process was by way of Stated Case, a position which was castigated by all stakeholders at the time.[3] This was remedied in 2010 when the summary application process was reinstated.

2 WHAT DECISIONS CAN BE APPEALED?

The starting point is to determine which decisions of the licensing board may be appealed. Section 131 provides that the decisions that can be appealed are set out in Schedule 5. Schedule 5 also indicates who may make the appeal in each circumstance. The Schedule is in two Parts, as set out in Table 20.1.

In each case, there is the potential to appeal the decision of the sheriff to the Court of Session on a point of law, and, with permission, from that place to the UK Supreme Court, although it is fair to say that examples of licensing cases in these upper tiers of the legal system are rare indeed.

Having reviewed these appeal rights, it is worth taking a moment to acknowledge those without appeal rights, which in particular is those persons ("any person") who have made a representation to a new licence application or a

1 SI 1999/929.
2 SSI 2010/416.
3 See, for example, "Lawyers fault stated case procedures" [2009] 41 SLLP 7; "Lawyers call for re-instatement of summary application appeals" [2009] 42 SLLP 4, in which Mairi Millar said: "'It is rare for licensing lawyers to agree unanimously on one issue, but this is one of those rare occasions where we are all in agreement: the stated case procedure does not work for licensing appeals and a straightforward return to the summary application is welcomed by all"; and Robert Skinner, "Appeals: Reasons for Change" [2009] 43 SLLP 21. The matter is also discussed by Jack Cummins in a case commentary for *Tesco Stores Ltd v Falkirk Licensing Board* [2010] 46 SLLP 28, at 32.

Table 20.1 Persons who may appeal

Decision	*Persons who can appeal*
Part 1: Appeals to the Sheriff Principal	
Refusal of a premises licence	The applicant
Refusal of a variation application	The applicant
Refusal of a transfer application under s 33 or s 34	The applicant
Refusal of a variation following transfer	The applicant
Suspension, revocation, variation or issue of a written warning following from a premises licence review	The premises licence holder or person seeking review
Refusal of application to revoke variation or suspension under s 40	The applicant
Refusal of extension of provisional period	The applicant
Refusal of a confirmation of a provisional premises licence	The applicant
Refusal of a temporary licence	The applicant
Refusal of extension of the period of effect of a temporary licence	The applicant
Refusal of an occasional licence	The applicant
Grant of an occasional licence	An objector under s 58(1)
Refusal of an extended hours application	The applicant
Part 2: Appeals to the Sheriff	
Refusal of a personal licence	The applicant
Suspension, revocation or endorsement of a personal licence	The personal licence holder

major variation application. This, of course, means an unhappy objector has no recourse to following the summary application route to appeal the decision made by a licensing board and must instead pursue judicial review, a course of action inaccessible to most for reasons of finance.[4] It is no coincidence that I cannot locate any record of a judicial review by an unhappy objector save *Buzzworks*. This is discussed further at Section 7.1 below.

3 JURISDICTION

Any appeal, under either Part 1 or Part 2 of Schedule 5, is to be made by way of summary application to the relevant sheriff court within the appropriate Sheriffdom. The Sheriffdoms of Scotland, and relevant sheriff courts, are shown in Table 20.2.

The Sheriff Principal, as referred to in the Schedule above, is the principal sheriff for the sheriffdom. Having licensing appeals assigned to these busy individuals is not always possible. Thankfully the Act allows for an appeal to be delegated by the Sheriff Principal to a sheriff.[5] This authorisation can be given "whether generally or specifically", meaning there can either be a direct

4 The process for judicial review is governed by chapter 58 of the Rules of the Court of Session 1994. This includes rules such as, inter alia, a 3-month deadline to raise the review from the date of the decision you wish to be reviewed; that the petitioner requires the permission of the court to proceed, and the petitioner must show "sufficient interest" in the petition.

5 2005 Act, s 132(4).

Table 20.2 List of sheriff courts by area

Sheriffdom	*Sheriff Courts*
Glasgow and Strathkelvin	Glasgow
Grampian, Highlands and Islands	Lochmaddy, Stornoway, Portree, Fort William, Inverness, Tain, Elgin, Wick, Kirkwall, Banff, Aberdeen, Peterhead
Lothian and Borders	Livingston, Edinburgh, Selkirk, Jedburgh
North Strathclyde	Campbeltown, Oban, Dunoon, Greenock, Dumbarton, Paisley
South Strathclyde, Dumfries and Galloway	Stranraer, Ayr, Hamilton, Airdrie, Lanark, Dumfries
Tayside, Central and Fife	Stirling, Falkirk, Alloa, Dunfermline, Perth, Kirkcaldy, Dundee, Forfar

delegation to a particular sheriff, or a scheme of delegation in place where licensing appeals are automatically delegated to particular sheriffs. There must be some decision or process in place.[6]

Typically, the sheriff court is the one in whose jurisdiction the “principal office” of the board is located:[7] meaning in normal circumstances the usual address where either (a) the administration of the licensing board is conducted, or sometimes (b) the address of the facility where the hearing took place, if there was one.

4 THE GROUNDS OF APPEAL

The grounds of appeal are found in section 131(3) and are that, in reaching the decision, the licensing board:

- erred in law,
- based its decision on an incorrect material fact,
- acted contrary to natural justice, or
- exercised its discretion in an unreasonable manner.

These are the same grounds as pertained to the 1976 Act, and so it is worth noting that much of the case law from that Act remains useful. There is a special further ground of appeal (which did not exist under the 1976 Act regime) in relation to a decision to revoke, suspend or vary a premises licence following a premises licence review hearing, or revoke, endorse or suspend a personal licence, which is:

- that the step taken is disproportionate in all the circumstances.

Whilst there is no scope in this book to forensically unpick these grounds, it may be worth stating that proportionality, which, as a ground appeal, was new to licensing law when adopted in the 2005 Act, should not be viewed as

6 An example of where there was no authorisation of any sort is in *Nelson v Renfrewshire Licensing Board*, Paisley Sheriff Court, 22 October 2013, unreported, on which see Chapter 14 at Section 2.1; and footnote 7 of that chapter.

7 As is required under s 131(6) of the 2005 Act.

equivalent to *Wednesbury*[8] unreasonableness and although it may be generally correct to indicate that proportionality is about the board making a fair and balanced decision, the concept is far more complex.[9]

If an appeal is to be lodged, it must be with the sheriff clerk no later than 21 days after the date of the decision that is being appealed, or within 21 days of the issue of a statement of reasons (save in relation to reviews and occasional licences – see the "review trap" discussion at 7.3 below). The "date of issue" of the statement of reasons is the date shown on the statement, that is, Part 12 of the prescribed form of the statement, which is headed "Date Statement of Reasons Issued",[10] as opposed to when it might be physically issued or indeed received. There is no provision to extend the deadline if an appeal is lodged late – the general dispensing power under Rule 2 of the 1999 Rules does not apply to appeals under the 2005 Act, so it is important to ensure any appeal is marked timeously.

5 LICENSING APPEAL PROCESS

The general civil procedural principles of Scots law apply in a summary application to the sheriff. An initial writ (Form 1) will be drafted by the appellant, and normally lodged together with a first inventory of productions with the relevant sheriff clerk's office to obtain a warrant to serve on the licensing board (and such other parties as may be relevant). Due to time pressures the initial writ may need to be skeletal and simply outline the basic thrust of the appeal, knowing that this can be fortified later. A hearing will be set for the first calling of the case during which the sheriff, all being well, will agree various dates including for formal answers to be provided by the licensing board to the condescendence and pleas-in-law made in the writ, a timeframe for adjustments to pleadings, and for other materials to be provided to all parties such as inventories of productions and a joint list of legal authorities. It is not unusual for the appeal diet to be fixed at this first hearing. The result of the timetable is that an over-arching document stating the position of both parties is ultimately produced and is referred to as the "record". There may be further procedural hearings before the sheriff, such as where an agreement has been reached between the parties and a joint motion made for a certain outcome, but ultimately if the case is proceeding then focus switches to the date which is set for the hearing.

5.1 The appeal hearing

The appeal hearing[11] generally consists of oral presentations made by each party or his solicitor/advocate to the sheriff or sheriff principal as appropriate, including liability for expenses, which generally follow success. It is important

8 *Associated Provincial Picture Houses Ltd v Wednesbury Corporation* [1948] 1 KB 223 (CA); itself, of course, a licensing case, focusing on the licensing regime for cinema premises as was in place at that time.

9 See Scott Blair, "The Contours of Proportionality: a learning curve" [2010] 47 SLLP 8 for his, as ever, impeccable insight; and, further, the discussion of Lord Reed in *Bank Mellat (No. 2) v HM Treasury* [2013] UKSC 38.

10 Licensing (Procedure) (Scotland) Regulations 2007 (SSI 2007/453) Sch 4.

11 Sometimes, a licensing appeal hearing might be referred to colloquially as a "proof" although

to appreciate that the appeal hearing is not a re-hearing of the case itself but is an examination of the decision-making and reasoning of the board. After hearing both sides, during which time questions might be asked of either party, the sheriff or sheriff principal will typically retire to consider and then make a decision (a period known as "avizandum").

Although evidence can sometimes be heard in a licensing appeal (such as where there is a factual dispute about what happened at the board hearing, or where it is suggested an incorrect material fact was relied on by evidencing the correct fact[12]), they are usually debates focused on the adequacy of the statement of reasons, and the most common ground of appeal is likely to be error of law based on inadequate reasoning.[13]

In most cases the decision is announced in writing, although in some cases an oral decision is made from the bench there and then, but that is rare.

5.2 The powers of the sheriff or sheriff principal

If the appeal is successful the sheriff or sheriff principal may, under section 131(5), make one of the following orders:

- remit the case back to the licensing board for reconsideration,
- reverse the decision, or
- substitute the decision for such other decision as he thinks appropriate, providing the alternative is one which would have been open to the board.

The term "remit" means that the sheriff has upheld the appeal but considers it appropriate to have the licensing board re-hear the case. A remitted appeal will almost always result in a different decision being reached by the licensing board, especially as the written judgment of the court will provide guidance for the licensing board to digest where it may have misled itself in the original hearing. Cases where a remitted decision has resulted in a further refusal are difficult to locate – having consulted with licensing peers I have not been made aware of any under the 2005 Act.

A full reversal might occur where the sheriff has upheld the appeal and believes that their error is too significant to be overcome by the board, or that for some reason the board would be unable to properly reach an alternative outcome.

The contrast between agreeing a full reversal, or a remit for consideration, was helpfully explored in the case of *Alldays Stores Ltd v Central Fife Divisional Licensing Board*,[14] and makes clear that, whilst a sheriff might be slow to step into the shoes of a statutory decision-making body like a licensing board, there is no mandatory or expected requirement to always remit, and indeed taking such a position would be fettering the discretion of the court; rather, it is for the court to decide on a case-by-case basis whether a full reversal is necessary.

A substitute decision is a rarer beast and might, for example, include a decision to grant a licence, but with a condition attached. Sheriffs are generally slow to make a decision like this where it is clear that Parliament has decreed

that term should really only be used where a court is engaged in hearing evidence or calling witnesses.

12 See Sheriff Holligan in *Habib v Central Fife Area Regulation Sub-committee* 2008 SLT (Sh Ct) 57.

13 The leading case on this is probably *Ritchie v Aberdeen City Council* 2011 SC 570.

14 [2007] 37 SLLP 34.

that such decisions are for boards to make. It might be more likely that a sheriff would remit the case, with an overt direction or suggestion as to a substitute.

In considering any of these outcomes, perhaps the most important point for lay practitioners to note is that the Scottish appeal system is not a hearing *de novo*, in other words, it is not a chance to run the case again, as mentioned above. The sheriff is not sitting as a replacement for the licensing board. The appeal hearing is purely an assessment of the lawfulness of the decision of the board and is therefore focused on those narrow technical grounds of appeal above. This is a subtle contrast to the English system which had, for some time, enjoyed a wider remit in re-hearing aspects of the original licensing case. That is, until the decision in *R (Hope and Glory Public House Ltd) v City of Westminster Magistrates' Court*,[15] which moved the English system much nearer the Scottish position, and was subsequently endorsed by *R (Developing Retail Ltd) v East Hampshire Magistrates' Court*.[16] In *Developing Retail Limited* the High Court judge said:

> "The magistrates' court is not considering any question of Wednesbury unreasonableness since it is not a process of judicial review, it is instead a fresh evidential hearing. This means that the task of the magistrates' court, having heard the evidence and specifically addressed the decision of the authority below, is to give a decision whether, because they disagree with the decision below in the light of the evidence, it is wrong. The magistrates therefore have power not merely to review the decision on the grounds of an error of law but also on its merits."

The English idea of a fresh evidential hearing, albeit one restricted by the *Hope and Glory* dicta and others,[17] is where the Scottish, and English and Welsh systems, clearly diverge. Our appeal cases are not fresh evidential hearings and our sheriffs do not re-open the merits of the licence application, but instead focus on the lawfulness of the decision-making and reasoning of the licensing board.

Finally, it is worth stating that another possible outcome is concession – perhaps by way of a joint minute between the parties, although the acceptance of this is still within the gift of the sheriff.

6 THE POWER OF "INTERIM RECALL"

Section 132(8) allows a sheriff principal to recall the suspension or revocation of a premises licence *ad interim* pending the result of the appeal on application by the licence holder, and if satisfied on the balance of convenience that it is appropriate to do so. The power of interim recall does not apply to any other outcome including outcomes under section 39 other than suspension of revocation: including, perhaps unfairly, variations which could have substantial detrimental effect on premises.[18]

The "balance of convenience" is not necessarily a blunt instrument as to

15 [2011] EWCA Civ 31.

16 [2011] EWHC 618 (Admin).

17 See, for example, *Mehrdad Kaivanpor v Director of Public Prosecutions* [2015] EWHC 4127 (Admin) and *Muck IT Ltd v Merritt and others* [2005] EWCA Civ 1124 for examples of the English courts re-examining the merits of a licensing case.

18 The most famous example of this is likely to be the decision by the Glasgow Licensing Board to vary the licence of the Arches so that the terminal hour was reduced from 3am to 12midnight: thus rendering the use of the venue as a nightclub impossible.

the financial inconvenience to the operator,[19] but that will depend on the individual case and merits thereof, as if not just the decision but the timing of the decision appears disproportionate then financial impact is of relevance to this balance, as was the case in *Tesco Stores Ltd v Midlothian Licensing Board*,[20] where the Sheriff was hyper-critical of a decision to impose a 7-day immediate suspension in the week prior to Christmas, when sales would be at their highest. In *Rentincome Ltd v Aberdeen City Licensing Board*,[21] Sheriff Miller accepted that the "relative strength" of the respective cases and an aim to do the "least damage in the meantime" to either party were factors in assessing the balance of convenience, including financial damage. In this case the board tried to argue that, as the premises could trade without alcohol, the damage was limited, but Sheriff Miller dismissed that as an unrealistic view of the wider impact the loss of alcohol sales would have on a late night entertainment business.

7 APPEALS: A CLOSER LOOK

There are a few bespoke elements of the appeal system which are worth a closer look: namely, objectors' rights; the immediacy of suspension and revocation; the review hearing "trap"; and whether the imposition of a condition in the grant or variation of a licence can be appealed.

7.1 Appeals: objectors' rights, such as they are

The 2005 Act gives a threadbare number of possibilities for an objector to appeal if the application should be granted. There are, in fact, only two: an objector to an occasional licence may object to the granting of the licence; and a person who has requested a premises licence review may appeal a decision to suspend, revoke or vary the licence or issue a written warning following the review. This is in contrast to the 1976 Act, s 17(5) in which objectors were provided the right to appeal to the sheriff against a decision of the board to grant, transfer or renew a licence. Indeed, not simply a competent objector could appeal but even an objector whose objection had been deemed incompetent and not heard "on the day" of the hearing, had an appeal route under the 1976 Act.[22]

As noted above, the unhappy objector is faced with only one remedy, namely judicial review. That would also be the case where an objector had their objection ruled out on the grounds of competency, whether such decision had been made by the clerk prior to any hearing or made by the board at a hearing.

7.2 Appeals: the immediacy of suspension and revocation

Under the 1976 Act, where a licence was suspended following a section 31 hearing, the licence remained "live" whilst any appeal was yet to be determined. This was heavily criticised on the basis that a nefarious licence holder could continue to trade in the most egregious of circumstances, and the result of such criticism

19 See Paul Romano, "Interim recall of suspensions and revocations: where lies the 'balance of convenience'"? [2010] 46 SLLP 13.

20 [2012] ScotSC 48.

21 Aberdeen Sheriff Court, 19 February 2020, unreported.

22 *Little v East Ayrshire Licensing Board* [1998] 10 SLLP 8.

was that the reverse is true under the 2005 Act. Under section 132(7), a decision of the board continues to have effect despite an appeal. This, of course, has a significant impact on the trade given the immediacy of the suspension or revocation, but that is where the interim recall provision comes in: see Section 6 above. It is worth noting here that, where a licence is suspended or revoked, there are alternative "remedies" to an appeal available: see Chapter 14 at Section 7.1 on the power to "review" a suspension due to a "change in circumstances", and Section 7.2 on recall of a revocation on the "fit and proper" ground.

7.3 Appeals: the deadline "trap" in reviews, occasional licences and extended hours applications

As is stated above, the timeline for lodging an appeal is 21 days from the date of the decision, or 21 days from the date of the issue of the statement of reasons under section 51 if one has been requested. This is not the case in respect of a decision following a review hearing, where the 21 days runs from the date of the hearing at which the decision to take a step under section 39 is taken, and the request or the issue of the statement of reasons is irrelevant. In relation to occasional licences and extended hours applications, the 21 days runs only from the date of decision, and the request for or issue of the statement of reasons is irrelevant. These booby traps are not thought to have been a purposeful act on the part of Parliament, but more of a drafting oversight when considering the interplay between the sections under which appeals can be brought: namely, by reference to section 51, which only captures applications under Part 3 (new licences and variations); and therefore omits section 61 (occasional licences) and section 70 (extended hours). In relation to reviews, this issue is also discussed in Chapter 14 at Section 8.

7.4 Appeals: can the imposition of a condition be appealed?

Conspicuous by its absence is any clear right of appeal in Schedule 5 to the imposition of a condition by the licensing board on a premises licence. It is accepted, of course, that there can be no right of appeal to the imposition of the mandatory conditions under Schedule 3 or the late-night conditions (where appropriate) as these are necessitated by operation of law, not of discretion. It is also accepted that a variation to impose a condition as an outcome following a review hearing can also be subject to an appeal. But what of a premises licence holder whose licence is granted or varied but with an additional condition imposed which is not necessarily to their liking?

This links to the "modification" power under section 23(7) under which the board may "propose" an amendment to an application before them where, if not for the proposal, they would refuse the application.[23] This proposal might include the imposition of a condition leaving the applicant with an invidious choice: accept a licence with the irksome condition attached; or have no licence at all.

There is a line of thought that where a licence is granted in this way, there is no right of appeal to deal with the condition, because a licence has been granted. The alternative view is that the ground of appeal does in fact apply

23 See Chapter 10 at Section 1 on the use of the "modification" power.

because, whilst there is a licence, it is not a licence in a form which is ultimately acceptable, albeit that the applicant was forced into having to accept some form of licence that was lesser or more restricted than the form desired.

In *Baillie v Wilson*,[24] a Motherwell publican appealed the imposition of a condition preventing the sale of spirits, a decision that had been imposed across all premises in the Motherwell licensing court jurisdiction which happened to be up for renewal at that time.[25] The court held the renewal of the licence with the condition attached did not amount to a renewal of the licence as sought. This was described as a "*vital difference*" and was held to be a refusal of the renewal. Whilst this case does not exactly sit with the provisions of the 2005 Act, the general principle that what was granted was not what was sought remains relevant. A key difference with the 2005 Act is the board can give the applicant the choice: a complete refusal; or a grant in terms which are less than those sought having forced the applicant to accept the latter as the better of two bad outcomes.

The matter was considered under the 1976 Act in the case of *Wolfson v Glasgow District Licensing Board*.[26] In this case an off-sale licence was granted to Mr Wolfson at the June quarterly meeting of 1978, but with a condition restricting the sale of spirits. The question of whether the grant constituted a grant given the imposition of the condition was ultimately appealed to the Court of Session. The court, following *Baillie*, looked at the severity of the restriction as relevant as to whether the "grant with condition" could amount to a refusal and therefore be capable of appeal, saying:

> "the restriction imposed affects the scope of the licence and is of a radical, compared to an administrative nature . . . In our opinion, by parity of reasoning, where there is an application for a full new licence and only a restricted licence is granted the same conclusion must be reached."[27]

What *Wolfson* appears to suggest to me is that, whilst a "grant with condition" could be capable of appeal, the terms of the condition are of some import: the more adverse the impact, the more likely it might be treated as a refusal in all but name.[28]

These earlier decisions are of interest in this context, but it is the presence of the quasi-Hobson's Choice in section 23(7) which is of special import.

24 1917 SC 55.

25 In an unavoidable link to the more recent "burger van" decision of *McCluskey & Others v North Lanarkshire Council* [2016] SC HAM 3, Lord Ormidale said (1917 SC 55, at pp 57–8): "I assume that the motive of the Magistrates of Motherwell in refusing authority to any of the licence-holders in the burgh to sell spirits was a good one. It was not suggested that it was not, and it may be readily admitted that in present circumstances many persons would maintain that it was a reasonable view to take that, if all facilities for the purchase of spirits were removed, it would be greatly to the advantage not only of Motherwell, but the country at large. But the magistrates must proceed strictly according to the statute, and in the statute, as I read it, there is no warrant given, either directly or impliedly, to the Magistrates at their option to veto the sale of spirits."

26 1981 SC 136.

27 Ibid at 138 and 140.

28 This was explored somewhat in the unreported case of *Hawthorn Leisure (Scotco) Ltd v South Ayrshire Licensing Board* (2018), in which a remit was agreed following imposition of conditions relating to noise and stewarding at the Red Lion in Prestwick, which were applied across the extent of the licence notwithstanding the variation related to additional hours. At the remitted hearing, the board agreed to "limit" the scope of the conditions to the extended portion of hours only.

Chapter 21

Gambling in Alcohol-Licensed Premises and Clubs

1 OVERVIEW

Before turning to the specific law of gambling in alcohol-licensed premises and clubs, it is important to contextualise the law of gambling generally and tease out some of the wider legal concepts. As of 1 September 2007, the vast majority of forms of gambling in Scotland are regulated by the Gambling Act 2005. This Act replaced a former archaic regime which was spread across a number of enactments, such as the Gaming Act 1968, the Betting, Gaming and Lotteries Act 1963 and the Lotteries and Amusements Act 1976. Although the gambling legislation is, of course, an entirely separate regime from liquor licensing, they are very much related and most licensing practitioners will become embroiled in gambling law at some point, even if only in applying for gaming machines permits or giving advice on a poker event. Further, it is the liquor licensing boards, and their staff, who deal with gambling matters. Finally, police involvement in gambling premises is usually from those officers within the licensing department.

The Gambling Act 2005 is constructed upon the basis of three gambling licensing objectives and has a tiered structure of three different kinds of licence: operating licences, premises licences and personal licences. This chapter is focused on gambling law as it pertains to alcohol-licensed premises and clubs and so only a general overview of these wider concepts is offered.

2 THE GAMBLING LICENSING OBJECTIVES

As with the Licensing (Scotland) Act 2005 and the English and Welsh Licensing Act 2003, the Gambling Act 2005 is underpinned by "objectives", which are set out "with admirable clarity"[1] as follows:

- preventing gambling from being a source of crime or disorder, being associated with crime or disorder or being used to support crime,
- ensuring that gambling is conducted in a fair and open way, and
- protecting children and other vulnerable persons from being harmed or exploited by gambling.

The licensing objectives are, in general terms, the undercurrent by which the vast majority of the functions of the Gambling Commission and the decision-making process of Scottish licensing boards are governed. However,

1 P Kolvin, *Gambling for Local Authorities* (Institute of Licensing, 2007) p 95.

one should take care not to suppose that the role of the licensing objectives under the Gambling Act 2005 is equivalent to the licensing objectives under the Licensing (Scotland) Act 2005. Although they share nomenclature, the gambling licensing objectives sometimes take a more subsidiary position in relation to certain aspects of the Gambling Act 2005: for example, the general duty to have regard to the objectives laid upon the Gambling Commission is not replicated for licensing boards in such a direct manner, and for certain types of application the gambling licensing objectives languish in a thoroughly secondary role.[2]

Another fruitful comparison is in relation to the Licensing (Scotland) Act 2005 requirement for the licensing policy statement to actively promote the licensing objectives,[3] whereas the equivalent requirement, the statement of principles under the Gambling Act 2005, makes no similar reference to the gambling licensing objectives.

3 OPERATING, PREMISES AND PERSONAL LICENCES

Operating licences are dealt with under Part 5 of the Gambling Act 2005 and their existence recognises the significant presence of "operators" in the gambling industry – business organisations that have a substantial impact on the industry and make up a large part of the economy of gambling. Many holders of alcohol licences will also have to be operating licence holders, but in particular casino and bingo operators. The operating licence is therefore partly aimed at the higher level of business management in terms of their operation and organisation, and not just about how they might go about running a specific set of business premises. It also acts as a check on the suitability of those persons and indicates that they have been deemed "fit and proper" although that specific term is not used in gambling law in the same way as we have discussed in Chapter 10 under the Licensing (Scotland) Act 2005. An operating licence does not of itself apply to a specific business premises but rather authorises a person or entity to provide certain facilities for gambling, which may or may not be from a set of premises. The requirements placed on applicants hoping to obtain an operating licence far exceed anything under any other licensing regime and specialist advice should certainly be sought. Applications for operating licences are dealt with by the Gambling Commission.

Whilst the operating licence deals with those "higher levels" of business management, section 150 of the Gambling Act 2005 provides for five different types of premises licence:

- casino premises licence[4]
- bingo premises licence

2 E.g. in relation to the consideration of an application for a family entertainment centre gaming permit, Sch 10 para 7 of the Gambling Act 2005 provides that licensing boards "need not (but may) have regard to the licensing objectives". A similar statement is used in Sch 14 para 8 in relation to prize gaming permits.

3 Licensing (Scotland) Act 2005, s 6(3).

4 There are different classes of casino licence: regional, large or small (a sub-variant of which is known as a "converted casino licence", which relates to a licensed casino existing before the Gambling Act 2005 came into force and "converted" to the new system at that time).

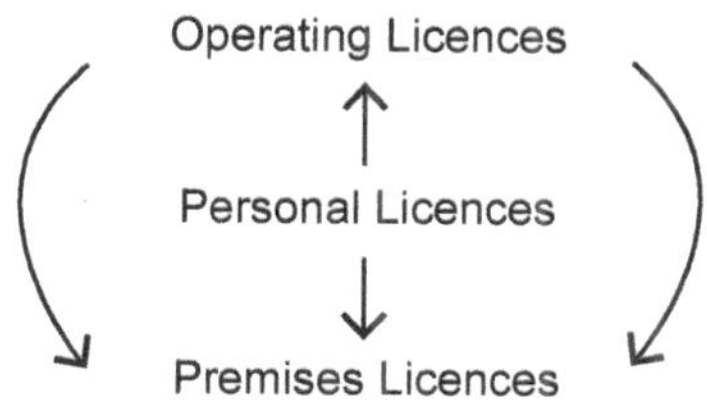

Figure 21.1 Links between types of licences

- adult gaming centre premises licence[5]
- family entertainment centre premises licence[6]
- betting premises licence.

A premises licence may not be in respect of anything other than one of the activities noted above: in other words, it must be a single premises licence for one of the activities and not a combination of two or more – and only one premises licence may be in force at any one premises.[7]

Personal licences under the Gambling Act 2005, which are also processed by the Gambling Commission, relate to individuals performing certain tasks on behalf of a gambling operator. This would include a premises manager in the sense we might be familiar with under the Licensing (Scotland) Act 2005, such as a casino manager, but also includes persons at the higher management level such as people tasked with ensuring regulatory compliance, or those in charge of IT provision and marketing.

It may be helpful to take a step back and view how these three forms of licence interact with each other. The best way to view this dynamic is to consider them in a diagram (Figure 21.1).

Persons holding personal licences will be employed (in the main part) in premises that hold premises licences or at the head of organisations holding operating licences, and in order to apply for a premises licence the applicant must first hold an operating licence. Personal licence applications under the Gambling Act 2005 frequently accompany new operating licence applications as the directors or controllers of the proposed business seek approval themselves. If the business falls into the category of a "small scale" operator, the personal licence requirement is not necessarily activated but is replaced by a similar process known as an "Annex A" application, which relates to an individual.

The alcohol-licensed trade interaction with the Gambling Act 2005 tends to be ancillary to the running of the pub, bar or club and therefore the need for operating licences, premises licences, or personal licences under that Act is rare. However, notable exceptions arise such as bowling alleys or leisure and holiday parks, which might have Adult Gaming Centre or Family Entertainment Centre licences.

5 An Adult Gaming Centre is an arcade premises offering gaming machines where only persons aged 18 or above are allowed.

6 A Family Entertainment Centre is an arcade premises offering gaming machines where persons of any age are allowed (albeit there are, of course, various restrictions concerning children and young persons).

7 Gambling Act 2005, s 152(1)(b). This does not mean that the same building could not have more than one gambling licence, of course. See paragraph 7.5 of the Gambling Commission Guidance to Licensing Authorities.

4 THE KEY DEFINITIONS OF THE GAMBLING ACT 2005

There are several key concepts which arise in the Gambling Act 2005 and these include: the definition of gambling; the definition of remote gambling; and the definition of providing facilities for gambling.

4.1 The definition of gambling

The starting point is the definition of "gambling" itself, which is to be found in section 3 and includes gaming, betting, and participation in a lottery. "Gaming" is defined in section 6 as playing a game of chance for a prize; "betting" is defined in section 9 as making or accepting a bet on the outcome of a race, competition or other event or process, making or accepting a bet on the likelihood of a thing occurring or not occurring, or making or accepting a bet on whether anything is true. "Lottery" is defined in section 14 and can be either a "simple" or "complex" lottery. Each of the definitions requires some further elaboration.

4.1.1 Gaming

This form of gambling is considered further in sections 6 to 8 of the Gambling Act 2005 and includes games of chance, casino games and equal chance gaming. "Games of chance" include a game that involves both an element of skill and an element of chance,[8] a game that involves an element of chance that can be eliminated by superlative skill, and a game that is presented as having an element of chance, so long as any of these games do not include sport. "Casino game" means a game of chance that is not equal chance gaming (otherwise known as bankers' games, such as blackjack). Finally, an "equal chance game" is a game which does not involve playing against a banker and where the chances are equally favourable to all participants (e.g. poker). Underpinning all of these forms of gaming is the end result: the "prize". A prize in this context can include money, money's worth, a prize provided by the person organising the gaming, or both a prize provided by the organiser and the aggregation of winnings through money staked.[9]

4.1.2 Betting

Including the definition given above, section 9 goes on to say that a bet made where the activity has completed and one party knows the outcome may still fall to be considered as a bet, and that a bet on likelihood may still fall to be a bet if the thing has already occurred or not, and one party knows this outcome. Betting also includes prize competitions where the punter has to "guess"[10] at

8 The interplay between "skill" and "chance" in relation to poker under the Gaming Act 1968 was famously considered in *R v Kelly* [2008] EWCA Crim 137; [2008] All ER 840; [2008], in which Mr Kelly unsuccessfully argued that poker was a game of skill, and not chance. Any ambiguity has been removed by the new definitions under the 2005 Act.

9 Gambling Act 2005, s 6(5). The traditional definition of "winnings" is, of course, a cash prize, but casino industries such as casino and bingo sectors have also sought to encourage a wider spectrum of high-end retail goods.

10 "Guess" in this context includes making a prediction based on skill or judgement and not just a random result: Gambling Act 2005, s 11(2).

an outcome, is required to pay and if his guess is accurate he wins a prize. The final form of betting is "pool betting", which is where all or part of the winnings is determined by the aggregate of stakes contributed and subsequently divided amongst the winners.[11] Schedule 1 to the Act makes further provision about betting arrangements.

4.1.3 Participation in a lottery

The Gambling Act 2005 has created two types of lottery: simple and complex. A simple lottery is one where entrants are required to pay to participate, prizes are allocated to one or more members of a class (i.e. those holding the winning numbers on a ticket), and the allocation process relies wholly on chance.[12] A complex lottery is effectively the same but where there is a series of allocation processes and the first of those processes relies solely on chance. Schedule 2 to the Act makes further provision about lottery arrangements.

The 2005 Act has also recognised that these three forms of gambling are not mutually exclusive and has provided for activities that may be betting and gaming, betting and lotteries, or lotteries and gaming. Sections 16 to 18 of the Act should be followed when an activity meets the definition of multiple forms of gambling in order to determine into which category the activity ultimately falls.

4.2 Definition of remote gambling

Remote gambling is defined in section 4 and is gambling by means of remote communication. This can include the internet, telephone, television, radio or any other kind of device or technology which facilitates communication (a generic description aimed at capturing the ever advancing march of technology and recognising that the popularity of this area of gaming has increased exponentially in recent years – indeed, the need to control internet and remote gambling was one of the driving forces behind the implementation of the 2005 Act).

4.3 Definition of providing facilities for gambling

Under the terms of section 5 of the Act, a person is deemed to be "providing facilities for gambling" if they invite another person to gamble in accordance with arrangements made by them; if they provide, operate or administer arrangements for gambling on behalf of someone else; if they participate in the operation or administration of gambling for others; or if they make facilities for remote gambling available for use.[13]

11 Gambling Act 2005, s 12.

12 "Chance" in the context of a lottery includes processes where the entrant has to use skill, knowledge or judgement, but only where the requirement "cannot reasonably be expected to prevent a significant proportion of persons who participate in the arrangement of which the process forms part from receiving a prize, and the requirement cannot reasonably be expected to prevent a significant proportion of persons who wish to participate in that arrangement from doing so": Gambling Act 2005, s 14(5).

13 See s 5(3) for the specific criteria for whether remote gambling provisions constitute facilities for gambling.

5 GAMBLING IN ALCOHOL-LICENSED PREMISES AND CLUBS

Any form of true gambling which occurs on alcohol-licensed premises is governed by the Gambling Act 2005 (although see comments below on the interplay with the premises licence operating plan). Under previous gambling regimes, a legal discussion of gambling in alcohol-licensed premises consisted, in the main, on the provision of gaming machines, or "amusements with prizes" (AWPs) as they were previously known. This was by way of a permit under section 34(1) or (5E) of the Gaming Act 1968. Other forms of traditional "gaming" in pubs include dominoes, bingo and so on, and these varying forms of entertainment have been an accepted form of gaming in licensed premises in Scotland for some time, and remain popular in different formats. The presence of "gaming" like dominoes was ratified in law at least as early as the decision in *Hoggan v Wood*,[14] where the court held that the game of dominoes was not unlawful, and did not become so by being played for a stake.

Aside from the seemingly evergreen pub pastimes of dominoes and perhaps cribbage, during the lifecycle of the 1976 Act it was fair to say that where "harder" forms of gambling such as poker nights or race nights were happening this was usually met with resistance from police. But this was not just a feature of business under the 1976 Act. Indeed, it has been accepted for some considerable time that gambling in licensed premises requires state intervention: the earliest law I was able to discern was an old Scots Act from 1621[15] which prohibited the "playing of cards or dice in inns". Card players would risk a fine, and dice players would risk loss of the "towns liberties".

The Gambling Act 2005 came into force on 1 September 2007 and has changed all of that and, it is generally fair to say, deregulated the forms and availability of gambling in alcohol-licensed premises and clubs. There are two main forms of gambling now allowed, and each of these is to a certain extent authorised by the Act itself without any further need for a permit or licence. These are gaming machines, and certain forms of equal chance gaming (which covers a number of games including poker and bingo), both of which we will examine in this chapter.

Another general point of context is that, whilst the Licensing (Scotland) Act 2005 brought traditional members' clubs into the licensing mainstream (see Chapter 11 at Section 2) with some notable exemptions, the Gambling Act 2005 has gone further in preserving the "special status" of clubs and as such there are different permits and rules. The interplay between permissions under the Licensing (Scotland) Act 2005 and the Gambling Act 2005 is something discussed in more detail below.

6 GAMING MACHINES IN ALCOHOL-LICENSED PREMISES

Gaming machines are one of the most popular forms of gambling in Great Britain and can be found in such diverse locations as casinos, clubs, pubs, entertainment centres and bingo halls. The Gambling Act 2005 makes provision for specific types of permits which will allow the use of such machines

14 (1889) 16 R (J) 95.
15 APS iv 613, c 14.

depending on the type of premises they are being used on. The Act also completely remodelled the definitions and categories of such machines, but before we look at the categories we should start by examining exactly what is meant by "gaming machine".

6.1 Definition of "gaming machine"

Section 235 states that "gaming machine" means:

> "a machine which is designed or adapted for use by individuals to gamble (whether or not it can also be used for other purposes)."

"Machine" means any apparatus which uses mechanical power, electrical power, or both.[16] The definition of gaming machine is therefore quite broad and, as such, the next provision in section 235 is to provide a list of machines which *do not* fall to be classed as gaming machines. These are as follows:

- A domestic or dual-use computer is not a gaming machine simply because it can be used to access online or remote gambling: this covers the use of, for example, personal devices at home where you might choose to access a gaming site (see below).
- A telephone or other communication device is not a gaming machine simply because it can be used to access online or remote gambling.
- A machine designed or adapted to take bets on future real events of itself is not a gaming machine.
- A machine which dispenses lottery tickets but does not determine the results of the lottery, and does not announce or display the results is not a gaming machine, unless there is an interval of at least one hour between the entry to the lottery and the announcement of the results.[17]
- A machine designed or adapted to play bingo is not a gaming machine, if used in accordance with the general conditions attached to the operating licence under section 75 or section 77 by section 85(2)(b) regarding the specification of the equipment.
- A machine designed or adapted to play bingo *by way of prize gaming* is not a gaming machine, if used in accordance with the general conditions attached to the operating licence under section 75 or section 77 by section 85(2)(b) regarding the specification of the equipment.
- A machine designed or adapted to play bingo *by way of prize gaming* is not a gaming machine, if made available for use in reliance on a family entertainment centre gaming machine permit and the code of practice is complied with.
- A machine is not to be classed as a gaming machine simply because it is designed or adapted to be controlled or operated by an individual who arranges for others to play a real game of chance or used in connection with a real game of chance the arrangements for which are controlled by an individual.
- A machine is not to be classed as a gaming machine simply because it is designed or adapted to enable individuals to play a real game of chance if

16 Gambling Act 2005, s 235(3)(a).

17 This particular provision, under s 235(2)(d)(ii) is fortified by the Gambling (Lottery Machine Interval) Order 2007 (SI 2007/2495).

it does not require to be controlled by the person arranging for the game to be played; if it is not designed for participation in a game the arrangements for which are controlled by an individual; and it is used in accordance with conditions under section 75 or section 77 and section 85(2)(b).

There is further provision in the Gambling Act 2005 (Gaming Machines) (Definitions) Regulations 2007,[18] in relation to computers. These regulations are provided for by section 235(3)(f) and (4). A "dual-use" computer is defined in the regulations as a computer capable of being used for a purpose which is not connected to gambling and either not knowingly adapted or presented in such a way that facilitates or draws attention to the possibility of using it to gamble or, where it is so adapted or presented, is only available for private use.[19]

A "domestic" computer is a computer that is capable of being used for a purpose unconnected to gambling, located in a private dwelling and used on a domestic occasion.

6.2 The gaming machine categories

Section 236 of the Act defines the various categories of gaming machine, which are listed as Categories A, B, C and D. The nature and appearance of these machines is discussed below. Section 236(2) makes provision for the sub-division of Category B. The definition of the categories is prescribed in regulations under section 236(1), namely the Categories of Gaming Machine Regulations 2007.[20] The Gambling Commission provides a number of tables to confirm the breakdown of maximum stakes and prizes for each category (and sub-category), which have been amended on a number of occasions since 2007. These are listed in the discussion of each category below.

Before considering each of the categories, it is necessary to be familiar with some of the terminology used to aid the definitions, *viz*: "prize", "prize-value" and "charge for use".

The term "prize" is defined in section 239 of the 2005 Act as:

> "any money, article, right or service won, whether or not described as a prize, but . . . does not include an opportunity to play the machine again".

"Prize value" is defined as:

> "the amount or value of any prize which can be won as a result of use of a gaming machine once".

Finally, "charge for use" in relation to any category of machine is defined as:

> "the amount a person pays for using a gaming machine once".

It is my view that the term "using a gaming machine" constitutes participation in a/the "game". In *Rosenbaum v Burgoyne*[21] it was held that each pull of a gaming machine handle constituted a separate game. In modern times,

18 SI 2007/2082.

19 "Private use" is defined in reg 1(2) as use by the owner of the computer, or use with the owner's permission, other than in a commercial arrangement. "Commercial arrangement" means any arrangement where the owner makes or receives (or expects) any payment or reward or benefit.

20 SI 2007/2158.

21 [1965] AC 430.

this may be equivalent to the press of the "start" or "spin" button for those machines without an arm: in other words, each separate act of participation on the part of the player[22] will constitute "using a gaming machine".[23] The individual categories are now considered.

6.2.1 *Gaming machines: Category A*

Category A machines are defined somewhat cryptically as any machine which is not Category B, C or D. These machines are perhaps best described as high-end super jackpot machines with unlimited stakes and prizes, and are only available to regional casinos[24] (and so are not discussed further here).

6.2.2 *Gaming machines: Category B*

Category B machines are slightly more complicated, as there are no less than five sub-divisions in this category as noted above. The definitions are as follows:

Category B1: this is a "high-end" jackpot or slot machine found in casinos. The maximum stake is £5 and the maximum prize is £10,000, with an option of a maximum £20,000 linked progressive jackpot on a premises only basis. There are limits on the number of these machines that can be used, depending on the type of premises, as follows:

- **2005 Act large casino**: a maximum of 150 machines of any category from B to D (subject to a machine/table ratio of 5:1)
- **2005 Act small casino**: a maximum of 80 machines of any category from B to D (subject to a machine/table ratio of 2:1)
- **1968 Act "converted" casino**: a maximum of 20 of any category from B to D; or alternatively an unlimited number of C and D machines.

Category B2 is not a jackpot/fruit machine but the type of machine commonly known as a "Fixed Odds Betting Terminal" (FOBT) and is generally found in betting offices, for example in the form of computerised roulette machines. The maximum stake is £2[25] and the maximum prize is £500. There are limits on the number of these machines that can be used, depending on the type of premises, as follows:

- **betting shops and tracks with pool betting**: a maximum of 4 machines of any category from B to D

22 *Armstrong v DPP* [1965] AC 1262.

23 Also of relevance to this point is the Gaming Machine (Circumstances of Use) Regulations 2007 (SI 2007/2319), reg 2(2), which states: "For the purposes of these Regulations a person is to be treated as using a gaming machine once, even where he uses the machine to gamble more than once, if the payment for each gamble is made before he is able to know the result of any of them" – see Section 8.1.

24 There are in fact no "regional" casinos in the United Kingdom. This was a licence type of which there was to be one only in the UK, and was proposed to be tendered for by local authorities. It was felt that Blackpool would win the right to allow such a licence, however Manchester City Council won the tender in 2008. It came to nought, though, as when Gordon Brown became Prime Minister he pulled the plug.

25 This was originally £100, and was reduced to £2 after several years of campaigning from pressure groups and politicians. The stake was reduced via the Gaming Machine (Miscellaneous Amendments and Revocation) Regulations 2018 (SI 2018/1402) and commenced as of 1 April 2019.

- **2005 Act large casino**: a maximum of 150 machines of any category from B to D (subject to a machine/table ratio of 5:1)
- **2005 Act small casino**: a maximum of 80 machines of any category from B to D (subject to a machine/table ratio of 2:1)
- **1968 Act "converted" casino**: a maximum of 20 of any category from B to D; or alternatively an unlimited number of C and D machines.

Category B3 is a form of higher end jackpot or slot machine style game. The maximum stake is £2 and the maximum jackpot is £500. There are limits on the number of these machines that can be used, depending on the type of premises, as follows:

- **bingo premises and AGCs**: a maximum of 20% of the total number of machines used on the premises
- **betting shops and tracks with pool betting**: a maximum of 4 machines of any category from B to D
- **2005 Act large casino**: a maximum of 150 machines of any category from B to D (subject to a machine/table ratio of 5:1)
- **2005 Act small casino**: a maximum of 80 machines of any category from B to D (subject to a machine/table ratio of 2:1)
- **1968 Act "converted" casino**: a maximum of 20 of any category from B to D; or alternatively an unlimited number of C and D machines.

Category B3A is not a slot or jackpot machine like those described above, although to the untrained eye will look remarkably similar. These machines enable a person to participate in a game which is actually a form of lottery, and are allowed to be used in members' clubs or miners' welfare institutes. The maximum stake is £2 and the maximum prize is £500. A premises may only have one such machine. These are sometimes conflated with unregulated lottery-ticket machines, so it is worth analysing the distinction.

A machine which issues pre-printed tickets or scratchcards, and which typically looks like a wall-mounted cigarette machine (for those who remember such things), is not any type of gaming machine and requires no permit or licence under the Gambling Act 2005. The tickets these machines will issue will either be a traditional scratchcard, where the purchaser scratches off a thin layer to reveal the outcome of the game, or a card with a pull-tab which, once removed, reveals whether the card is a winner or not. The key difference between this unregulated machine and a true B3A machine is that the outcome is not determined by the machine but on the luck of which pre-printed ticket is issued. With a B3A, the machine determines whether your play is a winning one at random and the tickets and outcome and format of the game are all represented virtually on the screen.

Category B4 is a higher class of familiar jackpot/fruit machine but with a lower jackpot than a B3. The maximum stake is £2 and the maximum prize is £400. There are limits on the number of these machines that can be used, depending on the type of premises, as follows:

- **members' clubs, commercial clubs, and miners' welfare clubs**: 3 machines
- **bingo premises and AGCs**: a maximum of 20% of the total number of machines used on the premises

- **betting shops and tracks with pool betting**: a maximum of 4 machines of any category from B to D
- **2005 Act large casino**: a maximum of 150 machines of any category from B to D (subject to a machine/table ratio of 5:1)
- **2005 Act small casino**: a maximum of 80 machines of any category from B to D (subject to a machine/table ratio of 2:1)
- **1968 Act "converted" casino**: a maximum of 20 of any category from B to D; or alternatively an unlimited number of C and D machines.

6.2.3 Gaming machines: Category C

Category C machines are typically jackpot/fruit machines. This category caters for machines on a vast number of premises including alcohol-licensed premises, for which there is an "automatic entitlement" of up to two machines, and a permit process to seek a higher number. The maximum stake is £1 and the maximum prize is £100 regardless of location. There are limits on the number of these machines that can be made available for use,[26] depending on the type of premises, as follows:

- **alcohol-licensed premises:** 2 with automatic entitlement, or a higher number where authorised by a Licensed Premises Gaming Machine Permit
- **members' clubs, commercial clubs, and miners' welfare clubs**: 3 machines
- **bingo premises, AGCs and FECs**: unlimited
- **betting shops and tracks with pool betting**: a maximum of 4 machines of any category from B to D
- **2005 Act large casino**: a maximum of 150 machines of any category from B to D (subject to a machine/table ratio of 5:1)
- **2005 Act small casino**: a maximum of 80 machines of any category from B to D (subject to a machine/table ratio of 2:1)
- **1968 Act "converted" casino**: a maximum of 20 of any category from B to D; or alternatively an unlimited number of C and D machines.

6.2.4 Gaming machines: Category D

Category D machines are low-level machines of varying types which might offer a small money prize, or a non-money prize like a toy or gift. The definition of "money prize" is a prize in the form of cash or a cheque (or a mixture of both), or a prize in the form of a document or ticket which enables the player to redeem its value on the premises in the form of cash or cheque.[27] "Non money-prize" is any other prize which does not meet this definition. The Gambling Commission breaks down the stakes and prizes for category D machines as shown in Table 21.1.[28]

Category D machines may be made available by casinos, betting premises,

26 It is theoretically possible that a pub, for example, might "house" more than the maximum number of machines allowed but so long as only that maximum is available to use.

27 SI 2007/2158, reg 3(6).

28 https://www.gamblingcommission.gov.uk/for-gambling-businesses/Compliance/Sector-specific-compliance/Arcades-and-machines/Gaming-machine-categories/D-gaming-machines.aspx

Table 21.1 Types of gaming machines (Category D)

	Maximum Stake	Maximum Prize
D money prize	10p	£5
D non-money prize (other than crane grab machine)	30p	£8
D non-money prize (crane grab machine)	£1	£50
D combined money and non-money prize (other than coin pusher or penny falls machines)	10p	£8 (of which no more than £5 may be a money prize)
D combined money and non-money prize (coin pusher or penny falls machine)	20p	£20 (of which no more than £10 may be a money prize)

adult gaming centres, miners' welfare institutes, members' clubs, alcohol-licensed premises and family entertainment centres. There are various types of gaming machines which fall into this category (and it should be noted that Category D includes machines where the outcome is determined by mechanical means rather than computer automation) and are therefore worthy of further exploration:

6.2.4A Category D gaming machines: jackpot machines

These are fruit machines or "one-armed bandit" style machines, albeit with lower stakes and prizes. These machines are effectively the same as Category C machines, that is, usually with some sort of theme and the action is based on nudges, holds and other special features in an effort to spin three or four identical fruits or icons. This outcome may in itself provide a prize, but often now allows access to a further "game within a game" which may allow for higher prizes.

6.2.4B Category D gaming machines: cranes

This is a machine where a mechanical arm is manipulated by the user in order to try and "grab" some form of prize, usually a soft toy like a Minion.[29] The crane is controlled by a joystick that the user positions over the prize of their choice, and then a button is pressed to lower the grabber. In order to win the prize, it must be successfully "grabbed" and lifted to a payout position in the corner of the machine.

6.2.4C Category D gaming machines: multi-slots

The best example of this type of machine is the motorised horse-racing or camel-racing games where a coin is placed in one of five or so slots, each slot representing one of the runners in the game. The "runners" are models, affixed to an apparatus that guides them along a pre-set course. The outcome is predetermined randomly at the time of the start of the "race".

29 Other soft toys are, of course, available.

6.2.4D Category D gaming machines: pushers

This type of machine usually consists of a moving deck, on which are pre-placed a number of coins (and sometimes other prizes) which seemingly defy gravity by perching on the ledge of the automated deck. The game player drops a coin into a slot on the top of the machine, hoping that it will fall behind those coins already on the deck, so that when the deck moves forward again it may "push" those coins on the edge over and into a tray for collection.

The Gambling Commission refers to the mechanised cranes, multi-slots and pushers as "Non-Complex" Category D machines.[30] Practitioners should also advise their clients that these types of machines must display on their face a notice stating:

> "This machine provides facilities for gambling"

7 SKILL MACHINES OR "'SKILL WITH PRIZES'"

There are a number of gaming machines used in alcohol-licensed premises which are not gambling machines. Under section 235, for a machine to be classed as a "gaming machine" it has to be able to be used to gamble. The Gambling Commission's Guidance to Local Authorities states:

> "there remains a distinction between skill machines and gaming machines, in that skill machines are unregulated".[31]

The Guidance goes on to say:

> "The Act does not cover machines that give prizes as a result of the application of pure skill by players. A skill with prizes machine is one on which the winning of a prize is determined only by the player's skill – any element of chance imparted by the action of the machine would cause it to be a gaming machine. An example of a skill game would be trivia game machines, popular in pubs and clubs, which require the player to answer general knowledge questions to win cash prizes. Other examples include racing games, such as F1 simulators, and shooting games. Many family entertainment centres have games that give prizes by redemption of tickets accumulated. Providing these machines give prizes according to the skill of the player, for example getting a high score shooting basketball, they will be exempt."[32]

Gaming machines and skill machines, or "skills with prizes" (SWPs) machines as they are also known, have been catered for as separate in Scots law for some time: in *Di Carlo v McIntyre*[33] a "penny-in-the-slot" machine, which released a ball which could be caught in a cup operated by the person playing the machine, was held to be a skills machine and not a gaming machine. Nowadays, the classic skills machine or SWP is a quiz machine as described in the quote above.

The matter should end there, but regrettably it may not be that simple. The definition of "gaming" in section 6 of the Act includes "games of chance", which in turn means:

30 Gambling Commission, "Machine Standards 'Non Complex' Category D" (June 2007).
31 Gambling Commission, Guidance to Local Authorities (5th edn) at para 16.2.
32 Ibid at para 16.32.
33 1914 SC (J) 61.

> "a game that involves both an element of skill and chance; a game that involves an element of chance that can be eliminated by superlative skill; and a game that is presented as having an element of chance; so long as any of these games do not include sport."

The question then is, do some "skill" machines have an element of skill and chance, or an element of chance which can be overcome by superlative skill? Here the waters get very murky indeed. Is there a "chance" element in the random generation of a trivia question in the classic pub quiz machine? If there is a run of particularly easy questions, is that down to "chance"?

This may yet be a matter for the courts, as Revenue & Customs waded into this particular debate in November 2008, relying on section 6 as a possible route by which a "skill" machine may be treated as a "gaming machine", as the tax payable on the gaming machine is considerably higher. BACTA had advised its members that skills machines should not have a prize exceeding £50. The higher the prize, the more attention this might attract from the Gambling Commission, who say:

> "the Commission considers that the higher the payout offered by this type of machine, the less likely the machine will be viable as a genuine skill machine simply because of the risk that very skilful players will win the top prize too frequently, making the machine commercially unviable."[34]

8 USE OF GAMING MACHINES

Having looked at the types of machines, we should also look at what the law says in relation to when these machines are legally "in use". Section 240 of the Gambling Act 2005 provides for regulations regarding the circumstances under which a gaming machine is "available for use". This term features no less than fifty-six times in the Gambling Act 2005 but is not of itself defined. The regulations under this section strike at the "circumstances" of use rather than the definition of "available for use" itself, and are the Gaming Machine (Circumstances of Use) Regulations 2007.[35] These regulations should also be read in conjunction with the Gaming Machine (Single Apparatus) Regulations 2007[36] and the Gaming Machine (Supply etc) Regulations 2007[37] as all three concern technical aspects of the machines themselves.

8.1 Circumstances of use

The Circumstances of Use Regulations impose certain requirements on gaming machines, most of which are highly technical and relate to the automation of the machines themselves. The first requirement is in relation to the display of information. Each machine must display the following:

- the category (or sub-category) of the machine,
- contact details for persons able to assist with problem gambling,
- warning that the machine is not to be used by persons aged under 18 (except Category D), and

34 Gambling Commission, Guidance to Licensing Authorities (5th edn) para 16.27.
35 SI 2007/2319.
36 SI 2007/2289.
37 SI 2007/2320.

- information about the proportion of stakes used to return prizes and the odds of winning.[38]

This information must be displayed at all times when the machine is available for use. The category must be displayed in a place readily visible to a person inspecting the machine; the remaining information must be displayed in a place readily visible to a person playing the machine. The other requirements are:

- A machine may not be made available for use if it is designed or adapted to take money by way of credit or debit card.
- A machine may not be made available for use if a person can gamble in an amount which is not a whole number of pence.
- Category A, B and C machines may not offer non-monetary prizes.
- Category D machines may not offer non-monetary prizes which are illegal to sell or supply to a child or young person.
- Payment limits must be observed.[39]
- Autoplay facilities may not use stored winnings which could otherwise be transferred to use as stakes unless the machine is adapted so that the player has to perform an action to move the stored winnings into the stake.[40]
- Residues may not be retained unless under £1 and the machine is not able to pay the correct denomination.
- Delivery of prizes for occasions when the prize is not dispensed by the machine being played must meet the requirements of the regulations.[41]

8.2 Single apparatus machines

The Single Apparatus Regulations provide that if a single piece of apparatus is a gaming machine and is made available for use to more than one person at a time, it is to be treated as one gaming machine for every person able to play it simultaneously.

8.3 Payment facilities in machines

The Supply Regulations simply provide that a gaming machine may not be supplied or installed if it has been adapted to facilitate payment by way of a credit or debit card, thereby bolstering the concurrent requirement in the Circumstances of Use Regulations.

8.4 Use of machines particular to alcohol-licensed premises

There are a few "ground rules" in relation to the use of gaming machines on alcohol-licensed premises. First, section 278(1)(a) of the Gambling Act 2005 states that machines may only be used by premises with an "on-licence", that is to say, a premises licence under the Licensing (Scotland) Act 2005 which features core hours for on-sales.[42]

38 This can be achieved by a notice on the machine indicating where such information may be found: SI 2007/2319, reg 3(3).

39 This area is highly technical and, as such, not discussed further here. See the regulations for further guidance.

40 For machines made prior to 1 March 2008 which had autoplay facilities not meeting these requirements, there was a grace period to allow continued use until 1 September 2008.

41 Again, this particular requirement is mainly technical and not covered further here.

42 Or, a "relevant Scottish licence" as defined in s 277(c) of the Gambling Act 2005.

Secondly, section 278(1)(b) then goes on to say that gaming machines may only be provided in premises that have a bar.[43] Under the Licensing (Scotland) Act 2005 there is no special rule concerning whether premises may have "a bar" or not, although it is not inconceivable that a licensing board could prevent premises from having a bar by imposing a local condition. In practice, however, this rule confirms it is unlawful to use machines in off-sale premises like shops and supermarkets (who would in any event be restricted because they do not have an on-sale licence) but also premises like restaurants or bistros which may serve alcohol for consumption on the premises but do not have an actual bar. In some cases, some premises have a "public bar" in the sense that I can walk in and lean on the bar and order a drink. In other premises, a bar is used as a holding area before people are ushered to a table to take a meal. In yet other premises, a bar might be simply a servery bar only used by staff and it is not anticipated that the public would use it to take refreshment.

Thirdly, and perhaps most interestingly, section 278(1)(c) provides that gaming machines may only be made available during the times when alcohol may be sold. This point was missed by many licensing stakeholders during the liquor transition and so it was not uncommon to find an operating plan purporting to allow the use of gaming machines outside the alcohol licensed hours, perhaps by way of some wording such as:

> "The premises may be open prior to the commencement of the licensed hours, from 9am, to cater for funeral receptions, club meetings or breakfasts. During this time gaming machines, background music and televised sport may be made available."

Practitioners should therefore avoid reference to gaming machines in such a way.[44]

9 GAMING MACHINES AND CHILDREN AND YOUNG PERSONS

There are special rules concerning the use of machines (or not) by children and young persons. Children are defined as persons aged 15 or younger, and young persons are defined as persons aged 16 or 17.[45] In short, Category D machines can be used by a person of any age and there is no restriction on the *location* of higher category machines on alcohol-licensed premises per se, only on the *use* of the machines. The contrast between C and D machines is sometimes poorly reflected in alcohol premises licences.

An example of the type of condition which some boards have attached to premises licences is couched in the following terms:

> "Children should not be permitted to operate any amusement with prizes or video machines which are located within the licensed premises."

These types of conditions were likely to have been imposed at the time of conversion and would have existed as a condition under the old 1976 Act children's certificate framework. This terminology is now contrary to the

43 Under the old Licensing (Scotland) Act 1976 this automatically removed "refreshment" and "restaurant" licensed premises from the equation as under the terms of that Act such premises were not allowed to have a bar.

44 See Chapter 8 at Section 3.6.12.

45 Gambling Act 2005, s 45.

gambling regime so consideration should be given to what form of wording should be used, if at all. In addition, the wording one can come across in alcohol premises licences is sometimes very poor in distinguishing the use of non-gambling machines and gambling machines.

The use of "video machines" is considered first. Arcade-style machines such as variants on the "space invaders" theme, "pacman" and racing games (i.e. motor racing) are not forms of gambling and there is no legal restriction on the use of these machines.[46] There is no legal mischief in a child or young person playing video games which happen to be located on an alcohol-licensed premises such as a leisure centre or bowling alley.

Another type of machine is the good old quiz machine, for example variants on the "Who Wants to be a Millionaire" game. These will no doubt be present in many licensed premises, from the classic pub quiz machine to machines in premises such as bowling alleys and entertainment complexes. Players pay, say, 50p a game and if they answer a series of general knowledge questions they can win a prize. These quiz machines are "skills machines" (see Section 7 above) and there is therefore no legal bar to children or young persons playing this type of machine.

Now consider what is traditionally considered as a gaming machine – a jackpot/fruit machine style machine. Alcohol-licensed premises are allowed both C and D machines. Category C machines can only be used by those aged 18 or over so any restriction on their use by children and young persons is clearly acceptable where it is appropriate.

Category D machines, however, have *no* age restriction – any person of any age is allowed to play them so there is no lawful basis to prevent use of these machines purely on age.

The main difficulty arises, therefore, when there is a mix of C and D machines. Happily, there is some guidance in the Gambling Commission Code of Practice for the use of gaming machines (of all categories) which proposes two conditions to their use:

- the use of the machines will be supervised, and
- the location of any ATM on the premises is far enough from a gaming machine that the player would have to cease gambling in order to get more money.

These are conditions of the Code, which are mandatory. The Code then goes on to list best practice (which is not a condition of the use of the machines) in relation to access by children and young persons. The code says that the provider should have procedures to ensure that there is no under-age gambling – in other words, that no child or young person uses Category C machines (or higher).

46 The use of such machines is exempted from the provisions of the Civic Government (Scotland) Act 1982 in relation to public entertainment: s 41(2)(g) of the 1982 Act states that a place of public entertainment does not include "premises in which machines for entertainment or amusement are being provided incidentally to the main purpose or use of the premises where that main purpose or use is not as a place of public entertainment". In his notes to the annotated 1982 statute, A Hadjucki, *Scottish Civic Government Licensing Law* (2nd edn, W Green, 2002) at p 82 suggests that this covers the use of a "single video machine (e.g. 'space invaders') or pinball machine in the corner of a café". There was a brief flirtation with the idea that such arcade machines may require a licence under the Cinematograph Act 1909 but happily that was rejected in *British Amusement Catering Trades Association v Greater London Council* [1987] 2 All ER 897.

This, in my view, does not mean that C machines cannot be located in an area to which children or young persons have access; simply that their use must be monitored. I do, however, think it is a good idea for the provider to consider the location of the machines so that C and D machines are not mixed together as this could cause confusion. Locating C machines separately would make the job of supervision easier, but it must be remembered that in many premises such as a bowling alley or entertainment facility there may be no area to which children and young persons do not have access due to the nature of the facility; and in some smaller alcohol-licensed premises there might simply be no room to accommodate machines separately, so this "best practice" can only really apply to premises which suit.[47]

10 PERMISSION FOR GAMING MACHINES IN ALCOHOL-LICENSED PREMISES

There are two main ways in which an alcohol licensed premises can provide gaming machines:

(a) by obtaining "automatic entitlement" for up to two machines; or
(b) by obtaining a "licensed premises gaming machine permit" which allows three or more machines.

10.1 Automatic entitlement for up to two gaming machines

The 2005 Act gives all alcohol-licensed premises (noting the conditions above) an automatic right to use up to two gaming machines of either C or D category.[48] All that is required to activate this right is a letter giving the relevant licensing board notice of the intent to use the automatic entitlement and payment of a processing fee of £50. The "activation" must come from the premises licence holder under the Licensing (Scotland) Act 2005.

There is no statutory form for this procedure, and all that is required is the covering letter and fee. However, some licensing boards in Scotland have decided to create a form for this purpose and therefore it is sensible to follow that process if there is one in place.

There is no actual permit or licence document in the case of automatic entitlement. There is no need to display anything at the premises to indicate the entitlement has been activated. That notwithstanding, some licensing boards have decided to create a document to indicate automatic entitlement has been activated. Practitioners should always check any such documentation to ensure that the terms of this "permit" are not at variance with the automatic entitlement itself. For example, the licensing board has no power to attach conditions to the automatic entitlement (although, remember that like any other form of permission allowing gaming machines, the Commission's code of practice must be observed).

47 Under 18s are not allowed in an area which is covered by an Adult Gaming Centre licence. They are allowed in an area covered by a Family Entertainment Centre licence, or Unlicensed Family Entertainment Centre Permit. Some premises may have one or all of these types of permissions, so the key is supervision, good signage and staff training.

48 Gambling Act 2005, s 282.

The automatic entitlement is indefinite and without any annual fee and the only reason a new entitlement would be required is if the identity of the liquor licence holder changes, for example by transfer of the premises licence, in which case a fresh entitlement request in the name of the new licence holder would be required.

Although the automatic entitlement is indefinite, it should not be taken for granted, as a licensing board has the power under section 284 to make an order disapplying the entitlement for premises if it thinks that:

- the entitlement is not consistent with the gambling licensing objectives,
- gaming has taken place under the entitlement but in breach of a condition of the code of practice,
- the premises are mainly or wholly used for gaming, or
- an offence under the Gambling Act 2005 has been committed on the premises.

If a licensing board resolves to take this approach, it must first give the licence holder 21 days' notice, consider any representations made by the licence holder, and hold a hearing if the licence holder requests one.[49]

10.2 Licensed premises gaming machine permit

Automatic entitlement only applies for premises wishing to provide one or two machines. For premises wishing to have three or more machines, this request is covered by a licensed premises gaming machine permit (LPGMP), which as the name suggests is a "true" permit and not an automatic right. These permits are regulated by section 283 of the Gambling Act 2005 but the principal law for the permits in Scotland is governed by the Licensed Premises Gaming Machine Permits (Scotland) Regulations 2007.[50]

Application for a LPGMP is made to the licensing board by a form which will be provided by the board and a fee of £150 for a new application.

The licensing board is required to consider the application having regard to the gambling licensing objectives, guidance issued by the Commission and "such other matters as it thinks relevant".[51] In practice, this means some licensing boards will request a plan of the premises showing the location of the machine, and yet others will "consult" with persons such as building control. It may grant the application, grant it in respect of a smaller number of machines or machines of a different category, or refuse the application. If the board proposes to refuse the application or proposes to grant it with fewer machines or machines of a different category than that sought, it must first give the applicant an opportunity to make representations.[52]

The LPGMP has an indefinite duration but attracts an annual fee of £50 that must be paid 30 days prior to the anniversary of the issue of the permit (or within 30 days from the date it is first granted). It may be varied and there is also provision for transfer of the permit if the liquor licence changes hands.

49 Gambling Act 2005, s 284(3).
50 SSI 2007/505.
51 Ibid reg 6.
52 Ibid reg 8.

Unlike with automatic entitlement, the LPGMP is a physical document and must be kept on the premises to which it relates and it is an offence to fail to produce it when asked to do so by a relevant person.[53]

The permit may be cancelled on the same grounds as automatic entitlement may be disapplied and, as with that procedure, the board must first give the licence holder 21 days' notice, consider any representations made by the licence holder, and hold a hearing if the licence holder requests one.[54] If the annual fee is not paid, the board has the power to cancel the permit without any need for notice or hearing and without further reason, although it may resolve to accept a late payment if the failure to pay is attributable to an administrative error.[55]

11 GAMING MACHINES AND GAMING IN CLUBS

Club premises have historically been allowed to use machines with higher stakes and jackpots. There are two types of permit available to clubs. These are club machine permits and club gaming permits. Before turning to these, it is necessary to look at what exactly is meant by a "club" under the Gambling Act 2005.

11.1 Members' clubs, commercial clubs and miners' welfare institutes

There are three types of distinct "club" catered for in the Gambling Act 2005: members' clubs, commercial clubs and miners' welfare institutes. Members' club is defined in section 266 as a club:

- established and conducted wholly or mainly for purposes other than the provision of facilities for gaming; including those
  - established and conducted wholly or mainly for the provision of facilities of a prescribed kind; and
  - facilities are not provided for any other kind of gaming within the club's activities;
- established and conducted for the benefits of its members (and not conducted as a commercial enterprise),
- not established to function within a limited period of time, and
- has at least 25 members.

The first two of these perhaps require some further elaboration. A members' club can either be a club which is conducted for non-gaming purposes, and in which the provision of gaming would be a secondary or ancillary feature (for example, a snooker club which provides gaming machines or the occasional poker tournament), or it can be a club which is specifically and solely conducted to provide facilities for one type of prescribed gaming, and no other. The prescribed types of gaming are bridge and whist.[56]

53 Police constable, enforcement officer, or relevant local authority officer such as a LSO.
54 SSI 2007/505, reg 16.
55 Ibid reg 17.
56 Gambling Act 2005 (Gaming in Clubs) Regulations 2007 (SI 2007/1942).

Commercial clubs, on the other hand, are defined in section 267 in the following terms:

- established and conducted wholly for purposes other than the provision of facilities for gaming; including those
  - established and conducted wholly or mainly for the provision of facilities of a prescribed kind; and
  - facilities are not provided for any other kind of gaming within the club's activities;
- not established to function within a limited period of time; and
- have at least 25 members.

As will be noted, the only difference between the definition of a members' club and a commercial club is that a members' club is not allowed to make a commercial profit.

The definition for a miners' welfare institute is to be found in section 268 and is an association:

- which is established and conducted for social and recreational purposes, and
- is either:
  (a) an association whose affairs are managed by a group of individuals of whom at least two-thirds are miners' representatives;[57] or
  (b) an association which operates on premises the use of which is regulated by a charitable trust funded by certain organisations.[58]

Certain classes of clubs may apply for special permits to provide for higher class gaming machines and other permissions – these are club machine permits and club gaming permits, to which we now turn.

11.2 Club machine permits

Club machine permits may be applied for by all classes of club. Club machine permits are provided for under section 273 of the Gambling Act 2005 which removes the offences under section 37 and section 242 of making a gaming machine available for use if done so in accordance with this permit. A club machine permit is a permit issued by the licensing board authorising premises to use up to three gaming machines that can be of Category B, C or D. The majority of such permits will be used to deploy Category B machines as, due to having a higher stake limit, they can achieve a higher return.

There are three general conditions for use of machines under a club machine permit and they are:

- in the case of members' clubs and miners' welfare institutes, each person to whom a machine is made available for use is either a member and has been for at least 48 hours, or is a *bona fide* guest of such a member,[59]
- no child or young person may use a Category B or C machine, and
- the gaming machine code of practice be complied with.

57 The definition of "miners' representatives" is found in s 268(3).
58 As defined in s 268(4).
59 Section 273(3).

Notice that in relation to the first of these, section 273(3) introduces the restriction of use for machines under a club machine permit to members and their *bona fide* guests to miners' welfare and members' clubs only – in other words, that the public can use machines if the premises are a commercial club.

The procedure for club machine permits is introduced by section 274 of the Gambling Act 2005 but is governed by the Club Gaming and Club Machine Permits (Scotland) Regulations 2007.[60] The identity of who may apply is not made abundantly clear when reading section 274 along with the regulations. Section 274 in fact states that the procedures for Scotland are to be found in section 285, which in turn provides for regulations to be made for the procedure for club permits where the applicant is the holder of a "relevant Scottish licence", which is subject to section 125 of the Licensing (Scotland) Act 2005.[61]

This phrase "relevant alcohol licence", the definition of which sits within the regulations, has never, unhappily, been updated since the Licensing (Scotland) Act 2005 came into effect and still refers to this as "any licence granted under section 9(1) of the 1976 Act provided it is not an off sale licence".[62]

Once satisfied that the applicant has *locus standi*, the application for a club machine permit is made to the relevant licensing board by way of application form and the appropriate fee, which is £200. Having lodged the application, applicants should remind themselves that they then have 7 days within which to lodge a copy of the application with the chief constable and the Gambling Commission – an aspect which is apt to be forgotten, so it is suggested that this should be done at the same time as the application itself is lodged.

The consultee may object to the application within a period of 28 days from the date the application was lodged with the board, meaning in effect a minimum period of 21 days depending on when it actually receives a copy. Objections must be lodged in writing and with reasons explaining the objection.

In considering the application the licensing board is to have regard to guidance issued by the Commission and to the gambling licensing objectives. Once the application is received, the board must either grant or refuse it. Reasons for refusal (which are in general underpinned by reference to the guidance and licensing objectives) are as follows:

- the applicant does not meet the definition of members' club, commercial club or miners' welfare institute,
- the premises are used wholly or mainly for children or young persons, or both,
- an offence or breach of condition has occurred in the course of gaming activities carried out by the applicant,

60 SSI 2007/504.

61 On the interplay between club permits and a "club" which sheds the s 125 status, see Chapter 11 at Section 2.4.1.

62 In *Licensing and Gambling Law in Scotland* (Avizandum, 2009), I stated it was unfortunate that Parliament did not look to future proof this description. 12 years hence, no one has bothered to fix this little error, which, whilst really inconsequential, is yet another example of the UK Parliament disconnect when it comes to ensuring Scottish licensing law is properly understood; and in fact is remarkably similar to the same error which pervaded the Part III registrations under the Gaming Act 1968, and how they interacted with entertainment licences under the Licensing (Scotland) Act 1976.

- a previous permit has been cancelled within the last 10 years, or
- an objection has been made.

The board must refuse the application if the first ground applies, and therefore by implication the other grounds will not lead to a compulsory refusal but may be used as a ground. If the board is of a mind to refuse an application, it must hold a hearing (unless the applicant and any objectors have consented otherwise).

Where an application is granted, the board must give notice of its decision to the applicant, the police and the Commission and issue the permit as soon as reasonably practicable. If the application is refused, the board must advise each party of this decision and state the reasons for refusal. The board must also keep a register of permits issued.[63]

Club machine permits have a duration of 10 years and applications for renewal must be lodged in a specific "window" no earlier than 3 months and no later than 6 weeks before the expiry date.[64] The renewal is by way of an application form, and attracts a fee of £200. There is also an annual fee of £50 to be paid, which must be given to the licensing board before each anniversary of the grant of the permit. If the annual fee is not paid, the board must cancel the permit, unless it is satisfied that the failure to pay was because of an administrative error.[65]

There is a variation procedure to change information in the permit but note that this will not include the identity of the holder. There is no transfer facility for club permits so if a new operator has taken over the premises a fresh application for the grant of a club machine permit will be required. The variation may be refused if the board is of the view that, had the application been for a new permit, it would be refused, and it can cancel the permit.[66]

The board may also cancel the permit if it thinks that the premises are used wholly or mainly by children, young persons or both, or that an offence has been committed or a condition breached. If the board is considering a cancellation, it must first give the permit holder 21 days' notice and must consider any representations made by the holder, and arrange for a hearing if the holder requires it. If the board does cancel a permit, it must give written notice of this, with reasons, to the holder and consultees.

An applicant may appeal a refused grant or renewal, or a cancellation, but the consultees have no power of appeal if an application is granted. Appeals must be lodged with the sheriff within 21 days from the day the applicant receives notice of the decision. Note that a permit will remain alive if refused at renewal, where an appeal has been lodged and is pending.[67]

11.3 Club gaming permits

The second type of club permit is the club gaming permit. Club gaming permits are covered by section 271, which provides that offences under ss 33, 37 and 242 shall not apply where a club gaming permit is in force. Club gaming

63 SSI 2007/504, reg 22.
64 Ibid reg 20(2).
65 Ibid reg 18(5) and (6).
66 Ibid reg 15(4).
67 Ibid reg 20(6).

permits may only be issued to members' clubs and miners' welfare institutes – commercial clubs are not included.

Like the club machine permit, the club gaming permit allows premises to provide up to three gaming machines of Category B, C or D, but also allows special games of chance to be provided.[68] These special games of chance are prescribed under the Gambling Act 2005 (Club Gaming Permits) (Authorised Gaming) Regulations 2007[69] and are pontoon and *chemin de fer*. Pontoon is a variant of blackjack which allows for the "banker" position to be passed from player to player and therefore escapes the definition of a "banker's game" in the way that a traditional casino blackjack game would be held. *Chemin de fer* is a version of baccarat which also allows for the "banker" position to be passed between the players, in that when the person currently in the bank position loses, the bank is then passed to another player. And unlike the traditional North American version of baccarat, *punto banco*, which is based solely on chance, chemin de fer is a game which involves both chance and skill.

Section 271(6) states that a person participating in gambling authorised by a club gaming permit must be a member of the club/institute for at least 48 hours prior to the commencement of participation, or a *bona fide* guest of such a member. Also note that section 271(4) places a condition that the public are excluded from areas where gaming under this type of permit is taking place, but this must be read in conjunction with section 272(2) which indicates that the definition of the "public" does not include *bona fide* guests of members.

The other difference between the two permits is that if a club gaming permit is in force, it removes the first condition under section 269 in relation to the provision of equal chance gaming, namely the limit placed on stakes and prizes as discussed below. In other words, if a club gaming permit is in place club premises can offer equal chance gaming with unlimited stakes and prizes. This is discussed further in Section 13 below.

The procedures for renewal, variation, cancellation and annual fees are identical to club machine permits as discussed above.

12 EQUAL CHANCE GAMING IN ALCOHOL-LICENSED PREMISES

The starting point here, of course, is to recall what is meant by "equal chance gaming". Equal chance gaming is described in section 8 of the Act and is a game which does not involve play against a banker and where the chances are equally favourable to all participants. This is most commonly associated with poker but may also include bingo (which I refer to separately in Section 14 below for special rules).

Equal chance gaming is allowed on alcohol-licensed premises by section 279, which removes the offences under section 33 and section 37 so long as the provisions which govern how the gaming is provided are met. There are five conditions laid down, which are:

- The gaming will match the prescribed stakes and limits.
- There can be no levy from stakes or prizes.

68 Gambling Act 2005, s 271(3)(c).
69 SI 2007/1945.

- There can be no participation fee.
- Games played on one premises are not linked to a game played on another set of premises.
- Children and young persons are excluded from participation.

The prescribed limits for stakes and prizes are laid down in the Gambling Act 2005 (Exempt Gaming in Alcohol-Licensed Premises) Regulations 2007.[70] These limits relate primarily to poker games and are a maximum stake per person of £5 per game, a maximum aggregate of stakes on one premises of £100 in any one day, and a maximum prize of £100. The regulations specifically remove the games of dominoes and cribbage from these limitations.

Unlike gaming machines, there is no restriction on the provision of equal chance gaming in relation to the times when alcohol may be sold: in other words, equal chance gaming can quite legally be provided for outside the core liquor licensing hours. From this point of view it could be quite acceptable to have "gaming" as an activity in a Licensing (Scotland) Act 2005 premises licence application taking place outwith the core hours where that refers to equal chance gaming, although I would submit that it would be a very rare occurrence for poker games to be played before 11am or after the core licensing hours have completed, and perhaps even rarer for a licensing board to approve of it.

13 EQUAL CHANCE GAMING IN CLUBS

As stated above, club premises are allowed to offer equal chance gaming under section 269. There are five conditions to be satisfied if this type of gaming is to be carried on:

- The gaming will match the prescribed stakes and prize limits.
- There is no levy from stakes or prizes.
- Any participation fees do not exceed prescribed limits.
- Games played on one premises are not linked to a game played on another set of premises.
- Participants in respect of all clubs except commercial clubs must be either a member of the club for at least 48 hours prior to participation, or a *bona fide* guest of said member.

Note again that the restriction on participation to members and their guests does not apply to commercial clubs: in other words, the public are allowed to participate in equal chance gaming on that type of premises.

The stakes and prize limits are prescribed under the Gambling Act 2005 (Exempt Gaming in Clubs) Regulations 2007[71] and relate to poker. The maximum amount an individual can stake in any one game is £10, the aggregate amount that may be staked at premises in one day is £250 and the aggregate amount that may be staked at premises over seven days is £1,000. The maximum prize that may be won in any one game is £250.

70 SI 2007/1940, as amended by the Gambling Act 2005 (Exempt Gaming in Alcohol-Licensed Premises) (Amendment) Regulations 2007 (SI 2007/2240) which removed references in the original instrument to a spooky "paragraph (4)", which did not exist.

71 SI 2007/1944.

Clubs are allowed to charge participation fees, prescribed under the same regulations. The level of fee depends on whether a club gaming permit is in place. If a club gaming permit is in force, the maximum fee is £3 per person for equal chance gaming and £20 for bridge and whist.[72] If there is no club gaming permit, the maximum participation fee is £1 for equal chance gaming and £18 for bridge and whist.

Finally, if a members' club or a miners' welfare institute holds a club gaming permit, then the first condition will not apply. This is a very significant point as unlimited equal chance gaming will allow these premises to hold poker tournaments with no limits on stakes, meaning persons can gamble as much as they like and there is therefore no cap on the amount of the prize that may be won.

14 BINGO IN ALCOHOL-LICENSED PREMISES

Section 281 of the Gambling Act 2005 makes specific provision for bingo in alcohol-licensed premises. There is no special permit or authorisation needed to allow bingo as it is a form of equal chance gaming, but one separate special rule applies in addition to the general conditions under section 279, namely that the licence holder may operate bingo nights so long as the stakes and prizes do not exceed £2,000 in a 7-day period. If this limit is breached, the licence holder must inform the Commission as soon as is reasonably practicable[73] and failure to do so without a reasonable excuse is an offence. As a form of equal chance gaming, the rules above apply. Pubs must ensure that no participation fee is charged, and they observe the limit of £5 per person per game in order to participate.

15 BINGO IN CLUBS

Section 275 makes provision for bingo in clubs and, again, so long as the £2,000 maximum on stakes and prizes is observed, bingo nights are perfectly legal on such premises without an additional permit or authorisation. The position on breaching the limit for clubs is the same as for alcohol-licensed premises and the general conditions on equal chance gaming in clubs under section 269 apply. As a form of equal chance gaming, clubs are allowed to charge participation fees for bingo, which are £1 per person, or £3 if a club gaming permit is in place.[74]

72 Ibid reg 5.
73 Gambling Act 2005, s 281(6).
74 Gambling Act 2005, s 269(4) and SI 2007/1944, reg 5.

Appendix A

Parliamentary History of the Licensing (Scotland) Act 2005

The Parliamentary history of the Act is as follows:

- 28 February 2005: Introduction (SP Bill 37 2005)
- Stage 1 (Local Government and Transport Committee)
  - 13 June 2005: 7th Report
  - 22 March 2005: 11th meeting
  - 12 April 2005: 12th meeting
  - 19 April 2005: 13th meeting
  - 26 April 2005: 14th meeting
  - 3 May 2005: 15th meeting
  - 17 May 2005: 17th meeting
- Stage 1 (Subordinate Legislation Committee)
  - 17 May 2005: 16th meeting
  - 24 May 2005: 17th meeting
- Stage 2 (Local Government and Transport Committee)
  - 20 September 2005: 24th meeting
  - 27 September 2005: 25th meeting
  - 3 October 2005: 26th meeting
- Stage 3 (Consideration by Parliament)
  - 22 June 2005: Debate and Parliamentary Vote
  - 21 December 2005: Royal Assent.

It is worth dipping in to the debate and vote on 22 June 2005 in order to get a flavour of the context and political views of the time, and to compare those views with how the licensing law has panned out in the last decade and more. I have therefore selected various passages which I think are of note or interest and make for illuminating reading. Readers should note that the ruling administration at the time of the passing of the 2005 Act was a Labour/Lib Dem coalition with an SNP opposition.

Tavish Scott (Liberal Democrat):

> "Too many Scots are in denial about the impact of alcohol on our everyday lives and about the fact that our cultural dependence on drink is as advanced as it is. For too many Scots, drink is the lifeblood, the shield, the excuse.
>
> Let me begin with the evidence in favour of reform, an enduring principle of this Parliament's legislative process. The cost of alcohol misuse to the national health service in Scotland is £110.5 million per year. According to the 2000 Scottish crime survey, nearly three quarters of the assailants in violent crimes were reported by the victim to be under the influence of drink. Young Scots aged between 16 and 24 drink more than any other age group, and the majority of 13 and 15-year-olds have drunk alcohol.

That is the reality that we are absolutely committed to tackling. The Licensing (Scotland) Bill alone is not the answer. Legislation does not change culture, nor does it change attitudes. That is why ministers across portfolios – in the Health Department and in the Education Department – are working together on a plan for action on alcohol. However, the bill will contribute to our efforts to reduce underage drinking, tackle binge drinking and protect and involve communities and local people and it will reform an outdated system.

The committee also raised concerns about the restriction of the police's role in new applications to the reporting of convictions for relevant offences. The police will, of course, continue to play a full part in the review of licences and they will be able to initiate a review at any time. However, we are prepared to consider further the role of the police in relation to applications for premises licences.

We also propose to amend the condition in the bill that requires on-sales premises to implement a non-differential pricing policy for 48 hours. We will extend the period to 72 hours, as recommended in some of the evidence that the committee heard."

Bruce Crawford (SNP):

"The role that the national licensing forum will play will be essential in winning over those who have expressed doubts about putting too much power into the hands of local licensing boards. Although it is right that licensing boards should be able to shape and decide policy based on local circumstances, it is also right that good guidance and advice will come from the centre to help to deliver a reasonable degree of consistency and equity of approach throughout Scotland.

Many licensed premises that are at the margins of what might be considered a successful business are the very establishments that might have the most difficulty in adapting successfully to the proposed new licensing regime.

However, we could have done more. This Parliament does not have control over issues such as advertising and labelling."

David Davidson (Conservative):

"I believe that the reform of our licensing system is long overdue. However, like other members, I am deeply concerned about the fact that ministers have chosen to provide for enabling powers, instead of exposing the regulations in advance for real scrutiny by the chamber and the Local Government and Transport Committee. I also have concerns about the costs to the trade, which I think have been underestimated in the production of the bill. I would like the minister to provide more clarification of what the trade will have to expect and what form of fees there will be, because that is a matter of extreme concern.

I would also like to hear what the minister has to say about personal licences. Unless there is full training, which he hinted would be available, there is not much point to them. We need a national registration scheme, so that we can identify easily who holds such licences. The register does not need to be expensive and could be attached to the driving licence database, for example."

Bristow Muldoon (Labour):

"The committee welcomed the bill and endorsed the Executive's objectives to simplify and modernise the legislation; to balance the rights of the majority who drink responsibly with the need to protect communities from the nuisance and crime associated with alcohol; to provide strong monitoring and enforcement; to make the system more inclusive; to support responsible members of the licensed trade; and to allow local flexibility. The bill also provides an opportunity to reduce alcohol-related health problems in Scotland.

Before I address the many problems associated with alcohol, I stress the importance of recognising that, consumed responsibly, alcohol can be an enjoyable part of many people's social lives. Through the provision of restaurants, pubs and clubs, the licensed and hospitality trade is an essential part of Scotland's economy. The production of alcohol, particularly whisky, is a major provider of employment and export income to Scotland. On the downside, alcohol is related to some serious social problems, ranging from homicide and deaths due to drink driving to assaults and much of the antisocial behaviour that afflicts many of our communities. The bill can contribute to addressing those issues."

Margaret Smith (Liberal Democrat):

"We welcome the simplification of the licensing process through the abolition of the outdated system in which there were seven types of licence. The bill will introduce just two types: the personal licence and the premises licence. The new system will take a case-by-case approach that will be backed up by an operating plan approved by the licensing board, which consists of elected councillors. We feel that that system is better equipped to deal with the hybrid quality of many of our licensed premises these days, particularly in cities such as Edinburgh and Glasgow."

Paul Martin (Labour):

"All too often, I hear of communities attending the licensing board or committee to be advised by the police authorities that there is nothing to report, although that has not been the local experience of the premises. There must be a standard format whereby all activities that take place in a certain premises are reported to ensure that the police report does not just say whether an offence has been detected, but creates a profile of a local facility in a community."

Brian Adam (SNP):

"The issue is about not just binge drinking or youth disorder, but the total health impact of increased alcohol consumption. If we cannot persuade society that it is not necessarily a good thing to drink in excess over either a short or a long period, we will guarantee that there will be even more health problems in the future. As a result, I think that this is a question not of responsible drinking but of the amount that individuals consume."

Margaret Smith (Labour) (in response to the above quote):

"I hope that the member agrees that the licensing system is the wrong place to look if we want to educate or re-educate people with regard to some of the issues that he has raised. Instead, we need a holistic approach that includes, for example, early intervention programmes in our schools to ensure that children and young people learn about drink in a responsible way and in a way that allows them to take a whole-life view of it. We should not address the matter simply by trying to stop them going into the local offie."

Bill Aitken (Conservative):

"I was convener of the licensing committee of the City of Glasgow District Council in the late 1970s, and the licensing board upon which I sat implemented the Licensing (Scotland) Act 1976. In those days, we had a serious problem with drinking in Glasgow. In fact, the street cabaret that one could see was one of the most depressing aspects of my childhood. However, we adopted a fairly liberal approach towards the Act and used the application of extension of permitted hours to force up standards.[1] It worked: there was a fairly spectacular drop in the number of people

1 It is striking to note the clear similarity in this comment, and that in the City of Glasgow Licensing board statement of policy released in 2018 in connection with the trial period proposed to allow certain nightclubs to open till 4am (para 5.3): "The Licensing Board will

who were arrested for being drunk and incapable and there was, for a time at any rate, an improvement in street behaviour. As I said, the circle has turned and we now have a problem of binge drinking.

I have said in the chamber before – I make no apology for repeating this – that law that is not enforced becomes bad law in its own right and meaningless in effect, and creates an unwelcome lack of confidence in the wider regime. We must consider the issue of enforcement. Unless the proper resources are focused and targeted at those who are the cause of the problem, I am not convinced that the bill will bring the result that we would all wish."

Patrick Harvie (Greens):

"Earlier, Bill Aitken talked about the five high-level objectives of the bill that are also intended to be the values of the licensing system. In welcoming those values, the only regret that I have is that alcohol is to be the only recreational drug to which we apply such a sensible approach. It would be beneficial if the same approach were taken to other recreational drugs that are currently illegal, many of which have higher social and health costs.

I want to say something about access for under-18s. First, at the lower end of the age range, I completely endorse Paul Martin's insistence on proper baby changing facilities, although I am happy to admit that I do so from a far more selfish point of view. If people were expected to change their babies on tables in bars I would rapidly find myself uncomfortable drinking my pint there. It is clear that the provision on baby changing facilities is needed.

I am unclear about the rationale for the opt-in approach. It seems to me that, in the bill, we do not have something that is at one extreme or the other – purely opt in or purely opt out. There is some useful stuff about encouraging licensees carefully to consider the implications of allowing under-18s access to their premises, but I worry about the implicit acceptance in the committee's report of the idea that large numbers of establishments are simply inappropriate for under-18s. I wonder whether we should question that assumption rather than signalling approval of it."

Donald Gorrie (Liberal Democrats):

"We have come a long way. In the first year or two of the Parliament, I was seized with licensing and alcohol problems as an issue – not personal, but political – and lodged various questions to ministers. They said that they had no plans to do anything about licensing, so I said, 'Right. I will propose a member's bill.' Partly as a result of that – people's opinions will depend on how cynical they are – the Executive hastily appointed a committee under Sheriff Principal Nicholson that produced an admirable report. On alcohol policy, I am now a member of the Sheriff Principal Nicholson party. I hope that members will lodge amendments that are based on his excellent critique of the bill. If they do not, I will. He hit many of the right points.

We must use the existing law and when we have the new law, we must use that. I discovered from asking questions previously that minimal use is made of the existing law that thou shalt not serve booze to somebody who is drunk. We have a nice law to which nobody pays attention.

Not everything in the bill is excellent. I was delighted to find that the report suggests the need for a national register of licensees, which seems an excellent idea.

launch a pilot scheme whereby it will consider granting a terminal licensed hour of 4am to nightclub premises in the city centre where the licence holder is able to demonstrate not only that the premises make a positive contribution to the late night economy, but are also able to evidence an investment in safety and security measures for both staff and customers, designed to promote the licensing objectives. The Licensing Board considers this to be an opportunity to reward and continue to encourage great practice in the nightclub trade."

However, it also mentions that the official reply to the suggestion was that it 'could be costly and might pose a range of other difficulties'. That could have come straight out of my tapes of 'Yes Minister'."

Kenny MacAskill (SNP):

"The fact is that we have a problem with alcohol in Scotland. I will not moralise about that because I have offended in spectacular fashion more than most and I fully accept my culpability. Although I seek to reform, I still transgress sometimes.

We need new licensing legislation because the current system is not working and needs to be changed. The system comes to some extent from the early part of the 20th century and we need to recognise that society has moved on. There are worries about liberalisation, but we must accept that there has to be movement. That does not mean that there has to be a free-for-all."

Michael McMahon (Labour):

"My colleagues on the Local Government and Transport Committee will be disappointed if I do not raise my pet subject. As I say, the use of alcohol in Scotland has changed over time; in fact, it has changed since Sheriff Principal Nicholson delivered his report. Because it has changed, he did not deliberate on the development of dial-a-drink services from our off-licences, a problem that has been raised with me by police. Such a service is not a bad thing, but it is evidently being used by young people to circumvent no-proof, no-sale initiatives. We must not overlook that."

Fergus Ewing (SNP):

"Lack of forethought seems to be the hallmark of the Executive's approach to formulating legislation. If the Executive could take one lesson from me, I would suggest that the Executive should kick binge legislating."

Appendix B

Timeline of All Amendments to the Licensing (Scotland) Act 2005, and All Associated Secondary Legislation

The following is a timeline which narrates:

(a) changes to the 2005 Act by way of secondary legislation (with a brief explanation of what the Order or Regulation relates to);
(b) changes to the 2005 Act by way of primary legislation;
(c) the issue of official Scottish Government guidance; and
(d) the issue of other official reports or documents pertaining into the 2005 Act up to publication of this book.

When the re-issue of the Liquor Licensing section of the *Stair Memorial Encyclopaedia* was released in 2009, the author John Batters said:

> "there has been a stream of orders and regulations which have made it difficult at any given time to produce an accurate summary of the law".[1]

Looking at the length of this Appendix, it is easy to agree with his wise words, and unsurprising to note that no attempt has been made to update Stair since that issue. The timeline is as follows:

- **28 November 2005** – *Licensing (Scotland) Act 2005*: this was the date the Act was given Royal Assent.
- **4 May 2006** – *SSI 2006/239, Licensing (Scotland) Act 2005 (Commencement No. 1 and Transitional Provisions) Order 2006*: this Order should have been the first to commence any aspect of the 2005 Act. However, due to a drafting error it had to be immediately repealed and replaced by SSI 2006/286 (below), an inauspicious start to say the least. Whilst making provision for "test purchasing" (discussed in detail at Appendix H) and enacting the relevant offences and exceptions under the 2005 Act, the draftsman had overlooked the special exemption under the 1976 Act allowing young persons to purchase alcohol with a meal.[2] This meant that such a young person, whilst not committing any offence under the 1976 Act, would have committed the new offence under the 2005 Act, before the Act itself was fully into force – so the whole Order was revoked somewhere shy of three weeks after it was enacted. Looking back, it did not herald well that the first ever SSI produced under the 2005 Act had to

1 *The Laws of Scotland: Stair Memorial Encylopaedia* (Liquor Licensing: Reissue) (Law Society of Scotland/LexisNexis, 2009) p 90.

2 Under the 2005 Act, young persons can consume beer or wine with a meal when purchased by an adult: see Chapter 19. Under the 1976 Act, the young person could purchase the alcohol themselves as well as consume it – as long as it was "beer, wine, made-wine, porter, cider or perry" (cf s 68(4) of the 1976 Act).

be strangled at birth because of a lack of comprehension of the licensing system.

- **25 May 2006** – *SSI 2006/286, Licensing (Scotland) Act 2005 (Commencement No. 2 and Transitional Provisions) Order 2006*: the Order that should have been! The Order is focused on the ability of the police to send a young person into a licensed premises in order to conduct a test purchase. This particular provision was commenced before everything else because certain police forces had already been conducting the exercise until reminded by the Lord Advocate that they did not have the power to do so.[3] This Order brought the relevant provisions into force, and even then this only applied to the then Fife Constabulary, which took effect as of 1 June 2006. The test purchasing provision, namely section 102 of the 2005 Act, appeared at Stage 3 of the Licensing (Scotland) Bill following lobbying by Fife Constabulary, which explains why they were given the power, which was agreed to be a "test pilot" of one year before being rolled out to the other forces but commenced on 1 September 2009 with the rest of the 2005 Act.[4]
- **31 January 2007** – *SSI 2007/33, Licensing Register (Scotland) Regulations 2007*: following a consultation carried out by the then Scottish Executive, which took place between October and December 2006 involving a variety of trade associations[5] as well as all licensing boards and local authorities, the content of the register was agreed and laid down in these regulations, which came into force on 1 February 2008 (this was the earliest date applications could be lodged under the 2005 Act). The regulations make provision for registers to be either in electronic or documentary form (or a combination of both), as well as all the details which must be contained within the register in relation to premises, personal and occasional licences (as well as details on transfers, variations and extended hours applications). It should also contain information on Closure Orders. Finally, the regulations require the licensing board to keep the information available for 5 years after relevant dates (e.g. when a licence was granted, closure order issued, and so on).
- **31 January 2007** – *SSI 2007/34, Licence Transfer (Prescribed Persons) (Scotland) Regulations 2007*: this resulted following the same period of consultation as noted above, in order to give flesh to the bones of section 34 of the Act. The Executive Note to the instrument states:

  > "The purpose of the instrument is to set out who other than the licence holder can make an application for the transfer of a premises licence. The licence holder's relationship with the transferee is defined by specified events, for example where the licence holder has died, it will be an executor who makes the application and where a business has been sold it will be the purchaser".

  The events covered relate to death, incapacity, insolvency, dissolution (but not dissolution of a company – see Chapter 12 Section 2.2.4), and finally "transfer of business", which turned out to be one of the most woeful provisions of the 2005 Act (see also Chapter 12).
- **31 January 2007** – *SSI 2007/35, Licensing (Closure Orders) (Scotland) Regulations 2007*: these regulations provide the statutory form required to be

3 Yet another example of poor comprehension of licensing law.

4 On the background to the test pilot, see "Scottish Pilot Project – Test Purchasing of Alcohol" Community Safety Committee, Fife Constabulary, 31 May 2006.

5 SLTA, BEDA, BBPA, BII, SGF, SRC, BHA and ACPOS were all included.

lodged by the police when requesting a closure order. The Executive Note confirms the forms were originally created by the police before being issued for consultation to the various trade groups during the period noted above. The standardisation of forms is discussed as follows:

> "The purpose of the instrument is to introduce a standardised proforma for applications to a Licensing Board for a Closure Order, for the Closure Order itself, and the request to end a closure order. In common with other aspects of the Licensing (Scotland) Act 2005, there is a wish for forms be in a standardised format to avoid the need for individual Licensing Boards and the Police to develop their own forms. Standardised forms created by regulations will help ensure a consistent approach to the use of Closure Orders."

Like much of the Act and attendant regulations, these came into force on 1 September 2009, and require that applications for closure orders or emergency closure orders must be in the prescribed format, which is a form laid down in Schedules to the Regulations. The regulations had to be amended later to confirm the exact time of commencement was 5am on 1 September 2009 (see below), a further oversight in the original version.

- **14 February 2007** – *SSI 2007/76, Licensing (Clubs) (Scotland) Regulations 2007*: one of the more technical secondary legislative examples arising from the 2005 Act is the creation of a series of special rules which apply to the definition of a members' club premises for the purposes of section 125 of the Act. This SSI was also consulted on with those noted above and in particular it (a) provides the definition for what constitutes a club under section 125, (b) disapplies certain parts of the Act as regards club premises, and (c) also creates special rules concerning occasional licences. Finally, there is a "modification" to section 147 of the 2005 Act which widens the definition of "references to selling alcohol or other goods to trade are references to selling the alcohol or goods to a person for the purposes of the person's trade" to "apply as if the expression 'selling alcohol or other goods to trade' included selling alcohol or goods to a person for the purposes of the business of the club". The modification allows the selling of alcohol to a person for the purposes of the business of a club without a licence, in the same way that a person may sell alcohol to someone for the purposes of trade without a licence.[6]
- **14 February 2007** – *SSI 2007/77, Personal Licence (Scotland) Regulations 2007*: another regulation subject to the same consultation as those above, this relates to the creation of the form of the personal licence, and the form of the application/renewal form to obtain/renew said licence. Provision is made for electronic application "if the Licensing Board to which the application is made so agrees".
- **20 February 2007** – *SSI 2007/93, Sale of Alcohol to Children and Young Persons (Scotland) Regulations 2007*: also consulted on as above, the purpose of this SSI was, according to the Executive Note, "to introduce a nationally accepted proof of age card that will be acceptable under the Act for the purposes of identifying a person's age with regard to the sale and purchase of alcohol". Evidently the British Retail Consortium had a significant part to play in the consultation process as it was their "Proof of Age Standards Scheme" (PASS) accredited cards which were decided upon as those to be

6 The law surrounding clubs is discussed in Chapter 11, Section 2.

formally recognised as appropriate ID (beyond the EU driving licence and passport already provided for on the face of the Act). This would later be added to, with additional acceptable documentation, under the Alcohol etc (Scotland) Act 2010. These regulations also specified the form of the notice to be displayed under section 110 of the 2005 Act concerning offences relating to children and young people. The regulations had to be amended later to confirm that the precise time of commencement was 5am on 1 September 2009 (see below), correcting yet another error.

- **20 February 2007** – *SSI 2007/95, Licensing (Training) (Scotland) Regulations 2007*: another in the swathe consulted on as noted above, this relates to the training of Licensing Standards Officers and the training of licensing board members, specifying the deadlines by which the relevant training must be undertaken (within 18 months of appointment in the case of a Licensing Standards Officer, and within 3 months of being elected or re-elected in the case of a licensing board member). In an interesting aside on costs, the Executive Note says: "There will be a cost on applicants wishing to undertake this qualification. These are not yet known as training still has to be designed and developed by awarding bodies. Costs will be determined by commercial training providers and competition in the market may keep costs to a minimum."
- **20 February 2007** – *SSI 2007/96, Occasional Licence (Scotland) Regulations 2007:* another of those involved in the October–December consultations with various bodies, this SSI came into force on 1 February 2008 and is certainly one of the simpler examples of secondary legislation under the 2005 Act in that it provides the templates for occasional licences, and the application form for occasional licences.
- **20 February 2007** – *SSI 2007/97, Licensing (Designated Airports) (Scotland) Order 2007*: as with those above, these regulations were consulted on in late 2006. The purpose is to confirm which Scottish airports are treated as exempt premises for the purposes of section 124(1) of the 2005 Act. The Explanatory Note states: "The Scottish Ministers may designate an airport in an order only if they consider it to be one at which there is a substantial amount of international passenger traffic." The Executive Note confirms that such consideration was given in respect of Inverness airport, added to the list since those airports listed under the 1976 Act: Aberdeen, Edinburgh, Glasgow, Glasgow Prestwick, and Sumburgh.
- **20 February 2007** – *SSI 2007/98, Licensing Qualification (Scotland) Regulations 2007*: further regulation subject to the late 2006 consultation as above, this relates to the training requirements for personal licence applicants (with reference to section 91 in Part 6 of the 2005 Act) and effectively confirms that a licensing qualification has to be one "accredited" by Scottish Ministers. The Executive Note states: "The qualification will be based on the framework for training developed by the National Licensing Forum. Ministers will only approve a qualification if it has been firstly accredited by the Scottish Qualifications Authority. The Scottish Executive has provided the Committee with a copy of the proposed specification for the qualification which accompanies these Regulations." The Explanatory Notes to section 91 of the 2005 Act state: "This section provides a power for the Scottish Ministers to set out in regulations the mandatory requirements for a qualification required to obtain a personal licence. Different qualifications

could be prescribed in relation to different types of licensed premises. For example, the premises manager for a particular type of licensed premises may be required to hold the appropriate qualification prescribed for that type of premises." This widely drawn provision was later restricted by the passing of SSI 2007/313 (see below) so that the different types of qualification are in fact restricted to either (a) off sales only or (b) all other licensed premises. Despite an early dalliance with a separate training course for on-sale premises and off-sale premises, in practice the separation has become redundant.

- **27 February 2007** – *SSI 2007/128, Licensing (Appointed Day and Transitional Provisions) (Scotland) Order 2007*: another of the late 2006 consultation batch of regulations, this is a mixed bag which provides for the following: (a) introduction of 3 years as the policy period for licensing board statement of licensing policies, to commence from 30 November 2007 (this period was subsequently raised to 5 years in order to tie in with local authority elections as a result of amendments in the Air Weapons and Licensing (Scotland) Act 2015 – see Chapter 4, Section 6 in relation to "policy periods"); (b) transitional arrangements for boards to be jointly constituted under both the 1976 and 2005 Acts during transition (as applications under both regimes would be lodged and processed) such as dispensation for members to deal with 1976 Act business even if not trained on 2005 Act business;[7] (c) certain early dispensations for local licensing fora;[8] and (d) a reversal of the previous limitation in SSI 2006/286 (noted above) regarding the power to conduct test purchasing by Fife Constabulary only.
- **27 February 2007** – *SSI 2007/129, Licensing (Scotland) Act 2005 (Commencement No. 3) Order 2007*: this Order commenced section 142 of the 2005 Act as of 1 May 2007, which relates to the issuing of guidance to licensing boards by Scottish Ministers; and separately a raft of other provisions also coming into effect as of 1 May 2007.[9]
- **16 April 2007**: The Scottish Executive Guidance to Licensing Boards is published. The Guidance, ninety pages or so, has been subject to continual criticism. Having been brought out over two years before the system even came into force, it was already out of date by commencement and has suffered constant opprobrium since then, particularly due to any lack of update in the decade-plus which has passed with significant amendment to the 2005 Act (as this timeline demonstrates). It was not until 2018 that the Scottish Government finally yielded and looked to conduct a wholesale update of the Guidance (discussed later). Although the 2007 Guidance was subject to infamy, the Act requires that boards had regard to it, and as such

7 As is required by Sch1 para 11(3) to the 2005 Act.

8 Two such dispensations were provided for: Licensing Standards Officers did not have to be members of the forum until 1 September 2009, thus providing breathing room for those areas where no officers had been appointed; and, secondly, that the requirement for quarterly meetings should not apply in 2007.

9 Sections 2–6, 7(2), 8, 10–14, 16 and 17, 19(1), 62, 66, 71, 90 and 91, 129, 134, 136, 139, 141, 143, 144 (so far as relating to paras 9 and 10 of Sch 6), 149 so far as relating to the following repeals in Sch 7: (a) ss 1, 2(1) and (3), 3, 6 and 7 of the Licensing (Scotland) Act 1976; (b) para 4 of Sch 8 to the Law Reform (Miscellaneous Provisions) (Scotland) Act 1990; (c) s 46 of, and para 106(2), (3) and (5) of Sch 13 to, the Local Government etc (Scotland) Act 1994; and (d) s 2 of the Licensing (Amendment) (Scotland) Act 1996.

significant elements of it remained relevant especially in certain appeal cases e.g. *Aldi Stores Ltd v Dundee Licensing Board.*[10] The Guidance is referred to throughout this book where relevant.

- **5 June 2007** – *SSI 2007/313, Licensing (Miscellaneous Amendments) (Scotland) Regulations 2007*: the reference to amendments in the title should not fill the reader with confidence and indeed this is another example of Parliament having to tidy up previous errors in no less than three of the SSIs noted above. As the Executive Note says: "This Scottish Statutory Instrument has been made in consequence of defects in S.S.I. 2007/35, 93 and 98. It clarifies the exact time of the coming into force of S.S.I.s 2007/35 and 93 which is 5.00am on 1 September 2009, the date and time which the Licensing (Scotland) Act 2005 comes into force. It also ensures that the provisions in S.S.I. 2007/98 allow for the policy intention that there can be a different licensing qualification for on sales and off sales premises."
- **7 June 2007** – *SSI 2007/324, Sports Grounds and Sporting Events (Designation) (Scotland) Amendment Order 2007*: not strictly a 2005 Act Order but relevant as it relates to the provision of alcohol. This relates to selling of alcohol at Murrayfield in the Six Nations. Since 1982 the Scottish Rugby Union had voluntarily agreed that Murrayfield would be captured by the prohibition of alcohol in stadia but this did not apply to international events. The amendment is in line with the licensing reform of the 2005 Act, but perhaps also as a result of the Rugby World Cup 2007 at which the anomalous situation of having alcohol allowed in Twickenham and the Millennium stadium but not Murrayfield would have occurred were it not for this Order. The Executive note states:

  > "The culture of rugby in Scotland has changed considerably over the last 25 years. The SRU has been at pains to dispel any elitist tag attributed to it. However as alcohol can be sold as part of a Murrayfield hospitality package to those who can afford such packages, the SRU has long expressed the view that this is inequitable and sends the wrong message to the thousands of rugby supporters from around the world coming to the stadium. At those non-international and club matches where alcohol can be sold, Murrayfield has not developed a drinking culture. Supporters come to the national stadium to watch rugby and have an occasional drink, not to drink and occasionally watch rugby."

  The Order therefore amends the Sports Grounds and Sporting Events (Designation) (Scotland) Order 2004,[11] removing Murrayfield, and Hampden, from the alcohol prohibition for international rugby matches. It also updated the name of Bayview Stadium to New Bayview Park.
- **21 June 2007** – *SSI 2007/336, Licensing Conditions (Late Opening Premises) (Scotland) Regulations 2007*: this brings us back to the swathe of proposed regulations consulted on with various trade bodies towards the end of 2006 (as noted above). In short, this is about imposing additional conditions on certain premises and arose primarily as a result of lobbying from the nightclub and late night entertainment industry concerned that a single premises licence approach would see a later terminal hour "creep" from hybrid bar and pub premises. The Executive Note says: "In policy terms we envisage certain nightclub and 'superpub' premises falling within this definition.

10 Dundee Sheriff Court, 12 August 2016, unreported.
11 SSI 2004/356.

The conditions are intended to create safeguards that will help protect the safety of customers and staff." The regulations therefore provide for various additional conditions which apply to certain premises that fit certain descriptions, all of which are discussed in Chapter 15 at Section 8; and also provides a definition for "adult entertainment", on which see Chapter 15 at Section 8.8.

- **30 August 2007** – *SSI 2007/397, Licensing (Training of Staff) (Scotland) Regulations 2007*: this SSI covers the minimum requirements for adherence to the staff training mandatory condition which is discussed in more detail at Chapter 15, Section 4.5. The proposal was subject to public consultation between October and December 2006 following the draft being drawn up by a Training Advisory Group which was established by the then Scottish Executive in May 2006. The Group was chaired by the then CEO of Alcohol Focus Scotland, Jack Law, and was made up of a diverse range of interested parties.[12]
- **9 October 2007** – *SSI 2007/452, Premises Licence (Scotland) Regulations 2007*: this is one of the most significant pieces of secondary legislation which affects the 2005 Act as it provides for the statutory form of the premises licence, the summary, the application form, the operating plan, and the matters required to be shown on the layout plan. This is another SSI subject to the late 2006 consultation with various parties. The Executive Note touches on the cost to applicants here not in terms of fees but in terms of professional advice relating to dealing with applications. The Regulatory Impact Assessment to the Licensing (Scotland) Bill said one of the benefits of the new licensing regime would be: "a reduction in legal costs incurred by individual businesses related to applications for licence renewals and extensions",[13] and that there would be "reduced hearings, time away from business and associated legal costs".[14] It goes to quantify this issue in more detail: "Over a ten year period the cost in terms of basic fees for any licensed premises would be £344. An average public house over a ten year period with a regular extension and children's certificate, including associated legal fees, could be facing a cost of between £6,548 and £51,548 depending on whether any decision made by the Licensing Board was contested. For a major operator owning 100 pubs, the figures would be between £660,000 and £1.5 million. These cost estimates do not include the unquantifiable costs of time spent by licensees and managers attending Licensing Board hearings in respect of applications, renewals and extensions. These costs are unquantifiable because Board practice varies, with some requiring attendance by the applicant and others accepting applications in certain circumstances".[15]
- **9 October 2007** – *SSI 2007/453, Licensing (Procedure) (Scotland) Regulations 2007*: these procedural regulations contain much of the meat of the day-to-day practice of licensing law in Scotland. This, like so many above, is one of

12 Alcohol Focus Scotland, SQA, ServeWise (which is the training arm of Alcohol Focus Scotland), BII, Edinburgh Licensing Board, ACPOS, SLTA, SBPA, SRC, BHA, Coal Industry Social Welfare Organisation, British Inland Waterways, South Ayrshire Council, South Ayrshire Licensing Board, City & Guilds, and City & Guilds Scotland.

13 Regulatory Impact Assessment, Licensing (Scotland) Bill (March 2005) para 24.

14 Ibid para 25.

15 Ibid para 37.

a series of regulations which were consulted upon with a number of organisations in late 2006. The Executive Note does not offer much other than to confirm that there would be costs to licensing boards in the procedural administration of the applications and processes. The regulations came into effect on 1 February 2008, the earliest date applications could be made under the 2005 Act. Much of the detail of these regulations is discussed in appropriate chapters, covering issues such as display of notices and who should be notified, and a variety of other matters.

- **9 October 2007** – *SSI 2007/454, Licensing (Transitional and Saving Provisions) (Scotland) Order 2007*: this Order was the primary facilitator of the "conversion" from the 1976 Act to the 2005 Act, and was subject to the winter consultation of 2006. The transitional period was 1 February 2008 to 1 September 2009. The Order created new powers for clerks to make all manner of decisions under the 1976 Act by way of delegated powers where previously those applications may have required to be dealt with at one of the quarterly hearings, and to some extent distilled the entire operation of the 1976 Act into this one Order whilst allowing for the continuation of licences and old Part III registrations. It also created the "special procedure" for 2005 Act premises licence applicants which held a current 1976 Act licence or club registration (otherwise known as "grandfather rights"), and made provision for deadlines for those applications in March, June, October 2008 and January 2009 depending on what month the old licence would have fallen to be renewed (regardless of year).
- **11 October 2007** – *SSI 2007/457, Licensing (Mandatory Conditions) (Scotland) Regulations 2007*: another of the regulations which were consulted on in the deep dark winter of 2006, this introduces two new conditions which apply to most premises licences, namely the Schedule 3 notice for display concerning access by children and young persons (on which see Chapter 15, Section 4.13), and a baby changing facility requirement (on which see Chapter 15, Section 4.14).
- **18 October 2007** – *SSI 2007/472, Licensing (Scotland) Act 2005 (Commencement No. 4) Order 2007*: this was the last of the commencement orders, bringing various provisions into effect and confirming that the remainder would come into force at the fateful time of 5am on the morning of 1 September 2009. At the same time the Order brings into effect various repeals.
- **15 November 2007** – *SSI 2007/513, Licensing (Relevant Offences) (Scotland) Regulations 2007*: section 129 of the 2005 Act states that certain offences are "relevant" for the purposes of the 2005 Act in that the police have a requirement to report on them in connection with licence applications. These regulations therefore provide the list of so-called "relevant" offences. In reaching this final list, the then Executive consulted with the public during June to September 2007 and then separately with ACPOS. The detail of these is looked at in more detail in Chapter 19 at Section 2.1 and Section 3.1.4. The list of Relevant Offences is contained in Appendix G.
- **28 November 2007** – *SSI 2007/545, Licensing (Vessels etc) (Scotland) Regulations 2007*: according to the Executive Note, the purpose of these regulations, which create certain special rules for vessels, was "to enable a proportionate application of the licensing provisions, without removing the responsibility of those selling alcohol on board such vessels from the provisions of the Act concerning selling to underage persons". Consultation

on these regulations took place between October and December 2006 involving the Maritime and Coastguard Agency, the British Marine Federation, the Scottish Inland Waterways Association, and ACPOS. The special treatment for vessels includes allowing the same premises manager to be named on two premises licences attached to vessels (as long as not permanently moored or berthed), and an excusal from lodging layout plans with a premises licence application. These special cases are considered in more forensic detail in Chapter 11, Section 7.

- **28 November 2007** – *SSI 2007/546, Licensing (Mandatory Conditions No. 2) (Scotland) Regulations 2007*: the "No. 2" regulations revised the mandatory condition pertaining to staff training to require a formal written record of the training having been done. The instrument also created a statutory form for the training record itself. These regulations also added the mandatory condition which relates to off-sale premises concerning the control of the area where alcohol is displayed.
- **4 December 2007** – *SSI 2007/553, Licensing (Fees) (Scotland) Regulations 2007*: this is the instrument which lays down all fees under the new system including the fee table for new premises licences based on rateable value, along with fees for personal licences and other applications such as variations and occasional licences under the Act.
- **20 December 2007** – *SSI 2007/573, Licensing (Transitional and Savings Provisions) (Scotland) Amendment Order 2007*: this Order created a number of time-limited rules to apply during the special period of transition from the old 1976 Act to the new 2005 Act such as dealing with certain types of applications which would still require to be submitted during the transitional period, under the 1976 Act, such as children's certificate renewals, and amending objection and public notification periods.
- **15 January 2008** – *SSI 2008/9, Act of Sederunt (Summary Applications, Statutory Applications and Appeals etc Rules) Amendment (Licensing (Scotland) Act 2005) 2008*: this much maligned Act of Sederunt created a new process for appeals under the 2005 Act by way of Stated Case. This was met with howls of derision, wailing and gnashing of teeth from solicitors and counsel alike, across the land, and was ultimately repealed and replaced with the summary application route.
- **February 2008**: publication by the Scottish Executive of "What all Licensees Need to Know about changes in the Scottish Alcohol Licensing Laws". This was a "practical guide" style document which was published by the Executive and a copy was posted to every known licensed premises in Scotland. The purpose of this was to try to put into layman's terms the provisions of the new system and to tell licensees what they had to do in order to convert their licence to the new system.
- **21 May 2008** – *SSI 2008/194, Licensing (Transitional Provisions) (Scotland) Order 2008*: this Order was to allow relief for provisional licence applicants under the old 1976 Act during transition by abolishing the requirement to produce the old-styled "section 23 certificates" relating to building control and food hygiene, until the holder proceeded to lodge Finalisation of the licence.
- **1 September 2008** – *SSI 2008/292, Licensing (Scotland) Act 2005 (Commencement No. 5) Order 2008*: this Order achieved one action: to bring into force the provisions of section 123 of the 2005 Act thus enabling the

additional application requirements relating to garages and forecourts, discussed in detail in Chapter 10 at Section 2.1.

- **23 June 2009** – *SSI 2009/270, Licensing (Mandatory Conditions) (Scotland) Regulations 2009*: this amends the previous noted condition above concerning alcohol display areas in off-sale premises by excluding "visitor attractions forming part of a manufacturing site and for visitor attractions that principally provide information about and promote the history and attributes of a particular alcoholic drink or a particular category of alcoholic drink". This relaxation followed lobbying from alcohol producers such as distilleries and breweries who argued successfully that the "single area" made no sense in a manufacturing context where the entire premises was given over to the manufacture and display of alcohol.
- **23 July 2009** – *SSI 2009/277, Licensing (Scotland) Act 2005 (Transitional Provisions) Order 2009*: these provisions created a "deemed personal licence" to allow for transitional relief during the transition period and created a "grace period" for non-personal licence holders to be named as such up to 1 November 2009 whilst waiting on their personal licence applications to be processed. This Order was made following representations from the trade, solicitors and others concerning the issue that personal licences would not be processed in time for the "big bang" date on 1 September 2009.
- **1 September 2009** – This date, of course, was when the 2005 Act finally came into force. It was therefore the date of the following Order, namely – *SSI 2009/248, Licensing (Scotland) Act 2005 (Consequential Provisions) Order 2009*: this Order cleaned the slate for the 2005 Act, repealing multiple old provisions, enacting various new ones, and amending a plethora of existing Acts and secondary legislation to update references to the 2005 Act.
- **June 2010**: the Regulatory Review Group published its review into the 2005 Act. This was the earliest scrutiny of the Act. The RRG said: "From the evidence presented it is clear that parts of the Act and its subordinate legislation are not operating as intended and this is causing unnecessary and unwelcome challenges both to Licensing Officers as well all sectors selling alcohol." The RRG looked into a number of failings of the legislation and made a number of recommendations. It is instructive to review the recommendation list in full:

> "i. The Scottish Government should review whether rateable value is the best scaling factor for the banding structure used for calculating licensing fees for premises licenses.
> ii. Councils should develop a transparent system which allows both Government and those applying for a license to examine the cost of running the Licensing Board and services in their area.
> iii. Licensing Boards should confirm that they are suitably resourced to carry out their task and they know and understand their function and role.
> iv. Local Licensing Forums should agree their remit and modus operandi across Scotland.
> v. Forms should be standardised across Scotland for all license applications.
> vi. Consideration be given to the idea of a national IT system and database for licensing.
> vii. Guidance should be altered to specify to what standard and in what professional manner certain parts of the application have to be completed.
> viii. New guidance should be issued for the whole Act which is clear and simple in terms of what the Act and associated regulations require.

ix. Variation issues should be re-examined to remove inconsistent anomalies.
x. A short term working group should be established, lasting for no more that 4 months and chaired by RRG, to look at and resolve the basic administrative issues around paperwork, variation of licenses, and guidance.
xi. A higher level Alcohol and Licensing Forum should be reintroduced to look at the more strategic and longer term issues around fees etc. as well as monitor the ongoing performance and issues of the Act and beyond in this area.
xii. There should be more consistency and transparency in issues around full cost recovery.
xiii. Where there has been significant consultation during the formation of legislation or where legislation is known to contain contentious elements, the Scottish Government should enable the provision of stakeholder steering or monitoring groups to follow legislation through its initial years of implementation.
xiv. In national issues driven centrally by Scottish Government but implemented by councils there is a strong argument to move to a standardised corporate approach across Scotland with a brokered position allowing individual councils to argue for exemption or adaption for local circumstances."

There have been calls for further post-legislative scrutiny but to date this 2010 review is the only one which has occurred. And now, the timeline continues:

- **6 August 2010** – the date of Royal Assent of the *Criminal Justice and Licensing (Scotland) Act 2010.* Less than one year into the new licensing regime and the Scottish Parliament was required to pass further primary legislation to amend and correct the 2005 Act in a number of areas. The changes brought about are discussed in detail in the relevant parts of the book, but Part 9 of this Act made sweeping changes, including: the introduction of the Disabled Access Statement (although it was some years before that was commenced); introducing the nebulous concept of "interested parties"; doing away with virtually all "knowingly allowing" offences under the Act; and creating new powers for LSOs (which again took some time to be commenced).
- **19 November 2010** – *SSI 2010/413, Criminal Justice and Licensing (Scotland) Act 2010 (Commencement No. 6, Transitional and Savings Provisions) Order 2010*: article 8 of this Order extended the shelf life of provisional licences to 4 years and commenced the majority of the licensing provisions in the 2010 Act.
- **15 December 2010** – the date of Royal Assent of the *Alcohol etc (Scotland) Act 2010.* Hot on the heels of the Criminal Justice and Licensing (Scotland) Act 2010 was this further piece of primary legislation. Where the former might be said to have been an attempt at tidying up various errors and issues, the latter was most certainly driven by further politicking and policy. The SPICe Briefing on the Bill dated 18 February 2010 (SP 10/13) is instructive on this point, confirming that the aim was "reducing drinking and alcohol related harm in Scotland" as opposed to technical reforms to try to make the system work better. The Bill was the original attempt at introducing minimum pricing but did not go forward at that time, as well as a purported "detrimental impact statement" which would have allowed licensing boards to raise the age of purchase in off-sales to 21, which also did not go forward. The Act as passed, however, did introduce provisions for a minimum price of multi-packs, the "Challenge 25" policy, and adopted NHS boards as statutory consultees, amongst other changes.
- **19 February 2011** – *SSI 2011/149, Alcohol etc (Scotland) Act 2010*

(Commencement) Order 2011: this Order brought into effect, as of 1 October 2011, a number of provisions from the relevant Act including the multi-pack ban, the "Challenge 25" policy, and consultation with NHS boards.

- **21 February 2011** – *SSI 2011/128, Licensing (Food Hygiene Requirements) (Scotland) Order 2011*: paragraph 3 of this Order refers to section 50 certificates and states: "For the purposes of section 50(7) of the Licensing (Scotland) Act 2005, a food hygiene certificate is a certificate signed on behalf of the appropriate authority, within the meaning of section 50(8)(c) of that Act, stating that the subject premises comply with all relevant requirements of the Specified Community provisions."[16] This Order was revoked a month later as ministers had to update references to updated food hygiene legislation.
- **21 February 2011** – *SSI 2011/130, Licensing (Local Licensing Forum) (Scotland) Order 2011*: this small and perfectly formed little Order simply increases the maximum number of members of a Licensing Forum from twenty to twenty-one. The explanation is found in the accompanying Executive Note, which enlightens thus:

> "Forum membership is not uniform across Scotland, most have more than 5 and some will have 20 members. The Government wished to avoid the need for any local licensing forum to lose a member who was volunteering their time due to the new requirement to include a Health Board nominee. Especially as in order to attract suitable members for the local licensing forum the local authority may have undertaken a public recruitment process. To prevent any such difficulties this order is to increase the maximum membership to 21 to accommodate the Health Board nominee."

- **23 February 2011** – *SSI 2011/150, Licensing (Scotland) Act 2005 (Consequential Provisions) Order 2011*: this Order makes a number of changes to update references in the Gambling Act 2005 and in particular to deal with gaming and club permits. It also updates the relevant legislation[17] to replace the statutory form of club machine and club gaming permits. The Order contained errors which were later amended on 10 March 2011 (see below).
- **23 February 2011** – *SSI 2011/151, Licensing (Minor Variations) (Scotland) Regulations 2011*: these Regulations created a number of new types of variations which are to be treated as minor variations. These are explained in Chapter 13, Section 2.
- **8 March 2011** – *SSI 2011/177, Licensing (Food Hygiene Requirements) (Scotland) (No. 2) Order 2011*: this Order revoked the earlier Food Hygiene Order which had referred to out-of-date food legislation. This Order clarifies the correct legislation at article 3, stating: "The requirements specified for the purposes of section 50(7) of the Licensing (Scotland) Act 2005 are the requirements specified in Schedule 2 to the Food Hygiene (Scotland) Regulations 2006."
- **10 March 2011** – *SSI 2011/187, Licensing (Scotland) Act 2005 (Consequential Provisions) Amendment Order 2011*: this amends SSI 2011/150 (as noted above) so that references to the 2005 Act are correct.

16 The "community provisions" referred to here relate to certain EU provisions which are listed in Schedule 2 to the Food Hygiene (Scotland) Regulations 2006 (SSI 2006/3).

17 Namely the Club Gaming and Club Machine Permits (Scotland) Regulations 2007 (SSI 2007/504).

- **10 October 2011** – *SSI 2011/354, Criminal Justice and Licensing (Scotland) Act 2010 (Commencement No. 9, Transitional and Savings Provisions) Order 2011*: this Order commenced, as of 1 November 2011, a number of amendments to the 2005 Act brought about by the CJLAS 2010 with particular regard to the controversial construct of "interested parties".
- **29 June 2012** – the *Alcohol (Minimum Pricing) (Scotland) Act 2012* was given Royal Assent on this date. See Chapter 15 Section 4.6.
- **8 November 2012** – *SSI 2012/304, Criminal Justice and Licensing (Scotland) Act 2010 (Incidental Provisions) Order 2012*: this Order updated the (at the time) yet to be commenced provisions for Disabled Access Statements to reflect the changes in equalities law under the Equality Act 2010 so that the definition of "disabled person" was updated.
- **19 December 2012** – "Further Options for Alcohol Licensing – Scottish Government Consultation": this consultation document arose principally as a result of a paper produced jointly by Alcohol Focus Scotland and Scottish Health Action on Alcohol Problems called "Re-thinking Alcohol Licensing" which was published in September 2011 and called for various reforms of licensing such as: more robust overprovision policies; amending the "children" licensing objective; extending the licensing policy period to 5 years; and reducing the off-sale terminal hour from 10pm to 8pm. The "Further Options" consultation conceded that "the pace of legislative change has created issues of its own. Not all aspects of the licensing regime are working effectively and stakeholders such as the police and local authorities have highlighted areas that require attention". The consultation ran with a number of the AFS/SHAAP proposals, but also made further suggestions such as the re-introduction of the fit and proper test and even a so-called "English language" ability test. The net result of the consultation was that the responses would go on to "inform" the Air Weapons and Licensing (Scotland) Act 2015 (see below).
- **May 2013** – "An evaluation of the implementation of, and compliance with, the objectives of the Licensing (Scotland) Act 2005": this NHS report looked to identify whether the changes in legislation had made any change to numbers of licences applied for, compliance with conditions relating to restriction of alcohol sale, display or supply, to explore the relationships and roles of LSOs and Forums; and a number of other matters. The study was conducted by way of telephone interviews, case studies, and a seminar. Concerns raised include a focus on the lack of penetration of public health objective; difficulties in sharing of data or quality of data; and concern over the decision in *Brightcrew* and board decisions being overturned on appeal:

  > "If all decisions have to relate specifically to the sale of alcohol, the view was that arguably it will become increasingly difficult to take action against breaches related to the public health objective (and indeed other objectives), as well as issues such as over-provision. Sheriffs were also overturning decisions made by Boards, which was also said to make Boards more reluctant to take action against premises."

- **18 June 2013** – "Personal Licence Holder – Modification to Guidance to Licensing Boards" (SG2013/21): this is an update to the Scottish Government Guidance to Licensing Boards pertaining to difficulties arising from the first ever 5-year "refresher" training deadline, which ultimately resulted in thousands of people losing their personal licence by not complying with the refresher training requirement in 2014.[18] This update essentially added three short paragraphs to the Guidance, as follows:

> "176A – All personal licences issued in the transition period 01 March 2008–31 August 2009, will be treated as being issued on 01 September 2009. Therefore, all those who were issued a personal licence between 01 March 2008 and 01 Sept 2009, must undergo refresher training, and submit evidence of this to the relevant licensing board before 01 December 2014. Holders of personal licences issued after 01 September 2009 will have until 5 years (and 3 months) of this later date e.g. if a personal licence is issued on, for example 01 June 2012, then the proof that the refresher training has been carried out must be submitted to the same licensing board before 01 September 2017."

- **25 June 2013** – "Alcohol etc (Scotland) Act 2010 – Guidance for Licensing Boards": this was the only substantive "addition" to the original 2007 Scottish (then Executive) Guidance to Licensing Boards, and was an attempt by the Scottish Government to provide practical guidance on how to interpret new provisions introduced by the Alcohol etc (Scotland) Act 2010 following a raft of complaints from licensing solicitors and trade bodies. In particular, the guidance provided several "working examples" of what was intended by the restrictions on multi-packs as well as amendments to the so-called "irresponsible promotions" mandatory conditions.
- **9 September 2013** – *SSI 2013/261, Personal Licence (Training) (Scotland) Regulations 2013*: these regulations sought to provide clarity on the "process" surrounding the training requirements such as the form of the training course and notification of said training requirements for personal licence holder 5-year "refresher" training. A working group of which I was a member was established to "update" the personal licence training course itself, and in doing so highlight the aspects which would require to be retrained as part of a refresher course session, and that course was subsequently "accredited" by Scottish Ministers.
- **18 June 2013** – *SSI 2013/199, Sale of Alcohol to Children and Young Persons (Scotland) Amendment Regulations 2013*: these Regulations introduced a number of new forms of ID which are considered acceptable for the purposes of age verification under the 2005 Act. These were:
  - a Defence Identity Card issued by the Ministry of Defence;
  - a national identity card issued by an EU state (other than the United Kingdom), Norway, Iceland, Liechtenstein or Switzerland; and
  - A Biometric Immigration Document.

  The creation of these new categories of ID follows responses which were received to the "Further Options for Alcohol Licensing" Consultation in 2012 (noted above). A Policy Note to the Regulations states:

  > "Representations were received from EU countries whose citizens can visit Scotland without a passport and therefore may not have ready access to any of the existing acceptable forms of identification."

- **10 February 2014** – the Scottish Government publishes a "Review of

18 The loss of several thousand licences saw considerable controversy raised in the press at that time. See further, Stephen McGowan, "Thousands of Licences at risk in Scotland under training rule", *Bar Magazine*, 1 August 2014; and Stephen McGowan, "Is this the end of the road for Personal Licences?", *Scottish Local Retailer*, 6 November 2013. These issues were to be repeated with 10-year renewals of personal licences in 2019.

Alcohol Licensing Fees". This 51-page document flows from the earlier Regulatory Review Group publication back in June 2010 (as noted above), the first proposal of which was that Government should review the fees and in particular tying premises licence fees to rateable value. The report made a number of findings, including a comment on occasional licences thus:

> "The analysis has shown that the activity most frequently cited as the most resource intensive was Applications for Occasional Licences, which had the lowest fee attached. The vast majority (30 out of 31) of Licensing Board respondents thought that the Occasional Licence fee was too low and did not reflect costs incurred."

With respect replacing the rateable value scheme, the report had proposed two alternatives: namely, a turnover based system and a square footage based system. The results of these two alternatives were summarised thus:

> "Some stakeholders were in favour of the turnover based system and the square footage based system, however both of these approaches were considered to be problematic and received more arguments against than in favour of their use. The turnover based system was considered to be the fairest as it linked fees directly with sales, however this approach would increase the administrative burden both for Boards, who may not have appropriate staff to administer such a regime, and for premises, particularly off-sales businesses who were not currently obliged to gather this data. Furthermore, premises were reluctant to disclose commercially sensitive information. The square footage based system was thought to be more proportionate and fairer to smaller businesses, however a system based on square footage was considered to be difficult for Licensing Boards to administer, while not necessarily equating to the amount of alcohol sold e.g. in the case of department stores."

- **4 August 2014** – "Alcohol Byelaws Circular", Scottish Government (LJ/02/2014): whilst not strictly law emanating from the 2005 Act, this circular pertaining to byelaws on public consumption of alcohol is of note as it updates model byelaws taking into account the 2005 Act, which local authorities can use/adopt in relation to public consumption prohibition byelaws they may wish to introduce locally. The circular states:

  > "The Scottish Government has no plans to introduce a general provision in primary legislation making it an offence to consume alcohol in any public place. Drinking in public may be quite acceptable and cause neither problem nor nuisance depending on the circumstances. To introduce byelaws covering whole local authority areas could, by increment, effectively introduce a general offence of drinking in public. The Scottish Government considers that this would be unacceptable."

- **2 April 2014** – a proposed Bill, sponsored by Labour MSP Dr Richard Simpson, is laid before the Scottish Parliament. The *Alcohol (Licensing, Public Health and Criminal Justice) (Scotland) Bill* failed on 16 January 2016 as the "general principles" of the Bill were not supported by a majority of the Health Committee, meaning it fell at the first hurdle. However, some of proposals in the Bill are of interest as they may yet have some legacy within licensing law.
- **4 August 2015** – Royal Assent is given to the *Air Weapons and Licensing (Scotland) Act 2015*. This Act may best be described as a "miscellaneous provisions" Act, amending as it did huge swathes of licensing law including

the 2005 Act. The 2015 Act, as far as alcohol licensing is concerned, is the resting home for many of the proposals put forward in the 2012 consultation noted above. Whilst not all recommendations from that consultation were taken forward, a number of provisions are to be found here including the re-introduction of the licensing objectives driven version of the "fit and proper" test, the amendment of a licensing objective to read "Protecting Children and Young Persons from Harm", greater reporting functions from licensing boards, as well as some softer amendments such as the inclusion of angostura bitters within the legal definition of "alcohol". The 2015 Act becomes the third primary piece of legislation to make sweeping changes to the 2005 Act.

- **13 November 2015** – *SSI 2015/382, Air Weapons and Licensing (Scotland) Act 2015 (Commencement No. 1) Order 2015*: this commenced the provisions requiring licensing boards to produce an Annual Functions Report and an Annual Financial Report (discussed in Chapter 4, Section 8 (on Functions Reports) and Section 9 (on Financial Reports)).
- **25 February 2016** – *SSI 2016/132, Air Weapons and Licensing (Scotland) Act 2015 (Commencement No. 4, Transitional and Saving Provisions) Order 2016*: this Order commenced the requirement for licensing boards to issue a statement of licensing policy every five years instead of every three years; and amended the definition of overprovision to (a) clarify that a board could treat its entire jurisdiction as a locality and (b) consider "such other matters as the Board thinks fit including, in particular, the licensed hours of licensed premises in the locality".
- **29 September 2016** – *SSI 2016/307, Air Weapons and Licensing (Scotland) Act 2015 (Commencement No. 5 and Saving Provisions) Order 2016*: this Order relates to the interplay between occasional licences and public entertainment licences (PEL) under the Civic Government (Scotland) Act 1982 and commenced the need to obtain a PEL even where an occasional licence is in force (or expected to be in force), from 1 November 2016.
- **29 November 2017** – *SSI 2017/424, Air Weapons and Licensing (Scotland) Act 2015 (Commencement No. 7) Order 2017*: this Order commenced as of 20 December 2017 the new section 9A of the 2005 Act, which, according to the Explanatory Note to the Order,

  > "requires Licensing Boards to prepare and publish an annual functions report in respect of the exercise of their functions under the 2005 Act during the financial year. They must do so no later than 3 months after the end of each financial year. The financial year is deemed to end on 31st March."

- **13 December 2017** – *SSI 2017/445, Criminal Justice and Licensing (Scotland) Act 2010 (Commencement No. 14 and Saving Provision) Order 2017*: this Order commenced the requirement to produce a Disabled Access Statement for applications lodged on or after 30 March 2018.
- **7 February 2018** – *SSI 2018/49, Premises Licence (Scotland) Amendment Regulations 2018*: these regulations provide the statutory form of a Disabled Access and Facilities statement for applications lodged on or after 30 March 2018.
- **27 February 2018** – *SSI 2018/88, Alcohol (Minimum Pricing) (Scotland) Act 2012 (Commencement No. 2) Order 2018*: this Order set the date of commencement for the minimum pricing condition at 1 May 2018.
- **21 March 2018** – *SSI 2018/102, Criminal Justice and Licensing (Scotland) Act*

2010 (Commencement No. 15 and Saving Provision) and the Air Weapons and Licensing (Scotland) Act 2015 (Commencement No. 8) Order 2018: this Order can be said to conduct a final bit of housekeeping concerning the vexed issue of "interested parties" in that it commences some final outstanding provisions regarding the notification of changes to connected persons, whilst formalising the deletion of the references to interested parties provisions which had already been provided for under section 59 of the Air Weapons and Licensing (Scotland) Act 2015. Brave Chapter 7, Section 3.1.1, if you dare, to attempt to fathom the concept of "interested parties".

- **26 April 2018** – *SSI 2018/135, Alcohol (Minimum Price per Unit) (Scotland) Order 2018*: this Order set the minimum price of alcohol in Scotland at 50p per unit.
- **23 August 2018** – *SSI 2018/256, Licensing (Fees) (Scotland) Amendment Regulations 2018*: these regulations introduce and set a fee of £50 for personal licence renewal applications.
- **5 September 2018** – *SSI 2018/267, Licensing Register (Scotland) Amendment Regulations 2018*: these Regulations updated the requirement for licensing boards to publish a publicly available register of details of licences so as to include what detail has been provided with Disabled Access and Facilities statements.
- **15 January 2019** – *SSI 2019/6, Licensing (Amendment) (EU Exit) (Scotland) Regulations 2019*: these regulations allow for the descriptors of forms of ID to be changed following Brexit, e.g. the adoption of a "UK driving licence" as an acceptable form of age verification.
- **16 May 2019** – *SSI 2019/177, Licensing (Personal Licences: Supplemental and Transitional Provision) (Scotland) Order 2019*: following difficulties arising from the 10-year personal licence renewal point, and concerns that timeous applications might not be processed by busy licensing boards, this Order creates a "deemed grant" for applications lodged competently to subsist past the "normal" expiration date if the board has not managed to determine the application by that date.
- **12 March 2020** – *SSI 2020/81, Alcohol (Minimum Price per Unit) (Scotland) Amendment Order 2020*: this Order put beyond doubt that the mandatory condition of minimum pricing does not apply to trade sales. See Chapter 11, Section 8 on sales to trade.

There have been no amendments to the 2005 Act since March 2020 save those under the Coronavirus (Scotland) Act 2020, which are explored in detail in Appendix I. It should be noted that attempts to finally publish the second edition of the Scottish Government Guidance to Licensing Boards in late 2019 and early 2020 were thwarted by the onset of the pandemic and it remains unclear if the updated Guidance will be issued in 2021.

Appendix C

References to the Licensing Objectives in the Licensing (Scotland) Act 2005 Act

As noted in Chapter 3, Section 2, the licensing objectives permeate the 2005 Act. The following table is a comprehensive note of their habitat.

Section no.	*Provision*
s 4	Introduction and definition of the licensing objectives
s 6(3)	Requirement for the Licensing Board Statement of Licensing Policy to seek to promote the licensing objectives
s 23(5)(c)	Provision for refusal of a premises licence application where the licensing board considers that the grant of the application would be inconsistent with one or more of the licensing objectives
s 23(5)(ba)	Provision for refusal of a premises licence application where the licensing board considers, having regard to the licensing objectives, that the applicant is not a fit and proper person
s 23(6)(b)	Requirement for the licensing board to take into account to any antisocial behaviour report provided by the chief constable in considering whether the application should be refused under any licensing objective with regard to s 23(5)(c)
s 23(8)(b)	Where the licensing board refuses a premises licence on the grounds of inconsistency with one or more of the licensing objectives, it must state which objective or objectives in question
s 24(8)(b)	Where an application has been lodged and the applicant gives notice of a new conviction prior to determination of the application
s 27(2)(a)	This creates a power for Scottish Ministers to add further mandatory conditions as they consider necessary or expedient for the purposes of any of the licensing objectives
s 27(6)	A licensing board may attach conditions to the grant of a premises licence as it considers necessary or expedient for the purpose of any of the licensing objectives
s 30(5)(b)	This creates a ground of refusal based on inconsistency with any of the licensing objectives with regard to an application for major variation of a premises licence
s 30(7)	Where a major variation is refused based on inconsistency with one or more of the licensing objectives, the objective or objectives must be stated
s 33(7)	This creates the right of the chief constable to object to a transfer application based on the licensing objectives

Section no.	*Provision*
s 33(10)	If a hearing is called regarding an application for transfer as a result of a police objection, the licensing board must refuse the application if satisfied that it is necessary to do so for the purposes of any of the licensing objectives
s 36(3)(za)	Grounds for review of a premises licence include, having regard to the licensing objectives, that the licence holder is not a fit and proper person to be the holder of a premises licence
s 36(3)(b)	Grounds for review of a premises licence include a catch-all "any other ground relevant to one or more of the licensing objectives"
s 36(5)(b)	An application for a premises licence review based on the licensing objectives must specify which objective or objectives the alleged ground of review relates to
s 37(4)(b)	Where the board initiate's its own premises licence review based on the licensing objectives, it must specify which objective or objectives the alleged ground of review relates to
s 39(1)	If a ground of review is established at a premises licence review hearing, the licensing board may take certain steps if it considers it necessary or appropriate for the purposes of any of the licensing objectives
s 39(2A)	If a board is satisfied that the licence holder is not fit and proper having regard to the licensing objectives, it must revoke the licence
s 44(5)(b)	Where a premises licence holder gives notice of a relevant conviction to the licensing board, and the board having intimated it to the police, the police may give a notice to the licensing board with a recommendation that they consider it necessary for the licence to be varied, suspended or revoked for the purposes of the licensing objectives
s 59(6)	If the licensing board considers that the grant of an occasional licence would be inconsistent with one or more of the licensing objectives, it may refuse the application
s 60(2)(a)	Scottish Ministers may add to mandatory conditions applicable to occasional licences as they consider necessary or expedient for the purposes of any of the licensing objectives
s 60(4)	A licensing board may attach conditions to the grant of an occasional licence as they consider necessary or expedient for the purposes of any of the licensing objectives
s 65(5)	In considering a premises licence, variation, occasional licence or extended hours application which proposes off-sales hours within the statutory maximum (10am to 10pm), in considering whether the granting of the application would be inconsistent with any of the licensing objectives, the Board must, in particular, consider the effect (if any) which the off-sales hours proposed in the application would have on the occurrence of antisocial behaviour.
s 69(2)	The chief constable may object to the grant of an extended hours application if he considers it necessary to do so for the purposes of any of the licensing objectives

Section no.	*Provision*
s 73(4)	The chief constable may include a recommendation to refuse a personal licence for the purposes of any of the licensing objectives when giving notice to the licensing board of the presence of relevant or foreign convictions
s 74(6)(a)	A licensing board must refuse a personal licence application if satisfied that it is necessary to do so for the purposes of the licensing objectives, having regard to the recommendation provided by the police under s 73(4)
s 74(6A)	The grounds of refusal for a personal licence are that, having regard to the licensing objectives, the applicant is not a fit and proper person to be the holder of a personal licence, or that it is otherwise necessary to refuse the application for the purposes of any of the licensing objectives (this also applies to renewal of personal licences under s 78)
s 75(7)(b)	The chief constable may include a recommendation to refuse a personal licence for the purposes of any of the licensing objectives when giving notice to the licensing board following notice of a relevant or foreign conviction being provided by the applicant subsequent to the lodgement of the application
s 83(5)(b)	The chief constable may include a recommendation to revoke, suspend or endorse a personal licence for the purposes of any of the licensing objectives when giving notice to the licensing board following notice of a relevant or foreign conviction being provided by a personal licence holder
s 83(8)(c)	At a hearing following receipt of confirmation of a relevant or foreign conviction, the licensing board may make an order revoking, suspending or endorsing a personal licence if satisfied that it is necessary to do so for the purposes of any of the licensing objectives
s 84(2)	During the course of a premises licence review hearing, a licensing board may make a finding that a personal licence holder who is or was working in the licensed premises has acted in a manner inconsistent with any of the licensing objectives
s 84(6)(b)	A finding under s 84(2) will result in a personal licence review hearing at which a licensing board may make an order revoking, suspending or endorsing a personal licence if it considers it necessary to do so for the purposes of any of the licensing objectives
s 84A	The chief constable may report conduct inconsistent with the licensing objectives
s 84B	A licensing standards officer may report conduct inconsistent with the licensing objectives
s 86(2)(b)	Following three endorsements being placed on a personal licence, a licensing board may make an order suspending or revoking that personal licence if it considers it necessary to do so for the purposes of any of the licensing objectives

Section no.	*Provision*
s 137(2)(a)	A police constable or licensing standards officer has a right of entry to any premises undergoing an application for a premises licence, variation, review, temporary licence, occasional licence or extended hours application, for the purposes of assessing the likely effect of the grant of the application on any of the licensing objectives [*or* (see below):]
s 137(2)(b)	*Or*, an inspection as noted under s 137(2)(a), if for a review proposal or application, the effect which the selling of alcohol in accordance with the premises licence is having on any of the licensing objectives

Appendix D

Scottish Health Boards as relevant to Licensing Boards under the Licensing (Scotland) Act 2005

NHS Health Board	*Licensing Board*
NHS Ayrshire & Arran	East Ayrshire Licensing Board, North Ayrshire Licensing Board and South Ayrshire Licensing Board
NHS Borders	Scottish Borders Licensing Board
NHS Dumfries & Galloway	Dumfries & Galloway Licensing Board (All divisions)
NHS Western Isles (Bòrd SSN nan Eilean Siar)	Western Isles Licensing Board
NHS Fife	Fife Licensing Board
NHS Forth Valley	Clackmannanshire Licensing Board, Falkirk Licensing Board, Stirling Licensing Board
NHS Grampian	Aberdeenshire Licensing Boards, Aberdeen City Licensing Board, Moray Licensing Board
NHS Greater Glasgow and Clyde	City of Glasgow Licensing Board, East Dunbartonshire Licensing Board, East Renfrewshire Licensing Board, Inverclyde Licensing Board, Renfrewshire Licensing Board, North Lanarkshire (certain parts), and South Lanarkshire (certain parts)
NHS Highland	Argyll & Bute Licensing Board, Highland Licensing Board
NHS Lanarkshire	North Lanarkshire Licensing Board, South Lanarkshire Licensing Board (All divisions)
NHS Lothian	City of Edinburgh Licensing Board, East Lothian Licensing Board, West Lothian Licensing Board, Midlothian Licensing Board
NHS Orkney	Orkney Licensing Board
NHS Shetland	Shetland Licensing Board
NHS Tayside	Angus Licensing Board, Dundee Licensing Board, and Perth & Kinross Licensing Board

Appendix E

Club Rules under the Licensing (Scotland) Acts 1976 and 2005: A Comparison

The 1976 Act rules under section 107(1) of that Act are provided here:

"(a) that the business and affairs of the club shall be under the management of a committee or governing body who shall be elected for not less than one year by the governing body of members and shall be subject in whole or in part or in a specified proportion to annual re-election, or of whom not more than one-third may be non-elected persons from outwith the club and the remainder shall be elected and subject to annual re-election as aforesaid;
(b) that no member of the committee or governing body and no manager or servant employed in the club shall have any personal interest in the sale of alcoholic liquor therein or in the profits arising from such sale;
(c) that the committee or governing body shall hold periodical meetings;
(d) that, unless the club is one to which subsection (4) below applies, all members of the club shall be elected by the whole body of members or by the committee or governing body, with or without specially added members;
(e) that, unless the club is one to which subsection (4) below applies, the names and addresses of persons proposed as ordinary members of the club shall be displayed in a conspicuous place in the club premises for at least a week before their election, and that an interval of not less than two weeks shall elapse between the nomination and election of ordinary members;
(f) that no alcoholic liquor shall be sold or supplied in the club to any person under 18;
(g) that no person under 18 shall be admitted a member of the club unless the club is one which is devoted primarily to some athletic purpose or to which subsection (4) below applies;
(h) that no persons shall be allowed to become honorary or temporary members of the club or be relieved of the payment of the regular entrance fee or subscription, except those possessing certain qualifications defined in the rules and subject to conditions and regulations prescribed therein;
(i) that there shall be a defined subscription payable in advance by members;
(j) that correct accounts and books shall be kept showing the financial affairs and intromissions of the club;
(k) that a visitor shall not be supplied with alcoholic liquor in the club premises unless on the invitation and in the company of a member and that the member shall, upon the admission of such visitor to the club premises or immediately upon his being supplied with such liquor, enter his own name and the name and address of the visitor in a book which shall be kept for the purpose and which shall show the date of each visit; and
(l) that no alcoholic liquor shall be sold or supplied in the club premises for consumption off the premises, except to a member of the club in person for consumption by him or to a person holding a licence or a wholesaler's excise licence for the sale of such liquor."

The equivalent rules, under the Licensing (Clubs) (Scotland) Regulations 2007,[1] are:

> **"Clubs prescribed for the purposes of section 125(1)**
>
> 2 (1) The description of club prescribed for the purposes of section 125(1) of the Act is a club–
>
> (a) which is not conducted for the purposes of making a profit; and
>
> (b) which has a written constitution and rules which make provision to the effect specified in paragraph (2).
>
> (2) That provision is that–
>
> (a) the business of the club is to be under the management of a committee or other governing body elected by the members of the club;
>
> (b) no person under 18 is to be admitted as a member of the club (unless the club is devoted primarily to some sporting purpose or is a students' union to which paragraph (3) applies);
>
> (c) no member of the committee or other governing body and no person employed by the club is to have any personal interest in the sale of alcohol on the club premises or in the profits arising from such sale;
>
> (d) other than when an occasional licence has effect, no person is to be supplied with alcohol on the club premises unless that person is–
>
> (i) a member of the club;
>
> (ii) a person who is on the premises at the invitation of a member of the club and is accompanied by that member; or
>
> (iii) a member of another club which falls within the description prescribed in paragraph (1);
>
> (e) where a person referred to in sub-paragraph (d)(ii) is supplied with alcohol on club premises when an occasional licence is not in effect, there is to be entered in a book kept for the purpose–
>
> (i) the date in question;
>
> (ii) the name and address of the person; and
>
> (iii) the name of the member accompanying the person;
>
> (f) correct accounts and books are to be kept showing the financial affairs and intromissions of the club;
>
> (g) the club has to have at least 25 members to be properly constituted; and
>
> (h) no person is to be allowed honorary or temporary membership of the club or to be relieved of the payment of the regular entrance fee or subscription–
>
> (i) except to allow temporary participation in the activity which is the prime purpose of the club; and
>
> (ii) except in accordance with specific provision set out in the club rules.
>
> (3) This paragraph applies to a students' union of–
>
> (a) a university; or
>
> (b) a further education college under the management of an education authority,
>
> which is recognised and certified as such by the Senate or Academic Council of the university or by the education authority, as the case may be.
>
> (4) Expressions used in paragraph (3) which are also used in the Education (Scotland) Act 1980 have the same meanings in that paragraph as in that Act."

1 SSI 2007/76.

Appendix F

List of Personal Licence Identification Codes

The codes used by licensing boards to identify the jurisdictional origin of a personal licence are as follows:

AC	Aberdeen City
AB	Aberdeenshire
AN	Angus Council
AR	Argyll & Bute
CC	Clackmannanshire
DG	Dumfries & Galloway
DC	Dundee City
EA	East Ayrshire
ED	East Dunbartonshire
EL	East Lothian
ER	East Renfrewshire
EC	Edinburgh City
FC	Falkirk
FI	Fife
GC	Glasgow City
HC	Highland
IC	Inverclyde
MC	Midlothian
MO	Moray
NA	North Ayrshire
NL	North Lanarkshire
OI	Orkney Islands
PK	Perth & Kinross
RC	Renfrewshire
SB	Scottish Borders
SI	Shetland Islands
SA	South Ayrshire

SL	South Lanarkshire
SC	Stirling
WD	West Dunbartonshire
WL	West Lothian
WI	Western Isles

Appendix G

List of Relevant Offences under the Licensing (Scotland) Act 2005

The relevant offences are prescribed in the Schedule to the Licensing (Relevant Offences) (Scotland) Regulations 2007[1] and are as follows:

"PART 1
VIOLENT AND SEXUAL OFFENCES

1. Any offence inferring personal violence.
2. Any offence which is a 'sexual offence' within the meaning of subsection (10) of section 210A of the Criminal Procedure (Scotland) Act 1995 (c 46), as read with subsection (11) of that section.

PART 2
OTHER STATUTORY OFFENCES

3. An offence under the Pharmacy Act 1954 (c 61).
4. An offence under the Betting, Gaming and Lotteries Act 1963 (c 2).
5. An offence under the Firearms Act 1968 (c 27).
6. An offence under section 1 of the Trade Descriptions Act 1968 (c 29) (false trade description of goods) in circumstances where the goods in question are or include alcohol.
7. An offence under section 13 of the Theatres Act 1968 (c 54) (performance of play in unlicensed premises).
8. An offence under section 7(2) of the Gaming Act 1968 (c 65) (allowing child to take part in gaming on premises licensed for the sale of alcohol).
9. An offence under any of the following provisions of the Misuse of Drugs Act 1971 (c 38)–
- (a) section 4(2) (production of a controlled drug);
- (b) section 4(3) (supply of a controlled drug);
- (c) section 5(2) (possession of a controlled drug);
- (d) section 5(3) (possession of a controlled drug with intent to supply);
- (e) section 8 (permitting activities to take place on premises);
- (f) section 23(4) (offence in connection with powers to search and obtain evidence).

10. An offence under the Immigration Act 1971 (c 77).
11. An offence under the Poisons Act 1972 (c 66).
12. An offence under the Health and Safety at Work etc Act 1974 (c 37).
13. An offence under the Lotteries and Amusements Act 1976 (c 32).
14. An offence under the Licensing (Scotland) Act 1976 (c 66).
15. An offence under either of the following provisions of the Customs and Excise Management Act 1979 (c 2)–
- (a) section 170 (disregarding subsection (1)(a)) (fraudulent evasion of duty etc);

1 SSI 2007/513.

(b) section 170B (taking preparatory steps for evasion of duty).

16. An offence under the Alcoholic Liquor Duties Act 1979 (c 4).

17. An offence under either of the following provisions of the Tobacco Products Duty Act 1979 (c 7)–

(a) section 8G (possession and sale of unmarked tobacco);

(b) section 8H (use of premises for sale of unmarked tobacco).

18. An offence under Part II of the Forgery and Counterfeiting Act 1981 (c 45).

19. An offence under any of the following provisions of the Civic Government (Scotland) Act 1982 (c 45)–

(a) section 7 (offences), so far as relating to public entertainment licences under section 41;

(b) section 21(1), (4), (5) or (6) (offences in relation to taxis and private hire cars);

(c) section 27D (provision of information to holder of knife dealer's licence);

(d) section 27F (powers of constables and authorised officers);

(e) section 27G (power to inspect documents);

(f) section 50 (drunkenness);

(g) section 57 (being in or on buildings etc with intent to commit theft);

(h) Part V (public processions).

20. An offence under the Cinemas Act 1985 (c 13).

21. An offence under Part I of the Food and Environment Protection Act 1985 (c 48).

22. An offence under either of the following provisions of Schedule 2B to the Gas Act 1986 (c 44)–

(a) paragraph 10 (injury to gas fittings and interference with meters);

(b) paragraph 11 (restoration of supply without consent).

23. An offence under the Company Directors Disqualification Act 1986 (c 46).

24. An offence under the Public Order Act 1986 (c 64).

25. An offence under the Crossbows Act 1987 (c 32).

26. An offence under the Firearms (Amendment) Act 1988 (c 45).

27. An offence under any of the following provisions of the Copyright, Designs and Patents Act 1988 (c 48)–

(a) section 107(1)(d)(iii) (public exhibition in the course of a business of article infringing copyright);

(b) section 107(3) (infringement of copyright by public performance of work etc);

(c) section 198(2) (broadcast etc of recording of performance made without sufficient consent);

(d) section 297(1) (fraudulent reception of transmission);

(e) section 297A(1) (supply of unauthorised decoder).

28. An offence under any of the following provisions of the Road Traffic Act 1988 (c 52)–

(a) section 3A (causing death by careless driving while under the influence of drink or drugs);

(b) section 4 (driving etc a vehicle when under the influence of drink or drugs);

(c) section 5 (driving etc a vehicle with alcohol concentration above prescribed limit);

(d) section 178 (taking motor vehicle without authority, etc).

29. An offence under either of the following provisions of the Electricity Act 1989 (c 29)–

(a) paragraph 3 of Schedule 6 (restoration of supply without consent);

(b) paragraph 8 of Schedule 6 (provision as to power of entry);

(c) paragraph 11 of Schedule 7 (interference with meters).

30. An offence under either of the following provisions of the Food Safety Act 1990 (c 16) in circumstances where the food in question is or includes alcohol–
- (a) section 14 (selling food or drink not of the nature, substance or quality demanded);
- (b) section 15 (falsely describing or presenting food or drink).

31. An offence under the National Lottery Etc Act 1993 (c 39).
32. An offence under section 92(1) or (2) of the Trade Marks Act 1994 (c 26) (unauthorised use of trade mark, etc in relation to goods) in circumstances where the goods in question are or include alcohol.
33. An offence under any of the following provisions of the Criminal Law (Consolidation) (Scotland) Act 1995 (c 39)–
- (a) section 19 (alcohol on vehicles);
- (b) section 20 (sporting events: control);
- (c) section 44 (false statements and declarations);
- (d) section 47 (prohibition of the carrying of offensive weapons);
- (e) section 49 (offence of having in public place article with blade or point);
- (f) section 49A (offence of having article with blade or point (or offensive weapon) on school premises).

34. An offence under section 3 of the Private Security Industry Act 2001 (c 12) (conduct prohibited without a licence).
35. An offence under the Proceeds of Crime Act 2002 (c 29).
36. An offence under the Building (Scotland) Act 2003 (asp 8).
37. An offence under the Antisocial Behaviour etc (Scotland) Act 2004 (asp 8).
38. An offence under the Breastfeeding etc (Scotland) Act 2005 (asp 1).
39. An offence under the Fire (Scotland) Act 2005 (asp 5).
40. An offence under either of the following provisions of the Smoking, Health and Social Care (Scotland) Act 2005 (asp 13)–
- (a) section 1 (offence of permitting others to smoke in no-smoking premises);
- (b) section 2 (offence of smoking in no-smoking premises).

41. An offence under the Licensing (Scotland) Act 2005 (asp 16).
42. An offence under the Prevention of Terrorism Act 2005 (c 2).
43. An offence under section 46 of the Gambling Act 2005 (c 19) (invitation to gamble).
44. An offence under the Terrorism Act 2006 (c 11).

PART 3
OTHER COMMON LAW OFFENCES

45. The offences at common law of –
- (a) theft;
- (b) theft by housebreaking;
- (c) fraud;
- (d) uttering;
- (e) fraud and uttering;
- (f) extortion;
- (g) abduction;
- (h) reset; and
- (i) conspiracy to defraud.

46. The offences at common law of –
- (a) wilful fireraising;
- (b) culpable and reckless fireraising;
- (c) culpable and reckless conduct; and
- (d) bestiality.

47. The offences at common law of –
- (a) perjury;

(b) subornation of perjury;
(c) attempting to pervert the course of justice;
(d) attempting to defeat the ends of justice;
(e) prevarication on oath;
(f) contempt of court; and
(g) prison breaking.

48. The offences at common law of –
(a) breach of the peace; and
(b) mobbing and rioting."

In addition to this list, regulation 2 provides further detail of more types of offence which are to be considered relevant, as follows:

"(b) any offence which –
(i) was provided for in an enactment which is no longer in force; and
(ii) was similar in nature to an offence specified in the Schedule;
(c) any offence in respect of aiding and abetting, inciting, counselling or procuring any offence referred to in paragraph (a) or (b); and
(d) any other offence in respect of which a sentence of imprisonment was imposed."

Appendix H

A Brief History of Test Purchasing

Test purchasing was originally piloted in Scotland in Fife back in 2007 and rolled out throughout Scotland in 2008. Depending on the police force in question, test purchases at that time were sometimes random but also "intelligence led": in other words, the police were using this power if they had received information that premises might not be adhering to the law.

There is a general practice advice document issued by the Scottish Parliament called "A Practical Guide to Test Purchasing in Scotland",[1] which the police would have regard to in carrying out a test purchase. This includes rules about how to go about the test itself – such as only using persons aged 16 or 17 and not "dressing up" that young person to look older than they are; nor can the young person lie about their age – but also includes advice in relation to the safety element of the practice to ensure the young persons involved are not at harm.

This document followed the early advice issued by Peter Wilson, the then Chief Constable of the Fife Constabulary in his guidance note following the test pilot powers being approved by the Scottish Parliament. In his report, he said:

> "In all such activities, it is important that standard operating procedures are both fair and ethical therefore Licencees have been assured that (a) all of the test purchasers utilised will be 16 years old and will look their age. There will be no alterations to appearance in an effort to have them look older than they are; and (b) they will all be briefed to tell the truth if asked any questions regarding their age."[2]

Independent test purchasers Serve Legal, who use 18- and 19-year-olds, indicated that, during the period August to October 2008, Scottish premises had a 67 per cent pass rate, compared with 71 per cent in southern England and 49 per cent in Northern Ireland. Several factors found to be affecting the pass rate included whether eye contact was made by the server, the impact of point-of-sale material, and that female test purchasers were less likely to be asked for ID.[3]

After 1 September 2009, the powers were used ad hoc; on a targeted basis; and also universally to test all premises in a given area. It was and is entirely up to the police to determine when a test purchase should be carried out, but

1 Available at: http://www.scotland.gov.uk/Resource/Doc/201135/0053738.pdf. This was released on 25 October 2007.

2 "Scottish Pilot Project – Test Purchasing of Alcohol", Fife Constabulary Community Safety Committee (31 May 2006) para 3.6.

3 Statistics provided courtesy of Ed Heaver of Serve Legal. See www.servelegal.co.uk for more information on independent test-purchasing.

the majority of police forces had been quite clear that they are not trying to catch licensees out, but instead to work with them and assure a high standard of service and training is being provided.

In the early days of the 2005 Act, failed test purchases had severe consequences for licence holders.[4] Most police forces operated a two-test practice: a failure in the first instance would result in a report being sent to the procurator fiscal, who may decide to prosecute, but a second failure, the licence holder having been advised of the first failure and warned about best practice, resulted not only in a report to the procurator fiscal but a request for a review hearing under the 2005 Act. There was therefore a spate of such reviews across the earlier part of the 2005 Act lifecycle.[5]

This approach then softened somewhat, with it becoming unusual through the 2010s for a licence review request being lodged by Police Scotland on the basis of just one or possibly two failed test purchases. It was more likely that such material would be put to a board as part of a wider review where perhaps there are further issues causing the police concern.

In March 2019 a Standard Operating Procedure (SOP) for test purchasing was issued by Police Scotland. This covered issues such as the health, welfare, selection and briefing of young persons, as well as practical dimensions like recovery of evidence. It refers to unpublished guidance by the Lord Advocate which indicates, *inter alia*, that test purchasing can only be deployed where intelligence exists, and can only be sanctioned by the Chief Constable.

The use of test purchasing appears to have ceased entirely as a result of regulatory complications surrounding the interplay between the practice of test purchasing, procedural issues identified in the SOP, and the Regulation of Investigatory Powers (Scotland) Act 2000.

4 Perhaps the last appeal under the 1976 Act arising as a result of a suspension following failed test purchases is *A M Landsburgh (St Andrews) Ltd v Fife Licensing Board* [2009] 42 SLLP 23, in which the Sheriff criticised the board heavily for placing little or no weight on the fact some tests had been passed, on the efforts made by the licence holder, or on "human error".

5 See "One in six fail under-age checks" [2007] 39 SLLP 5.

Appendix I

The Coronavirus (Scotland) Act 2020

1 OVERVIEW

In March 2020 both the Prime Minister, Boris Johnson, and the First Minister, Nicola Sturgeon, told us to "stop going to the pub", as the coronavirus pandemic took hold of society. This "instruction" was ultimately followed up with a legal closure of all licensed premises (save retail premises – see below). There can scarcely have been a more confusing and concerning time for us all, and for those of us who work within or with the hospitality industry, a bruising period commenced. The Scottish Government recognised some of the issues facing licensing practice, and the licensed trade, and sought to remedy them by creating temporary legislative easings. In this Appendix I am going to examine the temporary amendments to the Licensing (Scotland) Act 2005 which were introduced in the Coronavirus (Scotland) Act 2020, given Royal Assent on 6 April 2020.

I have elected to consider these changes in a vacuum, and although I make references scattered here and there as to the impact of the pandemic in the main body of the text, I have not sought to state the law as amended by the 2020 Act, instead reaching a view that the 2020 amendments should sit to one side, noting that they will fall off the statute books on 30 September 2021.[1] I have also elected not to try to capture the various additional laws which affected licensed premises across 2020 including, variously, curfews on trading hours and opening, the ill-fated creation of new terms such as "licensed cafe",[2] and additional guidance such as the ban on background music, and focus purely on the principal amendments to the 2005 Act itself. This appendix should therefore be taken as a snapshot of the amended 2005 Act, during the relevant period.

The amendments are contained, via section 6, in Schedule 5 to the 2020 Act. The key amendments to the 2005 Act might be grouped as follows:

- Amendments to the requirement to hold hearings
- Amendments to transfers and duration of licences

1 Section 12 of the 2020 Act provided that the amendments have an expiry date of 30 September 2020 but could be extended. This was subsequently carried out, most recently under the Coronavirus (Scotland) Acts (Amendment of Expiry Dates) Regulations 2021 (SSI 2021/152), which created a new expiry date of 30 September 2021. At the time of writing it is unclear if Parliament will have to introduce further primary legislation to extend this even further.

2 On which, see Stephen McGowan "We've gone from confusion to chaos on hospitality lockdown", *The Telegraph*, 9 October 2020, and "Covid in Scotland: Business owners 'in tears' over cafe status", BBC News, 9 October 2020.

- Amendments to provisional licences
- Amendments regarding home deliveries
- Amendments to minor variations regarding premises managers
- Amendments to extended hours applications
- Amendments regarding personal licences
- Amendments to licensing board procedures
- Amendments to LSO duties
- Amendments to Police notifications.

We will look at each of these in turn.

2 THE REQUIREMENT TO HOLD HEARINGS

One of the most obvious ways in which Coronavirus affected our lives in 2020 was the shutdown of numerous public events and gatherings, and this was to include local authority public meetings and, of course, hearings of the licensing board under the 2005 Act. The immediate result of this, in late March and into April 2020, was the cancellation of licensing board hearings all over Scotland, leaving many applications in licensing limbo. The 2020 Act sought to deal with this, to some extent, by allowing hearings to occur other than in person: thus, the "Zoom" hearing was born. Schedule 5 paragraph 1(2) inserted a new section 133(3C) to the 2005 Act in the following terms[3]:

> "(3C) The Board must give any person who would have been given the opportunity to be heard at the hearing the opportunity to be heard instead by whichever of the following means the person prefers—
> (a) telephone,
> (b) written representations, including by means of an electronic communication (as defined in section 15(1) of the Electronic Communications Act 2000),
> (c) video conference, if the Board has video conference facilities."

As boards across Scotland tried to do business, agents and applicants were invited to join hearings remotely, or to deal with their applications by written submissions or dialling in via phone. Although there were inevitable gremlins in some cases, clerks and committee services staff battled valiantly and many licensing boards were able to hold remote or virtual hearings.[4] The efficacy of such hearings as a permanent feature in the licensing landscape is likely to generate debate as those who have participated will have diverging views.[5]

The 2020 Act also goes on to make provision for relaxations relating to the timeframe of holding hearings, effectively saying that the deadline can be

3 An additional amendment focused on review hearings was also made at para 2(4) of Sch 5 to the 2020 Act.
4 See Junner, Audrey: "Licensing: Remote hearings – the future?", *Journal of the Law Society of Scotland*, 19 October 2020.
5 For my part, leaving the novelty aside, it was positive to be able to do business, but I missed the cut and thrust of appearing in person and meeting people face to face. I also found that the art of reading the mood of the board was curtailed in the virtual setting. A large part of licensing advocacy is, for me, the body language of the members, making eye contact, and building a rapport (or at least trying to). Those elements were more detached, and I found the experience the lesser for it. Some solicitors were positive about the lack of travel time, but for me the travelling to visit clients and all the boards of Scotland is an enjoyable aspect of the practice.

missed but "the Board must hold the hearing as soon as reasonably practicable after the end of that period", and this general rule applies to hearings dealing with premises licences, variations, transfers, reviews, occasional licences, extended hours, and personal licences.

3 AMENDMENTS TO TRANSFERS AND DURATION OF LICENCES

The 2020 Act created a relaxation to the "28-day rule" as regards transfers of licences, which is discussed in several parts of Chapter 12 but see also Chapter 7 at Section 2.1 and 2.1.3 on the duration of a premises licence. Under normal circumstances a licence is deemed to cease to have effect where no transfer application is lodged within 28 days of a prescribed event. The 2020 Act relaxed this by introduction of two new provisions, as follows:

> "[Section 28](5A) For the avoidance of doubt, a licensed premises does not cease to be used for the sale of alcohol, for the purposes of subsection (5)(b), if the premises cease to be used for the sale of alcohol for a temporary period for a reason relating to coronavirus."

> "[Section34](1A) If, for a reason relating to coronavirus, a person is unable to apply to the Licensing Board within the period set out in subsection (1), the Board may accept an application that is made after the end of that period."

The combined effect of this was to ensure that licences continued to have effect notwithstanding they were no longer trading; and that where a prescribed event occurred such as the death of a licence holder, and an application to transfer the licence was made outwith the normal 28-day period, the board could accept the "late" application with the catch-all provision that the lateness was due to the virus.

4 AMENDMENTS TO PROVISIONAL LICENCES

The normal currency of a provisional licence is 4 years although this can be extended – see Chapter 11 at Section 3.2 and 3.2.1. The 2020 Act added a further provision to require boards to grant a 6-month extension to the first "renewal" of a provisional licence at the 4-year point, where the delay to the completion of the works and confirmation of the licence was a "reason relating to coronavirus".[6] This was a useful safeguard, although I expect most licensing boards would have been sympathetic to this scenario in any event.

5 AMENDMENTS REGARDING HOME DELIVERIES

In the earliest stages of lockdown, as businesses reeled from the effect of forced closure, many sought to alter their business model to run what might otherwise have been a hospitality premises as a food retail premises, as such premises were exempt from the closure. This meant, for example, pubs reinventing

6 2020 Act, Sch 5 para 2(5)(b), which inserted a new s 45(7A) to the 2005 Act, to that effect.

themselves as local shops selling food and drink or even other retail goods, and restaurants becoming takeaway businesses only, doing home deliveries,[7] "click and collect"[8] services, and so on. In order to clarify any dubiety over these forms of business and how that linked to the premises licence, the following term was inserted by the 2020 Act to the mandatory condition regarding adherence to the operating plan:[9]

> "If food is sold on the premises but the operating plan contained in the licence does not contain an express term to the effect that food may be taken away, or delivered, from the premises for consumption off the premises, a term to that effect is to be implied into the operating plan."

This wording was to alleviate any concern that the absence of an express term would mean the operator was committing a criminal offence.[10] It will be interesting to see how the impact of the reversal of this provision will be managed by licensing boards. Many licensing boards do insist on wording in relation to the home delivery of alcohol, so that they can assess how the operator is managing such activity (and one will also now see reference to "click and collect" and other forms of purchasing arrangements which have grown in popularity). I would not be surprised to see a call to have this wording retained on the face of the 2005 Act as we near the repeal of the 2020 Act provision; and a rise in major variations to ensure licences are "future proofed" with wording to cover home delivery/click and collect and so on.

6 AMENDMENTS TO MINOR VARIATIONS REGARDING PREMISES MANAGERS

You will find a discussion of what I refer to as the "7 days and 6 weeks rule" in relation to the removal and nomination of premises managers in Chapter 13 at Section 3.3.2. The 2020 Act amends this to create a "28 days and 3 months plus" rule.[11] The usual notice period to advise a board a premises manager is no longer in place is extended to 28 days; and time to lodge a minor variation naming a new premises manager is extended from 6 weeks to 3 months, or later at the discretion of the licensing board if the reason for delay is due to coronavirus.

7 AMENDMENTS TO EXTENDED HOURS APPLICATIONS

The 2005 Act provides that police and LSO representations in relation to extended hours applications must be provided within 10 days of receipt of the notice of application – as discussed in Chapter 16 at Section 6. The 2020

7 On "home deliveries" generally, see Chapter 8 at Section 3.8 and footnote 41.

8 On "click and collect" generally, see Chapter 11 at Section 9.2.

9 Said condition being the one at Sch 3 para 3 to the 2005 Act.

10 See, *inter alia*, the author's articles "Coronavirus: Home Delivery Advice", *Scottish Licensed Trade News*, 19 March 2020; "Coronavirus and licensing", *Scottish Legal News*, 19 March 2020; and "Coronavirus: Which venues can still trade?", *Scottish Licensed Trade News*, 26 March 2020.

11 2020 Act, Sch 5 para 2(6).

Act amends this so that a report or representation can be submitted outwith the usual 10 days as a result of a reason relating to coronavirus; although the relevant officer has to intimate the lateness to the licensing board within the 10 days.[12]

8 AMENDMENTS REGARDING PERSONAL LICENCES

The 2020 Act introduced several administrative easings in relation to personal licences. First, a quasi "deemed grant" provision was inserted at section 77(2A) and (2B) so that a personal licence renewal lodged but not granted prior to the expiry date was deemed to run for a further 6-month period.[13] Secondly, the period in which a personal licence renewal application could be lodged[14] was amended to start 12 months prior to the expiry date, and up to the day before the date of expiry.[15] Lastly, in relation to the production of evidence of refresher training at the 5-year anniversary of the grant of the personal licence,[16] the 2020 Act allows the licensing board to extend these deadlines where satisfied that the non-compliance is as a result of a reason related to coronavirus.[17] It is left to the board to decide what the extension period may be, and more than one extension can be granted.

9 AMENDMENTS TO LICENSING BOARD AND FORUM PROCEDURES

The 2020 Act makes several technical amendments to ease or relax aspects of licensing board procedure and administration, and forum hearings.

- **Annual Functions Reports and Annual Financial Reports**: under normal circumstances these documents must be published within 3 months of the end of a local authority financial year.[18] The 2020 Act amends this "deadline" so that a board may, within 3 months of the end of that financial year, publish a statement that it will not be able to meet the deadline and the reason for the delay, along with an indication as to when it will be published; and the actual deadline for publication has been extended to 9 months after the end of the financial year.[19]
- **Power to relieve procedural failings**: the section 135 "slip rule" power, which is examined in Chapter 4 at Section 10, is amended so that a failure to comply with a procedural provision can be excused where "the failure is due to an excusable cause and that excusable cause relates to coronavirus", as well as the traditional "mistake, oversight or other excusable cause".[20]

12 2020 Act, Sch 5 para 2(7).
13 2020 Act, Sch 5 para 3(2).
14 On which generally, see Chapter 17 at Section 3.1.
15 2020 Act, Sch 5 para 3(3).
16 On which generally, see Chapter 17 at Section 3.2.
17 2020 Act, Sch 5 para 3(4).
18 On these requirements generally, see Chapter 4 at Section 8 on Annual Functions Reports and at Section 9 on Annual Financial Reports.
19 2020 Act, Sch 5 para 4(2) and (3).
20 2020 Act, Sch 5 para 4(4).

- **"Sub-committee" provisions**: the 2005 Act allows for a licensing board to establish a sub-committee to deal with certain matters, for example a sub-committee could be set up which would deal with review hearings. In practice, I cannot think of a single example of this in liquor licensing (although there are examples under how local authority licensing committee business is run under the Civic Government (Scotland) Act 1982) but in any event the 2020 Act creates a provision which would allow such a sub-committee to exercise the wider powers of the board. I don't see this provision as being of any practical use.
- **Licensing board member training**: under normal rules, a board member has to complete an approved training course within 3 months of being appointed, on which see Chapter 4 at Section 3. The 2020 Act eases this somewhat so that the evidence of training may be provided within 9 months, but goes further and also allows a board member to take part in business even where that evidence has not been produced, so long as the clerk has briefed the member (in person or otherwise) on:
  - the role of a member of the Board,
  - decision-making by public authorities, and
  - the different licences governed by this Act.
- **Forum hearings**: the 2020 Act allows some leeway with Forum meetings to the effect that they need not be held in public for a reason relating to coronavirus.[21]

10 AMENDMENTS TO LSO DUTIES

As with board member training, LSO related training requirements are relaxed by the 2020 Act. Under normal house rules an LSO is expected to pass the relevant training within 18 months or employment in that post must be terminated.[22] The 2020 Act allows the period of training to be extended where failure to comply is as a result of a reason relating to coronavirus; and more than one period of extension may be granted, but the extension(s) can only run for a maximum period of 12 months after the original 18-month deadline.[23]

Separately, relaxations are offered to allow late submission of reports with respect to occasional licences and personal licences, but the officer must tell the board within the usual reporting period that the report is going to be late. The board may take the late report into account if it is "reasonable to do so".[24]

11 AMENDMENTS TO POLICE NOTIFICATIONS

A series of amendments are made to provide additional time for the police to provide their various reports in relation to all application processes where the police deem it to be "reasonable in all the circumstances because of a reason

21 2020 Act, Sch 5 para 4(6).
22 See Chapter 6 at Section 2.1.
23 2020 Act, Sch 5 para 5(2).
24 2020 Act, Sch 5 para 5(3) and (4).

relating to coronavirus".[25] The general position is that the police must alert the board that they will not provide the report in time and indicate when they expect to be able to provide said report. This applies to the following:

- 21-day reporting period as regards premises licences and major variation applications,
- 21-day reporting period to provide/confirm details of convictions for premises licence applicants,
- 21-day reporting period to provide an antisocial behaviour report,
- 21-day reporting period as regards transfer applications,
- 21-reporting period following notification by a premises licence holder of a conviction,
- 21-day reporting period in relation to personal licence applications,
- 21-day reporting period in relation to notification by a personal licence holder of a conviction.

25 2020 Act, Sch 5 para 6.

Appendix J

Scottish Licensing Boards: Contact Details

Aberdeen
Aberdeen City Licensing Board
Legal Services
Aberdeen City Council
Business Hub 6 L1S
Marischal College
Aberdeen
AB10 1AB
Email: licensing@aberdeencity.gov.uk
Tel: 01224 522449

Aberdeenshire
Aberdeenshire Licensing Board
Aberdeenshire Council
Legal & Governance
Viewmount
Arduthie Road
Stonehaven
AB39 2DQ
Email: licapps@aberdeenshire.gov.uk
Tel: 01467 537329

Angus
Angus Licensing Board
Angus House
Orchardbank Business Park
Forfar
DD8 1AN
Email: LAWlicensing@angus.gov.uk
Tel: 01307 492299

Argyll & Bute
Argyll & Bute Licensing Board
Governance & Law
Argyll & Bute Council
Kilmory
Lochgilphead
PA31 8RT
Email: licensing@argyll-bute.gov.uk
Tel: 01546 604128

Clackmannanshire
Clackmannanshire Licensing Board
Clackmannanshire Council
Kilncraigs
Alloa
FK10 1EB
Email: licensing@clacks.gov.uk
Tel: 01259 452093

Dumfries & Galloway
Dumfries & Galloway Licensing Board
Municipal Chambers
Buccleuch Street
Dumfries
DG1 2AD
Email: licensing@dumgal.gov.uk
Tel: 01387 245923

Dundee
Dundee City Licensing Board
Dundee City Council
20 City Square
Dundee
DD1 3BY
Email: licensing.board@dundeecity.gov.uk
Tel: 01382 434444

East Ayrshire
East Ayrshire Licensing Board
London Road
Kilmarnock
KA3 7BU
Email: licensing@east-ayrshire.gov.uk
Tel: 01563 576005

East Dunbartonshire
East Dunbartonshire Licensing Board
12 Strathkelvin Place
Kirkintilloch
G66 1TJ
Email: Liquor.Licensing@Eastdunbarton.gov.uk
Tel: 0300 1234510

East Lothian
East Lothian Licensing Board
John Muir House
Haddington
East Lothian
EH41 3HA
Email: licensing@eastlothian.gov.uk
Tel: 01620 827827

East Renfrewshire
East Renfrewshire Licensing Board
East Renfrewshire Council
Eastwood Park
Rouken Glen Road
Giffnock
G46 6UG
Email: Christine.McAuley@eastrenfrewshire.gov.uk
Tel: 0141 5773005

Edinburgh
Edinburgh Licensing Board
249 High Street
Edinburgh
EH1 1YJ
Email: licensing@edinburgh.gov.uk
Tel: 0131 5294208

Falkirk
Falkirk Licensing Board
District Court Offices
Municipal Buildings
West Bridge Street
Falkirk
FK1 5RS
Email: licensing@falkirk.go.uk
Tel: 01324 501575

Fife
Fife Licensing Board
2nd Floor, Fife House
Glenrothes
KY7 5LT
Email: liquor.admin@fife.gov.uk
Tel: 0845 155 0000

Glasgow
City of Glasgow Licensing Board
City Chambers
Glasgow
G2 1DU
Email: LicensingBoard@glasgow.gov.uk
Tel: 0141 2875354

Highland – Caithness, Sutherland & Easter Ross
Council Offices
Caithness House
Market Place
Wick
KW1 4AB
Tel: 01955 609508

Highland – Lochaber
The Highland Council
Charles Kennedy Building
Archintore Road
Fort William
PH33 6RQ

Highland – Ross area (Civic Government)
The Highland Council
High Street
Dingwall
IV15 9NQ
Tel: 01349 868493

Highland – Skye area
The Highland Council
Tigh Na Sigire
Park Lane
Portree
IV51 9GP

Highland – South
The Highland Council
Town House
Inverness
IV1 1JJ

Highland – Sutherland & Easter Ross (Taxi & PHC Licensing only)
The Highland Council
Main Street
Golspie
KW10 6RB
Email for all **Highland** areas: licensing@highland.gov.uk

Inverclyde
Inverclyde Licensing Board
Inverclyde Council
Municipal Buildings
Greenock
PA15 1LY
Email: Fiona.Denver@inverclyde.gov.uk
Tel: 01475 712109

Midlothian
Midlothian Licensing Board
Midlothian House
Buccleuch Street
Dalkeith
EH22 1DN
Email: licensing@midlothian.gov.uk
Tel: 0131 270 7500

Moray
Moray Licensing Board
Council Offices
Elgin
IV30 1BX
Email: licensing@moray.gov.uk
Tel: 01343 563011

North Ayrshire
North Ayrshire Licensing Board
Licensing Section
Legal Services
North Ayrshire Council
Cunninghame House
Irvine
KA12 8EE
Email: licensing@north-ayrshire.gov.uk
Tel: 01294 324305

North Lanarkshire
North Lanarkshire Licensing Board
Civic Centre
Windmillhill Street
Motherwell
ML1 1AB
Email: licensingboard@northlan.gov.uk
Tel: 01698 403200

Orkney
Orkney Licensing Team
Council Offices
Kirkwall
Orkney
KW15 1NY
Email: licensing@orkney.gov.uk
Tel: 01856 873535

Perth & Kinross
Perth & Kinross Licensing Board
Pullar House
35 Kinnoull Street
Perth
PH1 5GD
Email: liquorlicensing@pkc.gov.uk
Tel: 01738 475180

Renfrewshire
Renfrewshire Licensing Board
Renfrewshire House
Cotton Street
Paisley
PA1 1TT
Email: licensing.cs@renfrewshire.gov.uk
Tel: 0300 300 0300

Scottish Borders
Scottish Borders Licensing Board
Council Headquarters
Newtown St Boswells
Melrose
TD6 0SA
Email: liquorandlicensing@scotborders.gcsx.gov.uk
Tel: 01835 826662

Shetland
Shetland Islands Area Licensing Board
Governance & Law
8 North Ness Business Park
Lerwick
Shetland
ZE1 0LZ
Email: legal.services@shetland.gov.uk
Tel: 01595 744550

South Ayrshire
South Ayrshire Licensing Board
County Buildings
Wellington Square
Ayr
KA7 1DR
Email: licensing@south-ayrshire.gov.uk
Tel: 01292 617682

South Lanarkshire
South Lanarkshire Licensing Board
Council Offices
Almada Street
Hamilton
ML3 0AA
Email: licensing@southlanarkshire.gov.uk
Tel: 0303 123 1015

Stirling
Stirling Licensing Board
Stirling Council
Room 9
Old Viewforth
Stirling
FK8 2EZ
Email: liquorlicensing@stirling.gov.uk
Tel: 01786 233612

West Dunbartonshire
West Dunbartonshire Licensing Board
Legal Democratic & Regulatory Services
Council Offices
Garshake Road
Dumbarton
G82 3PU
Email: licensing@west-dunbarton.gov.uk
Tel: 01389 738741

West Lothian
West Lothian Licensing Board
West Lothian Civic Centre
Howden Road South
Livingston
EH54 6FF
Email: licensingboard@westlothian.gov.uk
Tel: 01506 281632

Western Isles
Western Isles Licensing Board
Council Offices
Sandwick Road
Stornoway
Isle of Lewis
HS1 2BW
Email: iain.smith@cne-siar.gov.uk
Tel: 01851 822619

Appendix K

Convictions and Non-court Disposals for Offences under Licensing (Scotland) Act 2005, 2009–19

Table K.1 People convicted in Scottish courts for offences under Licensing (Scotland) 2005, sections 111 to 116, where main charge, 2009–19

	2009–10	*2010–11*	*2011–12*	*2012–13*	*2013–14*	*2014–15*	*2015–16*	*2016–17*	*2017–18*	*2018–19*
Total convicted	**9**	**56**	**66**	**66**	**52**	**64**	**51**	**10**	**12**	**9**
SECTION 111(1)	–	5	5	5	5	8	3	–	–	–
SECTION 111(2)	–	–	2	1	1	4	–	1	–	–
SECTION 112(1)	–	1	–	–	–	–	–	–	–	–
SECTION 113(1)	–	–	1	–	1	–	–	–	–	–
SECTION 114(1)	1	3	2	3	3	3	3	–	2	–
SECTION 114(1) & 141B	–	–	–	1	–	–	–	–	–	–
SECTION 115(1)(A)	5	23	27	28	19	28	17	1	4	2
SECTION 115(1)(B)	–	1	1	–	–	–	–	–	–	–
SECTION 115(2)	–	–	–	–	2	–	–	1	–	–
SECTION 116(1)	3	23	26	28	20	21	28	5	6	7
SECTION 116(2)	–	–	2	–	1	–	–	2	–	–

Table K.2 People given non-court disposals for offences under Licensing (Scotland) 2005, sections 111 to 116, 009–19

	2009–10	*2010–11*	*2011–12*	*2012–13*	*2013–14*	*2014–15*	*2015–16*	*2016–17*	*2017–18*	*2018–19*
Total	**198**	**599**	**735**	**957**	**1,164**	**891**	**779**	**612**	**476**	**465**
SECTION 111(1)	14	28	20	32	30	29	16	6	6	5
SECTION 111(2)	5	21	19	13	26	24	7	5	5	4
SECTION 112(1)	–	–	–	1	–	–	–	–	–	–
SECTION 112(2)	–	–	–	–	–	–	–	–	–	1
SECTION 113(1)	1	2	3	12	15	10	8	5	–	–
SECTION 114(1)	1	3	5	21	19	5	8	9	4	4
SECTION 114(1) & 141B	–	–	1	2	–	–	1	–	–	–
SECTION 115(1)(A)	74	262	290	329	399	299	237	206	177	159
SECTION 115(1)(B)	5	6	21	14	15	13	7	–	–	2
SECTION 115(2)	–	–	1	7	9	19	4	3	–	–
SECTION 115(2)& 141B	–	–	–	–	–	–	–	2	–	–
SECTION 116	–	1	–	–	–	–	–	–	1	–
SECTION 116(1)	95	260	363	487	601	470	465	359	259	274
SECTION 116(2)	3	16	12	39	50	22	26	17	24	16

Index